The Face of Nature

The Face of Nature

An environmental history of the Otago Peninsula

Jonathan West

Published by Otago University Press
Level 1, 398 Cumberland Street
Dunedin, New Zealand
university.press@otago.ac.nz
www.otago.ac.nz/press

First published 2017
Copyright © Jonathan West

The moral rights of the author have been asserted.

ISBN 978-1-927322-38-3

A catalogue record for this book is available from the National Library of New Zealand. This book is copyright. Except for the purpose of fair review, no part may be stored or transmitted in any form or by any means, electronic or mechanical, including recording or storage in any information retrieval system, without permission in writing from the publishers. No reproduction may be made, whether by photocopying or by any other means, unless a licence has been obtained from the publisher.

Editors: Imogen Coxhead, Paul Sorrell
Design/layout: Fiona Moffat
Indexer: Robin Briggs

Cover photograph © Arno Gasteiger
Frontispiece: The lighthouse at Taiaroa Head. © Ian Thomson

Printed in China through Asia Pacific Offset

Contents

Acknowledgements 7
Introduction 11

PART I: THE PRIMORDIAL PENINSULA AND PEOPLE

CHAPTER 1: He Whenua Hou: A new land 30

CHAPTER 2: Arrival and Adaptation 42

CHAPTER 3: Continuity and Change: Making southern Māori 62

PART II: THE WORLD WASHES ASHORE

CHAPTER 4: Takata Pora: The people of the ships, European exploration, Māori discovery 1770–1830 100

CHAPTER 5: 'Soon may the Wellerman come': Whaling at Ōtākou 1831–48 120

PART III: IMPROVING GOD'S CREATION

CHAPTER 6: 'A Desperate Struggle': British settlement on the Otago Peninsula 1848–61 160

CHAPTER 7: The Axe and the Lucifer Match: Boom-time settlement of the 1860s and 1870s 184

CHAPTER 8: 'The whole face of Nature is altered': 1881–1900 248

Conclusion 280
Notes 289
Bibliography 349
Index 369

William Hodgkins, Near Cape Saunders.

1870, watercolour. Hocken Collections, Uare Taoka o Hākena, University of Otago: 9,987 021

Acknowledgements

First and foremost my love and gratitude to my family, who have had to put up with rather a lot. Kate and our children have lived with me as I lived with this, and daily remind me that the present is more important than the past.

This book had its beginnings in a PhD, and I am grateful to the supervisors who took me on: Tom Brooking, who saw merit in a thesis on the environmental history of the Otago Peninsula, agreed that I might be the person to attempt it, and backed me to the end; and Janine Hayward, for her ever-keen eye and unflagging encouragement.

An environmental history must trespass over many fields, and so I have relied on the expertise of others wherever possible. Peter Johnson (botanist), John Jillett and Keith Probert (marine scientists) and Tony Harris (entomologist) were guides through the perils of the life sciences. Jill Hamel, Helen Leach and Ian Smith each tried to help me unearth archaeology.

New Zealand history is a small field, and some people know a great deal more than I about aspects of this study. Khyla Russell, Jim Williams, Edward Ellison, Bill Dacker, and Tahu and Megan Potiki have all helped shape my reading of Kāi Tahu whānui history. Michael Stevens, whose ability to refract the history of the world through that of his whānau never ceases to astound me, has been an especially invaluable touchstone. He mihi nui ki a koutou, ngā rangatira mā.

The late Hardwicke Knight was, among many things, a historian of the Peninsula, and though old and frustrated by his failing memory when I met him, still offered me many insights as well as access to his incomparable collection of early photographs, many now held in the Hocken Collections. Historian of early Otago Peter Entwisle provided detailed comments on the material that became chapters 4 and 5 while I worked on my PhD, and helpfully read parts of my book manuscript too. Environmental historian James Beattie has given valuable support and advice. I've especially appreciated his help in maintaining a connection as an associate to the University of Waikato history programme, which has helped me keep abreast of other research. David Haines has had to be more patient with my enthusiasm than most; he provided a final close read of the manuscript for which I am especially thankful.

Professor Tony Ballantyne has been very supportive, most especially in inviting me in 2014 to give a lecture at Toitū Otago Settlers Museum as part of the Global Dunedin series organised by the Centre for Research on Colonial Culture; preparing this talk crystallised some key themes of the present book. I am grateful also to Sean Fitzsimons and the University of Otago Geography Department for inviting me to give the Ron Lister Memorial Lecture for 2016, which afforded me the chance to think through my use of maps in this study. I thank Lala Frazer, of Save the Otago Peninsula, for helping ensure these talks were well attended, and more generally for her support of this work over many years.

My most particular thanks go to the extraordinary Atholl Anderson, emeritus professor at the Australian National University College of Asia and the Pacific, who has twice read a draft manuscript and whose unique expertise in archaeology and ethnography has saved me many blushes.

Any errors and omissions that remain are entirely my responsibility.

Dunedin is blessed with wonderful archives, libraries and museums, and over the years I have spent in them I have always been struck by the generosity and kindness shown to me. My grateful thanks go to the staff of Port Chalmers Maritime Museum, Otago Museum, Toitū Otago Settlers Museum, Archives New Zealand (Dunedin regional office), Land Information New Zealand (Dunedin office), Dunedin Public Libraries (McNab Collection), and the volunteers who staff Otago Peninsula Museum. In Wellington, my thanks go to the staff of Alexander Turnbull Library and the National Archives. I would most especially, however, like to thank the wonderful staff of the Hocken Collections, who were invariably generous with their time and knowledge as I endeavoured to navigate their invaluable archive. I am particularly appreciative of the time Anne Jackman, Anna Petersen and Karen Craw devoted to supplying so many of the paintings, photographs and maps that feature here.

Others who helped me greatly by providing images include Emma Burns, Kane Fleury, Fiona Glasgow and Rachel Wesley of Otago Museum; Paul Pope of Otago Peninsula Museum; and Alan Dove, John Huggett, Marchell Linzey, Keith Probert and Ian Smith. Ian Thomson has my especial thanks for graciously agreeing to the use of his beautiful photographs, as does Arno Gastieger for the glorious landscape that adorns the cover. I am also very grateful to Seonaigh Stevens, for permission to reproduce work in her possession.

Maps drawn for this book have been contributed by Craig Innes, Tracy Connolly, Chris Garden and Allan Kynaston; special mention in this regard to Brian Grant, who helped me make some maps of my own.

Friends and colleagues at the Waitangi Tribunal and the Office of Treaty Settlements have been very supportive. Tribunal librarian Jeff Abbott showed saintly patience with me as I asked for ever more time with other libraries' books. Hayden Wright was responsible for my seeking support from the Ministry of Culture and Heritage's New Zealand History Research Trust, without which I could not have taken the time to break the back of the manuscript. Thanks more generally to the Waitangi Tribunal for allowing me the time to work towards finishing this book.

Otago University Press has waited for this book for a long time. Wendy Harrex went out on a limb for me and agreed to publish, and Rachel Scott has been steadfast in her support of me and this project through to completion. My thanks to editors Imogen Coxhead and Paul Sorrell, and to Fiona Moffat for making such a beautiful book.

I owe the greatest debt to the late local historian Ian Church, whom I met while I was floundering in my PhD and he was in the middle of *Gaining a Foothold*, his extraordinary compilation of the early historical records of coastal Otago. Ian always welcomed me around for a talk, and when I arrived at his home he would invariably present me with a folder full of papers on people and places he thought I should know more about, all written up in his meticulous hand. Ian lent me many books while he lived, and before he died left me very many more, in the faith that I would use them. I dedicate my book to his memory.

© Aerial data sourced from LINZ

Introduction

The Otago Peninsula is a small finger of land poking out from the South Island's east coast into the Pacific Ocean. A place of great natural diversity and celebrated scenic beauty, it has a human history of equally exceptional depth and variety. The Peninsula's outward face juts forth to confront the rolling Pacific swells and wild southwest winds, which have smashed its lava tongues into cliffs and gouged out bays and estuaries from its softer rocks. The aspect it turns towards land is sunny and comparatively calm and encloses Otago Harbour and the city of Dunedin. Where the raw outer coast attracts wildlife, the hills and bays of the inner harbour are home to quiet suburbs and small villages. Stand atop any one of the Peninsula's volcanic cones and the drama of the contrast is breathtaking: a chain of hills folding into hills fringed by high cliffs, deep estuaries and white sandy beaches. Little wonder, perhaps, that the Peninsula has been at the centre of life in Otago for most of human history here.

The Otago Peninsula has always been among the places in Otago most important to Māori: they have lived there longest, and fought over it most bitterly. They shared it willingly with whalers and then reluctantly agreed to split it with the British. The Peninsula in the later nineteenth century was transformed from forest into one large dairy farm that fed a booming Dunedin city, and was home to many of its leading citizens, including the extraordinary entrepreneur and politician William Larnach. In the twenty-first century it has become the core of Dunedin's ecotourism industry and the city's claim as the wildlife capital of New Zealand. The Otago Peninsula is again the heart of Otago.

The Peninsula's enduring significance stems from the fact that it has attracted and held a succession of the forces that have been central to shaping human expansion into the third of the globe that is the Pacific Ocean. Here, natural forces combine with the forces of human history – the entanglements of empire, booming settler capitalism, the quest for national identity and an honourable home – to shape Otago, New Zealand, the wider Pacific, and even the entire earth.

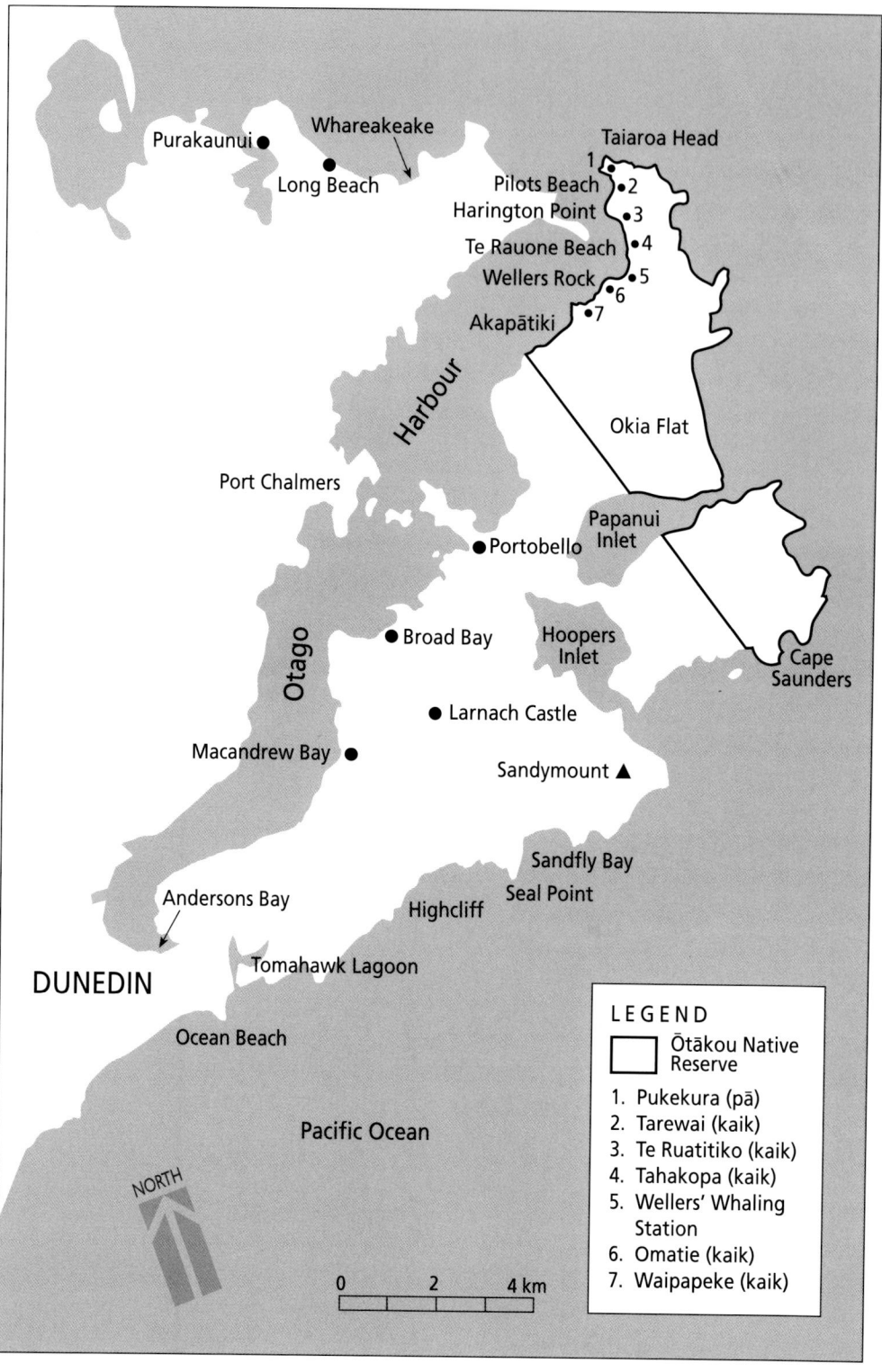

Looking south over Cape Saunders and Hoopers Inlet, towards Dunedin, and capturing the Peninsula's broken topography and varied shores. Photographer unknown, image courtesy of Ian Smith

New Zealand has long been seen as a Gondwanan ark – a place apart, cast adrift about 80 million years ago, which explains the peculiarity of its plants and animals.[1] Some geologists now claim that New Zealand drowned beneath the sea only some 20 million years ago, meaning that all our plants and animals later crossed the ocean to get here.[2] This claim is still contested.[3] Whether it is wholly or mostly true, we should now see New Zealand in a different way, as 'the fly-paper of the Pacific': animals and plants swirling around the globe on winds and ocean currents bump into New Zealand all the time.[4] Some successfully stick.

The yellow-eyed penguin, which famously still breeds around the Otago Peninsula, is a particular example. Saved from extermination by ongoing heroic efforts, along with the royal albatross it is now the backbone of the local economy. In 2009 scientists from Otago and elsewhere overturned what we thought we knew about the yellow-eyed penguin, *Megadyptes antipodes*.[5] Like most of our other surviving birds, it was believed to be a declining remnant of a once abundant species. It is in fact a very recent newcomer to the Otago Peninsula that arrived from the subantarctic islands only after its predecessor, a newly distinguished sort of penguin, *Megadyptes waitaha*, was exterminated by early Polynesian settlers – remembered here as Waitaha – within a few hundred years of their arrival in the late thirteenth century.[6]

Yellow-eyed penguins are no less precious or vulnerable for being newcomers. Their late arrival illuminates the importance of the ocean currents that, along with the prevailing westerlies, connect this place to the wider world; together they provide the pathways along which plants, animals and people have all come to New Zealand.

In southern Māori tradition, people's exploration of the sea began with a bird's feather, sent out over the ocean to discover whether the sky descended till it lay upon the water, or whether the sea continued beyond the horizon.[7] Shearwaters and petrels, especially the sooty shearwater – the tītī or muttonbird – might have been the most reliable guides to people's great migrations south. Fabulous numbers of the birds flew south in spring over East Polynesia, heading for their breeding grounds in New Zealand – and returned just as predictably each autumn.[8]

Lance Richdale, the man most famous for saving the Peninsula's albatrosses, once said of the sooty shearwater migration that from September 'an observer on any headland of the Otago Peninsula in New Zealand may see this species flying south in an endless stream'.[9] What Māori saw, though, is almost unimaginable. Where we see hundreds and thousands of birds, they would have seen hundreds *of* thousands, millions, even tens of millions. Such seabird populations once linked the ecosystems of the land and sea in a way we have only just begun to uncover.[10]

Māori tradition tells us that the first people to encounter the Otago coast came south out of the Pacific on the waka (canoe) *Uruao*, meaning 'squall', and called themselves Te Rapuwai, a name that commemorates how they splashed the water as they swam.[11] These people, who later came to call themselves Waitaha, considered that the Peninsula was formed by their atua (god) Kahukura, 'the main god of the migrators', who 'separated the good from the bad weather' and 'protected the frail canoes on the heaving waves'.[12]

The pattern of archaeological sites in Otago makes it plain that the Peninsula was at the centre of early Māori settlement from about the late thirteenth century on. Three of nine possible early village sites in Otago are found on the Peninsula, among many smaller sites.[13] Elsewhere in the south, early Māori settlers lived for only a few generations at most, until all the moa, seals and big seabird colonies in the vicinity had been eaten up and it was time to move on. After doing that for a few hundred years, there were no moa and few seals left; not only that, but the climate got much colder, and wetter.[14] Archaeologists paint a bleak picture of southern Māori life during the sixteenth and seventeenth centuries, even suggesting that the cold was such that people moved away from Foveaux Strait and the far south.[15]

The Otago Peninsula, though, remained an important home. It was at the core of the contest for the south between the iwi (tribe) Kāti Māmoe, who moved down from the North Island in the sixteenth century, and Kāi Tahu (southern dialect for Ngāi

Otago Harbour is seen to the west, Hoopers and Papanui inlets are lit in the east. Arno Gasteiger

Tahu). Hapū (subtribes) of Kāi Tahu such as Kāti Kurī began to come south about the turn of the eighteenth century. For the next century they would struggle over the south, beginning and ending with efforts to gain and maintain control over the Otago Peninsula.[16]

People – like seabirds and seals – were attracted to the Peninsula above all because of the food they could harvest from the rich ocean around it. They called Cape Saunders Poatiri, 'the fish-hook', for good reason. The edge of the continental shelf is only 10 kilometres from the tip of Cape Saunders – the closest it comes to shore on the east coast south of Kaikōura. Above the shelf's slope lies an important feeding area and biogeographic boundary (the so-called Subtropical Front, known locally as the Southland Front), where inshore water of subtropical origin meets offshore subantarctic water. Many species mass at this boundary – where, when I was a boy, the lights of squid boats were seen at night strung like shining beads to mark the unseen horizon. Inshore, currents and eddies combine to concentrate drifting zooplankton in the Peninsula's inlets and bays, making them nurseries for flatfish, and attracting shoals of feeding fish and great flocks of seabirds.[17]

Once the moa, seals and seabirds such as the Waitaha penguin were largely gone, southern Māori relied increasingly on the sea, which came to supply up to three quarters of their animal food. In this context, the yellow-eyed penguins' survival raises a question: Māori had just exterminated one sort of penguin, so why not another? This was perfect habitat for these birds, especially with the reduction in fur seals. The survival of yellow-eyed penguins perhaps reflects a significant shift in Māori culture, in which – having no alternative – they learnt to live more sustainably here. The Polynesians who became Māori, who had exterminated thousands of birds and several animal species as they spread out to colonise the Pacific, perhaps learnt to manage some significant resources.

Lieutenant James Cook described seals and yellow-eyed penguins as he sailed the *Endeavour* south off the Otago coast in March 1770. He did not land here, but he noted possibilities for a good harbour, the presence of seals and whales, and the fact that inhabitants were few.[18]

Cook's records of the resources of the Pacific, including the seals, whales, flax and timber of New Zealand, encouraged the British government to found Port Jackson (Sydney) at Botany Bay. However, the powerful British East India Company and the British whaling industry combined to clamp down on the new colony's capacity to exploit Pacific resources, and to compete with them for trade.[19] As a result, Sydney's governors were forbidden to allow shipbuilding or any kind of trade to Asia. They had no choice but to disobey. Sydney was a port town trapped inside the Blue Mountains. Its governors turned a blind eye to shipbuilding, and allowed Sydney merchants to explore the Pacific frontier.[20]

In the first years of the nineteenth century, therefore, ships out of Sydney quietly inspected the south of New Zealand. They came in the main for fur seals, whose pelts they sold in China and later in London. The first known sealing ship to enter Otago Harbour was the *Brothers* in 1810.[21] Seals had survived longer on the rocky islets around the Peninsula than anywhere further north, and the Peninsula's small remaining rookeries represented the high-tide mark for European sealing. But sealing in southern New Zealand lasted only a few years. Sealers very quickly stripped the shores, and though everyone from Sydney's governors down could see this happening, no one could successfully challenge the economic logic of plunder: taking everything you could, knowing that rivals would take what you left. Uncontrollable boom-and-bust exploitation has been a recurrent pattern in the history of the Otago Peninsula, and New Zealand, and elsewhere in Britain's colonies.

The sealers explored the coast and its resources, which enabled them to lead the turn to other trades in timber and flax. But there were too few Māori in Otago, and in the south more generally, to provide the labour force needed for these trades. For this reason, Otago was not yet important to Europeans. Even a little traffic with Europeans changed Māori life on the Peninsula, however. Māori gained pigs and, most important of all, potatoes – a vegetable that revolutionised their life just as it had done for the Scots and the Irish. Among other benefits, the ability to grow potatoes meant Māori could cluster at the harbours where European trade was most likely. Sealer John Boultbee reported in 1827 that the Peninsula settlements were the largest in the south.[22]

Trade with Europeans upset the balance of power in the Māori world. Basing himself strategically about Cook Strait, the Ngāti Toa rangatira (chief) Te Rauparaha gained guns first: he demolished Kāi Tahu power in Canterbury, and eyed the south.

Māori living on the Peninsula soon gained the guns to fight back, getting them from Sydney merchants the Weller Brothers in exchange for the right to establish a shore whaling station at Ōtākou, near the harbour mouth on the tip of the Otago Peninsula.[23] Māori from the Peninsula were then instrumental in fighting off Te Rauparaha, ensuring that he never threatened the far south, Murihiku.

Shore whaling was possible at Ōtākou because southern right whales followed regular winter migration paths along the east coast and would come into sheltered bays like Otago Harbour to nurse their calves. But whaling, like sealing, did not last long because the whalers exterminated whales so fast: during the 20-year whaling bonanza after 1830, over 40,000 right whales were killed in Australasia.[24] Whalers were a polyglot lot, mainly American at sea – but also British, French, even German – and mainly Australian ashore. No government could control whaling, even if they had wanted to. The whaling boom was global, and the entire Pacific basin was scoured for whales.[25]

Ōtākou was at the heart of the Wellers' empire, which dominated whaling on New Zealand's eastern seaboard in the 1830s. The Wellers' whaling base in Otago Harbour was one of the earliest and for a long time the biggest of such stations, the recourse of men and ships all along the coast. A new sort of settlement emerged at Ōtākou, where Māori and whalers mingled. Whalers became entangled with Māori in the trades ubiquitous to such ports: resupplying men wanting food, water and women; refitting ships needing wood, rope and men. Whalers and Māori worked together to send out cargo of the rawest materials – potatoes, pigs, the salted skins of clubbed seals, and the oil and bone of whale.

The character of the settlement remains contentious, and questions linger over how well Māori coped with the potent cocktail of 'sugar and tea and rum' brought by the 'Wellerman', as the whalers' shanty put it – not to mention muskets, measles and missionaries. Regardless, Māori and the newcomers gradually came to a mutual understanding and tacit trust through negotiating all manner of day-to-day exchanges: domestic affairs, sexual contact, dispute resolution and the terms of labour and property rights all had to be managed. Throughout the 1830s Māori and whalers traded in land, too, and common understandings developed of what was at stake for both parties. This experience stood Māori in good stead when, in 1844, they debated the sale of the Otago Block to the New Zealand Company.

The Otago Peninsula's importance to both Māori and the British was underlined in the debates over the sale, which was, in the words of historian Erik Olssen, the key 'rupture' in the history of Otago.[26] Māori eventually sold 160,000 hectares to the

New Zealand Company for £2400, providing the basis for the 'systematic colonisation' of the south. This sale secured the British a harbour and a hinterland on which to found organised settlement. It began a sequence of eight sales through which Māori sold almost all the South Island to the British in just 20 years, giving the new owners the base from which to entrench themselves, crush Māori resistance in the north, and make New Zealand.[27] The fate of the Otago Peninsula was at the heart of the debate in that first crucial southern land sale.

The question of who would own the Peninsula was bitterly disputed because of its obvious strategic importance at the entrance to Otago Harbour. Local leaders were deeply reluctant to relinquish any part of the Peninsula, but other chiefs with significant lands elsewhere were less adamant; in the end Māori retained only the Peninsula's northern tip. This land has remained a centre of the Māori presence in Otago.

Meanwhile, British settlers spread out over Otago. By 1860 Otago was home to some 12,000 people. A few of these trickled out onto the Peninsula's fringes, which surveyor Charles Kettle, in designing Dunedin, had designated as suburban areas.

Following the discovery of gold in 1861, everything changed. The city was awash with gold, and settlers surged to clear the forest and farm the land. For 20 years settlement on the Peninsula was carried forward on a wave of tremendous optimism. During this sustained boom the Peninsula's major roads were built – much of the work being carried out by prison labour, including that provided by the Taranaki war and Parihaka prisoners. Plans were laid to build a railway to Portobello, and there was a great deal of subdivision and massive land speculation. This activity was underpinned by cheap and abundant British credit, channelled into Otago by people such as banker and politician William Larnach.

By the late 1870s New Zealand was 'saturated with debt'. When the Bank of Glasgow, which had funnelled large amounts of British capital to New Zealand, suddenly went bust in 1878, it triggered a chain reaction in bank collapses and bankruptcies. The banks turned off cheap credit to Otago, and growth in the south slowed to a crawl for most of the rest of the century.[28] Still, Peninsula farming continued to consolidate. Led by Larnach, the Peninsula's settlers continued making the Peninsula into cow country, where dairy farming was 'the sole business of the district', churning out Dunedin's milk and butter.[29]

Dairying suited tight-knit communities of farming families who were highly educated, progressive and technically advanced. They were, on the whole, an extraordinary mix; as historian Hardwicke Knight has noted, in addition to their many farming achievements – notably New Zealand's first dairy factory – they could turn their hands to many things. They 'built, made furniture, could sink a mine shaft, construct water-wheels, build a limekiln, contract for works as large as Larnach's castle and the defence works at the heads, as well as make violins, milk churns, boats, and much else wherever one enquires into their activities'.[30]

Meanwhile, however, the Otago settlers shut Māori out: they were not welcome in politics, the economy or society. The small community at Ōtākou struggled. Their land was fairly poor – where it was not hill, it was mostly sand or swamp – and settlers owned and foreclosed access to their former lands. Perhaps their biggest single obstacle was that settler laws and settler banks refused to lend capital against the value of their property so that, unlike settler farmers, Māori could not rely on credit to develop their land.

These varying trajectories of Māori and British history on the Peninsula track changes in how the world was organised into property. Property systems provide blueprints for everything from religious belief to economics and politics. The settlers lived and breathed this: the distribution of land was for them *the* political, economic and moral issue.[31] This was just as true of Māori. The community at Ōtākou reorganised title to their lands to try to meet the demands of settler capitalism, allocating land to individuals in the first sitting of the Native Land Court in the South Island in 1868. They divided their land into narrow strips to ensure that each owner had access to both the land and the resources of the foreshore and sea. It was an attempt to compromise between two systems of property, and two ways of constructing an economy in relation to ecology. The settlers were horrified, however, to see Māori reproduce the thin strips of traditional Scottish peasant agriculture, and accurately predicted the problems Māori soon faced.

The ongoing dissonance in the legal status of Māori and settler land is shown in the fact that Peninsula rangatira Hori Kerei (H.K.) Taiaroa eventually had parliament pass the Taiaroa Land Act 1883 to allow him to deal with his land exactly as Europeans did.[32] Taiaroa, too, knew that property is so important that it forms the heart of law; and as historian William Cronon has observed, this understanding of property makes law 'the formal expression of a community's relationship with nature'.[33]

The settlers' view of the world as 'property' was central to their transformation of the Peninsula's lands and seas. The land was divided into farms, and owners poured enormous effort into controlling which plants grew where, and which animals ate them. Settlers brooked no interference over their own land; the rights and powers of private property in this age of laissez faire capitalism were almost absolute.

On the foreshore and at sea, however, settlers recognised no private property rights, to the consternation of Ōtākou Māori. Complaints about settlers 'plundering all the oysters and fish' from what Māori still considered their inshore fisheries were ignored.[34] By 1869 up to 60 commercial seine-net flounder fishermen operated in Otago Harbour year round.[35] As early as 1877, prescient settlers urged for 'the necessity of steps being taken to preserve the fisheries in the harbour from utter destruction'.[36] The state was quite prepared to regulate fisheries, but Otago Harbour was the first and worst case of settler overfishing: there, state interventions were generally too little or

By the 1970s many fences on the outer coast had become ramshackle and few cattle were to be seen. Hardwicke Knight photograph, 1970s, P2014-014/6-048

too late to prevent repeating the boom-and-bust exploitation that had already seen seals and whales exterminated. Oysters vanished, flatfish diminished, and inshore fisheries for the enormous hāpuku or groper disappeared.

By the end of the nineteenth century, the Peninsula was one of the most intensively and progressively farmed landscapes in New Zealand. In just 50 years the land had been laid bare and the harbour and other inlet fisheries hollowed out. The spate and scope of change was such that New Zealand's leading natural scientist, George Malcolm Thomson – who, at the turn of the twentieth century, 'knew Dunedin like a book' – looked out around the city in amazement, reflecting that already most of 'the indigenous flora and fauna' had vanished: 'The whole face of Nature is altered'.[37]

Since Thomson's 1899 observation, settlement has intensified in the southern suburbs and the harbourside bays. Overall, people have retreated from the hills and the Pacific side of the Peninsula, and the dense patchwork of dairy farms has given way to a thin scattering of sheep. Traces of the nineteenth century remain very visible in today's landscape. Stone walls still divide the paddocks, and gnarled macrocarpas loom over the ruins of old houses, byres and barns. Much of the Peninsula is a ghost landscape. As archaeologist Angela Middleton puts it, the patterns imposed on the land by the settlers of the nineteenth century are 'strikingly intact and beautifully preserved'.[38] This

Built in the 1880s, this cottage is typical of the timber structures on the northern Peninsula. It still stands near Papanui Inlet, on Weir Road. Photographer unknown, image courtesy of Ian Smith

The remains of an early dwelling on the Duckmanton farm, at Sheppard Road, Hoopers Inlet.
Otago Peninsula Museum: OPM 2013/34/46

is all the more extraordinary as the Peninsula immediately abuts Dunedin, one of New Zealand's significant cities.

The Peninsula has proved irresistible to scientists, writers, poets and painters searching for an understanding of this part of the world and people's place in it. Each generation has been drawn to wander and wonder over the Otago Peninsula. Some have been fascinated by its natural history, others by the many traces of human history still evident on and under its thin skin. It is to the Peninsula that the descendants of the settlers have turned in the search to understand themselves and their place here. This is perhaps what drove Colin McCahon to paint the Peninsula again and again in his effort to realise what it was that conveyed 'something logical, orderly and beautiful belonging to the land and not yet to its people. Not yet understood or communicated.'[39]

Otago historian Eileen Soper wrote of how women, especially, experienced the settlers' world as a 'habitat that must be continually altering – the natural demolished in order to give way to the civilized', and adding that 'whether she loved or hated the new land, no pioneer woman could be completely at peace while this process of destruction and reconstruction was taking place'.[40]

Today, the Peninsula that was reconstructed in the nineteenth century is being preserved as a living museum, a relict landscape in which an increasingly urban community works to preserve the remains of its rural history while encouraging a resurgence of indigenous life, most of which has come back to us from the sea.[41] Perhaps this effort will provide an answer to the question still at issue for New Zealand's settlers: how will we be at peace here?

This book explores what people and place have made of one another on the Otago Peninsula, from the first Polynesian settlement until the close of the nineteenth century, by which time the settlement of the Peninsula was at its zenith. It is intended as a rigorous local history – one that seeks to balance describing the ephemera of events with an explanation of the broad patterns of the past. It does not intend to present an argument that the Peninsula is a microcosm of New Zealand. It does, however, presume that the constellation of forces that shaped this particular place were also at work elsewhere in the archipelago, and in Britain's other colonies of settlement.[42] Elsewhere, those forces combined to have different effects.

The book is also an environmental history that attempts to uncover some of the links that integrate the Peninsula's natural environment and the economy, society, culture and politics that have characterised its human communities.[43] It proceeds from the premise that people and their world evolve in concert. People everywhere and always seek to make their world in their own image. This is most evident perhaps in the actions and attitudes of migrants: unsettled people most urgently need to make themselves at home. As people shaped the Otago Peninsula, they were themselves changed.

INTRODUCTION

Robin White, Oystercatchers. 1974, watercolour. Private collection

Larnach's farm steading was a model of its kind. The Dunedin City Council purchased 324 hectares of land here in 2008 to preserve this landscape, complete with such historic sites.
© Angela Middleton

Māori and British immigrants tried to create idealised societies and environments derived from their old world,[44] and the Otago Peninsula's environments responded in complex and often unpredictable ways to people's efforts to impose a cultural order. Its human inhabitants were intensely interested and intimately involved in the consequences of such changes. Their evolving responses to the process of encountering the Peninsula have been equally unpredictable, unintended and unforeseen. Neither the natural environment nor human communities are ever static; all have internal dynamics that drive ceaseless change, and when they intersect they change one another also.[45] As a result, encounter has made something different of both people and place on the Peninsula. What happened here, as elsewhere in New Zealand, was something nobody counted on.

Biogeographers study the history of life to explain what lives where and why; they suggest that if we understand New Zealand, 'the rest of the world falls into place'.[46] Perhaps the same is true of the environmental history of New Zealand. New Zealand's environmental history is generally exceptional for the sheer speed and comprehensiveness of change. Māori and Europeans arrived there very late, accompanied by some of the world's most influential organisms. Each also brought ideas, tools and technologies perfected over centuries of experience of settling new lands. Europeans, in particular, and the British above all, spread unprecedented

William Hodgkins, View of the Otago Harbour, *c. 1866, watercolour. Hodgkins, father of painter Frances Hodgkins, was a significant figure in the development of art in colonial Otago and New Zealand. His painting of the Peninsula landforms recapitulates the treatment by his contemporaries, such as George O'Brien, in making the hills much steeper than they are, something Colin McCahon was later also to do.* Hocken Collections, Uare Taoka o Hākena, University of Otago: 9,987 053

quantities of people, objects, organisms and capital around the world. As geographer Kenneth Cumberland observed: 'What in Europe took twenty centuries, and in North America four, has been accomplished in New Zealand within a single century – in little more than one full lifetime.'[47]

Following Cumberland, the speed and comprehensiveness of New Zealand's environmental transformations has been much remarked upon.[48] So, too, has the rapidity of the dispossession of southern Māori.[49] Ecological change has been especially complete on the eastern seaboard where the British settlers founded ports and cities such as Dunedin. Here, dramatic environmental change occurred in a new era of mass literacy, alongside an outpouring of print, paint and photography, enabling present-day historians to show how it happened.[50]

Less clear, however, is what gave these processes such momentum. This book suggests that a large part of the answer can be found in attending to how the distribution of property channelled the restless energy of colonial capitalism. Systems of property are perhaps the most organised expression of people's relationships with one another and their world. They are also therefore powerful causes of ecological and cultural change in their own right. Māori and settler systems of property and tenure of resources have each shaped where and how particular groups of people have made themselves at home; which elements of the Peninsula were harvested from or cultivated, and by whom; and which places became routes of travel or remained more or less wild. Uncovering the operation of property systems and tenure of resources reveals the patterns of human endeavour within nature's economy: they show us the blueprint of our desire, the circuits that channel our energy and our activity.

The British Empire of the nineteenth century was exceptional as an empire of mass settlement, underpinned by a colonising culture geared to create, develop and exchange property. Ideas and institutions of property, 'laws about possessory rights, individualised titles, transferability of title, and – most important – an insistence on improvement', were central to the ways in which settler colonies emerged from resource frontiers on the edges of the British Empire.[51] The British fine-tuned the capacity to transform land into property in the political economy of nineteenth-century New Zealand, obsessively tinkering with the statutory and policy settings that organised property.[52] The British – but especially the Scots – were pre-eminently defenders of the rights of private property, and of free markets.[53] The extraordinary effort that each individual farmer was prepared to pour into their own land, in order to produce a very narrow range of commodities for sale in Dunedin city or abroad, powered the speed and completeness of economic development and environmental transformation on the Peninsula.

But there is another trajectory of change, one only now beginning to be uncovered, which modulates the too-familiar tale of wholesale ecological loss. The sea is a source of ceaseless renewal to these islands. Life continues to wash ashore. Penguins, seals, sea lions, albatrosses and whales, all once (in some cases twice) extirpated from the shores of the Peninsula and its surrounding seas, have now returned. In some cases, at least, they are thriving. These processes of renewal, very visible on the Peninsula, provide a timely and telling reminder that we cannot understand these islands without thinking about the much larger sea surrounding them.

Historian Tom Brooking and geographer Eric Pawson have suggested New Zealand needs detailed, localised histories to act as 'the bedrock' of larger environmental histories.[54] Histories such as these ground the abstract questions we ask about people's relationships with the natural world so that they 'resolve themselves into small human actions at very particular times and places'.[55]

On the other hand, as Brooking and Pawson rightly insist, local studies must locate particular places within much wider processes and larger scales of time and space.[56] While New Zealand's isolation in the Pacific means that it is a rare case where a national environmental history makes any sense, as an archipelago of islands it is also ideally placed to help historians who feel we do too much national history.[57]

Perhaps the story of the Otago Peninsula also has something to say to all those striving to find what Māori call tūrangawaewae, a place to stand, an honourable home in these islands. As elsewhere in New Zealand, people have all but wiped out the area's native flora and fauna, yet now the Peninsula's landowners substantially depend on displaying what remains. All over the Peninsula, bits and pieces of native forest and scrub are fenced off, weeded and replanted. Slopes have been revegetated by farmers who now fleece flocks of people paying to peep at penguins. Farmers are also at the forefront of the effort to eradicate possums from the Peninsula. Sea lions have returned to breed on the Peninsula's beaches, and northern royal albatrosses, living in the world's only mainland breeding colony and caught right at the top of the cliff in every sense, soar above tourists in the adjacent carpark. Primordial New Zealand will reassert itself when we give it half a chance.

This book has three parts, each of which maps the development of a different set of relationships between people and the Otago Peninsula.

Part I: The Primordial Peninsula and People describes the evolution of the Otago Peninsula in deep time before discussing the arrival of Polynesians out of the Pacific. It explores the intertwined ecological, economic and cultural changes involved in the emergence, after Polynesian settlement, of the Māori communities for whom the Peninsula was such an important place.

Part II: The World Washes Ashore begins with the arrival of Europeans, the takata pora, 'people of the ships', which initiated a dialogue between Māori, the newcomers and the Peninsula environment based around a mutual desire to develop and exchange commodities.

Part III: Improving God's Creation discusses the environmental, social and ideological changes that took place in the wake of the sale of the Otago Block in 1844, and the concentrated British settlement that followed. British settlers initiated new property relations based on individual and exclusive ownership of land. These relations effected changes between British settlers and Māori, and between people and their respective portions of the Peninsula. The book traces these developments until the close of the nineteenth century, the point at which the environmental transformation of the Peninsula from forest to farm was essentially complete.

OVERLEAF: *Windshorn tree, Sandymount.* © Ian Thomson
PAGE 30: *Black swans at Papanui Inlet. The black swan flew to New Zealand one to two million years ago and evolved into a large bird, now named* Cygnus sumnerensis. *It was almost flightless by the time it was hunted to extinction by Māori soon after their arrival from Polynesia. British settlers introduced the smaller Australian black swans pictured here (*Cygnus atratus*) to Otago in the 1860s.* © Ian Thomson

Part I
THE PRIMORDIAL PENINSULA AND PEOPLE

CHAPTER 1: HE WHENUA HOU: A NEW LAND

Na Te Po, ko Te Ao
Na Te Ao, ko Te Aomarama
Na Te Aomarama, ko Te Aoturoa
Na Te Aoturoa, ko Te Koretewiwhia
Na Te Koretewiwhia, ko Te Koreterawea
Na Te Koreterawea, ko Te Koretetaumaua
Na Te Koretetaumaua, ko Te Korematua
Na Te Korematua, ko Te Maku

From the first glimmer of light
Emerged the long-standing light until light stood in all
 quarters
Encompassing all was a womb of emptiness
An intangible void intense in its search for procreation
Until it reached its ultimate boundaries and became a
parentless void with the potential for life

— The beginnings of a Kāi Tahu chant of creation, sung to children while in the womb[1]

Natural history of the Otago Peninsula

New Zealand's oldest rocks and life forms stem from Gondwana, the vast land that also gave birth to Australia, Africa, South America, India and Antarctica. Some 80 million years ago the continent geologists call Zealandia was one of the last fragments to break free, and it slowly tore open the Tasman Sea. By 65 million years ago Zealandia had become a vast eroded plain 10 times New Zealand's current size; when the seas began to rise, about 34 million years ago, they covered most – perhaps even all – of the land, in what is known as the 'Oligocene drowning'.[2] The seas only receded to about today's coastline some 13 million years ago.[3]

At that time the continental plate of the Otago region was being stretched and had begun to crack. Molten rock – magma – welled up and pooled in the chambers of the Dunedin volcano. Its eruptions occured in several series over three million years, centred on what is now Otago Harbour. The volcano's western rim is formed by the mountains Mopanui, Mihiwaka and Cargill, and its eastern edge is the Otago Peninsula.

The Otago Peninsula is a chain of basalt volcanic cones from which spread tongues of lava flows, now smashed into cliffs by the swells of the Pacific Ocean. Streams and the sea have together gouged softer ash-formed rock into valleys, bays and estuaries.[4] The Peninsula is therefore fairly rugged terrain, at best rolling and often steep; flat land is essentially confined to the marshes and sandy flats that enclose its estuaries. Its shores are varied and comprise cliffed rocky coasts, little bays, estuaries and long white-sand beaches, all surrounded by an especially rich ocean.[5]

The life that the Peninsula supports has changed with the climate as the world has cooled over the last 10 million years. This culminated in the Pleistocene glaciation of the past 2 million years, a series of glacial episodes in which ice sheets spread from the poles.[6] As they did so, sea levels fell to expose the continental shelf; winds blew the shelf's thick beds of sediments into clouds of dust that settled to form the dense yellow-brown clay of most Peninsula soils.[7] During the last major full-glacial episode, between 25,000 and 15,000 years ago, southern New Zealand became a barren, bare and eroding land. The Otago Peninsula and the Catlins coast, though, were refuges for forests, especially the tallest trees: red and silver beeches, and the podocarps – rimu, tōtara, kahikatea, mataī and miro.[8] Since the glaciers retreated, temperatures and sea levels have oscillated; the sea was at its highest about 6500 years ago. At this time the Peninsula became an island,[9] rejoining the mainland as quartz sand, carried north from the mouth of the Clutha River, was deposited to form the tombolo of sand upon which South Dunedin now sits. Māori traditions record that Ocean Beach was 'once a shoal' where 'the tides met'; and indeed storms still breached the sand dunes several times in the late nineteenth century.[10]

Overall the Otago Peninsula has experienced a cool, temperate maritime climate since the ice last receded.[11] New Zealand's weather comes from the west, driven by winds circling the pole. Air masses arrive after long ocean crossings that stabilise

CHAPTER 1: HE WHENUA HOU

John Buchanan, Otago Harbour. *This drawing of Otago Harbour delineates the peninsulas jutting out from either side of the harbour and the islands between them, the eroded remains of a ridge that once rose between Portobello and Port Chalmers.* c. 1859, wash on paper, 114 x 185mm. Hocken Collections, Uare Taoka o Hākena, University of Otago: A679 a9895

The Highcliff escarpment: the smashing force of the Pacific Ocean's swells has formed the sheer face of this 250-metre cliff. Photograph by Edgar Richard Williams. Alexander Turnbull Library: 1/4-097650-F

temperatures, so New Zealand does not experience the seasonal extremes found at the same latitudes in the northern hemisphere. However, air arriving here often bears a lot of moisture. The Southern Alps push this moist air higher, so that it cools, condenses and rains down upon the west of the South Island, which is much wetter than the east.[12] The climate is also wetter as one moves further south.

Even within a small area such as the Peninsula there are significant climatic differences. On the inner coast where it abuts Otago Harbour, the Peninsula is sheltered somewhat from the worst winter winds and exposed to the more benign northeast sea breezes of summer and autumn; there it is comparatively warm, sunny and sheltered 'with a micro-climate not bettered elsewhere on the Otago coast'.[13] The rugged outer coast is exposed to the full force of the Pacific Ocean and the frigid howling southwesterlies of winter and spring.[14]

Coastal Otago became wet and warm enough to support the establishment of a diverse conifer–broadleaved forest dominated principally by rimu.[15] In just a few thousand years before the arrival of human beings the Otago Peninsula became clothed in this forest, which would have extended inland as far as the eye could see.[16] The crowns of rimu, miro, mataī, tōtara and, in places, kahikatea, floated above the main canopy of many kinds of smaller trees, such as broadleaf, lemonwood, māhoe, kōhūhū, fuchsia, kōwhai, lancewood, narrow-leaved lacebark, lowland ribbonwood, patē, three-finger, ngaio, mānuka, kānuka and coprosma species.[17]

The mosaic of trees mirrored the broken topography of the Peninsula and the differentials in soils, water sources and exposure to strong, cold and salty southwesterly winds. Larger podocarps grew around the inner harbour hillsides and in gullies; drier soils on ridges supported broadleaf, tī, kānuka and other smaller trees and shrubs. Forest cover was probably broken only at the margins of the land and sea, where long, wind-swept beaches sheltering estuarine flats alternated with high-cliffed headlands. Sand dunes fronting the beaches were initially bound by the brilliantly orange pīkao (pīngao) which stabilised the sand, allowing the cover of flax, scrub and finally forest to take hold.

The Otago Peninsula was a very varied place, and so was the life that lived on and around it. Four species of moa roamed the Peninsula, ranging from the turkey-sized *Emeus crassus* to the massive, 250-kilogram *Dinornis robustus*.[18] Other big birds were here too: the giant rail, flightless goose and New Zealand swan.[19] The forest floor sheltered three kinds of kiwi (large spotted, little spotted and South Island brown), weka, the now-extinct quail and the remarkable parrot, the kākāpō – then among the most common birds. Other parrots such as kākā and parakeets flitted through forest alongside some 20 passerine (songbird) species. These included wrens, bellbirds, tūī, the South Island saddleback, kōkako and the now-extinct New Zealand crow. Besides the goose and swan, waterfowl included all four extant native ducks (paradise shelduck, blue, grey and brown teal) plus the extinct Finsch's duck. Falcons, hawks and

Few trees grow on the weather-beaten outer coast; those that do, like this macrocarpa on Cape Saunders, are tortured by strong, salt-laden winds. © Alan Dove

the massive Haast's eagle hunted by day; morepork and laughing owl preyed at night.[20] This range of species included most indigenous birds that still remain in southern New Zealand, and many others now extinct.

Seabirds were especially numerous. It is difficult to convey the scale of their abundance. People today may trumpet the Peninsula as a wildlife destination for tourists largely on the basis of the many seabirds there, but once shearwaters and petrels, albatrosses and mollymawks, shags and cormorants, penguins, prions, terns and gulls all flocked here in teeming breeding colonies of hundreds of thousands, if not millions of birds. Several species from each genus in this list bred here, and more visited – there were once five penguins, and at least that many each of petrels, shearwaters, shags and mollymawks or albatrosses.[21] Petrels and shearwaters had the biggest populations of all. New Zealand once supported numbers of these birds one or two orders of magnitude greater than those observed today: hundreds of millions, if not billions of birds.[22]

The best remaining illustrations of this lost world of seabirds are the subantarctic islands. The two main landmasses of The Snares, for example, which at a combined area of 330 hectares are mere specks in the surrounding sea, today support up to 2.75 million breeding pairs of petrels, fulmars and prions. This is a greater number of seabirds than exists today in the entirety of the British Isles.[23] Here is how the greatest New Zealand environmental historian, Herbert Guthrie-Smith, described his experience amid diving petrels at dusk on Big South Cape Island, near Rakiura (Stewart Island):

> *Now with the faster fall of Petrels from the sky – much as the congregation of an old-fashioned kirk follows the precentor's lead – bird after bird, pew after pew chimed in, louder and louder the commotion grew. From twos and threes, from dozens, from scores ... from tens of thousands of burrows, rose an intensifying babel of sound. By fullest dark, from that lonely island a roar ascended to the sky, an unceasing comminglement of sound, hour after hour sustained, seething, simmering, bubbling, the strangest, uncanniest, most unbirdlike epithalamium.*[24]

The Otago Peninsula too was once such a place. Seabirds' importance to its ecology is hard to overestimate.[25] By feeding from the ocean and defecating, shedding feathers or dying onshore, these birds linked the ecosystems of the sea to those of the land. They injected vast quantities of nutrients into soils around their colonies – on one estimate, as much as 30 per cent of the annual nutrient budget of all New Zealand – so sustaining plants, invertebrates and all manner of birds.[26]

Seabirds are attracted to the Peninsula because of the richness of the surrounding ocean. Three distinct water masses are found offshore from the Otago Peninsula; inshore, a shallow wedge of sediment-rich coastal water overrides the warm, salty Southland Current, which is met by cool subantarctic water above the slope dropping away from the continental shelf.[27]

The waters of the Southland Current derive from warm subtropical currents that eddy out from the tropical Pacific, are blown south and west into the Tasman Sea, strike Fiordland, and curl around to pour north along the South Island's east coast. This 'Southland Current' speeds up as it passes the Otago Peninsula, constricted into a narrowed band between land and the offshore subantarctic water mass above the continental slope that falls away from the shelf edge only 10 kilometres from the tip of Cape Saunders. Where the water masses meet is a major biogeographical boundary. Many species mass in this zone of increased productivity, making for a rich fishery.[28] The slope's food sources may be especially concentrated in and above the network of canyons that incise the continental slope off the Peninsula. As G.M. Thomson noted in 1912, fishermen 'find these deeps very excellent fishing-grounds'.[29] Recent research now confirms that a wide range of whale species frequent these canyons to feed from pelagic fish and squid, including deep-diving sperm whales, pilot whales, and the rarely seen Shepherd's beaked whale.[30]

Inshore, the northerly current's faster flow increases supply to significant populations of filter feeders on the sea floor. As the current spills around the Peninsula, an eddying backwash forms in the lee of Taiaroa Head, swirling around Blueskin Bay. The eddy gathers up vast swarms of drifting zooplankton such as the larvae of flounder, sprats and other inshore spawning fish, and crustaceans such as the white krill, *Nyctiphanes*, and the bright-red *Munida* or 'whale feed', the juvenile form of the squat lobster.[31]

CHAPTER 1: HE WHENUA HOU

A summer stranding of Munida *stains the shore at Portobello.* © Keith Probert

When the tide sweeps this rich soup into Otago Harbour, banks of plankton wash up to rot on shore, most commonly in summer.

These plankton are food for not just baleen whales but a great many fish besides, including pilchards, sprats and mackerels, which in turn attract predators like barracouta.[32] Dense shoals of feeding fish often form in a swarm of zooplankton; above all this broiling life myriad seabirds invariably feast. David Graham of the Portobello Fish Hatchery described such a sight off Cape Saunders in the early 1930s:

> *We observed these fish [pilchards] travelling north, a sight which can only be described in superlatives. As far as the eye could see these small fish were swimming in a northerly direction, accompanied by flocks of predatory birds, such as Mutton-birds, Mollymauks, Cape Pigeons, Gulls and others. There must have been hundreds and perhaps thousands of tonnes of this edible fish waiting for an enterprising fleet of fishing boats and canning factories ... They were so abundant that when the launch was moving it seemed as though we were speeding over a floor of silver.*[33]

This must suffice to suggest the plenitude that would have welcomed the first people to observe the Otago Peninsula: a complex and changing interface between land and sea, with many bays, white beaches and estuaries separated by cliffed headlands and backed by steep hills, all swathed in dense forest echoing with a constant chatter of bird song. Surrounding the land was a sea frothing with schooling fish, with a great nimbus of seabirds flying to and fro overhead and filling the sky.

A. *Limpets* (Cellana stigilis). *Harrington Point, Otago Harbour, 31 March 1978.* IV9238

B. *White whelk or ngaeo* (Haustrum lacunsum). *This was a type specimen originally used in 1878 by Frederick Hutton, leading figure among New Zealand's colonial scientists as (among other things) geologist, biologist, zoologist and curator of Otago Museum. Hutton was the first to attempt a comprehensive treatment of New Zealand mollusca.* IV7921

C. *Common toothed sea stars* (Diplodontias miliaris) *collected from 20–30 fathoms, outside 'the Heads', between Oamaru and Cape Saunders prior to 1899.* IV14194

D. *Spiny murex* (Poirieria zealandica). *Dredged off 'the Heads', May 1980.* IV9364

E. *Soft-skinned brittle star* (Ophiomyxa brevirima) *found at Broad Bay, Otago Harbour, 13 April 1975.* IV11101

F. *New Zealand sea cucumbers* (Australostichopus mollis). *Found east of Taiaroa Head in 30–150 fathoms, 1900.* IV9888

G. *Jumbo squid* (Dosidicus gigas). *Dunedin, unknown date.* IV27417

H. *Spiny dogfish* (Squalus acanthias). *Otago Harbour, 1896.* VT1793

I. *Southern pig fish* (Congiopodus leucopaecilus). *Otago Harbour?, Dunedin, unknown date.* VT1252

J. *Orca skull* (Orcinus orca). *This animal was killed by Ōtākou Māori some time before 1873, and obtained from them for the museum by Hon. Captain Fraser.* VT205

Photographs: Kane Fleury © Otago Museum

THE RICH MARINE LIFE around the Peninsula has been a focus of scientific study since the nineteenth century. As a result, Otago Museum holds a wide range of specimens from different habitats. These images suggest how their collection documents both the ecological significance of the diverse marine life found around the Peninsula and the history of science.

Seabirds may have provided another sort of link between far-flung ecosystems. It was perhaps the predictability and numbers of migratory seabirds on their annual southern migration that indicated the presence of land lying somewhere over the edge of the horizon to the first people to arrive here: the Polynesian colonisers of New Zealand.[34]

Southern Māori tradition associates the first exploration of the sea with a bird's feather, sent out to discover whether the sky descended till it lay upon the sea, or whether the sea continued beyond the horizon.[35] On its return, the feather's battered appearance indicated that there was a gap between the sea and sky, and so the first voyaging canoe was built, and named Huruhurumanu, for it was 'light as a bird's feather'.[36]

Shearwaters and petrels, especially the sooty shearwater – known to Māori as tītī and to Europeans as the muttonbird – might have been the most reliable guides to migration.[37] Fabulous numbers flew south in spring over East Polynesia, heading for New Zealand – and returned just as predictably each autumn. Millions of these birds make the same journey even today, so that throughout much of spring, when standing on a Peninsula headland, you 'may see this species flying south in an endless stream'.[38] It is possible to envisage Polynesian voyagers in large double canoes following these low-flying birds south over several weeks in spring,[39] when the chances of harnessing a prevailing northeasterly wind were greatest and the risk of encountering tropical cyclones smallest.[40] This would have been an incredible feat, shifting people, their plants and their animals over 3000 kilometres of open sea. Who were these people, and why might they have attempted this?

Origin and dispersal of the Polynesians

The islands of the Pacific were peopled in an extraordinary dispersal that spread east from Asia, moving out from Papua New Guinea and the rest of Near Oceania, and arriving by 2000 BC in Fiji, Tonga, Samoa and the other islands of Western Polynesia, where a common Polynesian culture developed.[41]

Polynesians then launched themselves across the Pacific to the archipelagos of Eastern Polynesia, including the Cook, Austral and Society islands. In perhaps as little as a few hundred years, they sprang forward again, this time towards New Zealand, whose islands were the last major landmasses on this planet to be discovered and settled by human beings.[42]

Polynesian voyagers migrated to find new landscapes that could be named, claimed, divided and inherited.[43] Intensive farmers and skilled fishermen, they kept pigs, dogs and fowl and cultivated 11 tree and eight root crops, including taro, breadfruit, yams, bananas and coconuts.[44] They took their stock and crops with them as they went, spreading this 'portmanteau biota' in an ecological whirlwind that profoundly changed the Pacific.[45]

Polynesian arrival meant decimation for most indigenous animals and plants and extinction for many. Seabird numbers, for example, outnumbered those of today by 100 or even 1000 to one, while more seabird species inhabited Oceania than are now found in all the world.[46] On island after island forests fell and erosion flowed as coastal fringes and valleys were fired to grow crops and establish tree plantations. These were deliberate modifications to make island ecosystems more inhabitable, since 'despite their famously salubrious climates, lack of disease-inducing organisms, and physical beauty, small oceanic islands are not naturally well suited to supporting large human populations'.[47]

The biggest leap of all in the Polynesian colonisation of the Pacific was the choice to sail south and west towards New Zealand across unknown seas, with the winds at the explorers' backs. Jeff Irwin has suggested that this reversed a strategy of exploring into the wind – to guarantee a short downwind voyage home to safety – that he considers had shaped Polynesian migration east across the Pacific; Atholl Anderson disagrees, arguing that Polynesians could not sail into the wind, and pointing out that all long-distance migration to the remote archipelagos of Hawai`i, Easter Island and New Zealand was downwind.[48] Certainly, reaching south towards New Zealand proved a voyage of no return.

New Zealand's environments, especially southern ones such as those of the Otago Peninsula, were very different from anything Polynesians had encountered previously. Here, they could grow none of the crops that had sustained them as they spread out across the Pacific. They had to subsist entirely on what they found. They changed not only their own ways of life, but also the new environment within which they were learning to survive. Through this process of continual adjustment, Polynesians became Māori.

OVERLEAF: *M. Elwes,* Otago Heads from Portobello, NZ *(detail).*

c. 1875, sepia wash on paper. Hocken Collections, Uare Taoka o Hākena, University of Otago: 7,654

Chapter 2: Arrival and Adaptation

E hine, e kimi ana i te huaki pouri
Kia puta mai koe ki te whariki tapu
I horahia ra e Kahukura, e Tu Te Rakiwhanoa.

Whakaroko mai ki ka taki
O te whenua e neneke ana
Te roa hoki i matata ka haehaetaka
Ka karaka atu to iwi ki a koe, e Hine
Whakamaurutia te mamae o roto nei

Ka whanau mai ki te tatau pounamu
I waihakatia e o tupuna
Hei turaka mohou i te ao tu nei.

E Hine, seek the opening of the womb
so that you may ascend onto the sacred mat
that has been lain by Kahukura and Tu Te Rakiwhanoa

Listen to the cries
of the shaking land
So long have the open wounds been gaping
Your people are calling to you
Soothe the pain we feel

You are born onto the tatau pounamu
shaped by your ancestors
as a standing place for you in the new world

— Waiata, Ngāi Tahu Deed of Settlement

How can we possibly know who first peopled Muaupoko, the Otago Peninsula? Māori offer us names without remains: stories without evidence, memories of what has mattered to identity and survival, passed from mind to mind. Archaeology unearths remains without names: evidence without stories, often what people discarded as rubbish.[1] Each kind of explanation has its own merits, but trying to reconcile them is a perilous exercise.[2] Moreover, many waves of settlement have washed over the Peninsula, and only fragments of its first people's tradition survive; archaeology, meanwhile, has had a painful learning curve on the Peninsula. Many sites were destroyed as they were dug up and little information was gained. Much must therefore remain uncertain.

Māori, however, have an emphatic explanation for their arrival on Muaupoko: they entwine their whakapapa, or ancestry, with its making. In Kāi Tahu cosmology, Aoraki, the first child, was born of Rakinui, the heavens, and Poharua Te Pō, 'the breath in the dark'. His parents later took other partners, and Aoraki and his siblings descended in anger on their father's new wife, Papatūānuku, the earth. They did not return: their waka was wrecked to become the South Island, and they its frozen high points, Aoraki/Mt Cook and other mountains.[3] Aoraki's mokopuna (grandson), Tū Te Rakiwhanoa, led the reshaping of the waka's wreckage to make land fit for habitation.[4] His kin Kahukura formed Muaupoko when he gouged out Otago Harbour and threw up the earth to form the hills on either side.[5]

In such ways, newly arrived Māori asserted their place in a vast and strange land. Their traditions are not history: they do not chronicle events so much as make them 'march to the beat of the timeless myth'.[6] The first waka made in Polynesian tradition are also those that bore the first settlers to New Zealand. In other words, 'Not only is there a tradition of migrations, there is also a migration of traditions' as Polynesians on the move rolled up their whakapapa and their histories and unfurled them on new lands.[7]

Newcomers to a territory also learnt the traditions of the existing inhabitants. Kahukura was never so prominent in the traditions of most Māori peoples but always remained important in the south, recorded as 'the great deity or tribal guardian' of Kāi Tahu, 'invoked in time of war'.[8] Kahukura first appears in the written record in Jules de Blosseville's brief 1823 account of southern Maori belief, where 'Kowkoula' 'governs the world during the day from the rising of the sun until its setting'.[9] Much later, Kāi Tahu kaumatua (elder) Hone Taare Tikao told early twentieth-century ethnographer Herries Beattie:

> *After the main beginning of the world and when people began to spread out, Kahukura became the main god of the migrators. He separated the good from the bad weather; he protected the frail canoes on the heaving waves; he sent fair winds to waft the canoes over favourable seas; he assisted them with rainbows, which showed the canoe-men their directions. The venturesome navigators regarded Kahukura with respect and gratitude, for his sign in the sky pointed the road into unknown seas.*[10]

The first possible person in southern Māori whakapapa to arrive in the south is Rākaihautū.[11] He came aboard the waka *Uruao*.[12] Rākaihautū lit the first fires of occupation in the south.[13] He explored the forests and found their foods, and used his kō or digging stick to hew out the western lakes and fiords.[14] His son Rakihouia sailed *Uruao* down the coast investigating the eastern sea and shore.[15] Tukete, the tohuka or priest aboard *Uruao*, cooked and ate weka, lifting the tapu from a land that 'had not been properly secured but was like the drifting flotsam on the sea'.[16] Names marked what mattered to them on their voyaging: for example, where eels might be caught, or birds' eggs collected.[17] According to Mataiha Tiremorehu, the first Kāi Tahu person to impart such information to Europeans, these people were named Te Rapuwai. Their 'numbers were great, even on the mountains'; they 'made the land open'.[18]

Later these people knew themselves as Waitaha, and their enduring presence in whakapapa anchors the mana of southern Māori; every major landmark in the south still bears a Waitaha name.[19] Waitaha whakapapa, or genealogy, all stems from Rākaihautū because he 'lit the fires' and named the land.[20] Naming places was critical to claiming them. As Atholl Anderson puts it, 'Traditional property business was thus a 'name-game' and so must be the analysis of its history.'[21] Rangatira named the land after aspects of themselves, and used these names in framing whakataukī or proverbs. In this way the land itself became a mnemonic that embodied ancestral memory.[22] For nothing was more important to Māori than knowing their whakapapa: the names of their ancestors.[23]

Whakapapa legitimated power, determined social status and shaped property rights. Edward Shortland, the first and among the most perceptive Europeans ever to analyse Kāi Tahu history, soon grasped that '[w]ith the New Zealander, genealogical questions are inseparable from investigations of claims to land'.[24] In 1843 when he heard recited the whakapapa of most southern Maori communities, he was 'so struck with the remarkable manner in which they coincided with each other, often when least expected, that I felt satisfied that dependence might be placed on their general accuracy'.[25]

Whakapapa are so consistent that they justify confidence in their chronologies. A comprehensive recent analysis of Māori waka whakapapa (genealogies traced from those arriving in the early canoes) has found that most are between 16 and 22 generations long, with peaks in frequency around 17 and 20 generations, and with few longer than 24 generations. By contrast, Herries Beattie found that whakapapa extending back to Rākaihautū were over 43 generations long, which Beattie himself considered was almost twice as long as 'the ordinary Maori genealogies'; this perhaps suggests that Rākaihautū was already an ancestral figure to the first arrivals.[26] If the consistency of the 'ordinary Maori geneaologies' is accepted as meaningful, and if each generation represents almost 30 years, then 'on the evidence of whakapapa', migration to New Zealand either began about the turn of the thirteenth century or in the fourteenth century.[27]

> ONE OF SOUTHERN Māori tradition's most famous waka is *Āraiteuru*, which was sent back to Hawaiki to collect kūmara. On return, *Āraiteuru* was blown down the coast before wrecking at Matakaea (Shag Point). The Otago coast itself is sometimes referred to as Te Tai o Ārai Te Uru,[28] and many place names celebrate the canoe's passage, including several on the Otago Peninsula. The most well known commemorates its kūmara kits, washed overboard to become Moeraki's boulders.[29] But a lack of associated whakapapa suggests to Kāi Tahu historian Te Maire Tau that this is a mythic explanation for the bringing of kūmara, rather than a true migration tradition.[30]
>
> The waka *Tākitimu* made the last migration under its captain Tamatea, but it was wrecked by enormous waves (now the ridge known as Maungātua) and became the Tākitimu mountains.[31] In the south this waka is associated with Kāti Māmoe, but it is prominent in many North Island and Pacific tribal histories too. Tradition states that after *Tākitimu*, the peoples of southern New Zealand had no more contact with their former Pacific homelands.[32]

Because it dwells on whakapapa and the deeds of named ancestors, Māori tradition gives us only hints about how early people lived in the south. For example, tradition, which often focuses on conflict, states that there was no significant early fighting.[33] This seems unsurprising, given how few people inhabited a large land with a lot of food available. Tradition also says that Waitaha encountered many moa.[34] Herries Beattie was told that moa had disappeared through a combination of floods, fires 'unwisely lighted' that 'got out of hand and burnt great areas of fern, bush, and scrub', and the fact that the newcomers from the north, Kāti Māmoe, 'instituted the practice of augmenting their food supply with the moa eggs'.[35]

Naming and claiming Muaupoko

Muaupoko, now widely used as the Māori name for the Otago Peninsula, means 'the front of the head'.[36] It is unclear when this name was bestowed, and it may even be spurious.[37] The sole historical record of it comes from Herries Beattie, who was informed in 1929 that it was the name for the Peninsula and the bays north of Otago Harbour, and that it was often twinned in pōwhiri with Murihiku, 'behind the tail', the name for the south of the island. Murihiku itself has been variously defined, but according to Matiaha (Matthias) Tiramorehu, it extended south from the Waitaki River and west to the Waiau River.[38] Regardless, the name Muaupoko has since become accepted by local Māori as the name for the Otago Peninsula. The name carries connotations of the senior and sacred, and it suggests the Peninsula's strategic place on the coast, guarding the throat of Otago Harbour and controlling access to the fisheries of the surrounding sea, and the swampy plains of the south.[39]

Of over one hundred recorded Māori place names on Muaupoko, a significant few were bestowed by the earliest peoples. Te Rapuwai is an urupā, or burial ground, on the western side of the heads, linked to the founder of that group; some Ōtākou people maintain whakapapa to Te Rapuwai.[40] Ōtākou itself is an old name brought from Hawaiki and given to the tidal current entering Otago Harbour. It came to name the 'oldest and largest' community in the south, the settlements backing onto the beaches tucked in the lee of Taiaroa Head.[41]

Oddly, however, the Otago Peninsula does not figure at all prominently in surviving settlement traditions. Herries Beattie was so indefatigable in cycling around the south to collect Māori tradition that they called him 'the man on a bike'; but he somewhat neglected the Peninsula because, from his home in Gore, it was 'out-of-the-way & hard to get at'; he was also told that 'all the old natives were dead'. He did visit in 1920, and 'though the result was small', concluded:

> *The Peninsula does not seem to be mentioned in traditions relative to the discovery of New Zealand by Maui; nor in the story of Rakaihautu's explorations (although Kaikarae (Kaikorai) is); nor in the legends that have gathered around Arai-te-uru – (although the Dunedin Town Belt is); nor in the few details we have of Waitaha or Katimamoe occupation (although we know it was occupied by first one and then the other of those tribes for centuries).*[42]

Beattie considered the Peninsula most attractive to Māori because of its proximity to fishing grounds and accessibility as a canoe building site. However, to confirm the early Māori occupation of the Peninsula, and to gain insight into its patterns and processes, we must understand what archaeologists and other scientists have discovered about the settlement of southern New Zealand.

Southern hunters: Polynesian arrival in southern New Zealand

When Polynesians arrived they explored New Zealand very quickly and thoroughly, exploding outwards in what archaeologist Atholl Anderson describes as 'an extremely rapid, undirected expansion – a star-burst pattern', in which they sought to stake claims to the best resources. Most settlers liked leeward southeastern New Zealand – the eastern South Island and the lower North Island.[43] It may have been colder, but it was also drier and the bush less dense than the West Coast rainforest to windward, while the sea was calmer with more and better-sheltered harbours. Many moa, seals and seabirds were there. Southern New Zealand was not, as used to be said, a hostile environment for a vulnerable and agriculturally dependent people:[44] it in fact provided 'the nearest thing possible to a leisured life in the central Pacific'.[45]

The settlers clustered beside coastal seal and seabird colonies, adjacent to rivers that offered inland access to moa. Groups of extended families formed village communities that were 'centres of extended foraging and interaction networks'.[46] The communities came together at their village homes in winter. This time together was critical. It maintained community cohesion, and it allowed links to other communities to be kept open. In winter the old and the young needed more care, equipment could be mended and made, and tradition maintained.[47] As the weather warmed, people scattered along the coast and inland up rivers to gather the foods and resources with which to survive the next winter.[48]

Excavations at Shag River Mouth, the best-preserved early village (some 60 kilometres north of present-day Dunedin), show that its few hundred inhabitants gorged on moa, seals and seabirds such as penguins, petrels and shags. They ate all of these animals out, exterminating all the big game in the vicinity. They burnt off the forest and scrub from the surrounding hills, which regrew as edible bracken.[49] This increased erosion and sedimentation, enlarged wetlands and attracted waterfowl.[50] Once the big game was gone the villagers ate more fish and shellfish, but within two generations of their arrival they had abandoned Shag River Mouth.[51]

Everything about the archaeological record suggests, therefore, that soon after arriving in New Zealand, some Polynesian settlers would have come to live on the Otago Peninsula.

The place of the Otago Peninsula in the pattern of early settlement

The Otago Peninsula was an important place early in Polynesian settlement. Indeed, of nine possible early villages that have been identified in Otago, like Shag River Mouth, three are on the Peninsula: at Harwood, Papanui Inlet and Little Papanui (see map opposite: numbers 18, 20 and 22 respectively).[52]

Several smaller sites in the vicinity are probably contemporaneous. All of these sites are by the sea, just behind beaches or on estuarine fringes near the mouth of the tidal flow, where they lie in the lee of headlands that give shelter from southerly winds. There is no apparent concern with defence in their siting, and no pā (fortified villages) are recorded from the time of early settlement.[53]

The sheer density of large and small sites confirms that the Peninsula was a focal point of regional settlement. But we know very little about the sites themselves. Some places the sea has washed away or conspired with the wind to bury beneath sand. Others have been overlain by European settlement. All too many were hunting grounds for Pākehā collecting Māori 'curios'. This was a popular pastime, and some curio hunters were passionately interested and very determined. There was also a ready market for Māori artefacts, like pounamu (greenstone) adzes and tiki, that was served by a number of more-or-less professional curio hunters.[54]

After 50 years of digging up the beaches surrounding Dunedin, J.W. Murdoch explained his motivations for this regrettable activity:

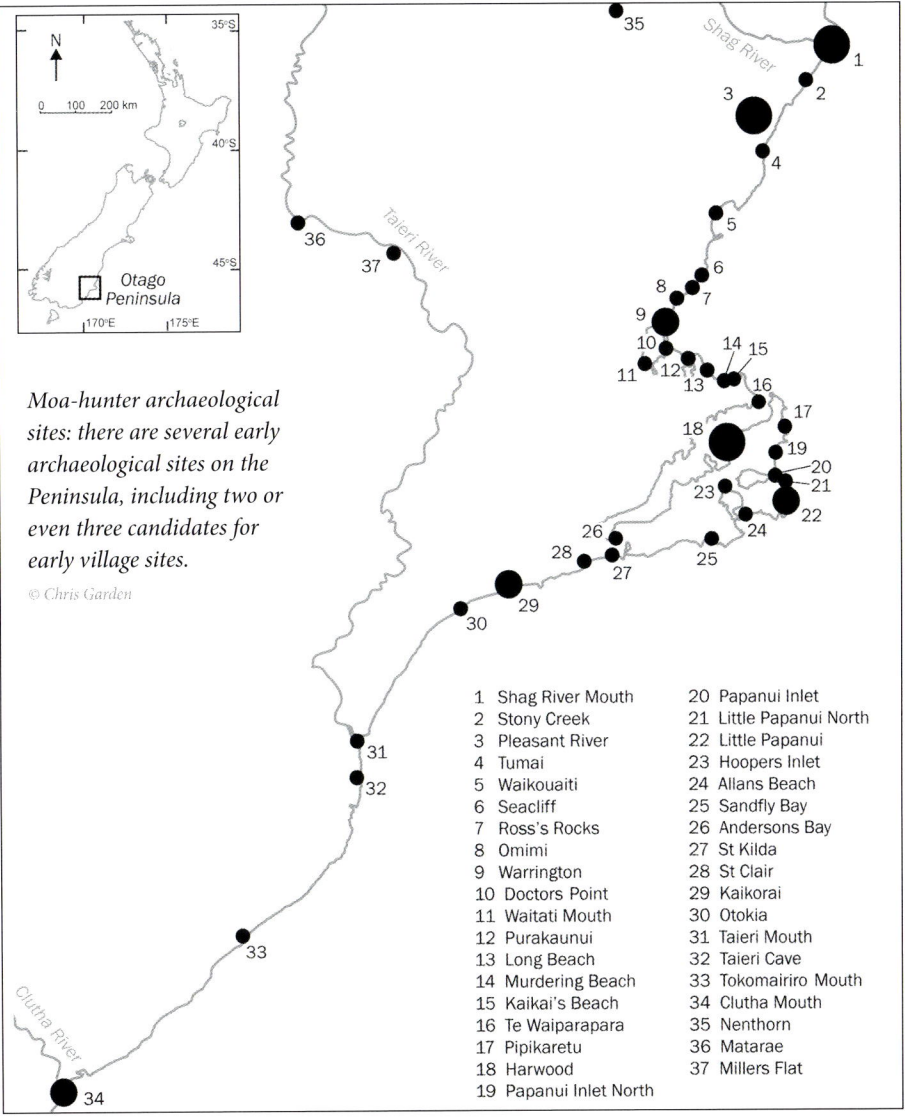

Moa-hunter archaeological sites: there are several early archaeological sites on the Peninsula, including two or even three candidates for early village sites.
© Chris Garden

1 Shag River Mouth
2 Stony Creek
3 Pleasant River
4 Tumai
5 Waikouaiti
6 Seacliff
7 Ross's Rocks
8 Omimi
9 Warrington
10 Doctors Point
11 Waitati Mouth
12 Purakaunui
13 Long Beach
14 Murdering Beach
15 Kaikai's Beach
16 Te Waiparapara
17 Pipikaretu
18 Harwood
19 Papanui Inlet North
20 Papanui Inlet
21 Little Papanui North
22 Little Papanui
23 Hoopers Inlet
24 Allans Beach
25 Sandfly Bay
26 Andersons Bay
27 St Kilda
28 St Clair
29 Kaikorai
30 Otokia
31 Taieri Mouth
32 Taieri Cave
33 Tokomairiro Mouth
34 Clutha Mouth
35 Nenthorn
36 Matarae
37 Millers Flat

VERY FEW of the Peninsula's many archaeological sites have been properly investigated.[55] But one recent investigation, by Shar Briden, obtained reliable radiocarbon dates from eroding midden at Sandfly Bay that indicate at least two distinct periods of occupation, the first probably in the fourteenth century and the second perhaps a hundred years later.[56] Fish, especially barracouta, and a variety of seabirds such as penguins, prions, petrels, shearwaters and shags dominated the midden. These species are most abundant at different times of the year, suggesting to Briden that the site was 'a multi-purpose camp occupied repeatedly at different times of the year'.[57]

> *It is safe to say that the Collector benefits both physically and mentally, he has frequently to tramp considerable distances on his hunting or fossicking expeditions, his eyesight is improved and rendered capable of spotting small articles amid a waste of sand, stones and shell heaps, his mind is exercised too, as he has to do a certain amount of gloating over a find, and to speculate and determine all sorts of things in connection therewith, whether the fish-hook just discovered is of human bone or otherwise, and so on.*[58]

Unfortunately, men such as Murdoch were interested only in the artefacts – their treasure – and paid scant attention to the 'waste' in which they were embedded. But to modern archaeology, context is everything: objects detached without detailed records of where they were found are almost meaningless. All the major occupation sites of the Otago Peninsula have been so badly disturbed or looted for artefacts that archaeologists have largely abandoned them as sources for systematic excavations.

What little we know of the 'Harwood' site on Akapātiki Flat suggests that it may well have been like Shag River Mouth, a village hub within a network of wider sites. But it is buried now under Harwood, the township named after Octavius Harwood who came to Ōtākou in the 1830s. Ever since arrival, Europeans have been finding evidence that people once lived on the flat, and inadvertent finds continue today. Harwood himself dug up hundreds of moa bones in making his garden. He was Oxford-educated and indulged a scientific curiosity; in his first letter from the Peninsula to his parents he wrote: 'I intend collection [of] all the curiosities on natural history possible, and turning them to some account.'[59] Over many years, he stuffed 'a fine collection of native birds'[60] and constructed many moa skeletons, selling some in 1872.[61]

His daughter inherited a shed 'full of boxes of moa bones all round the walls', and in 1922 presented Otago Museum with 10 more of her father's moa skeletons.[62] Ploughing the flat unearthed yet more moa, so that maps marked the area as 'strewn with moa bones'.[63]

Because of all this disturbance archaeologists have not bothered to excavate Harwood, and no house sites or graves have ever been found. But the late local historian and iconoclast Hardwicke Knight did some digging in the 1960s and described finding two cultural layers, the top containing moa, the bottom being almost entirely seal bone.[64] More digging in the 1970s found flakes of Nelson and Southland argillite.[65] Lucy Ann Harwood, Octavius's granddaughter, made the most spectacular find of all: when digging her garden she turned up three large and beautifully finished pounamu adzes.

> ON CURRENT ACCOUNTS there were nine different moa species. Four were found on the Peninsula and elsewhere in coastal Otago.[66] The most common was the relatively small 40–80-kilogram *Emeus crassus*, but the diverse hills, forests, shrublands and swamps also supported a few of the enormous 250-kilogram *Dinornis robustus*, as well as numbers of more middling moa like *Emeus curtus* and *Pachyornis elephantopus*.[67]

CHAPTER 2: ARRIVAL AND ADAPTATION

The records of Otago Museum describe Octavius Harwood's ten moa skeletons as 'said to be "individuals" but in poor state of preservation: & repaired with wood'. They were broken up by the museum, and the bones 'of any use' are now stored in 'like parts', such as these femurs and crania.

Photographs: Kane Fleury © Otago Museum, Otago Museum: AV3712–AV3714, AV3719–AV3723, AV4150–AV4153

THE ADZES Lucy Harwood unearthed are unusual, and were perhaps made while Māori master toolmakers were still learning about pounamu. They usually made adzes with these complex 'lugs' on the upper adze head by flaking basalt or argillite.[68] But pounamu has a felted crystalline structure that means it does not flake. Toolmakers found that pounamu can only be painstakingly ground down. Making large objects out of pounamu required great patience – and so most have simple and clean shapes. In other adzes of this form, the upper adze head is left rough to aid attaching the haft.[69] But these adzes also have a polish so fine that it may have been hard to actually use them. They are unmistakable emblems of wealth and power.

CHAPTER 2: ARRIVAL AND ADAPTATION

The Harwood adzes (detail opposite).

Photographs: Fiona Glasgow © Otago Museum,
Otago Museum: D49.480, D49.481, D49.482

The presence of so many moa tells us that Harwood must have been one of the first places used on the Peninsula. Moa would not have lasted at all long there. Paleoecologist Richard Holdaway suggests the Peninsula may have had a population of half a dozen breeding pairs of the largest moa, *Dinornis robustus*, for example, which would have represented a few months' food for a family.[70] Other roughly contemporaneous sites where moa were plausibly eaten include those at Papanui and Hoopers inlets, Andersons Bay, Pipikaretu Beach, Sandfly Bay and perhaps Little Papanui.[71]

The Peninsula's shores supported especially large breeding colonies of New Zealand fur seals. Sea lions hauled out there too.[72] Seals were probably the Peninsula's prime attraction: they were much more important food sources to Polynesian settlers than even moa, all in all making up over half the meat butchered in early Otago sites.[73] They were unrivalled sources of fat and energy, and second only to fish as a source of protein.[74] Historian James Belich was not really joking in suggesting that the title 'seal hunter' is more appropriate than 'moa hunter' for the first inhabitants.[75]

Seals' predictability made them easy prey. Seals congregate in breeding colonies to which they return each summer, feeding at night and spending their days lazing on rocky shores. From late October the bulls come ashore to prepare their breeding grounds and are followed soon after by the females, whose pups are mostly born in December. Mating is finished in January. Mothers cannot leave the breeding range because their pups suckle for up to 10 months before spreading out to ring the rookeries.[76] Tradition suggests that Māori focused on killing these congregations of young seals, which are reputedly more palatable than their parents.[77] Early European sealers certainly thought so: Benjamin Turner recorded that seals were 'very good eating, particularly the young ones cut out of the parents' bellies'.[78]

Fur seal mother with her pup. © *Marchell Linzey*

CHAPTER 2: ARRIVAL AND ADAPTATION

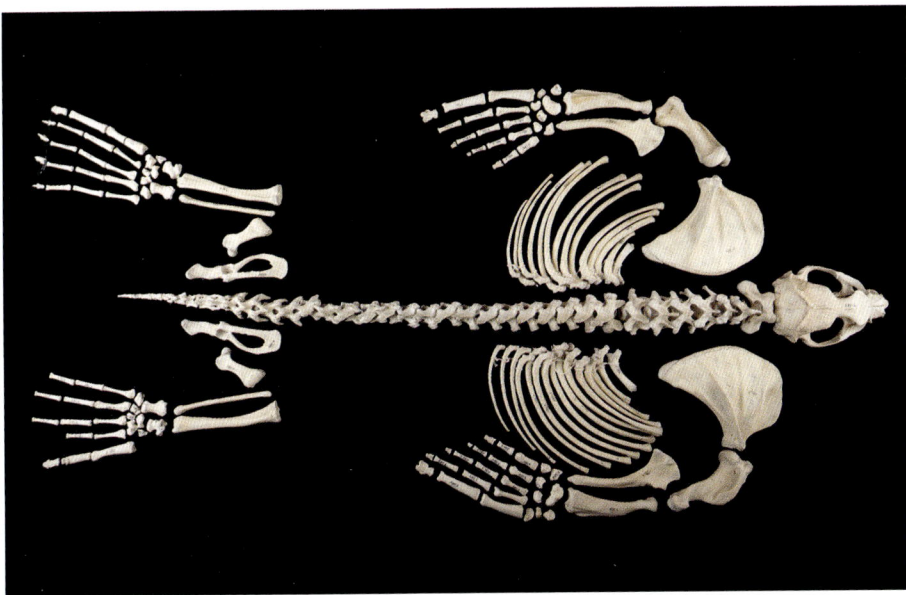

Skeleton of male fur seal remains found on the Otago Peninsula. Photograph: Kane Fleury © Otago Museum, Otago Museum: VT077

The Polynesian settlers in the south didn't just eat meat – though they came quite close. People can survive in perfect health on animal fat and protein. The fat is crucial, being much denser with energy than carbohydrates; humans will develop serious health issues when more than a third of their diet is made up of protein.[79] The Māori desire for fat was intense. Surgeon William Anderson, with Captain Cook at Queen Charlotte Sound in 1777, recorded that:

> *They also us'd to devour with the greatest eagerness large quantitys of stinking train [whale] oil and blubber of seals which we were melting at the tent and had kept near two months; and on board the Ships they were not content with emptying the lamps but absolutely swallow'd the cotton and stinking wick with equal voracity.*[80]

Plant foods were important too, and Māori developed many acidic plant accompaniments to help digest their fatty food.[81] Just three plants in the south provided carbohydrate: mamaku, a tree fern; aruhe or fern root; and tī or cabbage tree. Of these, mamaku cannot tolerate frost and was unimportant on the Peninsula;[82] aruhe was probably important everywhere, but its use is largely invisible to archaeology (save for examples of what are deemed to be fern-root beaters); while tī was especially important, probably from the start, since similar species of tī are cooked throughout Polynesia.[83] The roots and stems of tī were the principal source of carbohydrate, and also provided sweetness to flavour bitter foods or to make tasty treats, while tī shoots were an important green vegetable.[84]

PAPANUI INLET: A MAJOR MOA-HUNTER SITE?

It has long been suspected a 'major moa-hunter site' once existed near the mouth of Papanui Inlet, as indicated by material eroding from its edge.[85] While Harwood remains the only place on the Peninsula where moa remains have been found in numbers, unequivocally killed, butchered and eaten by people, *Dinornis giganteus* bones (among those of other moa), have been also found on the margins of Papanui Inlet. This is significant because these large rare birds would surely have been killed almost immediately after human arrival on the Peninsula.[86] Indeed, by 2001, Jill Hamel felt able to speculate the site had 'similar characteristics' to those of the large early villages. Since then many more artefacts have been brought to light, perhaps 1000 over the past decade. These objects have been rescued rather than systematically excavated, though archaeologist Shar Briden, who has worked closely with local Kāi Tahu, now has authority to begin to dig. This work will help answer the many questions about when people were there and what they were doing: was this another large early village site? Was it a later occupation? Were people living there year round, or visiting seasonally?

We can already be sure Papanui Inlet was a significant wood-working site, for many of the artefacts found so far are pieces of adzed wood, or carvers' wood-working tools. We do not yet know the full extent of what was being made. However, a range of remains are associated with waka, including a rare outrigger float, hull planks and paddle blade fragments, all mostly tōtara. The most spectacular taonga to be unearthed at the site is a large and wonderfully intact fishing canoe, over six metres long. The waka and other wooden artefacts have been preserved as a result of being embedded in and beneath a layer of peat. Even so, many are significantly degraded, and have survived only because water has plumped the wood's cells, whose walls would otherwise have long ago collapsed. To prevent it from drying out, the waka was covered in wet sacks when excavated and now remains in solution, while being conserved in a purpose-built conservation facility at Ōtākou Marae established by Dilys Johns, the University of Auckland and the Ministry for Culture and Heritage. Without immediate on-site expertise the waka and associated artefacts would have suffered irreversible damage.[87]

Three radiocarbon dates have been obtained from flax cordage found both in and outside the waka hull. These are very reliable dates, taken from short-lived materials with little inbuilt age found in close association with each other. The date range on flax fibre found underneath the hull was 1442–1464; that inside the hull was 1450–1488. This squarely dates the last use of the waka – which itself may be older – to the middle of the fifteenth century. It therefore predates the arrival of Kāti Māmoe, and represents a fairly early Waitaha occupation.[88]

Many of the stone tools recovered at Papanui are made from local stone sources, including many trachyte, basalt and 'Puddingstone' adzes. However, recently a pounamu adze has also been found, as have obsidian flakes from North Island sources. The early people working at Papanui must have moved a long way themselves, or maintained trading connections across significant distances.

It is interesting, in light of the ongoing discoveries at Papanui, to reflect on Herries Beattie's conclusion that the Peninsula's strongest assets, to Māori, were 'proximity to good fishing grounds, and accessibility as a canoe building centre'.[89]

CLOCKWISE FROM TOP LEFT: *This cluster of wooden artefacts, found in 2007, included waka planks and other hull fragments as well as pieces of paddle blade.* © Shar Briden. *The waka upside down and briefly out of water, in preparation for 3D scanning; The outside surface of a side strake, showing the holes drilled to lash it to the hull, making the waka deeper.* © Dilys Johns. *Adze marks are clearly visible along this part of the waka's hull.* © Shar Briden.

Umu tī above Akapātiki Flat. The dimples of numerous umu tī dot these slopes on either side of a creek from which water was likely drawn to generate steam in the earth ovens.
© Kevin Jones and Department of Conservation

On the slopes above Akapātiki Flat are the remains of many umu tī, enormous earth ovens used to cook the stems and roots of tī into a sweet starchy food called kāuru.[90] Umu tī were usually dug over 1.5 metres deep with a base up to 2 metres across. They were filled with hundreds and sometimes thousands of hot rocks on which water was poured to make the steam that cooked the kāuru.[91] Nearby creeks seem to have been dammed to pool the water needed to sustain high temperatures for many hours.[92] The intense heat crystallised the fructose sugars in which tī is richer than either sugar beet or sugar cane.[93] Cooking kāuru was obviously hard work and needed large-scale community effort and organisation, but it was worth it.[94] A kilo of kāuru provided a person with about 3000 calories – enough fuel for a day.[95] Tī groves, however, could only be harvested every four to five years, and kāuru did not keep well. Kāuru harvests were therefore occasions for inter-community feasting and exchange, known as kaihaukai.[96]

The communal effort required to operate umu tī, and their early dating elsewhere to the thirteenth and fourteenth centuries, suggests a correlation with 'the presence of organised villages'.[97] This density of umu tī at Akapātiki Flat is therefore a strong indication that Harwood might have been like Shag River Mouth: a large early village, the anchor point for a community that also maintained a network of campsites on and around the Peninsula.

Short and sometimes sharp: The impacts of early settlement

In little more than a hundred years, an ecological instant, Polynesian settlers pursued many animals to extinction and burnt off around half of New Zealand's forest cover, including most of the forest of the eastern South Island.[98] All the big birds – everything over 10 kilograms – vanished: all nine moa species were extinct within around 150 years, and with them went the massive Haast's eagle. A hawk, a swan, a goose, a pelican, a rail and a coot were exterminated too.[99]

The other large game, marine mammals such as sea lions and fur seals, were also wiped out around most of New Zealand, and in this case human hunting was the only cause. Fur seals lingered longer than moa, however, and still bred on the Peninsula's outer coasts until at least the end of the seventeenth century.[100]

At the other end of the ecological scale, exploding populations of kiore, the Polynesian rat, swept the forest floor in a 'grey tide that turned everthing edible into rat protein'.[101] Kiore exterminated small ground-nesting birds – smaller petrels, wrens and snipe – along with several lizards and frogs and an unknown number of large invertebrates, such as flightless forest-floor beetles.[102] Forests changed significantly, too, as kiore favoured eating the seeds of some species over others.[103] Kiore are much less efficient predators than some later mammal arrivals, but they got here first and killed off more species than any animal – excepting humans.[104]

In all, about 130 bird species bred on mainland New Zealand (North, South and Stewart islands and their inshore islands) prior to Polynesian arrival. About 40 were seabirds; the rest were the land and freshwater birds, many of which were endemic (unique to New Zealand) and often highly unusual. Nineteen of the 116 species to be found in the South Island existed only there. Within about 200 years, human and animal hunting, together with habitat loss, drove at least 26 of the South Island's birds to extinction. Many more bird species survived only in small relic populations.[105]

Why Polynesian settlers burnt most of the eastern South Island podocarp forests is a matter of debate. They may have lost control of some fires, as tradition suggests occurred in Canterbury, Central Otago and Southland.[106] It is said, for example, that one very dry summer a chief named Ue lit a fire that was fanned by a southwesterly gale into an uncontrollable and disastrous inferno that burned much of Murihiku and killed many people.[107] But there is no tradition of fires on the Peninsula, accidental or otherwise; and recent research suggests that lasting deforestation required multiple re-burns.[108]

Polynesian settlers had several possible reasons for using fire as a tool to burn forest. Forests throughout the Pacific were burnt to provide a range of 'edge habitats' and so increase resources.[109] South Island podocarp forests provided better habitats for birds than beech forests – but they were still not particularly rich in harvestable resources.[110] Burning probably increased food supplies and eased travel by providing a mosaic of bracken, tī trees, shrubs and remnant forest.[111] Māori probably had good reasons to burn many small areas of the Peninsula, such as to increase visibility around their villages and camps, or from headland lookouts, but it is unlikely that they burnt it wholesale.[112] If the forest was burnt, then it had regrown by the early nineteenth century, something that seldom occurred elsewhere.[113] All early European observations confirm substantial forest cover on the Peninsula.[114] And, as ecologist-turned-historian Geoff Park has stressed, Māori often retained such coastal forest even where cultivation was a viable alternative, because it 'could hardly be improved upon'.[115] The Peninsula's vegetation was already diverse, including tī, flax and ferns alongside fruiting podocarps, kōwhai and fuchsia, which supported a birdlife perhaps unparalleled on Otago's east coast.

It seems natural to ask how so few people, with limited means, could change everything so fast? In fact, this is the wrong question. Similar things have happened whenever people have encountered new environments. As Atholl Anderson emphasises, it 'is typical of colonisation everywhere and at all times' for migrants to cream off the richest resources, 'with pitiless energetic efficiency', in order to expand as fast as they can.[116] In this case, efficient human predators encountered a narrow band of large, naïve prey; so it is unsurprising that 'the first swing of the predator–prey pendulum pulled the clock off the wall'.[117]

When they arrived in these new and strange lands, Polynesian settlers had no option but to focus on obvious sources of energy such as moa and seals. They had only ever experienced a tropical climate with a relatively continuous supply of energy. By contrast, the Otago coast's temperate climate is seasonal, with pronounced periodic cycles of energy input shaped by the rise and fall of the sun and the waxing and waning of the moon. All species adapt their life patterns to harness these energy flows, and most species are only briefly abundant and often in quite particular places. Polynesians had to learn to match their lives to the rhythms of these flushes of seasonal abundance. In doing so, they became Māori.

The Polynesian settlement of the Otago Peninsula

If there is little substantive disagreement between the portrayals of Polynesian settlement provided by tradition and archaeology, this is largely because they seldom answer the same questions: Māori remembered what remained personally, politically and culturally significant in the present, while archaeology reconstructs past structures of economy and subsistence. Where they do examine the same issues – such as questions over the timing of arrival, where early settlement occurred, or whether return voyages ever took place – Māori tradition provides narrative recollections of specific events, whereas archaeology constructs models of what seems to best suit available evidence.

There is common ground, however. At least some of the early settlers, if perhaps not the very first, came as far south as Otago Peninsula. This is a tenet of both Māori tradition and archaeology. Despite an understandable preference for earlier dates among Māori, and a recent preference among archaeologists for later dates, an arrival date in the thirteenth century does little violence to either tradition or archaeological data.[118]

The model for early settlement derived from Shag River Mouth – that of a central village surrounded by outlying camps specialised to harvest resources from particular environments – fits the little we know about the settlement of the Peninsula fairly well: there are at least no points of outright contradiction, if only patchy confirmation.

The Otago Peninsula was a key focus point for settlers seeking concentrations of large prey: seals, above all, but also moa and other large waterfowl and seabirds. By the fifteenth century settlement had killed off all big birds, severely reduced the range and abundance of shore-based sea mammals, and diminished the vast numbers of smaller colonial seabirds. Smaller birds were also eaten by kiore, which in turn affected populations of invertebrates. The cascading ecological effects of removing this variety of fauna are poorly understood, though of course they are still being felt today.

Arguments from analogy must be treated cautiously, and differences acknowledged. In particular, as noted earlier, unlike most of the rest of the eastern South Island, there is no evidence that substantial forest cover was ever burnt on the Otago Peninsula. Seals continued breeding there for longer than in other inhabited areas, too. Their survival so late around the Peninsula clearly reflects in part the inaccessibility to people of the rough outer coasts and islets, and their especial appeal to seals. Like the survival of the population of newly arrived yellow-eyed penguins, however, it may require additional explanation.[119] After all, while Shag River Mouth became a place where people might halt a day or two at most en route to more productive areas, Māori continued to live on and around Akapātiki Flat. In fact, 'it is possible that Harwood is one of the most continuously occupied areas in New Zealand'.[120] And yet the forests – and, for some centuries, the seals – did not disappear. It seems, therefore, that the people on the Peninsula may have begun to adapt their behaviour, as part of a 'historic paradigmatic shift' in their culture.[121] Such ongoing adjustment to their altering environment was a key part of the process by which Polynesians became southern Māori.

Moa femurs.

Photograph: Kane Fleury © Otago Museum,
Otago Museum: AV4150–AV4153

CHAPTER 3: CONTINUITY AND CHANGE: MAKING SOUTHERN MĀORI

Ko Pukekura te mauka
Ko te Tai o Ōtākou te wai
Ko Muaupoko te whenua
Konei ka wahi tāoka o kā hapū no Ōtākou
Ko Kai Te Pahi, Kāti Moki, Kāti Taoka,
Kai Te Ruahikihiki hoki ka hapū

Pukekura is the mountain,
The tide of Ōtākou is the water
Muaupoko is the land,
These are the treasured places of Ōtākou,
Who belong to the hapū of Kai Te Pahi, Kāti Moki,
  Kāti Taoka
and Kai Te Ruahikihiki.[1]

By about the early fifteenth century, once moa and most of the other big game had gone from the south, Polynesian settlers had to devise 'a whole new strategy of life'.[2] They had to adapt their economy, their politics and their social organisation.[3] In the north settlers solved the problems posed by the disappearance of large game by increasing horticultural production, which drove social cohesion and underpinned the emergence of fortified pā as a means to protect stored food and defend cropland.[4] In the south the climate precluded this response; indeed, it got much colder, wetter and windier in the fifteenth and sixteenth centuries during the southern hemisphere's equivalent of the Little Ice Age.[5] How did people in the south cope?

Life on the move: Adapting to a depleted world

Not much is known for sure about the transition in Otago, between early Polynesian settlement and the traditional era of the Māori who encountered Europeans. But current archaeological orthodoxy has it that, for a long time – perhaps from the fifteenth through to the seventeenth centuries – Māori in the south could no longer maintain their large villages and had to live largely on the move.[6] Their communities fragmented; they ranged more widely in smaller, more mobile groups, spending most of the year in a succession of brief stays at seasonal camps. Population growth slowed – numbers may have even declined – while more marginal areas such as around Foveaux Strait may have been abandoned.[7]

Māori did eventually succeed in re-establishing village life. They did so by calibrating their lives to those of other species, by learning to harvest the short seasonal flushes of abundance. The sea became more important, too, and especially so while Māori learnt to live within the ecological constraints caused by the collapse of large game. Specialised fishing camps developed, such as that (in the fifteenth century) just north of the Peninsula at Purakaunui, where red cod were sought.[8] Nearby at Long Beach barracouta dominate the midden.[9] A similar pattern is evident in the small assemblage analysed from Taiaroa Head.[10]

Archaeologist Ian Smith calculates that Māori in Otago gained about three quarters of their energy from animals. Once moa and seals were largely gone, fish provided over half that, 10 times more than before.[11] Fish also became the principal source of protein.[12] Indeed, the overwhelming importance to Otago Māori of marine resources generally is shown in the fact that from the mid-sixteenth century onwards well over 80 per cent of their animal food came from fish, shellfish, marine and coastal birds, and the last seals.[13]

Māori fishermen in Otago always concentrated on just a few species. Barracouta consistently made up about half the total catch biomass; hāpuku, red cod and ling made up the bulk of the rest.[14] Two other trends are worth noting. First, hāpuku became much more important over time. Second, by about the middle of the eighteenth century, Māori in Otago caught these four species almost exclusively: together, Smith calculates, they constituted 99 per cent of harvested fish biomass.[15]

Māori now went to many if not most places with a single purpose in mind. At a smaller Papanui Beach site, for example, only marine resources are found – shellfish, fish, fur seals and some 20 seabird species, including five penguins, five petrels or shearwater, three albatross or mollymawk species, three shags, two ducks and a gull.[16] Albatross and mollymawk bone was particularly abundant, and is common in many Peninsula sites. These are large, meaty birds and their bones were the raw material for a range of tools, ornaments and musical instruments. No bush birds at all are recorded from this site, though the beach was then backed by forest.[17]

When southern Māori eventually succeeded in re-establishing permanent villages, these were the lynchpins of an entirely different way of life. As we have seen, Polynesian settlers based their villages besides big concentrations of moa and seal, ate them all, and then shifted the village to another colony. One of the processes through which Polynesians became Māori was by learning to maintain villages through gathering dispersed and seasonal flushes of finer-grained resources, such as small birds, rats, fish, eels and shellfish.[18] Māori developed new ways to preserve those foods, and maintained resource exchanges across extensive kin networks. Eventually, this ensured that food could be available when and where it was required, especially over the critical winter months when availability was lowest and the maintenance of energy requirements most difficult.

EARLY ARCHAIC MOA HUNTERS AND LATE CLASSIC MĀORI

Archaeological sites have tended to be crudely defined as belonging to either early 'Archaic' moa hunters or late 'Classic' Māori, with the period in between being almost invisible. This is in large part because most sites were dug up when there were no sophisticated dating techniques, and archaeologists tried to discern change over time through artefact analysis. It was thought that Archaic moa-hunter sites were defined by moa bone and artefacts analogous to Eastern Polynesian forms, such as a preponderance of large one-piece fish-hooks, while Classic Māori sites were distinguished by the lack of moa, two-piece fish-hooks and pounamu tools or ornaments.[19] Archaeologists have refined their analysis of material culture considerably, recognising the interplay of an object's intended use, its form and its raw material. But this means that artefacts are less reliable chronological markers, since we are often unsure how long 'early' or 'late' tools or ornaments were used, given the many reasons why people in different times and places might make very similar objects.[20] All in all, the binary division has not helped much to understand change in material culture, let alone in Māori society more broadly, precisely because it hinges on an unidentified and undescribed transition in which all the important changes took place. Nevertheless, it continues to be widely used.[21]

As Jill Hamel wryly says, 'living in nothing but constantly shifting campsites was apparently not seen as desirable'.[22] By re-establishing village life Māori gained 'a repository for both visible and invisible assets including stored food and equipment, elderly relatives, and large capital items such as canoes'.[23] Villages also enabled the living to guard the dead, and to protect places and objects of especial significance.[24] This explains the 'enormous determination' exerted 'to develop the social organisation and the pattern of seasonal gathering, preservation, and storage needed to support village life once again'.[25]

However, there are signs that this archaeological analysis depicts the difference and distance between early and late villages too starkly. The evidence that villages could not be maintained for some two centuries is largely negative: no village settlements in the south analogous to Shag River Mouth have been dated to the sixteenth or seventeenth centuries.[26] The period may have been much shorter – Jill Hamel has suggested a gap of 'perhaps one or two hundred years' in Otago, during which it is unlikely that there were 'any major disruptions of traditional society, given the strong continuities in subsistence strategies and artefact manufacture'.[27] And as Atholl Anderson has more recently observed, even then it is probable that each community managed to keep 'a preferred base camp or hamlet'.[28]

'Unearthing Māori Idols': Little Papanui and the history of archaeology

'Little Papanui', a place famous among archaeologists, is sited on Papanui Beach, a white-sand strand on the outer edge of Cape Saunders. The long history of excavations and interpretations of Little Papanui exemplifies the problems that the history of archaeology has left us as we try to understand change in the southern Māori world.

For over a century between the 1870s and the 1970s, Little Papanui attracted dozens of curio hunters and early archaeologists. By far the most diligent was David Teviotdale. Little Papanui has also played a significant role in reconstructions of the Māori past by a succession of key scholars in the history of archaeology in New Zealand, including Henry Skinner, Jack Golson, David Simmons, Atholl Anderson and Jill Hamel.[29] All of these scholars, however, relied on Teviotdale's records.

Teviotdale described evidence of occupation spread throughout sandbanks on either side of a small stream, and detected three different cultural layers. On this basis Henry Skinner, who did at least visit the site with Teviotdale, in 1960 concluded that Little Papanui was a periodically occupied 'important summer fishing camp'.[30] But David Simmons considered that Teviotdale's description of three layers at Little Papanui corresponded to his 'early', 'middle' and 'late' periods in prehistory, and assigned Archaic and Classic artefacts to lower and upper layers respectively.[31] This analysis influenced subsequent writers, so that in 1982 Anderson tentatively suggested that the site's lowest

'Charlie, yours truly & Dick several simple hooks and composite hooks were found here'. So David Teviotdale labelled this photograph of himself at work at Little Papanui, where he shovelled some thousand cubic metres of sand and even redirected a stream to sluice away the dunes in search of artefacts. Hocken Collections, Uare Taoka o Hākena, University of Otago: MS-0500/010: S17-528a

layers were remnants of an Archaic 'multi-function base camp', as he then saw Shag River Mouth. In 1996 he interpreted its lowest layers as a possible early transient village, as Shag River Mouth was now seen.[32] The middle layers, however, were perhaps a rare example of a small permanent base being maintained in the 'middle period'.[33] In 2004 Jill Hamel followed Simmons' analysis too, and treated Little Papanui as an important example of a site providing evidence of change.[34] She followed Anderson in suggesting that artefacts and faunal remains in lower layers were evidence of an early village, but considered that artefacts in its upper layers suggested the 'new sort of Classic village'.[35]

James Samson's 2003 PhD thesis had already argued, however, that all such analyses overlook the implications of Teviotdale's practice of selective curio recovery, his poor 'excavation' methods and his 'lack of meaningful provenance recording'.[36] Samson allows that the presence of some moa meant an early occupation, but concludes that otherwise we can say little: we do not know the duration of occupation at Little Papanui, and we know nothing of the nature of the occupation – for example, whether it was continuous or intermittent.[37] He also argues strongly that none of the artefacts are reliable chronological markers, and indeed that the collection does not provide any real evidence for significant changes in artefacts over time.[38] So he suggests that we should not seek answers to such questions, but rather look to see how the collection

DAVID TEVIOTDALE (1870–1958) was born to an Irish mother and a Scots father who followed the gold rush from Australia to Otago and raised him on the family farm at Hyde. After abandoning his own attempt to be a farmer, Teviotdale became a bookseller in Palmerston, and this gave him time to develop what became his lifelong passion: hunting for Māori curios. He began by spending his Sundays at Shag River Mouth. After he moved to Dunedin in 1924, he devoted himself above all to scouring the Otago Peninsula.

By this time the Peninsula was widely known for provoking 'visions of treasure-trove in the way of relics of the days of the Maori, curios and remains which have long been hidden …'[39] Teviotdale took the first of more than two hundred trips to Little Papanui on Boxing Day 1926. He was encouraged by Henry Skinner, curator at Otago University Museum, and was soon employed as his assistant. Later he became director of Southland Museum, but retained a relationship with Otago.

Under Skinner's tutelage, Teviotdale devoted himself to searching beaches all around the South Island, spending up to three days every week curio-hunting either in company with friends and fellow hunters or on his own. He became much more systematic in his methods, writing up his excursions and listing his finds; he also joined the Polynesian Society, and published 17 articles in its journal.

Teviotdale had begun with a gardening fork, graduated to a shovel, but at Little Papanui went so far as to use the goldmining techniques first learnt working alongside his father, and redirected the nearby stream into the sandbanks to sluice curios out of them. In this way he moved over 1000 cubic metres of sand and unearthed many thousands of artefacts.[40] In adopting these methods, Teviotdale was perhaps

CHAPTER 3: CONTINUITY AND CHANGE

influenced by Alfred Reynolds who, writing as 'Aparata Renata', described being the first curio hunter to use a spade to shift sand in singleminded pursuit of 'unearthing Maori idols'. Certainly Teviotdale, like Reynolds, had the dedication of a 'true fossicker' who 'can hardly spare time for his regular meals'.[41] None of these curio hunters considered it at all wrong to seek out and unearth Māori graves, loot the grave goods and display the bones of the dead – though they were well aware of the 'anger and vexation' this caused to Māori.[42]

Over time Otago Museum acquired the collected artefacts of Teviotdale and many other curio-hunters drawn to Little Papanui, and now holds an enormous 'collection of collections' from the site, comprising some 6282 pieces.[43] No one has systematically excavated the site since Teviotdale worked it, so subsequent analysis relies heavily on his diaries and records.

Chevronned whale ivory amulet (detail opposite): this finely detailed amulet, considered an early form, is among the more than 6000 objects unearthed at Little Papanui, mainly by Teviotdale, and now held in Otago Museum.

Photographs: Fiona Glasgow © Otago Museum, Otago Museum: D29-1

and associated records as a whole can aid evaluation of the way people lived at Little Papanui.

Teviotdale found several stone-lined fireplaces at the site; these, along with the many diverse artefacts he recovered, suggest permanent occupation at some point.[44] Perhaps the best clue as to why people lived there comes from the collection's many adzes, chisels and gouges.[45] These wood-working tools suggest that this was a place where canoes were made. According to Beattie's informants, the Peninsula was a centre for canoe-building, usually using local tōtara, a timber that is hard, durable and slow to rot in water.[46]

The gently shelving beach at Little Papanui would also have provided one of the best places to bring a canoe ashore on the Peninsula's outer coast, and there is a noticeably large quantity of fishing gear in Teviotdale's collection, including well over 1000 fish-hooks, lures and gorges.[47] This surely reflects the ongoing importance of the rich fishing grounds off Cape Saunders, known to Māori as Poatiri, 'the fish-hook'.

Teviotdale's diaries indicate that Māori focused on the immediate marine and rocky-shore environment. He noted the remains of seals, whales, fish, shellfish, penguins, albatrosses and other seabirds. Forest birds were also sought, as attested to by the large number of bird spears in the collection.[48] There is clear evidence that seals were hunted in large numbers: on 27 December 1927 Teviotdale recorded: 'This camp is remarkable for the number of seal bones in the middens. They are nearly as common as moa bones at Shag River.'[49]

The Little Papanui site illustrates the great limitations of the data provided by archaeology for the Peninsula. The depth and stratification recorded by Teviotdale, together with the many thousands of artefacts he and others unearthed, mean that it has always been regarded as an important site. But it has been variously identified as an early village, an intervening seasonal fishing camp and a late village.[50] In particular, it has been treated as a site in which we can see evidence of change. However, like Samson, I think we should emphasise continuity over change. As he puts it, people were probably 'living in the vicinity of Little Papanui, either continuously or intermittently, for approximately five to six centuries', and throughout that time 'the economy of the region was probably always based on fishing, sea mammal hunting, and the exploitation of ti'.[51]

This is not to deny that significant change occurred

> **O**ur special beaches on the Peninsula were Little Papanui near Cape Saunders lighthouse, and Pipikariti, some miles further towards the Otago Heads. Nearly always we had them to ourselves; it was unusual to meet other people, and we came to think of them as our own ground. At Pipikariti and other beaches Grandfather searched the beaches methodically, drawing his walking stick behind him to mark where he had gone, for what we children called Maori curios – adzes, fish-hooks of bone and shell, flint knives, drills, stone sinkers, greenstone and whale's tooth pendants. — Charles Brasch (Indirections, 18–19)

Successively the site of Pukekura pā, a lighthouse, settler fortifications built in the late nineteenth century to ward off the Russians, and now the Royal Albatross Centre, Taiaroa Head commands the entrance to Otago Harbour. © Kevin Jones and Department of Conservation

overall in southern Māori settlement patterns, in the discovery and development of resources, and in the attitudes that underpinned and reflected the relationships of Māori to their world. Two broad processes drove these cultural changes. First, this was a time of political ferment in the south, as the peoples we have come to know as Kāti Māmoe and Kāi Tahu moved from the North Island into Murihiku. Second, during this time Māori gradually adapted to the demanding rhythms of the southern environment. The remainder of this chapter examines these entwined processes.

Waitaha, Kāti Māmoe, Kāi Tahu:
The struggle for political power

Southern Māori trace descent from Waitaha, Kāti Māmoe and Kāi Tahu. Information about Kāti Māmoe and, especially, Kāi Tahu life in the south is much more detailed than for Waitaha. Indeed, the historical figures recorded in Kāi Tahu lore largely fall within two life spans, and most were contemporaries, so that when Kāi Tahu told early Europeans their traditions, they were describing events that their grandparents,

parents, and possibly even they themselves as children had witnessed.⁵² Such tradition is 'close to the production of documentary history'.⁵³

Kāti Māmoe and Kāi Tahu have their origins on the North Island east coast, and had some ancestral connections even before they arrived in the south.⁵⁴ Kāti Māmoe are descended from Hotu Māmoe, a woman who probably lived around the fifteenth century.⁵⁵ By the end of the sixteenth century some groups of Kāti Māmoe had begun to move into the South Island. They were pushed by growing population pressures in the North Island that precluded any easy expansion there, and were enticed across Cook Strait by the prospect of new foods and, especially, better access to pounamu. They knew the South Island as Te Wāhi Pounamu, 'the place of pounamu' (alternatively Te Wai Pounamu, 'the water of greenstone').⁵⁶

Kāti Māmoe had probably not long established their mana on the Otago Peninsula when further incursions from northern Māori began. The descendants of these latter groups later called themselves Ngāi Tahu or, in southern dialect, Kāi Tahu, after Tahu Pōtiki, an ancestral chief who lived around Hawke's Bay from whom they could all trace descent.

When these groups began to spill into the South Island they did not think of themselves as Kāi Tahu at all, but as members of the hapū Kāti Kurī, Ngāi Tuhaitara or Ngāti Irakehu. These hapū began to infiltrate Te Wai Pounamu from the Wellington area around the turn of the eighteenth century.⁵⁷ Some continued south, propelled by much the same reasons that had motivated the Kāti Māmoe migration one hundred years earlier.⁵⁸ Kāti Kurī were first to cross the strait, and they settled in the Marlborough Sounds before invading the Kaikōura area, where they wrested control of the land from Kāti Māmoe. Ngāi Tuhaitara arrived in Kaikōura, but pushed on to eventually dominate the Canterbury plains and coast from perhaps the 1730s.⁵⁹

One Kāti Kurī chief, Waitai, forged ahead of all others, and soon after the first crossings of Cook Strait led 300 men south, deep into enemy territory.⁶⁰ Waitai either built or successfully besieged Pukekura pā on Taiaroa Head, whose strategic location above the entrance to Otago Harbour is shown on page 71. The traditional history of Otago from this time on is turbulent, 'a marchland of political instability' as Anderson puts it, and the most protracted struggles of all were waged to gain and maintain control over the Otago Peninsula.⁶¹

Some idea of the swirling dislocations then occurring in the south is gained from the fact that Te Rakitauneke, a principal chief of Kāti Māmoe, successively occupied eight strongholds as he and his people retreated from the Kaikōura area in the face of the Kāi Tahu incursions. When he arrived in Otago, though, Te Rakitauneke decided to ally himself with Waitai and married his daughter to him; together they fought Waitaha and Te Rapuwai for control of the south.⁶² Te Rakitauneke was eventually buried at his last pā on Motupohue, or Bluff Hill.⁶³ After his death, Waitai and his Kāti Kurī people tried to encroach further on Kāti Māmoe territory, and were wiped out by the

It was here on Okia Flat, the swampy land at the back of Victory Beach, that Kāti Māmoe leader Whakatakenewa lured Tarewai to gather reeds in order to capture him. The distinctive 'Pyramids' formed as wave-washed rock stacks, but sand accretion has stranded them inland. They are wāhi tapu (sacred places) to Kāi Tāhu. W.A. Taylor, postcard. Hocken Collections, Uare Taoka o Hākena, University of Otago: Box-304-006; S17-026a

grandsons of Te Rakitauneke in Southland. Only two Kāti Kurī men returned north to tell their relatives of the resources of the south and what had happened to their kin.[64] Their reports, though, drew Kāi Tahu down into Canterbury, from where they later launched further incursions into Otago.[65]

At this stage, around the early eighteenth century, Kāti Māmoe were consolidating control over the south and came to dominate the Otago Peninsula, though in partnership with remnant Rapuwai and Waitaha. Meanwhile, the Kāi Tahu newcomers asserted their dominance over the north of Te Wai Pounamu.[66]

The border between the Kāti Māmoe and Kāi Tahu then lay near Taumutu, on the southern margins of Waihora (Lake Ellesmere) beside Banks Peninsula. Here the Kāti Kurī chief Te Ruahikihiki contemplated revenge for the killing of his father Manawa, slain in ambush while a guest of Kāti Māmoe.[67] His sons Moki and Taoka led Kāti Kurī hapū onto the Otago coast in force. These three leaders became the eponymous ancestors of the principal Kāi Tahu hapū of the Otago Peninsula – Ngāti Ruahikihiki, Ngāti Moki and Ngāti Taoka.

Moki settled peaceably enough at Pukekura pā, taking a Kāti Māmoe wife.[68] But Taoka, by all accounts bloodthirsty even by the standards of the time, tried to drive Kāti

Māmoe from the Otago coast; he built several pā as he moved south, the last at Katiki on the Moeraki peninsula.[69] However, Kāti Kurī themselves soon became embroiled in what is now known as 'the Otago feud', a long cycle of attacks and retaliations to decide the supremacy of mana on the Otago coast.[70] Traditions of the warrior Tarewai on the Otago Peninsula illustrate something of the causes and nature of these disputes.[71]

According to Ōtākou traditions, Tarewai was a warrior sent south to avenge the death of Waitai and other Kāi Tahu leaders.[72] By this time Moki had assumed the leadership of Pukekura pā. However, Kāti Māmoe, who also lived in and around the pā, still maintained control over the remainder of the Otago Peninsula. They had built a pā at Rangipipikao, close to Pukekura, to contain Moki and to protect their principal settlements around Papanui Inlet and at Aurakitaurira, on Papanui Beach. Though this sort of identification is risky, this is likely to represent at least one of the occupations of the site known to archaeologists as Little Papanui.[73]

Conflict broke out after the Kāi Tahu at Pukekura asserted a right to the Kāti Māmoe fishing grounds around Papanui. When this was disputed, the Pukekura people desecrated and spoiled the fishery by spreading the ash of burnt kelp on the water. One of the Kāti Māmoe leaders, Whakatakanewa, who was also a tohunga, chanted up a storm that wrecked some of the Pukekura canoes, prompting the Pukekura people to destroy some of the beached Papanui canoes in turn. Whakatakenewa then feigned friendship and gained Kāi Tahu's aid in gathering kākaho, or reeds, for a house to be built on Okia Flat. After the following celebratory feast, however, his people ambushed and killed most of the Kāi Tahu party.

Tarewai was taken alive and his tormentors intended to eat his heart. But he escaped to wage a one-man guerrilla war from the bush, while Whakatakenewa besieged Pukekura pā from Rangipipikao. Tarewai scaled the cliffs from Pilots Beach, a spot since known as Te Rereka-o-Tarewai, Tarewai's Leap, to re-enter Pukekura. He then led Kāi Tahu to a comprehensive victory, evicting his Kāti Māmoe opponents from Rangipipikao and harrying them as they retreated deep into Murihiku and even into the fiords of the West Coast.[74] According to Ōtākou tradition, these events occurred just before the rongopai, the peace between Kāti Māmoe and Kāi Tahu.

The rongopai effectively marks the transfer of political power over the Otago Peninsula from Kāti Māmoe to Kāi Tahu. Kāti Māmoe, recognising that Kāi Tahu had superior weapons and were better organised, sought peace.[75] The leading Kāti Māmoe chief, Te Rakiihia, approached his Kāi Tahu counterpart, Te Hautapunui-o-tu (Te Hau), and offered to share the mana of the land south of Kaiapoi, with a border around the Matau, or Clutha River.[76] The deal was confirmed, as was customary, by an exchange of women: Te Rakiihia married Te Hau's sister Hinehakiri, while Te Hau's son Honekai married Te Rakiihia's granddaughter Kohuai.[77] The peace was in effect by 1790.[78] It did not hold entirely on the Otago Peninsula, where the last small flickers of Kāti Māmoe recalcitrance erupted as the century drew to a close; the 'irreconcilables' were immediately forced to flee into the fiords, though some were later accepted back on the Peninsula.[79] As one Ōtākou elder later put it, 'that, according to me anyway, is how the mana of Kāi Tahu was brought down into this land; not by conquest but by agreement and familial support'.[80]

The Tarewai tradition illustrates that disputes could be sparked by conflict over control of resources – in this case the fishing grounds off Papanui. While the proximate causes of most disputes were slights to chiefly mana, the underlying causes were the political and economic necessity to acquire and control territory and resources. The Tarewai tradition also indicates how much costly fighting was required to gain undisputed mana over a place; Tarewai, as it happens, was later killed by Kāti Māmoe in the far south.[81] As the unions that sealed the rongopai indicate, the surest way to gain access to the land and its resources was not by fighting but by marriage. Kāti Māmoe women were much more valuable captives than men for this reason and, throughout the migration of Kāi Tahu into the South Island, their leaders married the women of their erstwhile enemies. Their children thereby gained their father's mana, his political and social standing, but also their mother's ancestral property rights to access land and resources.[82]

Southern Māori society: Whakapapa, power and property

Any explanation of Māori society must begin with whakapapa: the fundamental structure of Māoridom, the fabric that held the knowledge of the world together, placing everything and everyone in genealogical relationship.[83] Whakapapa were traced from both mother and father, and primarily interpreted through the distinction between tuakana, 'senior', and teina, 'junior'; rank was determined by proximity in descent from particular tupuna, or ancestors, so that junior members of a senior line of descent could outrank senior members of a junior line.[84]

Māori identified different layers of whakapapa groupings – most famously iwi (commonly glossed as tribe), hapū (subtribe or clan) and whānau (family), whose relationships are encapsulated in the alternative meanings of these words: iwi (bones) are the structures of society from which hapū (pregnant) life is generated, through whānau (birth).[85] Whakapapa determined social status within these groupings, defining who could be ariki (high chief) of an iwi or rangatira (chief) of a hapū, and in this way whakapapa was the primary source of mana, prestige, power and authority. With the right whakapapa one had status and power, and 'the main focus of power was the acquisition and use of property'.[86]

Whakapapa, above all, underpinned property rights to lands, fishing grounds and other resources; use and occupation were required to activate and confirm those rights and keep them alive; they might be transferred as a gift, or usurped by conquest, but whakapapa remained foundational to property rights.[87]

It was commonly argued by land-hungry British in the nineteenth century that Māori traditionally shared land 'in common' – and that therefore most lands and resources were not really owned at all. Many Pākehā – and some Māori for that matter – seem to believe much the same today. Yet nothing could be further from the truth. In fact, Māori had a very precise system of property allocation.

The building block of Māori property systems was a specific-use right to a discrete resource within an area. The area might be more or less loosely defined, but the resource was precise; one might, for example, take birds from a place, but not berries. Rights to resources were held exclusively, sometimes by whānau or even individuals.[88] Sometimes rights were held as common property by particular hapū, or even, perhaps, where harvest was most efficient on a very large scale, by an iwi.[89] But in each and every case, decisions about the use of a resource were exclusive to its particular owners. Rights to use resources always belonged to one person or a specific group; they were not shared, and they were certainly not common to all.[90] But because use rights were functional rather than spatial allocations,[91] they formed overlapping layers and became a 'crazy patchwork' across the landscape.[92]

The subtlety of this 'crazy patchwork' of property rights would have been hard for British settlers to understand even if they had wanted to, which they seldom did other than in the context of trying to buy land from Māori. It was further complicated, in that circumstance, by the fact that early land sales were, for Māori, political acts rather than economic ones, and by the fact that 'traditional' Māori political organisation did not stand still: then as now, it was fluid and dynamic.[93]

Most analysis of 'traditional' Māori socio-political organisation has centred on hapū as 'the essential political units' – independent kin groups whose identity and mana were bound up in their rangatira.[94] It is generally said that rangatira held authority over the tribal territory and other major property such as large canoes.[95] At least in the south, and certainly on the Otago Peninsula, however, this picture is complicated by the fact that hapū seldom lived together as communities. It was more common instead that 'a cluster of hapū' would combine as a community under the mana of a ruling rangatira.[96] He had the right to make political decisions about his people and their lands. For example, he could gift land, or allow other people onto it. In this light, all rights to land and resources could be expressed in terms of the mana of the rangatira.[97] In just this way Tame Parata described his grandfather Te Matahaere, leader of the community at Whareakeake just north of the Otago Peninsula, as the personification of his people's rights:

> He owned the country all the way up from Shag Point to Hawea and Wanaka. It was his hunting ground. He went up there to snare wekas and catch eels in the winter and in the summer came down to Shag Point. He went up in this way to keep up his title so that no party should dispute it. Nobody dared cross the range from the Waitaki to the country without asking his permission. If a chief did so there might be a long talk which would be accepted as it was a mistake but anyone below this rank was knocked on the head.[98]

This pattern of socio-political organisation, where communities of multiple hapū formed under a leading chief, was increasingly found throughout Māoridom, but became particularly pronounced in the south among Kāi Tahu, where by the eighteenth century 'the common form of community structure' was 'multi hapu settlement and, thus, multi-settlement hapu distributed over much of the tribal territory.'[99]

Several interrelated reasons explain why this pattern of socio-political organisation was increasingly important in the south.[100] Hapū migrating south initially sought to establish coherent tribal territories, but these groups fragmented and reformed as new entities. Some people stayed while others pushed on, and the newcomers intermingled with the existing inhabitants. Young fighting men dominated the southward migrations of Kāti Māmoe and Kāi Tahu. The beauty of Kāti Māmoe women was celebrated among Kāi Tahu,[101] and a large number of Kāi Tahu men married Kāti Māmoe women.[102] These women provided their children with valuable access, through whakapapa and ongoing occupation, to various bundles of rights to resources and land tenure, which is why some southern hapū were (and are) named for Kāti Māmoe women as well as Kāi Tahu men.[103] As the whakataukī (proverb) 'Na te rākau ke i riro ai te whenua' has it, 'it was a different stick the land fell to': not the taiaha of war, but of the bedroom.[104]

In Murihiku especially the result of such histories was, Anderson concluded, that 'Any family could possess a bundle of actual or potential rights of tenure and use, the constituents of which might be dispersed the length of the tribal territory.'[105] This pattern was an efficient response to widely scattered resources: it made economic sense for communities to contain diverse people with different property rights. In this way, communities could fragment throughout much of the year around a vast area, taking advantage of the temporary and localised places of abundance known as mahinga kai (sometimes rendered mahika kai in southern Māori), which they had painstakingly discovered, developed and defended, and returning to enjoy the fruits of their labour as they wintered at home. There they met the other families with whom they formed a community, who would also have returned home bearing a complementary set of foods and resources.

How did this pattern of political, social and economic organisation play out on and around the Otago Peninsula?

The territory of Ōtākou

By the late eighteenth century Kāi Tahu exerted undisputed control over the Otago Peninsula. From Ōtākou, which comprised Pukekura pā on Taiaroa Head and settlements strung along the harbour shore in its lee, the territory extended to Pūrehurehu, the headland at the end of Aramoana beach at the mouth of Otago Harbour, and encompassed the entire Otago Harbour basin, all of the Peninsula, south to the Matau, or Clutha River, and inland as far as the lakes district.[106]

However, the Ōtākou communities were a mixture of Waitaha, Kāti Māmoe and Kāi Tahu hapū. The common notion that Waitaha and Kāti Māmoe 'died out' or 'vanished' has absolutely no basis.[107] People of primarily Kāti Māmoe descent in fact retained significant political authority on the Otago Peninsula, though they often emphasised their Kāi Tahu lineage.[108] This is seen in the Ōtākou people's statement of identity at the beginning of this section, which lists the primary hapū of Ōtākou: Kai Te Pahi, Kāti Moki, Kāti Taoka and Kai Te Ruahikihiki. As noted, the latter three hapū are Kāti Kurī hapū, but the first is Kāti Māmoe.[109] All of these hapū are actually very closely connected – Te Ruahikihiki's son Moki married a Kāti Māmoe woman, and so did Moki's son and grandson.[110] The result of these connections was a particularly widespread distribution of potential property rights. As Harry Evison points out, 'a Ngai Te Ruahikihiki chief living at Otakou would have hereditary rights at Banks Peninsula, Taumutu, Arowhenua, and perhaps Foveaux Strait, and his family and adherents would share in these.'[111] It was the responsibility of such chiefs to ensure that their communities gathered the food, fibre and stone required to survive and thrive.[112]

The nature of occupation at Ōtākou: Following the seasonal round

Southern Māori learned to live within the cool southern environment by discovering the timing and placement of the seasonal energy surges of each species of bird, fish and plant, and then devising the means to harvest them efficiently. They developed methods to preserve, transport and store food, and each community contributed surpluses to trading networks, which exchanged and distributed resources missing from particular community environments. Each community therefore had its own annual round that ensured it could survive winter in some comfort in its own village.

For southern Māori, the New Year commenced anywhere between late May and early July with the onset of Tukurua, the cold winter season; it was marked by the rising over the horizon of the star Puaka in the constellation Orion.[113] If we follow the people of the Peninsula over a year from this point, we gain a good understanding of the general pattern of their lives.

As winter closed in groups would have been at their most concentrated, clustered together in settlements known as kāinga nohoanga tūturu. The most important of these, as at Ōtākou, were associated with urupā or burial grounds. The need to protect the remains of the community's ancestors committed the people to continuing residence there.[114] As in earlier times most settlements were on the coast, for much the same reasons: the coast provided a lot of different foods, eased transport and was a more benign place to be in winter. But moving during late winter and early spring was risky. Food was scarce then, and travel on stormy southern oceans or across flood-prone rivers was dangerous. During this time, when almost all the people were gathered

CHAPTER 3: CONTINUITY AND CHANGE

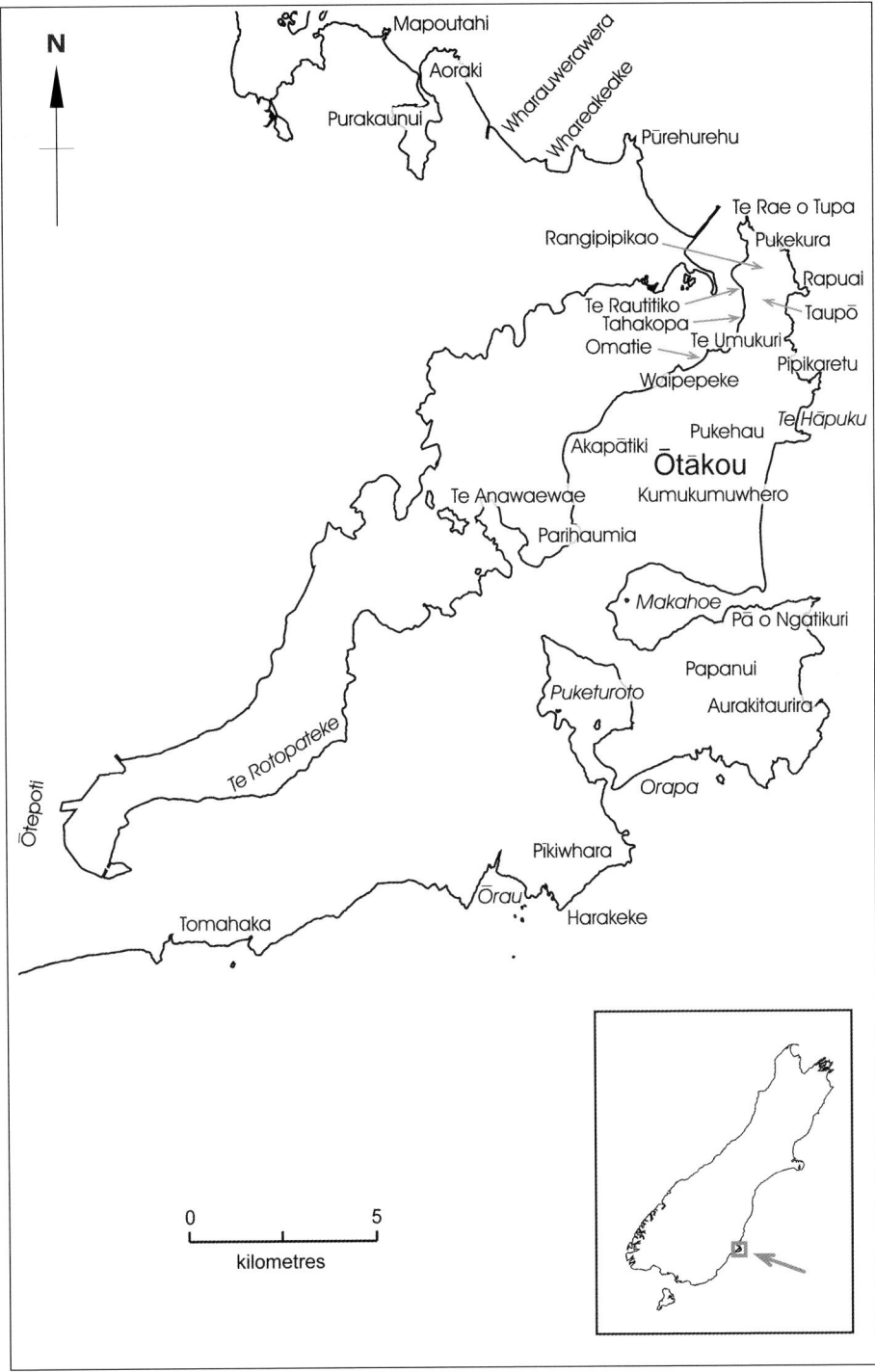

Some key Māori localities on the Otago Peninsula. © *Tracy Connolly*

together in their communities, stone tools, wooden implements and hunting and fishing equipment were manufactured or repaired by men; women made and mended clothing, rope and baskets; and the old moulded the minds of the young.

The winter diet was mainly preserved, stored food accumulated throughout the year, together with whatever could be gleaned locally. Dried aruhe or fern root was perforce the winter source of carbohydrate because kāuru could not be stored.[115] Europeans, at least, were to find this diet difficult, as aruhe can cause acute constipation. Fish were much harder to come by, since in winter many move offshore to spawn or find warmer water (inshore waters are especially cold in winter because of the influx of fresh water). Those fish that remained, such as flatfish like flounder and sole, were therefore predominantly late autumn and early winter foods: the season for taking them was properly from May to August, when large numbers were preserved by the pāwhara method, being dried in the sun or smoked.[116] Frostfish cast up on the beaches were also a winter food, as their name implies.[117]

Some people from the Peninsula ventured into the cold interior during the depths of winter. Between May and July, expeditions lasting several weeks travelled up the Taieri River into the Maniototo plain to catch weka and quail.[118] The weka were preserved on site and transported back to Ōtākou.[119] A hunter would call weka to him by blowing through a strand of the kāretu grass; the Peninsula place name 'Pipikaretu' commemorates this practice. They would then snare the bird in a noose attached to a pole.[120]

These were difficult and dangerous journeys: many people perished on the snow-laden and windswept inland plains,[121] but the weka were at their fattest then, and this sort of seasonal abundance was precious. Mass harvest of such plenitude was pointless without a means to preserve and transport it, however. Fatty foods like weka were preserved by tahā, pre-cooking, and packing them in their congealed fat in pōhā. Pōhā were blades of bull kelp inflated to form bags, wrapped in strips of tōtara bark and mounted on a harness that allowed them to be carried as a backpack.

Pōhā were an ingenious and very effective solution to the storage problems unique to the south (elsewhere in New Zealand, as in Polynesia, gourds and coconuts provided storage containers). They were of various sizes, but could be large enough to contain hundreds of birds (though more usually about 50).[122] As Shortland noted, they performed the function of casks, and though most often used for preserving birds – usually weka or tītī – any flesh, including seal, dog or human, might be safely kept in this way for some years.[123] Thomas Brunner described making 'a poha of ready-dressed wekas' in this way:

> *The natives here preserve the birds they catch during the winter months, when they are in excellent condition, in a rimu or sea-weed bag. They open the bird down the back, and take out all the bones; they then lay the flesh of the bird in a shallow platter made of the bark of the totara-tree, which is called a patua, when they cook the bird*

People from the Peninsula provided tōtara bark to enclose the kelp bags of pōhā. This example is particularly large, and was 'made to contain 326 birds (about 400lb)'. Hocken Collections, Uare Taoka o Hākena, University of Otago: O.W. 09/08/1927, p43; S10-279a

> by applying red-hot stones; they then place the cooked birds in the rimu bag, and pour over them the extracted fat, and tie tightly the mouth of the bag. I have tasted birds kept two years in this manner, and found them very good. They also keep eels and seals in the same way, using whale-oil for their preservation.[124]

Pōhā played a key role in trading food between disparate and far-flung groups. Shortland noted the long-distance trade in goods, both along the South Island's eastern seaboard and across Cook Strait, in which southern Māori sent north pōhā of tītī, as well as kāuru, kōtuku (white heron) feathers and taramea oil (used as scent), and received preserved kūmara, canoes and mats in return.[125]

Pōhā were absolutely critical to the development of southern Māori life. Without them Māori could not preserve, store or trade fatty foods, and as we have seen fat was their most important source of energy. Though most explanations stress population pressure as the reason Kāti Māmoe moved south, some traditions state that they were drawn by the delicious taste of the delicacies preserved in pōhā sent north by Waitaha in trade.[126]

Some forest birds were fattest in winter. Tūī and kererū were plentiful on the Otago Peninsula, and were in best condition after feeding from spring to autumn on nectar and then berries; if their feathers were soaked they could scarcely fly and could be shaken or clubbed from their perches. Sometimes on frosty mornings the birds were numb with cold and could be easily gathered.[127] Forest fowling lasted until about August; it ceased then because the birds were in their poorest condition and were about to mate.[128]

Shellfish, found around the Peninsula's extensive estuaries, sandy shores and rocky coasts, were staple foods. Paua, mussels, limpets, mudsnails, pipi and cockles were all harvested increasingly.[129] The large and flavoursome pink-and-blue tuaki, or cockles, were regarded as the principal regional speciality, the mana kai or kai wairua of the Peninsula; it is still considered an insult to bring tuaki to Ōtākou.[130] Tuaki are best harvested in spring and at particular points in the lunar cycle – at the full moon they are juicy and milky, at the new moon thin and sour.[131] In addition to being eaten fresh, cockles were dried and set aside for winter by the women.[132]

Spring, Koahu, arrived in late August to September.[133] From this point, as the weather warmed, many species began a flurry of feeding in order to come into better condition, attract mates and reproduce. People stirred, too. The most important local resources they sought were fish. As noted, the mainstays of the southern Māori fishery were pelagic (surface-dwelling) fish such as barracouta, red cod, blue cod, ling and hāpuku. All these fish return to inshore waters as the weather warms in spring; thin and hungry after spawning, they gorge on the exploding populations of plankton, squid and small shoaling fish such as pilchards.[134]

Southern Māori focused on fishing inshore coastal waters; there was little need to risk fishing further out. However, there is some evidence that Kāi Tahu did seek hāpuku, or groper, well out over the continental shelf. Hāpuku were the largest and most prestigious fish, and the second most economically significant. They could be found close inshore: a bay south of the heads was named Te Hapuku, and there was an especially good fishery around Cape Saunders even in the early twentieth century.[135] But further out over the shelf hāpuku formed large shoals. Elsdon Best was told by an Ōtākou informant (probably Hori Kerei Taiaroa) that Kāi Tahu canoes began to go out to these hāpuku fishing grounds in November or December; the larger vessels, destined for the more distant fisheries, required some 30 men as paddlers, and left in the middle of the night so as to reach their destination at the right time.[136]

The barracouta fishery was the most important. Barracouta were taken as they arrived from spring onwards, but were much fatter and tastier from March.[137] They were extremely easy to catch from a canoe, using a tackle of rod, line and lure (this was the only species Māori fished for using a rod). Through just thrashing a lure on the surface of the water, a fisherman might take thousands of fish a day at a rate of up to four a minute.[138]

In this 1860s reproduction of a sketch by John Barnicoat, c. 1844, whaleboats bring barracouta fishermen ashore. Fish dry on racks in the background, and signal flags to guide shipping into the harbour fly on Taiaroa Head. Hocken Collections, Uare Taoka o Hākena, University of Otago: Illustrated New Zealand, 18 March 1867, 1; S12-192a

The waters off the Otago Peninsula were ideal for barracouta fishing. Its headlands provided lookouts from which to spot schooling fish, and calm waters in their lee where thrashing lures were not masked by other surface disturbances.[139] The early whaler and settler William Haberfield recalled seeing as many as 20 double canoes setting out daily to fish for barracouta from the Peninsula settlements.[140] Women dried the fish on stages set out in the sun and wrapped them in mats to be stored on whata – storage shelves raised on poles high above the ground to protect food supplies from intruding people and pests.[141] Dried barracouta formed a staple of the Peninsula people's diet, and was an important item of trade.

Birds' eggs were also harvested in spring. Among other seabird eggs, Ōtākou Māori gathered karoro or black-backed gulls' eggs from October to January from around the cliffs on the seaward side of the heads, south to Pīkiwhara (Sandymount).[142] Scaling the cliff faces in search of nests defended by flocks of large angry birds was a dangerous task, much enjoyed by young men. According to Edward Ellison, nests were harvested every other day so that the eggs were guaranteed to be no more than two days old.[143]

Around November the rising of the star Rehua (Antares) heralded the start of Raumati, the summer season.[144] Travel on land was easier and the sea became less

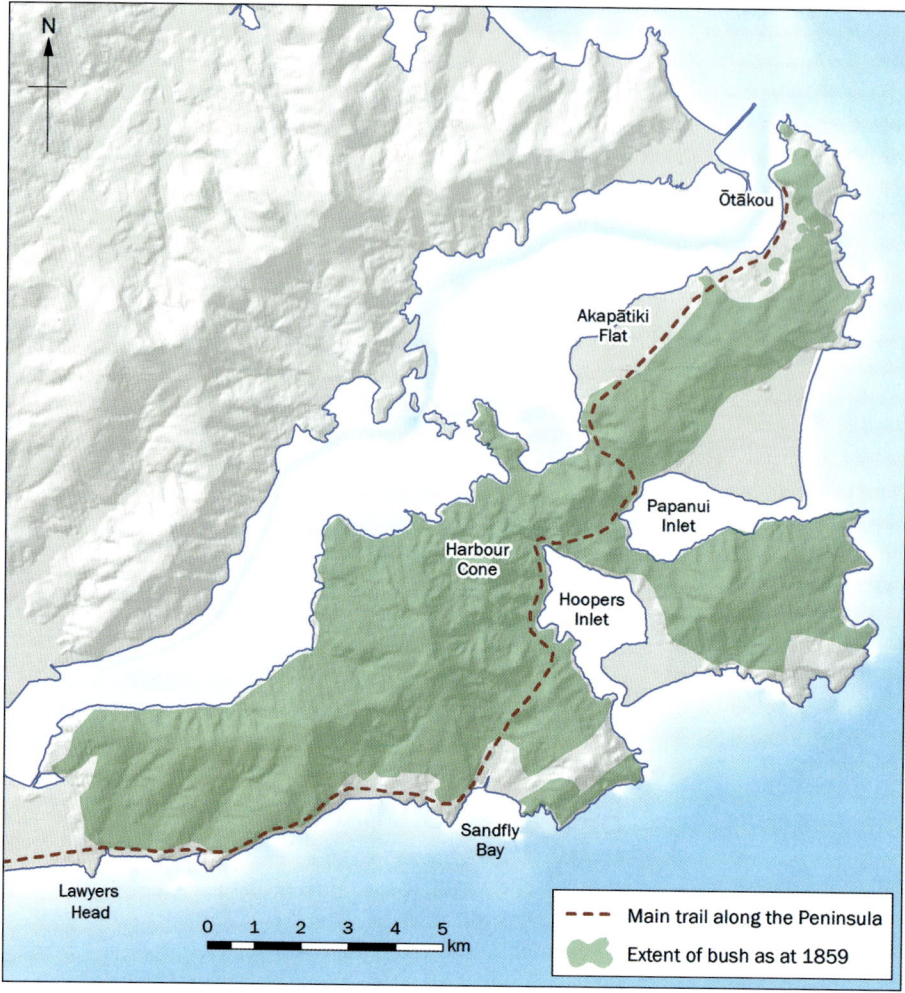

The track along the Peninsula and the distribution of bush in 1859.
© Redrawn by Chris Garden, from a map made by John Huggett

tempestuous. As the weather warmed, many more species became abundant. To take greatest advantage of this, the Ōtākou communities split into small family groups and scattered along the coast and inland. Most walked, on trails later described as 'little wider than a sheep track … worn down to a depth of some inches'.[145]

The track south from Ōtākou crossed to Papanui Inlet, passed over the neck to Hoopers Inlet, traversed the coast to Lawyers Head and exited onto the sand dunes fronting the swampy flats at the head of the harbour. From there it ran south over the intervening hills to the Taieri plain.[146]

Some people from Ōtākou would already have taken this route to where the Taieri River wound its slow way across the plain through many wetlands, notably the lakes

Waihola and Tatewai (the latter since drained). There Māori caught whitebait, lamprey eels and a variety of ducks.[147]

Whitebait are the juvenile forms of several species of *Galaxid*, fish that move down to the sea in autumn to spawn; their young swim back upstream in spring, at which time Māori caught enormous quantities of them in nets and cooked the bulk of the catch to be stored in kits for winter. Today's whitebait fisheries are shadows of the past: in the nineteenth century, Chinese on the West Coast reportedly mulched acres of their gardens with thick layers of whitebait.[148]

Eels became perhaps the most important resource of all,[149] and were by far the most common food mentioned in the lists Māori made of their mahika kai during the late nineteenth century.[150] Eels are very fatty, rich in energy, and provide all the essential fatty acids humans are unable to synthesise; it is, therefore, actually possible to live on eels alone.[151] Except for wholly marine species such as the conger, eels in New Zealand waters are diadromous – they inhabit both fresh- and saltwater at various stages in their life cycles. Māori developed detailed knowledge of those life cycles and a variety of harvest methods to take advantage of them.

Saltwater eels, or lamprey, known to Māori as kanakana, spend most of their lives at sea and only come up freshwater streams once in their lives to breed, in an annual spring migration. The Ōtākou people harvested thousands of kanakana struggling to ascend the waterfalls and rapids of the upper Silverstream and Taieri rivers.[152] The catch was floated downstream on mokihi.[153] These were small but buoyant craft made of bundled reeds, so easily constructed that they were effectively disposable but nevertheless capable of carrying considerable weights. They allowed rapid transport of people and goods across lakes and down rivers.[154] The dried kanakana joined the barracouta on whata at Ōtākou and, like them, were an important trade item.[155]

Freshwater eels teemed in the rivers, lakes, wetlands and lagoons of southern New Zealand. Science recognises two freshwater eels in New Zealand waters: the long-finned eel of rivers and streams, and the smaller short-finned eel of ponds, lakes and estuaries.[156] Māori had many names for different sorts – well over a dozen just in the south, and over 150 across New Zealand. These names demarcated first whether the eel was predominantly a fresh- or saltwater animal, and then its type, markings, shape, habitat and edibility.[157]

Southern Māori were almost always on the way to somewhere. Walking in hilly and forested southern New Zealand was essentially confined to ridgelines (where there is little or no food), riverbeds or lake margins. Waterways were therefore the arterial veins along which travellers almost always moved, and eels were easily the most reliable, sustaining and tasty fare to be found there. The early European travellers exploring the south were often kept alive only by the eeling prowess of their Māori guides.[158] Eeling methods used on the move included hī or bobbing, rapu or tickling (much as one can catch trout), and the use of a multi-pronged spear known as a matarau (a method still used today).

Freshwater eels were never plentiful on the Peninsula, and this was its greatest drawback in Māori eyes.[159] Yet eels were still very important to its inhabitants. Aside from their primary eel fishery on the Taieri, eels were also gathered locally from creeks draining into Otago Harbour, such as the Kaituna (now dried up); another favoured spot was the Kaikārae estuary south of Dunedin.[160]

Plant foods became important over spring and summer. Tutu berries and flax flowers were among the first summer foods to ripen.[161] Though the seeds in tutu berries are highly toxic (once famously killing an escaped elephant in Dunedin), southern Māori made a nutritious and – by all accounts – delicious drink from the berries after carefully straining the seeds out through fine flax cloth.[162]

As discussed in the previous chapter, the production of kāuru continued throughout summer, from the first ceremonies in October to the last cuttings in the autumn, after which gardening ended.[163] It was most intensive from December to January, when Edward Shortland noted that the task occupied most of a village.[164] There are signs that Māori had effectively begun to cultivate tī. The potential for cropping methods to develop around tī is clear, for the plant regenerates easily. According to Tikao, when the root and stem were taken for kāuru, the root tip and terminal shoot would be replanted so that each tree generated two clones. In this way groves of tī developed, many of whose qualities were artificially selected for by the particular hapū who had rights to harvest them.

Seals and to a lesser extent kake, the female sea lion, remained important food resources on the Otago Peninsula for a considerable time.[165] People probably continued to camp close by breeding seal colonies in order to 'crop' animals for immediate consumption.[166] According to Ian Smith, New Zealand's authority on marine mammal archaeology, one such camp was on Papanui Beach (about 300 metres along the shore from Little Papanui), probably occupied sometime between the fifteenth and seventeenth centuries, from which seals were cropped as required from the nearby Cape Saunders breeding colony.[167] People stayed there through winter and spring and possibly summer.[168] As Smith notes, the fact that 'at least one of the big game resources did not disappear completely' during the early occupation of the south suggests why the outer Peninsula might have remained an attractive base.[169]

As seals became scarcer, Smith suggests that a different hunting strategy emerged in which seasonal expeditions were made to harvest and preserve pups and juvenile seals in pōhā.[170] Late in the nineteenth century, Tame Parata told Frederick Chapman that his ancestors from the heads used to make annual expeditions to Cape Saunders to catch young seals.[171] Tare Wetere Te Kahu, on the other hand, told Chapman that Harekeke, the true 'Seal Point', north of Sandfly Bay, was 'where seals were got'.[172] In the early 1920s Herries Beattie was told that seals were harvested from a breeding colony at the heads themselves.[173] Much later, Edward Ellison suggested that similar expeditions sought sea lions from December to May around the mouth of Makahoe

The view over the mouth of Makahoe (Papanui Inlet) to Victory Beach and Okia Flat. Māori hunted sea lions here before the creatures disappeared from mainland New Zealand. In recent decades sea lions have returned to breed on the Otago Peninsula, and are often found on this beach. © Ian Thomson

(Papanui Inlet), where 'small parties of people' would kill the animals and cook the meat in large umu on the edge of Okia Flat, before carrying the cooked meat back to the villages at Ōtākou.[174]

When did seals cease breeding on and around the Otago Peninsula? Smith argues that the remains at the Papanui Beach site provide evidence that breeding continued 'until at least the end of the seventeenth century', but that because early Europeans did not go sealing there it must have ceased by the late eighteenth century.[175] However, the Papanui Beach site is not securely dated, and besides, it is only one of several Peninsula sites where seal remains are found. In addition, as discussed more fully in

Māori sought female sea lions for food, but it is unlikely they targeted male sea lions, which are powerful, fast and can be aggressive. Famed Kāi Tahu fighting chief Te Wera was given such a nasty fright by a male sea lion that a place on 'The Neck', on Stewart Island, was named for the event. © Ian Thomson

the next chapter, several sealing vessels did visit the Peninsula in the early nineteenth century. At least one thought it worthwhile to drop several gangs on Cape Saunders. Two thousand skins were taken in 1809–10 from the very small 'Isle of Wight', off the Otago coast just south of the Peninsula, by a few men over some weeks in the summer breeding season.[176]

Why did seals persist on and around the Peninsula? Perhaps the situation on the Peninsula was analogous to that on the Chatham Islands, where seal colonies survived despite being the most important food for people living beside them. Chris Lalas and Corey Bradshaw suggest that people there were perhaps too recent or too few to deplete the seals, or that the seals may have been replenished from colonies on uninhabitable nearshore islands. They emphasise that there are comparatively few such islands around mainland New Zealand, with the exception of Foveaux Strait, where of course seals also survived in numbers into historical times.[177]

In this light, however, it is interesting to consider the islands that Kāi Tahu included in lists of their mahika kai compiled in early 1880.[178] These lists were made as part of

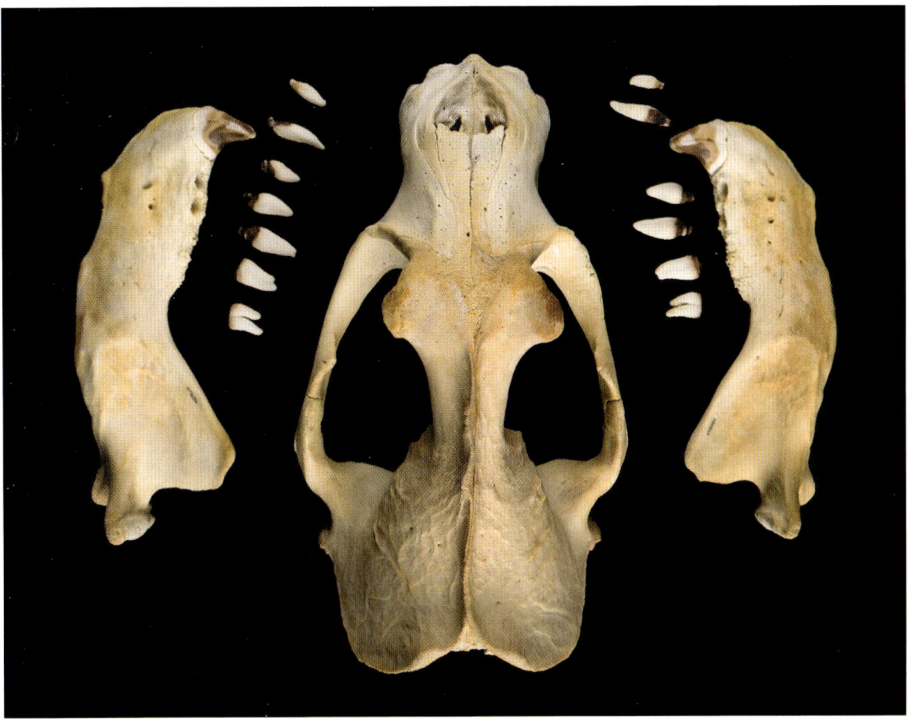

This male sea lion skull, part of an animal found at Papanui Inlet, suggests just how powerful its bite might be. Photograph: Kane Fleury © Otago Museum, Otago Museum

preparations for the Smith–Nairn Commission, in which Kāi Tahu contested the terms of the Otago and – especially – Kemp Block purchases. Most refer to the loss of mahika kai in the Kemp Block purchase. However, the first list names seven islands inside Otago Harbour and around the Peninsula that were 'never sold to Wakefield' in the Otago Block purchase; of these, three, on the outer coast, were wanted because each was 'a seal colony'.[179]

In sum, then, seals may have continued breeding on and around the Otago Peninsula for longer than allowed for by the limited archaeological evidence. This point should not, however, be pushed very far. Seals have rapidly recolonised Otago coasts since returning to breed on the Otago Peninsula in the 1970s, and Chris Lalas suggests that a stable population of some 20,000–30,000 animals is fast approaching.[180] Since early European sealers did not take seals from Otago in anything like those numbers, it is safe to say that Māori hunting had greatly reduced their abundance.

Ducks and shags were taken in large numbers from Otago Harbour and the inlets of the Peninsula, and were another principal focus of the expeditions from the Peninsula onto the Taieri plain.[181] They were best hunted during December and January, for in these weeks of their summer moult they could not fly. Pārera (grey duck), kukupako (scaup or black teal), pāteke (brown teal), tētē (grey teal) and kuruwhengi (shoveller) all flocked to the plain, drawn by the extensive wetlands created by the Taieri River. The helpless waterfowl were driven into snares or yards at the water's edge, each hapū having its own yard.[182]

Birding for the honeyeaters tūī, kākā and bellbird also commenced in about January and continued until July.[183] These birds primarily feed on nectar through late winter and early spring before switching to soft berries and insects in late summer and autumn.[184] All were plentiful on the Peninsula.[185] According to Alfred Reynolds (again writing as Aparata Renata): 'They started on the kowhai (*Sophora microphylla*). Some of these trees flower in June and July but most of them in September. Then they had the fuchsia and native flax. These three are all the honey flowers suitable for honey-birds' food on the Peninsula, as no rata ever grew on it.'[186] After the birds had fattened on sweet nectar and finished laying their clutches of eggs, Māori began to snare them at water troughs, or used spears made of a number of jointed sections that could be connected in varying combinations. This allowed the hunter to quickly construct the length of weapon needed on site – stalking birds while carrying long poles in dense and vine-entangled forest is not very feasible.

Ngahuru, or autumn, the fourth and final season in the southern Māori calendar, began at the rising of the star Whaanui, or Vega, in late February. Several important inland foods came into season around this time. Kiore were sought from the interior from about March to July, when they were plentiful and tasty and easily snared at night on their little tracks as they moved about in search of berries.[187] Kiwi and kākāpō were also caught inland throughout late summer and early autumn.[188]

Two more seasonal events were of paramount importance. First was the annual migration of freshwater eels to the sea at the new moon in late March or April. During this autumnal migration, or heke, Māori congregated at their favoured rivers and lagoons to construct pā tuna, eel weirs of brush or stone built out from the riverbanks. Hīnaki, tubular nets made of vines and flax, were set into the weirs, and the eels flooding downstream had little choice but to enter them.[189] Similar nets known as kaitara were used throughout the year, but outside the heke they needed to be baited to persuade the eels to enter.[190] Eels were dried in enormous quantities and kept for winter consumption.[191]

According to a historian of Kāi Tahu, Jim Williams, the people came to discern a pattern to the heke. Male short-finned eels migrate first, followed by the females. They are still arriving as the long-finned eels, first males and then females, begin their journey. The larger female eels bear as many as 30 million eggs, and Williams states that once these females arrived the channels were closed off, allowing the most important animals to pass freely to the sea to breed.[192] In another example of Māori awareness of

Animal remains at Little Papanui mostly derive from the sea, but many bird spear points were also found at the site. Such points were fixed to spears formed of segments that could be easily carried through bush and then assembled to the length required.

Photograph: Fiona Glasgow © Otago Museum,
Otago Museum: D29.406; D29.420; D29.429; D29.433;
D29.5998; D31.700; D31.1260; D31.1996; D31.2003;
D33.817; D33.1200; D33.1202; D33.1615; D41.540;
D41.541; D80.1165;; D80.1177; D80.1179; D80.1182

the cycles that governed their environment, drying eel was never hung out under the full moon, for at that time a saprophyte is activated that turns the flesh rancid. This was maramataka – moon knowledge.[193]

Shortly after the tuna heke ended the tītī season started. Tītī or muttonbirds are the plump chicks of the sooty shearwater that still breeds in great numbers on the small rocky islets scattered throughout Foveaux Strait. By the nineteenth century, if not before, tītī had become vital to Kāi Tahu: they were almost as important as eels as a source of fat and protein available over winter, and were without parallel as a prestige food item of trade. Up to two or three hundred thousand birds were being taken each year in the early nineteenth century.[194] People from as far afield as Kaikōura made hazardous journeys to and from the far south to harvest them and sustain their rights to the islands.[195] Great quantities were traded, too, some even sent across Cook Strait in exchange for resources lacking in the south.[196]

Several tītī colonies existed on the Otago Peninsula and some people stayed home to harvest them. Others from the Peninsula also manufactured pōhā using kelp from around Cape Saunders and southwards around the Clutha coast, and tōtara bark stripped from Peninsula trees; they supplied many of these pōhā to those going south to the main harvest on the tītī islands of Foveaux Strait – a practice that continued well into the twentieth century.[197] Te Matenga Taiaroa (father of H.K. Taiaroa) was one Ōtākou leader with rights to tītī there; in the 1820s two early European ships' captains met Taiaroa and his people on Stewart Island, where they were sealing before harvesting their tītī.[198] The Peninsula pōhā-makers would have been repaid when these hunters returned.

The close of the tītī season at the end of May signalled the end of major expeditions for the majority of the Peninsula people, and once more they congregated at home for winter.

Tenure to resources

The ways in which species were harvested illustrate important aspects of southern Māori tenure to resources. Many species' habitats, such as those of kiore, ducks (when in moult), kiwi or shellfish, were divided into family preserves. These were wakawaka, named for the tail of the pīwakawaka, the fantail, and which, radiating outwards from a central point, are suggestive of the traditional land divisions found throughout eastern Polynesia.[199] Wakawaka were favoured whenever competition for resources was highly inefficient: when species were found in discrete patches like cockles or, like rats, were taken using methods such as trap lines.[200] Control over discrete wakawaka ensured each family's access to the resource and, from the point of view of the wider community, ensured efficient harvesting by eliminating duplication of effort.

Other resources such as weka were fairly ubiquitous all year round in many areas, and accordingly there were no restrictions on weka harvesting. Aruhe was also fairly widely distributed, and although fern-root grounds were generally not strictly divided, the most senior families did reserve the very best areas.[201] Rank thus provided another mechanism for ecological control. Kiwi, for example, were especially prized for their feathers, and only the aristocracy were permitted to hunt them: one scholar suggests that for a common man to deliberately kill a kiwi meant certain death.[202]

Territories for each species were different, and distinct rights to different species might overlap in time and space.[203] Property rights, in other words, were closely adapted to reflect how a species could be most efficiently harvested. This system was underpinned by initimate knowledge of many other species: where and when they might best be found and harvested, and the uses they might then be put to.[204]

The consuming conflagration or the long-burning fire?

Whether Māori were ever in any sense 'conservationists' is a matter of some debate. There are two key broad questions: did Māori try to manage resources with a view to the long term? Did they ever succeed? Answers to these questions tend to be polarised. On the one hand, some have emphasised the extent of early species extinction and forest destruction, as well as ongoing declines in more vulnerable species, saying that even if Māori did belatedly attempt to preserve some resources (which is doubted), it is hard to see that they succeeded. On the other hand, others have stressed that Māori had an increasingly profound spiritual relationship with their environment as tangata whenua – those who kept the long-burning fires lit – from which arose an awareness of the need to act as kaitiaki, or guardians, of the land and its life.[205] In this view there was a shift from mining to harvesting, underpinned by 'an ideology that emphasized the restricted and therefore sustainable exploitation of the environment'.[206]

Māori cultural mechanisms for retiring resources from exploitation, such as rāhui, were noted as widespread from early European contact.[207] Rāhui were in effect injunctions against the use of an area, by some or all people. They were instituted for various reasons, often following deaths in an area, but also to set aside resources, perhaps when prey species were breeding or in poor condition.[208] According to Best, at least, some rāhui were specifically meant to restore the productiveness of land, forest or water.[209] This sense of rāhui is often now seen as having been common. Edward Ellison described his people's practices at Ōtākou to the Waitangi Tribunal in these terms: 'Strict tapu was placed on all kai [food] at certain times of the year. This was strictly adhered to as were the rohe potae pertaining to the various hunting grounds. Atua or protective gods were incorporated in the maintaining of these tapu. [The] [p]rincipal reasons [were] so as to assure that a resource was not overexploited.'[210]

Some examples of rāhui now seen as motivated by conservation seem to me to have been instituted for other reasons. For example, Mead instances as a conservation measure a description by the missionary Richard Taylor of kiekie (a plant used in weaving) being placed under rāhui until ready for use, at which point 'the entire population' went to harvest it, the 'first fruits' being offered to the chief who had laid down the rāhui'.[211] Similarly, Firth notes that it was forbidden to take ducks till the young had fledged; then those with rights all assembled, 'birds were caught in great numbers, and a feast was held'.[212] Such practices seem intended to focus the community's harvest at the point of peak productivity rather than to limit the harvest's effects on the resource. Any shift towards sustainability, in other words, may have been as much an incidental byproduct of rationalising economic activity as an end goal.

Atholl Anderson, moreover, warns against those who 'compress Maori environmental behaviour into an ethnographic present defined by historical snapshots of "rahui" and other forms of resource management'.[213] He himself considers that 'within their social rules of resource ownership and use', Māori always exploited resources as 'optimal foragers' who ate their way down the food chain, successively overexploiting the best and biggest resources 'without consideration' for 'the sustainability of any particular resource'.[214] For Anderson this is axiomatic, a key precept of evolutionary ecology being that people, like all animals, choose to use resources according to the return of energy on expenditure.

Other archaeologists propose more influential roles for 'cultural agency in ecological relations', and Anderson himself acknowledges that 'what constitutes a fundamental and satisfactory explanation of subsistence behavior in evolutionary ecology as a generality might be too simplistic for the behavioural flexibilities and emergent qualities of social organization, and information transfer in long-term human behavior'.[215] In other words, people may behave unlike other animals, being able to foresee the consequences of their actions and being subject to the shaping power of human culture.

The hard evidence, however, suggests that while extinctions slowed, some of the more vulnerable species continued to decline in range and abundance, especially in the north where the Māori population was much larger, but in the south also. Birds such as North Island kākā, bittern and takahē, as well as predators such as laughing owls, were sliding towards extinction before Europeans arrived.[216] Richard Holdaway and Trevor Worthy emphasise that in the nineteenth century southern Māori continued to travel into Fiordland in order to hunt takahē – presumably because these birds were now very rare and valuable – while living among abundant pukeko, a similar rail.[217] Likewise, the archaeological evidence shows that, in almost every site studied, shellfish found in middens become smaller over time, while some species disappear as people creamed off the larger animals.[218]

In my view, the most significant factor in why resources did not diminish more markedly in the south is that the population remained very low. So while in making the case for a measure of Māori resource management David Young suggests that in the south, 'owners placed rahui over shaggeries for their own use, not always without effect',[219] it is now clear that Stewart Island shag populations were extirpated over most of the coastal South Island, lingered in coastal Otago (it is thought mainly on offshore islands), and even recovered in the far south around Foveaux Strait. This pattern so precisely maps to the distribution of the human population as to leave no doubt about why these shags survived in some areas.[220]

That said, I do consider that Māori came to terms with the problems of resource management and conservation when they had finished 'fishing down the food web', and 'when there were no alternatives'.[221] As Raymond Firth concluded in his classic *Economics of the New Zealand Maori*, the system of prohibitions and imperatives at work in tapu, rāhui and the like 'definitely regulated the conduct of the people of the community towards their economic environment'. It provided 'a very useful reinforcement for rational rules'.[222] If Māori progressed towards a more sustainable use of some especially significant resources, then, as I have emphasised, it was only through the gradual imposition of 'rules of resource ownership and use'.

Establishing clear ownership and control of access to the most significant resources provided Māori communities with both means and motive to balance the conflicting imperatives of maximising and maintaining their harvests. This can be seen most clearly by returning to the muttonbird harvest from the tītī islands. This engaged the undivided attention of all hapū with rights for almost three months, from mid-March till the end of May. It has long been forbidden to visit the islands outside this season. While on the islands, strict protocols govern behaviour: the use of fire is tightly controlled; no living wood is cut; no damage to the ground or the burrows from which the chicks are plucked is permitted. Only those hapū with clearly defined rights to preserves are permitted on any particular island, and these preserves were and are defended vigorously against any intrusion. Thus Māori imposed tight controls that restricted access to a critical resource to a defined group of people, and defined when, where and how they could exploit them.[223]

Control is the essential prerequisite for care. Access to tītī was tightly controlled because they were so important, and because they were only abundant in specific places at specific times. But most other resources also had their own management regime prescribing who had a 'take' – a right to take – and when and where it could be exercised.

The control and maintenance of cockle beds at Ōtākou provides another example. As Boyd Russell told the Waitangi Tribunal, cockle beds at Ōtākou were divided into wakawaka:

> [T]he wakawaka in the harbour were demarcated by stakes driven into the bottom down to and just below the low tide level. Mr Russell remembered seeing stakes in a line running out to sea from the Otakou and Te Rauone Beaches during his own lifetime. Certain wakawaka belonged to specific whanau. Mr Russell is known in the district for attempting to maintain his family's once exclusive right to a certain area of shellfish near his house.[224]

Ownership and control of a resource provided an incentive to conserve and even enhance its habitat. Lagoons such as Waihora near Banks Peninsula were periodically opened to the sea every few years to flush out sediment and increase fish populations; this was a substantial and organised operation for ohu, or working bees, that involved 50–100 men.[225]

As Michael Stevens reasons, therefore, we can recognise that some resources were managed so as to maintain ongoing harvests 'without falling into the trap of depicting environmentally friendly noble savages'.[226] Furthermore, acknowledging the inevitability of early ecological impacts by the Polynesian settlers, and the very real difficulty in avoiding ongoing depletions, does not preclude a focus on the successes of Māori adaptation, by learning to live in what had become a difficult environment.

Conclusion

Māori culture developed from the lifeways brought by their migrant Polynesian ancestors; the forms it took were shaped by the relationships between people and place, human and landscape. The early settlers came prepared to follow a long-established way of life in which they identified the most accessible resources, plundered them and then moved on. Southern New Zealand was, however, the end of the line: there was nowhere to move on to. Many species were initially extirpated by humans and by kiore; the disappearance of the larger avifauna on the Peninsula can be clearly attributed to the direct impact of human hunting activity, while the reductions in smaller colonial seabirds and (most obviously) the reptile and insect fauna, were due to the introduction of kiore.

Even where people were the primary agents of extinction, they had little control over such processes; some extinctions were too quick to prevent, others too slow to perceive. For several species, the slide toward extinction continued right through to European contact. Yet, where a community of people could control access to significant resources, they harvested with an eye to the long term. As a result, in at least a few important instances, they learnt not only to live within the limits set by the environment but also to improve their world, dwelling in a landscape of their own making.

In some respects, the initial ecological impact on the Peninsula was less severe than in most other areas of the southeastern coast: there is no good evidence that Māori chose to clear any more than small patches of forest on the Peninsula, and seals survived to breed around its shores for longer than anywhere further north. As Atholl Anderson puts it, 'the environmental encounter ran in both directions. The growth of Maori society from Polynesian roots owed as much to the constraints and opportunities of the New Zealand environment as the latter was changed by it'.[227]

Māori learnt from bittersweet ecological experience. Māori social structures were mired in, and mirrored by, ownership of lands and resources. This was the foundation for ensuring access to the resources their communities required. Māori on the Peninsula thus overcame the inevitable impacts of initial settlement, and did without almost all the animals and plants that sustained them elsewhere in the Pacific and the rest of New Zealand. As they learnt to cope with a temperate climate, Māori living in the south, and on and around the Otago Peninsula, developed an almost entirely different way of life.[228]

OVERLEAF: *Louis Le Breton,* Mouillage d'Otago (Nouvelle Zélandia) *(detail). A whata, raised to keep food from rats, towers above a Māori settlement at Ōtākou, some of whose high-ridged houses show the whalers' influence. A sailor washes his clothes in Tahakopa Lagoon, now buried beneath sand drift.* 1846, tinted lithograph, hand-coloured, 181 x 310mm. Hocken Collections, Uare Taoka o Hākena, University of Otago: 91/40

Part II
THE WORLD WASHES ASHORE

AKATERE R large River often Dry. Dry in summer.

TIMAROU
Good place for boats

WAITAKI Large River Strong tide

OHAMARA good place for boats except during S.E. wind
MAKOTAKITA

ONEKAKA — good place for ships except during S.E. wind. Sydney Packet lost here.
MORAKI Good place for boats — Plenty of Natives.

Sandy Beach

WAIPAMA
Good harbour Deep water Anchorage.

MATAKI **WAITANUI** — rocks covered at high water.
MARANIHE Good for ships — Plenty of whites — Similar to beach at
WAIKAUITI R Good river, many whites
R — **WAIPUKE** small
POREAKENUI
PERIRA
TUPA
KAPUKETERET for boats
TARAKIPA
Rocks **OTAWAAKETO**

OTAGO
Shoal water
Schooners can get in.

Boat Bay

GEORGE'S SOUND Anchor
THOMPSON'S SOUND Good Harbour Anchor

Plenty of white Pine

TERA Good Harbour
KOREWA

WAIHORE Lagoon

MOTURATE
Nearly dry at the mouth. Good anchorage except in S.E. winds. One Schooner lost here. Plenty of Whalers huts

ANARERU Rocks **KOTAKA**
WAIMATAHU
OUAKA **OHITO POINT**
Plenty of wood **EREHAKA**
MAHAKA
TOTAKA
MAKATI
Plenty of wood Rock **CAROLINE**
TUREMAKA **HARBr**
WAIKAWA Good harbour strong tide
RUAPUN Bloody

PARAIKITE

WAKATEPA

Plenty of seals

KUTUKU The Place of Captn Cook

Seals

OTARA
MATARAK
TATAKI BAY

CHAPTER 4: TAKATA PORA:
THE PEOPLE OF THE SHIPS, EUROPEAN EXPLORATION, MĀORI DISCOVERY 1770–1830

How powerful must be the love of gain, when it can induce men to support the fatigues and privations which fall to the lot of the seal fishers!

— Jules de Blosseville[1]

*W*e cured ten thousand skins, for the fur, for the fur
Yes we cured ten thousand skins for the fur
Brackish water, putrid seal
We did all of us fall ill
For to die, for to die, for to die.

Come all you lads who sail upon the sea, sail the sea
Come all you jacks who sail upon the sea
Though the schooner Governor Bligh
Took on some who did not die
Never seal, never seal, never seal.[2]

Introducing the Otago Peninsula to the world

On Sunday 25 February 1770, on his first voyage to New Zealand, Lieutenant James Cook sailed the *Endeavour* south along the Otago coast with a fresh gale behind him. The weather, he wrote, was 'so hazey that we could see nothing distinct upon the land'. As darkness fell he hove to for the night, off a 'high bluff point' whose position he fixed and which he named Cape Saunders.[3] This was the first glimpse that the wider world had of the Otago Peninsula.

In the morning Cook saw aspects that interested him north of the cape, where 'the Shore seemed to form 2 or 3 Bays wherein there appeared to be good Anchorage & Shelter from SW, Westerly & NW winds'.[4] Though tempted to pursue these prospects of safe harbour, Cook was spurred by the desire to finally settle the debate of whether this was the Great Southern Continent or – as he already suspected – only an island. He decided to sail on.

In passing, Cook described land 'of a moderate height, full of hills which appear'd green & woody'.[5] Beating back to shore not far south of the Peninsula on the morning of Sunday 4 March, Cook saw 'several seals and whales and one Penguin', none of which had been noted off northern coasts.[6] That night a large fire was seen on shore; Joseph Banks believed as a result that there were people here, 'though probably very thinly scattered over the face of this very large country'.[7]

Cook never landed on or even near the Otago Peninsula. But his charts and these spare observations of seals and whales, the possibility of safe harbour and the scarcity of inhabitants drew the world there. Cook's charts and the journals he and his officers kept were the first historical records of most of New Zealand; they were scrutinised across Europe and America for signs of commercial opportunity, and remained for many years a constant source of reference for mariners and merchants.[8] As late as 1855 one captain reliant on Cook's charts floundered about for 11 days trying to find Otago Harbour.[9]

Cook sailed in the service of commerce and science, both of which underpinned empire. He looked to New Zealand for resources that could be rendered into commodities: things that were abundant, transportable and rare elsewhere. To discover and exploit such commodities was one reason why Cook fostered trading relationships with Māori. Another was that Cook recognised the importance of New Zealand, and of Māori, as a means of re-supply for British shipping.[10] On his return to England, he provided precisely the information most essential to continued commercial exploitation.[11]

Cook's information allowed, for the first time, a conception of the world as an integrated whole. It stimulated the British government of William Pitt to plan 'the creation of a great triangular commerce spanning the Pacific, with avenues to India and Europe'.[12] Above all, by opening the Pacific to British trade, the government hoped to gain access to South American silver and North American furs to trade for Indian cotton and spices and Chinese tea, silk and porcelain. Other Pacific resources noted by Cook were also seen as strategically significant, especially the whales and seals of the southern oceans and New Zealand's flax and timber.[13]

The penal colony at Port Jackson (Sydney) in Botany Bay was established as a crucial cog of this government strategy to expand British imperial interests into the Pacific. However, powerful elements of British society opposed the establishment of an economically self-sufficient jail in New South Wales, and these constrained the government's desire to open the Pacific to British trade. The influence of the East India Company was waning, but it still retained a monopoly on all trade into Britain from the lands and seas between the Cape of Good Hope and Cape Horn, as well as all trade into company ports such as Calcutta and Canton. At the same time, the increasingly powerful British whaling industry was implacably opposed to opening the way to any colonial competition.[14]

As a result New South Wales' early governors were instructed to forbid 'every sort of intercourse' between Botany Bay and the wider world, and 'not on any account [to] allow craft of any sort to be built' to allow 'such intercourse'.[15] But because Sydney remained abjectly dependent on Calcutta, the principal port of British India, for necessities such as food, livestock and tea, as well as for luxuries – 'china', fine furniture, and fashionable clothing – its governors had little choice but to turn a blind eye to ship-building, and to allow exploitation of the Pacific frontier.[16]

The British merchants operating out of India very much wanted return cargoes, but as New South Wales' Governor Phillip Gidley King lamented in 1803, 'we possess no known staple whatever'.[17] This was not quite correct. Sydney merchants had already begun to take advantage of the fact that soft, warm seal skins were one of the few commodities for which there was any demand in China.

Thanks to Cook, and the explorers who went to Dusky Sound in his wake, Sydney's merchants could anticipate finding a safe charted harbour there that provided timber, fresh food, potable water and 'great numbers' of seals, such as those Cook had killed there for meat, rigging repairs and lighting oil.[18] In 1792 the *Brittania* (a ship with a rare licence from the East India Company to operate in these waters) demonstrated the possibilities that sealing offered by depositing in Dusky Sound the first sealing gang employed in Australasia, before sailing away to Canton.[19] Over almost a year this gang accumulated 4500 seal skins, despite spending most of their time building a ship for fear the *Brittania* would not return for them.[20]

All the early governors of New South Wales disobeyed instructions and quietly encouraged colonial shipbuilding and sealing.[21] Small sealing ships were cheap and easily outfitted and, despite the appalling conditions, sealing suited the people of early Australia whose culture was, at its core, 'one of risk, of chance, of gambling'.[22] Both entrepreneurs and workers took their chances where the risks and rewards were greatest: they headed out to sea. But after only five years their first targets, the Bass Strait rookeries, were showing signs of exhaustion. The Sydney sealers, joined by a few English and American entrepreneurs, once again looked to New Zealand.[23]

A spasm of slaughter

In a few seasons of slaughter between 1803 and 1810, New Zealand's remaining seal rookeries were all but wiped out.[24] Sealers mainly killed fur seals, but also sea lions, the occasional leopard seal and, wherever possible, elephant seals, which also provided a rich source of oil.[25] In the first slaughters, tens of thousands of fur seals were taken from freshly discovered Foveaux Strait, followed by hundreds of thousands more from the rocky islands of the Southern Ocean, where single gangs sometimes killed tens of thousands of animals.[26]

Some seals escaped only because most of the Sydney merchants went bankrupt. The Chinese market for seal skins collapsed in 1807 due to oversupply; the next year England suffered a financial crisis, and in 1810 imposed a heavy duty on seal oil gathered by Australian vessels in New Zealand.[27] Even after oil or skins sold in Canton brought no profit they were still taken, for the Australian colonies had nothing else to offer the Asian markets and the ships would otherwise return empty.[28]

The rapid destruction of New Zealand's remaining seal rookeries was entirely predictable given that most northern hemisphere rookeries had already been annihilated, and their fate was widely foreseen. Governor King himself had identified the need for restrictions by 1803: he advised Whitehall that it would be expedient 'to restrain Individuals from resorting there in too great numbers and to fix certain times'. But King was powerless to enact, let alone enforce, anything meaningful.[29] The hopelessness of the situation is highlighted by Joseph Banks' suggestion, as a champion of Australian enterprise, that the locals chase the seals from the rocks so that only they knew where they were.[30] Any question of husbanding rookeries was purely academic, since captains and gangs operated in cut-throat competition; none could escape the logic that dictated that any rival would plunder what they did not. When the discovery of new felting processes opened markets for the skins in Europe, it was immediately recognised by one observer in Sydney that 'the increase in seals will be totally extinct within about three years' because of the surfeit of sealing vessels and the practice of killing both pups and parents.[31]

The Otago Peninsula marks the high-tide line of this first wave of sealing. Almost without exception sealers arrived from the south and looked no further: there is scant evidence that seals were ever taken north of the Peninsula. A scrap of inferential evidence suggests that some may have harvested seals from Cape Saunders as early as 1806 or 1807, but says nothing else save that they purportedly had friendly relations with Māori.[32]

Two small Australian vessels made the first definite visits: the *Brothers* left gangs on islets near the Peninsula late in the spring of 1809, and the *Sydney Cove* landed gangs on Cape Saunders in early 1810.[33] The *Brothers*' gangs killed over 2000 seals on the islets; it is not known how many the *Sydney Cove* gangs killed, but they thought it worth their while to work the Peninsula's shores. All this took place during the summer breeding season.[34] It suggests that fur seals still bred around the Peninsula and islets in the vicinity even after several hundred years of continuous Māori occupation.

Sealers and their ships initiated processes of environmental change that have gathered momentum to transform New Zealand almost beyond recognition. American historian Alfred Crosby suggests we should view European ships as 'viruses fastening to the side of a gigantic bacterium and injecting into it their own DNA, usurping its internal processes for their own purposes'.[35] Sealers introduced a surprising number of new species, including stock and pest animals, crops and weeds, viruses and bacteria. Yet Crosby's picture is incomplete; Māori had considerable influence over when, where and why most of these species became established. Willingly or unwittingly, Māori hosted the new organisms and mediated their environmental effects.[36] If European ships were 'viruses' then Māori communities were the medium in which they were cultured.

Sealing gangs were forbidden to fraternise with the natives on pain of forfeiting their pay – a 'lay' or proportion of the skins retrieved.[37] But sealers were men left for weeks, months and even years to survive on forbidding shores or barren islets. They always had too little food, and there were no women. From the very beginning some sealers, unsurprisingly, ventured to try the welcome of Māori.[38]

Māori living on the Otago Peninsula were forewarned well before sealers arrived. Already growing potatoes passed on by their southern relatives, they had inspected iron tools and heard about, if not seen, European ships. In Europeans, Ōtākou Māori encountered people, objects and ideas beyond all their experience, but were prepared to engage from the first. Their leaders had no reason to doubt their power to control encounters with small and isolated gangs of sealers, whom they called 'takata pora', the people of the ships.[39]

In Otago, as throughout New Zealand, Māori immediately grasped the transformative potential of some European goods, though in their eyes and hands new objects were inevitably something different. Māori made iron nails the first currency of trade, then rendered them into excellent chisels, gouges and fish-hooks. Iron axes, while valued for their efficiency in felling trees, were also prized weapons: at Bluff in 1813 the Sydney ropemaker Robert Williams believed he could buy a woman's son for a hatchet.[40]

The first sealers to come to the Peninsula perhaps had little choice: Māori could – and would – provide these hungry and lonely men with fresh food, water and shelter. First contacts were profitable to both Māori and the takata pora. They were most often amicable encounters, eagerly sought.⁴¹ The prospect of Māori hospitality even drew a few early sealing ships working eastern coasts to return to Otago Harbour, despite the paucity of their prey. In 1809 men straying from the *Brothers* had received a warm welcome at both Otago Harbour and at Whareakeake, or Murdering Beach, just to the north of the Peninsula.⁴² They included William Tucker, who later returned to Otago and lived at Whareakeake with a Māori woman for a few years; he became known to local Māori as 'Wioree', and introduced the first sheep and goats to southern Māori.⁴³

Encounters were fragile. It was all too easy for either side to unwittingly precipitate conflict. When the *Sydney Cove* anchored off the Otago Peninsula in 1810, several of its gangs harvested seals from Cape Saunders. After the sealers killed a chief, Te Wahie, reportedly for taking a knife and a shirt, the furious Māori attacked, and several violent and lethal affrays followed as the *Sydney Cove* and its gangs fled south from the Peninsula.⁴⁴ In March 1811 the Sydney papers reported 'several boats' crews in various employs having been barbarously murdered, and mostly devoured by the cannibal natives'.⁴⁵

During the quiet decade that followed the end of early sealing, Otago attracted only one or two captains forced to reprovision or refit vessels. These encounters were crucial to how Māori and takata pora began to comprehend one another. The reception of Captain Samuel Fowler and the crew of the brig *Matilda* on the southern coasts in 1814 suggests the volatility of early cross-cultural contacts, occasioned as Otago became drawn into the 'webs of empire' that the British, especially, were weaving, as their colonies and trades encompassed ever more of the world's peoples, objects and organisms.⁴⁶ Fowler had embarked from Sydney with a crew of Indian 'lascars' on a 'pleasant voyage' to 'Otaheite and the neighbouring islands and from thence to China'; he was in fact sealing on behalf of the ex-convict Sydney merchant Simeon Lord, and hoping to sell his harvest in Canton.⁴⁷

Their voyage was disastrous. On the southwest coast of Te Wai Pounamu Māori stole one of the ship's boats and captured six lascars deserting in another.⁴⁸ They kept three of these men, who taught them 'the manner of attacking the Europeans during the heavy rains when their guns could not be used, and also how to dive in order to cut the cables of the vessels during the night'.⁴⁹ North of the Otago Peninsula, a different group of Māori killed at least seven more sealers combing the coasts in search of the missing deserters.⁵⁰

When Fowler and what was left of his now emaciated crew sailed their battered brig into Otago Harbour in the late winter of 1814, they knew nothing of these events.⁵¹ And here, Māori cared for them. The chief 'Papuee' led his people in uprooting half-grown potatoes to feed the sailors, carried water casks to the ship a mile through dense flax, and mended the rigging with flax rope.⁵² On his return to Sydney, Captain Fowler published his views in light of 'divided opinion' about the disposition of Māori. He praised Papuee 'in the highest terms of regard and veneration … his countenance as benign as his manners are mild … he expressed the most friendly concern for the welfare of the captain and his people, and hoped if they should come that way again, he would call and acquaint him with their welfare.'[53]

Though Ōtākou Māori evidently wished to foster trade, it was not easy to negotiate peaceful exchanges. In 1817 the sealer William Tucker, previously hospitably received at Whareakeake, convinced Captain James Kelly of the *Sophia* to return there to trade for potatoes. But the sealers made the mistake of first dealing with the Ōtākou people under Te Matenga Taiaroa's father, Korako, rather than with Te Matahaere, chief of Whareakeake. Korako monopolised the sealers for days and refused to cooperate with the Māori from Whareakeake, who had gathered on the other side of the harbour to greet Tucker and share in 'the presents Taka [sic] was dispensing'.[54] Tucker's cooperation with Korako's attempt to usurp trade insulted and betrayed Te Mataheare.[55]

James Caddell, a survivor of the *Sydney Cove* who lived with southern Māori during this period, suggested: 'If one chief receives a less valuable present than that given to another or if a present be made to one of the common people, the anger of the first knows no bounds. This touchiness makes the position of a stranger, who negotiates with these people and who, whatever happens, must try to please everybody, most awkward.'[56]

By the time Kelly, Tucker and a few others eventually crossed to Whareakeake, Te Matahaere was furious; 'Ko te Matahaere i pouri tona ngakau' – 'Te Matahaere's heart was dark with anger.'[57] His people immediately attacked the small party. Only Kelly escaped alive to the *Sophia*. There he found many of the Ōtākou Māori still aboard and busy trading. Kelly proceeded to wreak a misplaced vengeance, killing or wounding Korako, burning the kaik at Te Rauone Beach – later described by Kelly as the 'beautiful city of Otago', a 'town of about 600 fine houses' – and destroying their fishing fleet of 42 canoes.[58]

Ōtākou Māori abandoned their burnt homes on Te Rauone Beach and rebuilt villages at either end. Soon after, the settlement at Whareakeake was disbanded and its people scattered across Murihiku, with some coming to Ōtākou.[59] The burning of the kaik on the foredunes at Ōtākou perhaps exacerbated the process of sand movement that, as we will see, came to completely swallow this once densely occupied area.[60]

For six years after Kelly's alarming reports were circulated in Australia, not one ship came to Ōtākou. A succession of violent encounters on southern coasts meanwhile cemented the reputation of southern Māori, in the Australian colonies and further abroad, as dangerous, untrustworthy cannibals.[61] The significance of this reputation can be overstressed; fear of cannibalism was undoubtedly prevalent, and even pervasive, but while seal populations and skin prices remained low the point was largely moot. Once duties dropped and prices rose appreciably after 1820, European interest in Murihiku resumed. Sealing then continued despite much smaller harvests, for southern Māori were eager to trade; a peace was brokered, and traffic in a variety of other commodities made profit possible.⁶² Ōtākou Māori did not forget Kelly, however, and the consequences of his attack upon them continued to influence events into the 1830s.

Māori imports: The incorporation of the world

Sealers brought Māori into contact with technology, ideas and organisms from the wider world. Māori assiduously cultivated their presence, and thereby initiated the process of entwining themselves, and the ecosystems of southern New Zealand, into the commercial market economy that was beginning to girdle the globe. Māori attitudes largely determined which aspects of the European biota brought here survived and thrived: plants and animals that they saw value in were tended and transported to places where new habitats were created for them. Sealers also cultivated some vegetables at their camps, but species ignored by Māori soon perished.⁶³

To Māori, the potato was by far the most significant new plant to arrive. Gangs of sealers carried seed potatoes and sometimes other crops to assure a reliable food supply. They introduced potatoes into the far south around 1803. In the minds of Kāi Tahu rangatira, potatoes were a potent way to attract regular contact with European shipping and gain iron: they were 'the means by which the ship people could be cultivated'.⁶⁴ Potatoes quickly became the primary medium of exchange in the growing trade between Māori and takata pora.⁶⁵

Murihiku Māori soon found the tubers meant much more. Potatoes are a fast-growing and reliable carbohydrate-rich crop, and they offered southern Māori higher yields of energy than traditional vegetable foods, for far less effort.⁶⁶ This was especially important given the loss of seals. At a stroke, therefore, southern Māori cultivation of potatoes both removed a primary limitation on population growth and provided Europeans with a compelling reason to trade with them.⁶⁷

Murihiku Māori had immediate success in growing potatoes, the generic name for which was mahetau – 'a string of sinkers'. Māori had long experience of extending kūmara cultivation beyond climatic boundaries, growing them in times and places where they would never survive naturally. Although hardier, potatoes shared similar requirements. In the early winter of 1813, on an abortive expedition to develop New Zealand flax, the Sydney ropemaker Robert Williams entered Bluff Harbour. He reported, 'The natives attend to cultivation of the potato with as much diligence and care as I have ever seen. A field of considerably more than 100 acres [40ha] presented one well cultivated bed, filled with rising crops of all ages, some of which were ready for digging, while others had been but newly planted.'⁶⁸

Williams' visit occurred no later than the end of June – an early and cold time of year both to have just planted frost-vulnerable potatoes in Bluff and to have a crop ready in the ground.[69] But Māori had already accumulated potato varieties that could be harvested at different times, and developed techniques to prolong their growing seasons.[70] The commonest variety was the tatairako or kāpana mangumangua, a firmly fleshed 'small rough kind ... streaked all through with black streaks like marble'[71] that set its tubers particularly late in the year.[72]

Elsdon Best recorded that Māori in the north grew at least two crops of potatoes each year. According to Best, 'in order to obtain a very early crop [Māori] planted seed tubers as early as June in scrub land or light bush, then felled the bush which was burned in early spring. The fire destroyed the haulm of the plants that had grown up through the felled timber, but a new growth soon followed, whereas exposure to frosts would have spoiled the crop.'[73]

James Caddell described similar methods in use in the south in the 1820s, and noted wryly that 'the Natives pay very little attention to any instructions which Europeans give them as they think their own method of doing things preferable'.[74]

Sealer John Boultbee observed techniques borrowed from growing kūmara, including planting potatoes three together with earth piled over them, so that the fields appeared to be full of 'mole hills'.[75] James Somerville, an early settler on the Peninsula, saw the same practice still in use much later, noting Māori at Ōtākou 'planted in hillocks; the way they planted them was to put a potato on the surface and with a grub hoe they drew up the soil all around about until they had made a good-sized heap'.[76]

By 1813 the Māori communities on and around the Peninsula were growing potatoes in this way on the gentle slopes rising to the low saddle south of Taiaroa Head, and just over the harbour mouth on the sand flats at Aramoana.[77] The ash-enriched, free-draining and sun-drenched soil on the harbour side of the Peninsula met the plant's requirements perfectly.

As rangatira organised their people to meet European demand for food, fresh water and hospitality, settlement patterns altered. Communities such as Ōtākou grew because they were clustered around the deep and sheltered anchorages Europeans favoured. More people now stayed at these villages, and for longer, driven above all by the need to cultivate and harvest their potatoes. This far south, only potatoes could be grown and stored in sufficient bulk to provide such a concentration of people with winter food and maintain a trade surplus. Potato cultivation therefore initiated self-reinforcing processes, or positive feedback loops, that increased the density of the Māori inhabitation of the Peninsula and focused it at the harbour mouth.[78] By the 1830s, when European ships came to Otago Harbour much more frequently, Māori at Ōtākou had developed an export economy increasingly based on supplying food and flax fibre to the takata pora, and their communities had become nodes within a transoceanic nexus of trades and exchanges.

European exports: The inadvertent arrivals of the European world

Almost all species brought by Europeans to ease their existence in the south required Māori care to survive. But Māori were also unwilling or unknowing hosts to inadvertent introductions. Only a few organisms were so adaptable that they needed no help from humans whatsoever and began to transform the wider environments lying beyond human habitation.

Prior to contact with the wider world Māori had coexisted with only seven parasites, none of which were particularly harmful. Māori could comprehend new parasites such as fleas, which became known as 'te Pākehā nohinohi', the 'little stranger', and rapidly infested their dwellings and clothing.[79] But no one then knew of the existence of bacteria or viruses. Long voyages followed by isolation in a temperate climate meant that Māori were almost free of such companions.[80] Epidemiological inexperience now made them extremely vulnerable. As Alfred Crosby puts it, 'Maori were as unprepared for continental pathogens as Adam and Eve were for deceitful serpents.'[81] The most problematic of the likely early infections were varieties of influenza, respiratory ailments (especially tuberculosis), and the venereal diseases syphilis and gonorrhoea.

For European ships' crews these diseases were unavoidable occupational hazards, and every ship brought such baggage.[82] Cook's crews first infected some Māori with venereal diseases in Queen Charlotte Sound, and by the mid-nineteenth century these were widespread throughout the Māori population, decreasing fertility and reproductive rates to the extent that the first Māori census of 1858 recorded 35 per cent sterility in women.[83] It may also have been Furneaux's men who, on Cook's second voyage, introduced the sickness known as rewharewha, which various early accounts suggest had devastating effects on Māori communities throughout much of New Zealand. Some of these diseases may have been spread into Murihiku by Māori moving south,[84] but it is probable that sealers introduced them to Māori communities on the Peninsula. Māori culture had no context for such baffling and frightening new sicknesses, which struck down the powerful and the insignificant alike.[85]

One new species needed little help from human beings once ashore. This was the Norway rat. Rats came with Cook and other early explorers, but again it was the sealers who spread them along southern coasts. Surrounded by enormous populations of naïve prey and capable of breeding several times in a year, nothing could stop Norway rats from increasing exponentially, just as kiore had done before them.

Having seen what happens when Norway rats are newly arrived on islands, we can imagine what happened next. Norway rats are comparatively large (200–300 grams) ground-dwelling predators which are comfortable in water, but which seldom climb trees.[86] They soon exerted enormous influence over the composition and structure of almost all ecosystems. On arrival in New Zealand, Norway rats had a wide range of available prey: ground-nesting or ground-dwelling birds (the New Zealand bittern, quail, rails and some wrens), as well as tuatara, lizards, frogs and large invertebrates.[87] Kiore predation had quite probably already killed off some of these species on Otago Peninsula – tuatara, for example – and Norway rats now extirpated the Peninsula's populations of more prey species in a quick pulse. Norway rats are around four times the size of kiore, and are therefore predators of much bigger birds. Colonies of burrow-breeding seabirds nesting on the Peninsula, such as petrels and shearwaters, must have disappeared or declined as Norway rats attacked adults, chicks and eggs.[88] Kiore too were now prey, and though they persisted on the Peninsula until at least the 1850s, their ecological niche was greatly circumscribed.[89]

Tentative trade returns: 1823–31

Otago Harbour was rediscovered by the world after the New South Wales government decided to renew efforts to develop New Zealand flax as a commodity.[90] Previous sporadic efforts to develop marketable hemp from the plant *Phormium tenax* had fallen away, since even after the British freed Pacific trade from the East India Company in 1813, a range of factors counted against flax as a viable commodity: the caution of the British navy (the principal customer); high duties on colonial produce; alternative profitable Pacific trades in sandalwood and sealing; British inexperience with the qualities of New Zealand flax; and reliance on Māori labour.[91] But the British were beginning to relinquish the straitjackets, and the Australian economy was growing; eastern Australia would soon become a fully fledged and booming colony of mass settlement.[92] Accordingly, Australian interest in New Zealand was rekindled in the early 1820s, before exploding from 1828.[93]

Captain William Edwardson took the *Snapper* to Foveaux Strait over the summer of 1822–23, under orders from the New South Wales government to investigate the prospects for trade in flax. Even though he returned with only a small cargo of flax, his voyage aroused considerable interest on both sides of the Tasman Sea. One reason for this was that Edwardson brought back a quantity of Māori 'curios', including birds' skins, woven and carved functional items, and preserved and tattooed heads, for which there was already an established market.[94] Edwardson also introduced southern Māori to pigs, and these soon became a significant trade commodity throughout Murihiku.[95]

Edwardson returned to Sydney with James Caddell, his wife Tokitoki (niece of Honekai), and Tuhawaiki (known to Edwardson as 'Jacky Snapper').[96] Caddell provided the critical interpretive link between the worlds of southern Māori and colonial Australia; with his help, the prospect of peaceful trade was embraced by both sides.

In 1823 the New South Wales government sent the *Mermaid* to Murihiku under Captain John Rudolphus Kent, to purchase more flax, with Caddell and the returning Māori on board. This voyage reopened contact between Ōtākou Māori and the wider world. At Ruapuke in June Kent met the Otago chief Te Matenga Taiaroa, who was visiting his relative Te Wera on his way home from his annual muttonbirding and sealing expedition. Taiaroa and Te Wera jostled to gain advantage from this encounter. Taiaroa impressed Kent, showing 'great ingenuity in understanding and imitating European ways'.[97] Needing Māori women to return to Sydney to clean his cargo of green flax, Kent was persuaded to ship Te Wera and his wife, along with another couple, but was then drawn north towards Ōtākou by Taiaroa's claim that the best shells to scrape flax with were found there.[98]

Kent thought Otago Harbour a new discovery, and named it Port Oxley. He described it as a 'commodious and well sheltered harbour, running in a southerly direction, navigable up about 5 miles[;] a sandy bar lies over the entrance, over which we carried 3 fathoms[;] the clearest channel is on the South side, as many sand banks lie inside, covered at high water'.[99] This first European description highlights a recurrent theme in early ship visits: the difficulty of both locating and entering the harbour, which was shielded from the east by the cryptic coasts of the Peninsula. It also suggests that two channels, known to Māori as Ōtākou and Aramoana, then connected the harbour to the outer sea.

When he arrived Kent saw 'two native settlements, one near the Harbour mouth, the other a short distance up the river but the inhabitants are few'.[100] It should be remembered that many Ōtākou Māori were away muttonbirding at the time.[101] Everybody was anxious. The Otākou people backed off the beach into the bush and waved their cloaks to signal their peaceful intent; the Europeans would not land until, with Caddell's help, each party was reassured of the other's intentions. The Europeans 'were met on the beach by two old men, who touched noses with us as customary enquiring from whence we came, and what was our business'.[102] The Ōtākou Māori were happy to trade what little dressed flax they had to hand, explaining that:

> *the natives to the Southward had told them a vessel would not come for flax, that it was not true the reports they had heard to that effect, and very justly observed the Southerns had told them so for the purpose of keeping all the trade within their own limits, but now when they found a vessel had come, and would come again, they meant to commence manufacturing, as soon as the warm weather set in, and would likewise inform all their friends accordingly.*[103]

When more Māori arrived from the north two days later, the lascar with them (a survivor from the attacks on the *Matilda*) declared that: 'Not knowing that the flax would ever become an object of trade, they seldom manufactured more than is required, to make their garments, but now that they saw a vessel come for it, he had no doubt but a great quantity could be procured, in a few months, as this party of natives would inform the other tribes, along the coast.'[104]

The desire of different Māori groups throughout the south to monopolise access to Europeans was clear to Kent: 'There is certainly a very great jealousy existing between the parties, and their only care at present seems to be in watching each others' motions.'[105] Kent reported that 'I was much pleased with the manner of our reception by these southern savages[;] they with great warmth told me they did not intend to kill any more white men now that we have become friends by commencing trade.'[106]

Peace held and trade continued under the authority of Te Whakataupuka, son of Honekai and Kohuwai and an embodiment of the truce between Kāti Māmoe and Kāi Tahu.[107] Te Whakataupuka forbade the killing of takata pora. He was supported in this stance by the other leaders of Murihiku, all his close relatives. They included the Otago people's foremost rangatira, Tahatu, described by the sealer John Boultbee as 'a man of peaceful habits, the reverse of Pahee [Te Pahi], his brother, who was a warrior'.[108] Māori desire for trade was matched by growing wariness of British power after Te Pahi's drowning in 1823 was attributed to atua displeasure at his recent killing of American sealers from the *General Gates*.[109] Their wariness was promptly reinforced in a more material fashion by the visit of British warship HMS *Tees* to Foveaux Strait in 1824.[110]

Māori dominated the flax trade, despite efforts to establish flax plantations and manufacture fibre in Australia, because New Zealand flax did not grow well in Australia and because the British failed to mechanise fibre production effectively, meaning that it required enormous amounts of labour.[111] John Marmon, in Otago with Kent in 1824, said that the crew attempted to work flax there, but that it turned black; it was 'most useful as the natives dressed it'.[112] Skilled Māori women produced perhaps 10 pounds (4.5kg) of fibre a day; at that rate only Māori could economically produce flax fibre fine enough to find a market.[113]

The reliance on Māori labour meant that the flax trade, like the timber trade, was focused on the more populous north of New Zealand. Knowledgeable captains such as Kent and James Herd, who each flirted with the south, perceived that sealing was falling away and established their trading settlements based on timber and flax in the Hokianga.[114] Such flax trade as occurred in the south still inaugurated a different kind of economic relationship both between Māori and tangata pora, and between Māori and their environment. Whereas commodities like potatoes met the fleeting demands of transitory visitors, flax products were exported to meet British demand for rope to rig ships and material to stuff mattresses. In response to its new commercial value, Māori began to alter their relationship with flax. Flax fibre bound traditional Māori society together – among many other items, their houses, clothes and fishing nets all required flax, and small, localised populations imposed only limited demands on flax resources. Commodity trades, however, offered the prospect of markets whose size and scope Māori could scarcely comprehend.

Te Whakataupuka had a counterpart in Kent, who led the development of trade in Murihiku. Kent perhaps ranks second to Cook as a mariner who advanced knowledge of New Zealand's coasts: he discovered 12 harbours, in most of which he established trade. He was later to marry Tiria, daughter of the first Māori king, Te Wherowhero.[115]

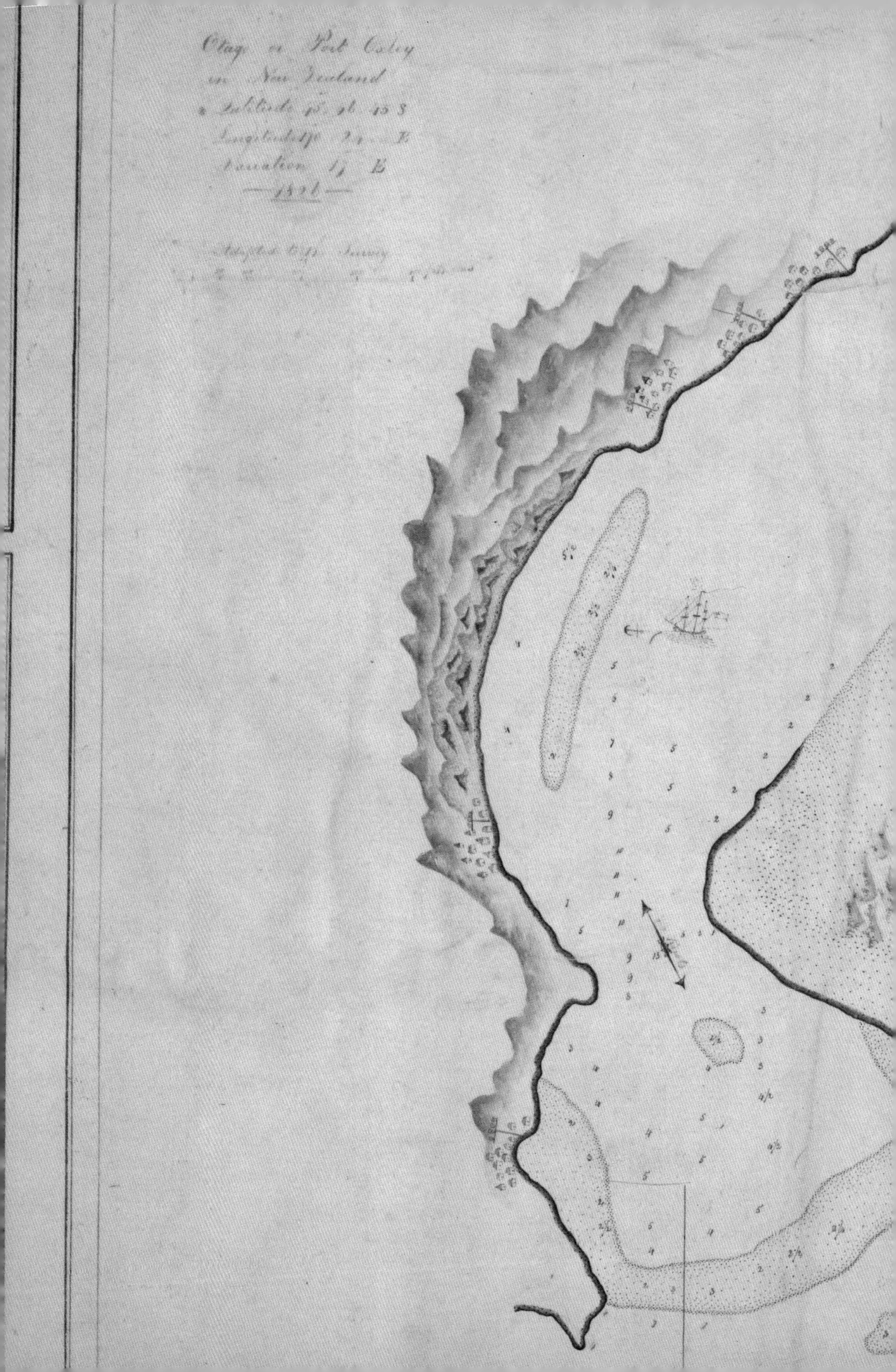

Otago or Port Oxley
in New Zealand
Latitude 45° 51′ 45″ S
Longitude 170° 24′ E
Variation 14° E
1844

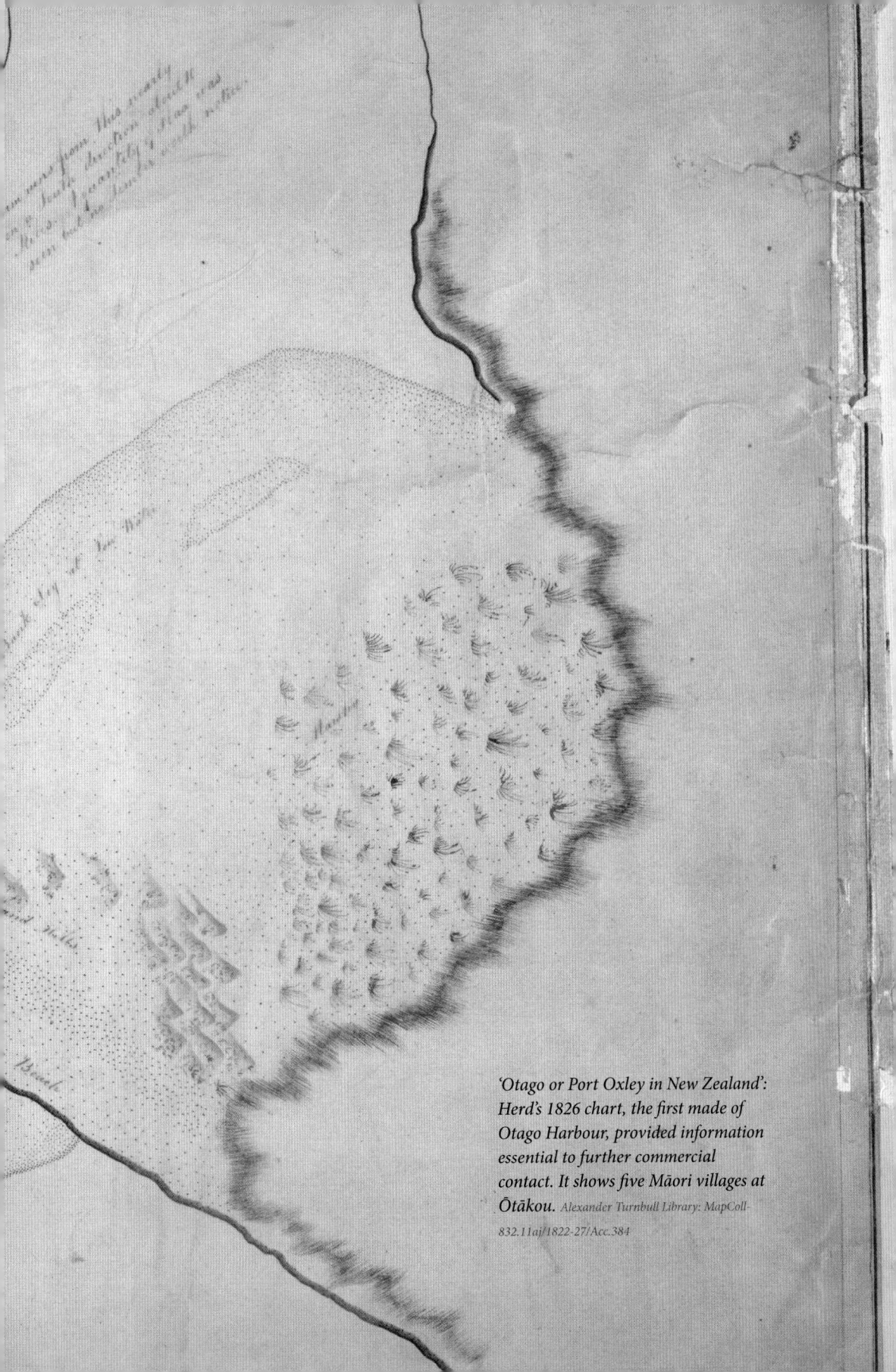

'Otago or Port Oxley in New Zealand': Herd's 1826 chart, the first made of Otago Harbour, provided information essential to further commercial contact. It shows five Māori villages at Ōtākou. *Alexander Turnbull Library: MapColl-832.11aj/1822-27/Acc.384*

Over the next few years Kent proceeded to establish a trading network based on flax that linked the principal Māori settlements of the south to Sydney.[116] According to Boultbee, by 1827 Kent had 'acquired an extensive knowledge of the language, which with his partiality for the people themselves, procured him considerable interest. He generally had 8 or 9 New Zealanders on board his vessel, who went to and from Sydney with him.' He also left agents on shore with the Māori communities at Akaroa, Foveaux Strait and perhaps Ōtākou, to organise cargo.[117]

It was probably Kent who persuaded Captain Herd, leader of the first New Zealand Company expedition, to abandon any thought of establishing a settlement in Port Pegasus on Stewart Island, when they met there in April of 1826.[118] After Kent told him of the qualities of Otago, Herd and Kent together visited Otago Harbour in May. Kent returned to Sydney with 10 tons of 'the very best quality' flax, while Herd's visit eventually publicised the existence of Otago Harbour in Sydney and Hobart, providing ship captains with the first detailed chart of the harbour's entrance and anchorage, an object essential to establishing regular contacts.[119]

Herd's chart reveals the influence on settlement patterns of increased European contact: it shows five villages along the waterfront inside the heads on the Otago Peninsula, where three years before Kent had seen only two villages.[120] One village, known traditionally as Tarewai, is marked at Pilots Beach; another, Te Ruatitiko, lies on Te Rauone Beach in the southern lee of Harington Point; and three more, Tahakopa, Omate and Waipapake, are strung close together just south of Wellers Rock.[121] Herd's chart also shows whata or raised storage platforms, and confirms the two channels inside the harbour entrance. It also hints at other possibilities: as mentioned earlier, the area behind Te Rauone Beach was burnt in 1817; on the chart this area is shaded brown, not blue like the rest of the landscape.

The New Zealand Company settlers' leader was Thomas Shepherd, nurseryman, surveyor and disciple of the revolutionary landscape designer Lancelot 'Capability' Brown.[122] Shepherd's journal of this visit makes valuable observations of Māori and their landscape.[123] At anchor inside the heads, he described 'an exceedingly good harbour much enclosed on all sides by sloaping [sic] hills of various heights which prevented any winds from Injuring the vessel'. Other than in the vicinity of the anchorage at Otākou, 'the hills were chiefly covered in trees'.[124] By contrast, when Shepherd arrived at the future site of Dunedin he observed that: 'It is singular the country should thus change all at once from woods to open land which very much resembles some parts in England. There is a complete division between the open land and the woods.'[125]

Shepherd was constrained by Herd's caution over the threat posed by local Māori, 'being ordered not to go too far into the woods', but still managed to scramble around Kamautaurua (Quarantine Island) and found 'on not more than 20 square yards 40 different shrubs'. He described the forest on the harbour's flanks as containing 'pine trees', but much inferior to those seen at Stewart Island. He concluded that there was 'a considerable quantity of timber fit for common purposes (no spars fit for masts), a greater variety of ornamental trees and shrubs than at any other place in New Zealand'.[126]

Shepherd differs from Herd, stating that there were 'four distinct parties at 4 different villages' (not five) that together comprised about 200 Māori, who visited the ship over two days to trade.[127] He felt that during their 'considerable trade' Māori 'dealt with us fairly'.[128] Shepherd hints at the wider range of products Māori had developed to provision shipping, describing their trade as 'a few tools for potatoes, flour, hogs, greens, fish, etc', as well as flax.[129]

Ōtākou Māori had evidently traded quickly with their relatives to the south to gain pigs, which were already a trading staple; indeed, unlike potatoes, pigs did not immediately form a crucial part of the southern Māori diet, probably because of their overriding value for trade.[130] Flour may have been a fern-root product, but could also have been wheat: Caddell had told Edwardson in 1824 that the Foveaux Strait Māori grew wheat, as well as cabbages, carrots and turnips.[131] Greens were now grown widely; the sealer John Boultbee, who has left us by far the most detailed account of Europeans' interactions with southern Māori, reported in 1827 that 'Almost at every place on the coast, where people have been in the habit of staying any time, are to be found greens growing wild'.[132]

Māori procured an increasing range of goods from Europeans in return. That year John Boultbee wrote that the 'principal trade' at Foveaux Strait was 'in flax and potatoes, which small vessels from Sydney obtain in barter for powder, ball, muskets, and other European articles, but the latter are most in request'. He also noted with some satisfaction that 'The father of a family will sell a daughter, or two, or three, if required, for a musket each! And it was in this manner that we acquired our little seraglio.'[133] Canoes were still used, but Māori had begun to step European sails, and had abandoned paddles for oars that provided greater leverage and allowed smaller crews.[134] Many Māori had also developed an addiction to nicotine and craved tobacco, and this habit spread rapidly among men, women and even children, despite high prices.[135] By 1843 Shortland was to find that tobacco 'supplies the place of small money in all parts of the country remote from the towns'.[136] Smoking strong tobacco through short, hot, clay pipes obviously exacerbated problems with tuberculosis.[137]

The other articles that Boultbee alludes to include blankets and European clothes, in which many Māori men now dressed, especially when meeting Europeans. This change suggests the high esteem in which things European were held. These clothes were seldom as warm or as functional as traditional cloaks, and wearing them also exposed Māori to the parasites and diseases of the former owners. Many European observers lamented seeing Māori in dirty, flea-ridden blankets – some even citing it as a cause of population decline.[138] Such observations, however, reflect a nostalgia for 'natives' in their 'natural state'. Thus Boultbee regarded Te Whakataupuka, who refused to ever wear European clothing, as 'the most complete model of strength, activity & elegance I had seen combined in any man'.[139]

Te Whakataupuka's attitudes to things European are interesting. He encouraged trade because of the wonder of the new weapons, tools and organisms, but he did not like takata pora themselves, who were 'selfish'. He allocated Codfish Island, to the west of Stewart Island, to Europeans as an island enclave, where they would not contaminate his communities.[140] The modern incarnation of Codfish Island as a sanctuary for native species unable to survive in settler company is thus more than a little ironic.[141]

Southern Māori rangatira had by now either been to, or heard eye-witness accounts of, Australia, and of their own ancestral homelands and beyond. The possibilities of an enormously enlarged world were opening to them: the potential gain in wealth and mana in managing exchanges with that world was immense. When Taiaroa and Karetai encountered John Boultbee in the south in 1827, they were fascinated by his demonstrations of writing in the sand and competed for his attention and affection, offering him clothing, women and anything else he might desire if he would only come to live at Otago. Boultbee agreed – but then a ship chanced by and returned him to Australia.[142]

In 1829 therefore, when some of the crew of the British whaler *Clarence* reportedly deserted at Ōtākou, Māori were eager to help sail the ship back to Hobart.[143] They seemed keen also to capture the American sealing ship *Rob Roy* when it visited in 1830 to trade for potatoes and flax.[144] However, there is no positive evidence that Otago Peninsula had any resident Europeans until the early 1830s, when whaling brought a sudden influx.

Southern rangatira now sought muskets above all else.[145] A few were used during the summer fighting season of 1825 to 1826, when the Kāi Tahu hapū in Otago became embroiled in a bitter internecine conflict on the eastern seaboard, which became known as the Kai Huānga ('Eat Relation') feud.[146] But many more soon arrived: the *Vittoria*, for example, took 120 muskets to trade on southern coasts in 1831.[147] Māori desire for muskets also stimulated a more permanent and substantial European presence in the south: Te Whakataupuka gained 60 muskets, 450kg each of powder and ball and sundry other merchandise, by becoming patron of Peter Williams' shore whaling station established at Preservation Inlet. These guns were required urgently. The uneven development of trade with Europeans had upset the balance of power in the Māori world. Basing himself strategically around Cook Strait, Te Rauparaha gained guns first: he demolished Kāi Tahu power in Canterbury, and eyed the south.[148]

This was the backdrop against which the leaders of Ōtākou considered the terms on which they would accept a proposal from Sydney entrepreneurs, the Weller brothers, to establish a shore whaling station on the Otago Peninsula.

Conclusion

Ōtākou Māori began to alter their lifeways to take advantage of the new tools, materials and organisms as trade with Europeans developed over the 1820s. Between 1823 and 1826 Ōtākou grew from two to five villages, immediately after trade was revived. Boultbee heard then that it was the largest and oldest settlement on southern coasts,[149] but just how large it was is hard to say. In 1826 Shepherd estimated that there were only 200 Māori present at the heads, albeit during the peak of the muttonbirding season.[150] If the 50 whare (houses) shown on Herd's chart are meant as an accurate count (the point is unclear), then perhaps there was only permanent accommodation in the various villages for about 400 people.[151]

As the European presence in the Pacific intensified, the frequency of encounter with Māori on and around the Otago Peninsula increased. Sealing and associated shipbuilding were important to the commercial development of New South Wales, after which colonial trade with New Zealand diversified. The visit of the ships of the first New Zealand Company to Ōtākou in 1826, searching for somewhere to disembark settlers and to exploit flax and timber, was a forerunner of things to come.

Throughout this time, however, the takata pora were fleeting visitors, people who brought an intermittent injection of objects and organisms, but who seldom stayed to create habitats for them. Those few takata pora who did linger had to find a niche within Māori society to survive. Similarly, bar the Norway rat and to a lesser extent pigs, the significant agents of environmental change that had accompanied the arrival of Europeans – their pathogens, plants and animals – relied on Māori hosts. Ōtākou Māori, meanwhile, remained secure in their own home on the Peninsula, but they began to look out over the ocean horizon to a newly widened world.[152]

Mouth of Japs - from the
Entrance to Otago
Harbour -

CHAPTER 5: 'SOON MAY THE WELLERMAN COME': WHALING AT ŌTĀKOU 1831–48

*There was a ship that put to sea
The name of the ship was the Billy of Tea
The winds blew up, her bow dipped down
O blow, my bully boys, blow.*

*Soon may the Wellerman come
And bring us sugar and tea and rum
One day, when the tonguin' is done
We'll take our leave and go.*

*She had not been two weeks from shore
When down on her a right whale bore
The captain called all hands and swore
He'd take that whale in tow.*

*Before the boat had hit the water
The whale's tail came up and caught her
All hands to the side, harpooned and fought her
When she dived down below.*

*No line was cut, no whale was freed
The Captain's mind was not of greed
But he belonged to the whaleman's creed
She took the ship in tow.*

*For forty days, or even more
The line went slack, then tight once more
All boats were lost (there were only four)
But still the whale did go.*

*As far as I know, the fight's still on
The line's not cut and the whale's not gone
The Wellerman makes his regular call
To the Captain, crew, and all.*   —ANON.[1]

The arrival of the Wellers' whaling station

Thomas Shepherd, in Otago Harbour in 1826, foresaw that 'a whale fishery would answer here. We see a number every day.'[2] The whales that Shepherd saw were southern right whales, so called because they were the 'right' whale to hunt.[3] Slow and placid, right whales could be caught along coasts and were so rich in oil that they seldom sank after death.[4] Most important of all, they were predictable. From May to October pods of females migrated north up the South Island's east coast, congregating to calve and nurse in sheltered waters like Otago Harbour. Whalers could lie in wait here, safe at anchor and protected from wild and stormy winter seas. They killed the calves first, because mothers did not leave even dead young.[5]

Whale oil was to the nineteenth century what petroleum has been since the twentieth. It greased the bearings of the Industrial Revolution, lit the lamps of Europe, heated homes, and was a crucial ingredient in the manufacture of any number of commodities, from candles and crayons to batteries and polishes.[6] 'Whale bone', or baleen, was variously used too in items from corsets to chairs, and 'made excellent buggy whips'.[7] Whaling was far more valuable than any other activity the Australian merchants could contemplate. However, as the East India Company monopoly fell away, the powerful British whaling lobby insisted on punitive duties on colonial oil that locked the Australian merchants out of whaling until the British government had overruled all opposition. In 1820 Britain lowered the duties as part of the decision to promote Australia as a fully functioning colony of settlement.[8]

Whalers had already enjoyed success with whaling around Australia, and the removal of the duty and the strength of the market prompted Sydney and Hobart merchants to establish shore whaling stations on Australian coasts. These shore stations required little initial capital to establish, and minimised risks to fragile, expensive shipping. As the 1820s ended, Australian entrepreneurs extended their operations to New Zealand.

The Sydney firm Weller and Co. was among the first to realise the possibilities New Zealand offered.[9] Perhaps prompted by Shepherd's descriptions of Otago Harbour, Joseph Brooks Weller, the eldest of three brothers, inspected the site in the autumn of 1831 and proposed to local Māori that Weller and Co. establish a shore whaling station at Ōtākou.[10]

The primary reason that Ōtākou Māori accepted the Wellers' proposal was probably to get guns.[11] The deal is not documented, but nor was it likely to be so soon after the infamous *Elizabeth* affair. In the spring of 1830 the Ngāti Toa rangatira Te Rauparaha had used the Sydney trader *Elizabeth*, under Captain William Stewart, as cover and lure from which to ambush and kill the paramount Kāi Tahu rangatira, the ariki Te Maiharanui and his family.[12] Captain Stewart's role was so controversial that it led London to appoint James Busby as British Resident to New Zealand. Meanwhile, bitterness lingering from the Kai Huānga ('Eat Relation') feud of 1825–

John Barnicoat, Otago, May 1, 1844. *The buildings of the Wellers' whaling station at Otākou. Harwood's store is the large central building with a prominent flag pole.*

Pencil on paper, 170 x 330mm. Hocken Collections, Uare Taoka o Hākena, University of Otago: A B263, #1930

28 meant that the Otago leaders declined pleas to ally with their northern relatives. The following fighting season Te Rauparaha sacked important Kāi Tahu settlements at Kaiapoi and Banks Peninsula.[13] Refugees poured into Otago. Te Whakataupuka led the unprecedented collective Kāi Tahu response with substantial arms secured by allowing Peter Williams to establish a whaling station at Preservation Inlet.[14] This sudden surge in Te Whakataupuka's power would not have wholly pleased the Ōtākou rangatira, and they had every reason to follow his lead.

The Wellers' guns probably helped Karetai and Taiaroa as they joined their southern relatives in Kāi Tahu counter-attacks against Te Rauparaha over the next two summers.[15] Despite being unable to achieve any decisive victory, Kāi Tahu were more or less successful; their taua (war parties) fended off Te Rauparaha, who never seriously threatened Ōtākou and the other settlements south of Banks Peninsula.[16] Kāi Tahu also plundered the whaling stations under Te Rauparaha's patronage in Cloudy Bay. This success was a crucial precondition for the Wellers to become securely established on the Otago Peninsula.

The Wellers built their settlement just up 'the river', as they called Otago Harbour, at the rocky point now named after them. The settlement soon after burned down, but the Wellers were committed and rebuilt immediately. Their station eventually centred on a large house for Joseph and Edward Weller (later Octavius Harwood's store), surrounded by whalers' cottages, stores and jetties. Strung along the beach in close proximity to the station were the Māori villages of Tahakopa and Te Ruatitiko, Omate and Ohinetu.

ABOVE: *Tahakopa kaik, or village, as drawn by John Barnicoat, consisted of small, low-roofed thatched houses, neatly fenced. Whaleboats and whata complete the scene.* John Barnicoat, May 1844; pencil on paper, 103 x 413mm. Hocken Collections, Uare Taoka o Hākena, University of Otago: #2076

BELOW: *John Barnicoat*, Mouth of Otago/Entrance to Otago Harbour. *The tryworks to render whales' blubber, and the jetty, of the Wellers' principal whaling station at Ōtākou.*

Pencil on paper, 103 x 413mm. Hocken Collections, Uare Taoka o Hākena, University of Otago: 94/272 a. #2121

When the surveyor John Barnicoat arrived here in 1844 in the company of Frederick Tuckett, who was seeking a suitable site for the Scottish settlement, he was drawn to sketch and describe in his diary the striking combination of Māori and whalers at Ōtākou. It was, he wrote, 'an interesting village with its strange mix of white + native inhabitations, whale boats + canoes, barrels by the hundreds, cellars, whale shears, gigantic remains of whales …'[17] His drawings capture this combination especially well.

Whaling on the Otago Peninsula initiated a new order. Whereas sealers and flax traders were occasional visitors, the Wellers' shore stations were substantial commercial operations. At their peak, over 80 men worked through the season at Ōtākou; from the mid-1830s bay-whaling ships brought influxes of hundreds more men who stayed for weeks, if not months at a time. During the 1830s Otago Harbour was the second busiest port in New Zealand after the Bay of Islands.[18]

The period between 1831 and 1848 was a window of time in which Māori and European coexisted on the Otago Peninsula in relative equality and intimate proximity. Māori men whaled for the Wellers and provided the labour to maintain the station. Māori women comforted the whalers throughout the season and occasionally formed more permanent partnerships. The station leaders married Māori women of mana, whose descendants often became significant figures in the community.[19] Māori supplied commodities that the Wellers could sell in Sydney, and protected them from potential attack by other Māori. In return the Wellers' station and store gave Māori reliable access to European goods, while their shipping directed and funnelled an export trade and allowed rangatira to visit Sydney regularly. Ōtākou became a small town attached to a flourishing port, with far-flung trade.

Māori and European fortunes entwined at Ōtākou, their shared world initially predicated on the exploitation of the whales. In the aftermath of the whales' destruction and the Wellers' subsequent abandonment of the station, however, some men remained and were soon joined by others. Between 1840 and 1848 there was a deepening of what had begun to develop during the whaling years – a mixed community with a new relationship to the environment of the Otago Peninsula.[20]

Through negotiating all manner of day-to-day exchanges, Māori and European gradually came to a mutual understanding and tacit trust. Domestic affairs, sexual contact, dispute resolution, the terms of labour and property rights all had to be managed. In the process, a community began to emerge that was created from the intersection of two cultures. This was the hinge between an old order and the imminence of something new for people and their place on the Otago Peninsula.

A town, a port and its trade: A new economic order

The Wellers initially prospered at Otago, and exported over 200 tuns of oil each year from 1834 until 1838. In 1835 they tried out 97 whales, retrieved 430 tuns of oil and cleaned 20 tons of 'bone', which combined might have fetched over £10,000 on the London market.[21] Prices almost doubled the following year after what George Weller, in the exuberant expectation of clearing a profit of £8600, described as the 'glorious news' of 'the total failure of the Davis Straits [Greenland] fishery'.[22] Such prospects prompted expansion, and the Wellers established two further 'fisheries' at Ōtākou above Pilots Beach and on Te Rauone Beach adjacent to Te Ruatitiko in 1836 and 1837,[23] and soon after set up stations at Taieri Island, Purakaunui, Timaru and Banks Peninsula.[24]

George ought to have considered more carefully the implications of the fact that, by his own admission, Sydney had gone 'Black Whaling mad', while 'no less than 60 sail of American whalers' were expected to join the shore stations on the southeast coast of New Zealand.[25] George's own trumpeting only helped prompt a flood of competition. American bay whalers were 'swarming' on the coast by 1836, and four or five fished Otago Harbour itself.[26] That year, John Hughes deserted the Wellers to establish his own station at Moeraki, while in 1837 Johnny Jones established the first of his rival stations at Waikouaiti (present-day Karitāne).[27] Nor were matters helped by the January 1837 publication in the *Australian* of the latitude and longitude of Otago, 'famous in point of obtaining right whales', together with precise descriptions of how to locate and enter the harbour.[28] French whalers joined the Americans from 1838.[29] Before the Scots settlers ever arrived, over 100 whaling ships had visited Otago coasts and more than 90 ships had entered the harbour.[30]

Whale numbers plummeted, and the Wellers' operations collapsed. The Ōtākou station was reduced from 11 whaleboats in 1835 to two by 1840, when only 10 tuns of oil were taken. Bay whalers had a similar lack of success.[31] Less oil and lower prices, combined with a series of shipwrecks and Edward's ill health, spelt the end for the Wellers' expansive enterprise. From 11 December 1841 the central Ōtākou station was advertised for sale in the *New Zealand Gazette* and *Wellington Spectator*.[32] The Wellers' woes continued: they were bankrupted in 1842 by the failure of their extensive land speculations in New South Wales.

Shore whaling at Ōtākou persisted a little longer; over the next few years one or two boats still put out from Otago Harbour as the occasion arose, while bay and deep-sea whalers continued to call in regularly. However, the character of occupation increasingly took on a new form, as whalers and Māori alike searched for other ways to sustain themselves.

Māori had formed much of the Wellers' labour force. Māori men worked both as shore whalers, and on bay whalers using the harbour as a base for the season. Edward Shortland estimated that Māori provided half the Wellers' whalers over the first four years, and one third thereafter.[33] They were employed on much the same terms as Europeans, sometimes rising through the ranks to become headsmen of their boats.[34] The Wellers also employed Māori as the general labour force for the station. Octavius Harwood, the Wellers' store clerk, controlled much of the day-to-day operation of

Octavius Harwood: the Weller Brothers' store clerk at Ōtākou kept a diary and account books that are the richest record of shore whaling in New Zealand. Harwood lived out his life on the Peninsula and died in 1900. Several of his children farmed on the Peninsula after him.

G.C. Thomson Collection, Hocken Collections, Uare Taoka o Hākena, University of Otago: P1951-003/1-093

the station after his arrival in 1838, in particular organising Māori labour. Between May and October of 1838 his journal describes Māori building and repairing houses, sheds, roads, fences, and even a sea wall made of whale heads. Māori fetched wood and water, removed sandbanks, dug ditches and took provisions to the outlying stations.[35] In summer when whaling ended the station ceased to be the focal point of Māori labour. Nevertheless, there was still considerable involvement between the two groups; Harwood, for example, employed Māori women to tend and harvest his potatoes.[36]

Harwood enforced punctuality and diligence by stopping the Māori employees' rations of 'grog', or even provisions and tobacco, for persistent absences.[37] He did much the same with the European whalers; when they went on strike 'on account of the meat' he stopped their grog, and Māori manned the boats instead.[38] Everyone waited to be paid off at season's end, running up credit in the interim; control over this truck system was another tool Harwood could use to enforce discipline.[39] Though some accounts have stressed a fear of Māori violence, Harwood never reported any eventuating, and according to his son Octavius Jr. 'was seldom afraid of the natives but there were times he felt great anxiety regarding many of the abandoned foreigners'.[40]

The Wellers' core business in New Zealand was always whaling, but they tried hard to diversify their operations. Their store exploited their position as the hub of shore whaling and became a trading post for men from rival shore stations, and bay and deep-sea whalers in need of provisioning. They exported a range of local resources: potatoes, pork, grain, timber, seal skins, muttonbirds, dried and smoked fish, flax, raupō 'coopers' flags' (leaves used between staves to make a barrel watertight) and Māori 'curios'.

Rangatira organised the labour and land of their people to increase the production of timber, flax, pigs and potatoes, selling either to the Wellers or to the bay-whalers' ships. By 1834 Māori had a substantial export trade, sending 30 tons of potatoes in a single shipment to Sydney in August that year.[41]

Māori leaders gained unprecedented access to the wider world. They regularly used the Wellers' ships as transport to and from Australia, and in doing so tried to establish friendly relationships with colonial commercial and political leaders. When Karetai visited Sydney in 1833, for example, he was at pains to stress that 'his countrymen want to live in peace, and be protected'.[42]

Māori also gained access to a panoply of European goods. Octavius Harwood's journal and accounts show that he dealt largely with Māori of mana, who negotiated exchanges not only for themselves but on behalf of their people. Something of their personalities shows through in their purchases. Karetai, who had a number of wives, traded potatoes and seal skins for iron pots, knives, clothes, blankets, boots, trousers, alcohol, tobacco and sugar. Taiaroa showed an early fondness for alcohol and fine clothes.[43] Trust and mutual esteem evidently developed in some cases. Tuhawaiki, for example, bought a whaleboat in 1842 on the promise of paying with three tons of flax and a ton of pork, which contract he faithfully fulfilled over the course of 1843.[44]

Sealing and whaling boats changed the structure of daily Māori life more than any other European technology. Māori clearly valued them, for they were easily their most expensive purchases.[45] Prices have been described as high,[46] but in fact varied considerably and on the whole were not exorbitant, given the scarcity of supply and the intense demand.[47] The Māori switch from canoes to European boats is evident in the changing composition of Kāi Tahu taua sailing north to engage Te Rauparaha. That of 1833 (the taua iti) consisted of six double canoes; that of 1834 (the taua nui), 29 vessels in a mixture of canoes and European boats; while Tuhawaiki's taua of 1839 was a flotilla of at least 10 boats.[48] Harwood described 'fishing double canoes' as common on his arrival in 1838, but by 1840 they were seen rotting on the shore at Ōtākou.[49]

By 1843 Shortland had difficulty convincing Māori to guide him on coastal trails now abandoned and overgrown for, as he remarked, where possible Māori had 'ceased to travel by land … since they have so generally obtained possession of whaling and sealing boats; for these are easily managed, and by few hands. The large double canoes they formerly had were too valuable a property to be possessed by any but the wealthy, and required a more numerous crew for their management.'[50]

Southern Māori had always drawn much if not most of their food from the sea and shore. The arrival of takata pora had focused their economy even more precisely on the

'Sketch of the Middle Island of New Zealand: Reduced from original Maori sketch made for Mr Halswell'. Unknown Otago Māori made this mariner's chart from memory in about 1841 for the New Zealand Company employee Edmund Halswell. Its distortions show the importance of harbours and river mouths, and it notes information important to the New Zealand Company. Otago is described as a harbour where schooners can reach the head of the harbour and there is 'Plenty of white pine'. Alexander Turnbull Library: MapColl-834ap/[1841-2?]/Acc.527

harbours that ships and boats frequented. Now, Māori took to crewing those ships in large numbers and, as Shortland noted, sailed boats to the virtual exclusion of coastal travel on foot. In short, Māori in the south were and remained a maritime people. The extent to which southern Māori looked out to sea before inland has perhaps been obscured by what Michael Stevens, making similar points, has called the 'long shadow' of the land wars and the land claims discourse of Treaty politics and the Waitangi Tribunal.[51] That Māori in the south understood their world as coastal – and shared that understanding with the takata pora – is seen in the map opposite, drawn in 1841 by a number of unknown Otago Māori for the New Zealand Company official Edmund Storr Halswell.[52]

Ōtākou Māori must have felt fairly secure and cautiously optimistic by the mid-1830s. Te Rauparaha's raids may have smashed the northern settlements, but they also welded Kāi Tahu into a much more cohesive entity and swelled the southern population, meaning that the Ōtākou rangatira were well placed to assume key leadership positions in the nascent iwi, as demonstrated in their roles in fending off Te Rauparaha.

Intimacy, however, entailed risk. As Ōtākou Māori intermingled with the Wellers and other whalers, more and more members of a foreign ecosystem entered their environment. The consequences proved swift and severe.

He Taru Tawhiti: '*Afflictions from afar*'[53]

A spate of epidemic diseases struck southern Māori from the mid-1830s. Whole communities fell ill, all at the same time, and many died. One series of incidents is particularly important, because it precipitated both a significant political union and the first and most deadly of the epidemics. In July 1834 the Wellers were alarmed by unprecedented threats to their station and to shipping in the harbour from the taua nui, returning from its campaign against Te Rauparaha. Trouble had been sparked by the presence in the harbour of one of Captain James Kelly's ships. Ōtākou Māori had neither forgotten nor forgiven Kelly's attack on them in 1817. Just the year before they had sent a letter warning Kelly never to send his ships to Ōtākou.[54] The sudden death of an infant further inflamed a tense situation. Māori blamed the Europeans, who now believed that Māori had decided to destroy both the whaling station and all the shipping in the harbour. Captain Anglem readied the Wellers' ship the *Lucy Ann* for defence, and threatened that Tuhawaiki, then visiting Sydney, would be hung if they were attacked. The success of this tactic then encouraged Captain Anglem to persuade Karetai and his family, along with another chief, to come aboard the *Lucy Ann*, at which point he promptly set sail for Sydney, taking them hostage.[55]

In Sydney Karetai and his family became 'guests' of the Reverend Samuel Marsden, who gave them Christian instruction and introduced Karetai to New South Wales Governor Bourke 'in order that he might tell his own story'.[56] Karetai told Marsden he wanted missionaries, not guns. The governor directed Marsden to buy him presents.[57] Other men had his ear: Joseph Weller, Captain Anglem, and Jacky Guard (whose whaling stations in Cloudy Bay had been plundered by the taua nui while he was shipwrecked in Taranaki, and his wife and children kidnapped) spread alarm in the Sydney papers, which breathlessly reported the 'terrible murders on the New Zealand coast' where 'massacre stalks abroad with impunity', and called for a 'crusade against the murderous and bloody savage'.[58] A letter written by Joseph Weller appeared in the *Sydney Herald* of 16 October 1834 arguing that were it not for the relatives of the rangatira held in Sydney, the station would have been burnt and pillaged.[59] The merchants petitioned the governor for aid, and he obliged by sending the warship HMS *Alligator* to Taranaki and arming the Wellers with swivel guns and a long gun.[60]

In December, however, a returning ship's captain reported in Sydney that 'the natives of Otago were very civil … so much so that Mr. Weller has resolved to remain a few months longer, in expectation that hostilities would cease between the natives and Europeans'.[61] It seems that the Wellers and the Otago Māori had renegotiated terms, and sealed their renewed understanding in the fashion familiar to both cultures through the marriage of Edward Weller and Paparu, Tahatu's daughter.[62] Personal ties now increasingly paralleled and cemented a strategic and commercial alignment of interests. Edward Weller learned to speak southern Māori and, after Paparu's death in childbirth in 1838, promptly formed another liaison with Taiaroa's daughter, Nikūru.[63] By 1836 George Weller felt able to advise Edward that if rival Sydney firm Campbell and Co. attempted to set up in the harbour as competition, he should 'let the Natives give him a benefit'.[64]

George did not know that measles had now struck Ōtākou Māori. While Karetai was detained in Sydney, the *Sydney Gazette* reported that a 'disease resembling measles has recently attacked infants in Sydney, and now prevails to some extent. The faculty speak of it as being of a trifling nature, and not liable to serious results if promptly attended to.'[65] What was trifling to Europeans was often fatal to Māori, but neither comprehended the risks they took in mingling.

Measles can only persist in and around clusters of people that constantly supply susceptible hosts, where it typically becomes a fairly innocuous childhood illness – for once the human host survives infection (typically after about two weeks), they are immunised for life.[66] Māori, however, had never encountered measles before. In February of 1835 Marsden reported that Karetai and his wife were still in Sydney, now 'very unwell, so much so indeed that I am afraid the woman will die of grief'.[67] They did not die, but when they were returned to Murihiku they brought the measles virus with them.[68]

Measles is breath-borne and extremely infectious. Typically, in a 'virgin soil' epidemic such as now occurred among southern Māori communities, almost everyone becomes sick, and many die.[69] In 1852 Karetai told the Reverend James Stack that the epidemic had carried off the bulk of the population at Otago and along the southern coast.[70] The epidemic's spread was exacerbated because Karetai and his companions were first landed in Foveaux Strait – and met there the Kāi Tahu taua assembled from all their various southern settlements to bring battle to Te Rauparaha. Three hundred men are said to have died on Measley Beach alone, including Te Whakataupuka, ariki of Murihiku. Of nine canoes that arrived there, only crew enough for one are said to have survived, and as they returned to their homes they spread the sickness everywhere.[71] The *Sydney Packet*, which sailed from Otago in August, dryly reported that 'Measles had shown itself among the New Zealanders and had carried some of them off'.[72] But William Palmer witnessed entire communities stricken so that no one could aid the sick, remembering:

> *on his visit to Otakou, the Maori so bad with the fell disease that, for want of attendance, they have crawled to the stream for water, and died on the spot ... One affecting instance he gives of a Maori father killing his young son and burying him in the sand, and who, when threatened to be brought to task for his crime, said the lad's mother had just died, and that he himself would be dead in a short time, and, as there would be no one to look after the child, this was the best thing he could do. The poor fellow predicted aright, for in less than forty-eight hours he too was lifeless.*[73]

Measles cripples the immune system, allowing other microbes to flourish. The lungs are then very vulnerable to pneumonia and pulmonary tuberculosis.[74] As remedy for the measles' fever, tohunga exposed their suffering people to cold air, or immersed them neck-deep in cold water.[75] These treatments were recipes for pneumonia, influenza and tuberculosis.[76] In November 1836 the *Sydney Herald* reported that measles had killed 'at least 600 of the natives' in the south.[77] That report also carried news of the incursions of another scourge – influenza – transmitted by the crew of the *Sydney Packet* when they visited Ōtākou about late October, leaving many Māori 'so affected by the new disorder that they are lying about half dead'.[78]

Like measles, the influenza virus is breath-spread and has a short period of incubation of only one or two days; it is highly infectious and spreads rapidly. The *Sydney Monitor* noted: 'Nearly the whole of the black and white inhabitants of New Zealand are suffering under an attack of influenza. Many of the natives have died from its effects.'[79]

Measles and influenza epidemics at least disappeared as quickly as they had come.[80] Tuberculosis, known to Māori as 'te mare', the cough, had an equally terrible onset, for newly exposed people have so little resistance that it races through lymph channels to infect numerous organs.[81] Soon after his arrival at Waikouaiti in 1840, the gloomy Wesleyan missionary James Watkin met a Māori man who had lost six children in quick succession to tuberculosis.[82] Tuberculosis struck the insignificant and the powerful indiscriminately, but, unlike the other diseases, it lingered and was the leading cause of mortality among Māori for decades to come. As Alfred Crosby has put it, endemic diseases such as tuberculosis and venereal disease 'provided the ground bass for Maori history in the nineteenth century'.[83] Reverend Johann Wohlers, the missionary who had the longest and deepest experience of southern Māori, considered tuberculosis their 'inherent disease'.[84] Tuberculosis also killed Europeans: Joseph Brooks Weller developed consumption – pulmonary tuberculosis – and died at Ōtākou in 1835, to be shipped home in a puncheon of rum. The following year Tahatu, principal chief at Ōtākou, was among the Māori victims.[85] Thus the two men who had struck the deal to allow the first European settlement on the Otago Peninsula shared the same fate.

The demographic impact of this series of diseases is very difficult to ascertain, and has been much debated. Accounts of European observers from the early 1840s and after almost all claimed that the Māori population centred on Ōtākou had once been much larger, perhaps as high as two or even three thousand, but suffered catastrophic decline from the early 1830s to reach the few hundreds they found. Several of the French officers who visited in 1840 stated this, including Élie le Guillou, surgeon-major of the *Zélée*: 'At the present time the population of Otago does not exceed two hundred, yet a scant ten years ago the total reached at least twelve hundred. This decrease may be attributed perhaps to migration, to a disease similar to measles, which was raging here four or five years ago and finally to a lack of suitable clothing …'[86]

Le Guillou's reasoning is clearly unsound – Ōtākou had had to cope with an influx of refugees, not an exodus, and Māori did not die en masse for want of suitable clothing. What, however, of the combined effects of measles and other epidemic diseases? Could their impacts explain his conclusion?

The most ferocious known measles epidemic occurred in Fiji in 1875; it occasioned 25 per cent mortality.[87] It seems likely enough that southern Kāi Tahu suffered something similar. This of course does not account for the effects of subsequent illness striking a debilitated community. Even fairly sceptical scholars such as Atholl Anderson have acknowledged it is plausible that the total Kāi Tahu population in the South Island may have been more than halved in only a few years.[88] But Ōtākou was the settlement most exposed to shipping, so it ought to have suffered the most. Peter Entwisle, who has provided the most substantive recent analysis, considers that by the early 1830s there were 'probably over 1000 Maori living in the whole extent of what is now the Dunedin district', with 'the greatest number' on the Peninsula.[89] Certainly, the Otago population should have swelled significantly from that observed in the mid-1820s, due to natural increase and the influx of refugees from Canterbury. Accepting Entwisle's figures, I think it reasonable to conclude that the Ōtākou Māori population peak in the early 1830s was a minimum of 500 to 600 people.[90] However, by the early 1840s, only 328 Māori lived in the entire district – and only 170 on the Peninsula at Ōtākou.[91]

What other effects did the epidemics have? Harry Evison, having estimated that the epidemics of the 1830s killed half of Kāi Tahu, concludes that these caused 'a sudden decline in the production of flax, potatoes, and other labour-intensive items'.[92]

But Evison provides no data. Nor have scholars such as Peter Entwisle, Bill Dacker and Michael Stevens assessed southern Māori economic capacity in the wake of the epidemics. As noted, Atholl Anderson also accepts considerable population decline in the total Kāi Tahu population, from a peak of 5000 to about 2000, but he doubts it can have been as devastating at Otago precisely because he claims that economic production at Ōtākou 'reached its peak during the period when measles and influenza were most virulent'.[93] As evidence for this claim Anderson suggests that Ōtākou Māori shipped between 25 and 60 tons of potatoes at 'regular intervals through the 1830s and early 1840s'.[94]

Only tentative conclusions about Māori capacity to engage in the new economy can be drawn from the best contemporary evidence, found in Sydney shipping records and the Wellers' correspondence. In the first years the Wellers experimented and shipped a wide variety of commodities: not just whale oil and bone, potatoes and flax, but also timber, raupō 'flags', seal skins, fish and even coal. But they soon focused on what was most profitable: oil and bone. Meanwhile, as Māori realised the size and significance of the market the Wellers had opened to them, they increased production for export of potatoes, especially, and to some extent flax also. Exports peaked in 1834, when the Wellers shipped 33.5 tons of potatoes as well as three tons and 33 bales of flax (however, as one cargo that comprised 30 tons of potatoes also called at Port Nicholson, the proportion stemming from Otago is unclear).[95] The Sydney harvest failed next year, and George Weller stressed the demand for both potatoes and flax in several letters in the autumn and winter of 1835.[96] Initially, Ōtākou Māori responded: a ton of their potatoes arrived in early May, and 10 tons more on 25 July.[97] George then wrote to Edward on 7 August and repeated a request for 50 or 60 tons of potatoes to arrive around the end of October.[98] However, the request could not be met. On 2 September Edward wrote to his brother explaining that he was far from being able to send such a large quantity: 'Potatoes are not to be procured,' he said, claiming that Captain Ridley of the *Susannah* had bought over 1000 baskets before him (if so, this might have amounted to some 15 tons).[99]

This purchase, as well as the five or 10 tons taken from Waikouaiti by the *Sydney Packet*, suggest that there was a reasonable potato crop harvested in 1835, perhaps just prior to the advent of measles.[100] On 12 September, Edward sent a terse note admitting that he could not send any bone because of 'the natives being ill and unable to clean it'.[101] In December he sent only 400 bags of potatoes,[102] and in January promised a cargo next year, assuring his brother of a plentiful harvest.[103] But in 1836 potato exports were almost non-existent.[104] True, this was the first year that bay whalers made extended stays in the harbour and sought supplies, but this does not account for the cessation of exports.[105] In 1837 they recovered somewhat: 12 tons arrived in Sydney on 22 August and another 600 bags on 12 December.[106] None at all were sent in 1838, but 20 tons were then shipped in both 1839 and 1840 (though probably not all of the latter came from Ōtākou). Very little flax – the most labour-intensive product – was exported over this time.

What can be made of these fluctuations in exports as evidence of the effects of disease? All that can be said with any safety is that potato exports almost ceased in 1836, after the onset of the epidemics – a decline all the more marked given the increases in exports in preceding years. Exports recovered within a few years, but did not return to pre-epidemic levels.

What of the effects of epidemic disease on Māori capacities to sustain their culture and social structures? Did Māori at Ōtākou suffer such a 'crippling impact' that it engendered cultural collapse? Were they a bewildered people propelled into accepting Christianity? Or rather, were they drawn to explore new forms of knowledge and explanations?[107]

Birth pangs of a new society: Social and cultural change among Māori

Throughout the nineteenth and for much of the twentieth centuries, it was almost universally believed that disease had so decimated Māori that it caused a cultural collapse in which Māori communities adopted Christianity in confusion and despair.[108] However, the demographic impact of disease is now generally downplayed by New Zealand historians as part of a larger argument emphasising that, far from experiencing cultural collapse, Māori adopted and adapted new technology and knowledge as required, while maintaining an essential cultural continuity. Māori adaptation of Christianity has been explained as an extension of – rather than a replacement for – traditional beliefs, and (on some accounts) as a means to achieving other ends, especially mana and literacy.[109]

Māori experiences differed widely, however, and it is still acknowledged by James Belich, for example, that the south is 'where the myths of fatal impact and conversion came most nearly and quickly true'.[110] Conversion to Christianity in the south was quick. It did follow closely behind rapid depopulation due to disease, but it also occurred alongside the pursuit of literacy and competition for mana. Can the effects of these influences be untangled?

Many accounts of the time stress the parlous state of the people at Ōtākou. Some bemoaned, in particular, the levels of male drunkenness and the apparently coerced prostitution of women. Both the journals of the Wesleyan missionary at Waikouaiti, Reverend James Watkin, and the accounts of French explorer Dumont d'Urville and his officers when they visited Otago Harbour at the end of March 1840, have been particularly influential. These accounts were long accepted fairly uncritically, and still persuade some, such as Peter Entwisle, that by 1840 Māori society at Ōtākou – not to mention European society – was in 'near terminal distress'.[111] Entwisle's arguments are classic 'fatal impact' fare: due to the epidemics, southern Māori society 'lost not only numbers but confidence in its own capacity to survive, and consequently coherence and the conviction of its own integrity'.[112] Other historians accept the loss of population but not these consequences. Harry Evison and Bill Dacker note that the nadir for southern Māori came later following the loss of their land. Others still, such as Atholl Anderson, occupy something of a middle ground, acknowledging demoralisation caused by disease and drink but not depicting collapse.[113]

Watkin's diatribes were aimed mainly at the Europeans at Ōtākou – 'the vilest class, Murderers, Adulterers, Whormongers and S[odomite]s'. He often acknowledged the superiority of Māori to the whalers, but he still excoriated them as 'a trying race, as stupid as asses, as rapacious as Jews' whom he did 'most thoroughly detest'. He condemned Māori 'Drunkenness and lewdness', too, castigating them especially for prostituting their women:

> One of the curses of this people is their giving their daughters and sisters to Foreigners for a consideration (small enough)! And many of them of a tender age often before any sign of puberty has appeared, it makes me sick at heart to contemplate such things, the consequences of which may be imagined. My hopes of the preservation of these tribes are faint indeed. Disease prevails, deaths are much more common than births ...[114]

Watkin was a miserable, tempted and fallen man, pent with fury and frustration. He was also a hypocrite. When in mid-1842 he went to Ōtākou, that 'modern Gemorrah', it was to fortify himself with four gallons of brandy, a cask of ale and a cask of porter (£6 8s), a box of cigars and 1lb tobacco (£2 17s) – and to indulge his cuckquean wife in a shawl (5s).[115] Other missionaries saw things differently. Against Watkin's intemperate railing about the effects of whalers on Māori, we might set Bishop Selwyn's view that 'the whalefishers impart a considerable amount of civilisation to the natives'.[116]

All in all, such anecdotal evidence does not take us very far. Harwood's account books tell a more precise story. They show that between 1841 and 1848 almost half of the money that Māori are recorded as spending at Octavius Harwood's store – which was where they got many of their tools, clothing and even food – was on alcohol.[117] The account books show that many Māori drank, and suggest that some became drunks. But as Wohlers, the other early missionary in the south, noted, the amounts they consumed were 'insignificantly small' when compared with the Europeans, who daily consumed quantities of raw spirits.[118]

So much for drunkenness; what of lewdness? The French with d'Urville were especially repulsed by the perceived filth and squalor of the Māori dressed in European clothing, which 'made them look like beggars in rags', and inhabiting 'wretched hovels'. They were disgusted, too, by prostitution, as 'troops' of women, 'riddled, it is said, with venereal disease', visited their ships overnight.[119]

The French explorers' jaundiced view in part reflects the fact that they had arrived amidst the dregs of the end of the off-season debauch. Their views on clothing and dirt display nostalgia for 'noble savages' and fond memories of Pacific maidens with warmer water to bathe in.[120] A wash completely transformed their superficial perceptions, as the officer Roquemaurel revealed: 'we found these filthy, ragged creatures, whom we had left crouching round a fire, transformed into maidens with their hair blowing in the breeze, laughing gaily as they helped our sailors wash their clothes.'[121]

Louis Le Breton's paintings (see example opposite) better portray the mingling of old and new elements in the society that had emerged at Ōtākou, with houses in both Māori and European styles in close proximity on the sandy foreshore, whata towering above them, canoes pulled up on shore, boats and ships afloat, and felled trees framing the scene.

The French accounts, or the experience of bay whalers, provide a partial view of the range of relationships that Māori women had with European whalers. As Atholl Anderson and Angela Wanhalla have each stressed, there was a continuum of relationships from prostitution, through exchange relationships, to Christian marriages.[122] Bay whalers and the French explorers were transient, and so therefore was the sexual hospitality afforded them by unattached young women. Relations with shore whalers, who stayed through the six months of the whaling season or longer, were much more domestic affairs. As one whaler recalled, 'the Maoris very jealously guarded the honour of their women. Each whaler had a Maori wife according to their custom.'[123] Edward Jerningham Wakefield noted that 'Regular bargains were struck between the experienced headsman and the relations of the girl selected and in most cases bargains were punctually adhered to.' Whalers expected these women to cook, wash and mend clothes, and generally keep a clean house. Her relatives expected payment throughout and at the end of the season.[124] This was a crucial arena of negotiation in which 'the middle ground' was (literally) born.[125]

Octavius Harwood, for example, partnered Titapu, daughter of the chief Pokene and Hinetaumai. 'King Bogany', as Harwood referred to him in land transactions, was an important Canterbury leader who resettled at Otago in the wake of Te Rauparaha's incursions.[126] The couple's relationship was evidently close, and Harwood raised as his own Titapu's son to a former partner. But in the winter of 1842 Titapu developed consumption. She was not alone; 'several natives died' on 1 May, and the whaleboats could not go out for some weeks for want of hands. She was attended by both Harwood and a French whaling doctor, but by 19 May Harwood was 'very much troubled' since Tetuk (as he called her) was 'almost dying'. Pokene warned Harwood on 12 June that 'he would be revenged if his daughter died', but there is no evidence of him doing so when Titapu passed away just two days later.[127]

Harwood's partnership with Titapu reflected wider patterns. In 1843 Watkin noted that Māori women generally had begun to force their partners to choose between marriage or separation.[128] The relationships that remained were often true partnerships with genuine affection. John Barnicoat recounted this delightful scolding a European man in Bluff was given after he disparaged Māori women:

CHAPTER 5: 'SOON MAY THE WELLERMAN COME'

Louis Le Breton, Port Otago 1840. *Ōtākou has become Port Otago: the harbour is thronged with seven ships and sailors cluster on the foreshore, which has been cleared to supply shipping with wood and to grow food for trade.* Watercolour with charcoal, 343 x 479mm. Hocken Collections, Uare Taoka o Hākena, University of Otago: DC Cl.452

By and by you go to Otago – to Waikawa – to Toutoe. You stay there three weeks – you stay five weeks – you stay two moons – you come back – you say – Hello! Where's the cow? Gone! – Where the bull? Gone! –Where the goats? Gone! –Where the chickens? Gone! The blankets gone the stock gone – all, all gone. – you get the Maori woman. By and by you go to Otago – to Waikawa – to Toutoe. You stay there three weeks – you stay five weeks – you stay two moons – you come back – you say – Hello! Where's the cow? Me say – All right! You say – Where the bull? Me say – All right! You say – Where the goats? Me say – All right! You say – Where the chickens? Me say, All right! The blankets are all right, the stock all right – All, All right – Ah very good the Maori woman.[129]

The voices of Māori women are almost entirely absent from the surviving archives of this time.[130] Yet this silence is far from true to life for, as Barnicoat remarked, this particular woman showed 'the characteristic talkativeness, livliness [sic] and shrewdness of her sex and people'.[131]

Some relationships can only be treated as love affairs. Kāi Tahu woman Patahi rebuffed Tuhawaiki's advances, defied her people and fled Ōtākou while she waited years for the return of her lover, Edwin Palmer. Palmer at last rejoined her as he had promised, the couple were accepted back and lived at Ōtākou for some years, having

139

two girls together.[132] Later, however, Palmer abandoned Patahi and took away his children when he married a European woman.[133]

Lives such as these complicate reports such as that of Frederick Tuckett, the stern Quaker who in 1844 chose Otago as the site for the Scots. Tuckett estimated then that two thirds of the younger women were living with Europeans and, not one to mince words, reported that the universal view was that southern Māori were now 'perishing like rotten sheep'.[134] Atholl Anderson has indeed suggested that the most significant cause of Māori population decline, even by 1840, was loss of women to Europeans, who 'left their communities' and 'brought up their children in predominantly European ways'.[135] Michael Stevens has countered that this shift was never total: 'even as they altered it, takata-pora nonetheless married in to a way of life. Kāi Tahu women did not simply marry out of one. Cultural practices proved durable throughout the substantial changes that reshaped the community in the mid-nineteenth-century'.[136] The children of these unions, though far from seamlessly integrated into Māori society, were yet Māori if they chose.[137]

The trauma of the epidemics lingered long in the cultural memory of southern Māori. Herries Beattie, who of all settlers knew southern Māori best, wrote in 1916 that '[s]ome of my friends laid great stress on the havoc wrought amongst [them by measles] in the thirties of last century'; they recalled deaths by the hundreds, and bodies 'left lying where they were for no one would go near them; in other cases they were not buried, but left in the *whares* which were set on fire'.[138]

In the event, Māori proved resilient: they did not disappear, nor did their society disintegrate or their culture collapse. At the time, however, Māori in the south themselves believed that they were vanishing. How can this not have been profoundly affecting? It would be surprising in such circumstances if the fabric of society at Ōtākou had not become fragile. Māori needed explanations for their predicament. As Judith Binney has argued, perhaps the movement towards Christianity can in large part be explained by the fact that Māori were afraid.[139]

THE WELLER BROTHERS' MEDICINE CHEST (pictured opposite). The Weller Brothers' medicine chest embodied the state of medical knowledge in the 1830s. It contains basic paraphernalia such as splints and dressings for binding people back together. A truss was used to treat hernia, perhaps caused by the terrible strains of towing a whale. Glass bottles contain a range of drugs and other medicines. Several were painkillers – extract of belladonna, tincture of henbane, or paregoric (opium). There are also expectorants and purgatives – emetic of tartar, ipecacuanha and rhurbarb – reflecting the idea that illness had to be evicted from the body. Balm of Gilead, meanwhile, was probably not the biblical herb, but Dr Samuel Solomon's quack cure-all which 'warms and enlivens the heart, raises the spirits and provides digestion, eases or cures nervous, hypochondriac, consumptive and female complaints, and lifts lassitude, debility and and weakness arising from juvenile imprudences'.

Photograph © Michael Hall

Certainly Watkin himself believed, like many other missionaries, that he could use fear of disease to achieve conversion.[140] Soon after arrival he noted that 'all sickness is ascribed to supernatural or perhaps infernal agency. Taipo being the supposed author of the disease whatever it may be. Taipo is a foreign word, its native place and etymology I cannot trace, but as it appears to mean the Devil and is of universal use I shall not disturb it.' Watkin instead preached that Māori were dying and their tohunga failing to save them because belief in their own atua was sinful.[141]

Some Māori do seem to have accepted that a new language of spirituality was needed to withstand the new diseases. Watkin reported a Māori belief that the Bible would restore life if placed on a dead person's chest; when he examined one such book, he found it was a copy of Norie's *Epitome of Practical Navigation*.[142] The argument that Watkin's books and Bibles were potent to Māori as medicine gains credence from the fact that medicine itself had seldom helped at Otago. The Wellers and Johnny Jones had doctors, as did visiting whaling ships, while Harwood also acted as a makeshift physician to whom many Māori had recourse,[143] but although Harwood 'gave physic' to Māori, they still died.

Watkin's success was quick: in 1843 virtually all the younger Māori chiefs of Otago, including the Peninsula villages, offered themselves for baptism and accepted the tapu of the Christian atua. Watkin had baptised 258 Kāi Tahu by the next year, and had 26 native teachers moving among the people to spread the new faith.[144] The old gods were not yet overthrown; it was not until 1865, for example, that the tapu of the shrine to Kahukura on the western harbour was removed by Piripi Te Kohe, a Ngāti Raukawa evangelist in the mould of Te Whiti, who was invited south by Raniera Ellison in the hope he could heal his wife Nani.[145] Te Kohe convinced the Ōtākou chiefs that their sicknesses were not the result of an inability to abide within the bounds laid down by the Christian atua, but were caused by their old gods such as Kahukura, who had turned upon them, and whose power had to be ritually broken.[146] H.K. Taiaroa's papers provide a detailed account of this 'Patunga Taipō' (which Megan Potiki translates as 'killing demons'), in which Te Kohe wrestled with Kahukura and was thrown high into the air before his astonished eyes, before directing cleansing rituals that combined eating kai gathered from sacred sites with Christian prayer.[147]

If conversion was less than complete, continued respect for their atua did not prevent all Māori embracing the new God with considerable fervour. Indeed, most Otago Māori were henceforth, in their own way, much better Christians than their European neighbours. Chiefs gave up their slaves, forsook multiple wives, made peace with their former enemies Ngāti Toa, and steadfastly refused to perform any work on the Lord's Day.[148] Christianity also slowly undermined fundamental tenets such as whakapapa and utu (for example, accidental deaths were no longer rectified by ritual killing), and hence gnawed at the traditional underpinnings of chiefly authority.[149]

This is not to deny that engagement with missionaries had other significant attractions. Foremost among them was the pull of literacy, which Māori accurately diagnosed as being the key to unlocking the European world.

When Watkin arrived at Waikouaiti in May 1840, Māori straight away flocked to him to learn to read and write. By November he was holding two writing classes each day, attended by 'all grades, old, young, chiefs, people', often including people from Ōtākou.[150] In 1844 the surveyor Barnicoat met Māori in Otago Harbour who wanted 'steel pens, ink and paper' in return for their fish and potatoes, had 'copybooks of very neat writing of which they seemed proud', and who wrote inscriptions on the gravemarkers of the recently deceased.[151] Evidently achieving literacy was a powerful motive for engaging with missionaries.

As Michael Stevens has pointed out, however, Kāi Tahu leaders were interested in writing well before they knew of Christianity (as shown in Karetai and Te Matenga Taiaroa's 1826 encounter with John Boultbee), and they had enthusiastically embraced Christian teachings disseminated orally by other Māori before they met any missionaries.[152]

Kāi Tahu scholar Te Maire Tau argues that his people abandoned the embedded system of explanation of the world via whakapapa because, like disease, 'potatoes, sheep, muskets and bullets all needed to be explained. At least as an all-encompassing explanation, whakapapa, the principle that held knowledge together, collapsed under its own inflexibility.'[153] If Tau is right that Māori recognised a need for new explanations, this in no way implies a cultural collapse, however.[154] It seems, rather, a sensible response to the fact that the conceptual structures of whakapapa could no longer satisfactorily explain to Māori the forces shaping their rapidly changing environment. For the environment, too, was becoming a middle ground, as the indigenous biota and introduced species jostled for space in new ecological niches carved out by human action.

A new world, 1831–48

Whaling initiated ecological changes that transformed southern Māori society and southern environments. Most obviously, the whalers virtually eradicated southern right whales from these waters. They brought many new plants, ranging from crops, garden plants and fruit trees to a wide assortment of weeds. Their animals included cattle, pigs, goats, sheep, poultry, dogs, cats and, inadvertently but inevitably, more Norway rats. Cats, rats and pigs soon spread over the landscape far beyond their point of entry at Ōtākou. Whalers totally transformed the environment of Ōtākou itself, and in doing so, turned the world of Ōtākou Māori inside out.

Whales were the most ecologically important animals in the ocean: their removal significantly affected the entire marine ecosystem, likely causing changes to the populations of almost all other ocean organisms.[155] It is, of course, impossible to be precise about what plucking whales out of the foodweb did to the ocean ecosystem. It is thought that some two thirds of the ocean's primary productivity was required to sustain great whale populations prior to their destruction; it is also thought that whales acted as a kind of ecosystem ballast by storing large amounts of biomass in relatively stable form.[156] In the whales' absence, other predators of krill such as seals and penguins may have boomed. Ecosystem perturbations may have been more frequent, and extreme. The loss of whales may also have reduced overall productivity, since deep-diving whales cycle nutrients up from the deep sea into the surface waters, where photosynthesis occurs. Further, primary production in the southern ocean is limited by availability of iron, which whale faeces once injected in significant amounts; this perhaps explains why krill have not dramatically increased with the removal of whales.[157]

When whales were brought to shore their vast bodies were flensed of blubber which, with the oil-rich tongue, was cut up and fed into the try pots. The upper harbour ran red with blood; the sand was saturated with the stench of oil, the air rank with the smell of burning and rotting flesh.[158] The decaying carcasses polluting the shore were food for birds, rats, pigs, dogs and insects. David Monro described nearby Waikouaiti: 'The whole beach was strewed with gigantic fragments of the bones of whales, and flocks of gulls, cormorants, and other sea-birds, and savage-looking pigs, prowled about to pick up the refuse. The place altogether, like other whaling stations, is a picture of the most perfect neglect ...'[159]

Unsurprisingly, d'Urville came to believe that rats were 'nowhere more numerous than in New Zealand'.[160] This was also a paradise for pigs, which were partial not just to whales but competed with people for cockles and potatoes. Such catholic diets helped pigs thrive: introduced to Otago in the 1820s, by 1830 they were soon 'like flocks of sheep'.[161] But their rooting among the cockle beds at Ōtākou made both pigs and shellfish less palatable. D'Urville and his officers found the cockles 'so horrible to taste that we were soon forced to abandon them', and the pigs 'nasty', 'briny', and 'absolutely revolting' because they fed on 'the shellfish that the sea throws up in huge quantities'.[162] The pigs had perhaps also been feeding on juvenile squat lobsters (*Munida gregaria*) or 'red krill', which was in abundant supply 'Several times a day … the surface of the water become[s] absolutely red from the enormous quantity of prawns that the incoming tide brings up and that the ebb carries back to the sea or throws up on to the beaches. Here and there in the bay there are masses of these prawns forming layers five or six inches thick, which give off a foetid smell.'[163] A further possibility though is that Māori supplied them with 'fishy pigs' as a deliberate insult.[164] Mrs Monson, a resident of Ōtākou who arrived in the early 1840s, later recalled: 'woe betide the man who sold a fishy pig to a ship. He was a marked man for the rest of his time in Otago. His neighbours sent him to Coventry in real earnest.'[165]

This possibility is buttressed by the fact that Māori were clearly aware of the ecological problems that pigs posed. Edward Shortland met Māori at the head of Otago Harbour in December 1843, and in an illuminating passage recorded how the Ōtākou Māori husbanded their pigs there:

> [I]t is the custom of this people to select, for pig runs, places distant from their ordinary cultivations, whither they transport a great part of their stock, when the crop is in the ground; leaving it to range at will till the season of storing the potatoes is past. They then catch as many as they require, and take them back to the plantations, in order that they may root up whatever food has been left in the ground.
>
> They now and then visit these pig-runs – as on the present occasion – to watch over the safety of their property, or to catch and mark the young ones; feasting at such times on the flesh of boars, which are killed by preference to prevent their becoming too numerous.
>
> It has sometimes happened that a party of Europeans, falling in with one of these preserves far away from any habitations, have taken it for granted that the pigs were wild, and, with this idea, have hunted and killed them, as if they had as much right to do so as any one else. Such heedless acts, however, have been a fruitful cause of complaint.[166]

The development of an economy incorporating root vegetables and pigs by the Ōtākou people reproduced something of the ancient agricultural complex of tropical Polynesia.[167] Moving the pigs back and forth between fern-root grounds and the potato plantations protected the cockles, ensured the fattened pigs' flavour, and thoroughly turned over the potato grounds, thus helping to maintain the soil. Killing boars to manage the population reflected an awareness that pigs were liable to become too much of a good thing and damage other valuable resources, such as fern-root grounds.[168]

Pig husbandry was a key domain over which the whalers and Māori had to negotiate terms. Māori marked their animals to identify them and discourage poaching. In 1839 the Wellers began to breed their own pigs on one of the islands up the harbour, a site that allowed them to keep their animals separate from those belonging to Māori.[169] But the problem of whalers poaching pigs continued until, apparently, matters came to a head around the winter of 1845. At this point, Māori threatened a general retaliation. The poachers were identified, however, and the whalers thereafter branded their pigs, too.[170]

The whaling station itself transformed Ōtākou. As land was cleared for cultivation, timber trees were picked out and the rest felled for firewood; by 1838 Harwood had to raft wood from further up the harbour.[171] Māori focused on growing potatoes, which were stored on whata and overwintered in clamps to guard against frost.[172] European farming was more diverse, especially after whaling fell away. Interspersed with bush the French saw 'cultivated fields', 'planted with potatoes, lettuces and turnips'.[173] According to the French, these fields 'almost all belonged to Europeans'.[174]

Octavius Harwood played a key role in establishing and diversifying these gardening and farming practices. His journal mentions planting his vegetable garden with cabbages, broccoli, peas, beans, cress and parsley. He established an orchard and indulged in 'a flowery garden'; his property was later described as including 'fruit trees and bushes in plenty'.[175] He also distributed seeds to other settlements.[176]

After 1840 Harwood assumed control over provisioning visiting bay whalers through the trading depot. In July 1841 he formed a partnership with Charles Schultze, who was based in Wellington and who supplied stock to the store and helped Harwood ship and sell his farm produce.[177]

Harwood had embarked on the first real attempt to emulate British farming on the Otago Peninsula, growing grain and root crops and running a range of stock. Edward Shortland calculated that by 1843 there were 12 acres (5ha) under cultivation at Ōtākou, where 50 sheep and 12 cattle were being run.[178] Harwood's journal also mentions rounding up cattle from Okia Flat, and lists pigs, sheep, goats and poultry among his animals.[179] Stock were frequently run loose, and the difficulty in recapturing cattle meant that wild herds formed – to the benefit of subsequent settlers in need of meat.[180] Cattle, pigs and goats thus began changing forest composition; their ongoing browsing has determined which species have survived in forest remnants. Other animals, not so often noticed, also arrived. Johnny Jones had many dogs and 200 cats (to catch rats) at his Waikouaiti whaling station alone.[181]

Harwood organised the burning of the 'grass' (pīkao and tussock) on the hills behind the station, and planted potatoes, barley and wheat.[182] People waxed lyrical about the quality of these potatoes. Tuckett exclaimed, 'I have not seen elsewhere in New Zealand such fine potatoes; supposing that I saw only a picked sample, they exceeded all other picked samples.'[183] Monro praised them, alongside 'very good' barley. He dismissed the wheat as 'almost universally smutty', however – clearly some crop pests were present from the very beginning of European agriculture.[184]

Harwood's efforts were soon emulated. After 1844 when the New Zealand Company purchased the Otago Block (as discussed in detail below), the European and Māori people at Ōtākou lived in expectation of the imminent arrival of settlers. Other people also drifted into the area to await them, so that by 1847 some 100 to 150 Europeans – more than ever before – lived on the tip of the Peninsula.[185] And, though these years are often brushed over, between 1844 and the settlers' belated arrival in 1848, some important developments occurred here.

The European population at Ōtākou were becoming true settlers, not seasonal migrants. They included at least a dozen couples and over 20 children.[186] The need to sustain these families changed the nature of the occupation and use of land. Archibald Anderson and Andrew Rowand expanded on Harwood's efforts to run stock and cultivate crops at Ōtākou and developed a farm named 'Kelvin Grove'.[187] The European settlers ventured to live further up the harbour margins; William Leslie settled in Portobello,[188] while John and James Anderson became the eponymous settlers of Andersons Bay.[189] And between 1846 and 1847 Charles Kettle led a large team of surveyors who laid out the proposed town of Dunedin and its vicinity, including properties and roads on the Peninsula. This last development is discussed in the next chapter.

Domesticity required European families to rely on more local resources. Like several others disappointed with their lack of progress at Waikouaiti, David Carey moved his family to Ōtākou in 1842 or 1843. There he leased land from Māori in exchange for cloth and 'trinkets'. He grew vegetables, hunted pigs, cut timber and fermented liquor from cabbage trees, products which not only fed his family but were traded to visiting ships for the essentials of the European diet – flour, salt, tea and sugar. Together with Charles Roebuck, he built a 20-ton ketch with Peninsula timber to trade with other coastal settlements. His wife Hannah learnt from Māori how to weave parapara (flax sandals), while Māori, for their part, learnt how European women cooked the new foods they were encountering.[190]

Kelvin Grove[191] was established as a cooperative arrangement between a former Codfish Island sealer, Archibald Anderson, who owned the stock but initially remained in Wellington, and Andrew Rowand, the farm manager at Ōtākou.[192] The farm included a homestead, outbuildings and stockyards, and Rowand attempted to run an operation based on 500 to 600 sheep for mutton and wool, some 70 cattle, run at first for meat and later for milk and butter, and several work horses; he also cropped potatoes, cabbages and lettuces. Rowand employed a housekeeper, a shepherd and an overseer.[193] Like Harwood's efforts, Kelvin Grove presaged the farming practices that British settlers attempted to impose on the Peninsula, more or less successfully, over the next 50 or so years.[194]

These early farming experiments faced tough constraints. Rowand was almost immediately forced to drive the sheep to the head of the harbour to find grazing, which took him nine days.[195] He could not move his cattle, however. He relied on supplying meat and dairy products to the community at Ōtākou, to visiting whaling ships, and to the surveyors who arrived in 1846.[196] Kelvin Grove had been handed on to Edward Stokes (formerly tutor to Johnny Jones's children) when the settlers arrived in 1848, and played an important role then in supplying them with milk, butter and vegetables; but Stokes, too, soon abandoned the land to join the settlers at Dunedin.[197] This combination of economic and environmental problems, especially the lack of reliable communications and poor land, haunted the development of the outer Peninsula.

The first agricultural practices on the Peninsula were important ecological experiments. When the apprehensive settlers of 1848 arrived, Captain Cargill's address to them pointed to 'the cultivations of the few squatters (mostly from Ross and Sutherland [i.e. Scots]) who have been waiting to join you, you have seen and partaken of the wheat, barley, oats and garden-stuffs you have been in the habit of raising, together with the sheep and cattle depastured on the hills you are to graze'. Here then was proof they and their animals and plants would thrive – especially as, armed with secure title, they might displace such 'squatters'.[198]

The whalers' farming showed Māori how to raise unfamiliar crops and animals. Māori, though, were quick to devise their own methods. James Hay recorded that Kāi Tahu on Banks Peninsula sowed their grain seed in the soil turned over as, day by day, they harvested potatoes; the grain was then harvested with sickles as it ripened. Māori had, Hay noted, 'an eye to saving labour'.[199]

Farming, too, had a variety of consequences for the local environment. New land for growing potatoes had regularly to be brought into cultivation because potatoes require large amounts of nitrogen (much more than kūmara, for example), and the Māori abhorrence of manuring land meant that fertility was rapidly exhausted; new land was therefore cultivated about every second year.[200] Hay describes Māori burning bush by cutting down all the smaller vegetation at ground level and piling it together with branches off the bigger trees: 'they generally got a capital burn, and got splendid crops of potatoes from the soil. If they wanted a second crop they left a few small ones on the ground.'[201]

Clearances left the shore settlements precariously situated on an unstable and increasingly active dune system.[202] When Shortland stayed with Harwood in 1843 he found that 'whenever the wind blew, it drifted with it a fine sand from the neighbouring beach, which penetrated everywhere, and was a source of much annoyance'.[203] Just a year later, Monro recorded that most of the 20 to 30 acres (8–12ha) around the whaling station 'consists of immense sand-banks like drifts of snow, without a blade of vegetation upon them, and shifting with every wind, so that you may see cottages half-buried, and garden fences completely overtopped'.[204] Over succeeding decades sand flooded over the land, spreading a few miles along the shore and another mile inland, and eventually covering as much as 1000 acres (400ha).[205]

Meanwhile, the shoreline eroded also. As early as 1837 the sea had washed over one of the stations; the oil had only been saved by a hasty retreat to higher ground.[206] Rain and sea washed away sandbanks by the station, sand swamped try pots, and kōwhai logs had to be dug out of the beach.[207] Harwood had a grotesque sea wall of whale heads built to stabilise the shore between Wellers Rock and his store.[208] This proved futile: by 1870 'a pretty broad slice of land' on which the whaling settlement had stood had 'been washed away by the sea', and Harwood's house, the sole survivor of the settlement, stood on the beach itself.[209]

Thus intensive settlement transformed the land around the whaling station. Direct human influence beyond the fringes of settlement was limited. The bulk of the whalers did not venture up the harbour to the station's hinterland, though the gentlemen – Edward Weller, Harwood and the doctors – would go shooting 'up the river' on a Sunday.[210] The more permanent settlers of the early 1840s did gather timber and pork all over the inner harboursides, and spent more time in the upper harbour. Māori, on the other hand, utilised the upper harbour and the outer coasts less than they had in the past, as their diminished population clustered around the whaling station. It is partially because Māori no longer lived on the great bulk of the Peninsula that it appeared to the influxes of British settlers as an untouched Arcadia. When David Monro visited in 1844 he admired:

> *an amphitheatre of wooded hills ... uniformly covered with trees, which clothe them from their summits to their bases, where they hang over and are reflected in the water ... The weather while we lay at Otago was most beautiful. The sky, a great part of the time, was without a cloud, and not a breeze ruffled the surface of the water, which reflected the surrounding wooded slopes, and every seabird that floated upon it, with mirror-like accuracy. For some hours after sunrise, the woods resounded with the rich and infinitely varied notes of thousands of tuis and other songsters. I never heard anything like it in any part of New Zealand. It completely agreed with Captain Cook's description of the music of the wooded banks of Queen Charlotte's Sound.*[211]

Monro had arrived as part of the party accompanying Frederick Tuckett, the surveyor entrusted by the New Zealand Company with the task of selecting the site for the proposed Scottish Free Church settlement to be called 'New Edinburgh'. Tuckett liked Ōtākou for its fine harbour, ample supplies of wood and access to a large, flat and fertile hinterland.[212] He chose to site the proposed company settlement here, and began to negotiate to buy the lands of the Māori living on the Otago Peninsula. This marked the key act in a succession of negotiations over property that had paved the way for Māori to contemplate such a crucial transaction, with a reasonable understanding of what selling land entailed in European eyes.

Perceptions of property: Selling Otago, 1831–44

Māori and British perceptions of property were different, but not so much as some recent writers suppose. As we have seen, Māori tenure of land, though held under the mana and political control of chiefs, was also overlain by a complex network of specific use rights distributed among communities of mixed tribal descent. The British, too, had a wide variety of agreed ways to legitimate title, and to distinguish layers of tenure and land uses. They not only distinguished Crown, private and common lands, but various separable uses of these – grazing rights, mining rights, fishing rights, lease of land and so forth. The whalers and Māori struck many bargains in which property rights were exchanged and rearranged in and around Ōtākou. Making these bargains stick in a community without mutually agreed authority required understanding and trust.

Meanwhile, differences over the mores surrounding property and making new uses of the environment made disputes inevitable. Outside assistance was helpful in negotiating these. While at Ōtākou, for example, Edward Shortland was called on to obtain compensation from a Māori man who had destroyed 'several 100 yards of bullock fence'. Shortland discovered that the Māori, who had built the fence, was provoked during a dispute over payment with his whaling employer, who cursed him and threatened to set dogs on him. Since the man's chopping down of the fence was seen as appropriate by his people, this left unresolved the matter of how the whalers could gain satisfaction.

Māori leaders, too, grasped the possibilities opened by the new forms of authority appearing in the European world. In 1842, for example, Māori at Ōtākou bought a whaleboat for 700 baskets of potatoes and 42 pigs. The purchasers included Karetai, Te Matahaere and Taiaroa's cousin Kohi. But Kohi soon believed his death was imminent and, fearing his young son would then be denied his inheritance, burnt the boat.[213] Furious, Karetai remonstrated with him; Te Matahaere burnt Kohi's house, and stripped and beat him. As Kohi's tuakana, or senior, it now fell to Te Matenga Taiaroa to obtain recompense. A protracted feud loomed. Taiaroa's solution was to persuade Kohi to allow himself to be strangled. Taiaroa then told the Reverend Watkin that Karetai and Te Mataheare had murdered Kohi and had Watkin write a letter seeking their arrest, which Taiaroa took north to the nearest enforcer of law, the police magistrate at Banks Peninsula.[214]

As Edward Shortland urged, we should observe 'the facility with which Taiaroa appeared to adopt our laws, while he was really only endeavouring to make use of them, as far as they served him to carry out his own ideas of what was befitting'.[215] Ōtākou Māori understood European systems of power and authority – they just preferred to choose for themselves when and how to abide by them.

It is in this light that we should consider the land sales of the late 1830s, when land hunger soared in expectation of Britain incorporating New Zealand into her empire.[216] The many transactions ranged from highly dubious to faithfully observed bargains. At one end of this scale, unscrupulous Australian merchants attempted to acquire enormous parcels of property for a pittance. The Wellers were especially keen purchasers, and by 1840 had claimed title to almost 3 million acres (approximately 1.2 million ha) of the South Island.[217] Taiaroa among others happily played along, repeatedly selling the same land. In transactions involving transient ships' captains, each party thought they were fleecing the other. The question, then, is not how well the parties understood each other, but how much they cared. Such land sales were little more than bets about who would have the power to enforce their own understandings of what was at stake. By contrast, transfers of mutually recognised rights to land went hand in hand with an expectation of an ongoing relationship. As Shortland realised, what shore whaling stations acquired was land to establish their station, and 'squatters rights' to extract resources from the sea adjacent to their 'purchase'. This form of tenure was known as 'he noho noa iho'. It was in no way a sale, but was almost identical to granting a squatting lease.[218] Smaller parcels of land were sold outright, and the Māori vendors acknowledged that they had relinquished the land.

The difference between the two sorts of transfer of rights is manifest in the prices paid and in the different ways that Māori subsequently treated the transactions. Thus, in 1839 the Wellers 'purchased' from Taiaroa and Karetai a vast swathe of land that they estimated at two million acres (approximately 0.8 million ha), including all of the Peninsula and much of coastal Otago, for £66 and 10 shillings – but were forced to 'repurchase' the land the very next year for £100.[219] In contrast, Harwood paid Taiaroa, Karetai and Pokene £100 for only one acre (0.4ha) around his house, and no Māori subsequently disputed his ownership of that land.[220]

All such land claims were, however, about to be put in question by proclamation of British sovereignty. In preparation for the acquisition of New Zealand by the Crown, Captain William Hobson was instructed on 14 August 1839 to investigate all claims to land and ascertain their entitlement for Crown grants.[221] Hobson was advised that if, as he had argued, the South Island was 'uninhabited, except by a very small number of persons in a savage state, incapable from their ignorance of entering intelligently into any treaties with the Crown', then he could assert British sovereignty by right of discovery. Under instruction from Governor Gipps of New South Wales, Hobson issued a declaration to this effect on 21 May 1840. The south was held to be empty land with too few inhabitants to matter.[222] In this decision there are both distant echoes of Cook's observations of an almost empty land, and the resonance of the impact of disease in depopulating the Peninsula and elsewhere.

When a copy of the Treaty of Waitangi was brought south to Ōtākou in June 1840 it was as an afterthought, a 'mere illusion and pretence' Hobson had felt, and one that he had believed was best avoided. The Māori at Ōtākou did not accord it much weight either. According to Harry Evison, only a man called Koroko signed aboard ship on 13 June. Karetai's name was added, but he did not sign.[223] Such signings of the treaty in the south did not signify acceptance of the transfer of sovereignty to the Crown for the British, for whom it was already a fait accompli, or Māori, for whom such a radical act could not have been legitimately done without the approval of the leading chiefs Karetai, Taiaroa and Tuhawaiki, acting with the consent of their people.

The treaty was not the primary basis of Kāi Tahu's continuous and vociferous complaint during the nineteenth century.[224] The Kāi Tahu claim was predicated on perceived injustices stemming from the critical land sales to the New Zealand Company and subsequently the Crown, beginning with the sale of the 'Otago Block' in 1844.

The British background to this sale is discussed in detail below. Here, it is sufficient to note that the purchasers were the New Zealand Company, represented in New Zealand by Edward Gibbon Wakefield's brother, Colonel William Wakefield. They wished to select at least 120,550 acres (48,784ha) of land for 'New Edinburgh', a proposed Scottish settlement to be based on small farming. They had gained Governor Fitzroy's approval to buy from Māori 150,000 acres (60,702ha) of land, at a place of their choosing, subject to close government supervision. The eventual Otago land sale on 31 July 1844 was the culmination of a complex process of selection, inspection and negotiation that involved three key groups of people: New Zealand Company representatives, government officials and Māori. Given the sale's significance, it is essential to consider what understandings each party brought to the transaction. How far did they share a common conception of what the sale entailed?

The British parties regarded this sale as extinguishing all prior right to the land and substituting secure, absolute and transferable titles ultimately derived from the Crown. The consensus of historians is that none of the Māori could have fully shared this view. As Alan Ward puts it, the past experience of Otago Māori in selling land 'did not create an understanding of sale in the sense in which it would be embodied in the later Crown purchases'.[225] Yet it is clear from the care and ceremony with which this sale was surrounded by both parties that Māori were well aware that this was a new and different sort of transfer of rights.

The process began with the surveyor Frederick Tuckett conducting a thorough search for a site along the southeastern seaboard of the South Island over April and May 1844. Fitzroy appointed John Jermyn Symonds to superintend Tuckett's progress, but the two promptly fell out and Symonds returned to Wellington to complain of Tuckett surveying Māori land without their permission. Meanwhile Tuckett settled on his site.

Tuckett's selection focused on Otago Harbour, spreading south and inland to include the Taieri and Molyneux plains. In the second week of June the parties assembled at Kopūtai (Port Chalmers) on the shores of Otago Harbour: Tuckett arrived from the south; Symonds returned from Wellington, accompanied by Daniel Wakefield (William Wakefield's younger brother and deputy); and Tuhawaiki, Taiaroa, Karetai and other chiefs came to meet them.[226]

Symonds' role was to ensure that there were no misunderstandings that might lead to a repeat of the Wairau affray. He insisted that the boundaries of the block that Tuckett had selected should be mutually observed and agreed. Tuckett refused, and on the morning of 18 June an irate Symonds returned to Wellington for the second time, having established only that Māori were very willing to sell the block, as roughly outlined, subject to whatever they reserved. In the interim, Tuckett continued to negotiate.[227]

The Peninsula was the focus of the most intense debate. At an initial meeting on 18 June the Māori stated their desire to retain the entire Peninsula, and various rangatira named purchase prices much higher than the £2000 Tuckett was authorised to offer – Tuhawaiki, for example, suggested a million pounds. Today this might seem a more reasonable figure than the paltry £2400 Māori settled for – which amounted to about only one penny per acre of land – but it must be remembered both that the

CHAPTER 5: 'SOON MAY THE WELLERMAN COME'

Sketch of the rural districts of New Edinburgh drawn by Frederick Tuckett 1844. Tuckett's sketch highlights how Otago Harbour was the central feature of the Otago Block purchase, providing access to the rural land on the Taieri and Tokomairiro plains. The Otago Peninsula's outer coast is still poorly understood. *Hocken Collections, Uare Taoka o Hākena, University of Otago: Hm /880/1844*

New Zealand Company became bankrupt only a few years later, because there was insufficient demand for their land, and that the Otago Māori were extremely keen to attract settlement as a market for their produce and a ready source of European goods. The real benefit of the sale to Māori – certainly in settler eyes, and probably in their own – would come with the arrival of settlers and the creation of a town.

Māori at last convinced Tuckett that they would not be parted from the northern quarter of the Peninsula, as well as smaller areas to the south at Taieri and Karoro. But they could not persuade Tuckett to let them retain the whole Peninsula. Tuckett was determined not to leave the Peninsula in Māori hands because it would inevitably have a strategic importance to the proposed town in its lee. He was anxious, too, not to leave Māori in control of Peninsula land occupied by squatters, least they should develop a rival settlement.[228]

The key features of the eventual deal were agreed on 20 June: a purchase price of £2400 was settled on for a roughly agreed block of land, the boundaries of which later proved to enclose 533,600 acres (244,033ha) (it was stated at the time to be 400,000 acres or 161,874ha).[229]

William Wakefield arrived on 16 July with the government officials Symonds, Commissioner of Land Claims William Spain, and Assistant Protector of Aborigines George Clarke. At the insistence of the government officials, all these men joined Tuckett and a party of Kāi Tahu in walking the boundaries of the purchase, which they did between 18 and 26 July. The boundaries thus agreed followed landmarks such as mountain ridgelines, and indeed seem to have matched traditional boundaries. Ōtākou leader Horomona Pohio later testified that it was Karetai, Taiaroa and Tuhawaiki who introduced the landmarks as boundary markers.[230]

The fate of the Peninsula was still at issue. Tuckett told Wakefield that he could not buy the Peninsula's northern quarter. Wakefield proved very reluctant to accept this. On the other hand, Karetai, and Koroko in particular, were determined to retain all of the Peninsula from Puketai (Andersons Bay). These were local chiefs with strong Kāti Māmoe ancestry. Chiefs whose central lands were not in question, such as Tuhawaiki and Taiaroa, were more willing to contemplate the sale.[231] Wakefield, however, threatened to call off proceedings unless most of the Peninsula was acquired.[232]

Parting with Ōtākou was out of the question. To convince Wakefield of this, on 27 July Tuhawaiki took Wakefield, Symonds and Clarke to the summit of Ohinetu Hill, above Omate.[233] As recalled by Clarke, his explanation there of why they would not sell Ōtākou was a masterful piece of rhetoric:

> *Look here, Karaka, here, and there, and there and yonder; those are all burial places, not ancestral burial places, but those of this generation. Our parents, uncles, aunts, brothers, sisters, children, they lie thick around us. We are but a poor remnant now, and the Pakeha will soon see us all die out, but even in my time, we Ngailaki were a large and powerful tribe, stretching from Cook Strait to Akaroa, and the Ngatimoe*

to the south of us were slaves. The wave which brought Rauparaha and his allies to the Strait, washed him over to the Southern Island. He went through us, fighting and burning and slaying. At Kaikoura, at Kaiapoi, and at other of our strongholds, hundreds and hundreds of our people fell, hundreds more were carried off as slaves, and hundreds died of cold and starvation in their flight. We are now dotted in families, few and far between, where we formerly lived as tribes. Our children are few, and we cannot rear them. But we had a worse enemy than even Rauparaha, and that was the visit of the Pakeha with his drink and his disease. You think us very corrupted, but the very scum of Port Jackson shipped as whalers or landed as sealers on this coast. They brought us new plagues, unknown to our fathers, till our people melted away. This was one of our largest settlements, and it was beyond even the reach of Rauparaha. We lived secure, and feared no enemy; but one year, when I was a youth, a ship came from Sydney, and she brought the measles among us. It was winter, as it is now. In a few months most of the inhabitants sickened and died. Whole families on this spot disappeared and left no one to represent them. My people lie all around us, and now you can tell Wide-awake (Wakefield) why we cannot part with this portion of our land, and why we were angry with Tuckett for cutting his lines about here.[234]

William Wakefield had to agree that Ōtākou Māori would retain the northern quarter of the Peninsula, where their villages and urupā were. Wakefield estimated this area at 10,000 acres (4046ha), though it proved to be only 6665 (2697ha).[235] In the Māori version, the deed of sale referred to these lands as 'Nga wenua kua kotia e matou mo a matou tamariki' – 'The portions of land that we have cut away entirely for us, for our children'.[236] In the Otago deed's English translation, and in the minds of the settlers who soon surrounded them, they became 'reserves'.

On 31 July 1844 all assembled on shore. Clarke explained the finality of the transaction to the Māori: that 'in disposing of their land they for ever surrendered their interest and title'. The boundaries were reiterated again, and agreed again, as Tuhawaiki, Te Matenga Taiaroa and Karetai each 'called out the boundary markers for his own territory in traditional style to the assembled'.[237] Karetai called the boundaries for the Otago Peninsula, and he also spoke for the Ōtākou people, stressing the need to respect each other's lands to avoid disputes.[238]

The deed was then read out in Māori and in English before being signed by five chiefs and marked by another 20, and the purchase money was given to Tuhawaiki, Taiaroa and Karetai for distribution to their people.[239]

The overwhelming impression given by the negotiations is that, as Harry Evison argues, the Kāi Tahu leaders 'were by now aware of the implications of selling land to Europeans'.[240] Certainly, this transaction was conducted by both sides with much more care than any other in the south. Telling signs that Māori understood the significance of the sale include the fact that the purchase's boundaries were walked, and the fact that Tuhawaiki unearthed his dead from Kopūtai and took them across the harbour to the unsold land on the Peninsula.[241]

Even so, there were subsequent disagreements about the sale, and Māori expressed a range of doubts about what had been conveyed. On 21 May 1880, in preparation for the Smith–Nairn Commission, the Ōtākou people gathered in council to 'detail, one by one, the names of the places where people camped within the Wakefield purchase'. H.K. Taiaroa was the scribe. As noted in chapter four, Taiaroa considered that Māori had retained some of the islands in and around the Otago Peninsula. The deed explicitly stated that Māori 'give up' eight named islands, which included islands in the harbour such as Kamautaurua (Quarantine Island) and Rakiriri (Goat Island).[242] But in evidence to the Smith–Nairn Commission in 1880, Taiaroa pointed out that seven other islands were 'Kihai i hokona kia Wairawake' (not sold to Wakefield), though he noted the government 'has claimed ownership' of two.[243] He also listed the channel of Otago Harbour, Papanui and Hoopers inlets and Tomahawk Lagoon as 'Awa moana, kaore i tukua kia Wairareke' ('sea rivers not ceded to Wakefield'). The resources noted for these seaways included whales, sharks and several fish and shellfish species.[244]

Taiaroa petitioned parliament for the award of Crown grants to the unsold islands in 1882.[245] The response was that he should seek to prove his title in the Native Land Court. It is unclear whether he did so. This attempt, however, speaks to the detail in which Otago Māori knew the terms of what they had agreed to sell (Taiaroa named no islands that were included in the deed as having been purchased), while suggesting that government officials considered that Māori only retained what had been explicitly 'reserved' to them.

Otago Māori also subsequently said that William Wakefield had promised them the 'tenths' (actually in effect an eleventh of the land, set aside by the government primarily to provide for Māori), as had been the case with previous New Zealand Company purchases at Wellington, Nelson and New Plymouth.[246] No such promise was written into the Otago deed; the company intended that the government should make any such arrangements. But Symonds, the government's representative at the sale, had made 'no express stipulation' with the Māori vendors, thinking it was 'beyond the comprehension of the aborigines'. He left this decision to the governor.

Governor Fitzroy did not issue any instructions regarding 'tenths', or make any other provision for further reserves. Richmond, the superintendent of New Munster (which included all of the South Island), wrote to inform Fitzroy that he would demand the tenths, but Fitzroy's reply was ambiguous.[247] Fitzroy intended to make further provision for Otago Māori, though it is unlikely that he had 'tenths' in mind (the tenths had proved universally unsatisfactory to Māori and to settlers), but he saw no need for haste.[248] As it transpired, Richmond died soon after, Grey replaced Fitzroy as governor, and the settlers did not arrive for another four years. By then Governor Grey had granted the settlers Crown title to all of the Otago Block, and neither he nor they entertained the idea of further reserves for Otago Māori.[249]

More generally, as historians Vincent O'Malley and Richard Boast have each concluded, Māori regarded such land sales as transactions akin to a treaty, marking the establishment of a relationship.[250] Tuckett himself captured this difference, writing, 'I have not yet effected the purchase, but the Maoris are gathering for the treaty …'.[251] The British settlers who arrived in the wake of the purchase, however, did not share this perception. The persistent efforts of Kāi Tahu leaders to establish relations with their settler counterparts proved singularly unsuccessful.

The sale of the Otago Block to the New Zealand Company in 1844 was by far the most significant event that shifted control over the Otago Peninsula from Māori to Europeans. Kemp's purchase of 1848 had a wider effect. According to the deed, at least, it sold the great bulk of Canturbury and the remainder of Otago. This sale left the Ōtākou Māori stranded on the northern tip of the Peninsula, confined to meagre portions of their once vast property: the way was thereby opened to British settlement, and the making of a new environment on the Otago Peninsula.

OVERLEAF: *'Map of the suburban lands in the settlement of Otago'. Kettle's mapping set the shape of central Dunedin and its relationship to the Peninsula. Suburban settlement is planned for the southern fringes and along the harbour and inlet margins. Sections sold in the colony, tinted pink, cluster close to town, with a number sold in Andersons Bay.* 1849, Hocken Collections, Uare Taoka o Hākena, University of Otago: S07-524a

Part III
IMPROVING GOD'S CREATION

CHAPTER 6: 'A Desperate Struggle': British settlement on the Otago Peninsula 1848–61

We were in the pursuit of health – and had an ill-defined notion that somehow or other, let but the preparatory or preliminary labour of settlement be once accomplished, our toils would vanish, and the Eden of perfect rest and peace into which we believed we had dropped, yield richly the fruits of this new earth, all but spontaneously to our hands, free of all those hard inevitable requirements, which Nature and Providence impose everywhere else. But, false or true, buoyed up by these dreams, we worked hard for a time with axe, grub-hoe, and spade, felling trees and uprooting flax and fern …

– James Barr, *The Old Identities*[1]

Transplanted dreams: The lowland clearances and the settlement of Otago

The dream of Otago was that people could come to be free and independent; for many if not most settlers, that meant owning land.[2] In this Otago was no different from other New World colonies, but it more particularly reflected Edward Gibbon Wakefield's vision that a better 'Britain of the south' could be created by 'systematic colonisation' that distributed land ownership properly. Wakefield's core idea was that land prices should be just dear enough to allow the middle classes to dominate property ownership. Their demand for labour would then ensure high wages, allowing workers rapid entry into the charmed sphere of land ownership.[3] The transition from wage labourer to capitalist landowner was the flywheel of Wakefield's economic model. It was a dynamic designed to avoid concentrating land ownership in a few aristocrats, as had happened in Britain, while not falling back into the past – 'a stagnant peasant semi-subsistent economy with a low division of labour and little market development'.[4]

Wakefield was a convicted felon who had eloped with one heiress and abducted another, but his ideas still held a powerful attraction. They seemed to offer a way out of the urban poverty and unrest plaguing Britain in the wake of the industrial revolution.[5] In *England and America*, Wakefield emphasised above all that the first rule of 'the art of colonisation' was to keep 'the power over waste land'. America, he argued, had founded its empire on secure land titles. They provided the lure that encouraged capital investment across oceans, and so unleashed excess British labour to make colonial 'waste land' productive.[6] In this way, Wakefield envisaged, land sales alone could fund a virtuous circle of ever-increasing immigration and infrastructure. In short, a Wakefieldian colony would be 'a self-financing example of free-enterprise capitalism'.[8]

Wakefield's message had a particular resonance in Scotland, which was in the throes of revolutionary changes in people's relationship to land. Traditionally, almost all rural Scots had had some direct access to land. In the sixteenth century about half the country remained common land, and access to and use of individually owned land was widely distributed. Most Scots lived in the lowlands, and almost half the people there were 'cotters' – a peasantry sustained by the use of small plots of land of perhaps a few hectares. Tenant farmers, the next largest rural class, allowed the cotters access to these plots in return for their otherwise unpaid labour at harvest time. But only a few landowners sat atop this social structure. Scotland had (and has) Western Europe's highest concentration of land ownership. By 1800 just 8000 Scots owned any land; but, in fact, some one hundred aristocratic families owned most of Scotland, as they still do today.[8]

Between about 1760 and 1840 the social fabric of lowland Scotland was entirely remade by two great and interlocking forces, now known as the industrial and agricultural revolutions. Scotland's population boomed, almost doubling in the two generations between 1755 and 1820 from 1.2 million to over 2 million.[9] The need to feed growing cities drove an agricultural revolution of intensive farming and cultivation, increasing yields of key crops such as wheat by about 75 per cent.[10]

Wealthy landowners who had imbibed the Scottish Enlightenment ideology of 'the age of improvement' drove this agricultural revolution. They abhorred the waste of labour and land perceived in traditional subsistence life. They enclosed the commons and forced most of their tenants to leave the land when their leases ended. The peasant cotters, who had no legal protections, were eliminated. Over about two generations, those people that remained in the countryside became mostly 'landless men and women servants';[11] those 'cleared' from the countryside became wage labourers in the new textile towns and port cities. It was explosive urbanisation, faster than ever experienced before by a European people.

Individual ownership of land was the flagbearer for the age of improvement. The verb 'improve' originally meant to put to a profit, and in particular applied to the enclosing of waste or common land.[12] 'Enclosure and consolidation altered the organisation, function and purposes of land from one in which several members of a community had rights of use to a new condition in which single occupants had complete control.'[13] In England it took several thousand acts of enclosure to hedge and fence off the common lands as exclusive private property. In Scotland, however, a single act of 1695 allowed the courts to divide common land. Any one neighbouring owner could instigate a division of common land and force all other interested people to court to defend their rights, where 'lawyers lent themselves to appropriate the poor man's grazing to the neighbouring baron', while 'the poor had no lawyers'.[14]

Environmental transformation went hand in hand with economic and social revolution. The landscape became a patchwork of neatly divided and highly productive individual farms.[15] Fencing was sign and symbol of the enclosures, which in Scotland had caused 'a more or less total revolution in the appearance of the landscape … In a way not found in most of England, it was geometrised by all these changes.'[16]

In Scottish lowland regions such as the Lothians, the result of this interlocking set of changes drove one writer to comment: 'everything here is abundant but people, who have been studiously swept from the land'. It was among such displaced landless lowland Scots that the dream of Otago first gained purchase.

George Rennie, a Scottish sculptor and politician from a distinguished farming and engineering family, first promoted the possibility of founding a Wakefieldian colony on the South Island's east coast in 1842.[17] Rennie sought to improve on Wakefield's model, but contributed little other than an added insistence on the need for 'contiguity' and 'concentration' of settlement. This emphasis especially appealed to members of the embryonic Scottish Free Church. In 1843 they adopted Rennie's scheme as a vehicle for their dreams of an exclusive – or, as the Reverend Thomas Burns described it to

Captain William Cargill, 'special' – little community blessed with the 'very delightful privileges of internal harmony and Christian unity'.[18] However, their insistence on religious exclusivity alienated and sidelined Rennie, and Cargill and Burns became, respectively, the political and spiritual leaders of the proposed settlement.

Cargill and Burns saw themselves as becoming patriarchs of a cohesive religious community far from the fractious religious discord of Scotland. Both men loathed the urban industrialisation that had transformed Scotland over their lifetimes, and feared the radical disruption of social hierarchy symbolised by the French Revolution. They shared a hope that, under their leadership, Otago might become what they believed Scotland ought to have been: a cohesive agrarian society founded on family-orientated Presbyterian small farmers.[19] Writing to Cargill on 30 January 1847, Burns set out his vision for the land they sought to found:

> [M]y prophetic eye wanders over the noble plains of Otago some generations hence to mark the future herds and flocks that cover the upland pastures far away to the ranges of the snowy mountains, whilst the lower-lying valleys are waving with the yellow corn and the pursuits of rural husbandry; the pretty farms, 'the busy mile,' and the happy smiling cottages by the wayside or nestling amid the trees in some bosky dingle or sylvan dell; and all this amongst a God-fearing people, with a bold peasantry, their country's pride, and an aristocracy whose highest honour it is to think that they are the disciples of Christ. But I awake; it is only a dream.[20]

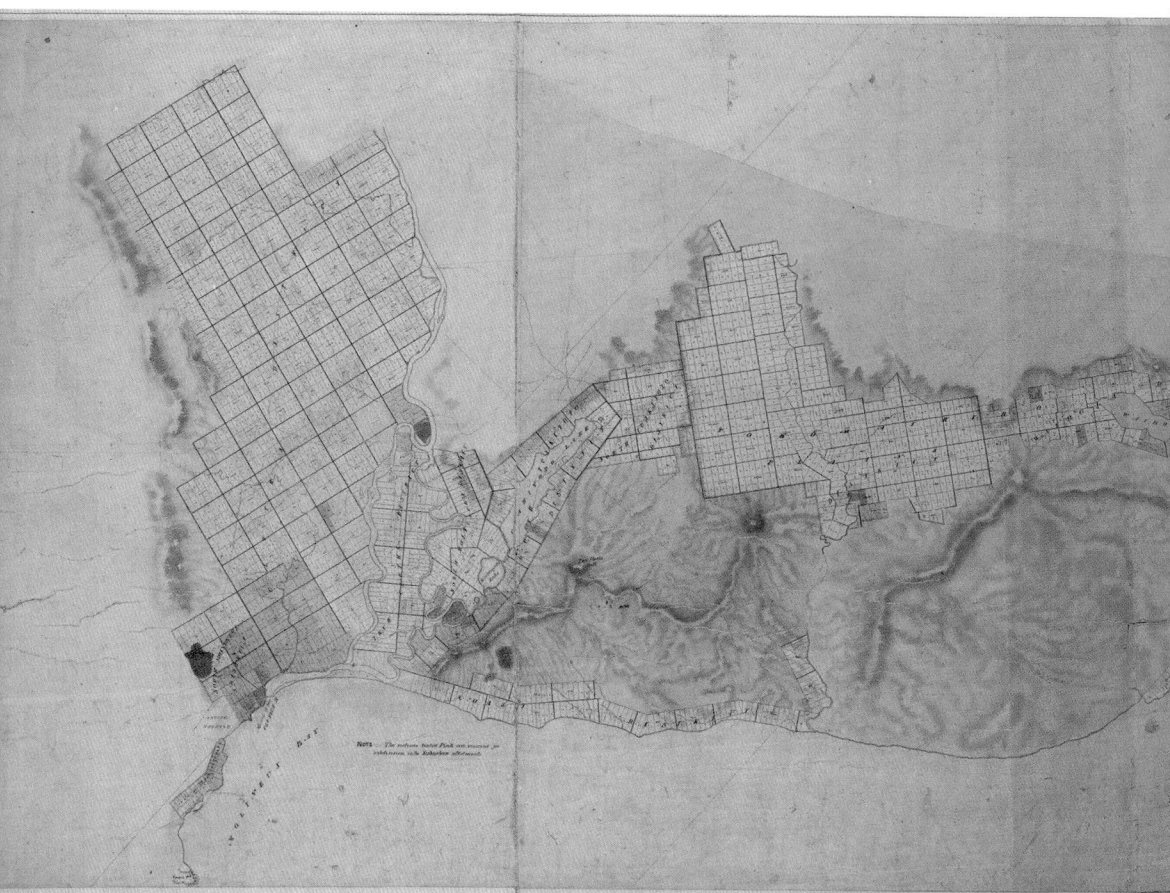

CHAPTER 6: 'A DESPERATE STRUGGLE'

It is too easy to scoff at dreams. Given the economic and ecological odds against which the settlers struggled, and which they themselves never really grasped, it is more remarkable how close they came to fulfilling their vision.[21]

Planning Arcadia: The survey of the Otago settlement

Wakefield's colonisation schemes depended on secure title underpinned by accurate surveys. In two years of intense effort in 1846 and 1847, Charles Kettle and his team surveyed the Otago Block and mapped out the form that the proposed Scots settlement was to take.[22] Kettle's work culminated in the 'Index Map of the Otakou Settlement'.[23]

Kettle's maps have shaped Otago more than any other documents, from specifying the layout of the Octagon to setting out the patterns of the southern plains' farms.

Kettle was told to follow Frederick Tuckett's choice of the head of the harbour as site for the principal settlement of Dunedin, and to reproduce there the characteristics

BELOW: *Charles Kettle's 1849 map of the suburban lands in the settlement of Otago, Middle Island, New Zealand. Kettle and his team of surveyors patterned the settlement much as Tuckett had envisioned. They spread a suburban fringe around Dunedin, at the head of Otago Harbour, and laid out agricultural settlement to the south on the Taieri and Tokomairiro plains.*
Hocken Collections, Uare Taoka o Hākena, University of Otago: Hl+/880/1849/a

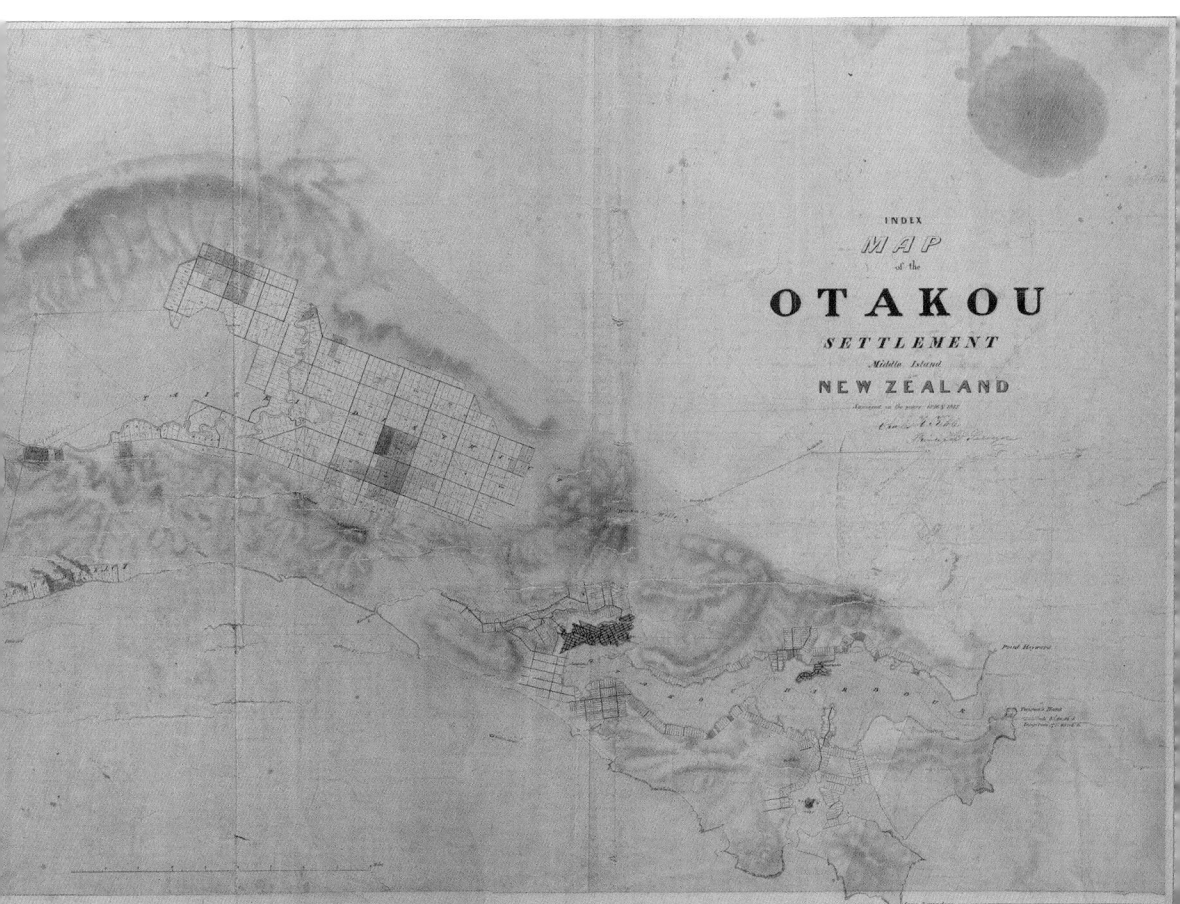

> THE FIRST QUESTION was where to site the town. Dunedin would have taken a very different form if William Mein Smith's advice on this question had been heeded. Mein Smith, who later designed Wellington, had visited Otago harbour in 1842. He thought the head of the harbour too far from the anchorage at Port Chalmers, and considered that the best town site was on the Otago Peninsula opposite the anchorage at Port Chalmers, in the vicinity of present-day Portobello and Broad Bay. Tuckett, however, preferred the head of the harbour.
>
> Before leaving Scotland Thomas Burns assessed some of the considerations for and against these locations in a letter to Cargill on 5 March 1845, questioning Tuckett's choice of 'the bleak side of a hill':
>
>> had he chosen the east side of the harbour, it would have been on the sunny side of the slope – a great point. I know the answer would have been that he would have planted us in the very heart of the Natives. Now, as to this I am not sure but that amalgamation in so small a number would be ultimately safer and better than what appears to be a permanent separate localization.[24]
>
> Mein Smith was right that getting goods between the town and the ships at Port Chalmers would be a terrible problem for early Dunedin. Today, Dunedin's people might agree with Burns' 'great point' as they look enviously across to the sunny Peninsula. For their part, Peninsula communities have always struggled to overcome relative separation from the settlement at Dunedin, none more so than the Māori community at Ōtākou. But there was not enough flat land to found a large town around Portobello, and siting the settlement there would have put town and port on different sides of the harbour, and made getting over to the agricultural land on the Taieri very hard.

of Edinburgh within a settlement divided into 2400 properties, split between town, suburban and rural sections of a quarter acre, 10 acres, and 50 acres (0.1, 4 and 20ha) respectively. He was to select the best 120,000 acres (48,562ha) for the Otago settlement; the rest of the Otago Block would revert to the Crown.

Kettle's mapping of the settlement was underpinned by New Zealand's first trigonometric survey, in which space is mapped by triangulating the relative locations of key high points. This was the most accurate way available to measure and map space.[25] It allowed Kettle to do 'no more than design the sections on the map', as they could be later 'laid off with facility whenever they are required'.[26]

Kettle envisaged that the Peninsula's southwestern fringe would become part of the town, and divided it into 10-acre (4ha) 'suburban' sections. This area has become the suburbs of Andersons Bay, Vauxhall and Waverley. Kettle also designated a suburban strip along the harbour to Portobello, around Harbour Cone, and along the margins of Hoopers and Papanui inlets. He thought the latter 'some very desirable sections', as besides access across the Peninsula to Otago Harbour, 'very deep channels communicating with the sea' at high tide would provide boats with entry to the inlets.

The survey and map were essential to settlement. The map provided the first detailed knowledge of much of the landscape; the Peninsula's outer coasts, for example, had remained essentially featureless in previous maps.[27] The plan produced by Kettle and his team of surveyors organised natural space into an image that could be used to generate cultural place.

Kettle has been frequently criticised for designing Dunedin without regard for the landscape.[28] Told to replicate the much-admired New Town of Edinburgh on its flat-topped hill, he in fact made considerable concessions to the topography he found here – a harbourside site surrounded by hills.[29] Dividing rugged and unruly landscape such as the Peninsula into neat patterns was never going to run quite according to plan, and some roadlines drawn up its steep slopes have remained 'paper roads' – but Kettle himself was very conscious that 'great care must be taken to obtain such lines of road as will render the section accessible – it would be manifestly imprudent to lay out broken country, without regarding hill or gully, into blocks of sections with straight roads not one of which perhaps would ever be available'.[30]

Given the constraints of his instructions, there is little to criticise in the way Kettle patterned Otago into properties. Those instructions in turn reflected the necessity of providing prospective property owners with full and exclusive ownership of clearly defined parcels of land. As we have seen, this was regarded as critical to efficient land use. But the first purpose for titles in the context of a new colony was to create something to sell. This is why the geometric grid is ubiquitous in colonial town planning: it created what the Australian geographer Paul Carter has called 'a container for real estate … its streets, conduits for auctioneers'.[31] Offering nominally equivalent units eased the establishment of a market and encouraged investors to buy land, sight unseen, from the far side of the world.[32] Of course, purchasers knew that grids are crude ways to partition land, trampling across topography, aspect, soils, availability of water and accessibility. In the case of Otago, at least, a lottery held before departure decided the order in which purchasers would get to choose their land when at last their ships hove to off the Otago Peninsula under 'a sultry, ethereal sky' in the autumn of 1848.[33]

The settlers' arrival: Anticipation and anxiety

Who were the settlers who looked to shore from the first ships, the *John Wickliffe* and *Phillip Laing*? Most were young married couples from what was now Scotland's industrial heartland, the villages and commercial towns between the Firth of Clyde and the Firth of Forth, and especially the city of Edinburgh.[34] Free Church adherents were even then not numerically dominant. Economic independence, not religious fervor, motivated most to emigrate.[35] Many of the first Otago settlers desired a return to a rural life that their parents or grandparents had abandoned in Scotland, and a reasonable number did have experience of rural life themselves: 12 per cent of the men on the first ships were farmers, and another 41 per cent were shepherds, ploughmen or labourers.[36] The rest of the men were largely tradesmen, storekeepers or artisans.[37] Few emigrants had any money to speak of; of the 247 passengers on the *Philip Laing*, for example, only 18 were wealthy enough to travel as cabin passengers, and of these five were ships' officers and eight were part of Burns' family.[38]

Thomas Ferens recorded the scene as the *John Wickliffe* entered the harbour on a fine autumn morning with a gentle northeast breeze. They were guided over the harbour bar by Pilot Driver and his Māori crew, and greeted by a mixed Māori and European welcoming party waving from the hills. It was, wrote Ferens,

> *a most delightful and picturesque domestic scene; heights on either side, we saw the native village on the native reserves, and further on a small village of Settlers and Whalers.*
>
> *The Cormorants rose out of the water as we approached, by thousands. The scenery as we gained Port Chalmers, where we anchord [sic], put me in remembrance of a great part of the Cumberland scenery, the imagination fired, and here will nature triumphant [sic] and bring the mind to rejoice, and adore the divine being.*[39]

Like Ferens, all the settlers were impressed with the beauty of Otago harbour at first sight – Burns describing it as 'one uninterrupted scene of most romantic beauty'. But some were understandably concerned by the steep forested slopes visible as they sailed up the harbour. Burns reassured them, pointing out that Kettle had laid out their farms on the Taieri and Molyneux plains.[40] Burns himself did not even sight the Taieri until 1850, and was among those who instead started by farming some of the only accessible land: the steep 'suburban' properties of the inner Peninsula.

Modelling the path of the righteous: Thomas Burns' farm

Thomas Burns' farm, Grants Braes at Andersons Bay, was named after the house his father occupied as manager of the Blantyre estates in Ayrshire. Burns wanted to model how British 'mixed farming', as practised in Scotland, could be recreated in Otago. He was committed to a settlement founded on agriculture, and was wary of the lure of pastoralism that would spread his flock too far and wide for him to minister to them. He exemplified the British obsession with property rights and the ideology of improvement.[41] This was arguably a particularly Scottish preoccupation for, as Sir John Sinclair asserted in 1814, 'In no country in Europe are the rights of proprietors so well defined and so carefully protected.'[42]

Improvement, Tony Ballantyne suggests, was 'the colonial keyword'.[43] For James Beattie and John Stenhouse, it was 'the ideological heart of ecological imperialism'.[44] Improving one's property fulfilled God's plans for both humanity and nature; empire was rendered as providence.[45] One of few settlers who had fully absorbed the new farming methods fostered by the Scottish Enlightenment, Burns intended his farm to exemplify to his fellow settlers the practicality and desirability of a scientific agriculture that improved both the land and the labourer.

Burns wanted to transplant British 'mixed farming' that combined rearing stock – most importantly cattle for meat and dairy products – with raising cereal and fodder crops. These practices had to be closely integrated to generate flows of several products, and to maintain soil fertility and control weeds without the need for fallow land. A typical Scottish rotation was to begin by planting oats after the land had lain in grass for about seven years, so that the grain benefited from compact soil and high nitrogen levels sustained by clover and manure. Clover was particularly critical as the key nitrogen-fixing plant, since a lack of nitrogen is the limiting factor on most crop yields.[46]

The adoption of new crops such as clover and turnips throughout the seventeenth and eighteenth centuries, as part of the agricultural revolution, had enabled higher stock densities, meaning that more animal dung was available to restore fertility and raise yields. Manure was spread as the animals grazed and, because the animals were typically housed indoors overnight, concentrated accumulations were also collected and distributed. A crop of turnips for winter fodder was typically followed by another grain crop – often barley, which likes a looser soil – before planting a final root crop. After this was harvested, the ground was ploughed and resown in grass and clover.[47]

Fencing allowed property owners to design the ecology of their land by maintaining strict divisions between different land users and uses. Fences bounded ecological processes in time and space, determining which plants grew where and when and which animals might eat them; Britain's quickset hawthorn hedges and drystone walls reflect the spread of this system, which is why they so clearly symbolised bounding the commons into private hands.[48] Establishing such control in this new environment was never going to be easy, however, but Burns was determined to show it was possible and profitable.

Burns was lucky in the ballot and had the luxury of choosing his land early; in July 1848 he selected suburban sections totalling 130 acres (52.6ha) at Andersons Bay.[49] He was impressed by its beauty, the aspect to the sun that promised fine tillage and pasture, the timber, the soil, the shells on the shore that could be burnt for lime – and, above all, the excellent access across the harbour.[50]

By the end of the year Burns had 50 acres (20ha) fenced off. Over the next few years he planted them in wheat, barley, oats, turnips and several varieties of potatoes, and cultivated a large garden where he grew onions, peas, cabbages, cauliflowers, carrots, celery, leeks, beans and rhubarb.[51] He ate the first food from this garden on New Year's

THE VISION OF THE LANDSCAPE that Thomas Burns and the settlers strove to create is seen in two similar paintings by surveyors: Edward Immyns Abbot's view of Dunedin from Little Paisley on the site of what is now the Southern Cemetery, and John Turnbull Thomson's depiction of a view from on or near Burns' land at Andersons Bay in 1856.

As James Beattie has noted, Thomson and Abbot have depicted how Dunedin's inhabitants wished to appear to the outside world: their town is peacefully laid out before the gaze of well-dressed sightseers; the hills have been flattened; the extent of native forest in the distance reduced; and the few plants framing the foreground are ornamental specimens of cabbage tree or flax, seemingly retained to emphasise the hillside swathed in pasture.[52]

The settlers survey clean fields, sturdy homes and warming fires while at their ease on a limpid Dunedin day. Abbot's image was lithographed and distributed in Britain to publicise the success of the colony.

RIGHT: *Edward Immyns Abbot,* Dunedin from Little Paisley, *1849, watercolour on paper, 177 x 275mm.* BELOW: *John Turnbull Thomson,* Dunedin, New Zealand, from Andersons Bay, *1856.* Hocken Collections, Uare Taoka o Hākena, University of Otago: #557; S06-458c

Day 1849 and, even allowing 'for the wonderment of our first fruits', had 'no hesitation in saying that vegetables of every description here are certainly super-excellent'.[53] After taking two or three crops, he planted the land in permanent pasture and ran cattle and sheep.[54] He then showed the way to market and shipped the settlement's first grain exports to Australia.[55]

Burns had demonstrated that agriculture was possible and potentially profitable – but he had numerous advantages. He had been raised to farm, being only a late and reluctant minister, and came equipped with the settlement's first bull and cow, along with many sorts of seeds. He was thoroughly familiar with modern farming techniques, for example gathering shells from Portobello to burn for lime, to be spread with grass and clover seed to reduce acidity and improve nitrogen uptake.[56]

A close and keen observer, Burns knew that settlers had much to learn about the alien environment and would have to adapt their methods accordingly. He kept meticulous meterological records. Three times a day, every day, for almost 20 years he recorded readings from his thermometer and barometer, noted the wind and described the weather; each morning he also recorded precipitation. He provided all of this information to the *Otago Journal* to be read by prospective immigrants, and to the *Otago Witness* for the benefit of established settlers.[57]

Burns was not above learning from Māori and, having noted that they planted their potatoes on headlands (presumably taking advantage of the more fertile soils derived from basalt), he selected his sections on top of the ridge with this in mind.[58] When he came to plant his potatoes, he did so 'Maori fashion', often employing Māori labour.[59] The land appeared as if 'covered over with large mole hills, which, with the stumps, gives it a very colonial appearance indeed'.[60]

Above all, Burns had money. He was the largest employer in the first three years of settlement. To prepare his acre of garden cost him just over £55 in wages; each 10-acre (4ha) section cost £10 to fence; clearing and planting one acre (0.4ha) in potatoes within a section cost him over £14.[61] He hoped to recoup his investment since, in the first flush of soil fertility, he expected to harvest about six tons of potatoes per acre, and planned to sell them at £3 to £4 a ton.[62]

Without start-up capital, farming was a different proposition. Writing home to his brother, Burns admitted how poor the prospects were for the majority of people striving to become farmers in the new settlement. He warned that 'No man who is above working for wages himself can embark as a settler in Otago without at the very least £500 in his pocket when he leaves the ship's side, and even then he would have to set an example by working like a horse.'[63]

Without such a sum, he wrote, men would be either driven into the labour market at a disadvantage or be forced to set out 'as some young men are doing, with a cow or pig or goat, and flour, trusting to shoot pigeons'. He foresaw that independence could be achieved after some years in this way, but only after 'making a desperate struggle for a livelihood in some crazy hut of tree branches and wet clay'.[64] This was precisely the struggle for subsistence that the majority of the Peninsula's early settlers faced during the 1850s as they moved out onto the land.

'A desperate struggle': Making the first farms, 1850–61

The prospect of hacking out a home and holding from the Peninsula's hills was daunting, and very few of the 12,000-odd settlers who arrived in Otago during the 1850s attempted it.[65] For those prepared to try, the first problem was getting there. A handful of families crossed the harbour from Port Chalmers to live at Portobello,[66] while slightly more followed Burns to Andersons Bay.[67] One, James Patrick, pushed on into the Tomahawk valley. He started off carrying provisions over the hill on his back, and brought his produce out the same way; eventually he bought a bullock and dragged a sledge to and from Dunedin.[68] The lucky ones, like the Somerville family, found a 'scarce' boat, and could spare £30 to buy it.[69] In 1860 all the settlers – 47 of them – backed a petition to the Otago Provincial Council, bemoaning their disadvantage: 'The land in our district being heavily timbered and generally of first-rate quality, would support a large and important population, produce a valuable export of grain, sawn timber, and firewood; and contribute in various ways to the general welfare and prosperity of the Province, if provided with a means of bringing its produce to market.'[70]

The settlers' families included up to a dozen children, and shelter was their first imperative.[71] Frustratingly, though surrounded by forest, the settlers had to wait for cut wood to season if they wanted to build a timber house that might help keep them warm. Burns, whose dignity precluded installing his family in a grass hut, did not wait long enough – the manse he had built for his family was floored with 'white pine' (kahikitea), which 'shrank fearfully making the room very cold'.[72] The settlers coped in the interim in shelters made 'on the pattern of a Maori whare'.[73] John McClay described his family's version at Andersons Bay as 'like the roof of an old thatch hut lifted off and set down on the ground'.[74] The settlers gradually erected simple houses, building 'with whatever was handiest'.[75] Many made 'wattle and daub' dwellings, with walls of saplings woven between fern-tree posts, packed with tussock and plastered with clay or lined with sheets of totara bark.[76] Raupō reeds tied onto mānuka rafters kept out all but the worst weather.[77]

Once settlers had a roof over their heads they set to work clearing land, beginning by preparing ground around the house for a garden. Women ran the gardens, which provided essential potatoes and other vegetables, fruit and the familiar flowers of home.[78] The letters and diaries of all the early settlers evince a pervasive yearning for such familiarity. Though they appreciated the beauty of their new surroundings, the language with which they described new sights, sounds and scents was wholly that of their old homes – the scent of bush lawyer resembled syringa, clematis and supplejack had 'white blossom like the convulvulus … the myrtle berry with its little unseen flower like white heath'.[79] Immigrants were urged to bring out 'some haws and some Scotch thistle and a bit of heather with a root', and these new arrivals were cared for assiduously: 'Mother … gathered up hundreds of young hawthorns she had grown from pips that the boys had gathered on the road.'[80] Unfortunately, many such introductions adapted too well and spread into the settlers' newly cleared land.

Clearing forest land involved felling all the larger trees, lopping off big branches, piling up as much of this vegetation as possible and waiting for summer and a suitable wind for a chance to burn it.[81] At this time timber was 'a weed to be eradicated', as the *New Zealand Journal* put it.[82] Bush land was preferred to fern land because it was thought more fertile – fern land was fairly acidic – but settlers soon discovered the value of burning, finding it 'essential to the full and immediate vigour of the soil'.[83]

The aim was a 'white burn', when all that remained was ash, but this was rare. As James Somerville recalled, '[i]t required the wind to keep the tree tops burning.'[84] Substantial logs were usually left, and tree stumps and root systems remained in the ground. Much of the Peninsula was also covered in a dense layer of boulders. While cattle could be run among stumps, roots and rocks, ploughing and harrowing were impossible and attempts to do so rendered useless many of the tools settlers had brought from home: not built to withstand the strain imposed by working new land, these quickly broke. Settlers found that kōwhai or mānuka made the best replacements for snapped tool handles. Like many early settlers, Garrett Hopper Clearwater, 'a splendid bush man, a Great Man with an axe', preferred American tools. He told John McLay's father that 'the axes and hoes from home were no good' and recommended turning the axes into grub hoes. He was right, McLay remembered, for they could then cut the roots.[85]

Land was cleared acre by acre, achingly slowly. By 1855 the Andersons Bay settlers had cleared a combined 238 acres (96ha). A year later, they had managed only another 24 acres (10ha).[86] The cumulative extent of their efforts is seen in Robert Gillies' *Topographical Sketch of Otago Peninsula 1859* (page 175), which shows the settlers' chipping away at the forest in Andersons Bay and Tomahawk Lagoon. Larger areas of bush, however, had been lost behind Te Rauone Beach and behind Sandfly Bay, where already the incursions of drifting sand are delineated.

Once cleared the land was fenced, largely in post-and-rail fences using hard and durable kōwhai and tōtara; kōwhai was abundant on the Peninsula, especially about Tomahawk, whose hills 'all looked bright yellow' from the flowers.[87]

Fenced land could be planted, and settlers adopted a basic crop rotation that typically alternated cereals and root crops before ending in sown grasses in an effort to maximise crop yields before the initial high fertility of the potash-enriched soil was exhausted.[88] Wheat was generally preferred because wheaten bread was 'the staff of life', and imported flour was expensive and not always available.[89] Wheat also

CHAPTER 6: 'A DESPERATE STRUGGLE'

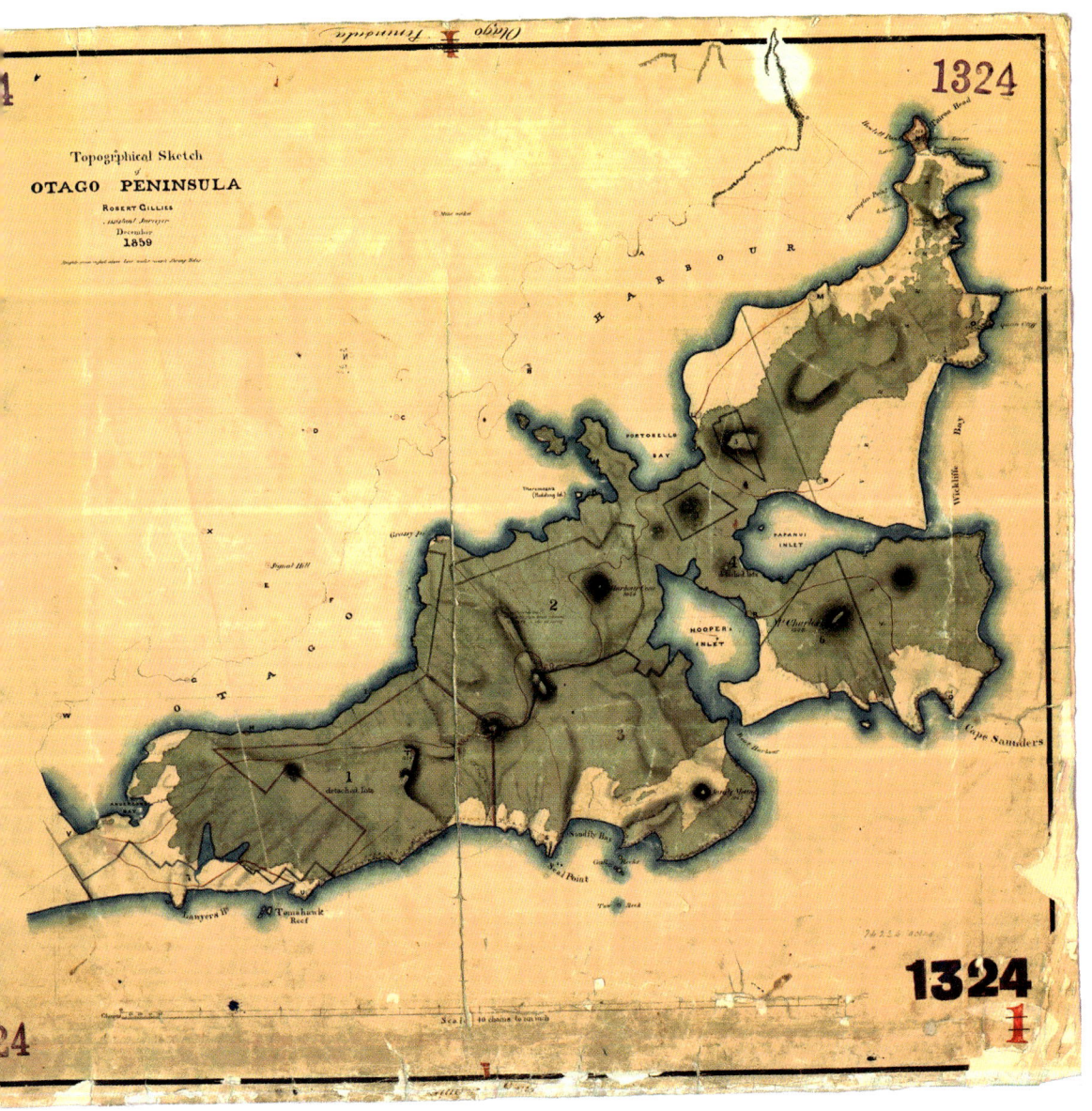

Robert Gillies, 'Topographical sketch of Otago Peninsula 1859'. Although settlement has begun to nibble at the forest fringes at Ōtākou and Andersons Bay, the sand is already on the move at Sandfly Bay, and this map suggests that the rest of the Peninsula was still clothed in forest.

Land Information New Zealand, SO 1324

commanded the highest prices – locally up to 12 shillings a bushel compared with eight for barley or five for oats.[90] However, Australian market dominance made prices volatile. When crops failed there, as in 1855, wheat was a profitable export, but the following year it was unsaleable in Australia and locally fetched only nine shillings a bushel.[91] Unsurprisingly, since most people were Scots and relied on horses, relatively large areas were also planted in oats despite their low market price. Barley was never grown in any quantity, despite the settlers' fondness for beer, and the *Otago Witness* frequently complained that the settlement had to import malt.[92]

The settlers' many crop variations reflected the fact that they were conducting simultaneous experiments while observing one another's results.[93] James Patrick, for example, sowed oats after felling, before laying down grass for three or four years. He then dug out the partially decayed stumps and took another three crops of oats. Neighbouring settler James King tried sowing oats with his grass, and let them stand for a few years.

Settlers were greatly encouraged by the fact that crop yields in the initial rotation were extremely high, though harvest was haphazard and it was difficult to mill grain into flour.[94] James Patrick reaped 60 bushels of wheat from his first acre; although average yields were seldom over 40 bushels, this still compared very favourably with Britain, where average yields were only 22 bushels per acre in 1840.[95]

All settlers ended their rotation by laying down grasses. They preferred perennial and Italian ryegrass, timothy and white clover. Cocksfoot, though less productive, often replaced ryegrass in this basic mixture on rougher ground, because it lasted longer. (Prior to the breeding programmes of the twentieth century, 'perennial' ryegrass did not really live up to its name.) Cocksfoot also better withstood trampling by cattle and, unlike the other grasses, maintained steady growth throughout winter.[96] Stock were then released onto the pasture.[97]

Most early settlers began with just a few cattle as a main source of income. Shorthorns, useful for both meat and milk, were favoured as an all-purpose animal. In the absence of fences, however, selective breeding was initially impossible and generic 'colonial cows' developed, in which Shorthorn and (less frequently) Ayrshire or Hereford blood predominated.[98] Alongside their cattle some settlers also had a few pigs, goats and poultry, as well as a horse or two.

The creation of every single farm on the Otago Peninsula required immense labour, and for most, 'mixed farming' of a subsistence sort was a matter of necessity – the land had to provide a substantially complete diet, because farm income was so low and town so far away. And if the settlers' initial hopes, captured so well by James Barr, proved futile – that this land would 'yield richly the fruits of this new earth, all but spontaneously to our hands' – there was meanwhile a lot of native game to be eaten.[99]

Spreading ripples: Settlers' ecological effects

Each settler homestead was a centre of spreading ripples of ecological change. Areas of cleared and planted land expanded around each house, while settlers and their stock roamed the forests beyond. But the wild flooded back, too, for the new fields provided opportunities for wild animals, weeds and native plants as much as stock and crops.

Early settlers derived a lot of food from the Peninsula forests and wetlands. Fresh from Britain, their records reveal that they revelled in the excellent hunting that every man could now enjoy.[100] Settlers shot tūī, kākā, weka, quail and pigeons in the bush, and paradise, grey and teal ducks at Tomahawk Lagoon and on the Akapātiki wetlands.[101]

Meanwhile, stock spread well beyond the settlements. Because there was initially no way to provide concentrated feed, all livestock – bar the cows in milk, for which a byre was built as a matter of priority – were turned into the bush to fend for themselves.[102] They formed herds of more-or-less wild cattle that often congregated as far away as Sandfly Bay and Cape Saunders, whence they could only be retrieved with great difficulty.[103] Māori and settler owners alike complained that their roaming cattle were treated as fair game by 'sportsmen' who nevertheless took care to remove the brands on the beasts they killed, so that the Peninsula in the late 1850s and early 1860s was 'covered with carcasses'.[104]

In the first years of settlement pigs also ran wild, and marauding swine often rooted out crops and gardens.[105] The law inherited from England required crop growers to attempt to fence out stock, if they were to claim damages, but fencing was prohibitively expensive. According to one settler this was the factor limiting crop growing, and was just one example of how, as the *Otago News* editor had it, 'the farmer finds his past knowledge almost useless, and all his old-fashioned ideas turned topsy-turvy by a new system of things'.[106]

Cats multiplied fast and went wild, too; as a boy in the 1850s John McLay found kittens in an old broadleaf at Andersons Bay.[107] Along with Norway rats, cats killed off the kiore that James Somerville's family had felt 'running over us in the bed when we were living in the tent' when they first went to Andersons Bay in 1849.[108] Writing in 1871, Peter Thomson noted that one might now 'look in vain' for these animals which, although common in the interior during the gold rush, might now only exist in Fiordland.[109]

But the wild bit back, too, as the existing fauna and flora found new opportunities in the farmers' disturbances. Insects, in particular, swarmed into the niches opened by the settlers. In 1850, for example, Burns watched in horror as 'myriads of caterpillars' descended on his first crop of wheat, heavy with grain, and utterly destroyed eight acres (3.2ha). Burns believed these caterpillars, which, he noted, 'pay periodical visits every few years', were from the 'common small black butterfly'.[110] But this is the day-flying magpie moth whose larva eats only plants of the Compositae or daisy family, often seen today on cineraria and ragwort. The caterpillars that had plagued Burns were probably armyworms.[111]

Other insects troubled settlers more personally. Before the bush was cleared and swamps were drained, both mosquitoes 'in the bush' and sandflies 'by the beaches' were far more common than they are now.[112] In summer, especially, they tormented settlers confined to coastal margins surrounded by bush and standing water.[113] Fleas were even more prevalent, 'infesting all domiciles alike', and spread 'over the whole face of the country'.[114] Possibly the worst insect pest was the native bluebottle blowfly which 'swarmed everywhere' so that:

> No woollen material could safely be left lying at rest for even a few minutes ... A working man took off his blue serge shirt and threw it down carelessly (and every man in those days was a working man and wore a blue shirt), and in a very short time when he went to pick it up he would discover to his annoyance and disgust that it was fly-blown, and not long after he would find it crawling with maggots.[115]

All woollen cloth and bed linen had to be wrapped in calico bags when not in use, and it was rare to see blankets not 'indelibly stained by burst eggs'.[116] The settlers were lucky that the native blowfly does not lay its eggs in the wool of living sheep and cause fly-strike. If it had, sheep farming here would have been much more difficult, and Otago might have lost what became its most important early export commodity.[117] The introduced European blowfly has now largely displaced the native fly; indeed, Alexander Bathgate recorded that settlers themselves took the European fly from town into the countryside in matchboxes, 'after it had been ascertained that they supplanted the [native] blow flies'.[118]

Some native birds were periodically crop pests too. Parakeets were the worst problem threatening the grain and fruit of early farmers cultivating in the midst of bush,[119] who 'had always the greatest difficulty' in saving their crops of wheat from flocks of hundreds of red- or yellow-crowned parakeets. These birds defied scarecrows and, though they rose from the crops at gunfire, they promptly settled again.[120] As a result some Peninsula settlers turned to bird-trapping and were seen to 'secure hundreds in their nets in a day in the late sixties'.[121] Like Burns' caterpillars, however, parakeets and other birds were generally occasional menaces, and settlers gradually came to understand and predict their behaviour. Observing one of their periodic plagues in 1878, a writer to the *Otago Witness* noted: 'Naturalists have observed attentively the phenomenon that when a failure takes place in the natural feed for these birds, there is a certainty of an invasion.'[122] Parakeets feed on the seed kernels of the podocarps, especially tōtara, and on berries such as fuchsia; all are subject to considerable variations in seeding.[123]

Kākā, with their varied diet of grubs, berries and honey, also descended on farmers' homesteads in leaner seasons. James Somerville recalled that when settlers found them 'very numerous', they were unusually thin and not good eating.[124] In 1855 and

1856 large numbers ate turnips and grain from the fields, and the damage they caused 'to [hay] stacks and thatched houses, tearing them open with their powerful bills, was something enormous … Settlers used to discuss how they were to protect their property against this serious pest, which it was believed would increase each year as the area of grain agriculture increased.' Yet next year, the kākā were gone. They returned in 1861 – but were never numerous again.[125]

One reason kākā disappeared was that, as noted above, settlers ate them.[126] Berry-feeding birds were best eaten in autumn, but because they were pests settlers shot and ate them all year round. One 'common recipe' called for 14 pigeons and a kākā to make a good soup.[127] Tūī were also favoured eating in autumn, when they were 'mere balls of fat' that had to be 'roasted off … to make them fit for pies and stews'.[128]

Settlers on the Peninsula were aware that these birds were disappearing fast. Initially, perhaps, they did need the food: town was for most a day away, and it could not always be relied on for supplies anyway. Regardless, there was no impetus among the settlers, individually or collectively, towards the preservation of wildlife: birds were seen as destined for extinction. Infamously, much the same was true of the settlers' attitude towards Māori at Ōtākou.

'An apparently doomed and expiring race': Ōtākou Māori and the settlers

When the first settlers arrived they were welcomed by Ōtākou Māori, and had reason to be grateful for their presence. Māori supplied the hungry settlers with fish and potatoes, and carried on this trade throughout the 1850s.[129] Māori boats provided local and coastal transport (sometimes going as far as Wellington), and Māori labour helped build houses and clear farms. Māori themselves benefited equally from the renewed market that the Scottish settlement provided. As one arrival on the *Philip Laing* recorded in a letter home, 'The natives are quiet, peaceful, harmless creatures. We shall probably wish we had more of them by-and-by.'[130]

Some settlers recognised that they had a lot to learn from Māori about this new land. Thomas Ferens, who spent the most time with Māori in the weeks after the first settlers arrived, quickly learned that tūī were 'very fat, round as a ball, and can be easily caught', while pigeons were 'exceedingly numerous, fat, and of excellent flavour'.[131] Māori showed the settlers how to supplement their food by baking fern root and eating fuchsia berries and the 'heart' of cabbage tree leaves.[132] They taught settlers the indicators provided by other species for daily weather or good and bad growing seasons, such as the activity of feeding pigeons, or the timing and abundance of plants' flowering and animals' seasonal movements.

Many such fruits of environmental engagement would have been hard won without Māori help – such as how to safely enjoy highly poisonous tutu berries, or when to eat the first fruit that the young John McClay tasted in New Zealand, 'bula bula' (poroporo) berries, with which his mother also made jam.[133] Children, who were more willing to befriend and learn from Māori, passed much of this knowledge on to their parents.

Settler gratitude for Māori aid faded fast. The settlers' leaders soon regarded Ōtākou Māori with kindly condescension at best, often sinking into outright contempt. Cargill's attitude is probably representative: he believed the Ōtākou Māori were 'the mere remnant of an apparently doomed and expiring race', and concluded that there were 'hardly enough of them left to show kindness to'.[134] Not that much kindness was shown.

Access to Dunedin markets was crucial for Ōtākou Māori. In the first few years of settlement they sold goods, primarily fish and potatoes, from the banks of the Toitū Stream (where today one finds Serpentine Avenue) where it debouched into the estuary.[135] John McLay remembered: 'We get plenty of Baracuda and Grouper brought to Dunedin by Maori boats. These are both large fish and we often get 4 Baracuda for one shilling and a large Grouper for 1/6d …'[136] Māori continued to supply fish throughout the 1850s, a correspondent to the press in 1859 noting that 'five or six boats two and three times a week come up to Dunedin from the heads full of fish'.[137]

Māori had erected whare on Rattray Street in which to stay while selling goods from their landing place at the Toitū estuary. But around 1851 the settlers, made uneasy by haka, evicted them.[138] 'All was very pleased they had left for ever this place', remembered McLay.[139] However, having boated their produce the length of the harbour, Māori often needed somewhere to stay overnight, to sell goods at market in the morning, or because the state of the tide or weather precluded going home.[140] Staying at an inn or hotel cut hard into profit margins. As James Adam noted in 1857, though 'detained by a foul wind for several days', rather than desecrate the Sabbath by sailing on a Sunday, Ōtākou Māori would remain in Dunedin 'in great discomfort to themselves',[141] and were reduced to using 'their boats, oars and sails' for shelter on the beach.

The Otago Provincial Council recognised the problem in April 1855, noting the 'urgent necessity … for the immediate erection of a suitable building … for the comfortable lodging of the natives'.[142] Cargill proposed renovating a building at the Toitū estuary, but did not allocate any money towards the project.[143] James Macandrew's (anti-Cargill) paper, the *Otago Colonist*, made much of the subsequent inaction: 'We have been asked time and time again by Maori where is the house promised them', an editorial on 17 July 1857 noted, but '[m]onths and years are passing away, and we are always going to do something; let us resolve that ere another year commences we shall have actually done something.' Māori were described as huddling under their boats on the waterfront in the snows of winter, 'frequently roused at night by vagabonds and plied with drink, for the most debasing and foul purposes'.[144]

That year Topi Patuki and over 100 Māori formally petitioned Cargill for aid:

We the undersigned of Otago, &c Beg that as your Servants are desiring of trading as much as possible with your White people; But having no place of accommodation in which to shelter ourselves from the inclemency of the weather Your Honour would take this into your most serious considerations; and cause to be erected some place of shelter for us out of the moneys set apart for Native purposes.[145]

The provincial government did nothing and, instead, the Crown funded the construction in 1859 of a two-storey stone hostelry at the Toitū estuary.[146] However, negotiations with the provincial government authorities broke down without settling the terms of subsequent arrangements – and the building was on provincial government land. They allowed it to be buried by earthworks when Dunedin developed in the wake of the gold rushes, and central government had to remove it in 1865. The building was meant to be resurrected elsewhere: it was not.[147] Ōtākou Māori had effectively lost access to the Dunedin market, just as it boomed.

Burns, meanwhile, was stung into action by Macandrew, and in 1857 the Dunedin Presbytery presented plans to the provincial government to raise the Māori, 'an interesting class, susceptible of improvement, and having the strongest claims upon our Christian sympathy', from their 'current degraded condition'.[148] Their proposal to offer small loans would have been especially helpful, but was not carried out. A school was proposed in which Māori were to be taught in English, so as 'to facilitate amalgamation', and which would adopt 'such mode of productive cultivation as they are directed to follow', including manuring their land, which was still abhorrent to them.[149] A schoolmaster, Baker, was engaged, but had no support and resigned after three years.[150] The presbytery then funded the appointment of German Lutheran missionary the Reverend J.F. Riemenschneider in 1862; a year later he felt forced to sever the connection with the presbytery, though he carried on his mission work at Ōtākou till his death in 1866, earning the lasting respect of the Māori community.[151] The school was not opened again till 1869, when it was funded by central government.[152] All the while the *Otago Witness* led attacks on the Ōtākou Māori as 'dirty, lazy, exacting, mean and covetous'.[153] Such concern as was shown by the Scots settlers was intermittent, highly patronising and totally ineffective. It did nothing to blur the reality that Māori were not welcome in Dunedin.

In 1844 Edward Shortland estimated that about 160 Māori were living at Ōtākou. In 1848 the count was 111; and by 1861 only 80.[154] In 16 years the population at Ōtākou had halved. The scale of the demographic collapse is further emphasised by Alexander Mackay's findings: of the 110 people Walter Mantell recorded at Ōtākou in 1852, only 17 had ancestral rights to own land there, the rest having arrived after the sale of Kemp's purchase.[155]

Unsurprisingly, Māori did not do much to develop their lands at this time. Locked in a small remnant of their territory, in an economy increasingly founded on the exploitation of large landholdings, Māori could not compete with the settlers. As Bill

Dacker has concluded: 'When European labourers arrived in increasing numbers, when larger European schooners began trading, when European agriculture was established on the vast acreages available to it, the demand for Maori produce and services dropped rapidly away.'[156] Māori participation in the settler economy stagnated. They continued growing some wheat and potatoes but did not increase their cultivations appreciably, while their numbers of horses, cattle and pigs all declined over the 1850s.[157]

British settlers not only displaced Māori, they began to erase their history from the landscape. The settlers did not need to be told by Edward Gibbon Wakefield that '*Names* of places, too, should be changed [for] they make part of the moral atmosphere of a country.'[158] Even prior to departure, Burns had written to Cargill arguing that the Māori names for their landscapes would have to go, since 'Purehurehu etc are rather "long nebbit", and would prove sort of clumsy stumbling blocks in the speech of our colonists, especially when they happened to be in a hurry – as will, no doubt, often happen, for some years to come!'[159]

Naming the land was an integral and inevitable part of the settler project of making themselves at home. There were three main reasons for settler names: to look backwards, commemorating home (as Cook first did by naming Cape Saunders after his admiralty patron); to mark an association with a place's first or most prominent people, as with Andersons Bay, Macandrew Bay or Mt Charles; or to describe the place, as with Sandymount or Harbour Cone. Changes in the name of one place capture the entire range: Parihaumia, named to mark an association with the atua of fern root, became Lime Burners Bay to the whalers, and was then named Portobello by James Christie, its first settler, before his departure in 1844; this name stuck, perhaps because Portobello had been Burns' vicarage in Scotland.[160]

Some Māori names were retained, but were often mangled or misplaced. More than anything, this rapid renaming in Otago reflected the fact that the British felt they had come to an empty land, a land whose few and vanishing inhabitants had no claim to a wilderness of 'waste land' they had failed to improve. Few settlers appreciated Māori names as markers of their history. Most were more like the rambler who, on visiting the 'Big stone' atop Highcliff, commented that 'had it been in the old country, there would have been no end of mythical stories about it. Some giant or hero, some Wallace, or Finn McCool ... would have chucked it from Signal Hill ... But there are few myths in the colonies; we are apt rather to look at things in a purely matter of fact light.'[161]

Māori probably did have just such mythical stories about this stone, although if so, they are forgotten. Now, the stone is a well-loved landmark and a pedestal for a memorial to soldiers from the Peninsula fallen in World War I.

Conclusion

The Otago settlement as a whole grew fairly rapidly over the 1850s. It was no instant metropolis, certainly, but it was not the struggling settlement that had to be rescued by gold, as it is sometimes described. Still, like the rest of New Zealand, it could not easily compete with cheaper and closer destinations such as Canada and America. Its immigrants were too few and too poor for Wakefield's flywheel of economic transformation to really spin. But all this was poised to change: with the discovery of gold in the province in 1861, a flood of people and capital propelled rapid settlement over the Peninsula.

N. Prentice, 'Block III Otago Peninsula 1863'. The initial cadastral survey of the land behind Sandfly Bay, over Sandymount and down to Hoopers Inlet. The road network mapped here has all been built subsequently, except for the road through Sandfly Bay, which in 1863 was already subject to sand drift and had been made a government reserve. *Land Information New Zealand: SO 1328*

CHAPTER 7: **THE AXE AND THE LUCIFER MATCH: BOOM-TIME SETTLEMENT OF THE 1860s AND 1870s**

[D]uring the last two or three years the axe and the lucifer match have been busy, cutting down and burning off; and now the whole surface is dotted with clearings, from which, at intervals, may be seen issuing heavy bodies of smoke, the result of further efforts of our hardy pioneers in turning the wilderness into fertile gardens and fields.

— Anonymous, 1865[1]

Wilbraham Liardet, Dunedin from the Portobello Road. *Civilisation was on the move in 1865: Dunedin had become a bustling town in the wake of the gold rush, backdrop to a smart buggy driving along a brand new road onto the Peninsula, while a Māori couple trudge towards town.*

1865, watercolour, pen and ink on paper, 249 x 375mm. Hocken Collections, Uare Taoka o Hākena, University of Otago: 86/152

Otago strikes gold

Otago changed forever in an instant when gold was discovered in 1861 in several strikes in the Clutha catchment. People and capital flooded into the region, drawn from all around New Zealand, Australia and even America. By the end of that year Otago's population probably exceeded 30,000.[2] Capital and goods began to flow in great quantities: imports totalled £859,753, while exports – mostly gold dust – soared to £849,149. Over the next decade some £21 million worth of gold flowed from the Otago diggings, the bulk of this capital distributed via Dunedin.[3]

Dunedin's transformation from small village to busy commercial centre sustained the development of the Peninsula. Many men left the area for the diggings; the few who struck it rich bought more land and stock when they returned,[4] stimulating the

'Crown Grant Index Map 1860'. Such maps, said Chief Surveyor John Turnbull Thomson that year, were 'the authentic groundwork of all titles to land – *plain, intelligible, and easily referred to*'. Here the holdings of the early land purchasers on the southern Peninsula are shown (inset), including those of the early settlers who feature in this chapter, such as the Reverend Thomas Burns and John Somerville. Quoted in *Otago Witness, 1 September 1860, 5 (emphasis in original). Archives New Zealand (Dunedin): DAAK 9431/D450/24. Archives New Zealand (Dunedin): DAAK 9431/D450/24

first thrust of settlement into areas such as Highcliff and Sandymount.[5] The boom also gave the Peninsula farmers access to much larger local markets, with higher prices for working bullocks, horses, stock and dairy products in particular.[6]

With a burgeoning city to serve, the Peninsula's population surged to 1269 by 1864, and 2425 by 1881.[7] There were more men than women (761 to 508 in 1864), but not in wildly disproportionate ratios because of the dominance of British farming families.[8] These families had bought almost all land on the Peninsula by the end of the 1860s, largely in smallholdings of less than 100 acres (40ha), purchased at between 10 shillings to £1 per acre.[9]

The rapid uptake of land was underpinned by Kettle's survey, which had allowed easy production of the Crown Grant Index map (previous page) in 1860. This map usefully shows who owned the original holdings Kettle had mapped on the Peninsula, and confirms how quickly these had been purchased. Secure title to the remainder of the Peninsula was made possible by surveys in 1863.

By 1869 farmers had fenced off over 6000 acres (2428ha) and planted two thirds of this in grass or crops; by 1880 almost double this area – around a third of the Peninsula – had become farmland, mainly devoted to dairying.

This chapter discusses the development of the Peninsula during the boom time: the kinds of communities and forms of social life that developed, and the dramatic environmental effects – about which some settlers were already expressing concern. In this we can discern the beginning of 'the colonisation of European minds within New Zealand, by the indigenous flora and fauna' – even as the settlers were intent on removing it.[10]

Although in 1880 two thirds of the Peninsula remained in bush, sand or swamp, considerable environmental changes had been wrought everywhere as plants, insects and animals flooded into the area.[11] At the crest of the boom in 1878, surveyor Robert Gillies remarked on its effects: 'The forms of life which we see around us now in New Zealand are not the forms which peopled and clothed our hills and valleys, woods and plains, even a quarter of a century ago. The change, though rapid, and in some cases complete, has been silent and continuous, and has escaped observation …'[12] Gillies was better placed than most to know what might have been lost, having mapped the Peninsula's forest in 1859. He lamented that 'the irrecallable past is gone without the data being preserved which now we wish we had, and it only remains for us to save the shreds and patches which linger in the minds of old settlers'.[13] Settlers were mostly too busy struggling to survive to document the cascading environmental changes occurring all around them, although they certainly paid attention to the incursions of pests and weeds.

'Turning the wilderness into fertile gardens and fields': The spread of farming and settlement

In 1879 the writer of the regular *Otago Witness* column, 'Chats with the farmers', visited William Stewart's farm Lilybank in the Tomahawk valley.[14] Stewart, a former grocer, had arrived at Otago in 1859 with his wife and seven children and had bought 100 acres (40ha) in the Tomahawk valley, with the intention of clearing the land with his sons and having his daughters make butter for market. William died in 1872, but one of his sons married another Peninsula farmer's daughter and continued to establish the farm.

By 1879 the family's plans had reached fruition. They had cleared 80 acres (32ha), burning all the broadleaf, tōtara and mataī 'which was then valueless', even though some of this was big timber: one felled mataī measured 10 feet (3m) in diameter. The remaining 20 acres (8ha) was still in bush, 'yearly becoming more valuable for fuel'. 'All the work on this farm' was 'subservient to the production of milk'. Besides some fruit

William Stewart's bluestone byre in the Tomahawk valley, as photographed by Hardwicke Knight in the 1970s. Made of locally quarried stone, such stone byres are a feature of the southern Peninsula. Hocken Collections, Uare Taoka o Hākena, University of Otago: P2014-014/6-040

trees, no particular attention was paid to 'planting or ornamental work of any kind'; the cows had a spacious bluestone byre, the family a comfortable brick home.

The Stewarts ran 30 cattle, half of which were Ayrshire cows; their only other animals were six horses to work the land. Oats were cropped for three years before ryegrass mixed with timothy and white clover was sown, with cocksfoot on the rougher ground. Each morning at 5.30am the family sent 30 gallons (136 litres) of milk to town; it was delivered by 9am and sold for 4d per quart in summer and 5d in winter.

By all accounts this was a typical Peninsula dairy farming operation, a pattern that was being repeated by many, though perhaps rarely so successfully since the Stewart family had the advantage of proximity to town, good land and a relatively large acreage.

Between 1861 and 1880 British settlers bought all the available land on the Peninsula, broke in the best of it and developed their properties. Many families, like that of William Stewart, created fairly finished farms. They formed small close-knit communities around churches and schools, bound by communal labour and codes of neighbourly assistance. Scots outnumbered English two to one, but by 1880 almost half the Peninsula's settlers were New Zealand born, as many of the young emigrants quickly gave birth to large families.[15]

A cadastral map from 1878 (opposite) depicts the pattern of property titles that the boom created on the Peninsula. It shows the settlers' portion of the Peninsula broken down into property parcels in line with the founders' intentions. Kettle's vision of Tomahawk and Andersons Bay as suburban lands divided into 10-acre (4ha) sections had been realised, and similar sections had been patterned around the inlets of the outer coast and over the land northeast of Portobello up to the edge of the Māori land. The bulk of the rural land was now in parcels of 30–60 acres (12–24ha).

The surveys that created these titles were carried out in the early 1860s in response to the sudden demand for land around Dunedin that arose in the wake of the gold rush.[16] Only some land above Seal Point and the slopes ascending from Broad Bay remained in larger parcels, and both were steep and difficult to access. The former was taken up by William Robertson, a man prominent in local politics whose innovative bent is best shown in the development of a water-powered flax mill on the property.[17] The latter parcel formed the core of William Larnach's estate, and Larnach expended enormous sums of taxpayer money to create the road that opened up his land.

The division of land on the Peninsula faithfully mirrored a founding premise of the Scottish settlement: that land ought to be allocated as the private property of yeoman small farmers who epitomised the rough-and-ready social equality that the settlers valorised: a sturdy, economically and socially independent citizenry of family farmers efficiently improving their properties.[18]

By the 1870s many of the Peninsula's settlers had cleared the bulk of their land, the necessary first 'improvement', and now faced the question of what their property could produce to sustain them. Some landholders around Andersons Bay and Portobello

CHAPTER 7: THE AXE AND THE LUCIFER MATCH

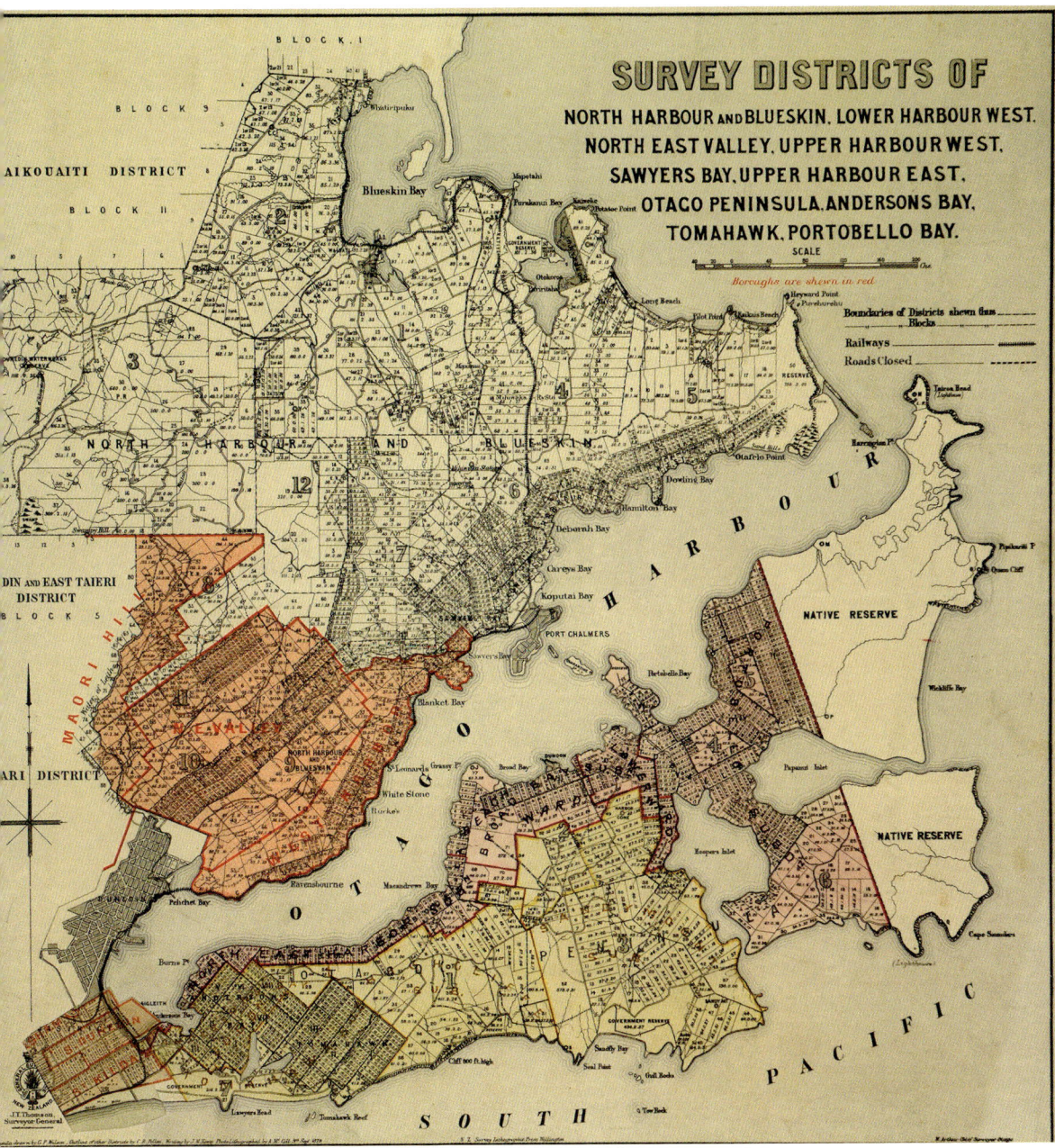

The 1878 cadastral map of the Peninsula is a vision of the future drawn on the crest of a wave of optimism. Only some of this has come to pass. The southern Peninsula suburbs are now outgrowths of Dunedin, as are the harbourside villages. The projected density of settlement around the inlets and up to Ōtākou never occurred, and settlement has retreated from the outer coast. *Archives New Zealand (Wellington): AAFV 997 76/ GAZ128A R22823017*

became market gardeners, but for almost all the answer was dairy farming. This choice was largely determined by the prevalence of terrain too steep for the plough, and by the size of most holdings, which precluded running sufficient sheep to be economically viable.[19] Sheep were preferred only in outlying areas where holdings were larger.

'Opening up the district in all directions': The development of transport

Access to the city and its markets was absolutely critical to the development of the Otago Peninsula. Throughout the remainder of the nineteenth century Peninsula residents directed a continuous stream of querulous complaint to local newspapers about the state of the roads, paucity of ferries and lack of rail.

From the 1860s until well into the twentieth century, Otago Peninsula politics was dominated by its road boards, which had the power to impose rates on property and set the dog tax, and to decide which roads should be built with that money. These were matters of great importance to all Peninsula residents, and membership of one of the road boards was the most sought-after and significant position of local influence.

The Portobello body (Portobello, Broad Bay and 'North East Harbour', i.e. Macandrew Bay) and Otago Peninsula body (Sandymount, Highcliff, Tomahawk and Andersons Bay) were the most influential road boards.[20] During the 1880s the two boards were split into four, and the Otago Heads Road Board and Tomahawk Road Board were formed.[21] Road boards retained their power even after provincial government was abolished in 1876 and the Peninsula became a county. The Peninsula County Council was effectively inoperative: it met annually, and then just to disburse funds to the road boards, which on the Peninsula carried out the duties elsewhere performed by county councils.[22] As Alexander Bathgate noted, on the Peninsula these boards were 'really the only governing body'.[23]

Though Peninsula residents were never satisfied, there was steady progress in extending the road network. The road to Andersons Bay and Tomahawk was completed and metalled by the winter of 1860, allowing the passage of wheeled traffic for the first time.[24] The tracks remained primitive in places, however, as illustrated in Hamilton's painting *Dunedin from the Track to Anderson's Bay*, which depicts a woman hitching up her long skirts to attempt the ramshackle 'Waverley' bridge (from which, if not the Walter Scott novel, the suburb is said to have derived its name).[25]

Such poor roads meant that only a few farmers were able to deliver their milk to Dunedin by cart.[26] Those further out had to rely on butter for their income and send it to town each week. Predictably, the first communities clustered around points of communication such as Andersons Bay, Tomahawk and Portobello.

The life of Samuel Gill after his arrival at Portobello in the 1860s illustrates the spread of settlement and its relationship to the gradual development of transport

Andrew Hamilton, Dunedin from the Track to Anderson's Bay.
1864, watercolour on paper, 180 x 306mm. Hocken Collections, Uare Taoka o Hākena, University of Otago: 12,240 a4288, Neg. #928

networks. Gill lived in a tent between 1863 and 1865 while clearing his own land and taking contracts to fell bush and 'grub' flax.[27] He recalled that 'there were then in Portobello no roads, no horses and no carts … neither were there butchers, bakers or grocers. We had to live a good deal on bread a week old and salt meat.' Gill gained a waterman's licence to carry passengers, and once a week for 20 years from 1865 took people and produce ('butter, eggs, fruit, poultry, pork, veal and vegetables') to Port Chalmers.[28]

Water transport was vital to the Peninsula economy. Each of the small settlements strung along the harbourside had a jetty that allowed the passenger craft and ferries plying the harbour to serve them.[29]

Ferry services began in 1859 with small steamers such as the *Pride of the Yarra* and the *Victoria*.[30] The *Pride of the Yarra* was first to service the Peninsula, running down the eastern channel from Dunedin to Portobello, across to Port Chalmers and back to Dunedin up the western channel each morning, before running the same route in reverse in the afternoon. Later, another route linked the southern suburbs of Waverley and Andersons Bay directly to Dunedin.[31] The owners of the *Victoria* initiated another activity that came to have some importance to the Peninsula, advertising its first excursion to the heads on Christmas Day 1859; over 150 people turned up for the inaugural trip, and such events became popular summer outings for Dunedin citizens throughout the nineteenth century.[32]

None of these small steamers lasted long. The *Pride of the Yarra* sank after colliding with another ferry, the *Favourite*, in 1863, in what is still the harbour's worst maritime accident; the *Victoria* was driven out of business by a flotilla of larger vessels that serviced increased flows of people and goods in the wake of the gold rush.[33]

In 1863 the first publicly listed ferry company, the Peninsula Steam Boat Company, was founded 'to establish a regular daily steam communication' between the Peninsula and Port Chalmers.[34] The company built the *Peninsula*, a paddle steamer, which ran twice daily from Port Chalmers to Dunedin; on Tuesdays and Fridays Portobello was included on its route. Competition from Johnny Jones's Harbour Steam Company soon killed the new company; Jones purchased the *Peninsula*, but abandoned the Portobello service.[35]

Regular service to the Peninsula was not resumed until the mid-1870s, when several ferries came into service. First was the *Golden Age*, which ran between the Peninsula bays and Dunedin twice a week for a few years from 1875. Another steamer, the *Jane*, ran a similar route, and also provided 'steam boat excursions' to the Māori kaik and Taiaroa Head on Sundays and public holidays.[36] The most important service was provided by the *Portobello*, which from 1878 to 1881 ran back and forth between

IN THE AFTERMATH OF THE TARANAKI WAR, 74 Ngāti Ruanui prisoners were sentenced to three (or in 12 cases, seven) years' penal servitude, and in 1869 were shipped to Dunedin, where they remained until 1872. During their period of forced labour 18 men died and were buried in unmarked graves in the Southern Cemetery. In 1879 another 137 people, all followers of the prophets Te Whiti and Tohu, founders of the Parihaka community, were exiled here. Until 1882 they worked as prison labour on the construction of the bay road and its sea walls around Portobello, on the High (Highcliff) Road, and at Fort Taiaroa.

The Māori prisoners were probably not kept in caves at Andersons Bay, as has been said. These caves housed explosives. Prisoners were kept at the Dunedin gaol or, if working too far away to return each night, in a prison hulk on the harbour.

The Otago Provincial Council recorded that the Ngāti Ruanui people spent 1870 labour days on the Andersons Bay road, 1762 on the Vauxhall Road and 119 on harbour works. It is hard to be sure where the Parihaka people were made to work, since they were not differentiated from general prison labour. But it is known that Parihaka prisoners worked on the bay roads, since this is recorded in the Portobello Road Board minutes and, occasionally, in the *Otago Witness*.

Portobello and Port Chalmers four times daily on a timetable designed to connect travellers with trains to Dunedin.[37] The success of this prompted Larnach to promote settlement at Waverley by launching the *Colleen*, which was to run between there and Dunedin at least six times daily: he also offered free travel to anyone buying sections there. The craft was poorly designed, however, and didn't sail well; the sections sold too slowly and the run was soon discontinued.[38]

Ferry services brought the Peninsula into closer contact with Dunedin and Port Chalmers. They were especially valuable for transporting freight goods, for which purpose the roads were effectively useless. But they were not a perfect substitute for reliable land transport, and improvement of the roads dominated Peninsula politics throughout these decades. As one prospective Peninsula representative reminded voters in 1872: 'Any person who was conversant with the peninsula must be aware that its great drawback was the want of roads.'[39]

Until the 1870s Andersons Bay was the terminus of organised land transport; the route through Highcliff and on to Portobello was merely a bridle track.[40] The settlers had every reason to demand a better road; those along the harbour at Macandrew Bay and Broad Bay had to boat their goods to town, and in order to reach Dunedin in time for Saturday's market, many had to leave the night before. Once there, bad weather might trap them in town for days, so that any potential profit was squandered on food and lodging.[41] As James Sim – who owned land on the slopes running from Highcliff down to Macandrew Bay, but who could not yet make a living from it – asked in 1867: 'What were they to do with their land, if they had not the Beach road, when there was a railway bringing produce from the Clutha in two or three hours?'[42]

While the burgeoning rail network was cutting transport time and freight costs for communities elsewhere throughout Otago, the Peninsula became frustratingly isolated. It urgently required better roads to connect it to Dunedin. The bay road along the harbourside was especially crucial. Like other large projects undertaken in Dunedin in the 1870s and 1880s, it was constructed by prison labour. Māori prisoners, some exiled to Dunedin in the wake of the wars in Taranaki and others evicted and exiled from Parihaka, did much of the construction work (see box).[43]

The causeway across Andersons Bay from 'Cuttens Corner' to Vauxhall Corner was completed by 1872; soon after, the bay road was opened as far as Macandrew Bay, and reached Portobello in 1878.[44] By then the 'High Road' through Highcliff and down to Portobello had been 'well macadamised'.[45]

As soon as the bay road was completed a mail coach began operating, and about 30 of the Peninsula farmers bought horses and spring carts, causing the steam boats to lose business and leave.[46] Horse-drawn buses were soon in operation also.[47] These improvements facilitated the development of the seaside settlements at North East Harbour (now Macandrew Bay), Company Bay and Broad Bay and stimulated speculative subdivision on the harbour front.

The Andersons Bay causeway. Completed in 1872, the bridge could be opened to allow watercraft into the bay. Copy print, n.d. Hocken Collections, Uare Taoka o Hākena, University of Otago: P2014-014/6-050

Andersons Bay in the 1870s. The fences are neater, but the buildings in the Andersons Bay subdivisions are still few. Photograph courtesy of Ian Smith

Six small 'townships' were created on paper by subdividing sections in Portobello and Broad Bay: Seatoun, Portobello, Lamlash, Dunoon, Oban and Granton. Together they comprised 502 quarter-acre (1000m^2) sections on the harbour. The land was sold at auction, largely to speculators who soon on-sold their purchases.[48] As a correspondent to the *Otago Witness* acidly remarked: 'From the very high prices obtained for the sections in the townships of Dunoon and Oban it is very probable that they were bought by persons who sooner or later intend residing on them.'[49] Samuel Gill recalled that 10 acres (4ha) at what became Lamlash had been on sale for years at £10 per acre, but sold in the rush for an extraordinary £1100. The 'boom' faded fast; Gill records a 'land boom company' buying Seatoun at £80 an acre, and trying to sell quarter-acre sections for £50. Within a few years they were being sold for £5.[50]

The enthusiasm of the 1870s generated equally ambitious schemes for infrastructure. For example, several Peninsula settlers, William Larnach prominent among them, attempted to raise private capital for a railway line along the harbour to Portobello. The line reached Andersons Bay in 1878 – and there construction halted, due to disagreements among the settlers over where the line should run, and the economic downturn of 1878.[51]

The new roads opened up the land for both settlement and recreation. James Sim, for example, who had worked as a wool sorter while building his family a two-storey house using timber felled as he cleared his 65 acres (26ha) of bush-clad land, was able to devote himself to farming at Highcliff full time from 1877.[52] Peter Thomson, the founding force behind the Dunedin Naturalists' Field Club, wrote a column for the *Otago Witness* called 'Rambles Round Dunedin', in which he described a series of visits to parts of the Peninsula in these decades.[53] In 1864 he set out on foot with the intention of reaching Sandfly Bay by way of Andersons Bay, Tomahawk and Highcliff. He was thwarted by thick bush, with only occasional clearings and a faint track. Just six years later he took a horse-drawn bus to the top of the hill above Andersons Bay and strolled along formed roads to look down into Sandfly Bay.[54] Five years had made a similar difference when Thomson took advantage of the advent of ferries up the harbour from Dunedin to revisit Portobello in 1869. He was

> *very much pleased and surprised to see the progress made by the settlers in the way of clearing the land and making roads. Instead of the muddy narrow bush track, through which it was difficult to make any but the slowest progress, there is now a series of well cut and well formed roads, with tolerably easy grades, opening up the district in all directions. And what was then a tract of almost impenetrable bush, with only a few small clearings, has been cut into right and left, and farm houses and all their accompaniments, and fields of heavy-looking grain crop, now stud the landscape.*[55]

The development of farming

In the wake of road construction the Peninsula's farmers created a mosaic of properties, each cut to a fairly standard pattern: of similar size, closely fenced and with a number of specific outbuildings. They mainly grazed cattle on grass and a narrow range of crops, ran a few horses, and sometimes raised pigs for household consumption, which they fed on the skim milk that resulted from butter-making.[56] Poultry were fairly universal and provided food and a little income from egg sales.[57] The few large holdings in the remote and difficult country around Mt Charles and Sandfly Bay specialised in sheep, but overall only about 20 farms ran any sheep at all.[58]

The development of this pattern of farming is evident in agricultural statistics. Cattle were utterly dominant: herds averaged around 20 milk cows, with five to 10 heifers and sometimes a bull. Stock density was around one head of cattle to 2–3 acres (0.8–1.2ha) of grass.[59]

Most farmers now favoured Ayrshire cattle[60] for reasons captured in verse by Joan White, from across the harbour at Mihiwaka:

> *If dairy farming be your aim,*
> *And if your land is steep,*
> *You'll find the Ayrshire cows the best*
> *In all respects to keep.*
>
> *Being light of frame they give more milk,*
> *And thrive upon less feed*
> *Than Durhams, Jerseys, Alderneys,*
> *Or any other breed.*[61]

Every farmer kept a few horses as draught animals and for light farm work and transport.[62] Horses were central to colonial life, especially prior to the spread of rail from the 1870s. Without horses to carry people and pull the plough, farms could not function. Peninsula farmers largely fed their working horses on green feed oats, oaten hay and grass hay.[63] In 1866 there were 164 horses and 231 acres (93ha) of oats on the Peninsula; in 1877 there were 696 horses, 442 acres of oats and 226 acres (178 and 91ha) of hay. Horses required as much as two acres of oats each, so it is fairly safe to say that they consumed most if not all the oats Peninsula farmers grew, as well as much of the hay; many farmers, especially those still establishing their land, would have had to buy horse feed.[64] Horses had deleterious effects, too, as explained by Murray Rose: 'To grow oats you needed horses. If you had horses you needed oats to feed the horses to grow the oats to sell to the cities to feed the horses of others. This was a vicious cycle that impoverished the soil, making it only suitable for browntop and biddy-bid.'[65]

Dairying required considerable investment in buildings and a close network of fences to separate pasture from feed crops. Cows needed a byre,[66] butter production

William Clarke Ferguson's stone steading on Braid (now Braidwood) Road, Sandymount.
Hardwicke Knight photograph, 1970s, Hocken Collections, Uare Taoka o Hākena, University of Otago: P2014-014/6-045

necessitated a dairy, feed and equipment required a barn, horses a stable and pigs a sty. Each dairy farm therefore had a similar patchwork of paddocks, and a predictable group of outbuildings built to fairly standard patterns, largely with local materials.[67] Barns built in the 1870s, for example, were generally simple timber frames clad in vertical weatherboards with iron roofs. By the 1870s, much of this timber came from Dunedin.[68]

Around Tomahawk, Highcliff and Sandymount local stone was available, and some farmers there were reasonably well off. Many invested in stone outbuildings using local basalt or bluestone. Dairies, in particular, were built in stone wherever possible to help keep the milk and butter at an even cool temperature. Perhaps the most prominent and exceptional stone outbuildings are on Alexander Mathieson's steading, built in the late 1870s and still owned and used by his descendants today.

Mathieson's imposing stone byre could house at least 70 cows in comfort and featured several notable improvements, such as direct feeding of the cows from lofts above the stalls, a tramway down the centre to carry steamed food from the boiler, a dung truck to gather manure, and conduits to carry liquid manure to storage tanks.[69]

Fences varied according to the environment. Most early fences were wooden, at first often piles of logs left on the land after burning, or the more durable post-and-rail construction. Posts were made from broadleaf or kōwhai, which lasted in the ground,

Mortise and tenon fencing on Clearwater's farm, between Hoopers and Papanui inlets, still standing in swampy ground in the 1970s. Hardwicke Knight photograph, 1970s. Hocken Collections, Uare Taoka o Hākena, University of Otago: P2014-014/6-041

and the rails (usually two or three, although Larnach used five) were also kōwhai.[70] Wooden fences were regarded as temporary, however, to be replaced by hedges or stone walls, as used in Britain[71] – symbols of the civilised landscape settlers sought to recreate. Early on, hedges of gorse or hawthorn were common, especially about Tomahawk, Andersons Bay and Macandrew Bay.[72] Networks of settler women were largely responsible for propagating and distributing precious gorse seed,[73] but settlers soon discovered this plant was difficult to control in the new environment.

Drystone walls were the most permanent solution and the most powerful symbol of improvement, and this helped justify the particularly arduous and painstaking work required in their construction. A well-built stone wall required skill and was a matter of pride. They were a logical use for the enormous amount of stone that Peninsula farmers unearthed, especially in the south and central Peninsula, as they cleared their land for the plough. This was a slow and sometimes expensive process. Richard Irving, for example, spent three weeks and £50 per acre picking out rocks on his Broad Bay farm.[74]

Fencing allows control of land, separating cropping and grazing areas, and delineating private and public property. It also marks divisions in attitudes that shaped land use, and hence ecology. The fence between a farmer's fields and the public roadside is often insubstantial – permeable to anything other than the animals it is designed to enclose or exclude – and often sharply divides different communities of plants and animals. At Alexander Stuart's farm, Clifton, for example, they ploughed in the old Scottish fashion, right up to the base of the stone walls. Beyond those walls a diverse mingling of native and exotic plants occurred.[75]

Dairying's pre-eminence meant that limited quantities of crops were grown. Early settler farmers took several crops from newly cleared land; by the early 1870s they straightaway sowed most cleared land in permanent pasture.[76] The grasses sown remained much as they were in the 1850s, dominated by ryegrasses, timothy, white clover and cocksfoot.[77] There were many variations on this basic theme, however. John Mathieson, for example, added a little 'cow grass' and cocksfoot into a generic mixture, but regretted the addition of cocksfoot, which overgrew the ryegrass and formed coarse and unpalatable tufts. His brother Alexander only used ryegrass, cocksfoot and clover.[78]

Some farms made extensive efforts to develop vegetable and fruit production. Alexander Stuart, for example, had been head gardener for the Duke of Buccleugh,

Some of the Peninsula's stone boundary walls on the south and central Peninsula have been carefully repaired and remain beautifully preserved; the macrocarpa windbreaks, however, have more often grown wild. © Ian Thomson

and after arriving at Dunedin and buying 130 acres (52ha) for £441 in 1863, began farming. Besides running the usual mixture of stock, he planted a wide range of vegetables: varieties of potatoes, cabbages, cauliflowers, lettuces, carrots and peas, as well as asparagus, beans, parsnips, leeks, celery and spinach.[79] Others, such as Alexander Clark who farmed at Hoopers Inlet, initially grew a lot of fruit, including apples, pears, plums, peaches and other stonefruit.[80]

Grain-growing virtually ceased. The Taieri plain and North Otago were now growing vast amounts of wheat for export and small Peninsula farmers could no longer compete.[81] By 1871 wheat production in Andersons Bay was 'inconsiderable, consisting of only a few patches' that were fed to poultry or made into flour for home use.[82] It lingered longer around Portobello, where 80 acres (32ha) were in wheat in 1870, but drought and bush fires in 1872 meant that only 20 acres (8ha) were planted, and by 1877 it was 'but little cultivated'.[83] Barley was never grown in quantity on the Peninsula; even in 1870 only 40 acres (16ha) were sown around Portobello, while no more than 10 acres (4ha) were ever grown in Andersons Bay and Tomahawk.[84]

Winter cattle-feed crops like turnips, carrots, mangolds, rape and beet were grown increasingly. Turnips and carrots were favoured, for they did not taint the milk.[85] Oats and potatoes were the only cash crops, but even they were of limited importance. Though some potatoes were sold in Dunedin, the bulk of crops were for local consumption.[86] And while some of the oats crop was threshed for grain, oats were more commonly grown for green feed and hay.[87]

Peninsula farmers did not stop growing grain because yields were too low – in fact they never fell below 35 bushels for any grain, and in good years oat yields reached 90 bushels in places and averaged 60.[88] Rather, their problem was low prices and growing competition. As we shall see, Peninsula farmers responded in innovative ways to these market pressures in an effort to sustain themselves and their communities.

'Plenty of hard work before me': The farmers' lot

What sort of life was led in making such a farm? For many farming families – especially those only just establishing their properties on more remote, isolated and usually poorer land – life was little easier than it had been for the very first settlers.

Walter Riddell's diary of 1865–71 provides perhaps the most detailed account we have of the continued struggle poorer farmers had for subsistence in those early years. Riddell and his family arrived in Otago in 1862 and bought land in 1864 at Sandymount, an area of the outer Peninsula that was then almost completely untouched. It took 10 days for the family just to carry their meagre possessions a mile from the end of the road through the bush to their property, where they intended to establish a small dairy farm.[89] Their arduous life in the years that followed is illustrated by comparing the hopeful tone of Riddell's New Year's entry for 1866 with his despondent reflections in 1871:

> *Jan 1st 1866: Was a fine day. I put up a bail for the cow & and then strolled through the bush for the rest of the day. I am entering another year with £83 debt on my head, with plenty of hard work before me, and if God grant me my health I will be a clear man in another year. I have increased in the year that has passed a house, an acre of land cleared, 15 hens, 2 cows and a son.*

> *Jan 7th 1871: Another New Year has arrived and I am still in existence, lonely & single handed to battle with the toil of getting bread for my family. Things are a great deal lower this year than ever they were, still hard up for money. We have 8 cows this year and can't keep going.*[90]

While land was gradually cleared, grassed and stocked, an income had to be found. Riddell's various employments demonstrate the sorts of industry then explored on the Peninsula. His diary details contract work for wealthier farmers, such as leading settler John Mathieson of Springfield Farm at Highcliff, for whom he sawed timber, cleared bush and fenced fields.[91] Like several others, Riddell also worked for James McDonald,

John Mathieson was a leading settler at Highcliff, with prominent roles on the Peninsula Road Board and the Peninsula Agricultural and Pastoral Association. This early photograph of his farm, Springfield, shows a homestead and cluster of outbuildings (including the Otago Peninsula Cheese Factory) built to last using local basalt. Hocken Collections, Uare Taoka o Hākena, University of Otago: S07-135f

The largest of James McDonald's three lime kilns, in operation from the 1860s until 1939.
Hardwicke Knight photograph, 1970s. Hocken Collections, Uare Taoka o Hākena, University of Otago: P2014-014/6-049; S17-036c

who pioneered burning limestone on the Peninsula. Beginning in 1865, McDonald erected three lime kilns near Sandymount, burning limestone quarried from a band some one kilometre wide and 20–30 metres deep that spans the Peninsula between Seal Point and Dowling Bay.[92] The caustic lime produced was unsuitable for agriculture and was used for making cement.[93] By 1882 the business was abandoned, having been eclipsed by quarries with better access to transport; although periodically reopened, the kilns finally ceased operation in 1939.[94]

Riddell was also a skilled craftsman and erected farm buildings for several neighbours, as well as a small but exquisite church at Pukehiki. For several years from 1871 he was employed by William Larnach and became foreman of works in the construction of Larnach's 'castle'.[95] Riddell prospered at last – but was able to spend only about a quarter of his time on his own farm.[96] Even with 11 days of labour from neighbours, it took him nine weeks to clear one acre.[97] His eventual rise to become manager of the Taieri and Peninsula Milk Supply Company is testament to his intelligence, skill and appetite for hard work.

Riddell's diary indicates how heavily each farmer relied on the help of his neighbours to clear bush, plough, plant, harvest and cover shortages in feed or stock. It also shows just how hard the settlers worked: Riddell described himself as '20 hours a day

CHAPTER 7: THE AXE AND THE LUCIFER MATCH

Pukehiki Church: testimony to Walter Riddell's building skills and sheer capacity for work.
© Alan Dove

KING OF THE CASTLE: WILLIAM LARNACH

From the 1860s many of the city's leading citizens either lived on the Peninsula or had summer houses built there. They included James Macandrew who, after his release from debtors' prison in 1863, moved to the house and 300-acre (121ha) farm in the bay that bears his name.[98] Macandrew developed large gardens there, and with less success attempted to establish Stewart Island oysters and trout. In 1871 George Grey Russell purchased part of this property and founded Glenfalloch ('hidden glen') as a 'gentleman's country residence'.

William Larnach, who built his castle on the crest of the Peninsula and developed a large estate and farm around it, was by far the most prominent Peninsula resident.[99] Larnach was a leading figure in national affairs. He was also easily the single most important person in the Peninsula's development. He represented the Peninsula residents as their local member of parliament, employed significant numbers of Peninsula people, helped them access credit in the city, promoted roads, subdivided townships, patronised local community organisations and events, and generally presided over Peninsula affairs.

Larnach had arrived in 1867 as chief colonial manager of the Bank of Otago, but quickly built a large and diverse commercial empire as 'a floater, promoter and director in very many companies'.[100] One of these, 'Guthrie and Larnach's New Zealand Timber and Woodware Factories Company, Limited: Ironmongers, Hardware Merchants and Sawmillers', became the largest trading company in Australasia in

Larnach Castle from the air. Larnach spared no expense whatsoever in constructing his 'castle', and he lavished great care on the plantings surrounding it. The Barker family has restored both to their former glory. © *Kevin Jones and Department of Conservation*

George O'Brien, Mount Charles, Otago Peninsula, from The Camp. *Romantic wilderness viewed from 'The Camp', as Larnach called his castle.* 1876, watercolour and opaque white on paper, 181 x 285mm (pasted to card). Hocken Collections, Uare Taoka o Hākena, University of Otago: 13,253

the 1870s.[101] Larnach epitomised the enthusiasm and optimism of the 1870s, his finest years. In 1870 he bought 100 bush-clad acres (40ha) at Sandymount, the last unsold Crown land in the district.[102] Larnach recalled how he had bid five guineas an acre at the auction, whereupon a settler had said, 'Let him have it, for a goat cannot get to it.' Larnach rapidly bought more land from neighbours, eventually forming an estate of some 1000 acres (400ha). Some neighbours sold up in the 1880s due to the depression, such as James Christie, who had attempted a failed harbourside subdivision.[103] The fact that James Sim sold his farm to Larnach in 1890 for £1850, at £25 per acre, suggests how well Peninsula farming held up during even the harder years.

Like Burns in the 1850s, Larnach provided a model of progressive farming for other settlers to emulate. His biographer, Fleur Snedden, suggests that he was the first dairy farmer on the Peninsula.[104] This is an exaggeration, but it is true that Larnach led the way in developing specialised dairying. The state of his dairy farm was a source of great personal pride, and his herd of stud Alderney cattle were much sought after, as was Larnach himself as a judge at agricultural and pastoral shows.[105] He was president of the Otago Peninsula Agricultural Society, and helped generate the impetus for its annual shows, which began in 1879.[106]

Larnach ran a fairly self-sufficient property, growing large quantities of fruit and vegetables, raising pigs and poultry, and indulging his special love of draught and bloodstock carriage horses. He built his castle largely of local stone dug from a quarry on his own property. In some respects – such as the composting of the solids from his servants' human waste, and the use of the resulting methane to light his chandeliers – he was well ahead of his time.[107] He built some of the drystone walls himself, and meticulously supervised the construction of wire fencing (some of the first used in the area).[108] He also, and unusually, included many native trees in his extensive plantings for shelter and ornament, so that a description in the *Otago Witness* in 1882 noted: 'Here we see English and Scotch firs and elms growing side by side with totara and cabbage trees', while 'myrtles, laurels, and other shrubs of European growth, hobnob with the native kaio, pepper, cabbage, and fern-trees'. According to this account, 'There is not a tree, shrub or plant indigenous to the whole colony, which is not cultivated with the utmost assiduity.' The 'reason why Mr Larnach's name should descend to posterity', this writer exclaimed, 'is the care and attention he has so signally bestowed in the cultivation of the native Flora'.[109]

Larnach drove development on the Peninsula in other ways. As a member of parliament he helped develop roads (those his own horses drove upon were noticeably favoured); he constructed hotels on both the high road and the beach road (the latter still stands and is commonly known as 'the White House'), to accommodate those for whom the journey between Dunedin and his home was too far to travel in a day.[110] He was also responsible for subdividing the suburban townships of both Portobello and Waverley. He spent lavishly and mainly employed local labour, with as many as 20 locals gaining a living in his employ.[111]

Larnach promoted his subdivision of Waverley, on the 'sunny side of the harbour', through offering purchasers free passes on the steam ferry Colleen, *which was to make at least six trips daily until a rail or tram link to Dunedin was opened.*[112] Hocken Collections, Uare Taoka o Hākena, University of Otago: 885.991/1881/bje

on my feet' in the effort to complete the church at Pukehiki.[113] On one occasion he joined the rest of the community and 'spent New Years Day at Mathieson's dancing and making a fool of ourselves'. He considered it 'wasted a good day'.[114]

The development of James Sim's farm, Pinkieburn, sited on the slope between Highcliff and Macandrew Bay, similarly illustrates the range of activity required for small farmers to make their living. From 1877, when he first began fulltime farming, until 1881, his accounts show that his primary source of income was butter, supplemented by the sale of eggs, potatoes, chaff, pork, fattened pigs, grazing and small amounts of wheat and oats.[115] Sim's butter was churned twice weekly by rotary horse-power and sold in Dunedin to Irvine and Stevenson, leading grocers in the city. Sim also negotiated exchanges with his neighbours, such as James Macandrew, John Mathieson and Cochrane Weir, to cover shortfalls in grazing and feed, or to enlarge herds of cattle and pigs.[116]

In 1879 Sim hosted the first Peninsula Agricultural and Pastoral Society show, which was attended by 600 people. As the *Otago Daily Times* reported after the second show, 'The Society do not pretend to much. Their object being merely to bring together the local stock, and afford the settlers a yearly opportunity of coming together to compare notes. Looked at from this point of view, the show may be called thoroughly successful.'[117]

This success was testament to their tight-knit communities, made more so by extensive inter-marriage between families. Communities formed where communication with the outside world was easiest, and centred on life structured by communal work, school and church attendance.[118] The rhythms of these communities were ordered by both natural and economic cycles (bar Sundays, the occasional sale day and New Year, there were no holidays). Weekly life was oriented around the Saturday market and church on Sunday; community events were oriented around the full moon when travel in the evening was simpler.[119]

The settlers' labour patterns followed the seasonal growth cycles of their plants and animals. They calved cows and sowed oats, grass and root crops through spring; milked cows, cut hay and harvested grains, potatoes and fodder crops through summer and autumn; and ploughed in winter and early spring to prepare the ground for the next round of crops.[120] The summer harvest, when crops had to be gathered quickly at their peak, was the time during which labour was most in demand.

As transport eased and communities formed, settlers explored alternative industries and modes of production, sometimes combining forces to form community ventures. A drop in the price of butter prompted eight Highcliff dairy farmers to form a co-operative, and in the spring of 1871 they established the Otago Peninsula Cheese Factory, the first of its kind in New Zealand.[121] The factory was built on John Mathieson's Highcliff farm. Almost 10,000lb (4.5 tonnes) of cheese was produced in its first year and sold in Dunedin, where it enjoyed a good reputation.[122] Fluctuating prices meant that profits proved meagre, however.[123] All the same, some other farmers were encouraged to join, and production at its peak reached at least 7.5 tonnes of Scottish-style 'Dunlop' cheese, made between October and March over the flush of the milking season.[124]

Farmers around Portobello founded another factory in 1877 at Harbour Cone, but this was destroyed by a large bush fire in 1881.[125] The Highcliff cheese factory meanwhile shifted to Pukehiki after John Mathieson's ill-fated effort to switch to sheep farming in

The inaugural Otago Peninsula Agricultural and Pastoral Society show, held in 1879 at James Sim's Highcliff farm, Pinkieburn. Notable features of the scene include the unfinished fields (complete with stump inside the circle of onlookers), the number and variety of buggies and carts, and the wire fencing now being incorporated into post-and-rail construction. Hocken Collections, Uare Taoka o Hākena, University of Otago: S07-135i – 29/5/C

CHAPTER 7: THE AXE AND THE LUCIFER MATCH

Farm work in the nineteenth century often required the community to pitch in, as shown in this scene of haymaking on Clearwater's farm, Cape Saunders. Otago Peninsula Museum: OPM 82 92/4

1875. Valiant efforts were made to find a more profitable market – cheeses were sent to several destinations in Australia in 1880 and 1881[126] – but in 1884 it was resolved to close the factory. The farmers' efforts were hampered by the 'long depression' which had set in towards the end of the 1870s, and which would not end until well into the 1890s.

Cooperation and innovation were not confined to dairying. In the 1870s several local farmers became shareholders in the short-lived Hoopers Inlet Gold Mining Company that attempted to exploit a small seam of gold-bearing quartz on the lower slopes of Harbour Cone; unfortunately the gold was too finely dispersed for mining to be economic.[127] William Robertson tried diversifying his farming by milling flax at Sandfly Bay, where he dammed a small creek to drive a millwheel;[128] and the Dickson family operated a small timber mill at Hoopers Inlet, building a tramway across the inlet to transport their timber.[129] But all these attempts at industry remained small-scale, and none lasted very long.

A place of pleasure and recreation

As the Peninsula became more accessible, it became an increasingly popular destination for sightseers in search of pleasure and recreation. The most famous venue was the Vauxhall Gardens, established above Andersons Bay in 1862 by Henry Farley.

The gardens were extensive and elaborate, costing as much as £10,000 to establish. Farley bought 23 acres (9ha) at Andersons Bay, had a jetty constructed and built a hotel, baths, summer houses, sports grounds, swings and roundabouts for children, and a rotunda for bands to play in during summer evening dances.[130] The rotunda can be seen in the large clearing in the left of Liardet's lithograph (above). A number of ferries and smaller craft plied their trade to the gardens and back in the early 1860s.[131] After the gold rush petered out the venture ceased to be economic, however, and no takers were found when it was auctioned in 1870; brick-making using local clay began on the land instead.[132]

As roads improved in the 1870s much of the harbour front of the Peninsula became devoted to servicing sightseers and holidaymakers. In 1878 a correspondent from Broad Bay noted: 'Harvest here consists chiefly in letting houses or apartments profitably to the summer visitors, who begin to arrive, if the season is good, early in December, and

Wilbraham Liardet, View of Otago Peninsula Opposite Dunedin, Showing Vauxhall Gardens. *The tastes that accompanied a goldmining boom were well catered for by the notorious Vauxhall 'pleasure gardens', to the left above Andersons Bay, where the band rotunda stood amid bush that reputedly gave cover to all manner of indiscretions. The number and variety of watercraft attest to the importance of water communication in the early settlement.* 1865, lithograph, 220 x 661mm. Hocken Collections, Uare Taoka o Hākena, University of Otago: 12,222

by the end of the month accommodation of any kind is at a premium.' Despite Broad Bay being 'admirably suited' to agriculture, '[o]f ordinary harvest work there is very little done here; the settlers "go in" for dairy produce or market gardening.'[133]

By 1880 the Peninsula was dominated by the people and ideals on which the Otago settlement had been founded: Scottish small-farming families had largely shaped the culture and economy of all the Peninsula communities. Settlers were sustained by the prolonged national economic boom that saw Dunedin become the largest and richest of New Zealand's cities. Sealed roads linked the Peninsula communities to the city and enabled the development of intensive and progressive farming. All this, however, was in stark contrast to the situation at Ōtākou.

When the tide rolled in upon us: The Ōtākou community

The Kāi Tahu communites scattered throughout the south faced a new world in the 1860s as British settlers flooded into the port towns and moved out onto the land. John Paratene captured their disquiet when he addressed Governor Gore Browne at Lyttelton in 1860. Kāi Tahu, he said, were now 'like a cormorant sitting on a rock, the tide rises, it flows over the rock, and the bird is compelled to fly. Do thou provide a dry resting place for us that we prosper.'[134] While war loomed in the north, Kāi Tahu leaders consistently pledged their loyalty to the authority of the British Crown and sought shelter under the law. As Te Matenga Taiaroa told a conference of chiefs at Kohimarama, also in 1860: 'I have nothing to suggest and only one thing to say. It is that Queen, that same Queen. It is that Governor, that same Governor. It is enough. Let that island be joined to this.'[135]

Kāi Tahu sought equality before the law, and representation in provincial politics. The Ōtākou rangatira Hoani Wetere Korako told the Otago settlers, 'We would like to have a place in Council that we may express our feelings to the European and also hear what they have to say.'[136] This request was not met.

Ōtākou Māori probably coped better than most southern Māori communities with the sudden advent of settler capitalism. In part this was because they had more land than most other communities. They also retained access to the Peninsula fisheries and, during the boom, there was demand for wage labour.

In 1867 the *Illustrated New Zealander* described Ōtākou Māori cultivating land to grow vegetables and grain and rearing pigs and poultry 'to a considerable extent'. The article stated that their 'principal avocation' was fishing for barracouta, supplying not only themselves but the Dunedin market as 'their staple trade'.[137] However, they were described by the *Otago Witness* in 1872 as 'seldom rewarded by success for the hardships they endured' in bringing fish to Dunedin.[138]

In the midst of a booming economy Ōtākou Māori were doing little better than holding their own, while simultaneously their economic options were being foreclosed. Gathering food in the traditional way by travelling to their mahika kai was becoming difficult as British settlers asserted property rights and improved their land. Drainage of key lakes such as Tatewai on the Taieri had begun by the 1860s.[139] Annual weka hunts on the Maniototo were halted by pastoral run proprietors' refusal to allow Māori access, and by 1880 the weka there had been extirpated, mostly poisoned by bait set for rabbits.[140] In many other cases traditional foods vanished with their habitats, such as waterfowl as lagoons and wetlands on Akapātiki Flat were drained and ploughed, and tī groves were destroyed.[141]

Emulating settler farming, and developing their remaining land to produce food for home consumption or sale at market were possible, but isolation and comparative inexperience were formidable obstacles for Ōtākou Māori. The communities had a limited capacity to compete with settlers' agricultural production. Initially, they did make an effort to do so. Murray Thomson recalled that his father Peter took on Kelvin Grove in 1862, leasing the land from Korako for £14 annually and planning to 'combine there a bit of farming and a fishing speculation'.[142] Thomson found a crop of wheat growing on the land, apparently sprouted from a 'very badly' harvested crop taken by Māori the previous year. The Māori practice with potatoes was to leave some in the soil to provide the next crop; it seems plausible they were applying the same method here.[143] After Thomson had cut this wheat, Māori claimed it on the grounds that they had sown it. Thomson refused them, and promptly threshed and sold the crop, pretending not to understand subsequent demands by Māori for the grain.[144] Clearly, Māori and settlers still had different views on property.

The most practical way for Māori to earn money was to work for wages, commonly through seasonal occupations such as shearing or harvesting. Fishing was possible for both food and trade, however, and became the focus of Māori efforts to maintain a commercial economy.

Competition for the fisheries

Māori believed that the sea held more promise than the land as the basis for a viable economy. They were keen to operate shipping transport, but the small single-masted schooners they had used in the 1840s as an integral part of coastal trading had all been wrecked. Replacing each one cost up to £200, a sum now beyond the means of almost all Māori.[145] Karetai had inherited the *Perseverance* after the death of Tuhawaiki, but it had foundered in 1847 in a storm at Otago Heads; Karetai wrote repeatedly to the government asking for a schooner or steamer.[146] He was unsuccessful.

Māori had advantages at sea. They had hard-won expertise on how, where and when fish could be caught, while settlers had yet to find the best fishing grounds and learn fishes' habits and feeding preferences. The gold rush opened a larger market that Māori surely hoped to profit from, but settler fishing expanded fast in the wake of the gold rush too; during the 1860s and 1870s the fishery around the Peninsula was easily the largest in New Zealand.[147]

Settlers established two distinct fisheries in the area. Small boats crewed by two men seine-netted in Otago Harbour and caught fish such as flounder, red cod and yellow-eyed mullet.[148] When the weather was poor, they turned to crayfish.[149] Richard Lewis, whose ketch was delivered from Victoria to Otago in 1862, was among the first fishermen.[150] Following his example, larger whaling boats usually crewed by three men ventured outside the harbour, often making for the coastal fisheries off Cape Saunders to catch hāpuku, red cod, ling, trevally and occasionally blue cod, moki and trumpeter.[151] According to Peter Thomson, writing in 1864, most of these fishermen lived 'in huts and tents on the Maori Reserve near the Heads and are generally on pretty good terms with their native neighbors'. Living at Ōtākou, he continued, 'gives them the advantage of being ready for work whenever the weather permits'.[152] Working outside the protection of the harbour was dangerous, of course, for once on the outer coast there was no shelter from stormy weather and it was a long pull back to safety.[153] Drowning was a very real risk.[154]

Fishing was profitable. In 1869, 11 boats and almost 30 fishermen were netting in the harbour and a similar number fished outside the heads. Together they caught £5000 to £6000 worth of fish and made about £75 each, less expenses.[155] The fishery continued to grow, and by 1876 the harbour alone sustained 16 boats and 40 men.[156]

The market was initially constrained by the settlers' conservatism – they still imported quantities of canned, salted or dried fish from 'Home'.[157] But once settlers were convinced that local fresh fish were palatable, the principal problem became supply. The lack of a fish market, the weather and the seasonal movements of fish often made this problematic. Over winter, stormy weather and the offshore migration of species such as hāpuku and barracouta meant that only red cod and flounder were regularly available in Dunedin shops; even then, there were some days every month without any fish at all.[158]

Settlers' understanding of the habits of local fish was in some measure gleaned from Māori on the Peninsula. Peter Thomson, who, as noted had lived among Ōtākou Māori briefly, alerted his readers in the *Otago Witness* of 29 October 1864 that he had 'noticed the Goai [kōwhai] in blossom – a sure sign that we may look for the baraccouta in a day or two' and, 'sure enough', soon after noted their arrival as forecast.[159] However, Māori guarded knowledge of their hāpuku fishing grounds carefully; in 1869 it was noted that the Otago settlers had still not yet discovered any 'reefs, banks, or natural spawning grounds'.[160]

Ōtākou Māori had more than enough knowledge and skill to compete with settlers in these fisheries, but it is clear that settlers dominated the fishing trade from the mid-1860s on, especially after the establishment at Port Chalmers of a fish-curing factory and small fishing companies.[161] Unlike isolated Ōtākou, Port Chalmers was connected to Dunedin by road and, from the mid-1870s, by rail too, and was the region's principal port. It was the best base for fishermen needing to bring their catch to market as quickly as possible, and to ship cured (smoked) fish elsewhere.

In addition, the Māori fishery was focused on barracouta, but the settlers were developing preferences for other fish.[162] In 1872 the *Press* reported that fishing companies had 'brought to light no less than fifty varieties of edible fish before unknown'.[163] The demand for barracouta dwindled. Perhaps, too, the settlers were becoming reluctant to deal with Māori in general. In December 1863 Māori from Ōtākou landed 'an enormous quantity' of crayfish in Dunedin. They tried hawking the live animals door to door, but despite being sold 'remarkable cheap ... something like a shilling a dozen', they struggled to find buyers and were forced to sell to the shops.[164]

View from Cape Saunders looking across Wairiri Bay to Matakitaki Point. Fishermen in small boats had to be very careful when working beyond the heads. Hocken Collections, Uare Taoka o Hākena, University of Otago: W.A. Taylor postcard, Box 304-007

While the Ōtākou communities never lost their connection to fishing, they did not compete again in the commercial fishery until the establishment of Otakou Fisheries by Raniera Ellison after World War Two.[165]

Problems with property: The subdivision of Ōtākou

Ōtākou Māori's efforts to organise production were complicated by problems with property. Māori elsewhere in Otago had so little land that some had to be provided for on the Peninsula. Growing numbers of 'half-caste' children also presented problems, as these children had to be accommodated within traditional property arrangements.[166] In 1876 H.K. Taiaroa complained to parliament that 'something had to be done for these half-castes, because their fathers had not taken notice of them, and had not provided for them. During all these years they had been living with, and had been brought up by, their Native mothers. Some of them had obtained land, but, on the contrary, others were simply squatting on what belonged to the Maoris.'[167]

Communal ownership of land disenfranchised Māori, as only male property owners able to demonstrate title to land could vote. Moreover, Māori could not exercise full control over their property, which greatly rankled leaders like H.K. Taiaroa. Until

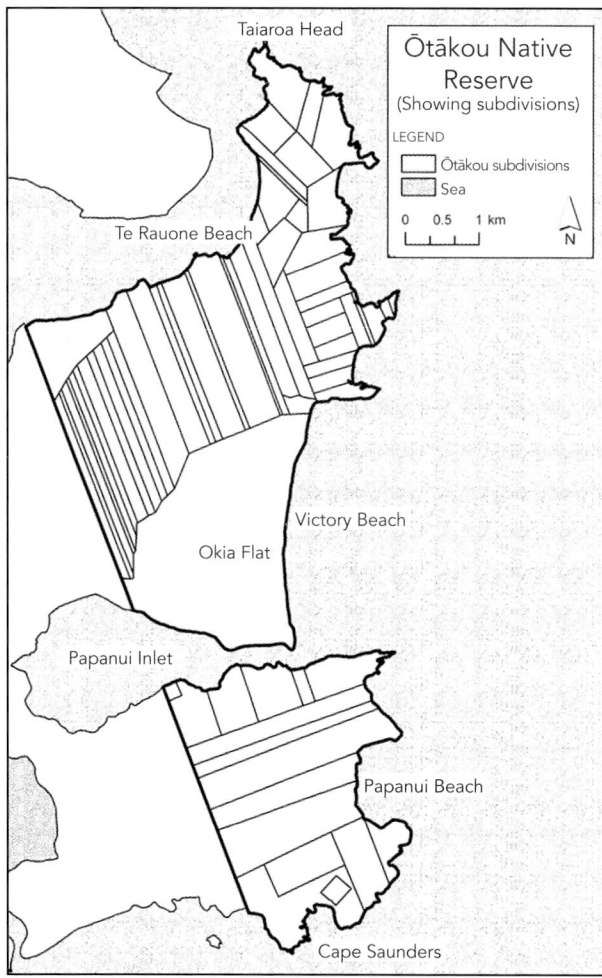

This map shows the narrow strips into which Māori chose to divide their lands to provide as many properties as possible with access to the foreshore. © Craig Innes, 2012. Land Information New Zealand

1862 Māori could legally lease or sell their land only to the Crown. This meant that the remnant ex-whaling population still occupying land at Ōtākou were illegal squatters. Taiaroa asked that chiefs be given authority to renegotiate their leases. The central government denied the request, fearing that the tribe as a whole would be deprived because of 'the improvidence of the chiefs'.[168] The Otago settlers certainly wanted the law enforced, and intervened on at least one occasion to try to prevent Māori organising any new leasing arrangements.[169] Peter Thomson's arrangement with Karetai, though, shows that some leases were renegotiated regardless. Meanwhile, pressure grew on Ōtākou Māori to individualise title to their land.

In 1862 the government passed the first of a series of laws to assimilate Māori land 'as nearly as possible to the ownership of land according to British law'.[170] Māori could now sell or lease their land to private individuals, but only after individualising title through the Native Land Court. Land held in common was useless as security against a loan, effectively precluding Māori from raising capital against the value of their land. The importance of this is hard to overstate: after all, settler capitalism, and settler farming, were completely dependent on a reliable supply of credit.[171]

Ōtākou Māori decided to do as the settlers advised, and allocate their land more precisely to gain better titles. In 1859 Te Matenga Taiaroa and Karetai divided the lands so that each held the mana over areas both at the heads and on Cape Saunders.[172] This was essentially a traditional arrangement: these leaders still held the lands as a trusteeship for their people. In 1868 the Ōtākou lands were brought before the Native Land Court. According to Bill Dacker, it was the Reverend Riemenschneider who persuaded Ōtākou Māori to go to the court, but whatever the case, it is likely that H.K. Taiaroa played the key role in the decision.[173] He and the Karetai family oversaw the initial division of the lands into large blocks along the lines already agreed by their fathers, and the subdivision of these into individual titles, typically with one owner named on each. The subdivisions were then confirmed by the court.[174]

Ōtākou Māori divided their land rather differently from settlers. In an echo of how Polynesians organised property on high Pacific atolls, the land was subdivided into strips, many of which ran from hilltop to shore. This provided access to a range of habitats from forest through littoral shore to the ocean, where each owner's property right was held to continue to at least low water.[175] Access to the sheltered harbour shoreline was especially important for providing kai moana (seafood) such as cockles, as well as enabling the use of boats for fishing and transport.

The subdivision was an attempt to reach a compromise between two systems of property and two ways of constructing an economy in relation to ecology. Māori had good reason to individualise their holdings, but it was also a decision made under duress. In the settlers' eyes Ōtākou Māori were guilty of two cardinal sins: their property rights were (mistakenly believed to be) held 'in common'; and they declined to stay on their reserve or to 'settle', instead persisting in harvesting their mahika kai. Individualisation of their property rights in land was seen as an essential cure. As historian John Weaver observes, 'improvement and property rights have had a reciprocal relationship since the Enlightenment. People who improved land deserved property rights. Property rights improved societies.'[176] The comments of Otago's commissioners for native reserves in 1858 show how tightly these ideas interlocked. As long as Ōtākou Māori held their land in common, the commisioners argued,

> *they had no individual interest in improvements … [Individualisation] would tend to settle them down on the soil … besides it seems to us a principle somewhat inherent in human nature that the possession of an individual Title to land has a tendency to increase the desire for improving the worldly circumstances and to encourage self-respect, and obedience and respect to the ordinances of Law and good Government, and as a means to these ends it has a tendency to increase the desire for mental improvement.*[177]

If the settlers were keen that Māori abandon the evils of 'beastly communism',[178] they were also uneasily aware that the Ōtākou area was an island of Māori customary land, not fully subject to their control. Under the Native Reserves Act 1856 commissioners were appointed to manage the leasing of Māori land, but 'had no power to deal with land' unless and until the owners consented 'to extinguish their original title and accept a title from the Crown'.[179] Commissioner of Crown Lands William Henry Cutten complained that, as a result, 'Europeans of good character and industrious habits have been prevented from settling in this neighbourhood. Thus the Natives have been deprived of the many benefits which would have arisen to them both pecuniarily and morally, had the nature of the reserve permitted their close contact with a civilized community.'[180]

Cutten believed, in fact, that if settlers had control they could plan a town at Ōtākou, where land would sell for 'more than the usual upset price of £50 per acre, and that probably £5,000 would be obtained for it in the course of one or two years'.[181]

With individual titles, Ōtākou Māori could now alienate their land, though a limit of 21 years was placed on the term of any lease. Such ongoing restrictions annoyed H.K. Taiaroa, member of parliament for southern Māori, who later had the Taiaroa Land Act 1883 passed to specifically allow himself (and only himself) to sell or lease his land exactly as European settlers did.[182]

British settlers associated individualised title with civilised land use – by which they meant farming. Māori intended their titles to allow owners to farm their land while maintaining access to the existing resources of the shore and sea. But within the confines of the Peninsula 'reserve' at least, this was not a workable compromise. Most properties were impractical for farming, being too small and with too little arable land.[183] In addition, as the Commissioner of Native Reserves in Otago, Charles Heaphy, commented, 'Many of the sections are so narrow in respect to their length, as to appear in the plan more like roads than country sections.' As a result, 'fences upon them could only be maintained at great disadvantage'.[184] Fencing the narrow strips was a major problem, and some owners leased parts of their land in order to meet the expense of bounding the rest.[185]

Control of fisheries

Different concepts of property also underlay conflict regarding control over fisheries. The settlers saw the sea as open to all and the foreshore as Crown owned. However, Māori, as we have seen, had long regarded fisheries as property. Now, having divided their lands, some owners staked their exclusive claims to the shore and sea fronting their land by fencing the beaches. Some of the fences used to define property rights to cockle beds at Ōtākou can be seen running out into the water in photographs taken in the early twentieth century (see opposite).

Foreshore fencing, Te Rauone Beach. Māori ran stakes out over the foreshore at Ōtākou to demarcate rights to foreshore resources, in particular their cockle beds. Otago Peninsula Museum, OP33/3

H.K. Taiaroa displayed an early understanding of the potential for dispute created by different attitudes to sea fisheries. In 1874 he had asked the House on what grounds the settlers throughout the country claimed the foreshore for public works, and queried whether this did not abrogate Māori property rights to their fisheries, as guaranteed under the Treaty of Waitangi.[186] By 1877 Taiaroa had specific grievances closer to home. On 8 November he demanded that Native Affairs Minister John Sheehan explain to parliament the authority for settler fishing in Mangahoe Inlet (Papanui), 'while the Native title thereto has not been extinguished', and asked that Europeans cease all fishing until 'some arrangement for the extinguishment of the Native title has been made'.[187] The inlet, Taiaroa said, was in the middle of his land, and he had applied for title to it. Settlers were meanwhile 'plundering all the oysters and fish from the place, and selling them in Dunedin'.[188]

Settlers seemed blind to the irony of their insistence that Māori abandon 'communism' and individualise title to land, while at the same time they overrode Māori property rights by treating fisheries and the foreshore as open-access commons. Sheehan acknowledged that Māori had been guaranteed their fisheries under the Treaty of Waitangi, but said the government could not stop Europeans from taking the inlet's seafood – though he did not know by what right they did so. He stated that when and if Taiaroa 'could prove his title to the property', then he could prosecute the Europeans for trespass.[189]

Meanwhile, Sheehan played a part in the very first legislation attempting to manage New Zealand's fisheries: the Fish Protection Act 1877. This act was in fact largely prompted by the very problems Taiaroa had highlighted: over-fishing flatfish in Otago Harbour and inlets such as Mangahoe, and a resulting influx of undersized and juvenile flounder in the Dunedin market. Peter Thomson, who daily noted the state of the Dunedin fish market, was drawing particular attention to this problem. In a series of articles published between 1876 and 1878 in the key organ for settler science, the *Transactions and Proceedings of the New Zealand Institute,* Thomson contended that flounder in the harbour and 'the various inlets up and down the coast' were overfished; he noted ongoing complaints that those brought to market were now too small, and predicted that if fishing continued at current rates, flounder would become rare.[190] The flounder fishery of Otago Harbour never fully recovered from the settlers' initial unbridled plunder. This was one impetus to the 1904 founding, largely at the instigation of George Malcolm Thomson, of the Portobello Marine Fish Hatchery on the shores of Otago Harbour.[191]

The Fish Protection Act was promoted by the Otago parliamentarian James Macandrew. It set minimum mesh and flounder fish size limits, and provided for fisheries to be set aside if necessary. Sheehan had an amendment added that explicitly protected Māori rights to fisheries under the Treaty of Waitangi. This may have been a reaction to the infamous ruling a few weeks prior, in 'Wi Parata v Bishop of Wellington', that the treaty was a legal non-entity because it had not been incorporated in statute.[192] However, Taiaroa's capacity to lay claim to the inlet itself was soon foreclosed by the Harbours Act 1878, which forbade the granting of any part of the seashore or land under the sea 'without the special sanction of an Act of the General Assembly'. This act 'put paid to any contention that the Crown's common law right to the foreshore was subject to customary usage'.[193] Thus the belief of Ōtākou Māori – that they owned not just the foreshore but the sea fisheries surrounding their land too – was overridden by the settlers' assumption that the resources of the foreshore and the sea were free for all.

Ōtākou Māori continued fishing, still went sealing on southern coasts, and even resumed whaling with others from Karitāne between 1869 and 1877, as numbers of southern right whales (as

Te Tuia Ki te Katikati
Te Whakekeu moe i a au
Te Whiuwhiu taku tatari
Kei Parakiwitini
E patu mai ra a Taiaroa
I te Kekerangi
E Takoru ra
Kei te Moana

Fleas with their biting
Disturb my sleep
How my bird snare swung
At Preservation Inlet
Where Taiaroa is killing the seals
That splash about in the ocean.

This is a waiata that Rawiri Te Maire Tau gave to the Waitangi Tribunal, which describes Te Matenga Taiaroa sealing at Preservation Inlet in the nineteenth century.[194]

well as some humpback, sperm and fin whales) were now returning to Otago coasts.[195] The venture began with two whaling boats setting out each day through the season, one from Ōtākou, the other from Waikouaiti (or Karitāne as it is now). Ten men from each settlement formed the crews, most of whom were Māori or 'half-caste', and all held shares in the cooperative. The first whale was caught in 1869, from which 10 tuns of oil were expected in addition to the bone; the Otago Museum offered £40 for the bone, but was declined. Given that oil fetched about £30 per tun at the time, the return on each whale was substantial. Thus encouraged, the cooperative expanded and more boats entered the industry.

As they had in the 1830s, the whalers killed the cow whales and their calves, prompting criticism from the *Otago Daily Times* that this threatened the industry's sustainability.[196] The concern was justified. The Ōtākou boats had their most success in 1872, taking six whales and selling oil and bone to the tune of £1218, but only five whales were taken in the years that followed, the last in 1876.[197] Southern right whales were not seen again off the Otago Peninsula for many years.

'The yoke of hired servitude'

Although whaling in winter fitted in well with the annual round of seasonal wage labour that now sustained Māori throughout the south,[198] this dependence on working for settlers was not what their leaders had envisaged. As James Stack remarked, 'Men who can trace their pedigree up to the creation and even beyond it shrink from the yoke of hired servitude'.[199] H.K. Taiaroa recalled with some bitterness that 'he had been compelled to commence work when quite a lad – to milk cows'.[200] In 1874 Kāi Tahu, in their petition to the government for redress for broken promises regarding their land sales, opened by stating that they were now totally dependent on the labour market for seasonal work: 'When they [the Europeans] want us and come upon us, we are able to gain a subsistence for ourselves and our children. Should this source fail as other springs do because dry we will become paupers in the presence of the present lords of the soil.'[201]

This was a recurrent theme throughout the remainder of the nineteenth century.[202] Chronic labour shortages in the 1860s meant that Māori labour was in ready demand. Work was available during the 1870s, too, despite the influx of workers in the wake of Vogel's assisted immigration schemes. The large amount of public works and a facility with trades such as shearing and harvesting and, for some, whaling, helped Ōtākou Māori to survive over this period. But after the brief burst of debt-boosted expansion in the late 1870s, the settlement was plunged into the long depression of the 1880s and early 1890s; employment became very hard to find.

From the 1870s onwards the Kāi Tahu leadership, in particular H.K. Taiaroa in his capacity as member of the House of Representatives for southern Māori, made intensive, expensive and unsuccessful efforts to regain land.[203] Five petitions to parliament during the 1870s testified to their need for land.[204] In 1881 Resident Magistrate and Commissioner of Native Reserves Alexander Mackay testified that economic conditions had begun to bite, and larger quantities of land were becoming imperative. He argued that Māori at Ōtākou and elsewhere could not be expected to subsist on such smallholdings when '[a] European finds even a hundred acres too small to be payable, and is frequently compelled by circumstances to have recourse to the money-lender, and probably in the end loses his farm ... small holdings in the present state of New Zealand are not conducive to prosperity ...'[205]

Disputes over land ownership flared within the reserves. Tare Wetere Te Kahu told the Smith–Nairn Commission of Inquiry in 1880 that 'they were still quarrelling' over land.[206] A few chiefly families, such as the Ellison and Taiaroa whānau, were able to expand their lands by leasing smaller holdings from poorer neighbours. They remained relatively prosperous and their children were well educated.[207] But very few had their advantages.

The Māori economy at Ōtākou was in a state of flux. They lacked experience of farming within a commercial market economy and had difficulty accessing capital to develop their lands. They had attempted to implement property arrangements to match the new conditions, but by emphasising the importance of access to the sea they created problems with fencing and cultivation, while the property arrangements they tried to impose on the foreshore and estuaries were simply ignored by settlers. Very little 'improvement' occurred in comparison to the land that settlers were assiduously clearing, fencing and stocking. As a result, very different environments developed.

The environmental impacts of settlement, 1861–80

'The spread of drifting sand'

On 25 September 1893 Hori Kerei Taiaroa rose to speak before the House of Representatives. His concern was the spread of drifting sand at Otakou. He remembered, he said,

> *the condition of this place in 1850, and there was very little drift-sand there at that time. In 1860 [actually 1868] the Natives entitled to that reserve applied to have it subdivided and individualised so that each person might be in a better position to deal with it and improve the land. Since 1873 the spread of drifting sand had greatly increased. He himself was a part-owner in that reserve, and some of them had applied to the other owners to fence their sub-divisions, and to take some steps to stop the drifting of the sand by growing grasses; but they had always replied that they would not do it, and there was no law to compel them to do so. The consequence was, it was still in the same condition now. When some of them fenced their land, the other owners refused to do it, and nothing could be done to stop the sand from covering*

over their fences. At the present time there were between 900 and 1,000 acres of land covered with sand-drift. The place was situated near the harbour, and there was a dispute as to where the sand came from – whether it came from the river, or was caused by the harbour-works, or whether it was from sand on the place itself, which was loose and was blown about … [208]

Taiaroa's minimisation of sand movement prior to the mid-1870s has to be read against the enormous acreage of ruined land confronting Ōtākou Māori by 1893. Sand movement and shoreline erosion was well under way before 1870. By then, sand had spread up the slope behind Te Rauone Beach, forming an enormous dune a kilometre long and three kilometres wide; it also spread south of Wellers Rock over the flat fronting the little valley of Omate.[209]

Peter Thomson described seeing the sand in southerly storms in the 1860s 'raised in thick clouds, and carried onward in tons, and spread over the grass and among the trees at the upper edge, where it lies, never to go back'.[210] The sand swallowed Pukehau, the small lagoon behind the beach where Te Matenga Taiaroa had lived in the 1850s.[211] He shifted his house, piece by piece, around the corner to the valley of Omate.[212] The sand drove Potiki and his people from Te Ruatitiko, which had been the largest of the kaik in the 1850s:[213] first the church was abandoned, then the village itself was buried.[214] A church, mission reserve and cemetery were then established at Omate on 10 acres (4ha) provided by Karetai, with Taiaroa donating much of the initial funding.[215] The church and school that Hoani Wetere Korako had built at Tahakopa was also abandoned, and Korako shifted to Te Taupō, on the hillside above Te Rauone Beach.[216]

By the late 1860s the land where the Wellers' station had stood was quite uninhabitable. Harwood's former store was surrounded by a sea of sand, and only a few forlorn ngaio trees stood amid the drifts. Early surveys suggest that the shoreline south of Te Rauone Beach was substantially eroded, possibly because the changing shape of Aramoana Spit narrowed the harbour entrance and pushed the harbour channel inshore.[217] At Omate in 1870, Thomson described how many of the buildings were long since gone as a result of decades of grazing and burning on marginal habitats:

[A] pretty broad slice of land on which they stood has been washed away by the sea, and what was once a pretty green flat, with a few old ngaio trees on it, is now a sandy waste. A little further on, Harwood's house stands on the beach, and a short way in was a fine garden, with fruit trees and bushes in plenty. But the sand has put horticulture to the flight, and the garden is now reduced to very small dimensions; the tops of the bushes may be seen sticking up through the sand. If it goes on as it has been doing, a very short interval will elapse ere the whole flat will become as barren as the beach below.[218]

H.K. Taiaroa's plea for government help to replant the dunes reflected his frustration over the difficulty he faced persuading individual landowners to contribute to the common cause, and illustrates the extent of intertwined change in property rights and

View from the sea of the Ōtākou sand drift at Te Rauone Beach. Hocken Collections, Uare Taoka o Hākena, University of Otago, SO7-136a

This photograph of the remains of the Wellers' whaling station surrounded by sand was taken from Omate by the schoolmaster Leask, probably in 1869 when he first took up his post.
Port Chalmers Regional Maritime Museum: #2929

Looking north from Omate to Wellers Rock, with the sand at Te Rauone Beach in the background. Hocken Collections, Uare Taoka o Hākena, University of Otago, S06-192b

political power. The mana of rangatira was not as closely identified with the mana of the community as before; as individuals no longer maintained their entitlement to land use through an ongoing contribution to the wider community, leaders found it increasingly difficult to direct communal activity.

Settlers faced the same problems with sand as farming intensified elsewhere on the Peninsula, and had similar difficulty organising their responses. By 1870 sand blown north over Lawyers Head coated the land between Tomahawk Lagoon and the ocean and had begun spilling into the valley behind. At the aptly named Sandfly Bay, Thomson saw sand 'flying from the shoulders of Sandymount in thick clouds [and] deposited on the beach at the entrance to the Inlet'.[219] Thomson elsewhere noted that by 1870, 'instead of nursing and encouraging the growth of grass and other vegetables on the sandhills', the settlers were allowing their cattle to 'trampl[e] over the loose surface', and were burning off the grass and scrub 'whenever they get a chance'.[220] As Thomson concluded, 'a process more mischievous and detrimental could hardly be carried on', as the settlers 'will very soon find out': it had already freed sand to encroach inland, swallowing the lagoon and marsh that had once formed 'an extensive flat' in the valley floor.[221]

'Half covered with weeds'

Bare and sandy land was an ideal nursery for weeds. Thistles were by far the worst, especially the Scotch thistle, which produces prodigious quantities of seed.[222] Between 1862 and 1870 the provincial government required property owners to control thistles on their land, but since there were no official means of identifying non-compliance, and the strictures did not apply to Crown lands or to Māori land,[223] their efforts were quite useless on the Peninsula.

During the 1860s Scotch thistle rapidly colonised much of the land around all of the Peninsula settlements. It spread south from Māori land, described as a 'complete nursery for seed', and north along the roadsides as settlement pushed out from Andersons Bay.[224] Alexander Begg, curator of the Botanic Gardens, described Ōtākou in 1864 as infested with these thistles. Twenty acres (8ha) immediately behind the former whaling station were so dense with these large and spiny plants that 'horses and cattle cannot pass', and scattered patches were spread all over the reserve and down the Peninsula as far as Seaton's farm near Portobello. Scotch thistle is a biennial plant and relies largely on regeneration from seed; it is therefore fairly susceptible to control. Begg estimated the cost of clearing the thistles at £400 in the first year, and a further £1000 per year for two to three years to keep new growth down.[225] Scots councillors, however, objected to spending such money on eradicating 'the stalwart, proud emblem' of their country.[226] They pointed to the Māori reserve as the primary source of the problem and the supposed reason they could do nothing to prevent the invasion. A petition from Peninsula settlers presented to the council in 1866 also blamed Māori, and demanded that the ordinance be amended to allow an inspector to identify culprits, rather than the law being operative only if settlers 'laid informations against their neighbours'.[227]

Just as Māori found it hard to compel people to control environmental problems for the common good, so too did settlers. They complained year after year in the press about the growing problem. They blamed Māori and, increasingly, that other irresponsible class: absentee owners.[228] In 1875, 30 settlers, most from Tomahawk, petitioned the provincial government to reinstate a thistle ordinance, arguing that otherwise '[t]hey ... will with every year get worse and no individual trouble or expense will be of any use.'[229]

The provincial government did impose another ordinance, specifically for the Peninsula, but there was no agreement over who ought to take responsibility for eradicating the weed. As noted earlier, political control over the Peninsula was effectively divided between the Peninsula and the Portobello road boards. In this case the Peninsula board, led by John Mathieson, wanted to enforce the ordinance, and sought the cooperation of the Portobello board, which declined, arguing that it was best left to individual settlers.[230] In the event, the entire system of provincial government was disbanded the following year, obviating the measure.[231] As a result, nothing was 'spreading faster or thriving better than "Scotchmen"', which had 'a monopoly of the soil as thorough, the land yielding almost no more return than when the Maori was lord in the land, as when the primeval forest was as yet unmolested by axe or lucifer'. [232]

Though none provoked consternation on the scale of 'Scotchmen', other weeds like Cape-weed and dandelion also arrived and thrived, 'usurping the soil', especially on 'older clearings and poorer lands', and causing a 'large amount of labour and trouble'.[233] It was frequently argued that the spread of weeds indicated 'poor farming'.[234] Certainly, farmers and their animals were the principal vectors for the spread of weeds. Seed sold to farmers typically contained many weeds, and few had the time and means to clean it.[235] And since Peninsula farmers grew oats to feed horses rather than humans, they were perhaps tempted to buy cheaper, weed-infested seed.[236] As well, forest clearance provided introduced weeds with ideal habitats. The result, as an *Otago Witness* editorial lamented, was that even 'the most thickly populated parts … really are more than half covered with weeds'.[237]

In 1872 Peter Thomson of the Dunedin Naturalists' Field Club wrote its first report.[238] He observed the spread of weeds along with other, related phenomena:

> *The spread of acclimatised weeds is much noticed by the members, – wither the dock, cape weed, thistles, or chickweed being found everywhere over the district.*
>
> *On the other hand, some of the native plants are becoming scarce, and will soon be extinct – clearing the land, the grazing of cattle, and the ravages of fire are the main causes of this. The larger native birds, too, are gradually dying out; there are very few in the bush near town, while cats and rats are common.*[239]

Thomson accurately summarised how the spread of settlement simplified habitats and caused biodiversity to plummet. Settlers' burns sent the forests' enormous accumulated biomass up in smoke; the nutrients left in the ash fuelled only a short flush of crop and grass growth, after which farmers and their stock effectively began to mine the soil.

'Falling and burning off': Clearing the forest

The shift from forest to grass and the introduction of stock were the most significant mechanisms of ecological change on the Peninsula between 1860 and 1900. Trees were a weed in the way of farming, and although some good timber was saved, most were hacked down and burnt. As Thomson wrote in 1865, 'there are many large trees, yet commercially speaking, it seldom pays to cut them for the sake of the timber, on account of the difficulty of getting at them, and of dragging them to a convenient place for a sawpit. So the plan adopted all round the locality is the simple one of falling and burning off.'[240]

As the amount of easily accessible wood diminished, the population of Dunedin increased and so did the need for fuel. Firewood had always been a valuable commodity in the city. Settlers often had large fireplaces and required prodigious amounts of wood to cook food, launder clothes and heat homes.[241] The supply of firewood was a real problem in winter and spring. As early as October 1850, Dunedin households paid over 14s for a cord (3.6m^3) of firewood, which might last only about three weeks.[242] As nearby bush was cleared the cost rose quickly, hitting 23s a cord by the winter of 1857.[243] For many households living on a labourer's wage of three shillings a day, purchasing wood was out of the question. The obvious and common recourse was to steal it from Crown land, where it might take a man a day's labour to cut a cord of wood.[244]

By the mid-1860s a 'considerable amount of firewood, posts and rails, &c' was being carted to town from Andersons Bay, although the favoured firewood, mānuka (actually kānuka more often than not), was rare there.[245] Several brick kilns that required a lot of local fuel also operated in the area, and by 1876 so little forest was left in the vicinity that fencing timber had become very scarce.[246]

Forest lasted only a little longer around Portobello. By the mid-1870s the constant demand for timber meant that podocarps were now picked out and pit-sawn, though the prohibitive cost of transporting timber to Dunedin meant that only a small local market could be served.[247] This, as much as a shortage of timber, prevented operations such as the Dicksons' sawmill from becoming anything more than small family concerns.[248] Now, instead of 'cutting down the bush indiscriminately ... the greater part of it is cut into cord-wood for sale'. Once 'mānuka' had been virtually removed, the settlers cut 'mixed wood' to supplement their incomes.[249] But transport was critical, and often their efforts were wasted. A visitor in 1878 observed:

> *Thousands of tons of stacked firewood are to be seen on the clearings, much of which is rotten. Where stones are not available, it is stacked to form fences, but it seems a sad waste considering the scarcity of this material in Dunedin. I suppose with increased water carriage it will pay to bring it to market, but in the mean time it is so much capital sunk.*[250]

In dry years fires to burn offcut bush sometimes burst out of control and 'raged for miles'.[251] On 14 October 1881, 'Black Friday' as it became remembered on the Peninsula, two fires escaped control after a strong, warm northwest wind sprang up. One, around Sandymount, burnt off about 15 acres (6ha) of bush, miles of log fencing and tons of hay; Larnach alone lost 1000 cords of firewood. The second, a conflagration around Harbour Cone, destroyed the cheese factory, numerous farm buildings and houses, and firewood and fencing. Many settlers, most of whom were uninsured, were reportedly 'half ruined'.[252]

CHAPTER 7: THE AXE AND THE LUCIFER MATCH

Turning forest to field was a gradual process, as clearly seen in these Burton Brothers images of early Portobello (see next page also), where tree remains are strewn over the lower slopes of Harbour Cone, and the remaining forest on the crown is being eaten into. Burton Brothers studio, maker unknown. Museum of New Zealand Te Papa Tongarewa: C.011778

'Portobello, Dunedin'. Burton Brothers studio, maker unknown. Museum of New Zealand Te Papa Tongarewa: C.011775

'Vast masses of debris': Problems with erosion

As the forests fell, the ways in which the soil interacted with sunlight, wind and water changed. Erosion increased markedly, streams dried up and disappeared, and lagoons were swamped with silt. The firing of forest, the loss of habitat and the intrusion of stock into forest remnants affected plant and animal species at all trophic levels.

Forests exert greater influence over their immediate environment than grasses do. In the nineteenth century it was widely thought that deforestation actually changed the climate. At a local level this was quite true.[253] Forest maintains a more constant air temperature and humidity than grassland by providing shelter from wind, sunlight and water. Forest also regulates soil temperature and hydrology – soil that the forest has of course largely created. Once laid down in exotic pastures or ploughed for crops, soil was exposed to far greater variation in these elemental variables, and was largely stripped of its microbial and invertebrate biota.[254] These changes in the ecosystems of the soil had considerable effects on landowners.

The removal of trees means that more water reaches the ground, and faster.[255] Under forest, water drips to the ground and seeps in slowly. Much of it is then sucked up by tree roots. The water that escapes the forest's clutches gradually accumulates into channels that become rivulets and streams. Under grass, however, much of the water simply runs off the surface, especially on steep slopes or when it is pugged and compacted by stock. This prevents the accumulation of water into perennial streams and promotes rapid floods of water in periods of high rainfall.[256]

Forest floors are shaded, spongy with leaf litter, and feel moist and cool. The surface under grass more often feels dry. But without forest, the soil itself is actually much wetter since, like any container, soil fills from the bottom up. Successive drying and wetting of topsoils exposed to rain, wind and sun causes the ground to swell and shrink, crack and fissure. When water reaches bedrock its flow across this impermeable layer, creating a plane of weakness above which saturated, heavy, fluid soil is liable to shear away. In the absence of forest, soil becomes saturated more often.[257]

The inevitable result on the Peninsula was that huge masses of soil slid downhill, either suddenly in a roar of mud and debris, or almost imperceptibly but no less inexorably.[258] Massive landslides and debris flows occurred above Portobello, around Hoopers Inlet and along the eastern flank of the ridge running towards Ōtākou – all areas underlain by weaker pyroclastic rocks.[259]

Some landowners to this day consider erosion a natural feature of these areas.[260] Geologists and soil scientists confirm that the region is inherently unstable. However, D.M. Leslie's studies of soil erosion found that landslides had 'virtually ceased' under forest, and concluded that settlers had activated major erosion events as newly cleared and grassed slopes evolved to reach a new equilibrium.[261] Michael Crozier's study of mass movement in the area likewise concluded that human settlement 'has in recent

Kerr's house after the slip. A river of mud has engulfed this house, on Weir Road between Portobello and Papanui Inlet. Otago Peninsula Museum, OPM 96 173/3

times so drastically upset the long established environmental balance that a vast redistribution of energy is currently taking place within the system'.[262]

The problem first became apparent in 1871 around Portobello, when landslips carried 'large portions of the soil on to the beaches', destroying many acres of pasture.[263] In 1877 the *Otago Witness* happily reported that as 'the stumps decay from our paddocks, the plough is being more used … giving the tilled lands that finished aspect they sadly need when encumbered by these unsightly relics of the bush'.[264] Early ploughing was often up and down the slope rather than along the contours, further exacerbating the erosion effects.[265] After heavy rain in early February 1877, large and sudden slips had caused havoc: some settlers had to flee from their houses to escape torrents of mud; roads and bridle tracks remained blocked for weeks with 'vast masses of *debris*', and 'such a state of ruin to outhouses, fences, gardens and pasture has fallen upon the inhabitants that a feeling of consternation pervades the entire district'.[266]

Other large slips had scoured out the southern slopes of Mt Charles, affecting several properties. But the biggest slips of all were at Sandymount, where one slide alone had carried off 10 acres (4 ha) of grass and potatoes, leaving only 'a mass of bare clay and stones'.[267]

The destruction of forests posed both short- and long-term problems. Besides immediate damage from erosion – smashed infrastructure, ruined crops and blocked roads – it created prime habitat for weeds. As well, without reliable streams farmers on the Peninsula lost the potential to regulate water supplies to stock and pasture. This last problem continues to limit farming significantly, and many areas face water shortages in summer.[268]

'Burnt bones': The impact of deforestation on wildlife

Fire incinerated much more than trees. Alfred Reynolds recalled 'thousands – nay, even millions – of birds being roasted alive by the extensive fires'; bigger birds left 'burnt bones … on the charred ground', but 'smaller birds were reduced to ashes, with nothing left to speak of their existence and fate'.[269] Most species had habitat enough to survive in pockets on the Peninsula, but kākā, quail, weka and white herons were among those that completely disappeared.[270]

The greatest losses to the biota were the least noticed. Most of the animal biomass of rainforest is composed of insects.[271] Few invertebrate species could escape fire, or adapt to pasture.[272] The transformation of the Peninsula would have exterminated thousands of species' populations. Each species' fate had implications for others. The loss of kōwhai – cut down for fences – reduced the food supply for kererū, tūī and bellbirds, all of which became less common.[273] Kōwhai in turn needed tūī, especially, as its principal pollinators.[274] Still stronger associations exist between plants that bear seeds within large fleshy fruits, and the birds that disperse the seed. Most New Zealand forest birds eat the fruit, and some 70 per cent of the 240 or so woody plants bear fruit that birds are attracted to.[275] The loss of big birds left trees with large fruits, like miro and matai, almost exclusively reliant on kererū for seed dispersal.[276]

The settlers singled out these larger trees, and were very fond of pigeon, too. Writing in 1910, Alfred Reynolds recalled that the kererū, 'always a bird to move about for its food, visited the Peninsula in great flocks' in the early 1860s. But shooting and predation by cats made short work of the flocks.[277] By the late 1860s, seeing a pigeon was a notable event. As Reynolds reported, 'I heard about some being in a pine bush about four miles distant. After a day's search I found two and shot them. From that time till last year I did not see or hear of any about.'[278]

The speed at which the settlers moved meant that these implications were not the immediate problem: kererū were killed off long before their food supply was imperilled, and most kōwhai were cleared before the long-term effects of the loss of pollinators were felt. Yet the need to reconstruct such relationships problematises how we can hope to maintain and regenerate species populations, now and in the future.

It is important to remember that a few species thrived. Reynolds considered that the bush wren (rifleman) and the fantail had maintained or even increased their numbers.[279] He noted, too, that waxeyes were 'still plentiful'. Reynolds was perhaps unaware that waxeyes were actually recent introductions, having been blown here from Australia only a few years before.²⁸⁰ Such recent arrivals generally coped better. Although settlers sometimes found these birds bothersome in the orchard, waxeyes were also helpful and were sometimes known as the 'blight-bird', for they also fed on the aphis species that blighted settlers' crops and fruit trees.²⁸¹ The worst aphis pest was American apple blight (now known as woolly apple aphid, *Eriosoma lanigerum*) which spread so fast that by 1861 the provincial government was fining settlers for not clearing trees of it.²⁸² It still 'hung about the boughs like hoar frost' on John Mathieson's orchard trees in 1878.²⁸³

As with weeds, settlers carried insect pests with them. Deforestation created prime conditions for some animals. In 1867 an early Portobello settler was driven to ask the Otago Acclimatisation Society for introduced frogs to cure his introduced slug infestation; by 1874 the *Otago Witness* reported that in older clearings slugs were increasing so fast that 'it is almost impossible to raise sufficient vegetables for home use, and it is only by going further into the bush on new land, that sufficient can be grown'.²⁸⁴

Of the few native invertebrates that thrived on pasture or crops, the worst was 'the grub' (the native grass grub). The larvae of Porina moths and crane flies also liked 'improved' pasture, while various 'caterpillars' (probably native armyworms) and 'grasshoppers' periodically threatened crops.²⁸⁵ These insects infuriated settlers in the late 1860s and early 1870s, when there were widespread worries about the 'steady increase in the damage' done by them.²⁸⁶ However, fears that insect pests would soon be an 'evil' of 'the most alarming proportions' proved largely transitory, with the marked exception of the grass grub.²⁸⁷ For this, the settlers thanked the rapid spread of introduced insectivorous birds.

'A true Britain of the South': Importing species

During the 1860s settlers indulged a passion for importing species, both privately and through government-funded acclimatisation societies. The Otago branch operated from 1864. Most of its importations were of familiar species from Britain, but some settlers operating on their own account were prepared to experiment with almost anything.²⁸⁸ During the heyday of unquestioned introductions, between 1869 and 1871, the Otago Acclimatisation Society received £500 per year from the provincial government. It brought in several shipments of small British birds, from which are descended most of the introduced birds that thrive around Dunedin today. These included starlings, song thrushes, blackbirds, 'hedge sparrows' (actually dunnocks), house sparrows, chaffinches, goldfinches, greenfinches, yellowhammers, robins and a nightingale.²⁸⁹ The society also introduced a wide variety of Australian birds, most of which failed to establish initially. Black swans, magpies and spur-winged plovers thrived, however, and are now common.²⁹⁰

Acclimatisation societies were more widespread and long lasting in New Zealand than anywhere else. Accused at times of thoughtlessly causing ecological ruin, they have had bad press for a long time. In the case of small birds, at least, there was some thought shown, however. The real need to check insects was the primary motive for their importation. According to Canterbury settler-scientist James Drummond, birds for importation were to be non-migratory, prolific breeders and, to cope with winter, able to eat seeds in addition to insects.[291] Sentiment was also significant. As the *Otago Witness* put it, the hope was to create 'a true Britain of the South, by stocking the woods and forests of New Zealand with the feathered songsters of the old land'.[292] As G.M. Thomson noted, the motive for introduction in practice was sometimes simply that 'those who suggested them knew them or of them in Australia or the old country'. Alexander Bathgate suggested that the Otago Acclimatisation Society too often acted in ignorance: when he queried the wisdom of introducing the grain-devouring, 'harsh-voiced' 'green linnet' – knowing this was likely to mean the greenfinch – he was informed that it was a harmless and beautiful songbird.[293]

Such carelessness reflected the early settlers' perception, as expressed in the *Otago Witness*, that 'to introduce birds, beasts and fishes into Otago was something like writing upon the blank page of a child's mind'.[294] Indeed, introductions were sometimes childlike in motive and means: European robins, for example, were introduced 'to show in the reality to Otago children, what they have so often seen in their picture books' – but the numerous robins brought all had their red breasts, and therefore were all male.[295]

While some British small birds did have unwelcome side-effects, they do seem to have performed their primary intended role of checking the 'blasting plagues of insects'.[296] Certainly, Peninsula farmers as elsewhere were delighted with the introductions of small (largely) insectivorous birds such as hedge sparrows, starlings, blackbirds and thrushes.[297] Many introduced species increased rapidly; by 1875 one journalist marvelled that in Portobello and Broad Bay, 'Blackbirds, thrushes, linnets, and finches may all be seen and heard. Starlings exist in thousands.'[298] Peninsula farmers approvingly noted large flocks of starlings feeding on larvae and grubs, and tolerated their occasional depredations of fruit crops.[299] In 1876 the freedom from insect pests was 'a source of great satisfaction' attributed to the 'feathered friends of the farmer', which were regarded as a clear benefit overall.[300]

Scientists such as Alexander Bathgate concurred. He felt that the spread of an 'Elater beetle' (*Conoderus exsul*) in Otago, which he thought had come in with grass seed, was 'a very strong argument (if any be needed) in favour of the urgent necessity for the introduction of British insectivorous birds'. He later described the effects of its larvae's depredations on the roots of the limited amount of grass then sown: 'it was no uncommon thing to see English grass wither up in large patches as though scorched by fire'.[301] Likewise, the spread of 'the great plague of aphis' was associated with a lack of ladybirds, of which only one species was then observed.[302] By 1897 Bathgate noted – in the context of castigating the acclimatisation societies for failing to track the results of their introductions to 'preserve evidence of their own usefulness' – that once the starlings became numerous such plagues were a thing of the past. He considered that starlings had also caused the disappearance of 'black hairy caterpillars' that had formerly made barley growing 'almost impossible' around Oamaru, and the 'almost total disappearance' of grasshoppers and cicadas around Dunedin.[303]

Everyone was pleased with the efforts of the Otago Acclimatisation Society, abetted by Larnach, to establish game birds such as pheasant and California quail on the Peninsula. This was a significant part of the project to create a 'better Britain', free from the restraints of aristocratic privilege that had barred all but the landowning elite from enjoying game animals. Pheasants were still shot there at the turn of the century.[304] But Peninsula farmers would 'never forgive them' for introducing house sparrows or greenfinches.[305] These birds joined native parakeets in devouring sown seed of crops and grasses, and attacking grain crops long before they were ripe.[306] Parakeets could be shot, but greenfinches were harder to deal with.[307] Farmers were forced to spend time guarding their crops, and often had to harvest early and hurriedly, thus reducing the crop's value.[308] In 1881 John Mathieson, who led a long campaign against the small bird pest, recorded his experience to date:

> *Two years ago there were a few linnets, which stripped a little of the grain and ate most of the turnip seed. Last year they ate the largest half of the grain and most of the seed turnips. This spring they went with most of the clovers and grain had to be sown extra thick to allow for what the birds would take. Turnip sowing was a vexation: they not only lifted all they could find, but pulled it up when braided; but by great perseverance with scares, &c., we saved some. They are now flocking on the grain, although quite green. I do not think we will be able to save any of it this year ... Now if in two years they have increased so as to make us importers of our seed grain, horse and fowl feed, &c., and almost without turnip and clover seed, how will the province fare in a like time hence? It is surely time to ask, Is there a remedy? and what is it? and how can it be applied?*

The most famously ill-advised introduction to Otago was of course the rabbit, brought in for food, sport and perhaps nostalgia.[309] By 1870 they were already 'thoroughly acclimatised' above Sandfly Bay, and numbers were increasing steadily. Wild cats and shooting, for the market and the table, were thought to keep their numbers down a little; certainly their effects on the Peninsula were far milder than in central Otago, where landholdings were considerably larger.[310]

Problems with introduced exotic fauna did help generate an increased awareness that the environment was not a blank slate that could be written upon at will. In fact, almost from the first, some settlers began to regret erasing quite so much of the life indigenous to Otago Peninsula.

CHAPTER 7: THE AXE AND THE LUCIFER MATCH

'Man the destroyer': The evolution of attitudes to the Peninsula environment

In 1872 a writer to the *Otago Witness* recalled how, looking out over Otago Harbour towards the Peninsula, he would 'muse on what we had come to, and what was to be accomplished, ere the beautiful wilderness stretched before us should blossom with the rose, and the conquest of art be complete over nature'.[311]

Settlers had extolled the Peninsula's beauty from the moment they saw it. In 1865 the Otago provincial government employed painter Nicholas Chevalier, on a retainer of £200, to produce scenic views for exhibition in Australia and Europe that would celebrate the beauty of the domain and perhaps entice emigrants. The *Otago Witness* recommended his employment as 'a public work' by which Otago's 'attractions as a beautiful and desirable land for settlement' would be promoted by this 'first introduction to the World of Taste'.[312]

Nicholas Chevalier, Sandfly Bay and Gull Rock, Near Dunedin. *The 1865 watercolour is already a romantic view.* 1865, watercolour on paper, 232 x 300mm. Gift of Mrs Caroline Chevalier, the artist's widow, England, 1919. Museum of New Zealand Te Papa Tongarewa: 1919-0002-14

Nicholas Chevalier, Sandfly Bay, Otago. *Chevalier's 1879 oil painting adds a fanciful Māori family, pausing on the path from the dark forest to the pastoral future ahead.* 1879, oil on canvas, 916 x 1221mm. Gift of Mr L. Owen Menck, 1962. Auckland Art Gallery Toi o Tāmaki: 1962/31

Chevalier initially produced a watercolour painting of the view of Sandymount from above Sandfly Bay (previous page). He painted a landscape in transition: in the foreground is a forest where kōwhai, festooned with vines, bloom gold, but some trees are already felled stumps. In his subsequent oil painting of the scene, *Sandfly Bay, Otago* (above) he exercised his imagination. The Māori family portrayed are fanciful figments, the man dressed in 'native' clothing that had long since been discarded in the south.[313] The eye, drawn to the distance, sees a pastoral landscape seemingly ready-made and awaiting the grazing of settlers' stock.

The settlers aimed to fulfil Thomas Burns' vision of 'the lower-lying valleys … waving with the yellow corn and the pursuits of rural husbandry; the pretty farms, "the busy mile", and the happy smiling cottages by the wayside or nestling amid the trees in some bosky dingle or sylvan dell'.[314] By the end of the 1870s some dared to believe it was in prospect. In 1878 a visitor gazing north along the Peninsula celebrated the view before him: 'The hill slopes of the Peninsula, as far as the eye will carry, are bespangled with the cottage homes of industrious settlers.'[315]

George O'Brien's watercolours evoke the progress towards this ordered harmony of humanity and nature. Compare his two views from Signal Hill of 1866 and 1872 (next page). The earlier shows a serene and untouched landscape of limpid tranquillity bathed in golden light, a vision of a world better than any O'Brien could ever have looked upon, for in reality, the Peninsula landscape at that time was 'raw as only a half-broken frontier can be – a wasteland of scars dotted with stark, as yet unassimilated buildings.'[316]

O'Brien's 1872 picture depicts a surveyor peering through his theodolite in the foreground. The atmosphere in this picture is crisper, as O'Brien, himself a surveyor, invites us to share the man's gaze as he precisely delineates the landscape. We see that the landscape, untouched in 1862, is now a mosaic of crops, pasture and forest from shore to hilltop.

This change was not wholly imagined. Peter Thomson, who often rambled around the Peninsula, on viewing Harbour Cone in 1870 commented:

> *Till within the last couple of years or so, it was one unbroken forest from base to summit, but the march of settlement has somewhat marred its beauty on the harbour side, as some large clearings have been made on it, reaching from the road to a short distance from the top. On the southern side, however, there has been much less clearing, although there too, it has begun, and the axe and fire are busy at work destroying the natural beauties of the locality.*[317]

O'Brien painted 'a future when man and landscape will again be in harmony' and foregrounds a landscape 'idyllically settled by men'.[318] He asks us to consider that the surveyor's gaze, which we follow into the landscape, is the instrument by which a future world of order and harmony can be constructed.

O'Brien's contemporaries thought his work an overly literal rendering of the landscape. One commented in 1876 on his view of *Dunedin from the Junction*: 'This painting is a remarkably accurate record of everything the eye could include at that date ... Indeed, the beholder might with very little effort imagine himself on the spot with the view before him. This accuracy is, however, quite destructive of artistic effect, but a few centuries hence the record will prove interesting.'[319]

If O'Brien's vision has proved 'interesting', it is not as an accurate record of the past, but as a revelation of the settlers' dreams for their future. Peter Entwisle suggests that O'Brien's paintings made manifest the pervasive dream of settler society, a dream 'so mundane in fact, that it could be mistaken for reality ... His works show us not how New Zealand was, but how it might have been – if the optimism of the colonising Victorian could have been translated into complete and unblemished fact.'[320] O'Brien's work is a form of prolepsis: a vision of the future as existing already, in the hope that it can be called into being. As such, it is a precise echo of Burns's dream of 'bosky dingle or sylvan dell' where an obedient God-fearing flock would dwell.

George O'Brien, View of Otago Heads and Port Chalmers from Signal Hill near Dunedin.
c. 1866, watercolour with pencil & opaque white on paper, 288 x 634mm. Hocken Collections, Uare Taoka o Hākena, University of Otago: 7,302

George O'Brien, Otago Heads from Signal Hill.
1872, watercolour, 466 x 615mm, Auckland Art Gallery Toi o Tāmaki: 1981/9/2

While the settlers' dream was of improvement and progress, they were not wholly indifferent to the native flora and fauna, nor – as several scholars have argued – did they hate and fear the bush. Many settlers expressed misgivings over the ways in which their activity was transforming landscapes like that of the Peninsula. Part of the settlers' problem was that the process of settlement was itself deeply unsettling. As Eileen Soper remarked of the effect on women, their world was a 'habitat that must be continually altering – the natural demolished in order to give way to the civilized', so that 'whether she loved or hated the new land, no pioneer woman could be completely at peace while this process of destruction and reconstruction was taking place'.[321]

'So unthinkingly marred': The rise of concern for the indigenous environment

The prevailing trope of New Zealand literature has long been that the settler has his progress and laments it too: a 'bitter price to pay/ for Man's Dominion – beauty swept away', as William Pember Reeves put it. That this attitude existed from the beginning is evident in the reminiscences of older settlers who had participated in the rapid surge of change and now felt able to reflect on the meanings these changes held for them. Their opinions represent the hesitant emergence of an emotional attachment to the indigenous environment as it had been.[322]

The rise of concern for the indigenous environment is usually only traced to around the last decade of the nineteenth century. However, as Paul Star has demonstrated, it is clearly evident considerably earlier in Otago, beginning in the 1860s and flourishing in the 1870s.[323] The reports of one *Otago Witness* agricultural correspondent provide a telling example. In 1873 he wrote, 'The grass crop is making encroachments on the bush every year. A short time longer and there will be no bush land in this district.' The next year he again reported that 'bush is fast disappearing, and anon will be a thing of the past'.[324] In 1875, however, he had this to say:

> *It is to be regretted that this magnificent forest which clad each spur and gully of the Peninsula is fast disappearing. If the work of destruction goes on at the present rate, in not many years hence few and faint traces of our indigenous vegetation, as far as the Peninsula is concerned, will exist. While no one will deny the necessity of the ground being cleared, many will deplore that the scene once so picturesque is being so unthinkingly marred, and even proprietors themselves may yet see and acknowledge that, even for personal benefit, its process of extermination has been all too complete.*[325]

Several of the city's leading citizens deplored the marring of the picturesque view. As we have seen, Peter Thomson had misgivings about the loss of forest; so too did Dunedin politician and naturalist Alexander Bathgate. In 1874 he reflected that clearings on the Peninsula 'are already too large and numerous for the beauty of the scene, but as the settlers on the sunny slopes of the "Peninsula" doubtless study more the growth of early potatoes than aesthetics, Dunedin must submit to lose in time a little of its loveliness. But it will only be a little, for man the destroyer cannot change the outline of the hills, nor wholly rob their sides of verdure.'[326]

The seeds of state intervention to preserve native forests germinated in such views. However, the line that could not be crossed is equally evident: proprietors had to be persuaded to preserve forest, and the only argument seen to have any force was to appeal to the landholder's 'personal benefit'. Various writers pointed out that there was little to be gained in clearing bush from land unsuitable for farming, and suggested that unless more attention was paid to planting trees, farmers would soon find themselves short of timber for shelter and fuel.[327]

Another factor that contributed to appreciation for indigenous flora and fauna was that the wholehearted affection for the familiar biota of 'Home' fell away. Experiences with rabbits, thistles, gorse and other problematic introductions qualified attachment to even the most emblematic exotic flora and fauna. The Otago Acclimatisation Society had released rabbits between 1866 and 1868, but by 1870, as angry letters in the press condemned them for doing so, chairman W.D. Murison felt compelled to deny the charges and demanded compensation, pointing out that the society required public sympathy and support.[328]

In 1868 the early New Zealand historian A.S. Thomson wrote, 'Every man loves the spot of ground he reclaims from the wilderness better than the place of his birth, and consequently the moral tie which binds the emigrant's heart to his native soil is annually weakened.'[329] By 1880 over half the Peninsula's settlers had either been born on the land or had grown up there. This was the only home they knew, and the only place they could love. As they aged, settlers could reflect on the changes they had witnessed, and desired to see some wilderness yet unclaimed.[330] There was perhaps more time for leisure, and a large proportion of the population now lived in urban Dunedin and only ventured to the Peninsula as visitors or holidaymakers.[331] For them, the Peninsula's forests and wildlife were key components of a landscape increasingly viewed for pleasure, not profit.

However, the degree of concern for the indigenous environment should not be exaggerated. Literate observers with the luxury of time to ponder the meanings of environmental change were few and far between. Quite why native animals, in particular, were disappearing was a much-debated question, but most explanations favoured inexorable laws of nature over the effects of human behaviour.

Some thought native species were senescent 'sport' species that were dying out naturally; others blamed climate change, disease or predation. Many believed that inferior native species, Māori included, were doomed to give way before civilisation. This doctrine of 'displacement' was advanced by Darwin, and many followed him in arguing that European species were superior competitors that evicted natives

CHAPTER 7: THE AXE AND THE LUCIFER MATCH

Light-mantled sooty albatross. These birds are rare visitors to the New Zealand mainland; these two were 'collected' at Taiaroa Head and purchased in 1899 as stuffed specimens by the Otago Museum. Otago Museum: AVO81-AVO82

when brought into competition with them.[332] As Paul Star points out, none of these explanations drew a link between declines in indigenous biota and loss of habitat.[333] There was no overarching concept of the 'environment' or of 'ecosystems' to guide scientific thought.[334]

The result was that even when regret was expressed at the passing of native species, it was accepted, in Walter Buller's words, as 'one of the inscrutable laws of Nature'.[335] If rare survivors were discovered, as in 1869 when 'stormy petrels' were found on rocks off Tomahawk, the *Otago Witness*'s plea was not that they be protected, but that some should be 'secured' – that is, shot and stuffed – for posterity in the museum.[336]

The settlers were keen to scrutinise nature in order to decipher her laws. The spread of notions concerning the 'balance of Nature' were significant in this respect. Some gradually recognised that people had caused pest problems.[337] Humanity, argued Canterbury settler-scientist R.M. Fereday, 'in his blindness, is ever breaking, or throwing out of gear, some wheel of the great cosmical machine, and disorder necessarily follows'.[338] Fereday, an entomologist, illustrated his point with reference to huge increases in pest insects in recent years, something he attributed to the loss of native insectivores and the spread of crops. This scientist's proposal, so common among his successors, was to engineer solutions to problems associated with British settlement by bringing still more of Britain to bear; he argued for the careful introduction of British insectivorous birds and predatory insects.[339]

Ideas of a balance of nature provided a new framework for considering the problems caused by settlement. They provoked a reassessment rather than a rejection of acclimatisation; the very consequences of early thoughtless introductions justified more importations. The *Dunedin Morning Herald* supported the acclimatisation society bringing in more birds, saying the 'economy of Nature must be preserved'. The *Herald* denied that 'we are actually interfering with this economy by introducing the birds of another clime'; while 'New Zealand was a waste wilderness, the Native birds probably sufficed to keep the balance true. But no sooner did settlement begin than the balance was destroyed.'[340]

The opinion that the indigenous biota was too weak and ineffectual to compete with the spread of civilization remained pervasive. As one character mused in John Turnbull Thomson's *Rambles with a Philosopher*: 'May we not anticipate that the brown tussock will succumb to the white clover, and the flax to the gorse and broom – that the tui will give place to the sparrow, the kakapo to the partridge? And why should we sigh at these changes since they are the inevitable conditions of life and progress?'[341]

The *Otago Witness* took the view that nothing was wholly bad; even the rabbit could be called 'God's pioneer of settlement'. Readers were comforted with the prediction that '[y]oung communities take these diseases as children take the measles, and get through all right after a feverish period and a drastic purge or two'.[342] (The choice of measles was unfortunate, given Otago's history with the disease.) But during the boom years, rapid progress underpinned faith that New Zealand's destiny was to recreate or even better British civilisation, and so in the process inevitably extinguish the indigenous. However, as we shall see in the final chapter, changing economic and environmental conditions in the 1880s and 1890s shook the settlers' faith in their preordained path.

Andersons Bay.
Hocken Collections, Uare Taoka o Hākena, University of Otago:
Box-220-001 S07-135e

CHAPTER 8: 'THE WHOLE FACE OF NATURE IS ALTERED': 1881–1900

If a Rip Van Winkle among naturalists could arise here, one who had known the natural conditions in 1849, and if he could be dropped down in Dunedin now, he would be astounded at the changes which had taken place during the interval in the aspect of Nature. A very large proportion of the indigenous flora and fauna has disappeared. The ferns and other delicate plants which formerly filled up the bush are nearly all gone, dried up and exterminated. The big trees have disappeared long ago. The undergrowth consists very largely of European plants, the birds are those of the old land, the whole face of Nature is altered.

– G.M. THOMSON, 'NOTES BY THE WAYSIDE' 1899[1]

An age of improvement?

In 1901 it was said of George Malcolm Thomson that 'he knew his Dunedin like a book'.[2] Thomson, a Scot, had lived in Dunedin since 1871 and become one of New Zealand's leading natural scientists and historians of environmental change. Few knew better than he the extent to which 'the whole face of Nature had been altered' by 50 years of British settlement.

Thomson had a particular fondness for the Otago Peninsula. In 1900 he reflected on some of the changes he had observed around Tomahawk Lagoon – 'a prettily situated sheet of water' when first he knew it, 'surrounded at its upper end, with bush and scrub ... fed by more than one perennial stream of clear water'. He had gone there to gather specimens of ferns and insects, 'not now to be got without rambling much further afield'. He lamented, 'the destruction of the bush has dried up the streams, and the poaching of cattle round its margins has converted part of the lake into a boggy swamp'. Settlement had scarred the place. Thomson called on the proprietors of the lands for change: 'Now that the age of destruction has passed, an era of improvement might well be inaugurated by the surrounding proprietors, and with a little care and some judicious planting, the spot might again be transformed into a place of beauty.'[3]

For 50 years the settlers around the lagoon had struggled to improve their properties. Thomson questioned the way in which they had so single-mindedly approached the task of hacking their farms from the wilderness, and characterised their labour as a long age of destruction. In his view, the era of improvement on the Peninsula had yet to begin. He suggested introducing white and yellow water lilies, the yellow flag iris and the yellow buttercup (*Ranunculus lingua*), together with 'many pretty marsh plants of temperate regions'. He envisaged the lagoon as a garden where a combination of indigenous and exotic plants would thrive and make the place beautiful. It was a plea to better tend to the ecology of the place; as a habitat on the boundary between fresh and salt water, it was, he said, 'an extremely rich repository of living organisms'.

Thomson's vision was that of a man who had learned to be devoted to the health and diversity of the life of this land. This concluding chapter explores the evolving dynamic expressed in his musings – the increasing tension between the economic imperatives faced by individual landowners, and the desire to protect the Peninsula environment. In doing so, it takes the survey of economic, environmental and cultural change on the Peninsula to the close of the nineteenth century. It contrasts the settlers' consolidation of progressive and intensive dairy farming against the ongoing struggles of the Māori community at Ōtākou.

The Otago Peninsula transformed: One large dairy farm

In 1887 a resident recently arrived at Portobello described the Peninsula's economy. Its industries, he noted, were:

> ... principally of the bucolic type. The splendid grass produces excellent beef, and nearly all the settlers follow dairy farming. Whether it pays or not I am not in a position to determine; but at present I cannot help hearing universal grumbling at the low prices of products. Splendid butter is sent from here to town and brings from 4½d per lb upwards. When I think of the extraordinary prices charged up country there seems to be a screw loose somewhere; so that the middlemen make a nice profit by fleecing at both ends. Bacon, potatoes, oats, &c. which are usually looked for in an agricultural district, are, I am informed, mostly imported from Dunedin. If this is true, wholly or in part, I may be excused for wondering what the Peninsula farmers are about. There is nothing in the soil or climate inimical to the growth of cereals or vegetables. Why they are not more extensively cultivated, I suppose, can only be excused on the score of difficulty. The country is, to put it mildly, rough and timbered.[4]

What *were* the Otago Peninsula farmers about? As this bemused correspondent reveals, Peninsula farmers now ran highly specialised enterprises producing only a few key products for market. The vast majority were dairy farmers, as shown in the figure below.[5]

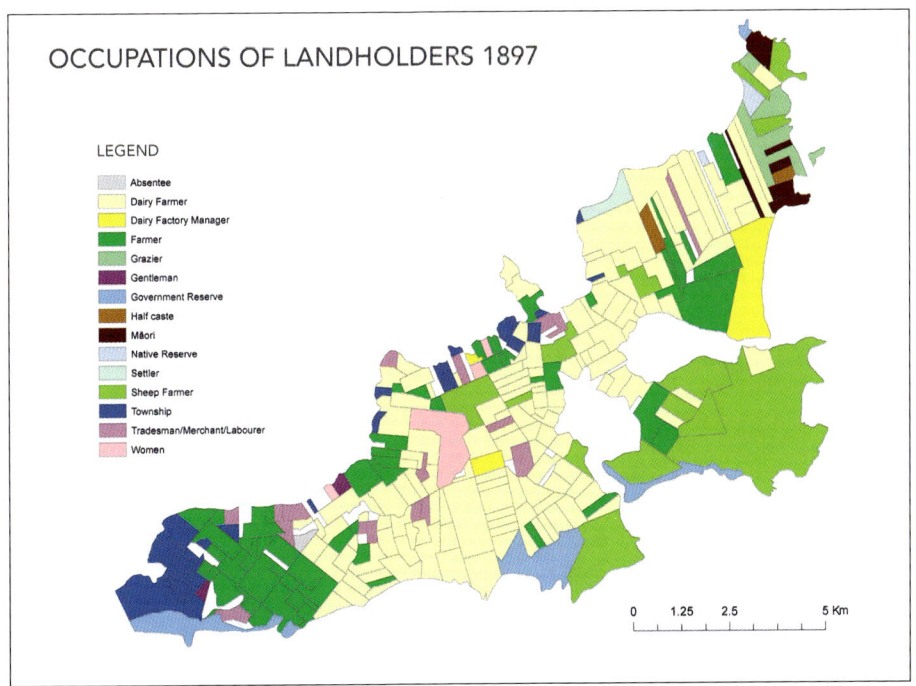

The occupation of each of the Peninsula's significant landholders, 1897. Dairy farming is dominant through the southern and central Peninsula. Map made by the author

Beginning in 1897 the newly established government Valuation Department recorded a wealth of information about the state of the Peninsula in the district valuation rolls. Valuation officers visited each Peninsula property and recorded the state of each title. They included data on the owner, occupier, occupation, acreage and improved and unimproved value, and the type, age, material and condition of buildings and fences; the area, age and condition of grass and crops; and the extent of ploughable land, bush, swamp, sand and stony land. The rolls provide a remarkably complete picture of the Peninsula's economy and environment at the turn of the century.

Some of the occupational categories – such as 'women', 'Maori', 'half caste', 'gentleman' and various tradesmen – tell us nothing about how the land was being used, though they do suggest the prejudices of the age. Larnach's large dairy farm and estate above Broad Bay is among the few holdings occupied by 'women', for Larnach, who would commit suicide in 1898, had already entrusted his property to his wife to avert its seizure in the event of bankruptcy.[6]

Dairy farms had a byre and a dairy – unless they were close enough to Dunedin to supply town milk, in which case only a byre was necessary. That the farmers in Andersons Bay and Tomahawk were running milking cows is confirmed by the distribution of farm buildings shown in the map of dairy farm outbuildings extant

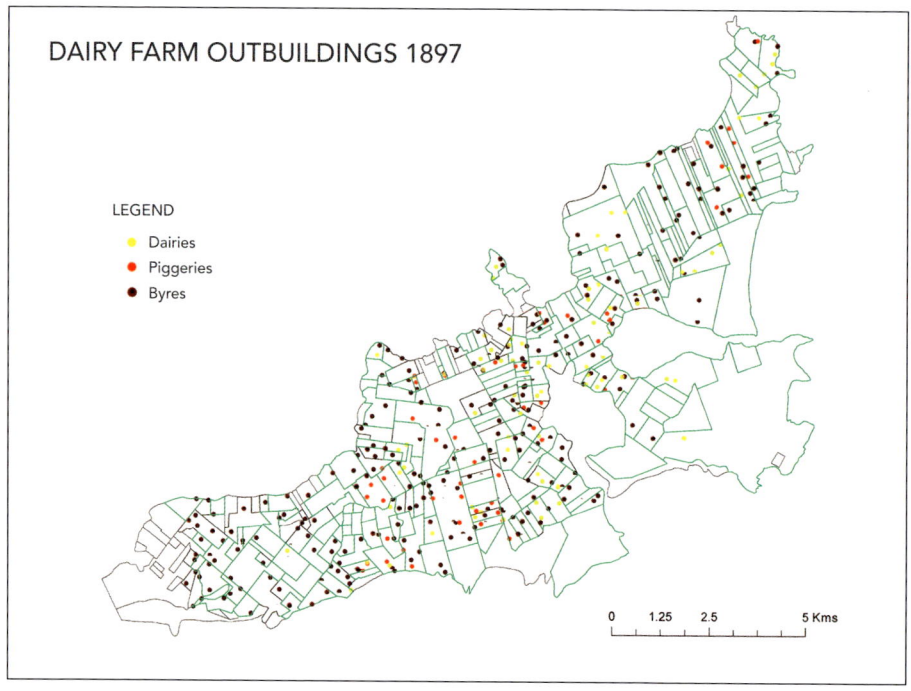

The distribution of dairy farm outbuildings demonstrates the relationship to town milk supply. Farms close enough to Dunedin to supply town milk had a byre but no dairy. Map made by the author

The Dickson brothers' station, Belmont. The Dickson brothers had the largest Peninsula holding. They farmed sheep and cattle around Hoopers Inlet and Cape Saunders, and operated a small timber mill. Hardwicke Knight Collection, courtesy of Ian Smith

in 1897 (see page 252), in which byres and piggeries can be seen scattered across Andersons Bay and Tomahawk.

Other than the harbourside townships and a few government reserves, the Peninsula was now a mosaic of dairy and sheep farms. Dairy farming was virtually the sole activity in the south and on the harbour side of the Peninsula as far as Akapātiki Flat. On the isolated and exposed outer coast around Sandymount, on Okia Flat, Cape Saunders and at Taiaroa Head, a small number of sheep farmers and graziers had established larger landholdings. A few of these, notably the Dickson brothers' station on Cape Saunders, also ran fat cattle.[7] On this difficult country, stock could only be carried at densities of around one sheep per acre.

The success of the first shipment of frozen meat for England on the *Dunedin* in 1882 had given sheep farming on the Peninsula some impetus.[8] Twelve farmers altogether ran 4654 sheep in 1881, compared to 1898, when 16 farmers ran flocks totalling 9227 sheep.[9] The following year sheep numbers crashed to 4007, and to 1496 in 1901.[10] This volatility probably reflects the fact that, despite the enthusiasm generated by the export of frozen meat, most farmers could make considerably more money from their dairy products. Some had kept a few sheep to tide them over the poor dairy prices of the 1880s and 1890s,[11] but when prices recovered many sold off their flocks, and by 1900 only 10 farmers carried sheep.[12]

Cattle were always more economically and environmentally significant on the Peninsula in the nineteenth century. The number of cattle – 4904 in 1881 – steadily increased to 6995 in 1900.[13] Over half of these were cows specifically bred for dairying. Ayrshire strains still predominated, but Alderney, Shorthorn and Jersey stock became more numerous.[14] Few farmers kept any steers, save for those, like the Dickson and Ryan families, who ran beef cattle on poorer, steeper country.[15]

By 1900 the Peninsula had the highest ratio of cattle to other stock of any area in Otago.[16] An astonishing 90 per cent of the Peninsula's 200-odd farmers were dairymen, and many owners of small properties also had a house cow or two. Peninsula farmers had become single-mindedly devoted to milk production and were highly specialised producers of milk, butter and sometimes cheese.

The reason for this specialised focus is largely explained by factors cited by the Portobello correspondent: the generally poor prices for farm produce over the decades of the long depression, the difficulties in transport, and the roughness of the country. All of these narrowed farmers' options, so that monocultures for market became the economic norm.

As a result the Peninsula environment was subject to the heavy ecological footprint of dairy cows, the needs and habits of which determined what plants were grown and when, what resources were sought, and how, why and where settlers permitted the indigenous biota to remain. Grass and fodder crops dominated the fields, while small bush remnants were typically retained to provide cattle with supplementary winter feed and shelter, timber to fence them in, and firewood.

Dairying is a particularly intensive form of farming, however, and the Otago Peninsula with its steep slopes and erosion-prone clay soils is not well suited to running cattle. But while small farmers on the Otago Peninsula were able to meet the daily demand for fresh dairy produce from Dunedin, market forces largely controlled farming practices.

The growing dominance of dairying occurred against a backdrop of the severe and prolonged national economic depression that lasted for 20 years from 1878 to 1896. The depression was triggered in 1878 by the collapse of the Bank of Glasgow, which had invested heavily in New Zealand. This sparked a credit crisis, and because international prices for agricultural products remained very low, the colony struggled to trade its way clear.[17] In New Zealand the depression's effects were worse in the south than the north, but the Peninsula dairy farmers were buffered somewhat because they served the substantial Dunedin market. Even when the Dunedin market itself stagnated – between 1875 and 1885 Dunedin's population increased by only 1762 people – the Peninsula's farmers were still able to stay afloat by selling dairy produce; as a result, most survived.

The Peninsula supplied the bulk of Dunedin's potatoes, and early varieties were particularly sought after.[18] About 70 farmers in all, around Highcliff and Sandymount, grew most of these.[19] Obtaining a satisfactory price was a primary problem and led to complaints about being forced to deal with 'middlemen' – the grocers and shopkeepers who marketed produce to the public. In 1890 these farmers formed the Peninsula Farmers Association, in an effort to develop a more certain market and a guaranteed minimum price. The association seems to have failed quickly, however.[20]

In 1882 a correspondent who had noted several farmers around Hoopers Inlet growing peaches and other stonefruit – 'going in heavy as orchardists' – predicted that the Peninsula would become 'one of our largest fruit-producing districts'.[21] He was wrong: during the 1880s both fruit growing and market gardening fell away markedly. In 1867 settlers had devoted 147 acres (59ha) to these pursuits; this had fallen to 110 acres (44ha) by 1890, and did not recover. Those orchards that remained were described as 'prolific in apples, pears, peaches, plums, and berries of all kinds', while vegetable gardens 'grew abundantly', producing specimens of 'a terrific size'.[22] A lack of demand, however, meant that 'year by year, [farmers] have become more indifferent to cultivating fruit and vegetables in large quantities'.[23] Excess fruit was often turned into wine, but 'being of Colonial manufacture there is no demand, and [it] is only used for home consumption'.[24]

Market gardening was the only other significant land use over this period, and was centred on Andersons Bay and, to a lesser extent, Portobello – the two key points of access to the Dunedin and Port Chalmers markets. The Chinese dominated market gardening in Andersons Bay and grew a wide range of produce: cauliflowers, red and white cabbages, celery, onions, parsnips, turnips, leeks, lettuces, radishes, peas, beans and herbs. Their success was reportedly due to their choice of flat land, their liberal use of horse manure (gathered for free from city stables), large amounts of labour (including continuous 'stirring' of the soil), extensive watering, and careful weeding.[25] The *Otago Witness* admitted that the European settlers had something to learn from the Chinese, and encouraged Europeans to copy their techniques, with the addition of 'ploughs, windmills, and other improved contrivances' to save labour.[26] When Chinese gardeners tried to establish 'a footing on this stronghold of European labour' further along the Peninsula, they were 'hunted off'.[27] In 1881 it was reported that 'for the first time in Portobello the Chinamen have succeeded in establishing themselves here. A number of them are being employed in clearing bush in the Native reserve, Cape Saunders.'[28]

The large Chinese market gardens that developed on the southern headlands of Andersons Bay are shown on the left of surveyor William Thompson Neill's 1901 mapping of the Peninsula, completed as part of a survey of Dunedin and its surrounds 'for the Intelligence Office' (see next page). Neill was later surveyor-general and his work was 'most minutely and carefully done': his maps, at a scale of 10 chains to the inch (roughly 80m to the centimetre), display the Peninsula in extraordinary detail. Each farm building is marked, as are fences, fields and patches of forest.[29] This map illustrates the mingling of suburban and rural development that had accompanied the intensification of farming on the Peninsula, and the growth of Dunedin. Notable

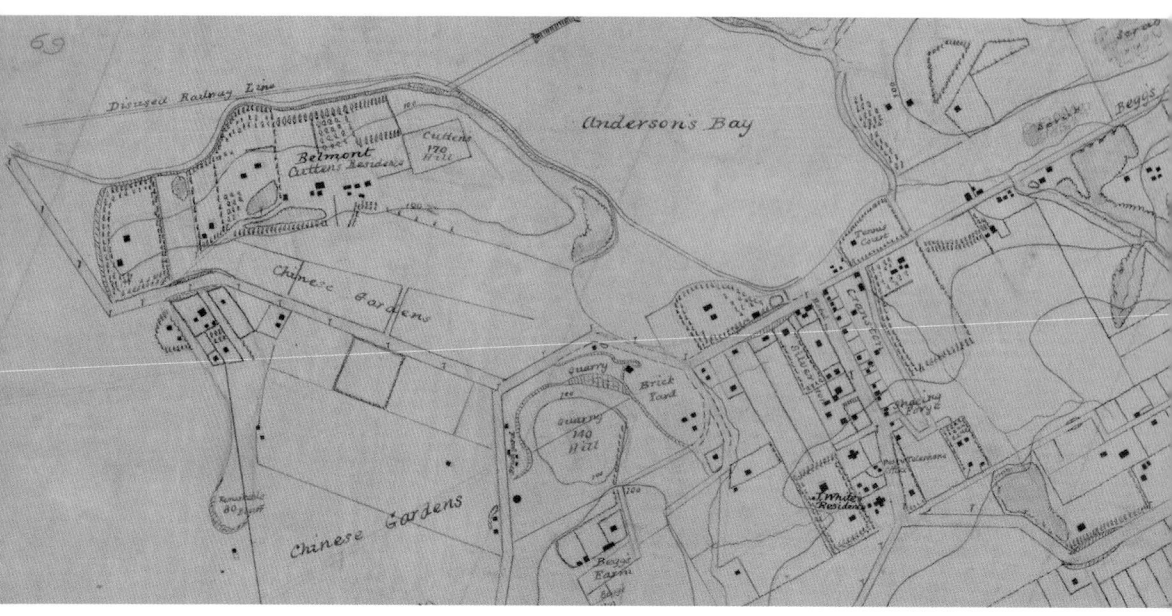

Above: *W.T. Neill's map of the Andersons Bay area: 'Sheet No. 14: Military topographical survey: Andersons Bay and part of Otago Peninsula dist' (detail).* Archives New Zealand (Dunedin): DAHG 23774 D591 644/c 14 R23188979

CHAPTER 8: 'THE WHOLE FACE OF NATURE IS ALTERED'

ABOVE: *W.T. Neill's map of Portobello: 'Sheet No. 18: Military topographical plan: Block II Otago Peninsula and Upper Harbour East Dist' (detail).* Archives New Zealand (Dunedin): DAHG 23771 D591 644/c 14 R22756747

ABOVE: *A panorama of Portobello, c. 1900. There are few buildings, but farmers have succeeded in turning the hillsides into clean paddocks.* Hocken Collections, Uare Taoka o Hākena, University of Otago: S07-136c

features include the causeway with its moveable bridge across Andersons Bay; the brickyards; the small patches of bush; the large residences such as Cutten's, White's and Scobie Mackenzie's; and the low housing density in the subdivisions of Oaklands, Shiel Hill, Craigleith, Vauxhall, Grants Braes and Waverley. By 1900 Andersons Bay had become one of the city's more fashionable outlying suburbs and was home to a high proportion of professional people and businessmen.[30] The richest of these maintained large residences with substantial grounds, such as Cutten's residence on the southern headland above the bay.

Other than Andersons Bay, only Portobello – which enjoyed reasonably regular ferry services – developed at all over these 20 years. As shown in Neill's map, however, Portobello was still no more than a small village, with a school, church, store and stables servicing the scattering of surrounding dairy farms.

Throughout the Peninsula only small patches of housing broke up the rural character of the landscape. Population growth in the rural areas had stagnated: in 1881 the Peninsula population was 2425; it peaked in the 1890s at 2701 and fell to 2561 by the turn of the century.[31] The speculative townships of the 1870s had stalled in the face of poor access: although transport costs continued to fall elsewhere as the regional rail network flourished, on the Peninsula there had been no major improvements to land transport links with the city.

Peninsula residents continued to push for change. A bridge across the harbour, linking Waverley to Jetty Street in Dunedin, was mooted in 1881 and remained under consideration for much of the decade, a bill having passed through parliament specifically to enable finance to be raised for it. The project was never begun, however: a prohibitively expensive exercise in a depression, it would have been of little benefit to the majority of the Peninsula's inhabitants.

The first telephone was installed in Andersons Bay in 1885, saving 'many weary trudges into town for the doctor',[32] but at the turn of the century, land transport patterns remained much as they had been in 1882, when a correspondent complained, 'The Peninsula railway has come to grief, the tramway hangs fire, the ferry-boat is laid up, and the bridge threatens a toll, so that the old devious path can alone be followed.'[33] As it happens, a toll *was* instituted on the Andersons Bay causeway in 1887. Its charges indicate the sort of traffic then current along the Peninsula: wheeled traffic 3d, horses 2d, cattle drive ½d per head, sheep, goats or pigs 3d per 20 animals, and 5 shillings for every vehicle 'propelled along the road by steam or light power including bicycles and tricycles'. This last peculiarity stemmed from a fear that cyclists would frighten horses.[34]

Two ferries plied the harbourside route during the 1880s – the *Sappho* (later renamed the *Edina*) and the *Kate* – but these struggled to provide more than an intermittent service.[35] More regular and dependable services resumed when ferries that had been brought in to serve the 1889 Dunedin and South Seas Exhibition were put into service.

G.P. Wilson, 'The survey districts of North Harbour and Blueskin, Lower Harbour West, North East Valley, Upper Harbour West, Tomahawk, Sawyers Bay, Andersons Bay, Portobello Bay, Otago Peninsula and Upper Harbour East'. The cadastre on the settlers' portion has not changed from that of 1878, but can now be contrasted with that of the Māori portion of the Peninsula, where the coastal road comes to an abrupt halt. Several large areas designated as suburban subdivisions – including much of Tomahawk, around Hoopers Inlet and the southern margins of Papanui Inlet – have instead become farms. Māori had not just leased most of their land but sold much of it too, especially around Papanui. Archives New Zealand (Wellington): R19708208 ACGT 18718 LSDrawer 43/ 7/20

The two important ones were the *Onslow* and the *Tarewai*. The *Onslow* was bought by David Seaton who, as mentioned earlier, already ran horse coaches between Dunedin and Portobello; throughout the 1890s he ran a regular and reliable daily ferry service on the Dunedin–Macandrew Bay–Broad Bay–Portobello line through the week, and weekend excursions to the Peninsula for Dunedin residents.[36] Over this decade, the locally built *Tarewai* linked Port Chalmers to Portobello, allowing children from the Peninsula to attend the Port Chalmers District High School and bringing doctors across from Port Chalmers to attend patients or deliver babies.[37]

The stagnating Peninsula population also reflected the rationalisation of landholdings, as many of the less-economic farms of fewer than 50 acres (20ha) were amalgamated into medium-sized dairy farms and larger sheep runs. Farmers sometimes bought out their neighbours, but more often expanded their holdings by leasing land.

The capacity for farmers to buy or lease Māori land or land designated 'suburban' was one reason why the farmed areas of the Peninsula expanded considerably, despite the difficult times. In 1880 about a third of the Peninsula – 3082 of 9719ha – was farmed.[38] Of this, 2313ha were planted by simply broadcasting grass seed on burnt-over ground, 410 ha were ploughed and sown with grass, and 359ha were in crops.

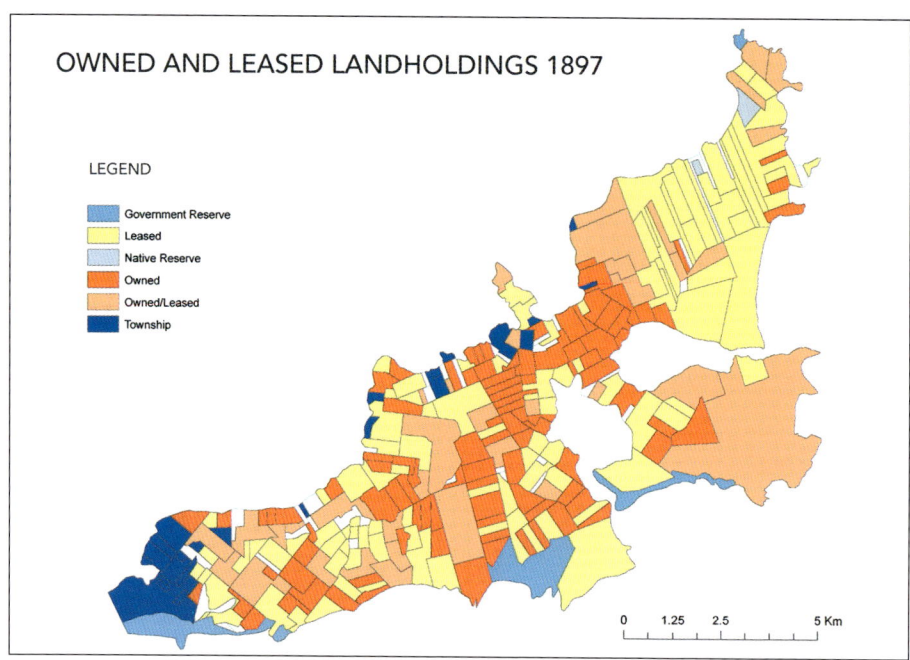

The Peninsula's landholdings in 1897 comprised a mix of owned and leased property, with many farmers owning core land and leasing subsidiary areas. Map made by the author

By the close of the century the extent of farmed land had doubled and 6326ha were in production. This comprised 4492ha of unploughed grassland, 1179ha of ploughed grassland and 655ha in crops.

Most settlers in the more established farming regions had now cleared the bulk of their land. Substantial patches of bush and tussock remained only in isolated or newly settled areas, such as Sandymount and Cape Saunders, where there were also stretches of sand, scrub and swamp that were essentially useless for agricultural or pastoral purposes.

Farmers cleared more trees during the deepening depression in the early 1880s, since burning forest and broadcasting grass seed in the ash-enriched virgin soil was a quick way to generate cash.[39] By the 1890s most accessible bush had been removed and, as economic conditions slowly improved, farmers focused on intensifying production. The ratio of ploughed to unploughed land increased and soon hit its effective limit:[40] by 1904 ploughed land totalled 2370ha (1795ha of ploughed pasture and 575ha of crops).[41]

Early visions for the Peninsula were of a mosaic of crops, grazing fields, orchards and gardens, but most properties now had well over four-fifths of their land sown in European grasses. Tussock and low scrublands remained only in outlying areas such as Okia and Akapātiki flats.

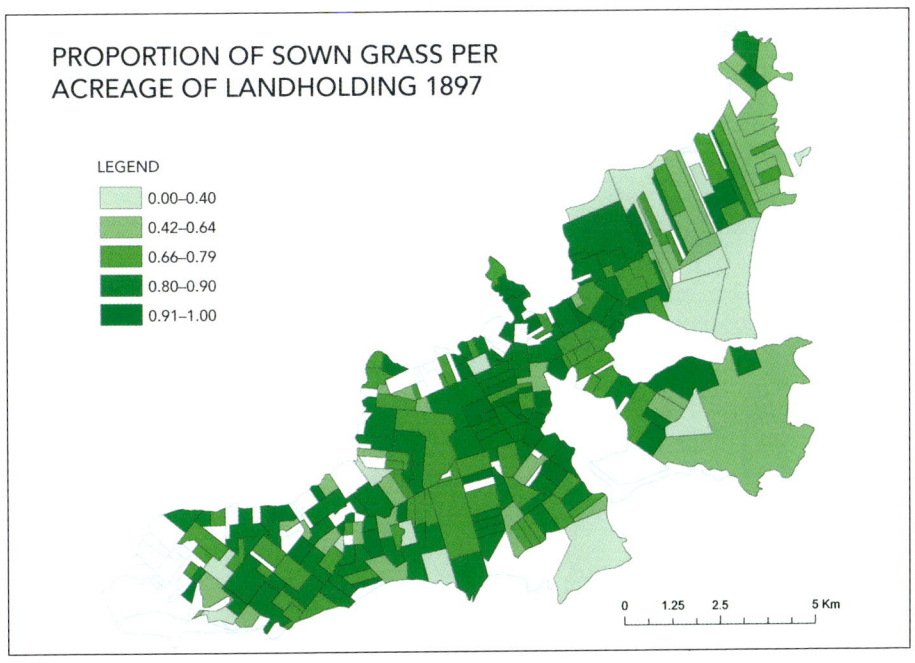

Ryegrass was preferred, with cocksfoot favoured on rougher ground. Map made by the author

Sandymount creamery, c. 1900. Sited at the heart of the dairying district, this was the first and largest of the Peninsula's creameries. Otago Peninsula Museum: OPM 86 139/1 Neg F. 765/9

Otago Peninsula dairy farmers pioneered the cooperative systems that still dominate the industry today and, as the dairying economy became established and matured, developed new modes of production and distribution. Several farmers were early shareholders in the Taieri and Peninsula Milk Supply Company, established in 1884 to streamline milk distribution to Dunedin.[42] More milk soon flowed into Dunedin than the city could ever consume, and in 1889 the company installed butter- and cheese-making equipment to cope with the excess.[43] The Pukehiki cheese factory had already changed to butter-making in 1885, though it was not successful and had ceased operations by the early 1890s.[44] The New Zealand Dairy Supply Company also operated in the area between 1891 and 1896, collecting 300–400 gallons (1300–1800 litres) of milk morning and evening from as far away as the heads;[45] and for a brief period in the late 1880s, milk was sent across the harbour from Portobello to the short-lived Roseville Dairy Company factory in Sawyers Bay.[46]

By the 1890s, despite low profits, most Peninsula farmers had acquired shares in the Taieri and Peninsula company, which repaid their faith in the last years of the nineteenth century by rapidly becoming the mainstay of the Otago dairy industry under the management of Walter Riddell.[47] The company regularly returned dividends of 8 per cent to its shareholders and paid consistent prices for milk (in 1899 it paid 3–4¾d per gallon for milk used for butter, and 4½–6¾d per gallon for town-supply milk).[48]

During the 1890s the company developed a network of creameries to which farmers took their milk each morning to be separated; the cream was then made into butter at the central factory in Dunedin. As a result, farmers gained higher and more predictable prices, and consumers a more consistent product. By 1897 four such creameries operated on the Peninsula: at Sandymount, Granton (a putative township near Portobello), Papanui Inlet and Ōtākou. Another opened in Highcliff in 1903. The Sandymount creamery opened first in 1893; it was supplied by up to 30 farmers and processed as much as 9000 litres of milk daily.[49]

The creameries provided a focal point where farmers, who transported their morning milk there by buggy, met and discussed their trials and fortunes. A sense of shared endeavour was generated – each farmer's success relied on the success of his neighbours, for only communal good fortune would keep the creamery open. Magda Wallscott recalled the days of the Ōtākou creamery: 'gossip and the day's news was exchanged … and it was quite a feature of the day for the women folk when Dad came back with all the news'.[50]

Ōtākou: A world apart?

Ōtākou Māori had lived among Europeans since the early 1830s. They had never been entirely alone at the end of the harbour. Resident whalers-turned-settlers had been joined by the men of the Pilot Station, then in 1864 by the lighthouse keepers at Taiaroa Head, and from 1885 by the men stationed at the barracks of Fort Taiaroa, founded in the Russian scare. By the 1890s, Hardwicke Knight suggested, a 'unique community' of over 100 people had formed 'at the Heads'.[51]

Ōtākou Māori were not well integrated into the settler economy. They were isolated at the mouth of the harbour, and suffered most from the lack of efficient communications. The road boards were disinclined to help them since Māori did not pay rates, and consequently there was almost no roading inside the reserve. Ferry services were occasional and mostly consisted of excursions by voyeuristic Dunedin residents, who were often disappointed not to find 'real' Māori. In 1897 a petition 'signed by nearly everyone in the district' asked the government to complete the road from Ōtākou to Portobello to 'greatly improve the means of communication between Dunedin and the Kaik'.[52]

Although Ōtākou Māori leaders such as H.K. Taiaroa were thoroughly involved in the colonial world, the structures connecting the community to the settler economy were weak, and the long depression proved a significant setback. Tame Parata summed up the situation in 1890, telling Alexander Mackay's Royal Commission into the Middle

Island Native Land Question: 'The people cannot live respectably and comfortably. Most of them are always in debt. Whatever they earn in the season goes to pay their creditors and in the wintertime they depend on the few potatoes and things they grow.'[53]

Mackay noted that a casual observer passing through settlements such as Ōtākou, on seeing 'the appearance of the people and the neat looking houses' might conclude that the people were thriving. In fact, 'in spite of their poverty they never relax their efforts to clothe and feed themselves like their European neighbours. The privations they are often forced to undergo in order to do this none but those who live amongst them can have any idea of.'[54] He went on to say that 'in building themselves a house they frequently build themselves out of a home'.[55] Mackay's observations might be borne in mind when examining the objects pictured in Mrs Karetai's house (see photograph opposite), which might have been found in any colonial settler dwelling.

Matters were perhaps at their worst among Ōtākou Māori in 1891, when collectively they cultivated less than five acres (2ha) and kept few animals.[56] It was not for want of effort. That year it was reported that 'Many of the young people, who earn money, spend it unsuccessfully in trying to cultivate and improve their land.'[57] The Kāi Tahu communities also raised large sums to support the tribe's claims against the state, in particular the claim to retain their mahika kai in the Kemp Purchase.

Access to mahika kai had been largely foreclosed and, according to Bill Dacker, even kai moana was now 'only a welcome addition to the diet of a few of the aged and indigent'.[58] Settlers shut Māori out of freshwater fisheries on the Taieri and Waitaki rivers to protect trout fishing; landowners accused Māori of trespassing on their lands. As Rawiri Te Maire told the commission: 'If they went fishing they were threatened to be put in jail, and if they went catching birds they were turned off.'[59]

Otago Māori continued to assert their rights to their former sea fisheries. In 1896, for example, H.K. Taiaroa was asked to seek that the law provide for Europeans to be excluded from Māori hāpuku and other fishing grounds because they had 'been used as such from a long time back'.[60] Similarly, in 1903, Tame Parata told parliament that 'along the coast of Otago' ancestral fishing grounds had been 'overrun and made use of by everybody, including Europeans in recent years'. He now asked that 'these reefs should be to some extent protected for the benefit of the Maoris'.[61]

At this point technology began to transform fishing. Curing facilities at Port Chalmers now provided a market for as much fish as could be caught. According to H.O. Bowman, by 1900 'Otago possessed thirteen of the twenty-eight fish curing works in New Zealand, and most of them were about Port Chalmers'.[62] This helped stimulate the advent of sustained trawling in larger boats, and the use of benzene-powered engines made travel beyond the harbour faster and more reliable.[63]

By the turn of the century settler fishermen had discovered the richest fishing grounds north and south of Otago heads, such as the North Reef, Two Lights and Hydra Rock. The location of these had long been a secret guarded by Māori hāpuku

CHAPTER 8: 'THE WHOLE FACE OF NATURE IS ALTERED'

Inside Mrs Karetai's house.

Photograph by John Halliday Scott. Hocken Collections, Uare Taoka o Hākena, University of Otago: Album 052, P2008-066-009b; S14-031e

fishermen, who visited reefs such as Two Lights, 19 kilometres offshore, by triangulating their position using landmarks on shore.[64] Taiaroa's correspondent in 1896 considered that these landmarks came 'within the meaning of the expression "mahinga kai" (food producing places) used in the Ngai Tahu Deed'.[65] According to David Graham, once the settlers discovered the reefs, they were rapidly overfished.[66] Otago Māori evidently considered that they had been elbowed out of the commercial fishery and their rights usurped; certainly, they no longer participated significantly in commercial fishing. In 1893 only two Māori fishermen made a living from flounder fishing at Papanui Inlet.[67]

Teone Ratara described the situation at Ōtākou to Alexander Mackay's commission, in fairly bleak terms:

Teone Ratara had a large family, and only 10 acres [4ha] of ground to support them on. He had very bad health, and was unable to work. The 10 acres of half-caste land was all he had, and that was situated in an out-of-the-way place where he could not cultivate it. No Government relief has been received in aid of the poor and indigent people. These people have been supported by their relatives, who could ill afford to do so ... No person had sufficient land to maintain himself and his family. Several persons were unprovided for, and had to obtain work to get a living. In fact, everyone had to seek employment during the shearing and harvest seasons to procure money to purchase food and clothing with, as the land did not support them; and sometimes work was not obtainable.[68]

The situation did improve somewhat. In 1896 Māori cultivated 37 acres (15ha), and had sown 507 acres (205ha) of grass. They had 26 sheep, 282 cattle and 44 pigs. Soon after the creamery opened in 1897, the *Otago Witness* reported that 'farmers are beginning to find the benefit of the creamery in their midst after having to drag their milk four miles along a soft beach'.[69] Dairy farming continued to develop quickly: the creamery took in 1200 gallons (5455 litres) of milk every day during the peak of the 1899 season.[70] Its presence greatly reduced the cost of getting milk to market.

Much of the farming in the area was being done by settlers. The valuation rolls of 1897 state that Māori occupied only 518 of the more than 6000 acres (2428ha) they had retained in 1848.[71] Remaining land was leased and provided a limited income to pay for fencing and the expense of pursuing Māori land claims.[72]

Bill Dacker suggests that, generally, those without land tended to drift away from the community and their Māori heritage.[73] This was easier for those with Pākehā ancestry, for they were more readily accepted elsewhere. The Māori community certainly dwindled throughout the 1880s, reaching its nadir in 1891 when only 22 Māori were recorded as living on the Peninsula. By 1901 numbers had increased to 92, 87 of whom were of mixed ancestry.

Most settlers in New Zealand still believed that Māori were destined to disappear, if not by dying outright then through amalgamation with the European population.[74] This doctrine was not seriously disputed until a succession of census returns, beginning in the 1890s, clearly showed the Māori population increasing.[75] In Otago however, where Māori remained all but invisible to most Europeans, this belief lingered long into the twentieth century.[76]

The analogy between Māori and New Zealand's indigenous plants and animals had long been drawn to buttress beliefs in displacement. The settlers argued that even Māori themselves believed they would disappear as the native rat had before the European rat and – some went so far as to say – as the flax had before clover.[77] Attempting to maintain this last example ought to have exposed the absurdity of arguing that displacement was an inevitable law of nature. However, by the end of the nineteenth century, displacement was essentially a historical fact: the indigenous had been replaced by introduced species. But just as with Māori, the plants and animals of New Zealand did not simply melt away: they were forcibly replaced.

The Ōtākou creamery made dairying more viable on the isolated Māori land. Farmers used both sleds and carts to bring milk to the creamery. The sleds were needed to cross the swathes of sand that in many places made the use of wheeled conveyances impossible. Otago Peninsula Museum: OPM 87 99

An age of improvement? The environmental impacts of settlement, 1881–1900

Dairy cows now determined which plants the settlers grew and which survived in the bush. Mustelids and ship rats, on the other hand, reshaped the fauna. Tree-nesting birds, previously fairly safe from Norway rats, were easy prey for stoats and the arboreal ship rat, which came later. Populations of the larger colonial seabirds now also collapsed. The destruction of native birds was obvious, and most remarked on. Change was so rapid and so complete that it was impossible for settlers to escape the knowledge that, in the space of just 50 years, they had entirely altered almost every aspect of their surroundings.

In 1900 the Otago Peninsula environment was radically different from that which the Scots and English settlers encountered in 1848. Almost all the native species that had greeted the settlers had been eradicated in most areas. The indigenous trees, shrubs, ferns and even mosses and lichens were largely gone, replaced by the exotic flora that is familiar today: grasses and clovers, with a smattering of macrocarpa, pine, hawthorn and gum trees and numerous weeds. Most of the native birds were gone; many species had been eradicated, and almost all the survivors were reduced in number. The introduced stock, birds and mammalian predators dominated the vertebrate fauna. Even the insects were almost wholly different. From the soil up, the land had been remade in the settlers' image.

Only about 4000 of Peninsula County's 24,016 acres (9718ha) were not occupied farmland or sites of urban development. Of that, close to 3000 acres (1200ha) remained in bush and the remainder in tussock.[78] Almost 75 per cent of the Peninsula land area was devoted to European agriculture.[79] Bush clearance had not yet peaked – by 1915 only 938 acres (379ha) remained – but there were probably fewer trees on the Peninsula than there are today.[80]

Native biota was only retained in small, fragmented patches in environments that farmers struggled to use, such as sand, swamp, stony ground, estuarine salt marshes and wetlands, scrub and tussock. These remnant environments persisted almost exclusively on the Peninsula's outer coast.

W.T. Neill's mapping of 1901 was the source for the 1922 map of the Peninsula reproduced here, which shows that most farmers had retained small patches of bush

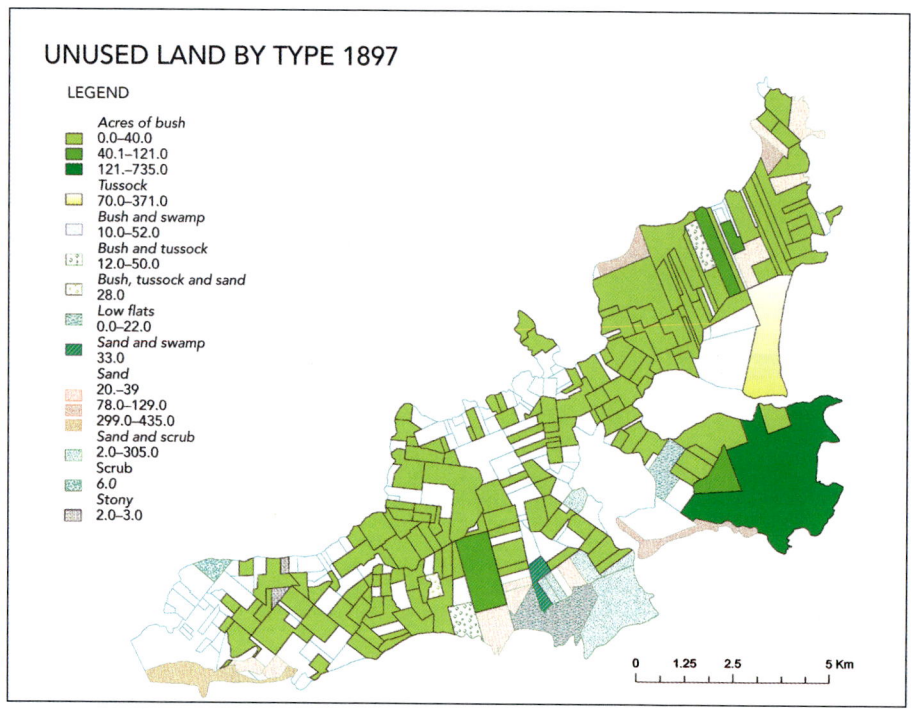

A range of difficult environments hampered farming development on the outer coast, including swamp, sand, scrub and tussock. Map made by the author

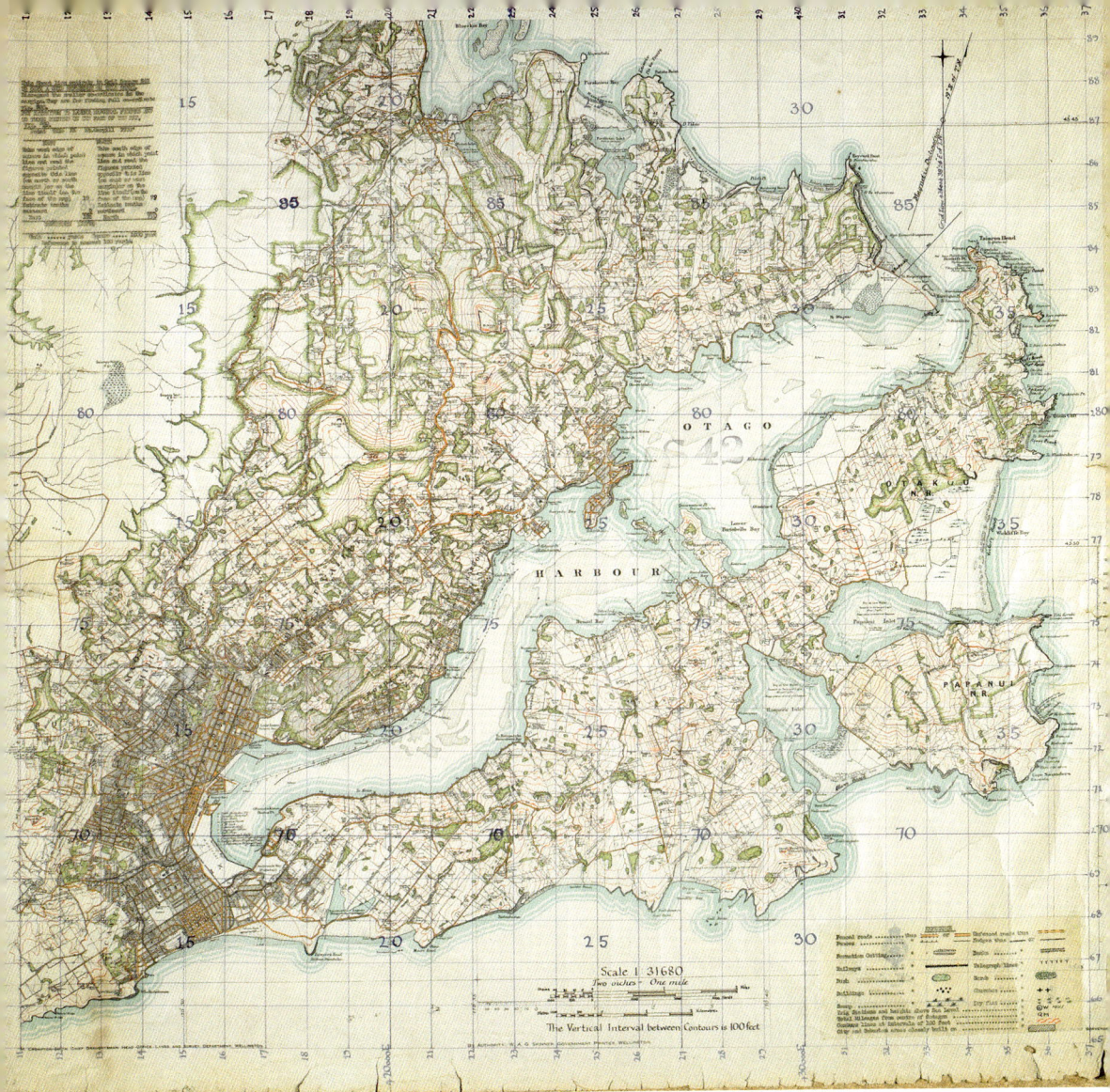

A topographical map showing Dunedin and surrounds, from surveys by W.T Neill, district surveyor, Wellington, Department of Lands and Survey, 1922. Hocken Collections, Uare Taoka o Hākena, University of Otago: S07-520b

on their property. These patches were scattered across the core dairying regions of Highcliff, Sandymount and Portobello. Larger areas of forest remained only on Māori land, in particular around the top of Mt Charles, on Cape Saunders and on the steep south-facing slopes above Okia Flat – areas where it would be difficult to establish grass and where shelter was at a premium.

Stock had the run of all these areas, however, and would have exerted considerable influence on the structure and composition of the forest. Cattle and sheep prefer softer ferns such as the hen and chicken fern *Asplenium bulbiferum*, and the broad-leaved trees and shrubs such as māhoe, three-finger, seven-finger, broadleaf, kōwhai, kaikōmako, raukawa, and putaputawētā or marble leaf. They will eventually remove almost all of the palatable vegetation from a forest understory, however: there is little they will not eat, save perhaps the twiggiest coprosmas.[81] By preventing regeneration, stock open up the bush, desiccating the forest floor, compacting the soil, lowering carrying capacity and removing habitat for species such as ferns.

Some native plants now disappeared completely, while others survived only in a few places. Data from the period itself is scanty, but by considering it in conjunction with the pattern found today, some reasonably informed guesses might be made as to the state of the vegetation. Peter Johnson has uncovered historical records of 13 native plants on the Peninsula that are not found today, including four ferns, seven herbs, a sedge and two woody plants.[82] Many others have long been rare. In 1900 Thomson described the disappearance of 'angelica' (probably *Gingidia montana*, native aniseed, or perhaps *Scandia geniculata*, climbing aniseed), known to the settlers as anise. This had been common around Andersons Bay but, as Burns had happily realised, was palatable to stock (rabbits also like it).[83] Thomson noted that it persisted only on the most inaccessible cliffs.[84] It was last recorded on the Peninsula in 1924.[85] This is a widespread pattern: 374 native vascular plants species survive on the Peninsula (just outnumbered by 331 naturalised and 48 planted species). Of the native species, 135 (36 per cent) are found in only one or two places.[86]

Thomson recognised that the actions of people were causing the decline of native plants. As a test case he used the Dunedin Town Belt where, although the larger trees had been excised, there had been no fire or grazing.[87] He concluded that in areas where the ground was not disturbed by man, introduced species were less likely to spread to any great extent, with 'a few striking exceptions': cocksfoot grass, broom, gorse and elderberry.[88] In contrast, 'wherever roads or tracks have been cut and the ground disturbed, introduced species of plants have mainly taken possession of the soil'.[89]

Native fauna struggled to adapt to the new environment. By 1885 only parakeets maintained a population sufficient to cause the settlers problems, when they engaged in a 'new departure in wickedness' by eating the buds of plum trees.[90] They did not last: in 1910 Reynolds reported that they had been extinct on the Peninsula for many years.[91] Large numbers of other birds disappeared from the Peninsula in this period. Reynolds mentions the complete disappearance of mohua and South Island robins from the forest; white herons, brown teal, paradise ducks and pūkeko from the waterways; and banded dotterels, snipe, gannets and fairy prions from the seabird colonies.[92]

Many other bird populations diminished markedly, including the forest-dwelling tūī, bellbirds, pigeons, brown creepers, pipits and moreporks; the grey duck; and the shore-dwelling black-backed gulls, red-billed gulls, terns, oystercatchers, sooty shearwaters, erect-crested penguins, little blue penguins, yellow-eyed penguins, Stewart Island shags and spotted shags.[93] Reynolds concluded:

CHAPTER 8: 'THE WHOLE FACE OF NATURE IS ALTERED'

Remnant forest at Hoopers Inlet. When Hardwicke Knight photographed the area in the 1970s, browsing stock had long since removed the undergrowth and continued to prevent any regeneration. Hocken Collections, Uare Taoka o Hākena, University of Otago: P2014-014/6-046

> ... *a summary of the birds that are extinct, nearly so, and increasing goes a long way to prove that all the native bird fauna of the Otago Peninsula is being sadly diminished. Very few species are holding their own, and practically none are increasing locally.*
>
> *The cultivation of the open country, the destruction of bush to carry on farming on good soil, the sawing out of timber trees that bore berries that were the principal food of many of our birds, the devastation caused by extensive forest fires, the increase of stoats, weasels, ferrets, and other imported vermin (and perhaps more will be imported by those who only guess at results) must in the long run mean the extermination of all our native birds. Ocean wanderers will hold out the longest, but even some of these, like the penguin, must soon be a thing of the past. The native grey duck, when thoroughly protected, is about the only bird we can hope to see as plentiful as formerly in special localities.*[94]

Birds disappeared in part because of the cumulative pressure exerted by the loss of forest and wetland, the fragmentation of what remained, and competition from introduced birds for food. However, predation was the primary cause.

New predators arrived on the Peninsula in the 1880s. Ferrets, weasels and stoats were brought to New Zealand in large numbers after a parliamentary joint committee concluded in 1881 that the rabbit problem had become so dire that no other solution seemed viable. It is important to realise how controversial the introduction of these mustelids was. Few settlers were as thoughtlessly flippant as 'Tally Ho', an *Otago Witness* correspondent who, in response to one Peninsula correspondent's worries over rabbits and thistles, argued that the introduction of foxes, stoats and weasels would eliminate rabbits, while the resulting increase in horses for fox hunting would deal to thistles.[95] The introduction of mustelids to southern New Zealand was a much debated and desperate last-resort measure that 'represented the victory of landholders' desperation over scientific foreboding, and of income over the environment'.[96] In 1882 the Otago Acclimatisation Society had decided, by the narrowest of margins, to refrain from spreading mustelids. They were soon firmly convinced that their introduction was wrong, but the damage was done – other individuals spread the predators, which were deemed protected species in the early 1880s.[97]

Mustelids generally prefer to eat rabbits rather than birds, and they have fairly large ranges. Today, female stoats range over an average of 83 hectares on the Peninsula, while male ferrets cover 163 hectares, so mustelid numbers on the Peninsula may not have been particularly high.[98] Nor were there many rabbits there – the first rabbit inspector was not appointed until 1886.[99] Rabbits were only problematic around Hoopers and Papanui inlets and, in particular, Sandymount – where in 1884 they were described as 'increasing', their 'depredations unlimited', and were controlled with guns, dogs and ferrets.[100] Elsewhere they 'never attained to anything like a pest'; the closely settled farmers were able, with 'the assistance of plenty of good cats, to keep bunny in subjection'.[101] Once landholdings became much larger in the twentieth century, rabbit numbers exploded.[102]

Mustelids are terribly efficient predators: they are pure carnivores, and primarily hunt at night by scent. Few of New Zealand's birds have any defences against them. Stoats would have had a devastating impact on the Peninsula's populations of hole-nesting forest birds, such as mohua and yellow-crowned parakeets,[103] while ferrets perhaps posed the greatest threat to colonial seabirds. Reynolds recorded that penguins once bred in their thousands, especially on Cape Saunders, but he now believed there were only a few score.[104]

The mustelids demolished the sooty shearwaters.[105] In 1910 Reynolds noted that these shearwaters formerly 'bred in hundreds of thousands from Tomahawk Cliffs, along the steeps of Highcliff (which is 800ft [243m] high), about Seal Point, Sandfly Bay, Sandymount, Cape Saunders, Papanui Inlet, and as far as Pipi Kariti [sic] near Cape Saunders. The sandy soil about Sandymount was their favourite breeding ground. A few still breed there.'[106] He lamented that 'the flocks about the coast here are certainly nothing to what they were a quarter of a century ago', attributing this decline to the clearance of bush, but most importantly to the fact that 'stoats, weasels, ferrets, and polecats destroy these birds by thousands'.[107] Recent studies have confirmed Reynolds' observations: sooty shearwater colonies can persist despite changes in habitat, but not in the face of prolonged predation from mustelids, cats and rats.[108] Though they are the largest and most aggressive of New Zealand's shearwaters, like the other petrels they have physiological and behavioural traits that render them vulnerable: they have a strong, musky odour, they nest in burrows, they lay only one egg, and most leave the egg or chick for long periods to feed.[109]

Sooty shearwaters were the last seabird species to breed on the Peninsula in anything approximating their former densities. Their loss represented a massive decline in bird biomass. Formerly, petrel numbers and their habit of nesting in huge concentrated colonies meant that they influenced the terrestrial environment more than any other group of vertebrates.[110] They underpinned the base of the terrestrial food chain, transferring immense amounts of nutrients from the sea to the land, which increased soil fertility and plant growth and sustained life from invertebrate populations up.[111] The scale of nutrient input in and around these colonies was enormous and prolonged – in the order of hundreds of kilograms of nitrogen and phosphorus each year for hundreds, perhaps thousands of years.[112]

Nowadays only a few petrels cling to Peninsula shores, at Taiaroa Head and north of Allans Beach. Their absence has greatly simplified and distorted the ecological webs that sustained the evolution of New Zealand's flora and fauna. Ironically, for much of the nineteenth and twentieth centuries farmers have maintained soil fertility and supplied key nutrients by replicating the petrels' role – importing and distributing the residue left by seabirds elsewhere.[113]

The loss of this last substantial element of the ecological links between ocean and land is symbolic of the broader intent and effects of European settlement. Owning and occupying a parcel of land involved extracting it from its embedded ecological context via a range of ideological and material processes. Land was first perceived as pieces of property created by the processes of surveying, planning and mapping. The pieces were then demarcated in ways that made their boundaries potent ecological divides, by defining where human energy was expended in exercising control over species, especially stock. Settlers struggled to cope with the other ecological influences to which such boundaries were irrelevant.

Nowhere is this clearer than in the impact of another newly arrived predator, the ship or black rat. By the mid-nineteenth century ship rats had displaced Norway rats from shipping and, once here, did the same over most of New Zealand's land mass.[114] Though smaller than the Norway rat, they are more agile and readily climb trees.[115] It was likely the ship rat and stoat predation of eggs, chicks and adults that exterminated or reduced Peninsula populations of several species of smaller tree-nesting birds, such as the robin, brown creeper and tomtit, and reduced the numbers of bellbirds and tūī.[116] Some introduced birds flourished: blackbirds and thrushes, for example, cope better with rats and cats, and in the absence of native birds had an abundance of food.[117] The trend towards introduced flora and fauna dominating the biota therefore accelerated. Rats' silent nocturnal slaughters, which so profoundly shaped the Peninsula ecosystems, seldom disturbed the settlers, for they did not in any way affect the mechanisms by which farmers gauged their own control – their fences, their stock and their plants.

As the Peninsula became closely settled, farmers were able to have an impact on some of those species that did disturb them, however. As a result, the introduced 'linnet' (or greenfinch), for example, was no longer a problem by the end of the century. Settlers eliminated them by a variety of means. John Mathieson, whom as we have seen took a particular interest in the problem, began by watching for them from a window, dropline in hand, and netting them when a good kill was in the offing. He demonstrated his success in killing several hundred linnets and sparrows to colleagues from the Peninsula Agricultural and Pastoral Society, who were so impressed they agreed to subsidise the purchase of three more nets.[118] But a more effective and less labour-intensive method of killing birds was soon resorted to: the spreading of poisoned grain.[119] This rapidly eliminated linnets, especially once the road boards organised the purchase and distribution of poisoned grain from the early 1890s.[120] Infuriated farmers thought that sparrows could distinguish the clean grain: sparrows seemed to one local observer to have largely superseded linnets by 1885.[121] Their depredations were as bad as ever: 'if no action is taken we may almost as well stop sowing any crops whatever. They destroy all crops except potatoes, and they may even attack them soon.'[122] Boys had always been encouraged to destroy these birds' eggs, and from the spring of 1897 the Peninsula Road Board offered a bounty of 2s per 100 sparrow and linnet heads or eggs.[123] By the end of the century the *Otago Witness* reported that the small bird nuisance was not 'quite so bad'.[124]

Settlers also began to have success in controlling sand drift on the southern Peninsula, through the introduction of sand-binding plants such as marram, lupin and broom. As James Beattie has shown, by the turn of the century New Zealand (and Australian) governments were prepared to legislate to prevent sand drift, though in doing so relied on local authority action.[125] Beginning in the mid-1890s, the Tomahawk Road Board directed intensive planting and fencing efforts to protect the road linking Musselburgh and Tomahawk Lagoon; £200 had been spent by 1900 and the drift arrested.[126] The larger sand drift at Ōtākou remained a significant problem for longer. Concerted efforts to address the issue may have been led by the Otago Harbour Board; certainly it was their engineer who, in a 1914 address to the Otago Institute, described marram and lupins 'spreading on the sandy slopes, so that in a few years the hillside may show green again and a new Otakou in days to come rise over the site of the first white settlement in Otago'.[127]

Peninsula farmers could clearly exert influence, but the ecology was far from being under their conscious control. Some species were simply too well adapted to colonising the disturbed ground that farmers were in the business of creating, for any control to

The north end of Allans Beach, refuge for a few surviving sooty shearwaters. © Ian Thomson

be effective. Easily the worst such weed in this period, from the farmers' perspective, was the Canadian thistle. In 1890 a *Witness* correspondent recorded that this thistle was probably first noticed in Otago 'about a score of years ago' when a few specimens were found 'growing on Mr Sanderson's ground, close to the Tomahawk lagoon'.[128] In the interim it had moved far down the Peninsula, seemingly spreading along the Andersons Bay roadside.

This thistle still plagues farmers on the Peninsula and in southern New Zealand generally. It is particularly difficult to control because (unlike the Scotch thistle) it is a perennial plant that spreads both by wind-blown seed and by sprouting from long rhizomes, all of which must be removed, since any part can propagate a new plant. It also became a common – even ubiquitous – element in agricultural seed. In 1888 three Peninsula farmers appeared before the Peninsula Road Board to urge the necessity of parliamentary action, as the thistle was 'becoming an intolerable evil and threatening in a few years to render the district uninhabitable'.[129] Though the road board resolved to petition the government, write to their MP William Larnach and coordinate action with the Portobello Road Board, nothing was done by way of legislative compulsion until the hotly contested Noxious Weeds Act of 1901 was finally pushed through after protracted debate.[130] In the meantime, farmers struggling with the effects of the depression often found it too much trouble to attempt to control the thistles, which needed persistent weeding and fallowing – both highly problematic activities on the hilly Peninsula. Gorse hedges were spreading for similar reasons, and although the road boards often required farmers to remove gorse from roadsides, this did little to slow its spread.[131]

Where farmers successfully targeted a species, as in the case of linnets or rabbits, their actions sometimes had unintended side effects. Birds other than linnets ate poisoned grain: this eradicated weka from the Maniototo, where Ōtākou Maori had sought them annually. On the Peninsula the grain killed pheasants, partridges and quail, the principal game birds that the acclimatisation society had worked so hard to import.[132] Of these, according to G.M. Thomson, by the turn of the century only quail lingered in small areas of Otago, including the Peninsula, where (perhaps because he associated poisoned grain with efforts to control rabbits) he wrongly thought no poisoned grain was spread.[133] Quail were 'very numerous in patches of bush' there in 1893, annoying settlers by eating grass and clover seed, and they could still be seen in numbers on the lower parts of the Peninsula in 1897.[134]

More acclimatisation failures occurred with the efforts to stock Tomahawk Lagoon with introduced trout and perch. These fish provided Dunedin anglers with local sport for a time, but succumbed to the effects on the lagoon of clearing the forest from the surrounding hills.[135] Thomson first saw the lagoon in the 1870s; in the early twentieth century he described what had happened since: 'its beauty has given place to an appearance of desolation and mud. Only a few years ago it was surrounded by a fine bush, and its waters were clear and sparkling, but the clearing of the ground has dried up the little streams which formerly kept up its supply, and now when heavy rain does come on, mud and clay are washed into it in quantity, and it is silting up in all parts.'[136]

Thomson noted also that the 'the poaching of cattle has destroyed much of the original flora' around the lagoon,[137] and had 'converted part of the lake into a boggy swamp'.[138] Reynolds in the early twentieth century lamented the fate of 'the big creeks [that] joined the bays and inlets', where paradise, grey and teal ducks were plentiful. None of these creeks are much more than periodic trickles today: their paths have been clogged by soil and pugged by cattle and sheep, so that they are seeping bogs.'[139]

Changed minds: At home in a newly made land?

After witnessing the dramatic environmental changes experienced on the Peninsula during the closing decades of the nineteenth century, Alfred Reynolds closed his lament to the disappearance of native birds from the Otago Peninsula by noting: 'The passing generation misses a lot of our beautiful birds, but the rising one cannot feel the want of their presence so keenly.'[140] Reynolds was obviously more concerned than most, but his conclusion points us towards two significant facts. First, that many of the older settlers of the nineteenth century mourned the loss of life they had witnessed and, in large measure, caused. Second, that the next generation, born after the period of bush clearances, were perhaps less likely to share these sentiments.

It was once thought that the early settlers hated and feared 'the bush'. But historians tracing the rise of environmental awareness in settler New Zealand now cite early and increasing concern about the fate of the life indigenous.[141] Some, such as David Young and James Beattie, have also argued that the Scots in New Zealand may have been more aware of the problems associated with environmental transformation, and more inclined to pay heed to ways in which settlement could be gentled.[142] This stemmed not only from the deforestation associated with the enclosures of Scotland, but also the highly educated character of many Scots émigrés. The latter certainly applies to several of the keenest observers of ecological change on the Peninsula and around Dunedin, such as G.M. Thomson (1848–1933), Alexander Bathgate (1845–1930) and Robert Gillies (1835–1886), all well-educated Scots.[143]

More attention should also be paid to the intra- and intergenerational differences that Reynolds' conclusion hints at. Most early settlers arrived on the Peninsula as young adults or children. The latter, in particular, only really knew New Zealand, and the period of most profound ecological change on and around the Peninsula coincided with their journeys from exhilarated youth to reflective old age.[144]

The reminiscences of the Scottish settler John McLay, written in 1916 when he was 75, display the changing emotional reactions of the young and old settler. McLay recalled, as a boy, watching his father and other men clear land for themselves and for the Reverend Thomas Burns: he 'did very much like to see the sawyers felling the big Totara pines – when they fell with a terrific crash, smashing all small trees to the ground'. At the same time, his love of clematis flowers in the bush meant that he 'often thought it was a sin' to cut the vines to bind shingles.[145] Having witnessed the deforestation of the Peninsula, he had come to feel that 'it is a cruel shame the ruthless hand of man should destroy God's beautiful work, all for the lust of money that sends so many to destruction and for the want of it – misery, sin and shame'. This awareness quite naturally coexisted alongside the knowledge that the forest had to be used – McLay next commenced a list of 'the names of some of the best trees for sawing timber'.[146]

This account, by a Scot who was not a well-read or highly literate man, suggests that many settlers, whether they had scientific pretensions or not, would have felt the loss of the forest. McLay's ambivalence is much the same as that which gnawed at Herbert Guthrie Smith's troubled heart, as he queried whether he had 'misunderstood the council [sic] of his Scottish forebears' in feeling urged to 'Destroy your fern! Clear off your woods!'; should he perhaps have heard them say, '"Oh, be content to leave alone. Admire, conserve, let well alone." Have I then for sixty years desecrated God's earth and dubbed it improvement?'[147]

Having not experienced the loss and destruction, the generation following this on the Peninsula could scarcely share such depths of doubt and conflicted emotions. This may help explain why, as David Young noted, the period between the late 1890s and the early 1900s was the most active in our conservation history until the 1960s.[148] It was the period when children who had grown up here from the days of early settlement came to power. New Zealand's very first conservation organisation, the Dunedin and Suburban Reserves Conservation Society, was established in 1888, largely through the efforts of Alexander Bathgate;[149] and around that time the government set aside three islands – Little Barrier, Resolution and Kapiti – as reserves to protect the wildlife.[150]

Reynolds pointed out that most people could not go to sanctuaries such as Resolution Island; he called for more protection around the places where people actually lived, and strove to awaken others' interest in native birds in order to prevent their disappearance from places like the Peninsula.[151] Such calls went unheeded for a long time.[152] Some suggest this was because the inherited doctrines of improvement, civilisation and progress remained dominant: clearance was still known as 'conversion', and might yet deliver a promised land.[153] Alex Calder, on the other hand, reminds us that the descrying of environmental destruction has been the dominant trope of our literature since at least the late nineteenth century. The primary problem, therefore, perhaps lay in the lack of purchase such attitudes – however widespread in the community – had in shaping the choices made by individual property owners.

Certainly no action was taken to preserve wildlife on the Peninsula until much later in the twentieth century, when the northern royal albatross, and then the yellow-eyed penguin, were saved from extirpation by the efforts of a few devoted individuals. Now, farmers are to the fore in preserving these birds. It pays them well to do so.

Reynolds' pessimism about the ultimate fate of the Peninsula's birdlife is probably still justified. His sentiments are more widely shared; we have succeeded in staving off the disappearance of a significant number of birds and have welcomed the reappearance of breeding seals and sea lions. Today, several bird species – among them the yellow-eyed and little blue penguins, the sooty shearwater and the royal albatross – retain small populations on the Peninsula, thanks to continuous and intensive predator control. In the long term, however, reliance on the capacity and willingness of human beings for protection is almost certainly not sustainable. On the New Zealand mainland at least, these species are perhaps but 'the living dead'.[154]

Conclusion

The Scots who predominantly settled on Otago Peninsula enjoyed relative economic prosperity. The settlers' goal to reproduce a mode of production – family small farming – determined how they approached the Otago Peninsula. Proximity to the harbour and the site of Dunedin, and an abundance of wood, ultimately determined the

Peninsula's fate: it was surveyed and allocated into properties according to the precepts of contiguity and concentration.

This system of property ignored the problem noted when the first settlers sailed into the harbour: these hills were too steep and the topography too broken for mixed farming. As it turned out, market forces dictated dairy farming as the most profitable pursuit on such smallholdings. The Peninsula's steep hillsides and slippery clay soils have been sliding into the sea ever since.

On their own terms, the settlers made what they saw as an empty, 'waste wilderness' into a 'better Britain'. This was primarily accomplished by the enclosure of land within precisely defined private properties, and the efficient improvement of these by extremely industrious owners. By 1900 the European lands had become a landscape of small farms generating fine dairy produce. The Peninsula had been comprehensively 'improved'.

Peninsula communities were hampered by the lack of transport that elsewhere expanded the hinterland of Dunedin and made large-scale agricultural production possible. Persistent but futile attempts by Peninsula residents to raise the capital to construct a railroad for themselves illustrate how keenly they felt this deficiency.

If some wondered at the wisdom of the settlers' means, none really questioned the validity of their goal to support communities of small farmers and small villages on the Peninsula. Yet in Thomson's inversion of the progress of settlement at the close of the century – characterising what had been done so far as the 'age of destruction' and calling for an 'era of improvement' – can be discerned the seeds of a concern: that the proprietors' single-minded pursuit of progress had for too long ignored the value of the environment before them. They had saved too few vestiges of the verdure that once clothed its hills.

Ōtākou Māori, relegated to their 'reserve' on the Peninsula, became increasingly marginalised. Here, as elsewhere, they adapted fast; for all the upheaval of the nineteenth century, incorporating modernity was for Kāi Tahu primarily an economic problem, not a cultural one. As Mackay had predicted, the 1880s and early 1890s were difficult years, although not, as he had feared, a 'drift into a state of semi starvation'.[155] Money was scarce, and mahika kai were vanishing fast. For most families the properties established in 1868 had proved uneconomic, much as the original smallholdings had for many British settlers. A few families had been able to increase their holdings; more were in danger of losing their land. As the depression eased, and with the opening of the creamery at Ōtākou, some families were able to reoccupy their land and operate dairy farms.[156] As farm sizes grew in the years ahead, however, many Māori landowners would struggle to retain their properties. In later decades, the settlers faced the same struggle.

John Buchanan, Otago Harbour, Portobello Bay.
1859, wash drawing. Hocken Collections, Uare Taoka o Hākena, University of Otago: A678

Conclusion

What a poor, curtailed, mutilated, sterile world we threaten our descendents with! Man and the rat sharing it – fit mates in many ways – in their desperate, deplorable, gnawing energy, in their ruthless destruction of every obstacle. – Herbert Guthrie-Smith, Sorrows and Joys of a New Zealand Naturalist 1936[1]

This book has described the entwining of human history with the ecology of the Otago Peninsula up to the end of the nineteenth century. By that time settlement of the Peninsula was complete: the forest was cleared, the farms established, and today's familiar infrastructure of roads, suburbs and villages was in place. The Peninsula has changed comparatively little since that time. In a raw, young country, it is an old and even relict landscape. It is an ideal site through which to understand our history in these islands.

The Peninsula is famous above all as a place where wildlife may be viewed in proximity to people, and this book's central concern has been to understand people's engagement with its environment. Seeking to integrate an analysis of economics, culture and ecology, it has emphasised the power of property in shaping how people interact with the world around them. Passion for property is often identified as a peculiarly British phenomenon and therefore central to colonisation, but it has been equally important to the histories of Māori on the Peninsula.

On arrival, both Māori and Europeans exploited a small band of easily accessible resources: large game, such as moa, seals and whales, predictable animals that could be found concentrated in the same places at the same times. But in the absence of agreed property rights, controlling exploitation was extremely difficult for both peoples. Despite the small numbers of humans involved, rapid extermination of these animals occurred. Both settler groups then had to generate new economies. From this point, Māori and Europeans moved on divergent trajectories.

Māori came from a tropical environment and had to start from scratch in the radically different temperate environment; the organisms they brought with them could not survive here, and much of their environmental knowledge was irrelevant. Over several hundred years southern Māori gradually shaped their economy in accordance with a deepening understanding of the patterns and rhythms of the species around them. Each community adapted a complex seasonal pattern of fission and fusion, ranging widely to gather flushes of fine-grained resources and reuniting to winter over.

Property rights were divided functionally more than geographically: various people had rights to use different resources from the same place. These use rights were primarily defined by ancestry. Members of a community knew what they were entitled to, and the community protected the rights of its individual members against encroachment by outsiders. Property rights were as tightly knit as the relationships among people.

The economy of each community was directed at the efficient harvest and transportation of resources to a critical point in time and space – the place where people chose to weather the winter together. For many Māori foraging across the Otago region, this was the Otago Peninsula. Because the Peninsula is one of the oldest, most southern and continuously and intensively occupied focal points of Māori settlement, it represents one of New Zealand's most complete examples of this pattern of cultural adjustment to a new environment.

Southern Māori depended on a rich knowledge of their environment for survival. Whether or not they exploited its resources 'sustainably' is a moot point, at best. I have endeavoured to establish that the preconditions for practising greater sustainability arose over time. I have stressed the significance of recognised mechanisms for asserting, upholding and transmitting agreed property rights, which established a close connection between the fortunes of a particular lineage and the resources on which their mana depended. The tight controls over access and use of the tītī islands, and the concerted community efforts to flush out lagoons such as Te Waihora (Lake Ellesmere), are two instances that provide some evidence of management with an eye to the future. But this should not be romanticised. If southern Māori learnt to live within the rhythms of the Otago Peninsula, it was because they had no choice.

Europeans came from a temperate climate relatively similar to that of the Otago region, and the crops and animals on which their culture subsisted were able to survive once a suitable habitat was created for them. The first Europeans came as transient visitors in search of the valuable resources that existed on and around the Peninsula. Seals, whales, flax and timber were the most important of these. Because of this transience, and the fact that demand for the resources was stimulated by their exchange value in imperial markets, these men were not motivated to control exploitation. Sealers, for example, knew that they would destroy the resource that sustained them, but in the absence of property rights it was a case of first in, first served.

Any restrictions that did arise were governed by the need to interact with Māori in order to gain access to resources. Dressed flax, a valuable commodity for making ropes, could only be procured from Māori, and this required the establishment and maintenance of relationships with Māori leaders. Those who achieved this successfully, such as ship's captain Kent, dominated the flax trade.

Shore whaling introduced a new level of interaction as whalers had to negotiate permission to establish a base for their onshore operations. They developed strategic political ties with Māori communities, strengthened by intermarriage. Through whaling, Māori began to be integrated into a commercial economy in which their labour and resources were traded for a range of goods. The most significant of these – potatoes, muskets and whaleboats – reshaped Māori economic and social structures on the Peninsula.

Whalers began the process of European settlement on the Peninsula, and negotiated crucial exchanges with Māori that developed shared understandings surrounding property systems, such as the organisation of labour, the exchange of goods, and rights to occupy and use land. Establishing a field of common understanding prepared the ground for organised British settlement and hastened its advent.

These interactions also drew Māori into contact with phenomena such as diseases and other invasive organisms – with unpredictable and sometimes disastrous consequences. This book has documented the impact of diseases on the Māori communities and attempted to reconcile contrasting interpretations in previous historiography. It has confirmed that several early epidemics did occur. The demographic and cultural impacts of these threatened Māori understandings of the world and stimulated their intense interest in European understandings, including European spirituality. Adopting Christianity was a crucial part of the process of cultural change that altered the role of Māori political leadership.

While Māori controlled the disposition of property rights, these changes did not alter the fundamentals of environmental interaction on the Otago Peninsula. People still harvested the resources that the existing ecology provided and, with the partial exception of tilling land for potatoes (still largely swidden agriculture where much of the original ecology would be allowed to reassert itself), little effort was directed towards creating a new ecological habitat that would produce a different set of resources.

In contrast, the British settlement on the Peninsula that followed the sale of the Otago Block was predicated on exactly that: British settlers had both the motives and the means to change the ecology of the area. They perceived beauty in this new world from the first, but believed they had an economic and moral imperative to own and 'improve' the land, and to establish farms that would form the 'Lord's Garden'.

Settler colonialism was a matter of dispossessing Māori of their land and turning that land to profit. This economic logic required legitimation, and found it in the doctrine of improvement, which saturated British culture – nowhere more so than in Scotland. In the minds of settlers, improvement was predicated on secure property rights: they did not proceed with settlement until Crown title was gained. In one of the earliest surveying cases in New Zealand in which triangulation was used to determine the parameters of the landscape the Peninsula was then mapped out as a set of neatly bounded land parcels. With the certainty of tenure, Peninsula farmers were secure in the knowledge that whenever they turned over a single inch of a field, their labour was precisely contained within their own property.

The Otago Peninsula landscape is a valuable setting in which to examine how settlers adapted their methods of agriculture. As a result of the early survey, attempts to establish small-farming communities occurred there in perhaps their most focused and prolonged form. Settlement was almost purely British and dominated by highly educated and hardworking Scots, who shared an intense interest in improving their farming practices. The newspapers of the time are filled with their suggestions on how best to transform New Zealand's environments.

The Peninsula became a sort of outdoor laboratory for the practice and development of colonial science. Because it was close to Dunedin and retained tracts of forest, wetlands and diverse coastal environments, it was of great interest to the more educated settlers, many of whom shared a keen interest in another defining passion of the age: natural history. The Dunedin Naturalists' Field Club, established in 1871, often visited the Peninsula. It is significant, as David Young and James Beattie have discussed, that many of these early naturalists were Scots.[2] The sustained interest of G.M. Thomson, who was to write an early (and for its time, magisterial) history of the acclimatisation of plants and animals in New Zealand, is particularly noteworthy, since Thomson was determined to dispel the notion that European arrivals inevitably displaced native species.

In the space of two short generations, the structure of a small-farming economy was imposed and the Peninsula was almost entirely deforested. The 'specialised production' characteristic of capitalism developed rapidly. More and more land was devoted to growing grass and fodder crops for dairy production, and less and less for cereal crops, orchards and market gardens. By the turn of the century the Peninsula was sometimes referred to as one large dairy farm.

By this time less than 20 per cent of the Peninsula's forest and tussock habitats remained, and then only in severely degraded form. Most indigenous life forms had either entirely disappeared or were greatly diminished. This environmental transformation is too often reduced to a focus on the loss of forest and birds. It was far more comprehensive than that: watercourses disappeared, soil structure altered, sand shifted, and many insects became scarce or disappeared altogether. Foreshore and inshore environments changed significantly, affected by increased erosion, sedimentation and the disappearance or reduction of fish and shellfish species. There was nothing inevitable about this: far from being displaced by a law of nature, the transformations were the result of vigorous labour expended to establish environments in which introduced stock and crops would flourish.

This trajectory of change is familiar, but it was far from even. As settlers cleared and planted land, indigenous and introduced species surged into the niches created and became pests and weeds. Settlers could kill off larger 'pest' animals, such as kākā,

Overgrown macrocarpa hedges line the way to Lovers Leap, Sandymount. © Ian Thomson

but smaller organisms such as insects plagued them and their companion animals and plants. Controlling these plagues impelled more introductions, from insectivorous birds to frogs and ladybirds, beginning a pattern that continues to the present.

Similar environmental transformations occurred on the remaining Māori land, albeit to a lesser extent, as Kāi Tahu attempted to adapt to the new economy. Their efforts were greatly hampered by the restrictions on their property arrangements imposed by central and provincial governments. Until 1862 Māori could legally only deal with the Crown, and the Crown was only interested in buying, not leasing their land. The provincial authorities meanwhile interfered with the lease arrangements that Ōtākou Māori had with the ex-whalers. As well, Māori were unable to raise capital against their land. Their property arrangements began to reflect an uneasy compromise between the ways in which their cultural traditions had determined their engagement with the environment, and the need to accommodate their economy within the broader context determined by settlers. The strips of land they eventually created were an attempt to allow each owner access to a range of forest, littoral and oceanic environments; in this sense, they strived for equality. Unlike the settler sections, however, there was no attempt at creating nominal equality by area: larger sections were allocated to the most significant people, and were the only parcels of land that were useful as individual farms. As a system of land ownership intended to sustain its proprietors, this was a failure: almost all of the land was leased to British settlers by the turn of the century.

This failure also reflected the refusal by settlers to countenance Māori systems of property, in particular their traditional tenure to resources such as shorelines, estuaries and wetlands. Māori leaders protested at this, and rallied their communities to fund ongoing campaigns to regain sufficient access to their lands and resources to re-establish a functional economy. This financially crippling effort went on for well over 100 years and was almost entirely in vain.

By the turn of the century the casual observer might have concluded that the British had successfully 'improved' the land into functional farms. Burns would have recognised in this landscape much of his longed-for 'pretty farms'. He surely could not have failed to be impressed by the evident labour with which this pastoral landscape had been created by its proprietors. He may have wondered, though, at the lack of cereals, the paucity of trees, the apparent subservience to milk production and dairy products.[3] He would still have recognised the people: most were of Scots descent and lived as family-farmers or in small, tight-knit communities. They were, in the main, Christian, law-abiding and comparatively well educated. They had learnt to love this land as their home – yet they had been changed in the process. The seeds of doubt over the doctrine of improvement had been sown in the settlers' experience of inhabiting such a rapidly transforming landscape. While the speed at which civilisation took hold was, therefore, most often a matter for celebration, it was also a deeply unsettling experience.

This book leaves to others the study of the twentieth century and the beginnings of the twenty-first. Two trends of the twentieth century are inescapable and have implicitly shaped this story, however. First, the twentieth century saw a spreading and intensifying desire to salvage the indigenous environment. As this book has shown, the seeds of that sentiment lay in the settlers' experiences of transformation in the previous century. Second, the Peninsula has become less and less economically valuable as farmland; today perhaps a dozen sheep farms, small by contemporary standards, cover the entire landmass, where once there were over 200 farms, the remnants of which are still discernible in their ruined buildings, crumbling drystone walls and shaggy macrocarpa windbreaks. The long retreat of the twentieth century means that this is a relict landscape, where the shapes of the past remain very visible.

Few of today's farmers sustain themselves by the production of meat and wool alone. Though mostly a matter of economic conditions, environmental factors have contributed to the current position: in particular, dairying is no longer seen as an appropriate use for such erosion-prone land.

Today the Peninsula economy is dominated by tourist ventures. It has become most valuable as a place where wildlife such as albatrosses, seals, sea lions and penguins may be seen close up in their 'natural' habitat.[4] The advent of breeding northern royal albatrosses, which returned when the loss of forest provided suitable nesting sites, symbolises the change; protected initially by the devotion of one man, Lance Richdale, they are now conserved through highly organised and intensive management. In hindsight, then, the dreams of the first British settlers as expressed in the property arrangements on the Peninsula have also failed: where its contemporary residents seek to make a living from the Peninsula environment, they now do so from the remnants of indigenous life left in the wake of nineteenth-century settlement.

Telling stories is the essence of history: we make sense of the past when it is retold as narrative.[5] The point of narrative is to chart an arc from beginning to end: stories construct spans of cause and effect across the abyss of the past. Dividing the seamless past into particular events and processes – the loss of some species, the arrival of others, the shifting sands of Otākou, the development of farming, the removal of forest – only makes meaningful sense within the context of a story, one shaped by its beginning in a peninsula ecology of stunning richness and diversity and its ending in a landscape of deep and rich human history. The concomitant of that human history has been irretrievable ecological destruction and loss. The British settlers who accomplished these twinned effects felt both pride and remorse. Regret is not simply a contemporary nostalgia.

The way in which we judge Alfred Reynolds, writing as Aparata Renata, as he describes searching for, finding, and shooting the last two kererū he ever expected to see on the Peninsula is, of course, coloured by the fact that kererū have returned. Expectations for the future also shape characterisations of the past. Reynolds believed the native birds of the Peninsula were doomed: a few of 'the ocean wanderers' might hold out, but the ecological tumult unleashed by humans and their multitude of companion species would, he believed, overwhelm all that had once made the Peninsula home.

This book aims to contribute to the knowledge of the Otago Peninsula's ecological and cultural past – knowledge that we will need if we are to avoid fulfilling Reynolds' fatalism. Many species on the Peninsula maintain a tenuous existence or are still in decline, despite all our efforts. In the long run, Reynolds might still be right. If human beings are to continue to call the Peninsula home, we must work very hard to make sure he is wrong.

The fate of the tītī, the sooty shearwater, provides a fitting closing allegory for what the Peninsula once was, what people have made of it, and what they may yet make of it in the future. Once present in teeming, breeding multitudes that came here after sweeping clear around the Pacific, migrating sooty shearwaters fertilised the soil by connecting the land to the ecosystems of the sea, and may have been among the birds that led Polynesians to these lands. Though the populations of most other shearwater species were greatly diminished by the impacts of Polynesian rats, kiore, sooty shearwater numbers were large enough to survive. As the people who had brought kiore here became Māori, they learned to treasure the sooty shearwaters as one of their most significant resources. The whalers traded for preserved tītī with Māori and endured the absence of their Māori wives for the weeks of harvest. When the European settlers arrived here in 1848 they were greeted by the sight of thousands of these seabirds lifting from the water, causing Thomas Ferens to write in excited anticipation, 'here will nature [be] triumphant and bring the mind to rejoice'.[6] Within 50 years of European settlement the shearwaters, once perhaps most numerous of such seabirds, had dwindled to small and scattered colonies and almost disappeared. Tītī remain a treasured resource today, and the annual harvest of these birds is one of very few examples of ongoing Māori control and authority over natural resources.

Recently a few birds have returned to the Peninsula to breed on the slopes behind beaches where people are replanting the hillsides in native bush. Life here comes from the sea, and it will continue to replenish the land. Nature has hardly been triumphant, nor can my mind bring itself to rejoice – but the surviving life on the Peninsula is still in our hands.

Notes

INTRODUCTION

1. Murray I. Dawson and Richard C. Winkworth, 'The New Zealand flora: "Moa's Ark" or "Fly-paper of the Pacific"?', *New Zealand Garden Journal*, vol. 11, no. 1, 2008, 20.
2. For an accessible introduction to this hypothesis, see Hamish Campbell, *The Zealandia Drowning Debate: Did New Zealand sink beneath the waves?* (Wellington: Bridget Williams E-Book, 2013); also George Gibbs, *Ghosts of Gondwana: The history of life in New Zealand* (Nelson: Craig Potton Publishing, 2006), especially 102–04; Tony Reay, 'Geology', in *The Natural History of Southern New Zealand*, eds John Darby et al. (Dunedin: University of Otago Press, 2003), 9; R. Ewan Fordyce, 'Fossils and the history of life', in *The Natural History of Southern New Zealand*, 39.
3. See generally Gibbs, *Ghosts of Gondwana*.
4. M.S. McGlone, 'Goodbye Gondwana', *Journal of Biogeography*, vol. 32, no. 5, 2005, 740.
5. Sanne Boessenkool et al., 'Relict or colonizer? Extinction and range expansion of penguins in southern New Zealand', *Proceedings of the Royal Society*, vol. 276, no. 1658, 2009, 815–21.
6. T. Higham, A. Anderson and C. Jacomb, 'Dating the first New Zealanders: The chronology of Wairau Bar', *Antiquity*, vol. 73, no. 280, 420–27; J.M. Wilmshurst, A.J. Anderson, T.F.G Higham and T.H. Worthy, 'Dating the late prehistoric dispersal of Polynesians to New Zealand using the commensal Pacific rat', *Proceedings of the National Academy of Sciences United States of America*, vol. 105, 2008, 7676–768.
7. Te Maire Tau, *Ngā Pikitūroa o Ngāi Tahu: The oral traditions of Ngāi Tahu* (Dunedin: University of Otago Press, 2003), 270, n. 313; Herries Beattie, *Traditions and Legends of the South Island Maori* (Christchurch: Cadsonbury Publications, 2004), 8.
8. M.S. McGlone, Atholl Anderson and R.N. Holdaway, 'An ecological approach to the settlement of New Zealand', in *The Origins of the First New Zealanders*, ed. D.G. Sutton (Auckland: Auckland University Press, 1994), 143–44.
9. Lance Richdale, quoted in ibid., 144.
10. Trevor H. Worthy and Richard N. Holdaway, *The Lost World of the Moa* (Christchurch: Canterbury University Press, 2002), 441, 444, 454; Scott A. Shaffer et al., 'Migratory shearwaters integrate oceanic resources across the Pacific Ocean in an endless summer', *Proceedings of the National Academy of Sciences of the United States of America*, vol. 103, no. 34, 2006, 12799–802; J.S. Harding et al., 'Incorporation into stream food webs of marine-derived nutrients from petrel breeding colonies', *Freshwater Biology*, vol. 49, 2004, 576–86; R.N. Holdaway, 'Otago Peninsula biodiversity: The past – contrast for the future' (paper presented at the Yellow-Eyed Penguin Trust 20th Anniversary Conference, Dunedin, 2007).
11. Herries Beattie recorded that all his southern Māori informants said that Te Rapuwai were the first people. See, for example, H. Beattie, 'Traditions and legends collected from the natives of Murihiku (Southland, New Zealand) Part I', *Journal of the Polynesian Society*, vol. 24, no. 95, 1915, 108.
12. Herries Beattie, *Tikao Talks* (Auckland: Penguin Books, 1990), 41; Herries Beattie, *Moriori: The Morioris of the South Island* (Christchurch: Cadsonbury Press, 1993), 27–31.
13. Jill Hamel, *The Archaeology of Otago* (Wellington: Department of Conservation,

2001), 19. As discussed subsequently, the inclusion of Papanui Inlet is a little speculative.
14. Atholl Anderson, 'Pieces of the past', in *Tangata Whenua: An illustrated history*, eds Atholl Anderson et al. (Wellington: Bridget Williams Books, 2014), 84; Atholl Anderson, 'Emerging societies', in ibid., 121–22.
15. Atholl Anderson, *Prodigious Birds: Moas and moa-hunting in prehistoric New Zealand* (Cambridge: Cambridge University Press, 1989), 180–81; Atholl Anderson, 'A fragile plenty: Pre-European Maori and the New Zealand environment', in *Environmental Histories of New Zealand*, eds Eric Pawson and Tom Brooking (Melbourne: Oxford University Press, 2002), 29; Anderson; 'Pieces of the past', 89; Anderson, 'Emerging societies', 124.
16. Atholl Anderson, *The Welcome of Strangers* (Dunedin: University of Otago Press, 1998), 41.
17. R.C. Murdoch, 'The effects of a headland eddy on surface macro-zooplankton assemblages north of Otago Peninsula, New Zealand', *Estuarine, Coastal and Shelf Science*, vol. 29, no. 4, 1989, 361–83; R.C. Murdoch et al., 'Evidence for an eddy over the continental shelf in the downstream lee of Otago Peninsula, New Zealand', *Estuarine, Coastal and Shelf Science*, vol. 30, no. 5, 1990, 489–507; D.S. Roper and J.B. Jillett, 'Seasonal occurrence and distribution of flatfish (Pisces: Pleuronectiformes) in inlets and shallow water along the Otago coast', *New Zealand Journal of Marine and Freshwater Research*, vol. 15, no. 1, 1981, 1–13.
18. Joseph Hooker, ed., *Journal of the Right Hon. Sir Joseph Banks* (London: Macmillan and Co., 1896), 218; John Beaglehole, ed., *The Journals of Captain James Cook: The voyage of the Endeavour 1768-1771* (Cambridge: Cambridge University Press, 1955), 260: entry for Sunday 4 March 1770.
19. D.R. Hainsworth, 'Exploiting the Pacific frontier: The New South Wales sealing industry 1800-1821', *The Journal of Pacific History*, vol. 2, no. 1, 1967, 67, 69.
20. James Broadbent, 'Fashioning a colonial culture', in *India, China, Australia: Trade and society 1788-1850*, ed. James Broadbent (Sydney: Historic Houses Trust of New South Wales, 2003), 25; Hainsworth, 'Exploiting the Pacific frontier', 60.
21. Ian Church, ed., *Gaining a Foothold: Historical records of Otago's eastern coast 1770-1839* (Dunedin: Friends of the Hocken Collections, 2008), 34–35; Peter Entwisle, *Behold the Moon: European occupation of the Dunedin district 1770-1848*, 2nd edn (Dunedin: Port Daniel Press, 2010), 35–42. Entwisle makes the case for a slightly earlier visit, most plausibly by the schooner *Unity*, under Captain Daniel Cooper the previous summer. The evidence for this is circumstantial, but includes the possibility that Hoopers Inlet and Mt Charles were named then to commemorate exploration by Cooper's chief officer Charles Hooper.
22. A. Charles Begg and Neil C. Begg, *The World of John Boultbee* (Christchurch: Whitcoulls Publishers, 1979), 107.
23. That munitions were the payment is the argument first made by McNab (1913), and followed by L.S. Rickard (1996) and Peter Entwisle (1998, 2006, 2010). See for example, Entwisle, *Behold the Moon*, 110.
24. Emma L. Carroll et al., 'Two intense decades of 19th century whaling precipitated rapid decline of right whales around New Zealand and east Australia', *PLoS ONE*, vol. 9, no. 4, 2014, e93789.
25. Several European nations were involved in nineteenth-century whaling, though Americans dominated. For the scale and scope of their activities, see T.D. Smith et al., 'Spatial and seasonal distribution of American whaling and whales in the age of sail', *PLoS ONE*, vol. 7, no. 4, 2012, e34905.
26. Erik Olssen, *A History of Otago* (Dunedin, John McIndoe, 1984), 29.
27. As Jim McAloon has argued, this point is significantly underplayed by New Zealand historians. See Jim McAloon, 'Gentlemanly capitalism and settler capitalists: Imperialism, dependent development and colonial wealth in the South Island of New Zealand', *Australian Economic History Review*, vol. 42, no. 2, 2002, 214.
28. W.J. Gardner, 'A colonial economy', in *The Oxford History of New Zealand*, 2nd edn, ed. Geoffrey W. Rice (Auckland: Oxford University Press, 1992), 70–77; Jim McAloon, 'The New Zealand economy, 1792–1914', in *The New Oxford History of New Zealand*, ed. Giselle Byrnes (Melbourne and Auckland: Oxford University Press, 2009), 211–12.
29. 'Peninsula County', *Otago Witness*, 23 February 1884, 9.
30. Hardwicke Knight, Manuscript notes for 'Otago Peninsula: A local history', Hocken Collections, not yet accessioned.
31. Gary Hawke, *The Making of New Zealand* (Wellington: Victoria University Press, 1981); Tom Brooking, *Lands for the People? The Highland Clearances and the colonisation of New Zealand: A biography of John Mckenzie* (Dunedin: University of Otago Press, 1996), 79–80.

32. New Zealand Acts as Enacted: www.nzlii.org/nz/legis/hist_act/tla188347v1883n3267/
33. William Cronon, 'Kennecott journey: The paths out of town', in *Uncommon Ground: Rethinking America's western past*, ed. William Cronon et al. (New York and London: Norton, 1993), 43.
34. NZPD, vol. 27, 1877, 65.
35. 'Report of the commissioners for the province of Otago', no. 2, in 'Papers relative to the fisheries of the colony' *AJHR*, 1869, D-15.
36. P. Thomson, 'Fish and their seasons', *Transactions and Proceedings of the New Zealand Institute*, vol. 9, 1876, 484–90; P. Thomson, 'The Dunedin fish supply', *Transactions and Proceedings of the New Zealand Institute*, vol. 10, 1877, 324.
37. G.M. Thomson, 'Notes by the wayside', *Otago Witness*, 28 September 1899, 62.
38. Angela Middleton, 'Hereweka/Harbour Cone: A relict landscape on the Otago Peninsula', *Australian Historical Archaeology*, vol. 30, 2012, 34.
39. Colin McCahon, 'Beginnings', *Landfall*, vol. 20, no. 4, 1966, 364.
40. Eileen Soper, *The Otago of Our Mothers* (Christchurch: Whitcombe & Tombs, 1948), 55.
41. See Middleton, 'Hereweka/Harbour Cone', 34–42.
42. Treating a particular place as a microcosm of the nation is a trap into which too many local histories fall. See Tony Ballantyne, 'On place, space, and mobility', in *Webs of Empire: Locating New Zealand's colonial past* (Wellington: Bridget Williams Books, 2012), 268–69.
43. William Cronon, 'Modes of prophecy and production: Placing nature in history', *The Journal of American History*, vol. 76, no. 4, 1990, 1123.
44. Peter Gibbons, 'Cultural colonisation and national identity', *New Zealand Journal of History*, vol. 36, no. 1, 2002, 8.
45. Arthur F. McEvoy, *The Fisherman's Problem: Ecology and law in the California fisheries, 1850–1980* (New York: Cambridge University Press, 1986), 14.
46. Gareth Nelson, quoted in Gibbs, *Ghosts of Gondwana*, 7.
47. Kenneth Cumberland, 'A century's change: Natural to cultural vegetation in New Zealand', *The Geographical Review*, vol. 31, no. 4, 1941, 529.
48. See, for example, Andrew Hill Clark, *The Invasion of New Zealand by People, Plants and Animals* (Piscataway: Rutgers University Press, 1949); Tom Brooking and Eric Pawson, *Seeds of Empire: The environmental transformation of New Zealand* (London: I.B. Tauris, 2011); Libby Robin and Tom Griffiths, 'Environmental history in Australasia', *Environment and History*, vol. 10, no. 4, 439–74.
49. Waitangi Tribunal, *The Ngai Tahu Report* (Wellington: Legislation Direct, 1991); Harry Evison, *The Long Dispute: Maori land rights and European colonisation in southern New Zealand* (Christchurch: Canterbury University Press, 1997).
50. All these points are well made by Paul Star, 'Environmental history and New Zealand history', *Environment and Nature in New Zealand*, vol. 4, no. 1, 2014: http://environmentalhistory-au-nz.org/2014/04/environmental-history-and-new-zealand-history
51. John Weaver, *The Great Land Rush and the Making of the Modern World, 1650–1900* (Montreal & Kingston: McGill-Queen's University Press, 2003), 88.
52. Weaver, *The Great Land Rush*, 64; Tom Brooking, 'Use it or lose it: Unravelling the land debate in late nineteenth-century New Zealand', *New Zealand Journal of History*, vol. 30, no. 2, 1996, 141–62, esp. 141–43; Brooking, *Lands for the People?*, 79–80. For the centrality of statute in shaping New Zealand's constitution and legal framework, especially in the context of land law, see Richard Boast, 'Maori fisheries 1986–1998: A reflection', *Victoria University of Wellington Law Review*, vol. 30, no. 1, 1999, 111, 120–21; Richard Boast, '"An expensive mistake": Law, courts, and confiscation on the New Zealand colonial frontier', in *Raupatu: The confiscation of Maori land*, eds Richard Boast and Richard Hill (Wellington: Victoria University Press, 2009), 148–49.
53. See, for example, T.M. Devine, *The Scottish Nation 1700–2000* (London: Penguin Books, 2000), 448–59.
54. Eric Pawson and Tom Brooking, 'Introduction', in Pawson and Brooking, *Environmental Histories of New Zealand*, 14.
55. Cronon, 'Kennecott journey', 47.
56. Pawson and Brooking, 'Introduction', 14.
57. See in particular Peter Gibbons, 'The far side of the search for identity', *New Zealand Journal of History*, vol. 37, no. 1, 2003, 45; Ballantyne, 'On place, space and mobility', 54.

PART I: THE PRIMORDIAL PENINSULA AND PEOPLE

CHAPTER 1:
HE WHENUA HOU: A NEW LAND

1. Te Maire Tau, 'The death of knowledge: Ghosts on the plains', *New Zealand Journal of History*, vol. 35, no. 2, 2001, 137.
2. Tony Reay, 'Geology', in *The Natural History of Southern New Zealand*, eds John Darby et al. (Dunedin: University of Otago Press, 2003), 9; R. Ewan Fordyce, 'Fossils and the history of life', in *The Natural History of Southern New Zealand*, 39; George Gibbs, *Ghosts of Gondwana: The history of life in New Zealand* (Nelson: Craig Potton Publishing, 2006), 102–04.
3. Reay, 'Geology', 9.
4. Stefan Olsson, 'The geology of the Portobello Peninsula: Proposal of an oversaturated lineage within the Dunedin volcano' (BSc diss., University of Otago, 2001), 2–7.
5. Patricia Grieg, 'Sand and plant community on Otago Peninsula: A study of three coastal areas and their vegetation' (Master's thesis, University of Otago, 1965), 13; J.P. Huggett, 'The historical geography of the Otago Peninsula' (Master's thesis, Victoria University, 1966), 2.
6. Reay, 'Geology', 15.
7. Peter Johnson, *Otago Peninsula Plants: An annotated list of vascular plants growing in wild places* (Portobello: Save the Otago Peninsula, 2004), 7.
8. Matt McGlone, Peter Wardle and Trevor Worthy, 'Environmental change since the last glaciation', in *The Natural History of Southern New Zealand*, 108, 111.
9. Jeremy Gibb, 'A New Zealand regional holocene eustatic sea-level curve and its application to determination of vertical tectonic movements: A contribution to Igcp-Project 200', *Royal Society of New Zealand Bulletin*, vol. 24, 1986, 392. It seems that rising seas flooded a forest. When early market gardeners and residents dug over the south Dunedin flats, they unearthed many hundreds of cubic metres of wood. In one account this was largely mānuka, but the early settler Murray Thomson recalled logs that were the remains of a forest of 'giant trees'. See Jane Davies, 'The prehistoric environment of the Dunedin area: The approach of salvage prehistory' (Master's thesis, University of Otago, 1980), 47–48; Alfred Eccles, ed., *A Pakeha's Recollections: The reminiscences of Murray Gladstone Thomson* (Wellington: A.H. and A.W. Reed, 1944), 116.
10. P. Thomson, 'On the sand hills, or dunes, in the neighbourhood of Dunedin', *Transactions and Proceedings of the New Zealand Institute*, vol. 3, 1870, 269; H.J.A. Aitken, *St Kilda: The first hundred years* (Dunedin: Borough of St Kilda, 1975), 75–76. My thanks to Doug Booth for this source.
11. For both a synopsis of the forces governing the local climate and an historical climate history, see Paula Brown, 'Trends and variability of temperature extremes in southern New Zealand' (PhD diss., University of Otago, 2006).
12. Jill Hamel, *The Archaeology of Otago* (Wellington: Department of Conservation, 2001), 4.
13. Peter Entwisle, *The Otago Peninsula: The historical case for its preservation* (Dunedin: Otago Peninsula Museum and Historical Society, 1980), 5.
14. Brown, 'Trends and variability of temperature extremes', 86–87; Grieg, 'Sand and plant community on Otago Peninsula', 14.
15. McGlone, Wardle and Worthy, 'Environmental change since the last glaciation', 126. McGlone elsewhere calls this a 'dense podocarp-angiosperm forest'. See M.S. McGlone, 'The origin of the indigenous grasslands of southeastern South Island in relation to pre-human woody ecosystems', *New Zealand Journal of Ecology*, vol. 25, no. 1, 2001, 8.
16. Hamel, *The Archaeology of Otago*, 7; McGlone, 'The origin of the indigenous grasslands of southeastern South Island', 8; Peter Johnson, 'Forest and scrub vegetation on Otago Peninsula', Unpublished report for Botany Division, Department of Scientific and Industrial Research, Dunedin, 1982, 2.
17. Huggett, 'The historical geography of the Otago Peninsula', 11; Johnson, 'Forest and scrub vegetation on Otago Peninsula', 8; Johnson, *Otago Peninsula Plants*, 8.
18. Moa taxonomy has continued to vary even in recent years. Currently there are thought to have been nine species, of which four inhabited the Peninsula: *Dinornis robustus*, *Emeus cratus*, *Emeus crassus* and *Pachyornis elephantopus*. See M. Bunce et al., 'The evolutionary history of the extinct ratite moa and New Zealand neogene paleogeography', *Proceedings of the National Academy of Sciences of the United States of America*, vol. 106, no. 49, 2009, 20646–51.
19. R. McGovern-Wilson, 'Small-bird exploitation: An archaeozoological approach to the study of fowling in southern New Zealand' (Master's thesis, University of Otago, 1986), 107–37. Including the goose in this list is a

little speculative – it has not been found in the Dunedin area, though found nearby both inland and on the Catlins coast. See Hamel, *The Archaeology of Otago*, 26.
20. These lists have been compiled from a number of archaeological and historical sources. For archaeological data, see primarily McGovern-Wilson, 'Small-bird exploitation'; Davies, 'The prehistoric environment of the Dunedin area'; Hamel, *The Archaeology of Otago*; Shar Briden, 'Archaeofauna from Sandfly Bay (I44/68), Otago Peninsula' (Postgraduate Diploma, University of Otago, 2005); also generally, Trevor H. Worthy and Richard N. Holdaway, *The Lost World of the Moa* (Christchurch: Canterbury University Press, 2002). For historical sources, see Aparata Renata, 'The native birds of the Otago Peninsula past and present', *Otago Witness*, 10 August 1910, 76; this article has been reproduced as Florence Enid Graham, 'The native birds of the Otago Peninsula past and present by Aparata Renata', 1910 (2001), HC, Misc-MS-1721. Current bird distribution data that distinguishes visiting from breeding birds are also useful. See C.J.R. Robertson et al., eds, *Atlas of Bird Distribution in New Zealand* (Wellington: Ornithological Society of New Zealand, 2007). Not all of the species listed here have been recorded in archaeological contexts on the Peninsula. However, as Hamel notes, 'the greater the quantity of midden analysed, the greater the number of birds identified'; very little midden on the Peninsula has been analysed, but at Long Beach, just a few kilometres to the north (as the bird flies), where Helen Leach and Jill Hamel conducted a thorough analysis of 50m², some 60 small-bird species were discovered. See Hamel, *The Archaeology of Otago*, 23.
21. The loose wording again reflects the lack of specific Peninsula data. See McGovern-Wilson, 'Small-bird exploitation', 51–53; Briden, 'Archaeofauna from Sandfly Bay', esp. 33; Davies, 'The prehistoric environment of the Dunedin area'; Hamel, *The Archaeology of Otago*, 23–26, and esp. 210.
22. Worthy and Holdaway, *The Lost World of the Moa*, 444.
23. David Young, *Our Islands, Our Selves: A history of conservation in New Zealand* (Dunedin: University of Otago Press, 2004), 29.
24. Herbert Guthrie-Smith, *Bird Life on Island and Shore* (Edinburgh and London: Blackwood and Sons, 1925), 128–29.
25. Worthy and Holdaway, *The Lost World of the Moa*, 441, 444, 454.
26. D.J. Hawke et al., 'Soil indicators of pre-European seabird breeding in New Zealand at sites identified by predator deposits', *Australian Journal of Soil Research*, vol. 37, 1999, 104; J.S. Harding et al., 'Incorporation into stream food webs of marine-derived nutrients from petrel breeding colonies', *Freshwater Biology*, vol. 49, 2004, 576–86; R.N. Holdaway, 'Otago Peninsula biodiversity: The past – contrast for the future' (paper presented at the Yellow-Eyed Penguin Trust 20th Anniversary Conference, Dunedin, 2007).
27. John Jillett, 'Physical oceonographic setting and water masses', in *The Natural History of Southern New Zealand*, 318–19.
28. John Jillett, 'Zooplankton associations off Otago Peninsula, south-eastern New Zealand, related to different water masses', *New Zealand Journal of Marine and Freshwater Research*, vol. 10, no. 4, 1976, 543–57.
29. G.M. Thomson, 'The natural history of Otago Harbour and the adjacent sea, together with a record of the researches carried on at the Portobello Marine Fishhatchery: Part 1', *Transactions and Proceedings of the New Zealand Institute*, vol. 45, 1913, 226.
30. Pers. comm. Will Rayment. Recent research also suggests the canyons have a rich benthic (seafloor) ecology. See Bryce Peebles, 'Otago submarine canyons: Mapping and Macrobenthos' Master's thesis, University of Otago, 2014).
31. R.C. Murdoch, 'The effects of a headland eddy on surface macro-zooplankton assemblages north of Otago Peninsula, New Zealand', *Estuarine, Coastal and Shelf Science*, vol. 29, no. 4, 1989, 361–83; R.C. Murdoch et al., 'Evidence for an eddy over the continental shelf in the downstream lee of Otago Peninsula, New Zealand', *Estuarine, Coastal and Shelf Science*, vol. 30, no. 5, 1990, 489–507; D.S. Roper and J.B. Jillett, 'Seasonal occurrence and distribution of flatfish (Pisces: Pleuronectiformes) in inlets and shallow water along the Otago coast', *New Zealand Journal of Marine and Freshwater Research*, vol. 15, no. 1, 1981, 1–13.
32. For the variety of fish feeding on *Munida*, see G.M. Thomson, 'The natural history of Otago Harbour and the adjacent sea together with a record of the researches carried on at the Portobello marine fish-hatchery, Part I', *Transactions and Proceedings of the New Zealand Institute*, vol. 45, 1913, 240.
33. David Graham, *A Treasury of New Zealand Fishes* (Wellington: A.H. & A.W. Reed, 1974), 104. Interestingly, however, pilchards are no

longer common on the southeast coast, and they are widely considered a northern fish. See George Habib, 'Report on Ngaitahu fisheries evidence', Wai 27, Document T4, 111
34. M.S. McGlone, Atholl Anderson and R.N. Holdaway, 'An ecological approach to the settlement of New Zealand', in *The Origins of the First New Zealanders*, ed. D.G. Sutton (Auckland: Auckland University Press, 1994), 144.
35. Te Maire Tau, *Ngā Pikitūroa o Ngāi Tahu: The oral traditions of Ngāi Tahu* (Dunedin: University of Otago Press, 2003), 270, n. 313; Herries Beattie, *Traditions and Legends of the South Island Maori* (Christchurch: Cadsonbury Publications, 2004), 8.
36. Tau, *Ngā Pikitūroa o Ngāi Tahu*, 313.
37. McGlone et al., 'An ecological approach to the settlement of New Zealand', 143–44.
38. Lance Richdale, quoted in ibid., 144.
39. Ben Finney, 'Experimental voyaging and Maori settlement', in *The Origins of the First New Zealanders*, 52–76. Modern 'prototypic' voyages meant to replicate those of the original Polynesian voyagers have typically sailed from Rarotonga in 17 to 22 days. There is some doubt, though, about the accuracy of these replica vessels, especially their sails. See K.R. Howe, *The Quest for Origins*, 2nd edn (Auckland: Penguin Books, 2008), 119; Atholl Anderson, 'Ancient origins', in *Tangata Whenua: An illustrated history*, ed. Atholl Anderson et al. (Wellington: Bridget Williams Books, 2014), 27–31.
40. McGlone et al., 'An ecological approach to the settlement of New Zealand', 143–44.
41. Patrick Kirch, *On the Road of the Winds* (Berkeley, Los Angeles, and London: University of California Press, 2000), 214, 230–38; Donald Denoon et al., eds, *The Cambridge History of the Pacific Islanders* (Cambridge: Cambridge University Press, 1997), 64; Margaret Orbell, *The Natural World of the Maori* (Auckland: Collins, 1985), 9; Atholl Anderson, 'Retrievable time: Prehistoric colonisation of South Polynesia from the outside in and the inside out', in *Disputed Histories*, eds Tony Ballantyne and Brian Moloughney (Dunedin: Otago University Press, 2006), 37.
42. The timing of Polynesian colonisation of Eastern Polynesia – and from there the extension to Hawai`i, Easter Island and New Zealand – remains controversial. For the debate, and different dates, see Anderson, 'Retrievable time', 37; Kirch, *On the Road of the Winds*, 230–45, 277–78.
43. Kirch, *On the Road of the Winds*, 304.
44. King, *The Penguin History of New Zealand*, 63.
45. Atholl Anderson, 'Faunal collapse, landscape change and settlement history in remote Oceania', *World Archaeology*, vol, 33, no. 3, 2002, 375–90; Kirch, *On the Road of the Winds*, 54.
46. David Steadman, 'Extinctions of Polynesian birds: Reciprocal impacts of birds and people', in *Historical Ecology in the Pacific Islands*, eds Patrick Kirch and Terry Hunt (New Haven and London: Yale University Press, 1991), 70; Jill Hamel et al., 'The human factor', in *The Natural History of Southern New Zealand*, 131.
47. Kirch, *On the Road of the Winds*, 304.
48. Anderson, 'Retrievable time', 35–37; Atholl Anderson, pers. comm.

Chapter 2:
Arrival and Adaptation

1. Michael King, *The Penguin History of New Zealand* (Auckland: Penguin Books, 2003), 67.
2. Atholl Anderson, 'Pieces of the past', in *Tangata Whenua: An illustrated history*, ed. Atholl Anderson et al. (Wellington: Bridget Williams Books, 2014), 70.
3. Atholl Anderson, *The Welcome of Strangers* (Dunedin: University of Otago Press, 1998), 4, 13; Jim Williams, '"E Paakahi Hakinga a Kai": An examination of pre-contact resource management practice in southern Te Wai Pounamu' (PhD diss., University of Otago, 2004), 19–20; Bill Dacker, *Te Mamae me te Aroha* (Dunedin: University of Otago Press, 1994), 5.
4. Anderson, *The Welcome of Strangers*, 13.
5. Michael Stevens, 'The names are in the land, our history is in the land' (BA diss., University of Otago, 1976), 19–20; Williams, 'E Paakahi Hakinga a Kai', 21; Department of Conservation and Te Rūnanga o Ngāi Tahu, 'Te Waihora joint management plan: Mahere tukutahi o te Waihora' (Christchurch: Department of Conservation and Te Rūnanga o Ngāi Tahu, 2005), 28.
6. Te Maire Tau, *Ngā Pikitūroa o Ngāi Tahu: The oral traditions of Ngāi Tahu* (Dunedin: University of Otago Press, 2003), 83.
7. Herries Beattie, *Traditions and Legends of the South Island Maori* (Christchurch: Cadsonbury Publications, 2004), 135. Also Khyla Russell, 'Landscape perceptions of Kāi Tahu' (PhD diss., University of Otago, 2000), 28.
8. James Cowan, *Legends of the Maori*, 2 vols. (Wellington: Fine Arts, 1930), vol. 1, 213.
9. Quotation from de Blosseville in McNab, *Murihiku and the Southern Islands*, 216.

10. Herries Beattie, *Tikao Talks* (Auckland: Penguin Books, 1990), 41; see also Herries Beattie, *Traditional Lifeways of the Southern Maori*, ed. Atholl Anderson (Dunedin: University of Otago Press, 1994), 401, 559; Robert McNab, *Murihiku and the Southern Islands* (Invercargill: William Smith, 1907), 216; Bill Dacker, 'He Raraka A Ka Awa, updated, annotated and sourced manuscript for the book, "Te Mamoe Me Te Aroha", originally published in 1994', HC, Misc-MS-1716, 21, n. 3; James Cowan, 'The life and wars of Te Wera', *Otago Daily Times*, 9 March 1906, 6.
11. Anderson, *The Welcome of Strangers*, 14. Though, as the text indicates, it is possible that Rākihautū was an ancestral figure of the first arrivals.
12. I have recounted the traditions largely as given by Herries Beattie and Te Maire Tau, between whom there is generally substantial agreement. See Beattie, *Traditions and Legends of the South Island Maori*, 13; Herries Beattie, *Moriori: The Morioris of the South Island* (Christchurch: Cadsonbury Publications, 1993), 27; Tau, *Ngā Pikitūroa o Ngāi Tahu*, 270.
13. Tau, *Ngā Pikitūroa o Ngāi Tahu*, 271.
14. Te Maire Tau and Atholl Anderson, eds, *Ngāi Tahu: A migration history: The Carrington text* (Wellington: Bridget Williams Books, 2008), 47.
15. Beattie, *Moriori*, 31.
16. Tau and Anderson, *Ngāi Tahu: A migration history*, 47.
17. Anderson, *The Welcome of Strangers*, 13–16.
18. Beattie recorded that his informants all agreed that Te Rapuwai were the first people. See Herries Beattie, 'Traditions and legends collected from the natives of Murihiku (Southland, New Zealand) Part I', *Journal of the Polynesian Society*, vol. 24, no. 95, 1915, 108; Herries Beattie, 'Traditions and legends collected from the natives of Murihiku (Southland, New Zealand) Part II', *Journal of the Polynesian Society*, vol. 24, no. 96, 1915, 130; Herries Beattie, *Maori Place Names of Otago* (Dunedin: Otago Daily Times and Witness Newspapers Co., 1944), 42; Beattie, *Moriori*, 50. See also Anderson, *The Welcome of Strangers*, 18; Williams, 'E Paakahi Hakinga a Kai', 38; Tau, *Ngā Pikitūroa o Ngāi Tahu*, 159–82; Tipene O'Regan, 'Ngai Tahu and the Crown: Partnership promised', in *Rural Canterbury: Celebrating its history*, eds Garth Cant and Russell Kirkpatrick (Wellington: Daphne Brasell Associates, 2001), 9.
19. Beattie, *Moriori*, 27–31.
20. Ibid.
21. Atholl Anderson, 'Kin and border: Traditional land boundaries in Eastern Polynesia and New Zealand with particular reference to the northern boundary of Ngai Tahu', Wai 785, Document Q2, 143.
22. Alan Clarke, *The Great Sacred Forest of Tane: Te Wao Tapu Nui a Tane: A natural pre-history of Aotearoa New Zealand* (Auckland: Reed Books, 2007), 42; Anderson, 'Kin and border', 47–48.
23. Atholl Anderson, 'Speaking of migration', in Anderson et al., *Tangata Whenua*, 62–63.
24. Edward Shortland, *The Southern Districts of New Zealand: A journal, with passing notices of the customs of the aborigines* (London: Longman, Brown, Green & Longmans, 1851), 92.
25. Ibid., 93.
26. Herries Beattie, 'Traditions and legends collected from the natives of Murihiku (Southland, New Zealand) Part VIII', *Journal of the Polynesian Society*, vol. 27, no. 107, 1918, 137, 147.
27. Anderson, 'Speaking of migration', 63–66.
28. Anderson, *The Welcome of Strangers*, 14–16.
29. Atholl Anderson, *When All the Moa Ovens Grew Cold* (Dunedin: Otago Heritage Books, 1983), 7; Anderson, *The Welcome of Strangers*, 14–16.
30. Tau, *Ngā Pikitūroa o Ngāi Tahu*, 177–78; Beattie, *Traditions and Legends of the South Island Maori*, 81.
31. Jeff Evans, *Ngā Waka o Nehera: The first voyaging canoes* (Auckland: Reed Books, 1997), 153–70; Beattie, *Moriori*, 40.
32. Tiaki Hikawera Matira, *Takitimu* (Christchurch: Kiwi Publishers, 1997), 40–44; Beattie, *Traditions and Legends of the South Island Maori*.
33. The belief that Kāi Tahu 'had brought the fighting in' was a common theme among Beattie's informants. See Herries Beattie, 'Traditions and legends collected from the natives of Murihiku (Southland, New Zealand) Part II', 134.
34. Beattie, *Moriori*, 49–50. Beattie's informants did not use the name 'moa', rather 'manu-nui' (big bird) as the generic name, with 'kiwi-nui' to refer to the smaller species, and 'poua' (old man) or 'poua-kai' (old glutton), for the larger species.
35. Ibid., 52.
36. Williams, 'E Paakahi Hakinga a Kai', 30; Russell, 'Landscape perceptions of Kāi Tahu'; Hardwicke Knight, *Otago Peninsula: A local history*, 3rd edn (Broad Bay, Dunedin: The author, 1979). Knight gives the name of the Otago Peninsula as Owarara. This is an error; that is the name for

36. the Portobello peninsula. Herries Beattie, *Maori Place-names of Otago: Hundreds of hitherto unpublished names with numerous authentic traditions told by the Maoris to Herries Beattie* (Christchurch: Cadsonbury Press, 1949), 8. Megan Potiki considers the name Muaupoko inauthentic, but acknowledges that it is now widely used by Māori to refer to the Peninsula: Megan Potiki, 'The Otago Peninsula, a unique identity', *Shima: The International Journal of Research into Island Cultures*, vol. 10, no. 1, 2016, 1–19. Understandings of the extent of Murihiku vary. This is the definition given by Matiaha (Matthias) Tiramorehu. For discussion see Michael J. Stevens, '"What's in a name?": Murihiku, colonial knowledge-making and "thin-culture"', *Journal of the Polynesian Society*, vol. 120, no. 4, 2011, 339.

37. Megan Potiki, 'The Otago peninsula, a unique identity', *Shima: The International Journal of Research into Island cultures*, vol. 10, no. 1, 2016, 1–19.

38. For discussion of the extent of Murihiku, see Michael Stevens, '"What's in a name?": Murihiku, colonial knowledge-making and "thin-culture"', *Journal of the Polynesian Society*, vol. 120, no. 4, 2011, 333–48. Also Herries Beattie, *Maori Place-names of Otago: Hundreds of hitherto unpublished names with numerous authentic traditions told by the Maoris to Herries Beattie* (Christchurch: Cadsonbury Press, 2001 [1944]), 79; Michael Stevens, 'Muttonbirds and modernity in Murihiku: Continuity and change in Kāi Tahu knowledge' (PhD diss., University of Otago, 2009), 2–10.

39. Michael Stevens, pers. comm., 2 September 2006. The Peninsula was certainly a key boundary by the time of the land sale in 1844. For the connotations of 'mua' see Atholl Anderson, 'Emerging societies', in Anderson et al., *Tangata Whenua*, 109. Note though that according to one of Beattie's informants, Murihiku was 'quite recently bestowed', and was, for example, not nearly so old a name as Rakiura. See Beattie, *Traditional Lifeways of the Southern Maori*, 444.

40. Stevens, 'The names are in the land', 24. This is the Ōtākou tradition. Others, however, give the founding ancestor as Puhirere, while Te Maire Tau disputes that there was a founding ancestor. See Tau, *Ngā Pikitūroa o Ngāi Tahu*, 177.

41. Beattie, *Maori Place Names of Otago*, 44; Beattie, *Tikao Talks*, 52. The name Ōtākou has generated considerable debate. It is first recorded in a lament sung in Māori before Cook's surgeon, David Samwell, in 1777, when it was recorded as 'Otagoo'. All early printed references used 'Otago', or variants of it. 'Otakou' does not appear in print until the 1840s. It is quite clear that southern Māori traditionally pronounced this name much as 'Otago' is pronounced today. See Peter Entwisle, *Behold the Moon: European occupation of the Dunedin district 1770–1848*, 2nd edn (Dunedin: Port Daniel Press, 2010), 164–67. Pukekura, 'Red Hill', which became the name for the pā on Taiaroa Head, is mentioned in waiata as being where Kupe shortened sail and took shelter. See Stevens, 'The names are in the land,' 7, 17; Beattie, *Maori Place Names of Otago*, 43; A.W. Reed, *The Reed Dictionary of New Zealand Place Names* (Auckland: Reed Books, 2002), 370.

42. Letter from Herries Beattie, Waimate, 6 January 1932. In W.H. Roberts, 'Unfiled letters from front of correspondence file', HC, MS-0439/012.

43. Atholl Anderson, 'Retrievable time: Prehistoric colonisation of South Polynesia from the outside in and the inside out', in *Disputed Histories*, eds Tony Ballantyne and Brian Moloughney (Dunedin: Otago University Press, 2006), 25–42; T.G.F. Higham, Atholl Anderson and C. Jacomb, 'Dating the first New Zealanders: The chronology of Wairau Bar', *Antiquity*, vol. 73, no. 280, 1999, 420–27.

44. Janet Davidson, *The Prehistory of New Zealand* (Auckland: Longman Paul, 1984).

45. Atholl Anderson, 'The chronology of colonisation in New Zealand', *Antiquity*, vol. 65, 1991, 792.

46. Atholl Anderson, 'Pieces of the past', 72.

47. Anderson and Smith, 'The transient village in southern New Zealand', 370.

48. It is always hard to be sure about year-round occupation, but it is suggested by midden contents that included species that would likely have been harvested in summer, such as trumpeter fish, seal pups and the chicks of little blue penguins. It is reasonable to infer generally that more limited movement occurred during winter. See Anderson and Smith, 'The transient village in southern New Zealand', 283–87, 360–63; Atholl Anderson, 'A fragile plenty: Pre-European Maori and the New Zealand environment', in *Environmental Histories of New Zealand*, eds Eric Pawson and Tom Brooking (Melbourne: Oxford University Press, 2002), 29.

49. See generally Anderson and Smith, 'The transient village in southern New Zealand'.

50. Atholl Anderson and R. McGovern-Wilson, 'The pattern of prehistoric Polynesian colonisation in New Zealand', *Journal of the Royal Society of New Zealand*, vol. 20, no. 1, 1990, 41–63.

51. Atholl Anderson and I.W.G. Smith, 'Shag River Mouth as an early southern village', in *Shag River Mouth: The archaeology of an early southern Maori village*, eds Atholl Anderson, Brian Allingham and I.W.G. Smith (Canberra: ANH Publications, 1996), 283, 364–67. Richard Walter, Ian Smith and Chris Jacomb have suggested that explaining the transient village as an efficient solution to economic imperatives underplays the importance of 'abstract models of culture'. They note that villages in the southern Cook Islands and early North Island were also shifted, despite these all being very different environments. See Richard Walter, I.W.G. Smith and C. Jacomb, 'Sedentism, subsistence and socio-political organization in prehistoric New Zealand', *World Archaeology*, vol. 38, no. 2, 2006, 280–87.
52. Hamel, *The Archaeology of Otago*, 19. This count includes the Papanui Inlet site. Though recent finds at Papanui Inlet increasingly suggest a substantial occupation, it has not yet been excavated, and the suggestion it might be a large early village site is speculative.
53. Ibid.
54. For discussion, see J.O. Samson, 'Cultures of collecting: Maori curio collecting in Murihiku, 1865–1975' (PhD diss., University of Otago, 2003).
55. Shar Briden, 'Archaeofauna from Sandfly Bay (I44/68), Otago Peninsula' (Postgraduate Diploma, University of Otago, 2005).
56. Ibid., 30–31.
57. Ibid., 33, 52, 62.
58. Murray Thomson, 'Papers relating to "Maori Curio" hunting', HC, MS-0326.
59. Octavius Harwood, Letter to parents, HC, MS 438/24.
60. Octavius Harwood, Jnr, 'Fragments of history of the Otago Peninsula, Larnach's Castle, etc.', HC, MS 0604 I+.
61. Ibid. The old site record form for Harwood, I44/76, gives this number of birds. Anderson notes Harwood advertising 40–50 skeletons, as well as knives: Atholl Anderson, *Prodigious Birds: Moas and moa-hunting in prehistoric New Zealand* (Cambridge: Cambridge University Press, 1989), 137.
62. *Otago Daily Times*, 12 September 1922, notes that Luch Harwood had recently presented the 'imperfect' skeletons found by her father.
63. Hardwicke Knight, *Otago Peninsula*, 13.
64. Pers. comm., Hardwicke Knight, 30 May 2006. Species information is derived from the old site record form, I44/76. The site record has this as: *Emeus crassus* and *Emeus huttoni* or *Anouslopterge* and *Emeus gravis* or *Pachyornis elephantopus*. I have provided the current species names.
65. See the site record form I44/391.
66. Trevor H. Worthy and Richard N. Holdaway, *The Lost World of the Moa* (Christchurch: Canterbury University Press, 2002), 78, 191–97. Worthy and Holdaway reported two families and 11 moa species in 2002. However, the taxonomy has been recently revised. See M. Bunce et al., 'The evolutionary history of the extinct ratite moa and New Zealand Neogene paleogeography', *Proceedings of the National Academy of Sciences of the United States of America*, vol. 106, no. 49, 2009, 20646–51; Samuel Turvey and R.N. Holdaway, 'Postnatal ontogeny, populations structure, and extinction of the giant moa Dinornis', *Journal of Morphology*, vol. 265, no. 1, 2005, 70–86.
67. Hamel, *The Archaeology of Otago*, 14.
68. Marianne Turner, 'Functional and technological explanations for the variation among early New Zealand adzes', *New Zealand Journal of Archaeology*, vol. 26, 2004, 60.
69. Later 'Classic' or 'traditional' Māori adzes were also often highly finished – but they were attached to the haft within a socket, and this technique required that the adze head have a smooth surface to prevent differential impacts that could split the haft timber during heavy work. See Helen Leach, 'The change from Archaic to Classic adze forms revisited', *Archaeology in New Zealand*, vol. 37, no. 4, 1994, 252. Jill Hamel, pers. comm., 25 April 2005. See also generally Walter, Smith and Jacomb, 'Sedentism, subsistence and socio-political organization in prehistoric New Zealand'.
70. R.N. Holdaway, 'Otago Peninsula biodiversity: The past – contrast for the future' (paper presented at the Yellow-Eyed Penguin Trust 20th Anniversary Conference, Dunedin, 2007.)
71. Moa bone has been found in these places and several more besides, but Māori used it for many tools and collected bone well after the birds became extinct. The sites listed are only those where it is likely moa were actually eaten. See generally Jane Davies, 'The prehistoric environment of the Dunedin area: The approach of salvage prehistory' (Master's thesis, University of Otago, 1980); Atholl Anderson, 'A review of economic patterns during the Archaic phase in southern New Zealand', *New Zealand Journal of Archaeology*, vol. 4, 1982, 53; David Teviotdale, 'The material culture of the moa hunters in Murihiku', *Journal of the Polynesian Society*, vol. 40, no. 162, 1932, 81–120; Anderson and

Smith, 'Shag River Mouth as an early southern village'. Also David Teviotdale, 'Diary relating to the excavation of camp sites [2/12/1928–1/12/1932]', HC, MS-500/C; Hamel, *The Archaeology of Otago*, 19; Hardwicke Knight, *Otago Peninsula*, 13–14; D.R. Simmons, *Little Papanui and Otago Prehistory* (Dunedin: Otago Museum Trust Board, 1967), 72.

72. Ian Smith, 'Maori impact on marine mammals', in *The Natural History of Southern New Zealand*, eds John Darby et al. (Dunedin: University of Otago Press, 2003), 137.
73. I.W.G. Smith, 'Estimating the magnitude of pre-European Maori marine harvest in two New Zealand study areas', *New Zealand Aquatic Environment and Biodiversity Report No. 82* (Wellington: Ministry of Fisheries, 2011), 25; Hamel, *The Archaeology of Otago*, 29.
74. I.W.G. Smith, 'The exploitation and cultural importance of sea mammals' (paper presented at the 9th Conference of the International Council of Archaeozoology, Durham, UK, 2002), 8.
75. James Belich, *Making Peoples* (Auckland: Penguin Books, 1996), 43.
76. Smith, 'The exploitation and cultural importance of sea mammals', 7–8; I.W.G. Smith, 'Maori impact on the marine megafauna: Pre-european distributions of New Zealand sea mammals', in *Saying So Doesn't Make it So: Papers in honour of B. Foss Leach*, ed. D.G. Sutton (Dunedin: New Zealand Archaeological Society, 1989), 90.
77. Hamel, *The Archaeology of Otago*, 30; Anderson and Smith, 'Shag River Mouth as an early southern village', 283.
78. 'Death of Mr. Benjamin Evans Turner', *Daily Southern Cross*, 6 October 1876, 3.
79. See Foss Leach, *Fishing in Pre-European New Zealand* (Wellington: New Zealand Journal of Archaeology, 2006), 235–40; Williams, 'E Paakahi Hakinga a Kai', 68.
80. John Beaglehole, ed., *The Journals of Captain James Cook: The voyage of the* Resolution *and* Discovery *1776–1780* (Cambridge: Cambridge University Press, 1955), 812; entry for Monday 25 February 1777.
81. Williams, 'E Paakahi Hakinga a Kai', 70, 172.
82. Helen Leach, 'Fern consumption in Aotearoa and its Oceanic precedents', *Journal of the Polynesian Society*, vol. 112, no. 2, 2003, 143.
83. Hardwicke Knight, 'Umu-ti', *Journal of the Polynesian Society*, vol. 75, no. 3, 1966, 345–46.
84. Williams, 'E Paakahi Hakinga a Kai', 192–95
85. Hamel, *The Archaeology of Otago*, 19.
86. Davies, 'The prehistoric environment of the Dunedin area: The approach of salvage prehistory', 73; Holdaway, 'Otago Peninsula biodiversity, 3.
87. D.A. Johns, 'Post-excavation treatment methods for waterlogged organic archaeological materials', in *The Oxford Handbook of Wetland Archaeology*, eds F. Menotti and A. O'Sullivan (Oxford: Oxford University Press, 2013).
88. Dilys Johns, Shar Briden, Rachel Wesley and Geoffrey Irwin, 'Excavation, analysis and conservation of a 15th century Māori waka (canoe) and associated artefacts from Papanui Inlet. *Journal of the Polynesian Society* (in press).
89. Letter from H Beattie, Waimate, 6 January 1932, in 'Unfiled letters from front of correspondence file', HC, MS-0439/012.
90. Hardwicke Knight, *Otago Peninsula*, 13.
91. Williams, 'E Paakahi Hakinga a Kai', 195–97; Hardwicke Knight, 'Umu-ti', 232–34.
92. Hardwicke Knight, *Otago Peninsula*, 13; Hamel, *The Archaeology of Otago*, 43.
93. Barry Fankhauser, 'The nutritive value and cooking of *Cordyline Australis* (ti kouka)', in Sutton, ed., *Saying So Doesn't Make it So*; Williams, 'E Paakahi Hakinga a Kai', 192–94.
94. 'Copy of report from E. Shortland, Esq., sub-protector of aborigines, to the chief protector', in Alexander Mackay, *A Compendium of the Official Documents Relative to Native Affairs in the South Island*, 2 vols. (Nelson: Government Printer, 1873), vol. 2, 125; Williams, 'E Paakahi Hakinga a Kai', 162; Hamel, *The Archaeology of Otago*, 47–48. Shortland stated that nearly the whole population of some villages would be employed making kāuru from December through February. Williams states that large groups of men only would travel to harvest kāuru. This evidence may reflect different practices at different places.
95. Williams, 'E Paakahi Hakinga a Kai', 194–95. As part of an overplayed argument that Māori in the south would have found food hard to come by, James Belich has noted, citing Fankhauser in support, that surviving on kāuru from tī alone would require eating 18.5 kilos of pith. See Belich, *Making Peoples*, 65. This is simply because kāuru is low in protein: it is not a complete diet in and of itself. Fankhauser in fact stresses that tī must have been a very important source of carbohydrate.
96. Williams, 'E Paakahi Hakinga a Kai', 165. According to Tikao, kāuru soon became mouldy.
97. Anderson, 'Pieces of the past', 82; Hamel, *The Archaeology of Otago*, 47–48, 73.
98. David B. McWethy et al., 'Rapid deforestation of South Island, New Zealand, by early Polynesian

fires', *The Holocene*, vol. 19, no. 6, 2009, 883–97; Anderson, 'A fragile plenty', 30–31; M.S. McGlone and J.M. Wilmshurst, 'Dating initial Māori environmental impact in New Zealand', *Quaternary International*, vol. 59, no. 1, 1999, 5–16; M.S. McGlone, 'Polynesian deforestation of New Zealand: A preliminary synthesis', *Archaeology in Oceania*, vol. 18, no. 1, 1983, 11–25.

99. Jill Hamel, 'Bird extinctions', in *The Natural History of Southern New Zealand*, 133.

100. Smith, 'Maori impact on the marine megafauna', 76–108; Ian Smith, 'Retreat and resilience: Fur seals and human settlement in New Zealand', in *The Exploitation and Cultural Importance of Sea Mammals*, ed. Gregory G. Monks (Oxford: Oxbow Books, 2005), 10.

101. Kerry-Jayne Wilson, *Flight of the Huia* (Christchurch: Canterbury University Press, 2004), 126; Alan Tennyson and Paul Martinson, *Extinct Birds* (Wellington: Te Papa Press, 2006), 10.

102. R.N. Holdaway, 'Introduced predators and avifaunal extinction in New Zealand', in *Extinctions in Near Time: Causes, contexts, and consequences*, ed. Ross D.E. MacPhee (New York: Kluwer Academic/Plenum Publishers, 2000); Wilson, *Flight of the Huia*, 126.

103. D.J. Campbell and Ian A.E. Atkinson, 'Effects of kiore (*Rattus exulans* Peale) on recruitment of indigenous coastal trees on northern offshore islands of New Zealand', *Journal of the Royal Society of New Zealand*, vol. 29, no. 4, 1999, 284–87.

104. Tennyson and Martinson, *Extinct Birds*, 10–11.

105. On bird extinctions, see generally Worthy and Holdaway, *The Lost World of the Moa*, 529–64; R.N. Holdaway, T.H. Worthy and A.J.T. Tennyson, 'A working list of breeding species of the New Zealand region at first contact', *New Zealand Journal of Zoology*, vol. 28, no. 2, 2001, 119–87; Trevor H. Worthy, 'What was on the menu? Avian extinction in New Zealand', *New Zealand Journal of Archaeology*, vol. 19, 1997, 125–60; R.N. Holdaway, 'New Zealand's pre-human avifauna and its vulnerability', *New Zealand Journal of Ecology*, vol. 12, supplement 1989, 11–25. The figures given for the South Island are derived from Worthy, 'What was on the menu?', table at 144. Worthy lists 118 species present in the South Island. I have adjusted this figure to 116 to reflect subsequent changes in moa taxonomy. Until 2002 it was thought there were 11 moa species, nine of which were considered to inhabit the South Island. It is now thought there were nine moa species, seven of which inhabited the South Island, and four of which would presumably have been found on the Otago Peninsula. See Bunce et al., 'The evolutionary history of the extinct ratite moa', 20646–51.

106. Early in his career Atholl Anderson favoured this possibility. See Atholl Anderson, 'Faunal depletion and subsistence change in the early prehistory of southern New Zealand', *Archaeology in Oceania*, vol. 18, no. 1, 1983, 6.

107. Beattie, *Traditions and Legends of the South Island Maori*, 23.

108. McWethy et al., 'Rapid deforestation of South Island', 894.

109. Hamel, *The Archaeology of Otago*, 7; McGlone, 'Polynesian deforestation of New Zealand', 11–25.

110. Anderson, 'Faunal depletion and subsistence change', 3; Anderson, 'A fragile plenty', 30.

111. Anderson, 'A fragile plenty', 30; Jill Hamel et al., 'The human factor', in *The Natural History of Southern New Zealand*, 133.

112. Murray Bathgate has argued that Māori did burn the Peninsula's forests. He cited traditional evidence of extensive fires, and suggested that early European accounts 'independently noted that the vegetation cover was open and consisted of low bush and scrub – indicative of a regenerating vegetation cover following the decline of local cultural activity in the area by 1840'. Murray Bathgate, 'Pre-European cultural interference on the forests of the southern part of the South Island', *Science Record*, vol. 17, 1967, 36. As explained in the text, I think he is wrong on both counts. His 'traditional' evidence is misplaced hearsay, and his description of early European accounts is misleading.

113. McWethy et al., 'Rapid deforestation of South Island', 892.

114. The first description is Thomas Shepherd's journal of 1826. See 'Journal of T. Shepherd', HC, MS-0440/06, 17–18. Dr David Monro, here with Frederick Tuckett in 1844, gives the most complete description: 'As far as we could see, looking down on the Peninsula, it appeared uniformly covered with wood.' See D. Monro, 'Notes of a journey through a part of the Middle Island of New Zealand', in Thomas M. Hocken, *Contributions to the Early History of New Zealand [Settlement of Otago]* (London: Sampson Low, Marston & Co., 1898), 244.

115. Geoff Park, *Ngā Uruora* (Wellington: Victoria University Press, 1995), 47.

116. Anderson, 'A fragile plenty', 33.

117. Anderson, 'Faunal depletion and subsistence change', 8.

118. The tendency among archaeologists to prefer such late dates is recent. In 2001 Jill Hamel advocated what was then considered a short prehistory – beginning 'about 1150'. Hamel, *The Archaeology of Otago*, 13.
119. Sanne Boessenkool et al, 'Relict or colonizer? Extinction and range expansion of penguins in southern New Zealand', *Proceedings of the Royal Society*, vol. 276, 2009, 815–21.
120. NZAA site record form I44/391.
121. Boessenkool et al, 'Relict or colonizer?', 815–21.

CHAPTER 3:
CONTINUITY AND CHANGE: MAKING SOUTHERN MĀORI

1. Mihi, or statement of identity, from Kāi Tahu exhibition, Toitū Otago Early Settlers Museum. Translation by Jim Williams, pers. comm., 12 June 2006. I have taken the liberty of adding macrons and of removing the gloss of hapū as 'subtribe'.
2. For quotation, see Jill Hamel, *The Archaeology of Otago* (Wellington: Department of Conservation, 2001), 73–74; for dating the period of moa extinction, see Atholl Anderson, 'Pieces of the past', in *Tangata Whenua: An illustrated history*, eds Atholl Anderson et al. (Wellington: Bridget Williams Books, 2014), 85, 509 (n. 92).
3. James Belich, *Making Peoples* (Auckland: Penguin Books, 1996), 67.
4. Michael King, *The Penguin History of New Zealand* (Auckland: Penguin Books, 2003), 71–72.
5. Atholl Anderson, 'Pieces of the past', 84; Anderson, 'Emerging societies', in *Tangata Whenua*, 121–22. Patrick Nunn has proposed a particularly sudden and severe decline in the climate. See Patrick Nunn and James Britton, 'Human–environment relationships in the Pacific Islands around A.D. 1300', *Environment and History*, vol. 7, no. 1, 2001, 3–22; Patrick Nunn, 'Revising ideas about environmental determinism: Human-environment relations in the Pacific Islands', *Asia Pacific Viewpoint*, vol. 44, no. 1, 2003, 63–72; Patrick Nunn, 'The A.D. 1300 event in the Pacific Basin', *Geographical Review*, vol. 97, no. 1, 2007, 1–23.
6. Atholl Anderson and I.W.G. Smith, 'The transient village in southern New Zealand', *World Archaeology*, vol. 27, no. 3, 1996, 369–70; Anderson, 'Pieces of the past', 86.
7. Atholl Anderson, *Prodigious Birds: Moas and moa-hunting in prehistoric New Zealand* (Cambridge: Cambridge University Press, 1989), 180–81; Atholl Anderson, 'A fragile plenty: Pre-European Māori and the New Zealand environment', in *Environmental Histories of New Zealand*, eds Eric Pawson and Tom Brooking (Melbourne: Oxford University Press, 2002), 29; Anderson; 'Pieces of the past', 89; Anderson, 'Emerging societies', 124.
8. Hamel, *The Archaeology of Otago*, 72; I.W.G. Smith, 'Nutritional perspectives on prehistoric marine fishing in New Zealand', *New Zealand Journal of Archaeology*, vol. 24, 2004, 16.
9. Hamel, *The Archaeology of Otago*, 75–76.
10. Smith, 'Nutritional perspectives on prehistoric marine fishing in New Zealand', 16.
11. I.W.G. Smith, 'Estimating the magnitude of pre-European Māori marine harvest in two New Zealand study areas', *New Zealand Aquatic Environment and Biodiversity Report No. 82* (Wellington: Ministry of Fisheries, 2011), 25.
12. Ibid., 25. Though most of the samples are small, in a few cases some thousands of individual fish were identified. Hamel, *The Archaeology of Otago*, 32–34, 76. There are gaps because of the selective preservation of evidence: for example, cartilaginous species like sharks and rays are missing. There are also odd gaps such as the paucity of material from freshwater fisheries for eels and kōkupu (in both adult and juvenile form) and estuarine fisheries for flatfish such as flounder and sole. For debate over the reasons for this, see George Habib, 'Ngaitahu claim to mahinga kai', report commissioned by the Waitangi Tribunal, Wai 27, Doument T4, 100–10; Atholl Anderson, 'Uniformity and regional variation in marine fish catches from prehistoric New Zealand', *Asian Perspectives*, vol. 36, no. 1, 1997, 12; Foss Leach, 'Fishing in pre-European New Zealand', *New Zealand Journal of Archaeology Special Publication: Archaeofauna* vol. 15 (Wellington, 2006). For the possibility that earlier excavation methods significantly underrepresented the diversity of recovered remains, see also Marshall I. Weisler, Chris Lalas and Paul Rivett, 'New fish records from an Archaic midden, South Island', *Archaeology in New Zealand*, vol. 42, no. 1, 1999, 37–42.
13. Smith, 'Estimating the magnitude of pre-European Māori marine harvest', 25.
14. Ibid., 14, 30–32; also, for a specific Peninsula site, see Shar Briden, 'Archaeofauna from Sandfly Bay (I44/68), Otago Peninsula' (Postgraduate Diploma, University of Otago, 2005), 55–56.
15. Smith, 'Estimating the magnitude of pre-European Māori marine harvest', 14.
16. Jane Davies, 'The prehistoric environment of the Dunedin area: The approach of salvage prehistory' (Master's thesis, University of Otago, 1980), 67–69.

17. R. McGovern-Wilson, 'Small-bird exploitation: an archaeozoological approach to the study of fowling in southern New Zealand' (Master's thesis, University of Otago, 1986), 51–53.
18. Tipene O'Regan, 'Ngāi Tahu and the Crown: Partnership promised', in *Rural Canterbury: Celebrating its history*, eds Garth Cant and Russell Kirkpatrick (Wellington: Daphne Brasell Associates, 2001), 8; Hamel, *The Archaeology of Otago*.
19. For the historical development and application of this approach in New Zealand, see Jack Golson, 'Culture change in prehistoric New Zealand', in *Anthropology in the South Seas*, eds J.D. Freeman and W.R. Geddes (New Plymouth: Thomas Avery & Sons, 1959), 62–70; Jan Hjarno, *Maori Fish-hooks in Southern New Zealand*, (Dunedin: Otago Museum Trust Board, 1967); Roger Duff, *The Moa-Hunter Period of Maori Culture*, 3rd edn (Wellington: E.C. Keating, Government Printer, 1977). For discussion of problems inherent in this approach, see J.O. Samson, 'Cultures of collecting: Māori curio collecting in Murihiku, 1865–1975' (PhD diss., University of Otago, 2003); Helen Leach, 'The change from Archaic to Classic adze forms revisited', *Archaeology in New Zealand*, vol. 37, no. 4, 1994, 248–54. For a summary evaluation, see Louise Furey, 'Material culture', in *Change Through Time: 50 years of New Zealand archaeology*, eds Louise Furey and Simon Holdaway (Auckland: New Zealand Archaeological Association, 2004), 29–54. For application to Otago sites, see Hamel, *The Archaeology of Otago*, esp. 74–75.
20. Samson, 'Cultures of collecting', 18.
21. Furey, 'Material culture', 37.
22. Hamel, *The Archaeology of Otago*, 91.
23. Anderson and Smith, 'The transient village in southern New Zealand', 370.
24. Ibid.; Jim Williams, '"E Paakahi Hakinga a Kai": An examination of pre-contact resource management practice in southern Te Wai Pounamu' (PhD diss., University of Otago, 2004), 123.
25. Hamel, *The Archaeology of Otago*, 91.
26. Anderson and Smith, 'The transient village in southern New Zealand', 369.
27. Hamel, *The Archaeology of Otago*, 86.
28. Ibid., 85; Atholl Anderson, 'Origins, settlement and society of pre-European south Polynesia', in *The New Oxford History of New Zealand*, ed. Giselle Byrnes (Melbourne: Oxford University Press, 2009), 37; Anderson, 'Pieces of the past', 89.
29. H.D. Skinner, 'Excavations at Little Papanui, Otago Peninsula', *Journal of the Polynesian Society*, vol. 69, no.3, 1960, 186–98; D.R. Simmons, *Little Papanui and Otago Prehistory* (Dunedin: Otago Museum Trust Board, 1967); Atholl Anderson, 'A review of economic patterns during the Archaic phase in southern New Zealand', *New Zealand Journal of Archaeology*, vol. 4, 1982, 45–75; Hamel, *The Archaeology of Otago*; Samson, 'Cultures of collecting'.
30. Skinner, 'Excavations at Little Papanui, Otago Peninsula', 188; Hamel, *Archaeology of Otago*, 74–75, 80.
31. Samson, 'Cultures of collecting', 270.
32. Anderson, 'A review of economic patterns', 65.
33. Atholl Anderson, *When All the Moa Ovens Grew Cold* (Dunedin: Otago Heritage Books, 1983), 27.
34. Hamel, *The Archaeology of Otago*, 73.
35. Ibid., 73–74, 79.
36. Ibid., 10.
37. Samson, 'Cultures of collecting', 269–70.
38. Ibid.
39. 'Rich in curios. Otago Peninsula. Fine site for excavation', *Evening Star*, 21 September 1929. Quoted in Samson, 'Cultures of collecting', 1.
40. Samson, 'Cultures of collecting', 231.
41. 'Unearthing Maori idols. War clubs, adzes, and bone implements, and what was learnt in the process. Part two', *Otago Witness*, 14 July 1892, 43.
42. Ibid.
43. Samson, 'Cultures of collecting', 13, 193.
44. Ibid.
45. Ibid., 273.
46. Letter from Herries Beattie, Waimate, 6 January 1932. In W.H. Roberts, 'Unfiled letters from front of correspondence file', HC, MS-0439/012.
47. Samson, 'Cultures of collecting', 274.
48. Ibid., 276, 279.
49. David Teviotdale, 'Diary relating to the excavation of camp sites [9/11/1926–18/11/1928]', HC, MS-500/B; Murray Bathgate, 'The Maori occupancy of Murihiku, 1000–1900 A.D.: A geographic study of change' (PhD diss., University of Otago, 1969), 146–47.
50. See variously Skinner, 'Excavations at Little Papanui', 188; Simmons, *Little Papanui and Otago Prehistory*; Anderson and Smith, 'The transient village in southern New Zealand', 360; Hamel, *The Archaeology of Otago*, 73–74, 79–80; Samson, 'Cultures of collecting'.
51. Samson, 'Cultures of collecting', 270.
52. Atholl Anderson, *The Welcome of Strangers* (Dunedin: University of Otago Press, 1998), 53,

58; Te Maire Tau and Atholl Anderson, eds, *Ngāi Tahu: A migration history: The Carrington text* (Wellington: Bridget Williams Books, 2008), 29.
53. Tau and Anderson, eds, *Ngāi Tahu*, 29.
54. Ibid., 26.
55. Anderson, *The Welcome of Strangers*, 23.
56. Ibid., 23, 146; Khyla Russell, 'Landscape perceptions of Kāi Tahu' (PhD diss., University of Otago, 2000), 19; Edward Shortland, *The Southern Districts of New Zealand: A journal, with passing notices of the customs of the aborigines* (London: Longman, Brown, Green & Longmans, 1851), 155. Shortland felt that this explanation was false – that Te Wai Pounamu was the name of a particular place where pounamu was found. But the Māori custom of naming a wider area after a particular spot (te tino) would explain this confusion. See Williams, 'E Paakahi Hakinga a Kai'.
57. James Stack, 'Sketch of the traditional history of the South Island Maoris', *Transactions and Proceedings of the New Zealand Institute*, vol. 10, 1877, 57–92; Anderson, *The Welcome of Strangers*, 25; Tau and Anderson, eds, *Ngāi Tahu*, 29.
58. Anderson, *The Welcome of Strangers*, 27–32.
59. Ibid., 35–38.
60. Tau and Anderson, eds, *Ngāi Tahu*, 71.
61. Anderson, *The Welcome of Strangers*, 41.
62. Ibid., 31; Anderson and Tau, eds, *Ngāi Tahu*, 72.
63. Anderson, *The Welcome of Strangers*, 41.
64. Ibid., 36, 41.
65. Tau and Anderson, eds, *Ngāi Tahu*, 71.
66. Anderson, *The Welcome of Strangers*, 41.
67. Ibid., 34–5.
68. Tau and Anderson, eds, *Ngāi Tahu*, 136.
69. Herries Beattie, *Traditions and Legends of the South Island Maori* (Christchurch: Cadsonbury Publications, 2004), 43, 55; Anderson, *The Welcome of Strangers*, 47–48.
70. This feud has often been described. For various accounts, see Beattie, *Traditions and Legends of the South Island Maori*, 43–46; Michael Stevens, 'The names are in the land, our history is in the land' (BA diss., University of Otago, 1976); Anderson, *The Welcome of Strangers*, 47–51; Tau and Anderson, eds, *Ngāi Tahu*, 136–42.
71. There is a significant and illuminating difference of opinion over the timing of the Tarewai tradition, as discussed by Anderson. One tradition places these events just prior to the truce organised by Rakiihia and Te Hau, and has Te Hau giving Pukekura pā to Tarewai after the truce. But in Ōtākou traditions the Tarewai traditions occurred earlier than that. Ōtākou people do not like the idea that Pukekura was at the disposal of a Canterbury chief. See Anderson, *The Welcome of Strangers*, 52–56, 222, nn.5 and 10.
72. Ibid., 52–53.
73. W.A. Taylor, *Lore and History of the South Island Maori* (Christchurch: Bascands Limited, 1950), 138. According to Taylor, the Kāti Kurī chief Te Wera, who had a particularly bloody and itinerant life, later dwelt at Aurakitaurira for a brief time – after he left Huriawa and prior to living at Moturata or Taieri Island. However, this suggestion does not appear in other traditional accounts, and Taylor is not regarded as especially reliable.
74. Stevens, 'The names are in the land, our history is in the land', 64–66, Anderson, *The Welcome of Strangers*, 54–55.
75. Stevens, 'The names are in the land, our history is in the land', 71; Anderson, *The Welcome of Strangers*, 50–57; Beattie, *Traditions and Legends of the South Island Maori*, 52.
76. Anderson, *The Welcome of Strangers*, 51.
77. Ibid.
78. Tau and Anderson, eds, *Ngāi Tahu*, 29; Te Maire Tau, *Ngā Pikitūroa o Ngāi Tahu: The oral traditions of Ngāi Tahu* (Dunedin: University of Otago Press, 2003), 197; Anderson, *The Welcome of Strangers*, 51.
79. Anderson, *The Welcome of Strangers*, 56–57, 62.
80. Stevens, 'The names are in the land, our history is in the land', 72.
81. Herries Beattie, 'Traditions and legends collected from the natives of Murihiku (Southland, New Zealand) Part IV', *Journal of the Polynesian Society*, vol. 25, no. 98, 1916, 60–61.
82. Williams, 'E Paakahi Hakinga a Kai', 23.
83. Te Maire Tau, 'The death of knowledge: Ghosts on the plains', *New Zealand Journal of History*, vol. 35, no. 2, 2001, 136.
84. Hugh Kawharu, 'Salvaging the remnant: New Zealand', in *Land Tenure in the Pacific*, ed. Ron Crocombe (Suva: University of the South Pacific, 1987) 143–44; Anderson, 'Emerging societies', 103–04.
85. Tau and Anderson, eds, *Ngāi Tahu*, 30–31.
86. Anderson, 'Origins, settlement and society of pre-European south Polynesia', 43.
87. Angela Ballara, *Iwi: The dynamics of Māori tribal organisation from c. 1769 to c. 1945* (Wellington: Victoria University Press, 1998), 194–200.
88. E.T. Durie, 'Custom law', discussion paper circulated by the New Zealand Law Commission, January 1994, 72; Judith Binney with Vincent O'Malley and Alan Ward, 'The coming of the Pakeha', in *Tangata Whenua: An illustrated history*, 213–14.

89. Ballara, *Iwi*, 195–96, 270–71; Durie, 'Custom law', 73.
90. Ballara, *Iwi*, 198–200; Anderson, 'Emerging societies', 112–13; Anderson, 'Origins, settlement and society of pre-European south Polynesia', 43–44. An especially common resource might be open to all, but particular people would still be recognised as having the right to decide otherwise and foreclose access. See Ballara, *Iwi*, 198.
91. See generally Stuart Banner, 'Two properties, one land: Law and space in nineteenth-century New Zealand', *Law and Social Inquiry*, vol. 24, no. 4, 1999, 807–52.
92. Ballara, *Iwi*, 195.
93. Ibid., 161–63, 204; Anderson, 'Emerging societies', 105–09, 127–28.
94. Durie, 'Custom law', 17; Ballara, *Iwi*, 163, 192–93.
95. Any number of scholars have asserted this, but for searching analysis of historical hapū formation and their roles in Māori political and economic life by the eighteenth century, see especially Ballara, *Iwi*, 161–214.
96. Ibid., 194.
97. Ibid., 204–06.
98. Tame Parata, 'Outline of the life of Te Matahaere', notes by F.R. Chapman, 27 December 1894, HC, MS-0412. Cited in Ian Church, ed., *Gaining a Foothold: Historical records of Otago eastern coast 1770–1839* (Dunedin: Friends of the Hocken Collections, 2008), 51.
99. Atholl Anderson, 'Evidence of Dr Atholl Anderson on mahinga kai', Wai 27, Document H1, 73; Anderson, 'Origins, settlement and society of pre-European south Polynesia', 44–45; Ballara, *Iwi*, 163–64, 200–01; Durie, 'Custom law', 72–74, 85.
100. Anderson, *The Welcome of Strangers*, 111–15.
101. Herries Beattie, *Our Southernmost Maoris* (Christchurch: Cadsonbury Publications, 1954; reprint, 1994), 85.
102. Williams, 'E Paakahi Hakinga a Kai', 80–81.
103. Ibid.
104. Ibid.
105. Atholl Anderson, 'Wakawaka and mahinga kai: Models of traditional land management in southern New Zealand', in *Oceanic Culture History: Essays in honour of Roger Green*, eds J.M. Davidson, G. Irwin, B.F. Leach, A. Pawley and D. Brown (Wellington: New Zealand Journal of Archaeology Special Publication, 1996), 635.
106. The boundary probably shifted somewhat depending on the waxing political power of Kāi Tahu, and on who was asked. One of Beattie's informants said that a post (poupoutunoa) at Clinton marked the boundary after the rongopai. Herries Beattie, 'Traditions and legends collected from the natives of Murihiku (Southland, New Zealand) Part V', *Journal of the Polynesian Society*, vol. 25, no. 99, 1916, 97. In 1880, however, Wiremu Potiki argued that Ōtākou territory extended south to the Mataura River. Anderson, *The Welcome of Strangers*, 108.
107. Several European writers have promoted this view of Kāti Māmoe as a 'lost' or 'vanished' tribe, whose remnants encountered Cook in Dusky Sound. Beattie's work ought to have ended this misconception, but it has unfortunately lingered in the works of historians such as the Begg brothers and John Hall Jones.
108. If I understand the matter correctly, Karetai, the prominent nineteenth-century leader at Ōtākou, could claim to have pre-eminent rights to the Otago Peninsula over and above his cousin Taiaroa (a disputed point), because even though Taiaroa descended from the senior tuakana line on their Kāi Tahu side, Karetai was descended on his mother's side from the Waitaha and Kāti Māmoe lines who had long occupied the Otago Peninsula (whereas Taiaroa had only married into those lines). The complications surrounding this issue were played out in the Native Land Court hearings of 1868. See Maori Land Court Minute Books, South Island Minute Books 1A, Reel 16.
109. Beattie records that Karetai was usually described as a 'half-and-half', that is, a mixture of Kāti Māmoe and Kāi Tahu, and that 'Kaitepahi' was his hapū on the Kāti Māmoe side. However, Anderson asserts that Ngāi Te Pahi, the hapū Karetai stated he belonged to in 1853, was a Te Ruahikihiki group hapū, and that Gāti Hawea, Karetai's choice of hapū in 1849, was his Kāti Māmoe side. Anderson, *The Welcome of Strangers*. The best documentary evidence of the continuing presence of Kāti Māmoe as a politically significant presence on the Otago Peninsula is perhaps the census taken by Strode in 1861. This listed the leading chiefs of Ōtākou together with their hapū affiliation. Six chiefs were recorded at Ōtākou, of whom three identified as 'Ngatiruahikihiki' (Kāi Tahu), and three as 'Ngatimamoe'. See 'Report from Mr. Assistant Native Secretary Strode', in Alexander Mackay, *A Compendium of the Official Documents Relative to Native Affairs in the South Island*, 2 vols. (Nelson: Government Printer, 1873), vol. 2, 134–35.

110. Tau and Anderson, eds, *Ngāi Tahu*, 152, 222, 226.
111. Harry Evison, *Te Wai Pounamu* (Wellington and Christchurch: Aoraki Press, 1993), 7.
112. These distinctions are largely based on Anderson, 'Evidence of Dr Atholl Anderson on mahinga kai', 73.
113. Williams, 'E Paakahi Hakinga a Kai', 102; Anderson, *The Welcome of Strangers*, 117.
114. Williams, 'E Paakahi Hakinga a Kai', 4.
115. Bill Dacker, *Te Mamae me te Aroha* (Dunedin: University of Otago Press, 1994), 7.
116. Herries Beattie, *Traditional Lifeways of the Southern Maori*, ed. Atholl Anderson (Dunedin: University of Otago Press, 1994), 312; George Habib, 'Report on Ngaitahu fisheries evidence', Wai 27, Document T4, 58; Michael Stevens, 'Muttonbirds and modernity in Murihiku: Continuity and change in Kāi Tahu knowledge' (PhD diss., University of Otago, 2009), 60.
117. Edward Ellison, 'Evidence of Edward Ellison on mahinga kai, Otakou area', Wai 27, Document H12.
118. Beattie, *Traditional Lifeways of the Southern Maori*; Ellison, 'Evidence of Edward Ellison on mahinga kai'; Anderson, *The Welcome of Strangers*, 143.
119. Williams, 'E Paakahi Hakinga a Kai', 115; Anderson, *The Welcome of Strangers*, 143; letter from Herries Beattie, Waimate, 6 January 1932.
120. Beattie, *Traditional Lifeways of the Southern Maori*, 174; Stevens, 'The names are in the land, our history is in the land'. Beattie gives a different name for this practice – whakakeokeo.
121. Anderson, *The Welcome of Strangers*, 143.
122. Ellison, 'Evidence of Edward Ellison on mahinga kai'.
123. Anderson, *The Welcome of Strangers*, 121–22.
124. Thomas Brunner, 'Journal of an expedition to explore the interior of the middle island of New Zealand', *Journal of the Royal Geographical Society of London*, 1850, 344–78 [358], in Stevens, 'The names are in the land, our history is in the land', 53.
125. Shortland, *The Southern Districts of New Zealand*, 224. 'Copy of report from E. Shortland, Esq., sub-protector of aborigines, to the chief protector', in Mackay, *A Compendium of the Official Documents Relative to Native Affairs in the South Island*, vol. 1, 225.
126. Williams, 'E Paakahi Hakinga a Kai', 23; Anderson, *The Welcome of Strangers*, 23.
127. Anderson, 'Evidence of Dr Atholl Anderson on mahinga kai', 70; Beattie, *Traditional Lifeways of the Southern Maori*, 175.
128. Dacker, *Te Mamae me te Aroha*, 7; Williams, 'E Paakahi Hakinga a Kai', 169.
129. I.W.G. Smith, 'Estimating the magnitude of pre-European Maori marine harvest in two New Zealand study areas', 17–18, 25; Letter from Herries Beattie, in Roberts, 'Unfiled letters from front of correspondence file'.
130. Williams, 'E Paakahi Hakinga a Kai', 169; Williams, pers. comm., 30 September 2007.
131. Khyla Russell, pers. comm., 30 August 2007.
132. Williams, 'E Paakahi Hakinga a Kai', 171.
133. Seasonality based on ibid., 100. Neither Anderson, *The Welcome of Strangers*, 117, nor Dacker, *Te Mamae me te Aroha*, 7, provide a name for spring.
134. David Graham, *A Treasury of New Zealand Fishes* (Wellington: A.H. & A.W. Reed, 1974), 107, 312–13; Leach, *Fishing in Pre-European New Zealand*, 47, 52, 67, 71, 89; Anderson, *The Welcome of Strangers*, 137.
135. Habib, 'Report on Ngaitahu fisheries evidence', 229; Ellison, 'Evidence of Edward Ellison on mahinga kai', Wai 27, Document H12.
136. Habib notes that while inshore hāpuku are scattered, they are only found in concentrated shoals offshore; for quotation, see Habib, 'Report on Ngaitahu fisheries evidence', 86.
137. Beattie, *Traditions and Legends of the South Island Maori*, 132; Graham, *A Treasury of New Zealand Fishes*, 313.
138. Anderson, *The Welcome of Strangers*, 136–37.
139. Hamel, *The Archaeology of Otago*, 33–34; Ellison, 'Evidence of Edward Ellison on mahinga kai'.
140. Habib, 'Report on Ngaitahu fisheries evidence', 105.
141. Anderson, *The Welcome of Strangers*, 120–21.
142. Ellison, 'Evidence of Edward Ellison on mahinga kai'; *Complete Book of New Zealand Birds*, ed. C.J.R. Robertson (Sydney: Reader's Digest, 1985), 221.
143. Ellison, 'Evidence of Edward Ellison on mahinga kai'.
144. Anderson, *The Welcome of Strangers*, 144.
145. Murray Thomson, *The Reminiscences of Murray Gladstone Thomson* (Wellington and Dunedin: A.H. and A.W. Reed, 1944).
146. Henry Duckworth, *The Early Years of Andersons Bay and Tomahawk*, 2nd edn (Dunedin: Otago Heritage Books, 1982).
147. Anderson, *The Welcome of Strangers*, 120.
148. Habib, 'Report on Ngaitahu fisheries evidence', 47–48.
149. Ibid., 46.
150. Williams, 'E Paakahi Hakinga a Kai', 163.
151. B.F. Leach and A.S. Boocock, *Prehistoric Fish Catches in New Zealand* (Oxford: Tempus Reparatum, 1993), 252.

152. Beattie, *Traditional Lifeways of the Southern Maori*, 325; Anderson, *The Welcome of Strangers*, 139.
153. Anderson, *The Welcome of Strangers*, 139.
154. Ibid., 118; Dacker, *Te Mamae me te Aroha*, 33.
155. Atholl Anderson, 'Evidence of Dr Atholl Anderson on Maori settlement at Otakou', Wai 27, Document C8a.
156. Habib, 'Report on Ngaitahu fisheries evidence', 45–46.
157. Ibid.; Williams, 'E Paakahi Hakinga a Kai', 111.
158. Anderson, *The Welcome of Strangers*, 138.
159. Letter from Herries Beattie, in Roberts, 'Unfiled letters from front of correspondence file'.
160. Ellison, 'Evidence of Edward Ellison on mahinga kai'.
161. Anderson, *The Welcome of Strangers*, 144.
162. Shortland, *The Southern Districts of New Zealand*, 191–92.
163. Ibid., 145.
164. Williams, 'E Paakahi Hakinga a Kai', 195.
165. Place names and oral testimony suggest that sea lions were sought at the mouth of Papanui Inlet. See Stevens, 'The names are in the land, our history is in the land'; Ellison, 'Evidence of Edward Ellison on mahinga kai'.
166. I.W.G. Smith, 'Historical documents, archaeology and 18th century seal hunting in New Zealand', 685.
167. Ian Smith, 'Sea mammal hunting and prehistoric subsistence in New Zealand' (PhD diss., University of Otago, 1985) 176–82, 312; Smith, 'Historical documents, archaeology and 18th century seal hunting in New Zealand', 679, 685.
168. Smith, 'Sea mammal hunting and prehistoric subsistence', 415–18; Smith, 'Historical documents, archaeology and 18th century seal hunting in New Zealand', 681.
169. Smith, 'Sea mammal hunting and prehistoric subsistence', 415–18.
170. Anderson, *The Welcome of Strangers*, 67. Tikao also reported to Beattie that seals were cooked whole in their skins. Smith notes that by his own admission Tikao knew little about seals, and considers this method 'rather unlikely'. He believed it more probable that seals were butchered and cooked in an earth oven, as also recorded by Beattie, and Ellison. Smith, 'Historical documents, archaeology and 18th century seal hunting in New Zealand', 675–77, 683–85.
171. F.R. Chapman, 'Notes on the depletion of the fur-seal in the southern seas', *Canadian Record of Science*, vol. 99, no. 27, 1893, 448. Other records also indicate young seals being taken in seasonal expeditions. Thomas Shepherd, for example, noted 'young seal' in the diet of Foveaux Strait Māori in 1826.
172. F.R. Chapman, 'Notebook entitled 'Gazetteer, Maori Names, South Island', HC, MS-0412.
173. Beattie, *Traditional Lifeways of the Southern Maori*, 156.
174. Ellison, 'Evidence of Edward Ellison on mahinga kai'. Place names on either side of the estuary mouth confirm such practices. See Stevens, 'The names are in the land, our history is in the land'.
175. Ian Smith, 'Retreat and resilience: Fur seals and human settlement in New Zealand', in *The Exploitation and Cultural Importance of Sea Mammals*, ed. Gregory G. Monks (Oxford: Oxbow Books, 2005), 10; I.W.G. Smith, 'Maori impact on the marine megafauna: Pre-European distributions of New Zealand sea mammals', in *Saying So Doesn't Make it So*, ed. D.G. Sutton (Dunedin: New Zealand Archaeological Society, 1989), 91, 103.
176. Peter Entwisle, *Taka: A vignette life of William Tucker 1784–1817* (Dunedin: Port Daniel Press, 2005), 66, 111, 114.
177. Chris Lalas and Corey J.A. Bradshaw, 'Folklore and chimerical numbers: Review of a millennium of interaction between fur seals and humans in the New Zealand region', *New Zealand Journal of Marine and Freshwater Research*, vol. 35, no. 3, 2001, 479–80.
178. For the context in which these lists were made, see most accessibly Jim Williams, 'Mahika kai: The husbanding of consumables by Māori in precontact Te Wāipounamu', *Journal of the Polynesian Society*, vol. 119, no. 2, 2010, 149–80.
179. George Habib, 'Report on the mahinga kai lists 1880', Wai 27, Document T4(b), 3. These three islands were named by H.K. Taiaroa as Ko Tāwheketū, Tokakaha and Te Here Kākaho. The first two were noted as lying 'off Ōrau', or Sandymount, and so suggests that these are the Gull Rocks. The third is 'off Tūmatakuru', and seems likely to be a different name for Wharekakahu, which is also on the outer coast off Allans Beach. See 'Mahinga kai list 1880 presented to Tipene O'Regan by Ministry of Agriculture and Fisheries', Wai 27, Document R 30, 2–3. Taiaroa petitioned parliament for title to these islands in 1882. See 'No. 419: Petition of H.K. Taiaroa', Reports of the Native Affairs Committee, 1882: http://nzetc.victoria.ac.nz/tm/scholarly/tei-Nat1882Repo-t1-g1-t99-g1-t1.html. Chasland also pointed out islands off the Otago Peninsula as being places where seals were harvested.

180. Chris Lalas, 'Recolonisation of Otago, southern New Zealand, by fur seals and sea lions: Unexpected patterns and consequences', in *Proceedings of the Conserv-Vision Conference, 2-4 July 2007*, eds Bruce Clarkson et al. (Hamilton: University of Waikato, 2008), 4.
181. Ellison, 'Evidence of Edward Ellison on mahinga kai'.
182. Williams, 'E Paakahi Hakinga a Kai', 144; Beattie, *Traditional Lifeways of the Southern Maori*, 505; Ellison, 'Evidence of Edward Ellison on mahinga kai'.
183. Atholl Anderson, 'Supporting papers to evidence of Dr Atholl Anderson on mahinga kai', Wai 27, Document H2; Dacker, *Te Mamae me te Aroha*, 7.
184. Robertson, ed., *Complete Book of New Zealand Birds*, 289-90.
185. As attested by numerous early European observations, including those of Monro, Shortland and the whalers' accounts, as well as by Renata, and by Māori tradition.
186. Aparata Renata, 'The native birds of the Otago Peninsula past and present', *Otago Witness*, 10 August 1910, 76.
187. Beattie, *Traditional Lifeways of the Southern Maori*, 510-11.
188. Williams, 'E Paakahi Hakinga a Kai', 164.
189. Beattie, *Traditional Lifeways of the Southern Maori*, 143-45, 316-26.
190. Ibid., 146.
191. Ibid., 144.
192. Williams, 'E Paakahi Hakinga a Kai', 223. check this is the old 193, wiata, Te Maire Tau
193. Ibid., 106.
194. Ibid, 205.
195. Ibid., 200.
196. Shortland, cited in ibid., 112.
197. Ellison, 'Evidence of Edward Ellison on mahinga kai'; Bill Dacker, *The People of the Place: Mahika kai* (Wellington: New Zealand 1990 Commission, 1990), 31.
198. John Rodolphus Kent, 'Journal of the proceedings of His Majesty's colonial cutter *Mermaid* from the 8th Day of May to the 15th Day of August inclusive', HC, MS 913, 39; Anderson, *The Welcome of Strangers*, 68.
199. Atholl Anderson has provided the clearest exposition of the possible distinctions between wakawaka and mahika kai. See Anderson, 'The evidence of Dr Atholl Anderson on mahinga kai'; Anderson, 'Wakawaka and mahinga kai', 631-40. Also Williams, 'E Paakahi Hakinga a Kai', 120.
200. William Cronon notes that Native Americans in New England developed a similar system of property rights, and there too similar differences emerged between Indians able to practise agriculture and those who sustained themselves by hunting and gathering. See William Cronon, *Changes in the Land: Indians, colonists, and the ecology of New England* (New York: Hill and Wang, 1983), 60-64.
201. Herries Beattie, *Tikao Talks* (Auckland: Penguin Books, 1990), 139.
202. Williams, 'E Paakahi Hakinga a Kai', 230.
203. Ibid., 120.
204. For the variety of resources sought, see Williams, 'E Paakahi Hakinga a Kai', 151; Dacker, *The People of the Place*, 6.
205. For representative samples see, on the one hand, Atholl Anderson, 'Prehistoric Polynesian impact on the New Zealand environment: Te Whenua Hou', in *Historical Ecology in the Pacific Islands: Prehistoric environmental and landscape change*, eds Patrick V. Kirch and Terry L. Hunt (New Haven: Yale University Press, 1997), 271-83; Anderson, 'A fragile plenty'; particularly stark is Richard Holdaway, 'Submission to the Waitangi Tribunal on Maori conservation of natural resources in the Pre-European and proto-historic period of New Zealand history', Wai 27, Document S17. On the other hand, see the works of Geoff Park, *Nga Uruora* (Wellington: Victoria University Press, 1995); Geoff Park, *Theatre Country: Essays on land & whenua* (Wellington: Victoria University Press, 2006). David Young attempts to balance these views in *Our Islands, Our Selves* (Dunedin: University of Otago Press, 2004), 38-56.
206. Belich, *Making Peoples*, 74.
207. For representative examples of this concept (and of others), see *Te Mātāpuenga: A compendium of references to the concepts and institutions of Māori customary law*, eds Richard Benton, Alex Frame and Paul Meredith (Wellington: Victoria University Press, 2013), 310-24.
208. For examples, see ibid., 312-18; Elsdon Best, 'Notes on the custom of rahui: Its application and manipulation, as also its supposed powers, its rites, invocations and superstitions', *Journal of the Polynesian Society*, vol. 13, no. 2, 1904, 83-88; Hirini Mead, *Tikanga Māori: Living by Māori values* (Wellington: Huia Publishers, 2003), 193-99.
209. Best, 'Notes on the custom of rahui', 86.
210. Ellison, 'Evidence of Edward Ellison on mahinga kai'.
211. Mead, *Tikanga Maori*, 197, citing Richard Taylor, *Te Ika a Maui: New Zealand and its inhabitants* (London: William McIntosh, 1870), 171-72.

212. Raymond Firth, *Economics of the New Zealand Maori* (Wellington: R.E. Owen, Government Printer, 1959), 261.
213. Anderson, 'A fragile plenty', 20.
214. For quotes see ibid., 36. Optimal foraging theory is a central tenet of the behavioural ecology which has so strongly shaped Anderson's research over several decades (and, after him, many other archaeologists in New Zealand). See for an early example, Atholl Anderson, 'Faunal depletion and subsistence change in the early prehistory of southern New Zealand', *Archaeology in Oceania*, vol. 18, no. 1, 1983, 1–10; For recent reflection on whether a more nuanced account of human motivation is required, see Atholl Anderson, 'Epilogue: Changing archaeological perspectives upon historical ecology in the Pacific islands', *Pacific Science*, vol. 63, no. 3, 2009, 752–54.
215. Anderson, 'Epilogue', 753–54.
216. Trevor H. Worthy and Richard N. Holdaway, *The Lost World of the Moa* (Christchurch: Canterbury University Press, 2002), 546–47, 563–64; R.N. Holdaway, 'Introduced predators and avifaunal extinction in New Zealand', in *Extinctions in Near Time: Causes, contexts, and consequences*, ed. Ross D.E. MacPhee (New York: Kluwer Academic/Plenum Publishers, 2000), 207; R.N. Holdaway, 'New Zealand's prehuman avifauna and its vulnerability', *New Zealand Journal of Ecology*, vol. 12 (supplement), 1989, 19.
217. Worthy and Holdaway, *The Lost World of the Moa*, 546–47.
218. A.J. Anderson, 'A model of prehistoric collecting on the rocky shore', *Journal of Archaeological Science*, vol. 8, 1981, 109–20. For a rare example of increased size in snapper, see B.F. Leach and A. Boocock, 'The impact of pre-European Māori fishermen on the New Zealand snapper, *Pagrus auratus*, in the vicinity of Rotokura, Tasman Bay', *New Zealand Journal of Archaeology*, vol. 16, 1994, 69–84.
219. Young, *Our Islands, Our Selves*, 50.
220. Nicholas J. Rawlence et al., 'Geographically contrasting biodiversity reductions in a widespread New Zealand seabird', *Molecular Ecology*, vol. 24, 2015, 4612–13.
221. Quotations from Anderson, 'Epilogue', 753; Richard Holdaway, 'Evidence of Richard N Holdaway on Maori conservation of natural resources in the pre-European and proto-historic periods of New Zealand history' Wai 27, Document S3, 3.
222. Firth, *Economics of the New Zealand Maori*, 263.
223. J.C. Kitson and H. Moller, 'Looking after your ground: Resource management practice by Rakiura Maori titi harvesters', *Papers and Proceedings of the Royal Society of Tasmania*, vol. 142, no. 1, 2008, 161–76; Henrik Moller, Jane C. Kitson and Theresa M. Downs, 'Knowing by doing: Learning for sustainable muttonbird harvesting', *New Zealand Journal of Zoology*, vol. 36, no. 3, 2009, 243–58; Williams, 'E Paakahi Hakinga a Kai', 204–05.
224. George Habib, Report on Ngai Tahu Fisheries Evidence, Wai 27, Document T4A, 158.
225. Ibid., 132.
226. Stevens, 'Muttonbirds and modernity in Murihiku', 52. For some views on whether Māori practised 'sustainable management', see Williams, 'E Paakahi Hakinga a Kai'; Alan Clarke, *The Great Sacred Forest of Tane, Te Wao Tapu Nui a Tane: A natural pre-history of Aotearoa New Zealand* (Auckland: Reed Books, 2007); Young, *Our Islands, Our Selves*, 38–56; Belich, *Making Peoples*, 74–75.
227. Anderson, *A Fragile Plenty*, 21.
228. Ibid., 56.

PART II: THE WORLD WASHES ASHORE

CHAPTER 4:
EUROPEAN EXPLORATION, MĀORI DISCOVERY:
FIRST CONTACTS 1770–1830

1. Jules de Blosseville, 'Nouvelles annales des voyages', extracts reproduced (in English) in Robert McNab, *Murihiku and the Southern Islands* (Invercargill: William Smith, 1907), 199–228, [220]. De Blosseville's accounts of southern Māori and sealers are based on information provided by Captain William Edwardson of the *Snapper* in 1823.
2. Frank Fyfe, 'The story of David Lowston, a pre-colonial NZ song', *The Maorilander: Journal of New Zealand folklore*, 1, 1970.
3. J.C. Beaglehole, ed., *The Journals of Captain James Cook on his Voyages of Discovery: The voyage of the Endeavour 1768–1771* (Cambridge: Cambridge University Press, 1955), entry for 25 February 1770, 257.
4. Beaglehole, ed., *The Journals of Captain James Cook*, entry for 26 February 1770, 258.
5. Ibid.
6. Ibid., entry for 4 March 1770, 259. Beaglehole notes (at n. 2) that Banks refers to the noise 'something like the shrieking of a goose' made by the bird, which identifies it as a yellow-eyed penguin. See also Ian Church, ed., *Gaining a*

Foothold: Historical records of Otago's eastern coast 1770–1839 (Dunedin: Friends of the Hocken Collections, 2008), 15.
7. Joseph Hooker, ed., *Journal of the Right Hon. Sir Joseph Banks* (London: Macmillan and Co., 1896), 218; Beaglehole, ed., *The Journals of Captain James Cook*, entry for 5 March 1770, 260. Harry Evison suggests that Māori saw Cook's ship to the south of Ōtākou, but provides no source for this assertion. See Harry Evison, *Te Wai Pounamu* (Wellington and Christchurch: Aoraki Press, 1993), 12.
8. Margaret Steven, *Trade, Tactics and Territory: Britain in the Pacific, 1783–1823* (Melbourne: Melbourne University Press, 1983), 22, 34, 39.
9. Thomas M. Hocken, *Contributions to the Early History of New Zealand [Settlement of Otago]* (London: Sampson Low, Marston & Co., 1898), 159.
10. Jim McAloon, 'Resource frontiers, environment, and settler capitalism', in *Environmental Histories of New Zealand*, eds Eric Pawson and Tom Brooking (Oxford: Oxford University Press, 2002), 53.
11. 'Additional instructions for Lt James Cook, appointed to command His Majesty's bark the Endeavour', in Beaglehole, ed., *The Journals of Captain James Cook*, introduction, cclxxxii–iii.
12. Alan Frost, *The Global Reach of Empire: Britain's maritime expansion in the Indian and Pacific Oceans 1764–1815* (Melbourne: The Miegunyah Press, 2003), 170, 177.
13. For the significance of New Zealand's flax and timber, see James Maria Matra's 'A proposal for establishing a settlement in New South Wales', in Robert McNab, ed., *Historical Records of New Zealand*, 2 vols (Wellington: Government Printer, 1908), vol. 1, 36–42.
14. D.R. Hainsworth, 'Exploiting the Pacific frontier: The New South Wales sealing industry 1800–1821', *The Journal of Pacific History*, vol. 2, no. 1, 1967, 67, 69.
15. Instructions to Phillip, 25 April 1787. Identical instructions were also given to Governors King, Bligh and Macquarie. See D.R. Hainsworth, *Builders and Adventurers: The traders and the emergence of the colony 1788–1821* (Melbourne: Cassell Press, 1968), 74.
16. James Broadbent, 'Fashioning a colonial culture', in James Broadbent, ed., *India, China, Australia: Trade and society 1788–1850*, (Sydney: Historic Houses Trust of New South Wales, 2003), 25; Hainsworth, 'Exploiting the Pacific frontier', 60.
17. McAloon, 'Resource frontiers, environment, and settler capitalism', 56.
18. See J.C. Beaglehole, ed., *The Voyage of the Resolution and Adventure 1772–1775* (Cambridge: Cambridge University Press, 1961), entry for 22 April 1773, 126.
19. Hainsworth, 'Exploiting the Pacific frontier', 60.
20. See Anne Salmond, *Between Worlds: Early exchanges between Maori and Europeans 1773–1815* (Auckland: Penguin Books, 1997), 287–88.
21. Steven, *Trade, Tactics and Territory*, 96–97.
22. Grace Karskens, 'The settler evolution: Space, place and memory in early colonial Australia', *Journal of the Association for the Study of Australian Literature*, vol. 13, no. 2, 2013, 6.
23. Rhys Richards, *Murihiku Re-viewed* (Wellington: Lithographic Services, 1995), 17.
24. Ibid., 28–29.
25. Ibid., 29.
26. Ibid., 18–19.
27. Ibid., 20.
28. Margaret Steven, 'Eastern trade', in Broadbent, ed., *India, China, Australia*, 49.
29. Cited in Tim Bonyhady, *The Colonial Earth* (Melbourne: Melbourne University Press, 2000), 10; Hainsworth, 'Exploiting the Pacific frontier', 66.
30. Steven, *Trade, Tactics and Territory*, 96.
31. McNab, *Murihiku and the Southern Islands*, 262; Richards, *Murihiku Re-viewed*, 36; Hainsworth, 'Exploiting the Pacific frontier', 68. Vincent O'Malley's assessment of this as 'idiotic indiscriminate slaughter' precisely misses the point that taking as many animals as possible was very rational behaviour for each individual sealer (earning a lay) and sealing captain. See Vincent O'Malley, *The Meeting Place: Māori and Pākehā encounters, 1642–1840* (Auckland: Auckland University Press, 2012), 88.
32. The Creed manuscript suggests that ships had visited for some time prior to the first trouble occurring in 1810. Charles Creed, MS papers 1187/201, Alexander Turnbull Library. For discussion, see Peter Entwisle, *Behold the Moon: The European occupation of the Dunedin district 1770–1848*, 2nd edn (Dunedin: Port Daniel Press, 2010), 27–30. Entwisle reproduces the Creed manuscript at pp. 193–96.
33. Peter Entwisle, *Taka: A vignette life of William Tucker 1784–1817* (Dunedin: Port Daniel Press, 2005), 70.
34. Church, ed., *Gaining a Foothold*, 32–39; Entwisle, *Behold the Moon*, 39–45; D.R. Hainsworth, 'Iron men in wooden ships: The Sydney sealers 1800–1820', *Labour History*, vol. 13, 1967, 23.

35. Alfred Crosby, *Ecological Imperialism*, 2nd edn (Cambridge: Cambridge University Press, 2004), 227.
36. As Tom Griffiths and Libby Robin among others have noted, Crosby generally removes too much human agency from this process. The 'displacement' of the indigenous comes to seem, as it did to some settlers in the nineteenth century, an expression of an immutable law of nature. See Tom Griffiths and Libby Robin, 'Introduction', in *Ecology and Empire: Environmental history and settler societies*, eds Tom Griffiths and Libby Robin (Edinburgh: Keele University Press, 1997), 2.
37. Hainsworth, 'Iron men in wooden ships', 20. For an account of the sealers' lay system as it operated on one ship in the south, the *Governor Bligh*, see McNab, ed., *Historical Records of New Zealand*, 558–60.
38. Entwisle, *Taka*, 63–66.
39. 'Takata pora' is the southern Māori equivalent of Pākehā – their name for all those people who were not Māori, a hitherto unnecessary distinction. 'Pākehā' was not in use in the south in this period, so its use is needlessly anachronistic; it only came to be used around the mid-nineteenth century. Different spellings and pronunciations of this name have been promoted – tangata pora, tagata bola. I have chosen 'takata pora', as it preserves something of the southern dialect's unique pronunciation without straying too far into speculation.
40. Evison, *Te Wai Pounamu*, 27–28; Michael King, *The Penguin History of New Zealand* (Auckland: Penguin Books, 2003), 105; 'Report on New Zealand flax, by R. Williams (ropemaker)', in McNab, ed., *Historical Records of New Zealand*, 463.
41. Peter Gibbons, 'The far side of the search for identity', *New Zealand Journal of History*, vol. 37, no. 1, 2003, 41.
42. Entwisle, *Behold the Moon*, 48–49.
43. See ibid., 63–68.
44. Ibid., 51.
45. *Sydney Gazette*, 30 March 1811, 2. In Church, ed., *Gaining a Foothold*, 53–54.
46. Tony Ballantyne, *Webs of Empire: Locating New Zealand's colonial past* (Wellington: Bridget Williams Books, 2012), esp. 13–15, 44–47, 124–36.
47. *Sydney Gazette*, 24 April 1813, 1; 14 August 1813, 2. In Church, ed., *Gaining a Foothold*, 63–64.
48. Entwisle, *Behold the Moon*, 59.
49. Ibid., 62; Extract from Jules de Blosseville, 'Essai sur les moeurs et les coutumes des habitans de la partie meridionale de Tavai-Poenammou', in McNab, *Murihiku and the Southern Islands*, 327–28. Thomas Shepherd's journal reveals that one of these men was still living in the Otago area in 1826, probably at Whareakeake (Murdering Beach).
50. Entwisle, *Behold the Moon*, 59.
51. Church, ed., *Gaining a Foothold*, 67, n. 50. See also Entwisle, *Behold the Moon*, 60.
52. Papuee's identity is mysterious, and scholars have suggested several candidates. See Richards, *Murihiku Re-viewed*; Atholl Anderson, *The Welcome of Strangers* (Dunedin: University of Otago Press, 1998), 67, 78; Entwisle, *Behold the Moon*, 60–61, n. 219.
53. *Sydney Gazette*, 2 December 1815, 2. In Church, ed., *Gaining a Foothold*, 67.
54. Charles Creed, MS papers 1187/201, Alexander Turnbull Library. Cited in Entwisle, *Behold the Moon*, 195.
55. Evison, *Te Wai Pounamu*, 9; Entwisle, *Taka*, 100.
56. Jules de Blosseville, 'Essay on the manners and customs of the inhabitants of the southern part of Tavai-Poenammou', in McNab, *Murihiku and the Southern Islands*, 211–18 [217].
57. Entwisle, *Taka*, 130.
58. The quotations I have used are taken from an article that originally appeared in the *Hobart Town Courier* on 12 April 1858, and was reprinted in the *Otago Witness* on 21 August 1858. See Entwisle, *Behold the Moon*, 215–18.
59. Entiwsle, *Behold the Moon*, 97–98, n. 368.
60. Ibid., 76.
61. Ibid., 76–83. Entwisle characterises all this violence as consequential from the theft of the shirt, hence 'The War of the Shirt'. He reasons that if through this incident 'relations hadn't been so generally soured deaths wouldn't have followed'. I consider that this conclusion stretches the evidence too far; for example, it doesn't account for why in 1813 the crew of the *Matilda* had good relations in Otago, scene of this incident, but were subject to murder and theft elsewhere.
62. Richards, *Murihiku Re-viewed*, 33.
63. See Anderson, *The Welcome of Strangers*, 74, 224, n. 14; Neil Clayton, 'Weeds, people and contested places: Selected themes from the history of New Zealanders and their weeds 1770–1940' (PhD diss., University of Otago, 2007), 203–04.
64. Anderson, *The Welcome of Strangers*, 75.
65. Ibid.; Belich, *Making Peoples* (Auckland: Penguin Books, 1996), 146.
66. Anderson, *The Welcome of Strangers*, 129.
67. Ibid., 73.

68. Elsdon Best, *Maori Agriculture* (Wellington: Te Papa Press, 1976), 285; McNab, *Murihiku and the Southern Islands*, 146–47. Michael Stevens rightly queries whether this 'extraordinary number' might not be an exaggeration or mistake. See Michael Stevens, 'Muttonbirds and modernity in Murihiku: Continuity and change in Kāi Tahu knowledge' (PhD diss., University of Otago, 2009), 86, n. 79.
69. McNab, *Murihiku and the Southern Islands*, 133–34.
70. A list held in the Hocken Collections distinguishes nine varieties of potato grown by southern Māori and differentiated by shape and colour. See 'Notebook of southern place names, waiata and vocabulary', HC, Misc-MS-0933/002.Also see Graham Harris, *Nga Riwai Maori – Maori potatoes* (Lower Hutt: The Open Polytechnic of New Zealand, 1999), 40.
71. Ross Gordon, ed., *Waikouaiti and Dunedin in 1850: Reminiscences of John McLay an early settler* (Dunedin: Self-published, 1998), 24.
72. For kāpana mangumangu, see G.M. Thomson, *The Naturalisation of Animals and Plants in New Zealand* (Cambridge: Cambridge University Press, 1922), 450–51; for tatairako, see Herries Beattie, 'Notebook entitled, "Further information about southern Maoris, mostly collected between 1900 and 1920" (1900–1920)', HC, MS-582/E/23; also James Barr, *The Old Identities* (Dunedin: Mills, Dick and Co., 1879), 50–51.
73. Best, *Maori Agriculture*, 285.
74. 'Journal of T. Shepherd', HC, MS-0440/06, 13.
75. A. Charles Begg and Neil C. Begg, *The World of John Boultbee* (Christchurch: Whitcoulls Publishers, 1979), 102–03.
76. James Somerville, 'Reminiscences of James Somerville', HC, AG-846/01, 18.
77. Herries Beattie, *Traditional Lifeways of the Southern Maori*, ed. Atholl Anderson (Dunedin: University of Otago Press, 1994), 463; Ian Church and Peter Entwisle have tried to ascertain the timing of Fowler's arrival via the record of half-grown potatoes. They place it in late July or early August. See Church, ed., *Gaining a Foothold*, 67, n. 50.
78. Anderson, *The Welcome of Strangers*, 72–75.
79. Murdoch Riley, *Maori Sayings and Proverbs* (Paraparaumu: Viking Sevenseas, 1990), 38–40.
80. J.R.H. Andrews, 'The parisitology of the Maori in pre-European times', *New Zealand Medical Journal*, vol. 84, 1976, 63–65. The seven parasites comprised five ectoparasites: head, body and (probably) pubic lice (respectively, *Pediculus humanus capitis, P. humanus humanus* and *P. Phthirus pubis*), the scabies mite (*Sarcptes scabei*) and *Demodex folliculorum* – a common mite cosmopolitan in humans worldwide; and two endoparasites, the worms known as 'iro', a threadworm (*Enterobius vermicularis*), and ngoiro (possibly *Ascaris lumbricoides*).
81. Crosby, *Ecological Imperialism*, 231.
82. Three men died of tuberculosis on Cook's first voyage. See ibid., 233. His difficulties with venereal disease are well documented.
83. Fenton's census of Māori taken in 1857–58, but going back to 1844, recorded 35 per cent absolute sterility in women. See D.I. Pool, *Te Iwi Maori: A New Zealand population past, present & projected* (Auckland: Auckland University Press, 1991), 50.
84. This possibility was suggested by the late Ian Church when he discovered references to a disease associated with the wreck of a ship captained by Rongotute, and realised that this could only refer to Cook (who was Tute throughout the Pacific). I helped him in hunting out archival and published evidence for it. We concluded that rewharewha was an epidemic disease affecting much of New Zealand, especially (but not only) the Cook Strait region, and specifically associated by Māori with Cook's second voyage and the failure to retaliate for the killings of Furneaux's men in the wake of the capture of the *Adventure*'s cutter. See Ian Church, 'The loss of the *Adventure*'s cutter and its aftermath', *Archaeology in New Zealand*, vol. 54, no. 2, 2011, 101–13.
85. This was because all sickness was due to the influence of atua; in particular, disease was seen as the manifestation of atua inhabiting humans to punish them for breach of tapu. Treatment therefore revolved not around treating symptoms, but on expelling the atua. See Edward Shortland, *The Southern Districts of New Zealand: A journal, with passing notices of the customs of the aborigines* (London: Longman, Brown, Green & Longmans, 1851), 30–31.
86. Kerry-Jayne Wilson, *Flight of the Huia* (Christchurch: Canterbury University Press, 2004), 136–37.
87. See ibid., 44, 137, 143; L. Sinclair et al., 'How did invertebrates respond to eradication of rats from Kapiti Island, New Zealand?', *New Zealand Journal of Zoology*, vol. 32, no. 4, 2005, 136; Alan Tennyson and Paul Martinson, *Extinct Birds* (Wellington: Te Papa Press, 2006), 12.
88. Wilson, *Flight of the Huia*, 252–53.
89. I.A.E. Atkinson, 'Spread of the ship rat (*Rattus r. rattus* L.) in New Zealand', *Journal of the Royal*

Society of New Zealand, vol. 3, no. 3, 1973, 458; G. Harper, K. Dickinson and P. Seddon, 'Habitat use by three rat species (Rattus spp.) on Stewart Island/Rakiura, New Zealand', *New Zealand Journal of Ecology*, vol. 29, no. 2, 2005, 252, 56–57; Worthy and Holdaway, *The Lost World of the Moa*, 553. James Somerville mentions their presence at Andersons Bay in the 1850s, but Peter Thomson writing in 1871 considered them long since disappeared. See P. Thomson, 'Work for field naturalists', *Transactions and Proceedings of the New Zealand Institute*, vol. 4, 1871, 140.

90. Richards, *Murihiku Re-viewed*, 33.
91. The development of the flax trade in New Zealand is best described by Roger Wigglesworth, 'The New Zealand timber and flax trade 1769–1840' (PhD diss., Massey University, 1981). For the early period to about 1822, see pp. 2–49 especially. See also 'Report on New Zealand flax, by R. Williams (ropemaker)', in McNab, ed., *Historical Records of New Zealand*, vol. 1, 475–76. The *Sydney Gazette*, 4 January 1827, 3, col. 2, reported on the largely unmet demand for flax: 'One hundred tons per annum could be worked up by that industrious rope-maker in Catherine Street, Mr Cowell'. Flax retailed in Sydney at up to £20 a ton. See Wigglesworth, 'The New Zealand timber and flax trade', 364; also Peter Entwisle, 'Edward Weller', in *The Advance Guard*, 3 vols., ed. G.J. Griffiths (Dunedin: Otago Daily Times, 1974), vol. 2, 35.
92. For example, in 1819 a restriction on ships under 350 tons carrying cargo back to Britain was lifted. This allowed Australian shipping to trade with Britain for the first time. In 1820 punitive duties on colonial whale oil and seal skins were slashed. See Rhys Richards, 'The first foreign sealing in New Zealand waters', in Rhys Richards, *Sealing in the Southern Oceans 1788–1833* (Porirua: Paremata Press, 2010), 182, 185 n. 32. The shackles on colonial entrepreneurs were fully loosened in the wake of Commissioner Bigge's report of 1823. Duties on New Zealand flax and timber landed in Sydney were lifted in 1825 and 1826. As Wigglesworth suggests, it is likely that Bigge's belief that trade with New Zealand needed strong government encouragement was known to Australian authorities prior to his reporting. This may have encouraged government-sponsored expeditions to open trade in timber in the north and in flax in the south. See Wigglesworth, 'The New Zealand timber and flax trade', 321.
93. James Belich, *Replenishing the Earth: The settler revolution and the rise of the Anglo-world, 1783–1939* (Oxford: Oxford University Press, 2009); Wigglesworth, 'The New Zealand timber and flax trade', 78–80.
94. Trade in Māori curios commenced with Cook's voyages and continued into the twentieth century. Joseph Banks, for example, inaugurated the trade in preserved heads, purchasing one in Queen Charlotte Sound in 1770. The early curio trade was fairly significant. Indeed, Peter Entwisle has gone so far as to suggest that Tucker may have inaugurated a new industry among Māori to serve this trade in 'curios' by promoting the making of tiki from adzes. Entwisle, *Behold the Moon*, 66.
95. McNab, *Murihiku*, 216; Boultbee notes Otago Māori bringing pigs south to trade for muskets in 1827.
96. Edwardson brought only about one ton of flax back to Sydney. Atholl Anderson suggests that Jacky Snapper might be Tuhawaiki. Anderson, *The Welcome of Strangers*, 67.
97. John Rodolphus Kent, 'Journal of the proceedings of His Majesty's colonial cutter *Mermaid* from the 8th Day of May to the 15th Day of August inclusive', HC, MS 913, 25 June, 39. Though born at Taumutu, Te Matenga Taiaroa had now established himself at Ōtākou under the authority of Tahatu, who was pre-eminent chief until the mid-1830s.
98. Kent, 'Journal', 2 July 1823, 50; Anderson, *The Welcome of Strangers*, 68.
99. Kent, 'Journal', 31 July 1823, 103–04.
100. Ibid.
101. Ibid., 2 July, 17 July 1823, 74–76.
102. Ibid., 17 July 1823, 76.
103. Ibid., 19 July 1823, 81.
104. Ibid.
105. Cited in Evison, *Te Wai Pounamu*, 34.
106. Kent, 'Journal', 14 June 1823, 30.
107. Evison, *Te Wai Pounamu*, 39. According to Atholl Anderson, Honekai died about 1815 and was succeeded by Te Whakataupuka. See Anderson, *The Welcome of Strangers*, 75. Evison claims that no Pākehā were killed 'on Murihiku coasts' after 1823: Evison, *Te Wai Pounamu*, 34. This ignores the killings in Fiordland of 1826, presumably by placing them north of Murihiku. Regardless, it has interesting parallels in the north of New Zealand, where in the 1820s leading Māori rangatira also decided to put a stop to violence towards Europeans. According to Samuel Marsden, for example, Hongi Hika declared that he would personally punish anyone harming Europeans. See Grant

Phillipson, 'Bay of Islands Maori and the Crown 1793–1853', Wai 1040, Document A1, 70.
108. Begg and Begg, *The World of John Boultbee*, 220–21. For discussion, see Evison, *Te Wai Pounamu*, 27, 31; 'Reminiscences of William Isaac Haberfield', in *Evening Star*, 14 February 1891. Also transcribed, with comment, in Church, ed., *Gaining a Foothold*, 257–63.
109. Te Pahi had recently killed men from the *General Gates*, as well as the youth Ebenezer Eton at Port William in 1823. Begg and Begg, *The World of John Boultbee*, 102; Evison, *Te Wai Pounamu*, 34; Anderson, *The Welcome of Strangers*, 76. According to Ian Church, the youth's name is listed on the ship's muster roll as Eton; the historians cited above give it as Denton. Ian Church, pers. comm., 1 October 2007.
110. Church, ed., *Gaining a Foothold*, 16, 109–11.
111. Wigglesworth, 'The New Zealand timber and flax trade', 26, 211–12; Australia sourced flax from Norfolk Island, where – it seems – Māori had introduced it during the prehistoric period. See Atholl Anderson, 'Pieces of the past' in *Tangata Whenua: An illustrated history*, eds Atholl Anderson et al. (Wellington: Bridget Williams Books, 2014), 74.
112. Cited in Entwisle, *Behold the Moon*, 92.
113. Wigglesworth, 'The New Zealand timber and flax trade', 211–12.
114. See especially and generally John O.C. Ross, *William Stewart: Sealing captain, trader and speculator* (Canberra: Roebuck Society, 1987).
115. Neil Begg, 'John Rudolphus Kent', in *Dictionary of New Zealand Biography*, vol. 1 (Wellington: Allen & Unwin and Department of Internal Affairs), 226–27.
116. The *Samuel* visited Ōtākou and Foveaux Strait in 1823 carrying muskets to trade for flax, returning with 800 seal skins also. Kent returned to Ōtākou several times over the following years to trade for dressed flax. He was here early in 1824 on the NSW government's *Elizabeth Henrietta* bringing a chief, 'Titohikau', and his wife from Sydney; again, later in 1824 in the *Mermaid*; and, according to Shepherd's diary, again in May of 1826 when Herd was also here. See *New Zealand Herald*, 9 October 1880, and *Sydney Gazette*, 1 July 1824, p. 2, col. 1, in Church, ed., *Gaining a Foothold*, 108–09, 111; Shepherd, 'Journal of T. Shepherd', 8 May 1826. Also Entwisle, *Behold the Moon*, 90–92.
117. For quotation and accounts of Kent's agents in Foveaux Strait, see Begg and Begg, *The World of John Boultbee*, 195, 197–98, 219; Richards, *Murihiku Re-viewed*, 38. For a record of Kent's agents at 'Tarkow' [Takapuneke], the Banks Peninsula home of Te Maiharanui, then head of Kāi Tahu, see Samuel Marsden, 'Additional observations', HC, MS 57/202, 18 April 1831. The suggestion that Kent may have had agents at Otago is speculative.
118. This meeting seems too extraordinary to have been coincidental. See generally Ross, *William Stewart*. At the same time another ship, the *Sally*, was also at Pegasus on a sealing voyage. One of its crew, Edwin Palmer, went north, probably to Otago (depending on the identification of 'Taieri Heads') with Te Whakataupuka and bought two pigs and 3500lb (1.5 tonnes) of potatoes for two muskets and an adze.
119. For the fact the ships were there at the same time, see Shepherd, 'Journal of T. Shepherd', 8 May 1826. For Kent's cargo, see *Sydney Gazette*, 4 January 1827, 3, in Church, ed., *Gaining a Foothold*, 131. For Herd's account of the harbour, see Church, ed., *Gaining a Foothold*, 127–28. Herd's accounts were widely available after they were published in 1838 in J.S. Pollack's accounts of voyaging in New Zealand.
120. As noted earlier, Ōtākou may also have grown after the abandonment of Whareakeake, probably in 1825.
121. The names and placement of these villages are found in several primary sources; for example, see Shepherd's journal, Harwood's records and Mantell's census. The settlement pattern is also summarised by Anderson, *The Welcome of Strangers*, 169. Anderson has Ruatitiko as Ruatiti, following Mantell. See also Murray Bathgate, 'The Maori occupancy of Murihiku, 1000–1900 A.D.: A geographic study of change', (PhD diss., University of Otago, 1969), 214–15 and Figure 22.
122. Geoff Park, *Theatre Country: Essays on land & whenua* (Wellington: Victoria University Press, 2006), 39.
123. There are frustrating difficulties with this source material. It seems that the version held in the Mitchell Library (copy in the Hocken G.C. Thomson Collection, MS-0440: 06) is likely to be the rough draft Shepherd kept on the voyage. Quotations are from this version unless specified. An alternative typescript version, with significant discrepancies, is also in the Hocken Collections, with the transcriber's note: 'In the original this paper has a line drawn through it as though it were not to be done.' Both versions are likely drafts of a missing final

report for the company. See Una Shepherd Price, *My Family of Shepherds* (Scone, NSW: privately published, 1988), 7.
124. Shepherd, 'Journal of T. Shepherd', HC, MS-0440/06. Entry for 4 May 1826. Spelling and grammar as in original.
125. Ibid., 6 May 1826.
126. Ibid.
127. Ibid.
128. Ibid. Edwin Palmer also said that he encountered 'about 2 or 300 natives' when at Taieri Heads – almost certainly Taiaroa Head – sometime late in 1826. See 'Reminiscences of Edwin Palmer', in Begg and Begg, *The World of John Boultbee*, 299–301.
129. Shepherd, Journal of Thomas Shepherd [typescript, alternative version].
130. Ray Hargreaves, 'An historical geography of New Zealand farming before the introduction of refrigeration' (PhD diss., University of Otago, 1966), 87.
131. Anderson, *The Welcome of Strangers*, 68. Edwardson reported in 1823 that Māori in Murihiku were growing 'potatoes, cabbages and other kitchen vegetables introduced by the Europeans'. Caddell adds carrots, turnips and wheat. As noted, Otago Māori may have grown wheat, too, since Shepherd reported trading for flour in 1826.
132. Begg and Begg, *The World of John Boultbee*, 87.
133. Ibid., 60, 102.
134. Anderson, *The Welcome of Strangers*, 76–77; Harry Morton, *The Whale's Wake* (Dunedin: University of Otago Press, 1982), 171.
135. Anderson, *The Welcome of Strangers*, 154; Johann Riemenscheider, 'On Maori habits of life', HC, MS 0303, 19. The prevalence of tobacco smoking among Māori was very often remarked upon. It was already valued in 1831 when the *Vittoria* visited. See Joseph Price, 'Extracts from the diary of Joseph Price', HC MS 0440/11. Price mentions that women considered 'an old cotton shirt or a quid of tobacco' as 'ample, nay munificent remuneration' for a night's warmth.
136. Shortland, *The Southern Districts of New Zealand*, 183.
137. Johann Reimenscheider, a missionary at Taiaroa Head in the mid-1860s, commented that '[t]he natives generally smoke much and they use only the strongest kinds of tobacco', using 'short clay pipes making the smoke very hot and sharp'. He added that children smoked also. See Riemenscheider, 'On Maori habits of life', 19.
138. For example Guillou, cited in Entwisle, *Behold the Moon*, 179–80.
139. Cited in Evison, *Te Wai Pounamu*, 46. See also Anderson, *The Welcome of Strangers*, 94–95.
140. Evison, *Te Wai Pounamu*, 39; Richards, *Murihiku Re-viewed*, 40.
141. This was a clever ploy in several respects – for example, it made the European men on Codfish Island reliant on Māori from the mainland for much of their food, rendering good behaviour all the more likely.
142. The surviving lascar lived at Whareakeake, just to the north, until at least 1823. The settlement at Whareakeake was disbanded at some point in the mid-1820s. According to a descendent of Te Matahaere, this was to gain better access to the Titi Islands in Foveaux Strait. Some of the people did move to the Peninsula settlements, according to Rawiri Te Maire. See 'Letter from Frederick Allen Green to Thomas Hocken, 23 October 1890', HC, MS-0482.
143. *Hobart Town Courier*, 16 January 1830, 2; Will Lawson, *Blue Gum Clippers and Whale Ships of Tasmania* (Hobart: Shiplovers' Society of Tasmania, 1986), 58, cited in Church, ed., *Gaining a Foothold*, 143–44.
144. Richards, *Murihiku Re-viewed*, 44.
145. Māori had attempted to gain a musket in 1773 at Dusky Sound, but Cook did not allow it. Anderson, *The Welcome of Strangers*, 210. By 1830 guns and associated equipment accounted for 40 per cent of Sydney exports to New Zealand. In 1831 they amounted to 68 per cent of the value of sales to Māori. See Morton, *The Whale's Wake*, 202.
146. Evison, *Te Wai Pounamu*, 35–36.
147. Ian Church, *Otago's Infant Years* (Dunedin: Otago Heritage Books, 2001), 24; Price, 'Extracts from the diary of Joseph Price'.
148. Evison, *Te Wai Pounamu*, 51, 63.
149. Begg and Begg, *The World of John Boultbee*, 107.
150. Anderson, *The Welcome of Strangers*, 196.
151. Ibid. Anderson arrives at this estimate by using 'Shepherd's count of whare (fifty one houses in six settlements)' combined with Elizabeth Durwood's estimate that eight people might have inhabited a house. Shepherd provided no such count – rather, Herd's chart depicts 51 houses (in five settlements). Entwisle, however, argues that Herd's depiction is not intended to be accurate, and that the houses marked are simply symbolic of the presence of a village. Certainly d'Urville and his officers recorded larger villages of 30 to 50 houses in 1840.
152. Anderson, *The Welcome of Strangers*, 76.

Chapter 5: 'Soon may the Wellerman come': Whaling at Ōtākou 1831–48

1. Richard Weller, *A Fortune Lost: The Joseph Weller family in New South Wales and New Zealand 1824–1890* (Sheffield, UK: self-published, 2003), 48.
2. Thomas Shepherd, 'Journal of Thomas Shepherd', HC, MS-0440/06, 18.
3. Harry Morton, *The Whale's Wake* (Dunedin: University of Otago Press, 1982), 23.
4. A. Charles Begg and Neil C. Begg, *The World of John Boultbee* (Christchurch: Whitcoulls Publishers, 1979), 26.
5. Morton, *The Whale's Wake*, 292.
6. Ibid., 52.
7. Ibid., 53.
8. Ibid., 121, 143.
9. For material on the Wellers, see in particular Ian Church, ed., *Gaining a Foothold: Historical records of Otago's eastern coast 1770–1839* (Dunedin: Friends of the Hocken Collections, 2008). This reproduces all the primary records. For discussion, see Peter Entwisle, *Behold the Moon: European occupation of the Dunedin district 1770–1848*, 2nd edn (Dunedin: Port Daniel Press, 2010); Weller, *A Fortune Lost*.
10. Entwisle, *Behold the Moon*, 106–07. There is convincing, albeit circumstantial, evidence that Joseph Brooks Weller visited Otago himself in 1831 as a passenger on the *Sir George Murray*, under Thomas McDonnell. Who if not he secured Māori agreement?
11. That munitions were the payment is the argument first made by McNab (1913) and followed by Rickard (1996) and Entwisle (1998, 2006, 2010). Not all have agreed; but we must presume that the Ōtākou rangatira would have required payment, and the similarity between the payment made to Te Whakataupuka for the establishment of the Preservation Inlet whaling station and the Wellers' first cargo is striking. The latter comprised '6 cases muskets, 10 barrels, 104 half-barrels gunpowder, 1 case axes, 2 iron boilers, 5 casks beef, 1 case whaling gear, 1 case whaling line, 1 pipe gin, 2 puncheons rum, 5 kegs tobacco, and stores'. *The Australian*, 30 September 1831, 3, col. 2. In Church, ed., *Gaining a Foothold*, 162.
12. Robert McNab, *The Old Whaling Days* (Auckland: Golden Press, 1913; reprint, 1974), 22–37.
13. Harry Evison, *Te Wai Pounamu* (Wellington and Christchurch: Aoraki Press, 1993), 52–60.
14. McNab, *The Old Whaling Days*, 89–90. In 1829 Peter Williams delivered two 12-pound carronades and two air-guns to Te Whakataupuka at Preservation Inlet. In 1832 he completed payment by delivering 60 muskets and 450kg each of powder and ball. See discussion in Te Maire Tau and Atholl Anderson, *Ngāi Tahu: A migration history* (Wellington: Bridget Williams Books, 2009), 171.
15. Evison, *Te Wai Pounamu*, 64–70.
16. Though in 1836 his kinsman Te Puoho led a taua down the West Coast and over the Southern Alps in an ill-fated attempt to directly engage Murihiku Māori. For details, see Atholl Anderson, *Te Puoho's Last Raid* (Dunedin: Otago Heritage Books, 1986); Evison, *Te Wai Pounamu*; Angela Ballara, *Taua* (Auckland: Penguin Books, 2003), 385–88.
17. J.W. Barnicoat, 'Diary, 17th June 1843–11th October 1844', HC, Misc-MS-1451-3, 19 April 1844, 14.
18. Ian Church, *Otago's Infant Years* (Dunedin: Otago Heritage Books, 2001), 10.
19. Morton, *The Whale's Wake*, 212.
20. Church, *Otago's Infant Years*, 10.
21. For oil-to-whale ratios, see Rhys Richards, *Murihiku Re-viewed* (Wellington: Lithographic Services, 1995), 64. George Weller's letter to his brother Edward of 23 July 1835 gives the price for oil in London as £26 to £27, with bone selling at £100 to £110. Church, ed., *Gaining a Foothold*, 211–12. However, leakage from casks was a great problem, and was one of the reasons why coopers, who constructed the casks, were indispensable and very highly paid. If it had all reached the London market, the Wellers' 430 tuns of oil and 20 tons of bone might have fetched over £13,000.
22. Letters from George Weller to Edward at Otago, 29 February 1836, 23 April 1836, 4 March 1837, in Church, ed., *Gaining a Foothold*, 230–32, 236–37, 269–72 respectively.
23. Entwisle, *Behold the Moon*, 86.
24. Church, ed., *Gaining a Foothold*, 5.
25. Letter from George Weller to Edward at Otago, 29 February 1836, in ibid., 230–32.
26. Quotation from Captain Parkinson of the *Bee* in Church, *Otago's Infant Years*, 33. This was the number of ships fishing in the harbour according to Shortland, though he mistakes the year as 1835. See Edward Shortland, *The Southern Districts of New Zealand: A journal, with passing notices of the customs of the aborigines* (London: Longman, Brown, Green & Longmans, 1851), 300–01 (Appendix VI).
27. Church, *Otago's Infant Years*, 12.
28. *The Australian*, 20 January 1837. Cited in Church, ed., *Gaining a Foothold*, 267–68.

29. Ian Church, 'French whalers at Otago 1838 to 1853', in *Pacific Journeys: Essays in honour of John Dunmore*, ed. Glynnis M. Cropp et al. (Wellington: Victoria University Press, 2005).
30. Church, *Otago's Infant Years*, 12.
31. Richards, *Murihiku Re-viewed*, 64.
32. The advertisement gives a clear indication of the extent of the Wellers' station. It describes 'Premises at Otago. These premises lately occupied by G & E Weller, at Otago, consisting of dwelling house, two storehouses, large carpenter's workshop and capital range of outhouses with large garden well stocked with fruit trees in bearing. Also a large blacksmiths shop. Also a yard for shipbuilding, with large work shed, saw pit, blocks, launching ways, steam box etc. There is a large quantity of seasoned timber lying in and near the yard. The above is a capital opportunity for parties wishing to establish themselves in the Middle Island.' See Weller, *A Fortune Lost*, 33.
33. Edward Shortland, 'Outwards Letter Book "a" 15 September 1842 to 13 March 1845', HC, MS 86A PC-0027.
34. The *Columbus*, for example, shipped four Māori from Ōtākou for the whaling season of 1838. See Church, ed., *Gaining a Foothold*, 305. Whalers were paid a 'lay', a share of overall proceeds, in proportion to their importance. According to Shortland, a chief headsman typically received 1:18, a headsman 1:28, boatsteerers 1:60, a cooper or carpenter 1:70 (or monthly wages), and an ordinary boatman 1:100. Shortland, *The Southern Districts of New Zealand*, 109.
35. 'Copy of Octavius Harwood journals', G.C. Thomson papers, HC, MS-0438/03.
36. Harwood's journal records employing 12 Māori women at 2s 6d a day to harvest potatoes.
37. For one such sequence see ibid., 30 September, 5 October, 6 October, 9 October 1838.
38. Ibid., 27 June, 2 July 1838.
39. Ibid., 20–21 October 1838.
40. Octavius Harwood, Jnr, 'Notes on the settlement of the Otago Peninsula', HC, MS 0604/025. Harwood himself recorded potentially violent disputes with Europeans, not Māori.
41. *Sydney Herald*, 25 August 1834, 3, col. 2. Cited in Church, ed., *Gaining a Foothold*, 194.
42. *Sydney Herald*, 11 November 1833, 2, col. 4. Cited in ibid., 180. Haberfield recorded that Tahatu had visited Sydney 'several times'. See HC, MS-0439; 183, 'Transcript of reminiscences of unidentified person' [Haberfield]. Karetai certainly went to Sydney at least twice, and Taiaroa at least once.
43. Octavius Harwood, 'Accounts ledger of store customers and any debts incurred', HC, MS-0604/003'.
44. Octavius Harwood, 'Accounts ledger', HC, MS-0604/003.
45. For a range of such transactions, see Octavius Harwood's journals and accounts; also Church, ed., *Gaining a Foothold*, 292; Atholl Anderson, *The Welcome of Strangers* (Dunedin, University of Otago Press, 1998), 129.
46. Shortland, *The Southern Districts of New Zealand*, 19.
47. In 1837, for example, Edward Weller sold sealing boats for 1000 baskets of potatoes each, which George complained left far too little profit from an outlay of £38. Actually, presuming for the sake of argument that a basket weighed 35 lb, and potatoes were worth £5 a ton to the Wellers in Sydney (George's lower estimate), the sale price of over £75 was reasonable. 'George Weller to Edward Weller, 16 October 1837', cited in Church, ed., *Gaining a Foothold*, 280–81.
48. In September 1839 Harwood noted that Tuhawaiki had arrived with 10 boats and 60–70 men. Harwood, 'Copy of Octavius Harwood journals', 8, 12 June 1839. The log of the Piraki whaling station mentions Tuhawaiki having 15 boats and (perhaps included and perhaps separate to this) Karetai having four boats. See entries for 31 October, 2 November, 18 November 1839. Cited in Church, ed., *Gaining a Foothold*, 388–89. This is presumably the source for Anderson's statement that some 20 boats were involved. Anderson, *The Welcome of Strangers*, 86, 125–26.
49. Harwood makes this comment in a note attached to an undated list in HC, MS-0439/14/2. Cited in Church, ed., *Gaining a Foothold*, 298, n. 210. For the largely complete abandonment of canoes by 1840, see Anderson, *The Welcome of Strangers*, 125–26.
50. Shortland, *The Southern Districts of New Zealand*, 171–72.
51. Michael Stevens, '"The ocean is our only highway and means of communication": Maritime culture in colonial southern New Zealand', *The Journal of New Zealand Studies*, no. 12, 2011, 155–56. Frances Steel, acknowledging that 'questions of land alienation, transformation and use go [to] the heart of New Zealand politics', argues for 'the timeliness of a "sea turn" in approaches to New Zealand colonial history'. See Frances Steel, 'Uncharted waters? Cultures of sea transport and mobility in New Zealand colonial history',

The Journal of New Zealand Studies, no. 12, 2011, 138.

52. Halswell was not long arrived as Protector of Aborigines and Commissioner for the Management of Native Reserves at Wellington, on behalf of the New Zealand Company. Phillip Barton, who made a study of Māori map-making, notes that all we know of how this map came to be made comes from two letters. In a letter of 11 November 1841 to the secretary of the New Zealand Company in London, Halswell writes: 'I have, at this time, some natives from the South with me, who are at work upon a map of the entire Middle [South] and Southern [Stewart] Islands, giving a minute description of every bay and harbour round the entire coasts, with their native names, which generally convey a correct idea of the headlands, soil, &c.' Edmund Storr Halswell, 'Report of E. Halswell, Esq., on the numbers and condition of the native population', *New Zealand Journal*, 14 May 1842, 111–13 [112]. Subsequently, a letter of 4 December 1841 to Henry Samuel Chapman, which Phillip Barton considers was probably from Thomas Mitchell Partridge, stated: 'I sent you by the Bailey a chart of the Middle Island drawn by some natives of Otago; it is of course a caricature but in many points useful.' 'Letter from a merchant of Wellington,' 4 December 1841, *New Zealand Journal*, 62 (28 May 1842), 125. See generally, Phillip Lionel Barton, 'Maori cartography and the European encounter', in *Cartography in the Traditional African, American, Arctic, Australian and Pacific Societies*, eds David Woodward and G. Malcolm Lewis (Chicago: University of Chicago Press, 1998), 494–532.
53. Murdoch Riley, *Maori Sayings and Proverbs* (Paraparaumu: Viking Sevenseas, 1990), 70–77.
54. On 21 May 1833 Joseph Brooks Weller wrote this note from Otago to Kelly: 'This is to certify that the natives of Otago have threatened to take your ship from Capt. Lovat stating that you had formerly killed or wounded several years ago some of their people and that would have revenge. Most of the people also deserted the vessel at the above Port.' G.M. Thomson, 'Notes on sealing and whaling', HC, MS-0439.
55. That they were hostages in the eyes of the Europeans is made clear in two letters: 'Letter from James Backhouse to Thomas Fowell Buxton, Sydney, 5 February 1835' and 'Letter from Samuel Marsden to T.F. Buxton, Parramatta, 11 February 1835', cited in Church, ed., *Gaining a Foothold*, 200–02. James Backhouse was a member of the Society of Friends, who had discussed the matter with Marsden, while Thomas Buxton was a prominent anti-slavery campaigner and member of parliament.
56. Karetai arrived in Sydney on 21 September 1834 on the *Joseph Weller*. In a letter dated 25 September, Marsden said: 'Since I began my letter a chief and his wife have arrived from the South Cape and are with me. His object is to get a missionary to reside at his settlement.' Robert McNab, ed., *Historical Records of New Zealand*, 2 vols (Wellington: Government Printer, 1908) vol. 1, 720. Stack records that Karetai received instruction. See James Stack, *More Maoriland Adventures of J.W. Stack* (Dunedin: A.H. and A.W. Reed, 1936), 114–15.
57. 'Rev. S. Marsden to ----, Parramatta, September 25th, 1834', in McNab, ed., *Historical Records*, vol. 1, 719–20.
58. *Sydney Gazette*, 26 August 1834. Cited in Church, ed., *Gaining a Foothold*, 196.
59. *Sydney Herald*, 16 October 1834. Cited in ibid., 197.
60. *Sydney Gazette*, 18 October 1834; 'George Weller to Edward at Otago, Sydney, 7 August 1835', in Church, ed., *Gaining a Foothold*, 199, 214.
61. *Sydney Herald*, 1 December 1834, 2, col. 7. Cited in ibid., 205.
62. Entwisle, *Behold the Moon*, 122–23, n. 492. G.C. Thomson later wrote that 'from the time of the Kelly mass. the Maori had no time for the Pakeha[;] the trouble in 1831 was mainly due to this and until Edward Weller married Nikaru the daughter of Taiaroa the Wellers went in fear of their lives.' See G.C. Thomson, 'Miscellaneous handwritten notes', HC, MS-0439/192.
63. Weller, *A Fortune Lost*, 22, 32.
64. 'Letter from George Weller to Edward at Otago, Sydney, 29 February 1836', in Church, ed., *Gaining a Foothold*, 230–33.
65. J.W. Donovan, 'Measles in Australia and New Zealand, 1834–1835', *The Medical Journal of Australia*, vol. 1, no. 5, 1970.
66. Andrew Cliff, Peter Haggett and Matthew Smallman-Raynor, *Measles: An historical geography of a major human viral disease* (Oxford and Cambridge: Blackwell Publishers, 1993), 31, 46.
67. 'Letter from Samuel Marsden to T.F. Buxton', in Church, ed., *Gaining a Foothold*, 201–02.
68. It has been argued that Tipu brought measles to Murihiku. See Bill Dacker, *Te Mamae Me Te Aroha* (Dunedin: University of Otago Press, 1994), 14; Anderson, *The Welcome of Strangers*. However, Karetai and his family must be

primarily identified as vectors because Karetai specifically told Stack that this had been the case. See Stack, *More Maoriland Adventures of J.W. Stack*, 114–15. See also Harry Evison, *The Long Dispute: European colonisation and Maori land rights in southern New Zealand* (Christchurch: Canterbury University Press, 1997), 69; Harry Evison, 'Karetai ?–1860', *Dictionary of New Zealand Biography*, vol. 1 (Wellington: Allen & Unwin and Department of Internal Affairs), 216–17; Virginia Perry, ed., *Eliza's Journal – A gentlewoman's experiences in the late 1850s* (Dunedin: Virginia Perry, 2004), 263.

69. Contemporaneous accounts of this epidemic at Ōtākou include reports in the *Sydney Herald*, 2 September 1835, *Sydney Herald*, 21 November 1836 and *Sydney Monitor*, 21 November 1836. There is also Edward Weller's remark, in a letter to George on 12 August 1835, that the Māori were too ill to clean bone, while measles was reported at Preservation Inlet in *The Australian*, 18 September 1835. There is a contemporary denial that measles was at Otago in the spring of 1835. On arrival in Sydney in September, Captain Ridley denied an account that Māori on board his ship had measles, stating 'that disorder had not existed at Otago for some months prior to his arrival there'. See *The Sydney Monitor*, 3 October 1835. Cited in Church, ed., *Gaining a Foothold*, 217. However, Ridley's denial that measles was affecting Otago, made in the context of the claim that his ship was carrying the disease, is unreliable, especially given that the *Sydney Packet*, which sailed from Otago on 25 August, had just reported its presence. See *Sydney Herald*, 2 September 1835. Cited in Church, ed., *Gaining a Foothold*, 216. This means that we cannot dismiss the subsequent Māori recollections recorded by Europeans, which all stress the scale of mortality. Evison's summary of these records includes an eyewitness to a subsequent epidemic at Pigeon Bay, Canterbury, in 1848–49, in which almost half the population purportedly perished. See Evison, *Te Wai Pounamu*, 101–02, n. 15.

70. Stack, *More Maoriland Adventures of J.W. Stack*, 114–15.

71. 'William Palmer's reminiscences', *Evening Star*, 4 July 1891. Māori memories of this epidemic are recorded by several early European residents or visitors, including Watkin, Jollie, Haberfield, Palmer and Shortland. Jollie, for example, recorded that '[m]easles, one of these diseases, was brought by ship to the Bluff, and carried to the Northward by Maoris along the coast, who voyaging by day and landing for the night at different pahs, left the disease behind, and still carried it forward until the principal Maori settlements were all infected. The mortality was so great that in some cases the survivors could not bury their dead.' R. Jollie, 'Recollections of early days in New Zealand, ca 1847', HC, MS 0440/14, 7. See also Anderson, *The Welcome of Strangers*, 193.

72. *Sydney Herald*, 2 September 1835, cited in Church, ed., *Gaining a Foothold*, 216.

73. Extract from 'William Palmer's reminiscences', *Evening Star*, 4 July 1891. Cited in Church, ed., *Gaining a Foothold*, 216. Also in Evison, *Te Wai Pounamu*, 85.

74. Michael Oldstone, *Viruses, Plagues, and History* (New York and Oxford: Oxford University Press, 1998), 73–76; P.H. Curson, *Times of Crisis: Epidemics in Sydney 1788–1900* (Sydney: Sydney University Press, 1985), 54–55. Curson notes that the effects of measles were exacerbated by interactions with malnutrition and other diseases, so that this epidemic triggered many deaths from diarrhoea, dysentery and broncho-pneumonia.

75. Evison, *Te Wai Pounamu*, 85.

76. It should be borne in mind that Europeans were not particularly effective in treating these diseases, either – they often treated tuberculosis by prescribing cold baths and wrapping in wet sheets. See Evison, *Te Wai Pounamu*, 85.

77. *Sydney Herald*, 21 November 1836, in Church, ed., *Gaining a Foothold*, 253.

78. For timing, see Church, *Otago's Infant Years*, 34. For effects, see *Sydney Herald*, 21 November 1836; *Sydney Monitor*, 21 November 1836, 2. In Church, ed., *Gaining a Foothold*, 252–53.

79. *Sydney Monitor*, 21 November 1836, 2. In Church, ed., *Gaining a Foothold*, 253.

80. Several historians have dated a measles epidemic to 1838. This might explain the lack of potato exports for that year, but there is no documentary evidence for it (and Harwood would surely have noted such in his journal), while it is highly unlikely that measles would have reoccurred so soon after the widespread 1835 epidemic conferred immunity on its survivors. The error seems to first appear in A.S. Thomson, *The Story of New Zealand*, 2 vols (London: John Murray, 1859; reprint, Capper Press, Christchurch), vol. 1, 212. As is the way of such errors, it is then repeated by others, of whom Alexander Mackay, *A Compendium of the Official Documents Relative to Native Affairs in the South Island*, 2 vols

(Nelson: Government Printer, 1873), vol. 1, part II, 25, has been most influential. There were subsequent but localised outbreaks of measles in 1848–49 at Pigeon Bay and Banks Peninsula, and at Aparima in the 1850s. For Pigeon Bay, see James Hay, *Reminiscences of Earliest Canterbury (Principally Banks Peninsula) and its Settlers* (Christchurch: Christchurch Press Company, 1915), 8–10, 49. For Aparima, see Bill Dacker, 'He Raraka A Ka Awa, updated, annotated and sourced manuscript for the book, "Te Mamoe Me Te Aroha", originally published in 1994', HC, Misc-MS-1716,47, n. 34. In reference to the latter, Beattie noted that part of the old village at Riverton where most of the people had died had since been called 'Te Whiu' (the plague). Herries Beattie, 'Traditions and Legends Collected from the Natives of Murihiku (Southland, New Zealand) Part V', *Journal of the Polynesian Society*, vol. 25, no. 99, 1916, 96.
81. Kenneth Kiple, ed., *Plague, Pox and Pestilence* (London: Weidenfield & Nicholson, 1997), 48.
82. 'Transcript of journal of Rev. James Watkin', HC, MS 0440/04.
83. Alfred Crosby, *Ecological Imperialism: The biological expansion of Europe, 900–1900* (Cambridge: Cambridge University Press, 1986), 242.
84. Quoted in Michael Stevens, 'Muttonbirds and modernity in Murihiku: Continuity and change in Kāi Tahu knowledge' (PhD diss., University of Otago, 2009), 202, n. 61.
85. Though Harwood recorded that he died in 1838. See G.C. Thomson papers, HC, MS-0438/45.
86. Élie le Guillou, *Voyage autour du monde de l'Astrolabe et de la Zélée sous les ordres du contre-amiral Dumont d'Urville pendant les annees 1837, 38, 39 et 40 par Élie le Guillou, chirurgien major de la Zélée*, trans. Basil Howard (Paris: J. Arago, Le Edition, 1844), 2.
87. It is telling that Ian Pool explained the exceptionally high 25 per cent mortality in Fiji in 1875 via unusual historical circumstances: it was due to measles spreading after the king's son returned, bearing the disease to a welcoming assembly of chiefs, who then spread it to all their districts. This, concluded Pool, occurred 'for reasons which would not have applied to New Zealand'. Ian Pool, *Te Iwi Maori: A New Zealand population past, present & projected* (Auckland: Auckland University Press, 1991), 123. For mortality in the Fiji epidemic, see Cliff, Haggett and Smallman-Raynor, *Measles*, 36.
88. Evison, *Te Wai Pounamu*, 86; Dacker, 'He Raraka a Ka Awa', 27, n. 15; Anderson, *The Welcome of Strangers*, 197–98.
89. Entwisle, *Behold the Moon*, 124–25; 172–81.
90. This is obviously something of a guess derived from weighing imponderables. However, while the Kai Huānga feud must have heightened mortality during the latter 1820s, there is no evidence of epidemics, and contact before whaling commenced was too infrequent to assume widespread venereal disease. Since Māori enjoyed the benefits of steel tools and potatoes, while people were accommodated in the wake of Te Rauparaha's incursions, it is reasonable to assume a substantial population increase at Ōtākou from that observed in 1826.
91. Entwisle, *Behold the Moon*, 180. These are Edward Shortland's figures for the summer of 1843–44.
92. Evison, *Te Wai Pounamu*, 86.
93. Anderson, *The Welcome of Strangers*, 192–94.
94. Atholl Anderson, 'Atholl Anderson's submission on Otakou', Wai 27, Document C8(a), 21; Anderson, *The Welcome of Strangers*.
95. Anderson, *The Welcome of Strangers*, 26–28.
96. Letters from George Weller to Edward at Otago, Sydney, 16 March, 9 May, 23 May, 23 July, 7 August 1835, cited in Church, ed., *Gaining a Foothold*, 206–15.
97. Church, *Otago's Infant Years*, 29.
98. Letter from George Weller to Edward at Otago, Sydney, 7 August 1835, cited in Church, ed.,*Gaining a Foothold*, 214–15.
99. Captain Ridley of the *Susannah* told Edward Weller that he had bought 300 baskets for his crew, but Edward believed it was 1000 baskets, and for sale in Sydney. Letter from Edward Weller to George Weller, Otago, 2 September 1835, cited in Church, ed., *Gaining a Foothold*, 215. The size of a basket is unclear and may have varied considerably. Shortland estimated a basket of potatoes at 35lb (15.8kg). See *Southern Districts*, 21. Boultbee also stated that 100 baskets of potatoes brought back from Otago weighed 35lb each. See Begg and Begg, *The World of John Boultbee*, 81. However, the 2262 baskets that arrived in Sydney 20 August 1837 weighed 12 ton, giving an average weight of about 12lb (5.4kg) per basket. Finally, Harwood's journal entry for 13 October 1839 recorded that he gave a Mr Cureton 13 baskets that weighed 2130lb (966kg), at an average weight therefore of 164lb (74kg).
100. The *Sydney Packet* was variously reported as having a cargo of five or 10 tons of potatoes. See *Sydney Herald*, 2 September 1835; *Sydney Herald*, 16 September 1835. Cited in Church, ed., *Gaining a Foothold*, 216.

101. Letter from Edward Weller to George Weller, Otago, 2 September 1835, cited in Church, ed., *Gaining a Foothold*, 215.
102. *The Australian*, 22 December 1835, cited in ibid., 223.
103. Edward Weller to George Weller, Otago, 27 January 1836, cited in ibid., 223–24.
104. The *Mediterranean Packet* delivered 51 baskets to Sydney – but had also called at Cloudy Bay and the Bay of Islands. There was demand in Sydney, too. George Weller asked for potatoes on February 1836. See George Weller to Edward Weller, 17 September 1836, cited in ibid., 247.
105. The *Genii*, for example, took on 460 baskets of potatoes over an extended stay in the harbour between June and October 1836. See various entries in Harwood's journal, cited in Church ed., *Gaining a Foothold*, 238–51.
106. *The Australian*, 29 August 1837, 2, col. 1, and 19 December 1837, 2, col. 1. Cited in ibid., 276, 284.
107. For the 'crippling impact' of epidemics on Māori, see James Belich, *Making Peoples* (Auckland: Penguin Books, 1996), 177.
108. The classic statement of this 'fatal impact' thesis in New Zealand is that of Harrison Wright, *New Zealand 1769–1840: Early years of Western contact* (Harvard: Harvard University Press, 1969). See also Judith Binney, 'Christianity and the Maoris to 1840: A comment', *New Zealand Journal of History*, vol. 3, no. 2, 1969, 150–54, 162–63.
109. Belich, *Making Peoples*, 173–78; Michael King, *The Penguin History of New Zealand* (Auckland: Penguin Books, 2003), 107, 148–50.
110. Belich, *Making Peoples*, 177, 227.
111. Entwisle, *Behold the Moon*, 134, also n. 556.
112. Ibid., 134.
113. A.H. McLintock, *The History of Otago* (Christchurch: Capper Press, 1949), 82–97, Hardwicke Knight, *Otago Peninsula: A local history* (Broad Bay, Dunedin: self published, 1979), 18–19; Entwisle, *Behold the Moon*, 132–36. For a different perspective see Dacker, 'He Raraka a Ka Awa', 64; Anderson, *The Welcome of Strangers*, 129.
114. 'Transcript of journal of Rev. James Watkin', HC, MS 0440/04, 23 July 1842.
115. Harwood, 'Accounts ledger'.
116. Cited in Anderson, *The Welcome of Strangers*, 214.
117. Leanna Parker, 'Re-conceptualizing the traditional economy: Indigenous people's participation in the nineteenth century fur trade in Canada and whaling industry in New Zealand' (PhD diss., University of Alberta, 2011), 292–93. According to Parker's analysis of Harwood's accounts, the exact figure Māori spent on alcohol is £221 0s 9d, which is 45.7 per cent of what Māori are known to have spent at the store, a total of £486 17s 6d.
118. Wohlers, cited in Stevens, 'Muttonbirds and modernity in Murihiku', 201; Harwood's journal describes drawing off vast quantities of rum for the whaling gangs – regularly dispensing amounts such as 30 gallons (136 litres) for a few weeks' consumption.
119. Olive Wright, *The Voyage of the* Astrolabe (Wellington: A.H. & A.W. Reed, 1955), 34.
120. See Joseph Banks on cleanliness, cited in *Tangata Whenua: An illustrated history*, eds Atholl Anderson et al. (Wellington: Bridget Williams Books, 2014), 144.
121. Wright, *The Voyage of the* Astrolabe, 65.
122. Anderson, *The Welcome of Strangers*, 129; Angela Wanhalla, *In/Visible Sight: The mixed-descent families of southern New Zealand* (Wellington: Bridget Williams Books, 2009), 7; Angela Wanhalla, *Matters of the Heart: A history of interracial marriage in New Zealand* (Auckland: Auckland University Press, 2013) 4–7.
123. F.A. Joseph, 'The old whaling station on Taieri Island: The last of the old whalers', *Otago Witness*, 22 April 1903, 13.
124. Wakefield, *Adventure in New Zealand*, vol. 1, 45.
125. Richard White, *The Middle Ground: Indians, empires, and republics in the Great Lakes region, 1650–1815* (New York: Cambridge University Press, 1991).
126. Church, *Otago's Infant Years*, 62, 'Photocopy of a deed of land sale between Harwood senior and King Bogany', in G.C. Thomson papers, HC, Misc-MS-0425.
127. 'Copy of Octavius Harwood journals', 1 May, 9 May, 19 May, 5 June, 12 June, 14 June, 15 June 1842.
128. Watkin, 'Transcript of journal of Rev. James Watkin', 9 September 1843.
129. J.W. Barnicoat, 'Diary', 8 May 1844, 24–25.
130. See David Haines, 'In search of the "whaheen": Ngāi Tahu women, shore whalers, and the meaning of sex in early New Zealand', in *Moving Subjects: Gender, mobility and intimacy in an age of global empire*, eds Tony Ballantyne and Antoinette M. Burton (Urbana and Chicago: University of Illinois Press, 2009), 58–60.
131. Barnicoat, 'Diary', 8 May 1844, 24.
132. Ibid., 25 September 1843. See Angela Wanhalla, 'Transgressing boundaries: A history of the mixed descent families of Maitapapa, Taieri, 1830–1940' (PhD diss., University of Otago, 2004), 64.

133. See Wanhalla, *In/Visible Sight*.
134. 'Mr. Tuckett's diary', in Thomas M. Hocken, *Contributions to the Early History of New Zealand [Settlement of Otago]* (London: Sampson Low, Marston & Co., 1898), 223.
135. Anderson, *The Welcome of Strangers*, 194; Atholl Anderson, *Race Against Time: The early Maori-Pakeha families and the development of the mixed-race population in southern New Zealand* (Dunedin: Hocken Library, University of Otago, 1991), 31.
136. Stevens, 'Muttonbirds and modernity in Murihiku', 130–31.
137. Angela Wanhalla, '"My piece of land at Taieri": Boundary formation and contestation at Taieri Native Reserve, 1844–1868', *New Zealand Journal of History*, vol. 41, no. 1, 2007, 44–60; Angela Wanhalla, 'Marrying "in": The geography of intermarriage on the Taieri, 1830s–1920s', in *Landscape/Community: Perspectives from New Zealand history*, eds Tony Ballantyne and Judith Bennett (Dunedin: University of Otago Press, 2005).
138. Herries Beattie, 'Traditions and legends collected from the natives of Murihiku', *Journal of the Polynesian Society*, vol. 25, no. 99, 96; Alfred Reynolds similarly attested that early settlers found many such skeletons on the Peninsula, lying as they had died, unattended and unburied; see *Otago Witness*, 3 August 1893, 35.
139. Binney, 'Christianity and the Maoris', 154.
140. Anderson et al., *Tangata Whenua*, 200.
141. Watkin, 'Transcript of journal of Rev. James Watkin', 5 June 1840.
142. Alfred Crosby, *Ecological Imperialism* (Cambridge: Cambridge University Press, 2004).
143. Watkin, 'Transcript of journal of Rev. James Watkin'. The first doctor was Dr Strang; Dr Crocombe succeeded him in 1838, but left after quarrelling with Edward Weller.
144. Anderson, *The Welcome of Strangers*, 202.
145. Stevens, 'Muttonbirds and modernity in Murihiku', 205–06.
146. Megan Potiki, 'Killing demons and cultural collisions', unpub. presentation at the University of Otago, 2014. Copy supplied to the author; Dacker, 'He Raraka a Ka Awa', 149–50; similar debates occurred around New Zealand. See Judith Binney with Vincent O'Malley and Alan Ward, 'The coming of the Pākehā', in Anderson et al., *Tangata Whenua*, 200.
147. Potiki, 'Killing demons and cultural collisions'.
148. Dacker, *Te Mamae me te Aroha*, 16.
149. Ibid; Dacker, 'He Raraka a Ka Awa'; T.A. Pybus, *Maori and Missionary: Early Christian missions in the South Island of New Zealand* (Christchurch: Cadsonbury Publications, 2002), 29.
150. Anderson, *The Welcome of Strangers*, 194.
151. Wanhalla, '"My piece of land at Taieri"'; Wanhalla, 'Marrying "in"'.
152. Stevens, 'Muttonbirds and modernity in Murihiku', 108; Deborah Montgomerie, 'Coming to terms: Ngai Tahu, Robeson County Indians and the Garden River band of Ojibwa, 1840–1940. Three studies of colonialism in action' (PhD diss., Duke University, 1993), 50–51.
153. Te Maire Tau, 'The death of knowledge: Ghosts on the plains', *New Zealand Journal of History*, vol. 35, no. 2, 2001, 145.
154. This critique of Tau draws on Stevens, 'Muttonbirds and modernity in Murihiku', 70.
155. A.B. MacDiarmid et al., 'Taking stock – The impacts of humans on New Zealand marine ecosystems since first settlement: Synthesis of major findings, and policy and management implications', *New Zealand Aquatic Environment and Biodiversity Report No. 170* (Wellington: Ministry for Primary Industries, 2016), 35–37.
156. Joe Roman et al., 'Whales as marine ecosystem engineers', *Frontiers in Ecology and the Environment*, vol. 12, no. 7, Sept. 2014, 379.
157. Ibid., 380–81.
158. See, for example, Edward Jerningham Wakefield, *Adventure in New Zealand, from 1839 to 1844: With some account of the beginning of the British colonization of the islands*, 2 vols (London: John Murray, 1845), vol. 1, 45–46.
159. David Monro, 'Notes on a journey through a part of the Middle Island of New Zealand', in Hocken, *Contributions to the Early History of New Zealand*, 241.
160. Some rats also fled ships smoked to kill them; see, for an example at Ōtākou, Church, ed. *Gaining a Foothold*, 312.
161. Crosby, *Ecological Imperialism*, 173–75.
162. Wright, *The Voyage of the* Astrolabe, 19–20, 26–27.
163. Ibid., 29. The French officer who attributed the pigs' foul taste to 'shellfish' did, however, clearly differentiate these from the 'prawns'.
164. Pigs raised by Māori were notoriously 'fishy', however, as this riddle told in Sydney and elsewhere reveals: 'Why is New Zealand pork like West India turtle? Give it up. Cause its flesh, fish and FOUL.' See Ray Hargreaves, 'An historical geography of New Zealand farming before the introduction of refrigeration' (PhD diss., University of Otago, 1966), 87, n. 50.
165. See 'Otago Early Settlers' Association', *Otago Witness*, 7 September 1904, 11.

166. Shortland, *The Southern Districts of New Zealand*, 175.
167. Anderson, *The Welcome of Strangers*, 208.
168. According to Julius von Haast, all the pigs at Taramakau were destroyed when they began digging up valuable fern-root grounds. Cited in ibid., 227, n. 12.
169. Harwood, 'Copy of Octavius Harwood journals', 5 October 1839, 17 December 1841.
170. Daphne Elliot, 'Carey, David, 1814–1896, and Hannah, 1817–1888', in Otago Daily Times Historical Biography Competition, HC, MS-0891, 8–9.
171. Though blubber from which the oil had been extracted was also used as fuel, the demand for wood was still high, as evidenced by the 'rafts' of firewood taken on board by bay whalers like the *Genii*, under Captain Cattlin, which stayed in Otago Harbour from June to October 1836. In that time it took 11 whales, and traded three muskets, some lead, an adze and two buckets with Māori for 490 baskets of potatoes, as well as shipping firewood and fresh water. For the captain's log while at Otago, see Church, ed., *Gaining a Foothold*, 238–52.
172. Ibid., 18. De Blosseville recorded that Māori stored their potatoes as the Irish did, in pits. Robert McNab, *Murihiku and the Southern Islands* (Invercargill: William Smith, 1907), 215.
173. Wright, *The Voyage of the Astrolabe*, 19.
174. Ibid.
175. Harwood, 'Copy of Octavius Harwood journals', 21 November 1838, 13 December 1838, 21 January 1839, 22 October 1840, 23 June 1841. P. Thomson, 'On the sand hills, or dunes, in the neighbourhood of Dunedin', *Transactions and Proceedings of the New Zealand Institute*, vol. 3, 1870, 267. According to Octavius Harwood, Jnr, his father sent plums to Watkin. See Octavius Harwood, Jnr, 'Note on whaling', HC, MS 0604/024.
176. Church, *Otago's Infant Years*, 62.
177. 'Agreement of partnership between Harwood and Charles Schultze', HC, MS-0438/074.
178. Shortland, 'Outwards letter book "a" 15 September 1842 to 13 March 1845'. George Weller mentions in a letter dated 25 July 1835 that he sent six sheep and a dozen fowls to the station. See Church, ed., *Gaining a Foothold*, 211–12. Chickens may have arrived much earlier. The Creed Manuscript mentions that Hoani Tawiri brought live white fowls to Waikouaiti after an attack on a European sealing gang to the south; this was one of the *General Gates'* gangs, and the attack occurred in either 1821 or 1822. This introduction may not have been significant: there may have been no rooster with the chickens, or Māori may have eaten them all.
179. Harwood, 'Copy of Octavius Harwood journals', 27 December 1840, 9 February 1841.
180. Thomas Burns, *Early Otago and the Genesis of Dunedin: The letters of Reverend T. Burns* (Dunedin: R.J. Stark & Co., 1916); James Somerville, 'Reminiscences of James Somerville', HC, AG-846/01, 45; Eileen Soper, *The Otago of Our Mothers* (Christchurch: Whitcombe & Tombs, 1948), 47.
181. Morton, *The Whale's Wake*, 182; Hocken, *Contributions to the Early History of New Zealand*, 241; Wakefield, *Adventure in New Zealand*, vol. 1, 6–7; Thomson, 'Papers on sealing and whaling'. Wakefield wrote: 'The great nurseries for good [pig-hunting] dogs have been the whaling stations, where they bred them for fighting.'
182. Harwood, 'Copy of Octavius Harwood journals', 22 January 1841. See 'C.W. Schultze to Harwood, Kai Warra, Wellington 26 April 1846', in 'Miscellaneous Letters', in G.C. Thomson papers, HC, MS-0438/096 .
183. Hocken, *Contributions to the Early History of New Zealand*, 213.
184. Ibid., 244.
185. Charles Kettle, Letter to Colonel William Wakefield, 25 January 1847, in 'Letter book of Charles Henry Kettle chief surveyor of the settlement of Otago', HC, MS-0083. Kettle reveals not only the population, but their typical occupation: 'It is a notorious fact that there are more spirits drunk in Otakou than at any other place in New Zealand where there is an equal population. I have ascertained that during the last six weeks there were 200 gallons (909 litres) consumed at what is called the port, where there are about 100 people living – there are no less than 6 public houses.' Later in the same letter, however, Kettle states that there are about 150 people at Ōtākou. For discussion of the fluctuations in population over this period, see Entwisle, *Behold the Moon*, 160–62.
186. Many of these people arrived having abandoned Johnny Jones' settlement at Waikouaiti. This included families such as the Careys, the Monsons and the Colemans. According to the obituary of Mrs Woolsey, née Coleman, there were 34 families at Ōtākou by 1848. See 'Obituary', *Otago Daily Times*, 21 October 1929.
187. Jill Hamel, *The Archaeology of Otago* (Wellington: Department of Conservation, 2001), 105.

188. Octavius Harwood, Jnr, 'Fragments of history of the Otago Peninsula, Larnach's Castle, etc.', HC, MS 0604 I+. According to Octavius Harwood, Jnr, Christie of Sydney settled in 1840 at the bay 'known to the Maoris as Hereweka and to the Sea going men as Lime burners Bay and renamed it Portobello after his birthplace near Edinburgh in Scotland'. He kept drapery and provisions for sale that he received from Octavius Harwood's store. Harwood Jnr explained Christie abandoning his stock on 'account of his wife taken a trip to Stewarts Island for supply of mutton birds for the winter before his departure from New Zealand in 1844 back to Sydney. This was his last words, goodbye groper, goodbye barracooter and God bless the Pigeons.'
189. Hocken, *Contributions to the Early History of New Zealand*, 62–64, 80; Entwisle, *Behold the Moon*, 156.
190. Elliot, 'Carey, David, 1814–1896, and Hannah, 1817–1888', 7–10.
191. The precise location of the Kelvin Grove homestead is uncertain, since it has been buried by sand. However, 'Kelvin Grove' is marked on McLeod's map of 1868, and the house is described by Murray Thompson as being 'midway between Harrington Point … and the Black Rock' and was 'about 400 yards back from the beach'. See Alfred Eccles, ed., *A Pakeha's Recollections: The reminiscences of Murray Gladstone Thomson* (Wellington: A.H. and A.W. Reed, 1944), 29.
192. Hamel, *The Archaeology of Otago*, 105; Entwisle, *Behold the Moon*.
193. Papers relating to Murray Gladstone Thomson, HC, MS-0439/084.
194. Eccles, ed., *A Pakeha's Recollections*, 28; Wendy Hinton, 'Pre-settlement Otago from Moeraki to Molyneux' (BA diss., University of Otago, 1976), 70. Hinton gives the stock numbers sent to the farm in 1844 as 30 cows, two horses and 500 ewes. According to an advertisement in the *Otago News*, 7 March 1849, when the stock were sold, they numbered 77 cattle, 'the greater part in milk or calving', as well as several horses and about 600 sheep.
195. Alma Rutherford, 'Archibald Anderson 1817–1910', in Otago Daily Times Historical Biography Competition, HC, MS-0891; Hardwicke Knight, writing as 'Sam Fossicker', *Otago Daily Times*, 8 November 1975. Hardwicke Knight states that Rowand considered Kelvin Grove 'an impossible place', and let the 'Methodists' use it as a mission house. Murray Thomson recalled finding missionary material there when he arrived with his father in 1862.
196. Hardwicke Knight, *Otago Daily Times*, 8 November 1975. Rowand was something of a scoundrel; selling stock to American whaling captains is understandable, but he then attempted to abscond with all the proceeds, only to drown when his ship, the *Leven*, sank off Akaroa. See Rutherford, 'Archibald Anderson 1810–1917', 6.
197. Stokes advertised the stock for sale in the *Otago News* from 7 March 1849. Harwood offered to buy the farm for £50 but Stokes declined, believing several parties to be interested. However, I have been unable to discover whether anyone occupied the land between this time and 1862, when Peter Thomson took up a lease there. See 'Miscellaneous Letters', HC, MS 0438/105, 12 July 1849.
198. *Otago Journal*, no. 3, November 1848, 38–39. Cargill's address to the newly arrived settlers stressed their commonality with the established residents: both were Scots, wanting to grow the same crops and raise the same stock. The key difference was that the residents were 'squatters' who could be rightfully displaced.
199. Graham Harris, *Nga Riwai Maori – Maori Potatoes* (Lower Hutt: The Open Polytechnic of New Zealand, 1999), 27; B.A. McKenzie, 'Processed and new crops', in *New Zealand Pasture and Crop Science*, eds James White and John Hodgson (Auckland: Oxford University Press, 1999), 265.
200. Hay, *Reminiscences of Earliest Canterbury*, 16.
201. Ibid., 16–17.
202. One French officer, Dubouzet, noted that 'there is plenty of vegetation beyond the sand dunes which lie all around the anchorage'. Cited in Wright, *Voyage of the* Astrolabe, 25.
203. Shortland, *The Southern Districts of New Zealand*, 9.
204. Monro, in D. Monro, 'Notes of a journey through a part of the Middle Island of New Zealand', in Hocken, *Contributions to the Early History of New Zealand*, 243–44.
205. Peter Thomson, 'On the sand hills, or dunes, in the neighbourhood of Dunedin', *Transactions and Proceedings of the New Zealand Institute*, vol. 3, 1870, 269; 'Otago Heads native reserve', NZPD, 25 September 1891, vol. 82, 6 Sept.–6 Oct., 602–03.
206. Church, *Otago's Infant Years*, 37.
207. 26 January 1839, in Church, ed., *Gaining a Foothold*, 356.
208. Harwood, 'Copy of Octavius Harwood journals', 18 May 1838. Hocken, *Contributions to the Early History of New Zealand*, 244. According to Harwood's journal, the wall was between

the beach and the coopers' workshop. The location of Edward Weller's 'Big House', later Harwood's store and tavern, is shown in early images. A photograph from the late 1860s shows the store at the foot of the slope just south of Wellers Rock, surrounded by drifting sand. This location is also confirmed by reconstructions from the field books of William Davison, who made a survey of the upper harbour coastline in 1844, and used the flagpole atop the store as a point of reference. These references indicate that the store was at grid point 32210 87207, based on the modern topographical map 'Dunedin and surrounds' I/J44, 1:50 000. See Matthew Campbell, 'Premliminary investigation of the archaeology of whaling stations on the southern coast' (MA thesis, University of Otago, 1992), 111, 125.
209. Thomson, 'On the sand hills, or dunes, in the neighbourhood of Dunedin', 267.
210. As recorded in Harwood's journal, and in letters home to his family. For example, in a letter written home on 18 March 1838, soon after arrival here, Harwood recorded: 'Game is so abundant here that I have been out with Mr Wr and in the course of a few hours filled the boat with all kinds of water fowl.' Church, ed., *Gaining a Foothold*, 298. For a representative sample of these shooting excursions, see also Harwood's journal entries for 1838: 3 June; 24 June; 5 August; 4 November; 2 December; 9 December; 17 December; 30 December. Harwood, 'Copy of Octavius Harwood journals'.
211. Monro, 'Notes of a journey through a part of the Middle Island of New Zealand', 243–44.
212. 'Mr. Tuckett's diary', Appendix A, in Hocken, *Contributions to the Early History of New Zealand*, 213; 'Letter from Mr. Tuckett to Dr. Hodgkinson, Otakou, August 16, 1844. Port of New Edinburgh', Appendix B, in ibid., 227.
213. Ibid., 19–20.
214. Ibid., 20–23.
215. Ibid., 24–25.
216. Dacker records 29 transactions occurring between 1829 (the Preservation Inlet whaling station) and 1840, of which 22 occurred between 1838 and 1840. See Dacker, 'He Raraka a Ka Awa', 55.
217. Weller, *A Fortune Lost*, 19–20.
218. Shortland, *The Southern Districts of New Zealand*, 86–87.
219. 'The memorial of Edward Weller of Sydney [NSW] merchant' to Sir George Gipps, 4 February 1841. In G.C. Thomson papers, HC, MS-0440/20, 6. Cited in Church, ed., *Gaining a Foothold*, 321–22. 'Letter from Edward Weller to George Weller, Otago, 15 January 1840', cited in ibid., 402–03.
220. Extract from 'The memorial of Octavius Harwood … to His Excellency Captain Robert Fitzroy … governor', cited in Church, ed., *Gaining a Foothold*, 401.
221. 'Instructions from the Colonial Office to Captain Hobson, regarding land in New Zealand 14 August 1839', cited in ibid., 403–04.
222. Ibid., 5; Dacker, 'He Raraka a Ka Awa', 57, n. 71.
223. Evison, *Te Wai Pounamu*, 45–47, 127–34; Harry Evison, *The Ngai Tahu Deeds* (Christchurch: Canterbury University Press, 2006), 36. Harwood was away at the time, but simply noted on return that 'Herald, Sloop of War, had been in and left a paper for the Natives' perusal.'
224. Evison, *The Ngai Tahu Deeds*, 38.
225. Alan Ward, 'A report on the historical evidence: The Ngai Tahu claim', Wai 27, Document T1, 7.
226. This summary of the events that surrounded the land sale is largely drawn from the authoritative account provided by the evidence presented to and summarised by the Waitangi Tribunal. For another useful perspective, see Evison, *Te Wai Pounamu*; Evison, *The Ngai Tahu Deeds*.
227. The course of negotiations are well summarised in Ward, 'A report on the historical evidence', 87–97.
228. Evison, *Te Wai Pounamu*, 205.
229. Waitangi Tribunal, *Ngai Tahu Land Report* (Wellington: Waitangi Tribunal, 1990), 1.
230. Evison, *The Ngai Tahu Deeds*, 56.
231. Herries Beattie, 'Notebook entitled, "Further information about Southern Maoris, mostly collected between 1900 and 1920" (1900–1920)', HC, MS-582/E/23.
232. This is substantiated by the testimony of both Horomona Pohio and Rawiri Te Maire Tau to the Smith–Nairn Commission in 1880. In addition, H.K. Taiaroa told Mackay that Hoani Wetere Korako wanted to fix the boundary there also. See 'Middle Island land native claims, report by Mr. Commissioner Mackay relating to', *AJHR*, Wellington: Government Printer, 1891, 38.
233. Ward, 'A report on the historical evidence', 96.
234. George Clarke, *Notes on Early Life in New Zealand* (Hobart: the author, 1903), 62–63. There are numerous points of interest in this speech, the only record of which is in George Clarke's memoirs published in 1903. The accuracy of the speech is therefore open to question, though Clarke was purportedly fluent in Māori, and it agrees with his evidence given to the Smith–Nairn Commission of 1880. See Ward, 'A report on the historical evidence', 107.

It is worth noting Tuhawaiki's pervasive sense of despair at his people's prospects, and the emphasis on the rapidity and scale of measles' impact. Indeed, William Wakefield considered the chief motive for the sale was Māori belief that their people were dying out.
235. Ward, 'A report on the historical evidence', 53.
236. Evison, *Te Wai Pounamu*, 206.
237. Evison, *The Ngai Tahu Deeds*, 56.
238. Symonds to Richmond, 2 September 1844; William Wakefield to Harington, 31 August 1844, in 'Supporting documents to evidence of Ann Rosemary Parsonson in respect of the Ōtākou tenths', Wai 27, Document C2-7, 1–2 and C2-11, 57–58. Also Alan Ward, 'A report on the historical evidence', 96; Evison, *The Ngai Tahu Deeds*, 57.
239. Peter Tremewan, *Selling Otago* (Dunedin: Otago Heritage Books, 1994), 37. Their relative importance is revealed in the money awarded. Tuhawaiki received £1000, Taiaroa and Karetai £300 each.
240. Ibid.
241. Alan Ward, 'A report on the historical evidence', 95–97.
242. Besides the two main islands in Otago Harbour, the other islands named as purchased were 'Okaihe' (St Michael's Mount, or Green Island) and Moturata (Taieri Island). The remainder – Paparoa, Matoketoke, Hakinikini and Aonui – are named on the 'Sketch showing the New Edinburgh purchase', and are no more than small coastal reefs and rocks between the Taieri and Tokomairiro river mouths.
243. George Habib, 'Report on Ngai Tahu 1880 list of settlements and food resources as compiled by H.K. Taiaroa', Document T4(b), Wai 27, 3; 'Mahinga kai list 1880', Document R30, Wai 27, 2–3.
244. Murray Bathgate, 'Evidence of Dr Murray Bathgate on the archaeological and early documentary record concerning Maori fishing in the South Island', Document S2, Wai 27, 171; Jim Williams, '"E Paakahi Hakinga a Kai": An examination of pre-contact resource management practice in southern Te Wai Pounamu' (PhD diss., University of Otago, 2004), 274–75.
245. In Taiaroa's petition, the unsold islands are named as '(1.) Kapukepuke kite Waiparapara, (2.) Te Pao Titere Moana, (3.) Tawake Tu, (4.) Tu Kakaha, (5.) Pounui Ahine, (6.) Te Here Kakaho, (7.) Kapo, (8.) Tuhiraki'. These are (by my reckoning) what are now known as the Aramoana Spit, Pudding Island, the Gull Rocks, Bird Island, Wharekakahu, and the two small islets inside Papanui Inlet, respectively.
246. The first documented claim for the tenths, however, was Topi Patuki's petition to the Queen in 1867. Considerable correspondence from Otago Māori to government officials over the previous years contained no reference to tenths. For discussion, see Ward, 'A report on the historical evidence', 100–02.
247. Waitangi Tribunal, *Ngai Tahu Land Report*, 14; Despatch no. 7, 'J.J. Symonds to the superintendant of the southern division Wellington, 2nd Sept 1844'. See Mackay, *A Compendium of the Official Documents Relative to Native Affairs in the South Island*, 102–03; 'Despatch from his honour the superintendant of New Munster (copy of), dated 12th June 1844', in ibid., 100A.
248. Ward, 'A report on the historical evidence', 110.
249. Ibid., 111.
250. Vincent O'Malley, *The Meeting Place: Māori and Pākehā encounters, 1642–1840* (Auckland: Auckland University Press, 2012), 137–54; R. Boast, 'The Law and Maori', in *A New Zealand Legal History*, eds P. Spiller, J. Finn and R. Boast (Wellington: Brookers, 1995), 133. See also Ward, 'A report on the historical evidence', 12–14. It was certainly conducted with much more ceremony and care by both Māori and the British than the signing of the Treaty of Waitangi at Ōtākou.
251. Letter from Frederick Tuckett, 14 June 1844. 'Copies of papers relating to Frederick Tuckett 1842–1849 & 1887–1891', HC, PC-1049.

PART III: IMPROVING GOD'S CREATION

Chapter 6: British Settlement on the Otago Peninsula: 1848–61

1. James Barr, *The Old Identities* (Dunedin: Mills, Dick and Co., 1879), 50–51.
2. James Belich, *Replenishing the Earth: The settler revolution and the rise of the Anglo-world, 1783–1939* (Oxford: Oxford University Press, 2009), 131, 155–57; Alexander Bathgate, *Colonial Experiences or Sketches of People and Places in the Province of Otago* (Glasgow: James Maclehose, 1874), 196–97; Barr, *The Old Identities*, 192, 248.
3. John E. Martin, '"A small nation on the move": Wakefield's theory of colonisation and the relationship between state and labour

in the mid-nineteenth century', in *Edward Gibbon Wakefield and the Colonial Dream: A reconsideration* [Friends of the Turnbull Library] (Wellington: GP Publications, 1997), 111–12.
4. Ibid., 110.
5. Erik Olssen, *A History of Otago* (Dunedin: John McIndoe, 1984), 31.
6. Andro Linklater, *Owning the Earth: The transforming history of land ownership* (London: Bloomsbury, 2014), 234–39.
7. Ibid., 239.
8. T.M. Devine, *To the Ends of the Earth: Scotland's global diaspora 1750–2010* (London: Allen Lane and Penguin Books, 2011)
9. T.M. Devine, 'The transformation of agriculture: Cultivation and clearance', in *The Transformation of Scotland: The economy since 1700*, eds T.M. Devine et al. (Edinburgh: Edinburgh University Press, 2005), 71, 77.
10. On this transformation, see T.M. Devine, *The Transformation of Rural Scotland: Social change and the agrarian economy, 1660–1815* (Edinburgh: Edinburgh University Press, 1994), 35–41; Devine, 'The transformation of agriculture', 71; T.M. Devine, 'Social responses to agrarian "improvement": The highland and lowland clearances in Scotland', in *Scottish Society 1500–1800*, eds Robert Allen Houston and Ian D. Whyte (Cambridge: Cambridge University Press, 2005), 148; Vaughan Wood, 'Soil fertility management in nineteenth century New Zealand agriculture' (PhD diss., University of Otago, 2003), 37.
11. T.M. Devine, 'Industrialisation', in *The Transformation of Scotland*, eds Devine et al., 38.
12. Richard Drayton, *Nature's Government: Science, imperialism, and the 'improvement' of the world* (New Haven: Yale University Press, 2000), 45.
13. Devine, 'Social responses to agrarian "improvement"', 148.
14. Quoting Cosmo Innes (1798–1874), Professor of Universal History and Greek and Roman Antiquities at the University of Edinburgh, in Andy Wightman, *The Poor Have No Lawyers: Who owns Scotland and how they got it* (Edinburgh: Berlin Limited, 2013), 1. In this, the Scottish system prefigured the problems that beset Māori when confronted with the Native Land Court.
15. Devine, 'Industrialisation', 38; Devine, 'The transformation of agriculture', 81.
16. I.G. Simmons, *An Environmental History of Great Britain: From 10,000 years ago to the present* (Edinburgh: Edinburgh University Press, 2001), 129.
17. The definitive account of the genesis of the Otago scheme is still A.H. McLintock, *The History of Otago: The origins and growth of a Wakefield class settlement* (Dunedin: Otago Centennial Historical Publications, 1949), 149–238.
18. Burns to Cargill, 22 March 1845, cited in McLintock, *The History of Otago*, 172–73.
19. James Beattie, 'Lusting after a lost Arcadia: European environmental perception in the Dunedin area, 1840–1860' (BA diss., University of Otago, 1999), 3–4.
20. The Reverend Thomas Burns to Captain John Cargill, 30 January 1847. See Ernest Northcroft Merrington, *A Great Coloniser: The Rev. Dr. Thomas Burns* (Dunedin: The Otago Daily Times and Witness Newspapers Co., 1929), 266.
21. Tom Brooking, *And Captain of their Souls* (Dunedin: Otago Heritage Books, 1984), 146–54; Tom Brooking, 'The great escape: Wakefield and the Scottish settlement of Otago', in *Edward Gibbon Wakefield and the Colonial Dream*, 129.
22. Charles Kettle, 'Letter book of Charles Henry Kettle chief surveyor of the settlement of Otago', HC, MS-0083.
23. McLintock, *The History of Otago*, 144–45. Kettle's instructions highlight the naivety of the settlers' expectations. He was told that he was not only to map the area, setting aside suitable reserves for various purposes, but also to buoy the channel for shipping and, last but far from least, construct a road between Kopūtai (Port Chalmers) and Dunedin. Kettle accomplished much of this but, unsurprisingly, he did not build the road.
24. Merrington, *A Great Coloniser*, 117.
25. Brad Patterson, 'Charles Henry Kettle', in *Dictionary of New Zealand Biography*, vol.1 (Wellington: Allen & Unwin and Department of Internal Affairs), 226–27. For general discussion see John Weaver, *The Great Land Rush and the Making of the Modern World, 1650–1900* (Montreal & Kingston: McGill-Queen's University Press, 2003), 226–39.
26. Kettle, 8 September 1847, 'Letter book of Charles Henry Kettle'. Mt Charles, highest point on the Peninsula and a dominant feature on the outer coast, commemorates Kettle.
27. See, for example, Tuckett's map of 1844. Kettle's letter book describes his work surveying the outer coast. 'Letter book of Charles Henry Kettle'.
28. See, for example, Giselle Byrnes, *Boundary Markers: Land surveying and the colonisation of New Zealand* (Wellington: Bridget Williams Books, 2001), 57–58. Byrnes cites the 'Scot'

Alexander Bathgate as authority, without noting that Bathgate was a long-term resident of Dunedin who regarded it as a fable.
29. Peter Entwisle, 'Charles Kettle's plan for old Dunedin: Identifying and preserving its values', HC, Misc-MS-1930.
30. Kettle, 4 December 1847, 'Letter book of Charles Henry Kettle'.
31. Geoff Park, *Theatre Country: Essays on land & whenua* (Wellington: Victoria University Press, 2006), 37. For discussions of the grid as cultural tool of colonisation see Paul Carter, *The Road to Botany Bay* (Chicago: The University of Chicago Press, 1989); also Byrnes, *Boundary Markers*, 55–62.
32. Byrnes, *Boundary Markers*, 56–57.
33. Thomas Ferens, quoted in McLintock, *The History of Otago*, 244.
34. Brad Patterson, Tom Brooking and Jim McAloon, *Unpacking the Kists: The Scots in New Zealand* (Dunedin: Otago University Press, 2003) 66, 68.
35. Brooking, *And Captain of their Souls*, 56; Tom Brooking, '"Tam McCanny and Kitty Clydeside" – the Scots in New Zealand', in *The Scots Abroad – Labour, capital, enterprise, 1750-1914*, ed. R.A. Cage (London: Croom Helm, 1985), 159.
36. Brooking, *And Captain of their Souls*, 91, 118.
37. Olssen, *A History of Otago*, 235; McLintock, *The History of Otago*, 34.
38. Merrington, *A Great Coloniser*, 157.
39. Thomas Ferens, 'Transcript of journal of Thomas Ferens on the "John Wickcliffe"', 23 March 1848, HC, MS-0440/016.
40. Merrington, *A Great Coloniser*, 169–70.
41. Drayton, *Nature's Government*. On New Zealand, see James Beattie and John Stenhouse, 'Empire, environment and religion: God and the natural world in nineteenth-century New Zealand', *Environment and History*, vol. 13, no. 4, 2007, 413–46; Tony Ballantyne, 'Culture and colonization: Revisiting the place of writing in colonial New Zealand', *Journal of New Zealand Studies*, vol. 9, 2010, 14.
42. Quoted in Tom Devine, *The Scottish Nation 1700-2000* (London: Penguin Books, 2000).
43. Ballantyne, 'Culture and colonization', 14.
44. Beattie and Stenhouse, 'Empire, environment and religion', 431.
45. For discussions of improvement in the context of empire, see Drayton, *Nature's Government*. In the New Zealand context, see Tom Brooking, 'Use it or lose it: Unravelling the land debate in late nineteenth-century New Zealand', *New Zealand Journal of History*, vol. 30, no. 2, 1996, 141–62; Beattie and Stenhouse 'Empire, environment and religion'; Ballantyne, 'Culture and colonization'.
46. Wood, 'Soil fertility management in nineteenth century New Zealand agriculture', 36.
47. Ibid., 37–38.
48. Simmons, *An Environmental History of Great Britain*, 124.
49. Thomas Burns, 'Diary of Reverend Thomas Burns 1848–1851', Toitū Otago Settlers Museum, C 017. Merrington, *A Great Coloniser*, 208.
50. Thomas Burns, *Early Otago and the Genesis of Dunedin: The letters of Reverend T. Burns* (Dunedin: R.J. Stark & Co., 1916).
51. Burns, 'Diary of Reverend Thomas Burns'.
52. Beattie, 'Lusting after a lost Arcadia'.
53. Burns, *Early Otago and the Genesis of Dunedin*.
54. Ross Gordon, ed., *Waikouaiti and Dunedin in 1850 – Reminiscences of John McLay an Early Settler* (Dunedin: Ross Gordon, 1998); 46, Hardwicke Knight, *Otago Peninsula: A local history* (Broad Bay, Dunedin: self-published, 1979), 44.
55. Merrington, *A Great Coloniser*, 209.
56. Burns, 'Diary of Reverend Thomas Burns'.
57. See Paula Brown, 'Trends and variability of temperature extremes in southern New Zealand' (PhD diss., University of Otago, 2006).
58. Burns, *Early Otago and the Genesis of Dunedin*. 'Burns to secretary of London committee of Otago Association, 28 January 1849', *The Otago Journal*, no.1, Jan. 1848, 4.
59. Burns, 'Diary of Reverend Thomas Burns'; Burns, *Early Otago and the Genesis of Dunedin*.
60. Anonymous, 'Letter from Dunedin 29 October 1849', *The Otago Journal*, no. 6, Nov. 1850, 90.
61. Burns, *Early Otago and the Genesis of Dunedin*.
62. Ibid.
63. Ibid. Burns' estimate is corroborated by an 1852 report produced by the agricultural committee of the Otago Agricultural Association on the economics of establishing a 50-acre (20ha) farm for those 'who would employ labour at the outset to a considerable extent'. This was reproduced in *The Otago Journal*, no. 8, Aug. 1852, 115. The report argued that £506 would be expended as an initial outlay, with £273 the return in the first year. The very few who did arrive with such a sum, such as William Henry Cutten, quickly rose to prominence.
64. Ibid.
65. Olssen, *A History of Otago*, 33–34, Ian Church, *Otago's Infant Years* (Dunedin: Otago Heritage Books, 2001), 224. Church estimated the population of Otago as of 31 December 1860 at

12,026. *The Statistics of New Zealand*, however, gives the population in 1860 as 12,691.
66. The electoral roll lists William Geary, Charles Edwards, James Seaton, Archibald Shand and William Winton as resident in Portobello. William Geary Jnr is listed at 'Popanui'. The Seaton, Winton and Geary families remained prominent in the history of the area. Geary had worked for the Wellers as a cooper. James Seaton and William Winton began farming at Portobello in 1848. Hardwicke Knight, *Otago Peninsula*, 37.
67. The electoral roll for 1857 published in the *Otago Provincial Gazette* names 30 voters with properties purchased on the Peninsula. Seventeen are listed as owners in Andersons Bay, three at Ocean Beach, three on the Upper Harbour, six at Portobello, and one at 'Poponui' [sic]. Some half dozen of these 30 owners did not occupy their properties at this stage, however. Duckworth lists very early settlers at Andersons Bay. John Anderson, for whom the bay was named, left with his family in 1846. Duckworth describes settlement at Tomahawk beginning with James Patrick in 1857 (though Patrick is not listed on the electoral roll for that year). See Henry Duckworth, *The Early Years of Andersons Bay and Tomahawk*, 2nd edn (Dunedin: Otago Heritage Books, 1982), 10–11, 52.
68. Duckworth, *The Early Years of Andersons Bay and Tomahawk*, 52.
69. James Somerville, 'Reminiscences of James Somerville', HC, AG-846/01.
70. *Votes and Proceedings of the Provincial Council, Province of Otago, New Zealand. Session IX, 1860* (Dunedin: Otago Provincial Council, 1860). Appendix, xxiii; memorial enclosed, xxiv.
71. Eileen Soper, *The Otago of Our Mothers* (Christchurch: Whitcombe & Tombs, 1948), 51.
72. Ibid.
73. Ibid., 35.
74. Gordon, ed., *Waikouaiti and Dunedin in 1850 – Reminiscences of John McLay*, 30.
75. Somerville, 'Reminiscences of James Somerville'; Duckworth, *The Early Years of Andersons Bay and Tomahawk*, 31.
76. Duckworth, *The Early Years of Andersons Bay and Tomahawk*, 12; Somerville, 'Reminiscences of James Somerville', 30–31.
77. Duckworth, *The Early Years of Andersons Bay and Tomahawk*, 12.
78. Soper, *The Otago of Our Mothers*, 40; Gordon, ed., '*Waikouaiti and Dunedin in 1850 – Reminiscences of John McLay*', 31.
79. Soper, *The Otago of Our Mothers*, 31.
80. Ibid., 40–41.
81. Somerville, 'Reminiscences of James Somerville', 34–35.
82. *The New Zealand Journal*, vol. 4, no. 81, 18 Feb. 1843, 47.
83. David Howden, *The Otago Journal*, no. 7, May 1851, 108.
84. Somerville, 'Reminiscences of James Somerville', 30.
85. H. Thompson and I. Thompson, *Clearwaters of New Zealand 1838–1986* (Invercargill: Sycamore Print, 1986), 4. Other settlers provided prospective emigrants with similar advice. See 'Letter from Mr. Edward Atkinson, Otago, 31 June 1848'. *The Otago Journal*, no. 3, 46.
86. *Otago Gazette*, vol. 1, 24; *Otago Witness*, 11 July 1856 (Supplement).
87. Gordon, ed., *Waikouaiti and Dunedin in 1850 – Reminiscences of John McLay*, 26, 30, 38.
88. For James Patrick's variation, see *Otago Witness*, 9 March 1878, 20. For James King's, see *Otago Witness*, 3 May 1879, 4.
89. Soper, *The Otago of Our Mothers*, 47–48; Burns, *Early Otago and the Genesis of Dunedin*.
90. *Otago Gazette*, vol. 1, 24, 57; vol. 2, 83. A bushel is equivalent to 8 gallons or 36 litres.
91. Ibid., vol. 2, 83, 159. Olssen, *A History of Otago*, 50.
92. For a representative example, see *Otago Witness*, 20 February 1869, 13–14.
93. This is a point made wonderfully well by Peter Holland, *At Home in the Howling Wilderness: Settlers and the environment in southern New Zealand* (Auckland: Auckland University Press, 2013).
94. Harvesting was done by hand using reaping hooks, threshing with flails, and then riddling in the wind to remove the chaff. Settlers at Andersons Bay bought a small flourmill early on, which rendered fairly coarse wholemeal flour. See Peter White, 'Early days of the White family at Tomahawk', HS, Misc-MS-1109, 1–2; Duckworth, *History of Andersons Bay and Tomahawk*, 14.
95. *Otago Witness*, 11 July 1857 (Supplement); *Otago Witness,* 9 March 1878, 20. See also Wood, 'Soil fertility management in nineteenth century New Zealand agriculture', 123.
96. *Otago Witness*, 24 August 1878, 3; 9 March 1878, 20; 3 May 1879, 4. For general discussion, see Tom Brooking and Eric Pawson, *Seeds of Empire: The environmental transformation of New Zealand* (London: IB Tauris, 2011), 122–27; J.P. Huggett, 'The historical geography of the Otago Peninsula' (MA thesis, Victoria

University, 1966), 80–81.
97. Huggett, 'The historical geography of the Otago Peninsula', 80.
98. Ray Hargreaves, 'An historical geography of New Zealand farming before the introduction of refrigeration' (PhD diss., University of Otago, 1966), 164. Burns' was the first Ayrshire bull in the settlement, landed from the *Philip Laing* in 1848.
99. Barr, *The Old Identities*, 51.
100. For a small sample, see 'Letter from George Ross, 3 October 1848', *The Otago Journal*, no. 4, 58; 'Letter, 14 April 1848', *The Otago Journal*, no. 5, 71; 'Letter, 20 October 1849', *The Otago Journal*, no. 6, 87; 'Letter, 17 September 1849', *The Otago Journal*, no. 6, 90.
101. White, 'Early days of the White family at Tomahawk', 30; Duckworth, *The Early Years of Andersons Bay and Tomahawk*, 3, 30; *Otago Witness*, 13 April 1910, 89.
102. Somerville, 'Reminiscences of James Somerville', 31; Gordon, ed., *Waikouaiti and Dunedin in 1850 – Reminiscences of John McLay*, 32.
103. Duckworth, *The Early Years of Andersons Bay and Tomahawk*, 29; Somerville, 'Reminiscences of James Somerville', 45.
104. Duckworth, *The Early Years of Andersons Bay and Tomahawk*, 29; Bill Dacker, 'He Raraka A Ka Awa, updated, annotated and sourced manuscript for the book, "Te Mamoe Me Te Aroha", originally published in 1994', HC, Misc-MS-1716, 103; Letters to the Editor: James Christie, *Otago Witness*, 17 May 1862, 6.
105. See John Cargill, 'Letter to editor', *Otago News*, no. 26, 1 September 1849. Also the editorial in reply. Also *Otago News*, no. 31, 6 October 1849, 3.
106. John Cargill, 'Letter to editor', *Otago News*, no. 26, 1 September 1849; editorial, *Otago News*, no. 27, 8 September 1849, 2.
107. Gordon, ed., *Waikouaiti and Dunedin in 1850 – Reminiscences of John McLay*, 42.
108. Somerville, 'Reminiscences of James Somerville', 32; Robert Gillies, 'Notes on some changes in the fauna of Otago', *Transactions and Proceedings of the New Zealand Institute*, vol. 10, 1878, 319.
109. P. Thomson, 'Work for field naturalists', *Transactions and Proceedings of the New Zealand Institute*, vol. 4, 1871, 140.
110. Burns, *Early Otago and the Genesis of Dunedin: The Letters of Reverend T. Burns*; 'Diary of Reverend Thomas Burns', Sept. 1850; Alexander Bathgate, 'On the Lepidoptera of Otago', *Transactions and Proceedings of the New Zealand Institute*, vol. 3, 1870, 138. I thank Anthony Harris of Otago Museum for this and all other insect identifications.
111. Bathgate, 'On the Lepidoptera of Otago', 138. Bathgate also believed that these 'black hairy caterpillars' were those of the magpie moth. But Bathgate described it eating 'grass and herbage', which definitively rules out this moth.
112. Gillies, 'Notes on some changes in the fauna of Otago', 310, 314; Soper, *The Otago of Our Mothers*, 42.
113. Gordon, ed., *Waikouaiti and Dunedin in 1850 – Reminiscences of John McLay*, 30, 32, 40.
114. Gillies, 'Notes on some changes in the fauna of Otago', 312–13.
115. Ibid., 307.
116. Soper, *The Otago of Our Mothers*, 308; Gillies, 'Notes on some changes in the fauna of Otago', 42–43.
117. Gillies, 'Notes on some changes in the fauna of Otago', 310; W.T.L. Travers, 'Notes upon a New Zealand flesh-fly', *Transactions and Proceedings of the New Zealand Institute*, vol. 3, 1870, 118–19.
118. Alexander Bathgate, 'Notes on acclimatisation in New Zealand', *Transactions and Proceedings of the New Zealand Institute*, vol. 30, 1897, 277; Alexander Bathgate, 'Acclimatisation', *Otago Witness*, 5 August 1897, 54.
119. Gillies, 'Notes on some changes in the fauna of Otago', 315; Aparata Renata, 'The native birds of the Otago Peninsula past and present', *Otago Witness*, 10 August 1910, 76; White, 'Early days of the White family at Tomahawk', 30; Soper, *The Otago of Our Mothers*, 2; Duckworth, *The Early Years of Andersons Bay and Tomahawk*, 43.
120. Gillies, 'Notes on some changes in the fauna of Otago', 315.
121. Renata, 'The native birds of the Otago Peninsula past and present'.
122. *Otago Witness*, 30 March 1878, 20.
123. Renata, 'The native birds of the Otago Peninsula past and present'.
124. Somerville, 'Reminiscences of James Somerville', 33; T.H. Potts, 'On the birds of NZ (ii)', *Transactions and Proceedings of the New Zealand Institute*, vol. 3, 1870, 84.
125. Gillies, 'Notes on some changes in the fauna of Otago', 315–16; Duckworth, *The Early Years of Andersons Bay and Tomahawk*, 30.
126. Potts, 'On the birds of NZ (ii)', 84.
127. Gillies, 'Notes on some changes in the fauna of Otago', 316.
128. Renata, 'The native birds of the Otago Peninsula, past and present'.
129. Somerville, 'Reminiscences of James Somerville', 22, William Ayson, *Pioneering in Otago: The recollections of William Ayson*

(Dunedin: Reeds, n.d.), 26; Ferens, 'Transcript of journal of Thomas Ferens on the "John Wickcliffe"', 52–53.
130. Atholl Anderson, *The Welcome of Strangers* (Dunedin: University of Otago Press, 1998), 217.
131. Ferens, 'Transcript of journal', 71–72.
132. Soper, *The Otago of Our Mothers*, 48.
133. Ibid; Gordon, ed., *Waikouaiti and Dunedin in 1850 – Reminiscences of John McLay*, 51-2. Poroporo berries are highly poisonous unless fully ripe. The *Otago News* reprinted this reference to 'pura-pura' from Earp's handbook, *Wild Fruits of New Zealand*: 'The only guide to their fitness for the purposes of eating or preserving is the experience of the natives, who know the precise time at which they should be gathered, so as to be in perfection. The pura-pura is beginning to be highly esteemed for preserving.' *Otago News*, no. 44, 5 January 1849, 2–3.
134. Bill Dacker, *Te Mamae me Te Aroha* (Dunedin: University of Otago Press, 1994), 43.
135. Ibid., 31.
136. Gordon, ed., *Waikouaiti and Dunedin in 1850 – Reminiscences of John McLay*, 19.
137. *Lyttelton Times*, 26 March 1859, 4. It is very likely, though not certain, that these were Kāi Tahu fishermen. See Tony Walzl, 'Ngāi Tahu fishing, 1840–1908', S7, Wai 27, 14.
138. Gordon, ed., *Waikouaiti and Dunedin in 1850 – Reminiscences of John McLay*, 25.
139. Ibid.
140. This was not always so. When the Reverend James Stack stayed at Ōtākou in 1852 he was boated up to Dunedin by Māori fishermen with a freshly caught load of barracouta, and returned to Port Chalmers with them that evening. See James Stack, *More Maoriland Adventures of J.W. Stack* (Dunedin: A.H. and A.W. Reed, 1936), 16-19. However, given that settlers in Macandrew Bay and Broad Bay often had great trouble dealing with tides and weather, and were much closer to their market, this was probably an exception that proved the rule. See 'General road board', *Otago Witness*, 9 March 1867, 9.
141. James Adam, *Emigration to New Zealand: Description of the province of Otago, New Zealand* (Edinburgh: Bell and Bradfute, 1857), 14.
142. Cited in *Otago Colonist*, 17 July 1857, 4–5.
143. Ibid.
144. Ibid.
145. Topi Patuki and others, 10 September 1857. Cited in Tony Walzl, 'Ngai Tahu fishing 1840–1908', doc S7, Wai 27, 16.
146. The hostelry is often confused with the Princes Street Reserve, around which revolves a long controversy. The key points are that in 1853 Commissioner of Crown Lands Walter Mantell gained Governor Grey's approval to create a landing reserve for Māori on land that the provincial government had set aside for public uses. But the site was unsuitable as a landing place and the provincial government (which did not even know the reserve had been designated until 1858) leased the land to local businesses. In the 1860s the provincial government had the land and accumulated rents of several thousand pounds awarded to them. Kāi Tahu took this matter to successive courts, and lost, though the provincial government settled regardless, paying £5000, while Taiaroa and Topi Patuki were also awarded £5000 by the central government. The matter was still a central grievance in the Kāi Tahu claim in the late twentieth century, however. For discussion, see Waitangi Tribunal, *The Ngai Tahu Report* (Wellington: Legislation Direct, 1991), 347–86, esp. 348-50; Dacker, *Te Mamae Me Te Aroha*, 42.
147. Waitangi Tribunal, *The Ngai Tahu Report*, 350–51.
148. 'Report of the committee of the presbytery of Otago in the condition of the aboriginal and half caste population', New Zealand Archives, Dunedin, 1857.
149. Ibid.
150. Renatus Kempthorne, *Maori Christianity in Te Waipounamu: A history* (Christchurch: Te Hui Amorangi, 2000), 66.
151. T.A. Pybus, *Maori and Missionary: Early Christian missions in the South Island of New Zealand* (Christchurch: Cadsonbury Publications, 2002), 138–41.
152. Dacker, *Te Mamae Me Te Aroha*, 42.
153. Kempthorne, *Maori Christianity*, 96.
154. Thomas Burns provided the count in 1848, Mantell conducted a census in 1852, and the magistrate Chetham Strode took a census in 1861.
155. 'Middle Island native claims (further reports by Mr. Commissioner Mackay relating to)', *AJHR*, 1891, G-7A, 3; Bill Dacker, 'The effects of loss of land at Otakou', F1, Wai 27 30.
156. Dacker, 'He Raraka a Ka Awa', 103.
157. See Alexander Mackay, *A Compendium of the Official Documents Relative to Native Affairs in the South Island* (Nelson: Government Printer, 1873), vol. 2, 135. Also *Otago Witness*, 11 July 1857 (Supplement). It is peculiar that Mantell noted no cultivation or stock at Ōtākou whatsoever in his census of 1853. Given the

documented sale of potatoes at this time, for example, this suggests that he did not look very hard. It also therefore throws a little doubt over the accuracy of his population figures, which show 109 people spread between 'Takopa', 'Te Ruatiti', Pukekura and 'Owenua' (not 110 as reported by Mackay). See HC, AG-653/172.
158. Giselle Byrnes, '"A dead sheet covered with meaningless words?" Place names and the cultural colonisation of Tauranga', *New Zealand Journal of History*, vol. 36, no. 1, 2002, 28.
159. Merrington, *A Great Coloniser*, 132.
160. Thomas. M. Hocken, *Contributions to the Early History of New Zealand [Settlement of Otago]* (London: Sampson Low, Marston & Co., 1898), 80; Octavius Harwood, Jnr, 'Fragments of history of the Otago Peninsula, Larnach's Castle, etc.', HC, MS 0604 I+.
161. *Otago Witness*, 4 March 1865, 22.

CHAPTER 7:
THE AXE AND THE LUCIFER MATCH: BOOM-TIME SETTLEMENT OF THE 1860S AND 1870S

1. *Otago Witness*, 4 March 1865, 22.
2. The census of December 1861 returned 27,269 people, but it was estimated that this left out 'about 3000 gold miners who were in tents in different gullies, or on the roads'. See Census of New Zealand, 1861.
3. Erik Olssen, *A History of Otago* (Dunedin: John McIndoe, 1984), 66.
4. Henry Duckworth, *The Early Years of Andersons Bay and Tomahawk*, 2nd edn. (Dunedin: Otago Heritage Books, 1982), 33. Among these lucky few miners was the Te Ati Awa man Raniera Erihana (also known as Dan Ellison), who took 300 ounces of gold from the Shotover in a day. Ellison's wealth, and his marriage to Nani Weller, grand-daughter of Taiaroa and Edward Weller, cemented his family's position as large landowners on the Peninsula. See Atholl Anderson, *The Welcome of Strangers* (Dunedin: University of Otago Press, 1998), 204.
5. J.P. Huggett, 'The historical geography of the Otago Peninsula' (Master's thesis, Victoria University, 1966), 67.
6. Duckworth, *The Early Years of Andersons Bay and Tomahawk*, 29, 33. Wheat prices actually fell despite the gold rush because of a recovery in Australian production. Oat prices rose dramatically because oats fed the horses needed to transport people and goods to the goldfields. Imported oats cost 6s 9d in 1863, more than wheat. Yet by 1865 even oats sold for only 3s 9d, once American grain exports resumed at the end of the Civil War. This reveals the crucial importance of external forces on the small New Zealand market's prices. See Vaughan Wood, 'Soil fertility management in nineteenth century New Zealand agriculture' (PhD diss., University of Otago, 2003), 308, 318.
7. Statistics of New Zealand 1864 and Statistics of the Colony of New Zealand 1881.
8. *Otago Provincial Government Gazette*, vol. 8, 1864, 150.
9. Huggett, 'The historical geography of the Otago Peninsula', 89.
10. Paul Star, 'New Zealand's changing natural history', *New Zealand Journal of History*, vol. 32, no. 1, 1998, 64.
11. Huggett, 'The historical geography of the Otago Peninsula', 89.
12. Robert Gillies, 'Notes on some changes in the fauna of Otago', *Transactions and Proceedings of the New Zealand Institute*, vol. 10, 1878, 306.
13. Ibid., 307.
14. 'Chats with the farmers: A visit to Lilybank, the farm of Mr. William Stewart, Tomahawk Valley, Peninsula', *Otago Witness*, 3 May 1879, 4.
15. The census for 1878 records that 47.9 per cent of European inhabitants had been born here. Scots-born numbered 26.1 per cent, English 13.6 per cent. Census of New Zealand 1878, 1881.
16. The earliest Survey Office (SO) plans date from 1863, and show that cadastral surveys of much of the Peninsula were completed that year.
17. See the description in Pakeha, 'Rambles round Dunedin: The Peninsula–Sandfly–Seal Point–Gull Rocks, etc', *Otago Witness*, 24 December 1870.
18. For extended discussions of the importance of yeoman small farming as an ideological trope, and as a powerful political force in nineteenth-century New Zealand, see the works of Tom Brooking, especially 'Use it or lose it; Unravelling the land debate in nineteenth-century New Zealand', *New Zealand Journal of History*, vol. 30, no. 2, 1996, 141–62; and *Lands for the People? The Highland Clearances and the colonisation of New Zealand: A biography of John Mckenzie* (Dunedin: University of Otago Press, 1996). Rollo Arnold's works also develop similar themes.
19. In 1875 the agricultural correspondent from Portobello and Broad Bay noted that his districts 'are almost exclusively engaged in

20. Portobello Road Board Enabling Act 1882.
21. The Otago Heads Road Board was created by the Road Boards Act 1882 Amendment Act 1884 s10. I have not been able to uncover exactly how and when the Tomahawk board was created (note, too, that it also appears to have had an earlier incarnation in the 1860s). See, for example, *Otago Daily Times*, 24 December 1868, 4.
22. See, for example, 'Peninsula County Council', *Otago Daily Times*, 20 January 1877, 3; 'Peninsula County Council', *Otago Daily Times*, 1 April 1878, 3.
23. Alexander Bathgate, 'A plea for the establishment of Arbor Day', *Otago Witness*, 22 October 1891, 36.
24. *Otago Witness*, 6 August 1859, 3; 26 May 1860, 5.
25. James Somerville, 'Reminiscences of James Somerville', HC, AG-846/01, 37.
26. William Stewart was one such early farmer in the Tomahawk valley. 'Chats with the farmers', *Otago Witness*, 3 May 1879, 4.
27. Samuel Gill, 'Farming at Portobello', in *Early Otago: Pioneer reminiscences recorded by the Port Chalmers Old Identities Association*, ed. Ian Church (Unpub., 1973), 11.
28. Ibid.
29. Jetties were built at Andersons Bay, Vauxhall Gardens, Waverley, Burns Point, Johnstons, Glenfalloch, Macandrew Bay, Company Bay, Broad Bay, Ross Point, Portobello, Ōtākou and Harington Point. See F.H. McCluskey, *Down the Bay: The history of the ferries on Otago Harbour* (Wellington: New Zealand Ship & Marine Society, 1995), frontispiece map.
30. Ibid., 15–20. McCluskey provides an extremely helpful discussion of ferries on Otago Harbour, but see also Huggett, 'The historical geography of the Otago Peninsula', 70; 'Early reminiscences', *Otago Daily Times*, 25 January 1930, 10.
31. The *Lady Barkly* ran five-shilling return sightseeing trips to Harington Point in 1862–63; the *Bruce* ran special excursions over Christmas and New Year to the heads in 1864–65, and again in 1868; the *Lady Bowen* took passengers and freight between Dunedin and Taiaroa Head via Portobello between 1870 and 1874; the *Golden Age* had run excursions throughout the 1860s, and from 1875 ran between the Peninsula bays, Port Chalmers and Dunedin twice weekly; the *Jane* carried passengers and cargo between Portobello and Port Chalmers from 1874, and from 1875 extended her daily run to include Dunedin. She also ran summer excursions to the heads during 1879–80. See McCluskey, *Down the Bay*, 24–26, 29–31, 49–50, 59–60.
32. Ibid., 20.
33. Ibid., 17, 20, 24–26, 29–31, 38–40, 43–47, 51–53, 59–71.
34. Ibid., 51.
35. Ibid., 51–53.
36. Ibid., 59. In 1881, however, the *Jane* was removed from this popular service to be converted into a gold dredge on the Clutha.
37. Ibid., 61–63.
38. Ibid., 69–71.
39. W.A. Tolmie, *Otago Daily Times*, 27 March 1872, 2.
40. Ibid.; 'General Road Board', *Otago Witness*, 8 June 1867, 13; Huggett, 'The historical geography of the Otago Peninsula', 69.
41. 'General Road Board', *Otago Witness*, 9 March 1867, 9.
42. Ibid.; '"A place called Pinkieburn": Sim family history and account book', Toitū Otago Settlers Museum, OSM 2000/08/01-03.
43. For discussion of the work of Māori prisoners while in Dunedin and the Peninsula, especially in the 1870s, see Jane Reeves, 'Maori prisoners in Dunedin 1869–1872 and 1879–1881' (BA Hons diss., University of Otago, 1989), 13–14, 44–49, 61–62, 74.
44. Hardwicke Knight, *Otago Peninsula: A local history* (Broad Bay, Dunedin: Self-published, 1979), 47–48, 52; Reeves, 'Maori prisoners in Dunedin', 14; 'Andersons Bay Road', *Otago Witness*, 6 July 1872, 16.
45. 'A trip to the Peninsula (from our travelling reporter)', *Otago Witness*, 10 August 1878, 6.
46. Gill, 'Farming at Portobello', 12.
47. Huggett, 'The historical geography of the Otago Peninsula', 68–69.
48. Karina Hogg, '"Newlands" a new home: The development of a community at Portobello 1848–1882' (BA diss., University of Otago, 1991), esp. 18–37.
49. See 'Broad Bay', *Otago Witness*, 10 March 1877, 7.
50. See Gill, 'Farming at Portobello', 12; Hardwicke Knight, *Otago Peninsula*, 120.
51. Hardwicke Knight, *Otago Peninsula*, 45, 123–24; *Otago Witness*, 2 January 1875, 13.

[Note: item continued from previous page begins with:] the production of dairy commodities ... This restricted production is caused by the nature of the land, which is very hilly, and in some places so steep as to be altogether unsuitable for tillage.' 'The crops, their condition and extent: Portobello and Broad Bay', *Otago Witness*, 20 February 1875.

52. '"A place called Pinkieburn": Sim family history and account book'.
53. Paul Star provides some biographical detail on Peter Thomson. See Paul Star, 'New Zealand's changing natural history: Evidence from Dunedin 1868–1875', *New Zealand Journal of History*, vol. 32, no. 1, 1998, 59–69.
54. Pakeha, 'Rambles round Dunedin: Andersons Bay, Tomahawk, Sebastopol, and back', *Otago Witness*, 17 December 1864; Pakeha, 'Rambles round Dunedin: The Peninsula–Sandfly–Seal Point–Gull Rocks, etc', *Otago Witness*, 24 December 1870.
55. Pakeha, 'Rambles round Dunedin: Portobello, Hooper's Inlet, Papanui, etc', *Otago Witness*, 17 April 1869.
56. Huggett, 'The historical geography of the Otago Peninsula', 92, 157.
57. Ibid., 92–93.
58. Ibid., 102.
59. Ibid., 93. These estimates are confirmed by the figures given in 'Chats with the farmers', which generally suggests that half to two thirds of the cattle were cows in milk.
60. See Ray Hargreaves, 'An historical geography of New Zealand farming before the introduction of refrigeration' (PhD diss., University of Otago, 1966), 357. The series 'Chats with the farmers', which ran in the *Otago Witness*, provides invaluable insights into the operations of several Peninsula farmers, especially those in Tomahawk. James Patrick, Alexander Mathieson, William Stewart, James King (all of Tomahawk), John Mathieson (Highcliff) and Richard Irving (Broad Bay) each discussed the history and development of their farms in the 1870s. By this stage, Alexander Mathieson, John Mathieson, Richard Irving and John King all ran 'colonial cows' crossed with Ayrshire bulls, while William Stewart had disposed of his colonial cows and ran pure Ayrshires. A few farmers preferred pure Shorthorns.
61. Cited in Ian Church, *Blueskin Days: A history of Waitati, Evansdale, Warrington and surrounding districts* (Waitati: Blueskin History Steering Committee, 2007).
62. Huggett, 'The historical geography of the Otago Peninsula', 157.
63. 'Peninsula county', *Otago Witness*, 23 February 1884, 9; 'Harvest prospects', *Otago Witness*, 10 February 1898, 14.
64. Huggett, 'The historical geography of the Otago Peninsula', 92–93. On William Grey's farm, in Milburn, 20 acres (8ha) of oats were required to feed a working team of four, two hackneys, a brood mare and four colts. 'Farm and station: The farm competition, Mr William Grey's farm, Milburn', *Otago Witness*, 11 October 1894, 6.
65. Murray Rose, 'What's new pussycat? A look at farms and farming life', in *Work'n'Pastimes: 150 years of pain and pleasure, labour and leisure*, ed. Norma Bethune (Dunedin: New Zealand Society of Genealogists, 1998), 194.
66. *Otago Witness*, 24 August 1878, 3; *Otago Witness*, 1 February 1879, 3.
67. Huggett, 'The historical geography of the Otago Peninsula', 93–94.
68. Ibid., 94.
69. Ibid., 95; Otagonian, 'Rambles in the Peninsula', *Otago Witness*, 1 April 1882; Hardwicke Knight, *Otago Peninsula*, 49.
70. Huggett, 'The historical geography of the Otago Peninsula', 98; Hardwicke Knight, *Otago Peninsula*, 107; Hardwicke Knight, *The Ordeal of William Larnach* (Dunedin: Self-published, 1993), 21; Ross Gordon, ed., *Waikouaiti and Dunedin in 1850 – Reminiscences of John McLay an early settler* (Dunedin: Ross Gordon, 1998), 26.
71. Hargreaves, 'An historical geography of New Zealand farming before the introduction of refrigeration', 279–80.
72. This is evident in the District Valuation Rolls 1897, when these fence types still commonly existed there. It is presumed that they were survivors of earlier planting because of the ubiquity of wire fencing by that time.
73. For this and other little-known contributions of settler women to environmental transformaton, see Annette Bainbridge, 'Birth, death, and marriage in the garden: Canterbury colonial women gardeners, 1850–1914' (MA thesis, University of Waikato, 2015), 92–93.
74. 'Chats with the farmers: A visit to Mr. Richard Irving's farm, Johnston Lea, Peninsula', *Otago Witness*, 1 February 1879.
75. For an American parallel, see William Cronon, *Changes in the Land: Indians, colonists, and the ecology of New England* (New York: Hill and Wang, 1983), 130–38.
76. 'The crops, their condition and extent: Portobello', *Otago Witness*, 24 February 1872; 'The crops, their condition and extent: Portobello and Broad Bay', *Otago Witness*, 21 February 1874.
77. This is the description given by William Stewart, who farmed at Tomahawk. See 'Chats with the farmers: A visit to Lilybank, the farm of Mr. William Stewart, Tomahawk Valley, Peninsula', *Otago Witness*, 3 May 1879.
78. See 'Chats with the farmers: A visit to

Springfield, the farm of Mr. John Mathieson, Peninsula', *Otago Witness*, 24 August 1878; 'Chats with the farmers: A visit to the farm of Mr. Alexander Mathieson, Tomahawk, Peninsula', *Otago Witness*, 9 March 1878.
79. Stuart, 'Dairy and recipe book pages'.
80. 'Rural rambles', *Otago Witness*, 25 November 1882, 27.
81. Vaughan Wood provides an excellent discussion of wheat-growing in Otago through the nineteenth century. See Wood, 'Soil fertility management in nineteenth century New Zealand agriculture'.
82. 'The crops, their condition and extent: Andersons Bay', *Otago Witness*, 4 March 1871; 'The crops, their condition and extent: Andersons Bay', *Otago Witness*, 15 February 1873; 'The crops, their condition and extent: Andersons Bay', *Otago Witness*, 9 March 1876. See also Huggett, 'The historical geography of the Otago Peninsula', 91.
83. 'The crops, their condition and extent: Portobello and Broad Bay', *Otago Witness*, 26 February 1870; 'The crops, their condition and extent: Portobello and Broad Bay', *Otago Witness*, 24 February 1872; 'The crops, their condition and extent: Portobello and Broad Bay', *Otago Witness*, 14 April 1877. For bush fires, see 'Bush fires', *Otago Witness*, 28 December 1872, 16.
84. 'The crops, their condition and extent: Andersons Bay', *Otago Witness*, 4 March 1871.
85. 'The crops, their condition and extent: Portobello and Broad Bay', *Otago Witness*, 26 February 1870; 'The crops, their condition and extent: Andersons Bay and Tomahawk', *Otago Witness*, 4 March 1871.
86. 'The crops, their condition and extent: Portobello and Broad Bay', *Otago Witness*, 21 February 1874.
87. Huggett, 'The historical geography of the Otago Peninsula', 91.
88. 'The crops, their condition and extent: Andersons Bay and Tomahawk', *Otago Witness*, 18 March 1876.
89. Walter Riddell's diary, 28 March 1865, Dunedin: McNab New Zealand Collection (Dunedin Public Library), Z920 Rid. 15928. Alexander Stuart, another pioneer Peninsula farmer of the 1860s, lists the sorts of tools that were a settler's basic equipment. In 1863 he spent almost £8 on an axe, adze, crosscut saw, handsaws, a hammer, iron rings, wedges, a spirit level, tape line, oil stone, spade, iron bucket, pick, a spoke shave, files, and spare adze and axe handles. See Alexander Stuart, 'Diary and recipe book pages', HC, Misc-MS-0607.
90. Walter Riddell's diary, 28 March 1865; 1 January 1866; 7 January 1871.
91. Hardwicke Knight, *Otago Peninsula*, 83; Walter Riddell's diary, 5 August 1865; 9, 30 September 1865.
92. Huggett, 'The historical geography of the Otago Peninsula', 109–11, Hardwicke Knight, *Otago Peninsula*, 84. When Peter Thomson visited in 1870, McDonald stated he produced 150 bags per day, or double that if necessary. See 'Rambles round Dunedin: Portobello–Harbour Cone–Peninsula lime works', *Otago Witness*, 9 April 1870, 8.
93. Huggett, 'The historical geography of the Otago Peninsula', 110.
94. 'Rural rambles: Peninsula', *Otago Witness*, 25 November 1882, 27; McDonald switched the primary focus of his lime industry to Milburn. He was still reported as using Peninsula 'hydraulic lime' as an ingredient in his cement works in 1887. However, in 1888 he declared bankruptcy. See 'Our industries. Mr McDonald's cement works', *Otago Witness*, 18 March 1887, 14; 'Creditors meeting', *Otago Witness*, 18 May 1888, 17. Others then took over the Peninsula kilns. Alex McTainsh, whose grandfather Peter McTainsh worked under McDonald, recorded that John Riddell (son of Walter) worked the kilns in the early years of the twentieth century ('about 1906'). 'Otago Daily Times: Letter, 1974, from Alex E. McTainsh', HC, Misc-MS-0653.
95. Fleur Snedden, *King of the Castle: A biography of William Larnach* (Auckland: David Bateman, 1997), 79.
96. Huggett, 'The historical geography of the Otago Peninsula', 85–87.
97. Walter Riddell's diary, 11 May 1866.
98. Brian and Diane Miller, *Macandrew Bay: A history of a community on the Otago Peninsula* (Dunedin: Lifelogs, 2009), 28–29.
99. Snedden, *King of the Castle*, 77, 132–34. Snedden states that Larnach had 410 hectares (1013 acres). For the use of the local stone and a very helpful description of the property, see 'Suburban residences: The Camp; the residence of W.J.M. Larnach, esq., C.M.G.', *Otago Witness*, 13 May 1882, 26.
100. Snedden, *King of the Castle*, 146.
101. Ibid., 72.
102. *Otago Witness*, 12 October 1888, 15.
103. Miller and Miller, *Macandrew Bay*, 26.
104. Snedden, *King of the Castle*, 85.
105. Ibid., 77, 84–85.

106. 'Otago Peninsula Agricultural Society', *Otago Witness*, 1 January 1879, 4.
107. Snedden, *King of the Castle*, 79.
108. Ibid., 85.
109. *Otago Witness*, 13 May 1882, 26.
110. Snedden, *King of the Castle*, 87, 132–34.
111. There have been numerous estimates of the expense of the estate. The cost of the castle alone has been estimated at £125,000. See Hardwicke Knight, *Otago Peninsula*, 83. But as Snedden points out, these estimates are all highly speculative.
112. This ferry was poorly designed, however, and proved a failure. This greatly hampered the development of Waverley; section prices fell 25 per cent when she was taken out of service, and irate purchasers demanded the difference in value be refunded. See McCluskey, *Down the Bay*, 134; *Otago Witness*, 17 February 1872, 15.
113. Walter Riddell's diary, 22 February 1868.
114. Ibid., 4 January 1868.
115. '"A place called Pinkieburn": Sim family history and account book'.
116. Ibid.
117. 'Peninsula Agricultural and Pastoral Society', *Otago Daily Times*, 8 January 1880.
118. A good discussion of the dynamics of such small communities is provided by Rollo Arnold, 'Community in rural Victorian New Zealand', *New Zealand Journal of History*, vol. 24, no. 1, 1990, 3–21. Arnold disposes of Miles Fairburn's claim that nineteenth-century New Zealand was an atomised society, characterised by 'the rootless condition of the colonial population'. See Miles Fairburn, 'Local community or atomized society: The social structure of nineteenth-century New Zealand', *New Zealand Journal of History*, vol. 16, no. 2, 1982, esp. 146–50. The Peninsula was certainly not 'atomised', as any wander through its cemeteries full of the same names confirms.
119. Rollo Arnold, *New Zealand's Burning: The settler's world in the mid 1880s* (Wellington: Victoria University Press, 1994), 115. For example: 'Portobello: From our own correspondent', *Otago Witness*, 19 July 1884, 11. 'The night was beautiful, being clear moonlight, and as a consequence there was a grand turnout, indeed the church was literally crammed …'
120. Anthony Lynch, 'The garden of Otago: A history of small-scale farming in the Clutha area 1848–70' (Master's thesis, University of Otago, 1989), 101–06.
121. Otago Peninsula Cheese Factory Co. Ltd, 'Minute book of the Otago Peninsula Cheese Factory Co. Ltd', HC, MS-0186-A. The enterprise went through several name changes, being called at various times the Peninsula Cheesemaking Company, the Peninsula Pioneer Cheese Company and the Pioneer Cheese Company. See Hardwicke Knight, *Otago Peninsula*, 66. Huggett provides a good description of the factory's operations. The basic principle was that each farmer bought shares at £1 in the company, each share being equivalent to 10 quarts of morning milk he was then obliged to supply. The original shareholders were James Beattie, John McGregor, Walter Riddell, Thomas Inglis, John Mathieson, Alexander Stuart and Richard Irving. See Huggett, 'The historical geography of the Otago Peninsula', 103–08.
122. 'Minute book of the Otago Peninsula Cheese Factory Co. Ltd'.
123. Ibid.
124. Huggett, 'The historical geography of the Otago Peninsula', 108–09.
125. Ibid., 106–07; Hardwicke Knight, *Otago Peninsula*, 60–62.
126. 'Minute book of the Otago Peninsula Cheese Factory Co. Ltd'.
127. Huggett, 'The historical geography of the Otago Peninsula', 111; Hardwicke Knight, *Otago Peninsula*, 62–64.
128. Huggett, 'The historical geography of the Otago Peninsula', 111–12; Hardwicke Knight, *Otago Peninsula*, 130.
129. Hardwicke Knight, *Otago Peninsula*, 70.
130. Ibid., 45.
131. These included the *Nugget* (Farley's own ferry); the *Lady of the Lake* (which ran hourly from 11am until 4pm, and from 7pm to midnight on gala evenings between 1864 and 1865); the *Golden Age* (in the summer months); the *Minerva* (briefly in 1864); and the *Iron Age*. In 1864 Farley also advertised that 'Farley's Line of Red Flag whale boats' would run to the gardens every quarter hour from 6am. See McCluskey, *Down the Bay*.
132. Hardwicke Knight, *Otago Peninsula*, 45.
133. 'Broad Bay', *Otago Witness*, 10 March 1877, 7.
134. Cited in Bill Dacker, 'The prejudicial effects of landlessness at Otakou', Document F11, Wai 27, 3.
135. Ibid., 6.
136. Ibid., 10.
137. *The Illustrated New Zealander*, 18 March 1867, cited in the Waitangi Tribunal, *The Ngai Tahu Sea Fisheries Report* (Wellington: Legislation Direct, 1992), 116.

138. *Otago Witness*, 16 November 1872.
139. Angela Wanhalla, 'Transgressing boundaries: A history of the mixed descent families of Maitapapa, Taieri, 1830–1940' (PhD diss., University of Otago, 2004), 191.
140. Bill Dacker, *Te Mamae Me Te Aroha* (Dunedin: University of Otago Press, 1994), 35–36.
141. Ibid., 36.
142. Murray Thomson, *The Reminiscences of Murray Gladstone Thomson* (Wellington and Dunedin: A.H. and A.W. Reed, 1944), 28–31; 'Papers relating to Murray Gladstone Thomson', HC, MS-0439/084. Murray Thomson described two acres enclosed by a fence and containing 'a House and Offices'.
143. Hargreaves, 'An historical geography of New Zealand farming before the introduction of refrigeration', 71. Hargreaves argues that this practice led to Māori potatoes degenerating, as instead of the finest examples being saved for reproduction, it was often the smaller and less successful potatoes that were left to seed the next crop.
144. Thomson, *The Reminiscences of Murray Gladstone Thomson*, 31.
145. David Johnson, *Hooked: The story of the New Zealand fishing industry* (Christchurch: Hazard Press, 2004), 34.
146. Peter Tremewan, *Selling Otago* (Dunedin: Otago Heritage Books, 1994), 48.
147. Specific information on settlers' fishing activities postdates the gold rush, but they must have begun earlier, as the *Otago Witness* (11 September 1863, 5) reported the complaint that fish had been scarce in the market for several weeks as a result of fishermen leaving to seek gold.
148. 'Further papers relative to the fisheries of the colony', *AJHR*, 1869, D15.
149. Ibid. See also Johnson, *Hooked*, 25. For crayfish, see 'The fishing trade', *Otago Witness*, 29 October 1864, 19.
150. Johnson, *Hooked*, 24.
151. 'Further papers relative to the fisheries of the colony', *AJHR*, 1869, D15. P. Thomson, 'Fish and their seasons', *Transactions and Proceedings of the New Zealand Institute*, vol. 9, 1876, 489; P. Thomson, 'The Dunedin fish supply', *Transactions and Proceedings of the New Zealand Institute*, vol. 10, 1877, 324; Peter Thomson, 'Our fish supply', *Transactions and Proceedings of the New Zealand Institute*, vol. 11, 1878, 386; Johnson, *Hooked*, 24.
152. 'Fish O', *Otago Daily Times*, 24 June 1864.
153. Several newspaper articles detail the risks entailed, and the price sometimes paid in lives and equipment. See 'A day among the barracouta', *Otago Witness*, 16 July 1864, 16; 'The fishing trade', *Otago Witness*, 29 October 1864, 19; *Otago Daily Times*, 29 July 1876.
154. See, for example, 'A perilous cruise', *Otago Witness*, 17 September 1864, 7; 'The fishing trade', *Otago Witness*, 29 October 1864, 19; 'Fatal accident', *Otago Witness*, 29 July 1876, 16.
155. 'New Zealand fisheries', *Otago Witness*, 22 April 1871, 1.
156. Thomson, 'Fish and their seasons', 484–90.
157. Johnson, *Hooked*, 22.
158. Thomson, 'Fish and their seasons', 484–90; Thomson, 'The Dunedin fish supply', 324–30; Thomson, 'Our fish supply', 380–89.
159. Peter Thomson, *Otago Witness*, 29 October 1864, 19.
160. 'Further papers relative to the fisheries of the colony', *AJHR*, 1869, D15.
161. Tony Walzl, 'Ngai Tahu fishing, 1840–1908', S7, Wai 27, 44–45; *Otago Witness*, 26 December 1874, 12; A.B. MacDiarmid, P. Cleaver and B. Stirling, 'Historical evidence for the state and exploitation of the marine fish and invertebrate resources in the Hauraki Gulf and along the Otago–Catlins shelf 1769–1850', *New Zealand Aquatic and Environment and Biodiversity Report* (draft), September 2012, 29–30.
162. MacDiarmid, Cleaver and Stirling, 'Historical evidence for the state and exploitation of the marine fish and invertebrate resources', 30.
163. *Press*, 1 October 1872, 2.
164. Johnson, *Hooked*, 22. In 1864 Peter Thomson reported that crayfish used to be sold for six to 12 shillings a dozen, depending on their size. See *Otago Witness*, 29 October 1864, 19.
165. Eric Schwimmer, 'Rani Ellison: Maori crayfish tycoon', *Te Ao Hou*, no. 20, 1957, 32–36.
166. Angela Wanhalla, '"My piece of land at Taieri": Boundary formation and contestation at Taieri Native Reserve, 1844–1868', *New Zealand Journal of History*, vol. 41, no. 1, 2007, 44–60.
167. *NZPD*, vol. 20, 1876, 454.
168. 'Evidence of Tony Walzl on Ngai Tahu reserves 1848–1890', M14, Wai 27, 36–37.
169. G.C. Thomson papers, 'Agreement by Maori chiefs not to disturb European settlers at Otakou', HC, MS 0438/109.
170. As stated in the Preamble to the Native Lands Act 1862.
171. This problem unfortunately continues to bedevil Māori land held in multiple ownership.
172. Dacker, 'The prejudicial effects of landlessness at Otakou'.
173. Bill Dacker, 'He Raraka A Ka Awa, updated, annotated and sourced manuscript for the

book "Te Mamoe Me Te Aroha", originally published in 1994', HC, Misc-MS-1716, 131.
174. This was the decision-making process according to H.K. Taiaroa, in his evidence before the Native Land Court in 1868. 'South Island Native Land Court minute books 1a', HC, 1868. For another discussion, see Dacker, *Te Mamae Me Te Aroha*, 45–46.
175. Susan Hanham, '"Where land meets water": Rights to the foreshore of Otaakau Maori reserve' (Master's thesis, University of Otago, 1996), 81, 149; Dacker, *Te Mamae Me Te Aroha*, 46.
176. John Weaver, *The Great Land Rush and the Making of the Modern World, 1650–1900* (Montreal & Kingston: McGill-Queen's University Press, 2003), 28.
177. 'Reports of commissioners of native reserves', *AJHR*, 1858, E-4, 13.
178. A now infamous phrase first used by C.W. Richmond, 3 August 1860, *NZPD*, 1858–60, 185–86. See also Evelyn Stokes, *The Individualisation of Maori Interests in Land* (Hamilton: Te Maataahauraki Institute, 2002), 2.
179. W.H. Cutten, Commissioner for Crown Lands, 'Report on native reserves', in Alexander Mackay, *A Compendium of the Official Documents Relative to Native Affairs in the South Island* (Nelson: Government Printer, 1873), vol. 1, 119.
180. Ibid, 116.
181. Ibid, 119.
182. See New Zealand Statutes 1883, 408.
183. Dacker, *Te Mamae Me Te Aroha*, 36.
184. 'Reports from the Commissioner: Major Heaphy, V.C., to the Hon. The Native Minister: Report on the native reserves in the province of Otago', *AJHR*, 1870, vol. 7, D, no.16, 24.
185. Dacker, *Te Mamae Me Te Aroha*, 34.
186. *NZPD*, vol. 16, 1874, 508.
187. Ibid., vol. 27, 1877, 65.
188. Ibid.
189. Ibid.
190. Thomson, 'Fish and their seasons', 484–90; Thomson, 'The Dunedin fish supply', 327–30; Thomson, 'Our fish supply', 380–89.
191. MacDiarmid et al., 'Historical evidence for the state and exploitation of the marine fish and invertebrate resources', 51.
192. Waitangi Tribunal, *Ngai Tahu Sea Fisheries Report*, 58, 137–38.
193. Waitangi Tribunal, *Report of the Waitangi Tribunal on the Muriwhenua Fishing Claim* (Wellington: Brookers, 1988), s 5.1.4.
194. 'Mahinga kai, evidence from the Tuahuriri area, including the submissions of Rawiri Te Maire Tau and Henare Rakiihia Tau', Document H6, Wai 27, 29.
195. For all information on the resumption of whaling, I am indebted to unpublished material collated by Ian Church.
196. *Otago Daily Times*, 14 August 1871.
197. However, Ian Church records that one last whale was harpooned by a Māori crew in February 1881. In total, as many as 24 whales were taken by the whalers at Karitāne and Ōtākou (including one taken by a boat from Purakaunui), while an American whaler also took a sperm whale.
198. *Otago Daily Times*, 12 January 1872.
199. Stack, cited in Alan Ward, 'A report on the historical evidence: The Ngai Tahu claim, Wai 27', T1, Wai 27, 338.
200. Cited in Alexander Mackay, 'Middle Island native claims (report by Mr. Commissioner Mackay relating to)', *AJHR*, 1891, G7, 43.
201. Kāi Tahu petition 1874. Quoted in Dacker, *Te Mamae Me Te Aroha*.
202. See, for example, Alexander Mackay, 'Middle Island native claims (further reports by Mr. Commissioner Mackay relating to)', *AJHR*, 1891, G8, 5.
203. For example, in 1873 H.K. Taiaroa was given £3000 to pursue land claims. In 1891 he estimated the cost of the Ōtākou claim at £3200, a sum he sought to have returned. See Bill Dacker, 'The effects of loss of land at Otakou', F1, Wai 27, 68–69.
204. Kāi Tahu petitioned parliament in 1872, 1874, 1875, 1876 and 1878. The Smith–Nairn Commission of 1880 eventually heard their case, but its funding was withdrawn midway through the process and only an interim report, albeit one which supported Kāi Tahu, could be tabled. See Alexander Mackay, 'Middle Island native claims (report by Mr. Commissioner Mackay relating to)', *AJHR*, 1891, G7, 3-4; Dacker, *Te Mamae Me Te Aroha*, 66.
205. 'Mr. Alexander Mackay. N.C. to the under secretary, Native Department', *AJHR*, 1881, G8, 16–17.
206. Dacker, *Te Mamae Me Te Aroha*, 44.
207. Ibid., 79–80.
208. 'Otago Heads Native Reserve', *NZPD*, 25 September 1893, vol. 82 (6 Sept.–6 Oct.), 602–03.
209. P. Thomson, 'On the sand hills, or dunes, in the neighbourhood of Dunedin', *Transactions and Proceedings of the New Zealand Institute*, vol. 3, 1870, 266.

210. Ibid.
211. Ibid., 268.
212. Hardwicke Knight, *Otago Peninsula*, 24. Burns recorded that Taiaroa had lived at Tahakopa, which lay close by the lagoon. Mantell also recorded him as living at 'Takopa' in 1853.
213. 'Census of the Middle Island natives made by Mr. Commissioner Mantell in 1848 and 1853', *AJHR*, 1886, 3.
214. T.A. Pybus, *Maori and Missionary: Early Christian missions in the South Island of New Zealand* (Christchurch: Cadsonbury Publications, 2002), 138; Hardwicke Knight, *Otago Peninsula*, 24. Pybus recorded: 'Ruatitiko being gradually depopulated by reason of the sand drifts, & the Church was also suffering from the same cause, being partly buried in the sand, the chief [Taiaroa] opened his house at Omati for Christian services.'
215. Renatus Kempthorne, *Maori Christianity in Te Waipounamu: A history* (Christchurch: Te Hui Amorangi, 2000), 80.
216. Reverend Thomas Pybus, 'Various manuscript notes on Otakou and Port Chalmers (c. 1939)', HC, MS 534/017; Thomson, 'On the sand hills, or dunes, in the neighbourhood of Dunedin', 268.
217. Matthew Campbell, 'Premliminary investigation of the archaeology of whaling stations on the southern coast' (Master's thesis, University of Otago, 1992), 124; Hardwicke Knight, *Otago Peninsula*, 23–24.
218. Thomson, 'On the sand hills, or dunes, in the neighbourhood of Dunedin', 267.
219. Ibid., 265.
220. Peter Thomson, 'Rambles round Dunedin. The Peninsula—Sandfly—Seal Point—Gull Rocks, etc.', *Otago Witness*, 24 December 1870, 9.
221. Ibid.
222. Department of Agriculture, *Department of Agriculture Annual Report* (Wellington: Samuel Costall: Government Printer, 1894), 64.
223. For an excellent discussion of the various provincial ordinances regarding thistles at this time, see Neil Clayton, 'Weeds, people and contested places: Selected themes from the history of New Zealanders and their weeds 1770–1940' (PhD diss., University of Otago, 2007), 165–81. Also Hargreaves, 'An historical geography of New Zealand farming before the introduction of refrigeration', 271.
224. Alexander Begg reported to the provincial government in 1867 that he had 'found thistles in great abundance extending eight miles [13km] up from the Maori reserve (where they first originated) and yearly spreading'. See 'Papers and returns – Report from government gardener [Alexander Begg] respecting the eradication of thistles – 4 May 1867', Archives New Zealand, R19002184, AAAC 701 D500 27/e 39.
225. 'Alexander Begg, botanical gardens, 27 April 1864 to the secretary of public works', in *Otago Witness*, 7 May, 1864, 14.
226. 'Provincial Council', *Otago Witness*, 16 December, 1865, 4.
227. 'Provincial Council', *Otago Witness*, 24 November 1866, 7.
228. These reports make plain that thistles became a serious problem in the 1870s. See, for example, 'The crops, their condition and extent: Portobello and Broad Bay', *Otago Witness*, 15 February 1873, describing thistles growing in sawyers' clearings and by roadsides 'as thick as they can stand, and higher than a man's head'; 'The crops, their condition and extent: Andersons Bay and Tomahawk', *Otago Witness*, 21 February 1874, describing thistle seed on the wind as 'snow adrift'. In 1877 this correspondent examined a Scotch thistle and found it had 87 heads, with one head alone found to contain 367 seeds. 'The crops, their condition and extent: Andersons Bay and Tomahawk', *Otago Witness*, 14 April 1877.
229. Inhabitants of the Otago Peninsula, 'Petitions presented: Inhabitants of the Otago Peninsula'.
230. 'Session 34 May–June 1875', Dunedin: Archives New Zealand, 1875. The notion that thistles might aid uncultivated land was widespread at the time, though disputed. Some also felt that thistles would die out on their own, given time, as the land became 'thistle sick'. This was not so. See 'The crops, their condition and extent: Portobello and Broad Bay', *Otago Witness*, 14 April 1877.
231. 'Portobello Road Board', *Otago Witness*, 11 December 1875, 10; 'Peninsula Road Board', 22 January 1876, 17.
232. Clayton, 'Weeds, people and contested places', 181.
233. 'The crops, their condition and extent: Andersons Bay and Tomahawk', *Otago Witness*, 18 March 1876, 9.
234. See 'The crops, their condition and extent: Portobello and Broad Bay', *Otago Witness*, 15 February 1873; 'The crops, their condition and extent: Portobello and Broad Bay', *Otago Witness*, 21 February 1874; 'The crops, their condition and extent: Portobello', *Otago Witness*, 14 April 1877, 10.

235. 'The crops, their condition and extent: Portobello and Broad Bay', *Otago Witness*, 15 February 1873. For discussion, see Clayton 'Weeds, people and contested places', esp. 142 and 158.
236. The writer of 'Station, farm, & garden: Agricultural seeds no. IV', *Otago Witness*, 1 April 1882, despaired that 'the indifference shown by our farmers as to the quality of the seed is proverbial', and argued this was one cause of New Zealand seed being refused in overseas markets. The New South Wales government examined 'grass and clover' seed imported from New Zealand in 1892 and found it to comprise 40 per cent perennial ryegrass, 20 per cent creeping trefoil, and 40 per cent miscellaneous species, including 'goose grass, dock, sorrel, silver grass, plantain, wild amaranth, Yorkshire fog, and other useless weeds and grasses'. Their findings were concerning enough to be reported here. See Department of Agriculture Annual Report 1893, 49–50.
237. *Otago Witness*, 22 December 1872.
238. 'A day with the Field Naturalist Club', *Otago Witness*, 30 March 1872, 10.
239. *Otago Witness*, 3 August 1872, 6.
240. *Otago Witness*, 4 March 1865, 22.
241. My estimate that households burnt 10 cords is probably conservative. Rollo Arnold has estimated that settlers in the mid-1880s burnt 5 tons of wood per head. This equates to about 9 cords per head (for conversion of cords to tons, I rely on a request for tenders issued by the army, which considered 71 cubic feet of hard wood equivalent to a ton. *Otago Witness*, 21 December 1861, 3). Arnold's estimate includes all uses for firewood, not just domestic. Arnold, *New Zealand's Burning*, 137.
242. For the varying price of a cord of firewood, see the *Otago News*, no. 4, 9 April 1849 ('12s or so'); *Otago News*, no. 57, 6 April 1850 ('9s and 10s 6d'); *Otago News*, no. 83, 5 October 1850 ('at least 14s').
243. *Otago Witness*, 18 July 1857, 4.
244. This practice prompted Cargill to evict squatters from the Dunedin Town Belt in 1850. But for the prevalence of stealing wood from the Town Belt, even among the well-to-do, see 'Rambles round Dunedin: The Town Belt', *Otago Witness*, 12 August 1865, 12. The writer states that one member of the executive had taken over 150 cords. A settler's letter states that a man could cut a cord in a day: 'Letter from W. Duff to W.R. Douglas, 4 May 1849', *Otago Journal*, no. 3, 1848, 74.
245. 'Rambles round Dunedin: The Peninsula to the Big Stone', *Otago Witness*, 4 March 1865.
246. 'The crops, their condition and extent: Andersons Bay and Tomahawk', *Otago Witness* 18 March 1876; 14 April 1877.
247. Hardwicke Knight, *Otago Peninsula*, 70–71.
248. Ibid., 70–71, 128.
249. 'The crops, their condition and extent: Portobello and Broad Bay', *Otago Witness*, 21 February 1874; 18 March 1876, 10.
250. *Otago Witness*, 10 August 1878, 6.
251. Ibid.; 'The crops, their condition and extent: Portobello', *Otago Witness*, 24 February 1872.
252. 'Sandymount: From our own correspondent', *Otago Witness*, 22 October 1881; 'The bush fires on the Peninsula', *Otago Witness*, 22 October 1881; see also Huggett, 'The historical geography of the Otago Peninsula', 78; Hardwicke Knight, *Otago Peninsula*, 62.
253. For research in the New Zealand context, see R.J. Davies-Colley, G.W. Payne and M. van Elswijk, 'Microclimate gradients across a forest edge', *New Zealand Journal of Ecology*, vol. 24, no. 2, 2000, 111–21.
254. Davies-Colley et al. found that wind exposure inside forest was only some 20 per cent of that in open pasture. Compared to pasture soils, the forest floor was much shadier, cooler and moister during the day, and warmer and drier at night, with little temperature variation. Soils under pasture, in contrast, followed atmospheric conditions much more closely. See ibid., esp. 115–19.
255. M. Crozier stationed a series of rain gauges inside and outside a remnant patch of forest on the Peninsula from 1967 to 1969. He found that rain gauges outside the forest always recorded more rain, while those furthest inside the forest almost always recorded least rain. See Michael Crozier, 'Mass-movement in eastern Otago: The relationship of slope instability to environmental factors and its importance to slope development on the Otago Peninsula' (PhD diss., University of Otago, 1970), Figure 31.
256. Ibid., 107–15.
257. Ibid., 112–14, 22.
258. Ibid., 112–14.
259. See D.M. Leslie, *Landslide Potential on Otago Peninsula*, ed. Department of Scientific and Industrial Research New Zealand Soil Bureau (Wellington: New Zealand Soil Bureau, Department of Scientific and Industrial Research, 1974). Leslie found that of 504 landslides identified in 1970, 297 occurred where the basement lithology (the underlying

rock) was pyroclastic, as opposed to flow rock, despite pyroclastic rock covering only about a quarter of the Peninsula. 97 per cent of slides occurred on hill land between 12 and 28 degrees.
260. For a useful discussion of contrasting attitudes to erosion on the Peninsula see Marion Read, 'The "construction" of landscape: A case study of the Otago Peninsula, Aotearoa/New Zealand' (PhD diss., Lincoln University, 2005), 157–60.
261. Leslie, *Landslide Potential on Otago Peninsula*, 17–18. He states that a 'marked increase in landslide frequency' had occurred.
262. Crozier, 'Mass-movement in eastern Otago', 90–91, 99, 103.
263. 'The crops, their condition and extent: Portobello and Broad Bay', *Otago Witness*, 4 March 1871.
264. 'The crops, their condition and extent: Portobello', *Otago Witness*, 14 April 1877.
265. Read, 'The "construction" of landscape', 157. According to a farmer Read interviewed, this was the method early farmers used.
266. 'Portobello 7th February', *Otago Witness*, 17 February 1877, 7; 'Otago Peninsula after the floods', *Otago Witness*, 10 March 1877; 'The Portobello Road Board', *Otago Witness*, 10 March 1877, 10.
267. 'Otago Peninsula after the floods', *Otago Witness*, 10 March 1877.
268. Huggett, 'The historical geography of the Otago Peninsula', 96.
269. Aparata Renata, 'Something about our native birds', *Otago Witness*, 22 March 1894, 50.
270. Aparata Renata, 'The native birds of the Otago Peninsula, past and present', *Otago Witness*, 10 August 1910, 76. The lack of records is unsurprising, given the settlers' priorities. Thus the *Otago Witness*' reviewer of T.H. Potts' article about losses of native birds criticised Potts' worries, and noted: 'The quail is the only bird, valuable as an article of food, which has become scarce during the last few years.' *Otago Witness*, 2 July 1870, 4.
271. Geoff Park, *Nga Uruora* (Wellington: Victoria University Press, 1995), 112.
272. Tony Harris, pers. comm., 30 September 2007. For a useful if brief survey of changes in soil fauna, see G.W. Yeates, 'Impact of historical changes in land use on the soil fauna', *New Zealand Journal of Ecology*, vol. 15, no. 1, 1991, 99–106.
273. Early settlers noted that the Peninsula generally was abundant in kōwhai, and that it dominated the slopes above Tomahawk. The Clearwaters considered that Mt Charles was mostly kōwhai and broadleaf. Richard Holdaway has suggested that kōwhai may have been much more abundant in southeastern New Zealand prior to Polynesian burning. See Duckworth, *The Early Years of Andersons Bay and Tomahawk*; John McLay, 'Reminiscences of John McLay', Toitū Otago Early Settlers Museum, n.d., 26–30; H. Thompson and I. Thompson, *Clearwaters of New Zealand 1838–1986* (Invercargill: Sycamore Print, 1986); Aparata Renata, 'The native birds of the Otago Peninsula past and present', *Otago Witness*, 10 August 1910, 76; R.N. Holdaway, 'New Zealand's pre-human avifauna and its vulnerability', *New Zealand Journal of Ecology*, vol. 12, supplement, 1989, 14.
274. The accepted view within New Zealand ecology is that pollination is dominated by a generalised insect pollination fauna, notably species from the orders Diptera (flies), Hymenoptera (bees), Cleoptera (beetles) and Lepidoptera (moths and butterflies). Some have argued that it is unlikely that any New Zealand plant has been threatened by the loss of bird pollinators. However, more recent research has argued that the role of birds has been underestimated, even for small-flowering flora whose blooms are traditionally regarded, on morphological grounds, as adapted to insect pollination. It has also been argued that the role of insects has been overestimated for other plants; kōwhai, with large, bright yellow bell-shaped flowers, is clearly adapted to bird pollination. Anderson noted that though insects visited kōwhai flowers to feed, very few actually successfully cross-pollinated the plant. She concluded that only tūī could be said to routinely achieve kōwhai pollination. See M.N. Clout and J.R. Hay, 'The importance of birds as browsers, pollinators and seed dispersers in New Zealand forests', *New Zealand Journal of Ecology*, vol. 12, 1989, 29, 31; Isabel Castro and Alastair W. Robertson, 'Honeyeaters and the New Zealand forest flora: The utilisation and profitability of small flowers', *New Zealand Journal of Ecology*, vol. 21, no. 2, 1997; Sarah Anderson, 'The relative importance of birds and insects as pollinators of the New Zealand flora', *New Zealand Journal of Ecology*, vol. 27, no. 2, 2003, esp. 84–89.
275. Clout and Hay, 'The importance of birds as browsers, pollinators and seed dispersers in New Zealand forests', 29–32.
276. Ibid., 31.

277. Gillies, 'Notes on some changes in the fauna of Otago', 316.
278. Aparata Renata, 'The native birds of the Otago Peninsula, past and present', *Otago Witness*, 10 August 1910, 76.
279. Ibid.
280. James Drummond, 'In touch with nature: An Australian in New Zealand', *Otago Witness*, 21 October 1898, 15. Drummond relates that silvereyes (waxeyes) (*Zosterops*) arrived in about 1856, being blown over from Australia and landing first on Dog Island, Foveaux Strait, where the lighthouse keeper found scores of them dead. According to Drummond, the birds quickly spread north from that point.
281. Ibid.
282. No other such measure occurred for an insect pest until 1884, when the Codlin moth was targeted. See Paul Star, 'From acclimatisation to preservation: Colonists and the natural world in southern New Zealand 1860-1894' (PhD diss., University of Otago, 1997), 304; Gillies, 'Notes on some changes in the fauna of Otago', 313-14. The blight was eventually deterred by grafting stock from an American variety, 'Northern Spy', which was largely invulnerable to the blight because of its hard bark and very firm wood. G.M. Thomson, *The Naturalisation of Animals and Plants in New Zealand* (Cambridge: Cambridge University Press, 1922), 330.
283. 'The crops, their condition and extent: Andersons Bay and Tomahawk', *Otago Witness*, 4 March 1871; 15 February 1873; 'Chats with the farmers: A visit to Springfield, the farm of Mr. John Mathieson, Peninsula', *Otago Witness*, 24 August 1878.
284. Acclimatisation society', *Otago Witness*, 2 August 1867, 17; 'The crops, their condition and extent: Portobello and Broad Bay', *Otago Witness*, 21 February 1874.
285. Fereday stated that the worst insect pests comprised five moths, two beetles and various aphides. See R.W. Fereday, 'On the direct injuries to vegetation in New Zealand by various insects, especially with reference to larvae of moths and beetles feeding upon the field crops; and the expediency of introducing insectivorous birds as a remedy', *Transactions and Proceedings of the New Zealand Institute*, vol. 5, 1872, 290-92. The worst aphides have already been mentioned. Fereday mentions only an introduced moth (*Sesia tipuliformis*) which attacks currants. Anthony Harris has tentatively identified the other moths (the larvae of which were usually the pest) as the Porina moth (Weisana sp. family Hepialidae) the larvae of which attacked pasture, cutworm and armyworm caterpillars (family Noctuidae), and the magpie moth (*Nyctimera annulata*). The beetles are the grass grubs (in northern New Zealand, this is more commonly *Costelytra zealandica*). See also T.C. Bourner et al., 'Towards greener pastures: Pathogens and pasture pests', *New Zealand Journal of Ecology*, vol. 20, no. 1, 1996, 101.
286. For such concern as expressed on the Peninsula, see 'The crops, their condition and extent: Andersons Bay and Tomahawk', *Otago Witness*, 21 February 1874.
287. 'The crops, their condition and extent', *Otago Witness*, 21 February 1874.
288. Star, 'New Zealand's changing natural history', 60.
289. Ibid., 63-64.
290. G.M. Thomson, 'Notes by the wayside', *Otago Witness*, 21 September 1899, 62.
291. James Drummond, *Our Feathered Immigrants: Evidence for and against introduced birds in New Zealand; together with notes on the native fauna* (Wellington: John Mackay, Government Printer, 1907), 3.
292. *Otago Witness*, 11 March 1871.
293. Alexander Bathgate, 'Acclimatisation in New Zealand', *Otago Witness*, 5 August 1897, 54.
294. *Otago Witness*, 12 September 1874, 13.
295. *Otago Witness*, 4 March 1871, 6; G.M. Thomson, 'Notes by the wayside', *Otago Witness*, 21 September 1899, 62.
296. Drummond, *Our Feathered Immigrants*, 2.
297. 'The crops, their condition and extent: Portobello and Broad Bay', *Otago Witness*, 21 February 1874; 20 February 1875; 18 March 1876.
298. 'The crops, their condition and extent: Portobello and Broad Bay', *Otago Witness*, 20 February 1875.
299. 'The crops, their condition and extent: Portobello and Broad Bay', *Otago Witness*, 18 March 1876.
300. Ibid., 9; 'The crops, their condition and extent', *Otago Witness*, 20 February 1875.
301. Alexander Bathgate, 'Acclimatisation in New Zealand', *Otago Witness*, 5 August 1897, 54.
302. Alexander Bathgate, 'On the Lepidoptera of Otago', *Transactions and Proceedings of the New Zealand Institute*, vol, 3, 1870, 137-38.
303. Alexander Bathgate, 'Acclimatisation in New Zealand', *Otago Witness*, 5 August 1897, 54.
304. 'Otago Acclimatisation Society', *Otago Witness*, 27 May 1865, 4; 'Acclimatisation', *Otago Witness*, 3 July 1875; 'Acclimatisation', *Otago Witness*, 16 October 1875, 6; G.M. Thomson,

'Notes by the wayside', *Otago Witness*, 21 September 1899, 21.

305. Star, 'New Zealand's changing natural history', 64, n. 23.
306. 'Chats with the farmers: A visit to the farm of Mr. James King, Tomahawk, Peninsula', *Otago Witness*, 3 May 1879.
307. 'Chats with the farmers: A visit to Springfield, farm of Mr. John Mathieson, Peninsula', *Otago Witness*, 24 August 1878.
308. 'Chats with the farmers: A visit to the farm of Mr. James Patrick, Tomahawk, Peninsula', *Otago Witness*, 9 March 1878; 'Chats with the farmers: A visit to the farm of Mr. Alexander Mathieson, Tomahawk, Peninsula', *Otago Witness*, 9 March 1878; 'Chats with the farmers: A visit to Springfield, farm of Mr. John Mathieson, Peninsula', *Otago Witness*, 24 August 1878; 'Chats with the farmers: A visit to the farm of Mr. James King, Tomahawk, Peninsula', *Otago Witness*, 3 May 1879.
309. Hargreaves, 'An historical geography of New Zealand farming before the introduction of refrigeration', 317–18. A column in the *Otago Witness*, 30 October 1863, 6, contained tender advice on how to feed and care for rabbits. Larnach seems to have been responsible for the introduction of hares, among other game. He released several onto his estate in 1873. See 'Acclimatisation society report', *Otago Witness*, 12 September 1874, 4. He also released quail and nightingales. 'Acclimatisation in New Zealand', *Otago Witness*, 5 August 1897, 54.
310. 'Rambles round Dunedin: The Peninsula–Sandfly–Seal Point–Gull Rocks etc', *Otago Witness*, 24 December 1870. The first record of rabbits in Otago was made when Tuckett encountered them in 1844. It is very hard to document the spread of cats; only a few scattered references are made to them. John McLay noted that Thomas Robertson, who farmed at Tomahawk, had a 'big yellow tom cat', and one day found kittens in an old broadleaf. See McLay, 'Reminiscences of John McLay', 40, 42.
311. *Otago Witness*, 16 March 1872, 16.
312. *Otago Witness*, 2 December 1865, 15.
313. Chevalier's imaginative additions are revealed by a comparison of the more finished painting shown here with the prepatory picture, *Sandfly Bay and Gull Rock, Nr Dunedin, 1865*, which preceded it. See Melvin Day, *Nicholas Chevalier Artist: His life and work with special reference to his career in Australia and New Zealand* (Wellington: Millwood Publications, 1981), Plate 1.
314. The Reverend Thomas Burns to Captain John Cargill, 30 January 1847. See Ernest Northcroft Merrington, *A Great Coloniser: The Rev. Dr. Thomas Burns* (Dunedin: The Otago Daily Times and Witness Newspapers Co., 1929), 266.
315. *Otago Witness*, 10 August 1878.
316. Roger Collins and Peter Entwisle, *Pavilioned in Splendour: George O'Brien's vision of colonial New Zealand* (Dunedin: Dunedin Public Art Gallery, 1986), 10.
317. 'Rambles round Dunedin: Portobello–Harbour Cone–Peninsula lime works', *Otago Witness*, 9 April 1870, 8.
318. Collins and Entwisle, *Pavilioned in Splendour*, 10.
319. Anonymous, *Otago Daily Times*, 3 November, 3. Quoted in Collins and Entwisle, *Pavilioned in Splendour*, 36.
320. Ibid., 11.
321. Eileen Soper, *The Otago of Our Mothers* (Christchurch: Whitcombe & Tombs, 1948), 55.
322. In arguing thus I am following in the footsteps of Paul Star, who has made precisely this argument for Otago generally. I am indebted to him for developing it in so lucid and comprehensive a form. The Peninsula provides some fine examples of the 'counter-revolution' that Star argues for. See Star, 'From acclimatisation to preservation'.
323. Ibid., 58; Star, 'New Zealand's changing natural history', 69.
324. 'The crops, their condition and extent: Andersons Bay and Tomahawk', *Otago Witness*, 15 February 1873, 15; 21 February 1874, 5.
325. *Otago Witness*, 20 February 1875, 10.
326. Alexander Bathgate, *Colonial Experiences* (Glasgow: James Maclehose, 1874), 14.
327. 'The crops, their condition and extent: Andersons Bay and Tomahawk', *Otago Witness*, 18 March 1876, 9. The correspondent advised planting 'the gullies and steeper hillsides, which are almost valueless for any other purpose' with eucalyptus. This would provide timber for fences, many of which were already in 'an advanced state of decay'. In 1877 another writer to the *Otago Witness* expressed similar sentiments about the suddenly 'dry and barren' appearance of land 'so steep and rocky as to be quite useless', and suggested establishing reserves where 'natural beauties' could be preserved. *Otago Witness*, 10 March 1877.
328. *Otago Witness*, 27 August 1870; 3 September 1870. See Star, 'From acclimatisation to preservation', 255–58 for discussion. Likewise, Neil Clayton has argued that ambivalence

towards live fences arose in the 1870s as farmers counted the costs of keeping gorse, in particular, under control. This attitude was slower to surface on the Peninsula. The Portobello and Broad Bay correspondent lauded the planting of live fences by several proprietors in 1875, arguing they were a 'most decided and permanent improvement, as they will afford shelter to the insectivorous birds now being rapidly propagated, besides being more sightly than posts and rails'. The Andersons Bay correspondent, meanwhile, bemoaned their lack. 'The crops, their condition and extent: Portobello and Broad Bay', *Otago Witness*, 20 February 1875, 10; 'The crops, their condition and extent: Andersons Bay and Tomahawk', *Otago Witness*, 18 March 1876.

329. Quoted in David Young, *Our Islands, Our Selves* (Dunedin: University of Otago Press, 2004), 70.
330. Thus Thomas Potts noted that change must be obvious to the older rural settlers. See T.H. Potts, 'Out in the open (A budget of scraps of natural history)', *New Zealand Country Journal*, vol. 3, 1878, 139–46.
331. By the early 1880s 40 per cent of New Zealand's population lived in towns, and there were now more New Zealand-born settlers than immigrants. See Star, 'From acclimatisation to preservation', 218–21.
332. For discussion of the prevalence and development of this belief in settler society, see Ross Galbreath, *Working for Wildlife: A history of the New Zealand Wildlife Service* (Wellington: Bridget Williams Books and Department of Internal Affairs, 1993), 65–108.
333. Star, 'From acclimatisation to preservation', 60.
334. Ibid., 11–12.
335. See Walter Buller, 'Address by the president, Wellington Philosophical Society', *Transactions and Proceedings of the New Zealand Institute*, vol. 17, 1884, 443–46.
336. 'News of the week', *Otago Witness*, 11 December 1869, 14.
337. Several of these leading figures – T.L. Potts, W.T.L. Travers and R.M. Fereday, for example – were settler-scientists from Canterbury.
338. Fereday, 'On the direct injuries to vegetation in New Zealand by various insects', 289.
339. Ibid., 294.
340. *Dunedin Morning Herald*, 21 April 1881. Cited in Star, 'From acclimatisation to preservation', 272.
341. Cited in ibid., 85.
342. Editorial, *Otago Witness*, 1 May 1880, 5.

CHAPTER 8:
'THE WHOLE FACE OF NATURE IS ALTERED': 1881–1900

1. G.M. Thomson, 'Notes by the wayside', *Otago Witness*, 28 September 1899, 62.
2. George Griffiths, 'Mr G.M. Thomson, who knows his Dunedin like a book', *Hocken Bulletin*, 48, September 2004.
3. G.M. Thomson, 'Notes by the wayside', *Otago Witness*, 5 June 1899, 62.
4. 'Portobello', *Otago Witness*, 2 December 1887, 17.
5. The data in this and subsequent figures is derived from a combination of two sources. The data on the state of each holding is contained in the 'District Valuation Rolls 1897', CAIH D121 83-90, Archives New Zealand, Dunedin Regional Office. These are the records provided by the valuation officers who visited each property on the Peninsula. There are eight rolls, each representing a riding on the Peninsula (Otago Heads, Portobello, Broad Bay, Highcliff, Sandymount, North East Harbour, Andersons Bay, Tomahawk). The landholdings were originally mapped by John Huggett by matching the titles recorded in the rolls with those shown on the cadastral map of 1896. There are eight holdings with discrepancies between Huggett's map of a holding and the data I accumulated relative to that holding, where Huggett either missed or misinterpreted a relevant title record. However, I chose not to remap the holdings, as I had by this time committed myself to the use of Huggett's map.
6. 'District Valuation Rolls 1897', CAIH D121 83-90, Archives New Zealand, Dunedin Regional Office.
7. J.P. Huggett, 'The historical geography of the Otago Peninsula' (Master's thesis, Victoria University, 1966), 161.
8. 'The settlers here are quite jubilant over the result of the venture per ship *Dunedin* … and you hear of nothing but "mutton" talked of.' 'Portobello: From our own correspondent', *Otago Witness*, 10 June 1882, 13.
9. Huggett, 'The historical geography of the Otago Peninsula', 142–43, 60–64. Dept of Agriculture Reports for 1899 and 1900.
10. Huggett, 'The historical geography of the Otago Peninsula', 164. Dept of Agriculture Report 1901.
11. Huggett, 'The historical geography of the Otago Peninsula', 160–64.
12. Ibid., 159.

13. New Zealand Statistics; New Zealand Agriculture Dept Annual Report 1900.
14. Dept of Agriculture Reports; Huggett, 'The historical geography of the Otago Peninsula', 167; 'Peninsula County agricultural statistics', *Otago Witness*, 23 February 1884, 9.
15. Huggett, 'The historical geography of the Otago Peninsula', 166.
16. Ibid., 165.
17. Keith Sinclair, *A History of New Zealand*, rev. edn. (Auckland: Penguin Books, 2000), 167–68.
18. 'Harvest prospects', *Otago Witness*, 10 February 1898, 14; Huggett, 'The historical geography of the Otago Peninsula', 155.
19. 'Peninsula County: No. 1.–Highcliffe: J.M.; No. 2.–Sandymount: B.M.; No. 4.–Sandymount: A.McK.', *Otago Witness*, 23 February 1884, 9; 'Peninsula Farmers Association', *Otago Witness*, 27 November 1890, 6. Derwents and Kidneys (fluke and ashleaf) seem to have been the principal varieties, though 'American early, pink eyes, cups' are also recorded.
20. 'Peninsula Farmers Association', *Otago Witness*, 27 November 1890, 6. At least, no mention of it is made again in the *Otago Witness*.
21. 'Rural rambles: Peninsula', *Otago Witness*, 25 November 1882, 27.
22. 'Rambles in the Peninsula', *Otago Witness*, 1 April 1882, 7.
23. Ibid.
24. Ibid.
25. 'The garden: Chinese market gardening', *Otago Witness*, 1 June 1878, 21.
26. Ibid.
27. *Otago Witness*, 10 August 1878, 6.
28. *Otago Witness*, 14 May, 18. Nineteen Chinese were recorded as resident on the Peninsula in the census of 1881.
29. Annual report of the Department of Lands and Survey', *AJHR*, C-1, 1901, xi. The plans are now held in the Dunedin office of Archives New Zealand.
30. Huggett, 'The historical geography of the Otago Peninsula', 194–97.
31. Census data for 1881, 1891, 1896, 1901.
32. 'Peninsula', *Otago Witness*, 12 September 1885, 13.
33. 'Rural rambles. Peninsula', *Otago Witness*, 25 November 1882, 27. See 'Waverley toll. To the editor', *Otago Witness*, 14 July 1892, 11; Minutes of the Portobello Road Board, quoted in Huggett, 'The historical geography of the Otago Peninsula', 190.
34. See 'Waverley toll. To the editor', *Otago Witness*, 14 July 1892, 11; Minutes of the Portobello Road Board, quoted in Huggett, 'The historical geography of the Otago Peninsula', 190.
35. F.H. McCluskey, *Down the Bay: The history of the ferries on Otago Harbour* (Wellington: New Zealand Ship & Marine Society, 1995), 74–75, 77–78.
36. McCluskey, *Down the Bay*, 80–83. Towards the end of 1899 a new timetable provided for twice-daily trips between Portobello and Dunedin, six days a week.
37. Ibid., 90–91.
38. Statistics of the Colony of New Zealand 1881.
39. Huggett, 'The historical geography of the Otago Peninsula', 153.
40. Ibid., 151.
41. Statistics of the Colony of New Zealand 1904.
42. Ibid., 144.
43. Ibid.
44. Ibid., 174.
45. 'Otakou: October 16', *Otago Witness*, 22 October 1891, 21; 'Portobello', *Otago Witness*, 5 November 1891, 21. Most of the farmers at Ōtākou, who were more isolated than the rest, used this service. The carrying contract stimulated the beginning of organised passenger transport, too: David Seaton took people and their luggage on his ferry in addition to the milk.
46. McCluskey, *Down the Bay*, 74–78; Huggett, 'The historical geography of the Otago Peninsula', 169.
47. Huggett, 'The historical geography of the Otago Peninsula', 145–46.
48. Ibid., 180.
49. Hardwicke Knight, *Otago Peninsula: A local history* (Broad Bay, Dunedin: The author, 1979), 96.
50. 'Notebook mainly containing notes on Pukekura, Octavius Harwood', HC, Louise Magdelene Teowaina Wallscott Papers, MS 2431/066.
51. Hardwicke Knight, *Otago Peninsula*, 26.
52. 'Otakou', *Otago Witness*, 1 July 1897, 30.
53. Quoted in David Armstrong, 'Evidence of David A. Armstrong on the Crown's reserve policy concerning Ngai Tahu, 1890–1944', Wai 27, M16, 7.
54. Alexander Mackay, 'Middle Island native claims (Further reports by Mr. Commissioner Mackay relating to)', *AJHR*, 1891, G7a, 4.
55. Ibid.
56. Alexander Mackay, 'Middle Island native claims (report by Mr. Commissioner Mackay relating to)', *AJHR*, 1891, G7, 10.
57. Ibid., 37.

58. Bill Dacker, 'The prejudicial effects of the lack of land with particular reference to the Otakou block', F1, Wai 27, 40.
59. Mackay, 'Middle Island native claims (report by Mr. Commissioner Mackay relating to)', *AJHR*, 1891, G7, 47.
60. Tony Walzl, 'Ngai Tahu fishing, 1840–1908', S7, Wai 27, 98.
61. Quoted in Walzl, 'Ngai Tahu fishing', 102.
62. Cited in Matthew J. Carter, 'People, place and space: The maritime cultural landscape of Otago Harbour' (Master's thesis, University of Otago, 2011), 71.
63. A.B. Macdiarmid et al., 'Historical evidence for the state and exploitation of the marine fish and invertebrate resources in the Hauraki Gulf and along the Otago–Catlins shelf 1769–1950', *New Zealand Aquatic Environment and Biodiversity Report* (draft), 2012, 26, 39.
64. In evidence to the Waitangi Tribunal, Kāi Tahu produced 'marks' books dating to the mid-nineteenth century, documenting how these reefs could be located several kilometres offshore by locating the intersection of lines 'drawn' in the mind's eye from onshore landmarks. See Waitangi Tribunal, *The Ngai Tahu Sea Fisheries Report*, 45.
65. Quoted in Walzl, 'Ngai Tahu fishing', 98.
66. David Graham, *A Treasury of New Zealand Fishes* (Wellington: A.H. & A.W. Reed, 1974), 227–28.
67. *Otago Witness*, 3 August 1893.
68. Mackay, 'Middle Island native claims (report by Mr. Commissioner Mackay relating to)', *AJHR*, 1891, G7, 44.
69. 'Otakou', *Otago Witness*, 16 December 1897, 50.
70. *Otago Witness*, 23 November 1899, 34.
71. District Valuation Rolls 1897.
72. Mackay, 'Middle Island native claims (report by Mr. Commissioner Mackay relating to)', *AJHR*, 1891, G7, 44.
73. Dacker, 'The prejudicial effects of the lack of land', 29.
74. Ross Galbreath, *Working for Wildlife: A history of the New Zealand Wildlife Service* (Wellington: Bridget Williams Books and Department of Internal Affairs, 1993), 354–55.
75. Ibid., 360–61.
76. In the standard histories of Otago, McClintock's *History of Otago* (1948) and Olssen's *A History of Otago* (1984), Māori disappear from the story of the twentieth century.
77. For discussion of the generation of this 'proverb', see Galbreath, *Working for Wildlife*, 87–94, 354–55.
78. In 1896 the Department of Agriculture's Annual Report stated that 1144ha were still in native bush, with 490ha in 'native grasses'. In 1900 the report stated that 1608ha were in tussock, apparently conflating the area in bush with that in tussock.
79. Department of Agriculture Annual Report for 1900.
80. Huggett, 'The historical geography of the Otago Peninsula', 149.
81. Peter Johnson, pers. comm., 17 January 2008.
82. Peter Johnson, *Otago Peninsula Plants: An annotated list of vascular plants growing in wild places* (Portobello: Save the Otago Peninsula (STOP), 2004), 12.
83. G.M. Thomson, 'Notes by the wayside', *Otago Witness*, 26 December 1900, 70; 'Extracts from letters of settlers: Dunedin 20 October 1849', *Otago Journal*, no. 6, 1850, 87.
84. Johnson, *Otago Peninsula Plants*, 30.
85. Ibid.
86. Ibid., 10, 13.
87. G.M. Thomson, 'Botany', in *Dunedin and its Neighbourhood*, ed. Alexander Bathgate (Dunedin: Otago Daily Times and Witness Company, 1904), 34–35.
88. Ibid., 35.
89. Ibid.
90. 'Portobello: From our own correspondent', *Otago Witness*, 22 August 1885, 14; 'Broad Bay', *Otago Witness*, 31 October 1885, 12.
91. Aparata Renata, 'The native birds of the Otago Peninsula past and present', *Otago Witness*, 10 August 1910, 76.
92. Ibid.
93. Florence Enid Graham, 'The native birds of the Otago Peninsula past and present by Aparata Renata', 1910 (2001), HC, Misc-MS-1721. I have transposed Renata's names into those used today.
94. Ibid.
95. 'Thistles and rabbits: To the editor', *Otago Witness*, 5 June 1875, 5.
96. Paul Star, 'From acclimatisation to preservation: Colonists and the natural world in southern New Zealand 1860–1894' (PhD diss., University of Otago, 1997), 314.
97. For discussion, see ibid., 314–29.
98. G.P. Smith et al., 'Diet of feral ferrets (*Mustela furo*) from pastoral habitats in Otago and Southland, New Zealand', *New Zealand Journal of Zoology*, vol. 22, no. 4, 1995, 363–69; H. Moller and N. Alterio, 'Home range and spatial organisation of stoats (*Mustela erminea*), ferrets (*Mustela furo*) and feral house

cats (*Felis catus*) on coastal grasslands, Otago Peninsula, New Zealand: Implications for yellow-eyed penguin (*Megadyptes antipodes*) conservation', *New Zealand Journal of Zoology*, vol. 26, no. 3, 1999, 165–74, esp. 165.
99. 'Broad Bay', *Otago Witness*, 4 June 1886, 14.
100. Aparata Renata, 'Rural rambles: Otago Peninsula', *Otago Witness*, 3 August 1893, 35; 'Peninsula County: Sandymount', *Otago Witness*, 23 February 1884, 9.
101. 'Portobello: From our own correspondent', *Otago Witness* 22 August 1885, 14; 'Peninsula County: Highcliffe', 23 February 1884, 9; 'Peninsula County: Portobello', 23 February 1884, 9.
102. Brian Clearwater recalls that 16,000 rabbits were trapped on Mt Charles one winter when he was young, in the 1940s or early 1950s. Pers. comm., 24 April 2007.
103. Kerry-Jayne Wilson, *Flight of the Huia* (Christchurch: Canterbury University Press, 2004), 191–92.
104. Renata, 'The native birds of the Otago Peninsula past and present'.
105. Chris Jones, 'Sooty shearwater (*Puffinus griseus*) breeding colonies on mainland South Island, New Zealand: Evidence of decline and predictors of persistence', *New Zealand Journal of Zoology*, vol. 27, no. 4, 2000, 327–34.
106. Renata, 'The native birds of the Otago Peninsula, past and present'.
107. Aparata Renata, 'Rural rambles: The Otago Peninsula', *Otago Witness*, 27 July 1893, 35; Renata, 'The native birds of the Otago Peninsula, past and present'.
108. Jones, 'Sooty shearwater (*Puffinus griseus*) breeding colonies on mainland South Island', 327.
109. T.H. Worthy and R.N. Holdaway, *The Lost World of the Moa* (Christchurch: Canterbury University Press, 2002), 441.
110. Ibid., 44, 441. Some idea of their former abundance is gained from the present population of 2.75 million breeding pairs of petrels, fulmars and prions on the 328 hectares of The Snares.
111. Ibid., 26, 516–17.
112. D.J. Hawke et al., 'Soil indicators of pre-European seabird breeding in New Zealand at sites identified by predator deposits', *Australian Journal of Soil Research*, vol. 37, 1999, 104.
113. Ibid; Worthy and Holdaway, *The Lost World of the Moa*, 517.
114. The timing of its arrival is uncertain. Atkinson states that it was not recorded as present in southern New Zealand until 1894. Given the uncertainty, it is probably safest to assume that it had arrived a little earlier. For discussion of the spread of ship rats in New Zealand, see I.A.E. Atkinson, 'Spread of the ship rat (*Rattus r. rattus* L.) in New Zealand', *Journal of the Royal Society of New Zealand*, vol. 3, no. 3, 1973, 457–72.
115. Wilson, *Flight of the Huia*, 137, 82.
116. John Innes, 'Advances in New Zealand mammalogy 1990–2000: European rats', *Journal of the Royal Society of New Zealand*, vol. 31, no. 1, 2001, 117–18.
117. Wilson, *Flight of the Huia*, 149; Renata, 'The native birds of the Otago Peninsula past and present'.
118. 'Peninsula: Otago Peninsula Agricultural and Pastoral Society', *Otago Witness*, 2 September 1882, 12.
119. I am not sure what poisons were used, though W. Sanderson informed the Otago Peninsula Agricultural and Pastoral Society of his success using strychnine in 1881. See 'Otago Peninsula Agricultural and Pastoral Society', *Otago Witness*, 19 March 1881, 12. Phosphorus was used as the poison to treat grain for rabbit control. In 1884 a Sandymount correspondent noted that small birds were doing less damage, 'as most farmers have resorted to dressing the seed'. 'Peninsula County', *Otago Witness*, 23 February 1884, 9.
120. 'Portobello', *Otago Witness*, 10 July 1890, 19; 'Peninsula Road Board', *Otago Witness*, 11 June 1891, 13; 'Portobello Road Board', *Otago Witness*, 30 June 1892, 21.
121. 'Broad Bay', *Otago Witness*, 31 October 1885, 12; 'Peninsula Road Board', *Otago Witness*, 11 June 1891, 13.
122. 'Portobello', *Otago Witness*, 10 July 1890, 19.
123. 'Peninsula', *Otago Witness*, 23 December 1897, 30.
124. 'Harvest prospects', *Otago Witness*, 10 February 1898, 14.
125. James Beattie, *Empire and Environmental Anxiety: Health, science, art and conservation in South Asia and Australasia, 1800–1920* (Cambridge: Palgrave Macmillan, 2011), 193–96.
126. Ibid., 189; 'Board meeting', *Otago Witness*, 2 May 1895, 23; 'Peninsula', *Otago Witness*, 16 August 1900, 32.
127. 'The Otago Institute', *Otago Witness*, 24 June 1914, 7.
128. *Otago Witness*, 20 February 1890, 7.
129. 'Peninsula Road Board', *Otago Witness*, 9 March 1888, 16.

130. For discussion, see Neil Clayton, 'Weeds, people and contested places: Selected themes from the history of New Zealanders and their weeds 1770–1940' (PhD diss., University of Otago, 2007), 264–85.
131. For example, 'Peninsula Road Board', *Otago Witness*, 9 March 1888, 16.
132. G.M. Thomson, *The Naturalisation of Animals and Plants in New Zealand* (Cambridge: Cambridge University Press, 1922), 116. Thomson and Bathgate both stressed that the survival of introduced species was difficult to predict: the history of acclimatisation saw many more failures than successes. Thomson, *The Naturalisation of Animals and Plants in New Zealand*, 114; Alexander Bathgate, 'Acclimatisation in New Zealand', *Otago Witness*, 5 August 1897, 54.
133. G.M. Thomson, 'Notes by the wayside', *Otago Witness*, 21 September 1899, 62.
134. 'Aparata Renata, 'Rural rambles: The Otago Peninsula', *Otago Witness*, 3 August 1893; Thomson, *The Naturalisation of Animals and Plants in New Zealand*, 125.
135. 'Otago Acclimatisation Society', *Otago Witness*, 8 November 1879, 21; *Otago Witness*, 26 May 1892, 31.
136. Thomson, 'Botany', 46.
137. Ibid., 45.
138. Cited in Michael Crozier, 'Mass-movement in eastern Otago: The relationship of slope instability to environmental factors and its importance to slope development on the Otago Peninsula' (PhD diss., University of Otago, 1970), 109.
139. Renata, 'The native birds of the Otago Peninsula, past and present'. See also Crozier, 'Mass-movement in eastern Otago', 109–10 for discussion.
140. Renata, 'The native birds of the Otago Peninsula past and present'.
141. See generally Star, 'From acclimatisation to preservation'; David Young, *Our Islands, Our Selves* (Dunedin: University of Otago Press, 2004), 80; Clayton, 'Weeds, people and contested places'.
142. Young, *Our Islands, Our Selves*; James Beattie, 'W.L. Lindsay, Scottish environmentalism and the "improvement" of nineteenth-century New Zealand', in *Landscape/Community: Perspectives from New Zealand history*, eds Tony Ballantyne and Judith Bennett (Dunedin: University of Otago Press, 2005); James Beattie and John Stenhouse, 'Empire, environment and religion: God and the natural world in nineteenth-century New Zealand', *Environment and History*, vol. 13, 2007, 413–46.
143. Tom Brooking, '"Green Scots and golden Irish": The environmental impact of Scottish and Irish settlers in New Zealand – some preliminary ruminations', *Journal of Irish and Scottish Studies*, vol. 3, no. 1, 2009, esp. 44–45; on G.M. Thomson, see Ross Galbreath, *Scholars and Gentlemen Both: G.M. & Allan Thomson in New Zealand science and education* (Wellington: Royal Society of New Zealand, 2002). On Bathgate, see Jennifer Henderson, 'Far south fancies: Alexander Bathgate and his ideal society' (MA thesis, University of Otago, 2007).
144. This applies to several of the key observers of change on the Peninsula and around Dunedin that I have found most useful – G.M. Thomson, Alexander Bathgate and Robert Gillies, for example. In other areas of New Zealand the timing of bush clearance obviously differed, and so would settlers' responses.
145. John McLay, 'Reminiscences of John McLay', Toitū Otago Early Settlers Museum, n.d., 32–35.
146. Ibid., 25–26.
147. Herbert Guthrie-Smith, *Tutira – The story of a New Zealand sheep station* (Seattle and London: University of Washington Press, 1921), xxiii.
148. Young, *Our Islands, Our Selves*, 88.
149. Ibid., 96.
150. Ibid., 88.
151. Aparata Renata, 'Something about our native birds', *Otago Witness*, 22 March 1894, 50.
152. This lack of protection for areas that people actually inhabit arguably remains a problem today. There is a lack of a middle ground between national parks and wilderness areas, in which people are tolerated only as visitors to a 'pristine' environment; and there are other environments in which, at least until recently, no protections were afforded the environment. This is a theme of Geoff Park's work, and it is something I have discussed also. See Jonathan West, 'Running wild', in *Wild Heart: The possibility of wilderness in Aotearoa New Zealand*, eds Richard Reeves and Mick Abbott (Dunedin: Otago University Press, 2012).
153. Young, *Our Islands, Our Selves*, 72, 104.
154. Worthy and Holdaway, *The Lost World of the Moa*, 564.
155. Alexander Mackay, 'To the under secretary, Native Department', *AJHR*, 1881, G8, 16.
156. Bill Dacker, *Te Mamae Me Te Aroha* (Dunedin: University of Otago Press, 1994), 89.

Conclusion

1. Herbert Guthrie-Smith, *Sorrows and Joys of a New Zealand Naturalist* (Wellington: A.H. & A.W. Reed, 1936), 218.
2. David Young, *Our Islands, Our Selves* (Dunedin: University of Otago Press, 2004); James Beattie, 'W.L. Lindsay, Scottish environmentalism and the "improvement" of nineteenth-century New Zealand', in *Landscape/Community: Perspectives from New Zealand history*, eds Tony Ballantyne and Judith Bennett (Dunedin: University of Otago Press, 2005).
3. The Reverend Thomas Burns to Captain John Cargill, 30 January 1847. See Ernest Northcroft Merrington, *A Great Coloniser: The Rev. Dr. Thomas Burns* (Dunedin: The Otago Daily Times and Witness Newspapers Co., 1929), 266.
4. Clem Tisdell, 'The economic importance of wildlife conservation – 20 years on' (paper presented at the Yellow-Eyed Penguin Trust 20th Anniversary Conference, Dunedin, 2007). Tisdell estimated direct revenue gains of $60 million for Dunedin through albatross and penguin tourism alone. Annually, some 160,000 people visited the Royal Albatross Centre at Taiaroa Head and over 100,000 visited Peninsula penguin colonies.
5. William Cronon, 'Modes of prophecy and production', *Journal of American History*, vol. 76, no. 4 (1990).
6. Thomas Ferens, 'Transcript of journal of Thomas Ferens on the "John Wickcliffe"', 23 March 1848, HC, MS-0440/016.

BIBLIOGRAPHY

PRIMARY SOURCES

UNPUBLISHED

Misc-MS-0933/002, Mrs Ulva L. Belsham papers, 'Notebook of southern placenames, waiata, and vocabulary'. Dunedin: Hocken Collections

Misc-MS-0425, G.C. Thomson papers, 'Photocopy of a deed of land sale between Harwood senior and King Bogany'. Dunedin: Hocken Collections

MS-0439/009, G.C. Thomson papers, 'Correspondence file T to Z'. Dunedin: Hocken Collections

MS-0439/051, G.C. Thomson papers, 'Transcripts of items relating to New Zealand from early Sydney newspapers'. Dunedin: Hocken Collections

MS-0438/074, G.C. Thomson papers, 'Agreement of partnership between Harwood and Charles Schultze'. Dunedin: Hocken Collections

MS-0438/096, G.C. Thomson papers, 'Miscellaneous letters'. Dunedin: Hocken Collections

MS-0438/109, G.C. Thomson papers, 'Agreement by Maori leaders not to disturb European settlers at Otakou'. Dunedin: Hocken Collections

MS-2558/016, Child papers, 'Research notes, mostly of extracts from early Otago newspapers'. Dunedin: Hocken Collections

CAIH D121 83-90, 'Peninsula County valuation rolls 1897–1907'. Archives New Zealand, Dunedin Regional Office

Bannerman, Jane. 'Jane Bannerman, reminiscences of her life to 1855'. Dunedin: Hocken Collections, MS-0536-2

Barnicoat, J.W. 'Diary, 17th June 1843 – 11th October 1844'. Dunedin: Hocken Collections, Misc-MS-1451-3

Beattie, Herries. 'Notebook containing information on Maori history'. Dunedin: Hocken Collections, MS-582/E/10

———. 'Nature and general Maori information gathered between 1920 and 1940 from Maoris, supplementary to previous notes printed, Bk1'. Dunedin: Hocken Collections, MS-582/E/11

———. 'General Maori information. Being items remaining in my notebooks and not published and now collected together. Bk II'. Dunedin: Hocken Collections, MS-582/E/12

———. 'Kahu, John. Maori notebook, 1880'. Dunedin: Hocken Collections, MS-582/F/11

———. 'Newspaper clippings'. Dunedin: Hocken Collections, MS-582/A/1

———. 'Newspaper clippings'. Dunedin: Hocken Collections, MS-582/A/2

———. 'Newspaper clippings'. Dunedin: Hocken Collections, MS-582/A/3

———. 'Newspaper clippings'. Dunedin: Hocken Collections, MS-582/A/4

———. 'Newspaper clippings'. Dunedin: Hocken Collections, MS-582/A/5

———. 'Newspaper clippings'. Dunedin: Hocken Collections, MS-582/A/9

———. 'Newspaper clippings'. Dunedin: Hocken Collections, MS-582/A/13

Burns, Thomas. 'Diary of Reverend Thomas Burns 1848–1851'. Dunedin: Toitū Otago Settlers Museum, C 017

Chapman, F.R. 'History of the canoe Arai-Te-Uru'. Dunedin: Hocken Collections, MS-0416/009

———. 'Notes on South Island place names, mostly in Otago'. Dunedin: Hocken Collections, PC-0290

———. 'Outline of the life of Te Matahaere'. Dunedin: Hocken Collections, MS- 04120, 1894

———. 'Notebook entitled "Gazetteer, Maori names, South Island"'. Dunedin: Hocken Collections, MS-0412

Dunedin Naturalists' Field Club. 'Minute books 1872–1882'. Dunedin: Hocken Collections, MS-0533/001

Ferens, Thomas. 'Transcript of journal of Thomas Ferens on the "John Wickcliffe"'. Dunedin: Hocken Collections, MS-0440/016

Green, F.A. 'Letter from Frederick Allen Green to Thomas Hocken, 23 October 1890'. Dunedin: Hocken Collections, MS-0482

Harwood, Octavius. 'Accounts ledger of store customers and any debts incurred'. Dunedin: Hocken Collections, MS-0604/003

———. 'Copy of Octavius Harwood journals 1838–1842'. G.C. Thomson papers. Dunedin: Hocken Collections, MS-0438/03

———. 'Letter to parents 1838'. Dunedin: Hocken Collections, MS 438/24

Harwood, Octavius Jnr. 'Fragments of history of the Otago Peninsula, Larnach's Castle, etc'. Dunedin: Hocken Collections, MS 0604 I+

———. 'Notes on the settlement of the Otago Peninsula'. Dunedin: Hocken Collections, MS 0604/025

Hocken, T.M. 'Notes on Pilot Driver'. Dunedin: Hocken Collections, MS 0451 034/13

Jollie, R. 'Recollections of early days in New Zealand, ca. 1847'. Dunedin: Hocken Collections, MS 0440/14

Kent, John Rodolphus. 'Journal of the proceedings of His Majesty's colonial cutter *Mermaid* from the 8th Day of May to the 15th Day of August inclusive'. Dunedin: Hocken Collections, MS 913

Kettle, Charles. 'Letter book of Charles Henry Kettle chief surveyor of the settlement of Otago'. Dunedin: Hocken Collections, MS-0083

McLay, John. 'My young life in Otago: Part one of reminiscences'. John McLay Papers, Toitū Otago Settlers Museum, copy 70: 1–43

McLay, John. 'My young life in Otago: Part two of reminiscences'. John McLay Papers, Toitū Otago Settlers Museum, copy 70: 44–51

Mantell, Walter. 'Outline journal, Kaiapoi to Otago 1848–1848'. Dunedin: Hocken Collections, Misc-MS 0552

Marsden, Samuel. 'Additional observations.' Dunedin: Hocken Collections, MS 57/202

Native Land Court. 'South Island Native Land Court minute books 1a'. In *Maori Land Court Minute Books*. Dunedin: Hocken Collections, 1868

New Zealand archaeological site record forms: NZMS 260 I/44-J/44 series

Otago Peninsula Cheese Factory Co. Ltd. 'Minute book of the Otago Peninsula Cheese Factory Co. Ltd 1871–1884'. Dunedin: Hocken Collections, MS-0186-A

'Otago Peninsula: Volume 1, clippings 1957-86'. Dunedin: Dunedin Public Library, 1988

Otago Acclimatisation Society records. 'Otago Acclimatisation Society records'. Dunedin: Hocken Collections, MS-338

Price, Joseph. 'Extracts from the diary of Joseph Price'. Dunedin: Hocken Collections, MS 0440/11

Records of the Otago Provincial Government, multiple-number subject files (AAAC/D500). Archives New Zealand, Dunedin Regional Office

Riddell, Walter. 'Walter Riddell's diary'. Dunedin: McNab New Zealand Collection (Dunedin Public Library), Z920 Rid. 15928

Riemenscheider, Johann. 'On Maori habits of life'. Dunedin: Hocken Collections, MS 0303, 1865

Roberts, W.H.S. 'Papers relating to Maori nomenclature'. Dunedin: Hocken Collections, MS-1206/030

———. 'Unfiled letters from front of correspondence file'. Dunedin: Hocken Collections, MS-0439/012

'Reminscences of Phillip Ryan'. G.C. Thomson papers. Dunedin: Hocken Collections, MS-0439/03 (I-Z)

Shepherd, Thomas. 'Journal of T. Shepherd 1826'. Dunedin: Hocken Collections, MS-0440/06

———. 'Journal of Thomas Shepherd [typescript, alternative version]'. G.C. Thomson papers. Dunedin: Hocken Collections, MS-0439/12

Shortland, Edward. 'Outwards letter book "a" 15 September 1842 to 13 March 1845'. Dunedin: Hocken Collections, MS 86A PC-0027

'Sim family history and account book'. Dunedin: Toitū Otago Settlers Museum, OSM 2000/08/01-03

Somerville, James. 'Reminiscences of James Somerville'. Dunedin: Hocken Collections, AG-846/01

Stuart, Alexander. 'Dairy and recipe book pages'. Dunedin: Hocken Collections, Misc-MS-0607

Taylor, Richard. '"Rongotute" in MS notes on New Zealand and its inhabitants', GNZMSS 297/27, notebook 7:113. Auckland: Auckland Public Library

Teviotdale, David. 'Diary relating to the excavation of camp sites [9/11/1926–18/11/1928]'. Dunedin: Hocken Collections, MS-500/B

———. 'Diary relating to the excavation of camp sites [2/12/1928–1/12/1932]'. Dunedin: Hocken Collections, MS-500/C

———. 'Diary relating to the excavation of camp sites [9/11/1932–2/1/1936]'. Dunedin: Hocken Collections, MS-500/D

———. 'Diary relating to the excavation of camp sites [8/1/1936–13/8/1937]'. Dunedin: Hocken Collections, MS-500/E

———. 'Notes on excavations at Little Papanui by David Teviotdale [c. 1928]'. Dunedin: Hocken Collections, MS-500/M
Thomson, G.C. 'Correspondence file T–Z'. Dunedin: Hocken Collections, MS-0439/09
———. 'Papers on southern Maori history'. Dunedin: Hocken Collections, MS-0439/177
———. 'Paper on the Otakou whaling station in the early 1830s'. Dunedin: Hocken Collections, MS-0439/176
———. 'Papers on sealing and whaling'. Dunedin: Hocken Collections, MS-0439/178
Thomson, Murray. 'Papers relating to "Maori curio" hunting'. Dunedin: Hocken Collections, MS-0326
———. 'Papers relating to Murray Gladstone Thomson'. Dunedin: Hocken Collections, MS-0439/084
Wallscott, Louise Magdelene. 'Notebook entitled, "Notes Otakou, Otago 'Tenths'"'. Dunedin: Hocken Collections, MS-2431/052
———. 'Notebook mainly containing notes on Pukekura, Octavius Harwood'. Dunedin: Hocken Collections, MS-2431/066
———. 'Rough notes on the history of the Peninsula, Taieri and Otakou'. Dunedin: Hocken Collections, MS-2431/138
Watkin, Rev. James. 'Diary of the Reverend James Watkin 1840–1844 (transcript)'. Dunedin: Hocken Collections, MS-0440/004
White, John. 'The ancient history of the Maori: His notes for Ancient history of the Maori by John White'. Wellington: Alexander Turnbull Library, Reel 6, MS copy micro 447
White, Peter. 'Early days of the White Family at Tomahawk'. Dunedin: Hocken Collections, Misc-MS-1109

Published – Official

Appendices to the Journals of the House of Representatives of New Zealand (AJHR)
Census of New Zealand
New Zealand Parliamentary Debates (NZPD)
Otago Provincial Government Gazette, 1855–76
Otago Provincial Government Records, 1857–76
Statistics of New Zealand 1869
Statistics of the Colony of New Zealand 1882; 1883; 1886; 1890; 1896; 1900; 1904
Department of Agriculture. 'Department of Agriculture annual report'. Wellington: Samuel Costall: Government Printer, 1894–1900
Mackay, Alexander. *A Compendium of the Official Documents Relative to Native Affairs in the South Island*. 2 vols. Nelson: Government Printer, 1873

Waitangi Tribunal. *The Ngai Tahu Report*. Wellington: Legislation Direct, 1991
———. *The Ngai Tahu Sea Fisheries Report*. Wellington: Legislation Direct, 1992
———. *The Ngai Tahu Ancillary Claims Report*. Wellington: GP Publications, 1995
———. *The Muriwhenua Land Report*. Wellington: GP Publications, 1997

Newspapers and Periodicals

Evening Star, 1890–1900
New Zealand Gazette, 1855
Otago Daily Times, 1861–1975
Otago Colonist, 1856–57
Otago Journal, 1848–52
Otago News, 1849–51
Otago Provincial Gazette, 1855–76
Otago Witness, 1855–1931
New Zealand Country Journal: A record of information connected with agricultural, pastoral and horticultural pursuits and rural sports in New Zealand. Christchurch: Canterbury Agricultural and Pastoral Association. Vol. 1, 1877 – vol. 24, 1900

SECONDARY SOURCES

Unpublished – Theses and Essays

Allen, David. 'Paper roads and walkways on the Otago Peninsula'. BA diss., University of Otago, 1993
Bainbridge, Annette. 'Birth, death, and marriage in the garden: Canterbury colonial women gardeners, 1850–1914'. MA thesis, University of Waikato, 2015
Bardsley, W.E. 'Origin of the Dunedin beach sands'. BSc diss., University of Otago, 1972
Bathgate, Murray. 'The Maori occupancy of Murihiku, 1000–1900 A.D.: A geographic study of change'. PhD, University of Otago, 1969
Beattie, James. 'Lusting after a lost Arcadia: European environmental perception in the Dunedin area, 1840–1860'. BA diss., University of Otago, 1999
Briden, Shar. 'Archaeofauna from Sandfly Bay (I44/68), Otago Peninsula'. Postgraduate Dip., University of Otago, 2005
Brown, Paula. 'Trends and variability of temperature extremes in southern New Zealand'. PhD, University of Otago, 2006
Campbell, Matthew. 'Preliminary investigation of the archaeology of whaling stations on the southern coast'. MA, University of Otago, 1992

Carter, Matthew J. 'People, place and space: The maritime cultural landscape of Otago Harbour'. Master's thesis, University of Otago, 2011

Clayton, Neil. 'Weeds, people and contested places: Selected themes from the history of New Zealanders and their weeds 1770–1940'. PhD, University of Otago, 2007

Clayton, Neil. 'Settlers, politicians and scientists: Environmental anxiety in a New Zealand colony'. BA diss., University of Otago, 1998

Crozier, Michael. 'Mass-movement in eastern Otago: The relationship of slope instability to environmental factors and its importance to slope development on the Otago Peninsula'. PhD, University of Otago, 1970

Davies, Jane. 'The prehistoric environment of the Dunedin area: The approach of salvage prehistory'. MA, University of Otago, 1980

Galbreath, Ross. 'Colonisation, science, and conservation: The development of colonial attitudes toward the native life of New Zealand with particular reference to the career of the colonial scientist Walter Lawry Buller (1838–1906)'. PhD, University of Waikato, 1989

Grieg, Patricia. 'Sand and plant community on Otago Peninsula: A study of three coastal areas and their vegetation'. MSc, University of Otago, 1965

Hanham, Susan. '"Where land meets water": Rights to the foreshore of Otaakau Maori reserve'. MSc, University of Otago, 1996

Hargreaves, Ray. 'An historical geography of New Zealand farming before the introduction of refrigeration'. PhD, University of Otago, 1966

Hinton, Wendy. 'Pre-settlement Otago from Moeraki to Molyneux'. BA diss., University of Otago, 1976

Hogg, Karina. '"Newlands" a new home: The development of a community at Portobello 1848–1882'. BA diss., University of Otago, 1991

Huggett, J.P. 'The historical geography of the Otago Peninsula'. MA, Victoria University, 1966

Kooyman, Brian. 'Moa and moa hunting: An archaeological analysis of big game hunting in New Zealand'. PhD, University of Otago, 1985

Lynch, Anthony. 'The garden of Otago: A history of small-scale farming in the Clutha area 1848–70'. MA, University of Otago, 1989

Martin, Ulrike. 'Eruptions and deposition of volcaniclastic rocks in the Dunedin volcanic complex, Otago Peninsula, New Zealand'. PhD, University of Otago, 2000

McGovern-Wilson, R. 'Small-bird exploitation: An archaeozoological approach to the study of fowling in southern New Zealand'. MA, University of Otago, 1986

Montgomerie, Deborah. 'Coming to terms: Ngai Tahu, Robeson County Indians and the Garden River band of Ojibwa, 1840–1940. Three studies of colonialism in action'. PhD, Duke University, 1993

Ohlemuller, Ralf. 'Indigenous forest fragments: Modelling present-day species richness and potential natural vegetation'. PhD, University of Otago, 2003

Olsson, Stefan. 'The geology of the Portobello Peninsula: Proposal of an oversaturated lineage within the Dunedin volcano'. BSc diss., University of Otago, 2001

Parker, Leanna. 'Re-conceptualizing the traditional economy: Indigenous people's participation in the nineteenth century fur trade in Canada and whaling industry in New Zealand'. PhD, University of Alberta, 2011

Petchey, Peter. 'Otago water wheels: The industrial archaeology of water wheels in Otago'. MA, University of Otago, 1996

Read, Marion. 'The "construction" of landscape: A case study of the Otago Peninsula, Aotearoa/New Zealand'. PhD, Lincoln University, 2005

Reeves, Jane. 'Maori prisoners in Dunedin 1869–1872 and 1879–1881'. BA diss., University of Otago, 1989

Russell, Khyla. 'Landscape perceptions of Kai Tahu'. PhD, University of Otago, 2000

Samson, J.O. 'Cultures of collecting: Maori curio collecting in Murihiku, 1865–1975'. PhD, University of Otago, 2003

Smith, Ian. 'Sea mammal hunting and prehistoric subsistence in New Zealand'. PhD, University of Otago, 1985

Star, Paul. 'From acclimatisation to preservation: Colonists and the natural world in southern New Zealand 1860–1894'. PhD, University of Otago, 1997

Stevens, Michael. 'The names are in the land, our history is in the land'. BA diss., University of Otago, 1976

Tau, Te Maire. 'Kurakura Ngai Tahu'. MA, University of Canterbury, 1995

Wanhalla, Angela. 'Transgressing boundaries: A history of the mixed descent families of Maitapapa, Taieri, 1830–1940'. PhD, University of Otago, 2004

Wigglesworth, Roger. 'The New Zealand timber and flax trade 1769–1840'. PhD, Massey University, 1981

Williams, Jim. '"E Paakahi Hakinga a Kai": An examination of pre-contact resource management practice in southern Te Wai Pounamu'. PhD, University of Otago, 2004

Wilson, Geoff. 'The urge to clear the "bush": A study of native forest clearance in the Catlins district of New Zealand, 1861–1990'. PhD, University of Otago, 1991

Wood, Vaughan. 'Soil fertility management in nineteenth century New Zealand agriculture'. PhD, University of Otago, 2003

Unpublished – Other

Anderson, Atholl. 'Kin and border: Traditional land boundaries in Eastern Polynesia and New Zealand with particular reference to the northern boundary of Ngai Tahu'. Wai 785, Document Q2

———. 'Atholl Anderson's submission on Otakou'. Wai 27, Document C8(a)

———. 'Mahinga kai, the submission of Atholl Anderson'. Wai 27, Document H1

———. 'Figures and tables presented with the submission of Atholl Anderson on mahinga kai'. Wai 27, Document H3

Beattie, Herries. 'Southern Maoris'. Dunedin: Hocken Collections, n.d.

Croot, Charles. 'James Seaton, M.H.R. An historical biography'. Dunedin: Hocken Collections, 1973

Dacker, Bill. 'He Raraka a Ka Awa'. Dunedin: Hocken Collections, 2000.

———. 'The effects of loss of land at Otakou'. Wai 27, Document F11

Durie, Eddie. 'Custom law'. Waitangi Tribunal Library, unpub., 1994

Elliot, Daphne. 'Carey, David, 1814–1896, and Hannah, 1817–1888'. In Otago Daily Times Historical Biography Competition. Dunedin: Hocken Collections, 1973

Ellison, Edward. 'Mahinga kai: Evidence of Edward Ellison (Otakou)'. Wai 27, Document H12

Entwisle, Peter. 'Saving the romantic city – Charles Kettle's plan for old Dunedin'. Dunedin: Hocken Collections, Misc-MS- 1930

Gill, Samuel. 'Farming at Portobello'. In *Early Otago: Pioneer reminiscences recorded by the Port Chalmers Old Identities Association*, ed. Ian Church, 10–12. Unpub., 1973

Habib, George. 'Ngaitahu claim to mahinga kai'. Dunedin: Hocken Collections, AG-653/485, 1989

———. 'Report on Ngaitahu fisheries evidence'. Dunedin: Hocken Collections, AG-653/484, 1989

Hamel, Jill. 'Contact at Parihaumia: Report to the New Zealand Historic Places Trust'. Dunedin: Hocken Collections, 2005

Hargreaves, R. 'The mapping of Otago'. Dunedin: Hocken Collections, 1947

Higgins, David, and William Goomes. 'Mahinga kai, evidence on sea fishery including the submissions of David Thomas Higgins and William Albert Grennell Goomes'. Dunedin: Hocken Collections, AG-653/175

Holdaway, Richard. 'Otago Peninsula biodiversity: The past – contrast for the future'. Paper presented at the Yellow-Eyed Penguin Trust 20th Anniversary Conference, Dunedin, 2007

———. 'Submission to the Waitangi Tribunal on Maori conservation of natural resources in the pre-European and proto-historic period of New Zealand history'. Wai 27, Document S17

Johnson, Peter. 'Forest and scrub vegetation on Otago Peninsula'. Unpublished report for Botany Division, Department of Scientific and Industrial Research, Dunedin, 1982

———. 'Sandymount, Otago Peninsula, botanical report'. Unpublished report for Botany Division, Department of Scientific and Industrial Research, Dunedin, 1990

———. 'Taiaroa Bush, Otago Peninsula – Botanical report'. Unpublished report for Botany Division, Department of Scientific and Industrial Research, Dunedin, 1979

———. 'The Pyramids, Otago Peninsula: Botanical report'. Unpublished report for Botany Division, Department of Scientific and Industrial Research, Dunedin, 1986

———. 'Wickliffe Bay, Otago Peninsula – Botanical report'. Unpublished report for Botany Division, Department of Scientific and Industrial Research, Dunedin, 1980

Knight, Hardwicke. 'Sam Fossicker remembers'. Dunedin: Hocken Collections, 1968

MacDiarmid, A.B.P. Cleaver and B. Stirling, 'Historical evidence for the state and exploitation of the marine fish and invertebrate resources in the Hauraki Gulf and along the Otago–Catlins shelf 1769–1850'. *New Zealand Aquatic and Environment and Biodiversity Report* (Draft), September 2012

Mitchell, Eleanor. 'James Seaton's Story 1822–1882'. Dunedin: Hocken Collections, n.d.

Parsonson, Ann. 'In respect of the Otakou tenths: Evidence of Ann Rosemary Parsonson'. Wai 27, Document C1

———. 'Supporting papers to the evidence of Dr Ann Parsonson'. Wai 27, Document C2

Phillipson, Grant. 'Bay of Islands Maori and the Crown 1793–1853'. Wai 1040, Document A1

Potiki, Megan. 'Killing demons and cultural collisions'. Unpublished presentation at the University of Otago, 2014

Renata, Aparata [Alfred Reynolds], 'Native birds of the Otago Peninsula past and present'. Dunedin: Hocken Collections, Misc MS 1721

Rutherford, Alma. 'Archibald Anderson 1817–1910'. In Otago Daily Times Historical Biography Competition. Dunedin: Hocken Collections, MS-0891

Star, Paul. 'Settlement and sentiment in New Zealand, circa 1900'. Paper presented at the Environmental History Symposium. Christchurch, 2000

———. 'Settling into New Zealand landscapes'. Dunedin: Otago University History Department, 1997

Walzl, Tony. 'Ngai Tahu fishing 1840–1908'. Wai 27, Document S7.

Ward, Alan. 'A report on the historical evidence: The Ngai Tahu claim, Wai 27'. Wai 27, Document T1

Published

Aitken, H.J.A. *St Kilda: The first hundred years*. Dunedin: Borough of St Kilda, 1975

Allen, Melinda S. and Lisa A. Nagoaka. '"In the footsteps of Von Haast ... the discoveries something grand": The emergence of zooarchaeology in New Zealand'. In *Change through Time: 50 years of archaeology in New Zealand*, ed. Louise Furey, 193–214. Auckland: New Zealand Archaeological Association, 2004

Anderson, Atholl, Judith Binney and Aroha Harris, *Tangata Whenua: An illustrated history*. Wellington: Bridget Williams Books, 2014

Anderson, Atholl. 'Epilogue: Changing archaeological perspectives upon historical ecology in the Pacific Islands'. *Pacific Science*, vol. 63, no. 3 (2009): 752–54

———. 'Origins, settlement and society of pre-European south Polynesia'. In *The New Oxford History of New Zealand*, ed. Giselle Byrnes, 21–46. Melbourne: Oxford University Press, 2009

———. 'Retrievable time: Prehistoric colonisation of south Polynesia from the outside in and the inside out'. In *Disputed Histories*, eds Tony Ballantyne and Brian Moloughney, 25–42. Dunedin: Otago University Press, 2006

———. 'Faunal collapse, landscape change and settlement history in remote Oceania'. *World Archaeology*, vol. 33, no. 3 (2002): 375–90

———. 'A fragile plenty: Pre-European Maori and the New Zealand environment'. In *Environmental Histories of New Zealand*, eds Eric Pawson and Tom Brooking, 19–34. Melbourne: Oxford University Press, 2002

———. 'The origins of muttonbirding in New Zealand'. *New Zealand Journal of Archaeology*, vol. 22 (2001): 5–14

———. 'Defining the period of moa extinction'. *Archaeology in New Zealand*, vol. 4 (2000): 195–200

———. 'Differential reliability of 14c AMS ages of *Rattus exulans* bone gelatin in South Pacific prehistory'. *Journal of the Royal Society of New Zealand*, vol. 30 (2000): 243–61

———. *The Welcome of Strangers*. Dunedin: University of Otago Press, 1998

———. 'Uniformity and regional variation in marine fish catches from prehistoric New Zealand'. *Asian Perspectives*, vol. 36, no. 1 (1997): 1–26

———. '"Was *Rattus exulans* in New Zealand 2000 years ago?" AMS radiocarbon ages from the Shag River Mouth'. *Archaeology in Oceania*, vol. 31 (1996): 174–84

———. 'Wakawaka and mahinga kai: Models of traditional land management in southern New Zealand'. In *Oceanic Culture History: Essays in honour of Roger Green*, eds J.M. Davidson, G. Irwin, B.F. Leach, A. Pawley and D. Brown, 631–40. Wellington: New Zealand Journal of Archaeology Special Publication, 1996

———. *Race Against Time: The early Maori-Pakeha families and the development of the mixed-race population in southern New Zealand*. Dunedin: Hocken Library, 1991

———. 'The chronology of colonisation in New Zealand'. *Antiquity*, vol. 65 (1991): 767–95

———. 'Mechanics of overkill in the extinction of New Zealand moas'. *Journal of Archaeological Science*, vol. 16 (1989): 137–51

———. 'On evidence for the survival of moa in European Fiordland'. *New Zealand Journal of Ecology*, vol. 12, supplement (1989): 39–44

———. *Prodigious Birds: Moas and moa-hunting in prehistoric New Zealand*. Cambridge: Cambridge University Press, 1989

———. *Te Puoho's Last Raid*. Dunedin, Otago Heritage Books, 1986

———. *When All the Moa-ovens Grew Cold*. Dunedin: Otago Heritage Books, 1983

———. 'Faunal depletion and subsistence change in the early prehistory of southern New Zealand'. *Archaeology in Oceania*, vol. 18, no. 1 (1983): 1–10

———. 'A review of economic patterns during the Archaic phase in southern New Zealand'. *New Zealand Journal of Archaeology*, vol. 4 (1982): 45–75

———. 'A model of prehistoric collecting on the rocky shore'. *Journal of Archaeological Science*, vol. 8 (1981): 109–20

Anderson, Atholl, and I.W.G. Smith. 'The transient village in southern New Zealand'. *World Archaeology*, vol. 27 (1996): 359–71

Anderson, Atholl, Brian Allingham and Ian Smith, eds. *Shag River Mouth: The archaeology of an early southern Maori village*. Canberra: ANH Publications, 1996

Anderson, Atholl, R.N. Holdaway and C. Jacomb. 'Less is moa'. *Science*, vol. 289, no. 5484 (2000): 1472–76

Anderson, Atholl, and R. McGovern-Wilson. 'The pattern of prehistoric Polynesian colonisation in New Zealand'. *Journal of the Royal Society of New Zealand*, vol. 20 (1990): 41–63

Anderson, Atholl, and I.W.G. Smith. 'Introduction and history of investigations'. In *Shag River Mouth: The archaeology of an early southern Maori village*, eds Atholl Anderson, Brian Allingham and I.W.G. Smith, 1–13. Canberra: ANH Publications, 1996

———. 'Shag River Mouth as an early southern village'. In *Shag River Mouth: The archaeology of an early southern Maori village*, eds Atholl Anderson, Brian Allingham and I.W.G. Smith, 276–91. Canberra: ANH Publications, 1996

Anderson, Sarah. 'The relative importance of birds and insects as pollinators of the New Zealand flora'. *New Zealand Journal of Ecology*, vol. 27, no. 2 (2003): 83–94

Andrews, J.R.H. 'The parisitology of the Maori in pre-European times'. *New Zealand Medical Journal*, vol. 84 (1976): 62–65

———. 'The parasites of man in New Zealand: A review'. *New Zealand Journal of Zoology*, vol. 3 (1976): 59–67

Anonymous. 'Is the thistle a nuisance, or is it beneficial to the farmer?' *New Zealand Country Journal*, vol. 4, no. 1 (1894): 94

Arnold, Rollo. *Settler Kaponga 1881–1914: A fragment of the western world*. Wellington: Victoria University Press, 1997

———. *New Zealand's Burning: The settler's world in the mid 1880s*. Wellington: Victoria University Press, 1994

———. 'Community in rural Victorian New Zealand'. *New Zealand Journal of History*, vol. 24, no. 1 (1990): 3–21

Asdal, Kristin. 'The problematic nature of nature: The post-constructivist challenge to environmental history'. *History and Theory*, vol. 42, Dec. (2003): 60–74

Asher, George, and David Naulls. *Maori Land*. Wellington: New Zealand Planning Council, 1987

Atkinson, I.A.E. 'Spread of the ship rat (*Rattus r. rattus* L.) in New Zealand'. *Journal of the Royal Society of New Zealand*, vol. 3, no. 3 (1973): 457–72

Atkinson, I., and D. Towns. 'Advances in New Zealand mammology 1990–2000: Pacific rat'. *Journal of the Royal Society of New Zealand*, vol. 31, no. 1 (2001): 99–109

Ayson, William. *Pioneering in Otago: The recollections of William Ayson*. Dunedin: Reeds, n.d.

Ballantyne, Brian, and Sue Hanham. 'Use of the New Zealand foreshore: Oral evidence of Maori rights in Otago'. *Asia Pacific Viewpoint*, vol. 37, no. 3 (1996): 255–68

Ballantyne, Tony. 'On place, space, and mobility'. In *Webs of Empire: Locating New Zealand's colonial past*, 264–82. Wellington: Bridget Williams Books, 2012

———. 'Culture and colonization: Revisiting the place of writing in colonial New Zealand'. *Journal of New Zealand Studies*, vol. 9 (2010): 1–22.

Ballantyne, Tony, and Brian Moloughney, eds. *Disputed Histories*. Dunedin: Otago University Press, 2006

Ballara, Angela. *Taua*. Auckland: Penguin Books, 2003

———. *Iwi: The dynamics of Māori tribal organisation from c. 1769 to c. 1945*. Wellington: Victoria University Press, 1998

Banner, Stuart. 'Two properties, one land: Law and space in nineteenth-century New Zealand'. *Law and Social Inquiry*, vol. 24, no. 4 (1999): 807–52

———. 'Transitions between property regimes'. *The Journal of Legal Studies*, vol. 31, no. 2 (part 2) (2002): 359–71

Barber, Ian. 'Sea, land and fish: Spatial relationships and the archaeology of South Island Maori fishing'. *World Archaeology*, vol. 35, no. 3 (2003): 434–48

———. 'Loss, change, and monumental landscaping: Towards a new interpretation of the "classic" Maori emergence'. *Current Anthropology*, vol. 37, no. 5 (1996): 868–80

Barnard, Alan, and James Woodburn. 'Introduction'. In *Hunters and Gatherers: Property, power and ideology*, eds Tim Ingold, David Riches and James Woodburn, 4–32. New York: Berg Publishers, 1988

Barr, James. *The Old Identities*. Dunedin: Mills, Dick and Co., 1879

Barton, Phillip Lionel. 'Maori cartography and the European encounter'. In *Cartography in the Traditional African, American, Arctic, Australian and Pacific Societies*, eds David Woodward and G. Malcolm Lewis, 494–532. Chicago: University of Chicago Press, 1998

Bathgate, A. 'Some changes in the fauna and flora of Otago in the last sixty years'. *N.Z. Journal of Science and Technology*, vol. 4, no. 6 (1922): 273–83

———. 'Notes on acclimatisation in New Zealand'. *Transactions and Proceedings of the New Zealand Institute*, vol. 30 (1897): 266–79

———. *Colonial Experiences*. Glasgow: James Maclehose, 1874

———. 'On the Lepidoptera of Otago'. *Transactions and Proceedings of the New Zealand Institute*, vol. 3 (1870): 137–41

Bathgate, Murray. 'Pre-European cultural interference on the forests of the southern part of the South Island'. *Science Record*, vol. 17 (1967): 34–6

Beaglehole, J.C. *The Voyage of the* Resolution *and* Adventure *1772–1775*. Cambridge: Cambridge University Press, 1961

Beattie, Herries. *Traditions and Legends of the South Island Maori*. Christchurch: Cadsonbury Publications, 2004

———. *Traditional Lifeways of the Southern Maori*. Ed. Atholl Anderson. Dunedin: University of Otago Press, 1994

———. *Our Southernmost Maoris*. Christchurch: Cadsonbury Publications, 1954. Repr., 1994

———. *Moriori: The Moriorios of the South Island*. Christchurch: Cadsonbury Publications, 1993

———. *Tikao Talks*. Auckland: Penguin Books, 1990

———. *Maori Place Names of Otago*. Dunedin: Otago Daily Times and Witness Newspapers Co., 1944

———. 'Nature-Lore of the southern Maori'. *Transactions and Proceedings of the New Zealand Institute*, vol. 52 (1920): 53–77

———. 'Traditions and legends collected from the natives of Murihiku (Southland, New Zealand) Part VIII'. *Journal of the Polynesian Society*, vol. 27, no. 107 (1918): 137–61

———. 'Traditions and legends collected from the natives of Murihiku (Southland, New Zealand) Part V'. *Journal of the Polynesian Society*, vol. 25, no. 99 (1916): 89–98

———. 'Traditions and legends collected from the natives of Murihiku (Southland, New Zealand) Part IV'. *Journal of the Polynesian Society*, vol. 25, no. 98 (1916): 53–65

———. 'Traditions and legends collected from the natives of Murihiku (Southland, New Zealand) Part II'. *Journal of the Polynesian Society*, vol. 24, no. 96 (1915): 140–51

———. 'Traditions and legends collected from the natives of Murihiku (Southland, New Zealand) Part I'. *Journal of the Polynesian Society*, vol. 24, no. 95 (1915): 98–112

Beattie, James. *Empire and Environmental Anxiety: Health, science, art and conservation in South Asia and Australasia, 1800–1920*. Cambridge: Palgrave Macmillan, 2011

———. 'Environmental anxiety in New Zealand, 1840–1941: Climate change, soil erosion, sand drift, flooding and forest conservation'. *Environment and History*, vol. 9, no. 4 (2003): 379–92

———. 'W.L. Lindsay, Scottish environmentalism and the 'improvement' of nineteenth-century New Zealand'. In *Landscape/Community: Perspectives from New Zealand history*, eds Tony Ballantyne and Judith Bennett, 43–56. Dunedin: University of Otago Press, 2005

Beattie, James, and John Stenhouse. 'Empire, environment and religion: God and the natural world in nineteenth-century New Zealand'. *Environment and History*, vol. 13 (2007): 413–46

Beavan Athfield, Nancy, Bruce McFadgen and Roger Sparks. 'Reliability of bone gelatin AMS dating: *Rattus exulans* and marine shell radiocarbon dates from Pauatahanui midden sites in Wellington, New Zealand'. *Radiocarbon*, vol. 41, no. 2 (1999): 119–26

Begg, A. Charles, and Neil. C. Begg. *The World of John Boultbee*. Christchurch: Whitcoulls Publishers, 1979

Belich, James. *Making Peoples*. Auckland: Penguin Books, 1996

———. *Replenishing the Earth: The settler revolution and the rise of the Anglo-world, 1783–1939*. Oxford: Oxford University Press, 2009

Benton, Richard, Alex Frame and Paul Meredith, eds. *Te Mātāpuenga: A compendium of references to the concepts and institutions of Māori customary law*. Wellington: Victoria University Press, 2013

Best, Elsdon. *Maori Agriculture*. Wellington: Te Papa Press, 1976

———. 'Forest lore of the Maori'. *Dominion Museum Bulletin*, no. 14 (1942)

———. 'Maori medical lore: Notes on sickness and disease among the Maori people of New Zealand, and their treatment of the sick; together with some account of various beliefs, superstitions and rites pertaining to sickness, and the treatment thereof, as collected from the Tuhoe tribe'. *Journal of the Polynesian Society*, vol. 13, no. 4 (1904): 213–37

———. 'Notes on the custom of rahui: Its application and manipulation, as also its supposed powers, its rites, invocations and superstitions'. *Journal of the Polynesian Society*, vol. 13, no. 2 (1904): 83–88

Binney, Judith. 'Maori oral narratives, Pakeha written texts'. *New Zealand Journal of History*, vol. 38, no. 2 (2004): 203–14

———. 'Christianity and the Maoris to 1840: A comment'. *New Zealand Journal of History*, vol. 3, no. 2 (1969): 143–62

Boast, Richard, '"An expensive mistake": Law, courts, and confiscation on the New Zealand colonial frontier'. In *Raupatu: The confiscation of Maori land*, eds Richard Boast and Richard Hill.

Wellington: Victoria University Press, 2009

———. *Buying the Land, Selling the Land: Governments and Maori land in the North Island 1865–1921*. Wellington: Victoria University Press, 2008

———. 'Maori fisheries 1986–1998: A reflection'. *Victoria University of Wellington Law Review*, vol. 30, no. 1 (1999): 111–34.

Boast, R. 'The law and Maori'. In *A New Zealand Legal History*, eds P. Spiller, J. Finn and R. Boast. Wellington: Brookers, 1995

Boast, Richard, Andrew Eruti, Doug McPhail and Norman F. Smith. *Maori Land Law*. Wellington: Butterworths, 1999

Boessenkool, Sanne, et al. 'Relict or colonizer? Extinction and range expansion of penguins in southern New Zealand'. *Proceedings of the Royal Society*, vol. 276, no. 1658 (2009): 815–21

Bonyhady, Tim. *The Colonial Earth*. Melbourne: Melbourne University Press, 2000

Bourner, T.C., T.R. Glare, M. O'Callaghan and T.A. Jackson. 'Towards greener pastures: Pathogens and pasture pests'. *New Zealand Journal of Ecology*, vol. 20, no. 1 (1996): 101–07

Brasch, Charles, *Indirections: A memoir 1909–1947*, ed. James Bertram, Wellington: Oxford University Press, 1980

Brey, Sharron, Graeme Thomas and Victor MacGill. *Under the Eye of the Saddle Hill Taniwha*. Dunedin: Nga Tutukitanga o Taieri, n.d.

Broadbent, James. 'Fashioning a colonial culture'. In *India, China, Australia: Trade and society 1788–1850*, ed. James Broadbent, 15–30. Sydney: Historic Houses Trust of New South Wales, 2003

Brook, F.J. 'Prehistoric predation of the landsnail *Placostylus ambagiosus* Suter (Stylommatophora Bulimulidae), and evidence for the timing of the establishment of rats in northernmost New Zealand'. *Journal of the Royal Society of New Zealand*, vol. 30 (2000): 227–41

Brooking, Tom. 'The great escape: Wakefield and the Scottish settlement of Otago'. In *Edward Gibbon Wakefield and the Colonial Dream: A reconsideration* [Friends of the Turnbull Library], 123–32. Wellington: GP Publications, 1997

———. *Lands for the People? The Highland Clearances and the colonisation of New Zealand: A biography of John McKenzie*. Dunedin: University of Otago Press, 1996

———. 'Use it or lose it: Unravelling the land debate in nineteenth-century New Zealand'. *New Zealand Journal of History*, vol. 30, no. 2 (1996): 141–62

———. '"Tam McCanny and Kitty Clydeside" – the Scots in New Zealand'. In *The Scots Abroad: Labour, capital, enterprise, 1750–1914*, ed. R.A. Cage, 156–90. London: Croom Helm, 1985

———. *And Captain of their Souls: An interpretative essay on the life and times of Captain William Cargill*. Dunedin: Otago Heritage Books, 1984

Brooking, Tom, and Eric Pawson. 'Writing New Zealand's environmental histories'. *History Now*, vol. 5, no. 2 (1999): 28–32

Brunner, Thomas, 'Journal of an expedition to explore the interior of the middle island of New Zealand', *The Journal of the Royal Geographic Society of London*, vol. 20 (1850): 344–78

Buchanan, John 'The botany of Otago'. *Transactions and Proceedings of the New Zealand Institute*, vol. 1 (1868): 181–212

Bunce, M. et al., 'The evolutionary history of the extinct ratite moa and New Zealand Neogene paleogeography'. *Proceedings of the National Academy of Sciences of the United States of America*, vol. 106, no. 49 (2009): 20646–51

Burke, Peter. *Eyewitnessing: The uses of images as historical evidence*. Ithaca: Cornell University Press, 2001

Burns, Thomas. *Early Otago and the Genesis of Dunedin: The letters of Reverend T. Burns*. Dunedin: R.J. Stark & Co., 1916

Byrnes, Giselle. '"A dead sheet covered with meaningless words?" Place names and the cultural colonisation of Tauranga'. *The New Zealand Journal of History*, vol. 36, no. 1 (2002): 18–35

———. *Boundary Markers: Land surveying and the colonisation of New Zealand*. Wellington: Bridget Williams Books, 2001

———. '"The imperfect authority of the eye": Shortland's southern journey and the calligraphy of colonisation'. *History and Anthropology*, vol. 8, nos. 1–4 (1994): 207–35

Campbell, D.J., and Ian A.E. Atkinson. 'Effects of kiore (*Rattus exulans* Peale) on recruitment of indigenous coastal trees on northern offshore islands of New Zealand'. *Journal of the Royal Society of New Zealand*, vol. 29, no. 4 (1999): 265–90

Campbell, Hamish. *The Zealandia Drowning Debate: Did New Zealand sink beneath the waves?* Wellington: Bridget Williams E-book, 2013

Cant, Garth, and Russell Kirkpatrick, eds. *Rural Canterbury: Celebrating its history*. Wellington: Daphne Brasell Associates and Lincoln University Press, 2001

Carmichael, Ann. 'Measles: The red menace'. In *Plague, Pox and Pestilence*, ed. Kenneth Kiple, 80–85. London: Weidenfeld and Nicholson, 1997

Carroll, Emma L., et al. 'Two intense decades of 19th-century whaling precipitated rapid decline of right whales around New Zealand and East Australia'. *PLoS ONE*, vol. 9. no. 4 (2014): e93789

Carson, Mike. 'Ti ovens in Polynesia: Ethnological and archaeological perspectives'. *Journal of the Polynesian Society*, vol. 111, no. 4 (2002): 339–70

Carter, Paul. *The Road to Botany Bay*. Chicago: University of Chicago Press, 1989

Castro, Isabel, and Alastair W. Robertson. 'Honeyeaters and the New Zealand forest flora: The utilisation and profitability of small flowers'. *New Zealand Journal of Ecology*, vol. 21, no. 2 (1997): 169–79

Chapman, Frederick. 'Notes on the depletion of the fur-seal in the southern seas'. *Canadian Record of Science*, vol. 99, no. 27 (1893): 446–59

Church, Ian. 'The loss of the *Adventure*'s cutter and its aftermath'. *Archaeology in New Zealand*, vol. 54, no. 2 (2011): 101–13

———. ed. *Gaining a Foothold: Historical records of Otago's eastern coast 1770–1839*. Dunedin: Friends of the Hocken Collections, 2008

———. *Blueskin Days: A history of Waitati, Evansdale, Warrington and surrounding districts*. Waitati: Blueskin History Steering Committee, 2007

———. 'French whalers at Otago 1838 to 1853'. In *Pacific Journeys: Essays in honour of John Dunmore*, eds Glynnis M. Cropp, Noele R. Watts, Roger D.J. Collins and K.R. Howe, 152–64. Wellington: Victoria University Press, 2005

———. *Otago's Infant Years*. Dunedin: Otago Heritage Books, 2001

———. ed. *Early Otago: Pioneer reminiscences recorded by the Port Chalmers Old Identities Association*. Port Chalmers: Port Chalmers Old Identities Association, 1973

Clark, Andrew. *The Invasion of New Zealand by People, Plants and Animals: The South Island*. New Brunswick: Rutgers University Press, 1949

Clarke, Alan. *The Great Sacred Forest of Tane, Te Wao Tapu Nui a Tane: A natural pre-history of Aotearoa New Zealand*. Auckland: Reed Books, 2007

Clarke, George. *Notes on Early Life in New Zealand*. Hobart: The author, 1903

Cliff, Andrew, Peter Haggett and Matthew Smallman-Raynor. *Measles: An historical geography of a major human viral disease*. Oxford and Cambridge: Blackwell Publishers, 1993

Clout, M.N., and J.R. Hay. 'The importance of birds as browsers, pollinators and seed dispersers in New Zealand forests'. *New Zealand Journal of Ecology*, vol. 12 (1989): 27–33

Cockayne, Leonard. 'Observations concerning evolution, derived from ecological studies in New Zealand'. *Transactions and Proceedings of the New Zealand Institute*, vol. 44 (1911): 1–50

Collins, Roger, and Peter Entwisle. *Pavilioned in Splendour: George O'Brien's vision of colonial New Zealand*. Dunedin: Dunedin Public Art Gallery, 1986

Cook, James. *The Journals*. Ed. Philip Edwards. London: Penguin Books, 2003

Cowan, James. *Legends of the Maori*, 2 vols. Wellington: Fine Arts, 1930

———. 'The life and wars of Te Wera'. *Otago Daily Times*, 9 March 1906, 6

Cronon, William. 'Kennecott journey: The paths out of town'. in *Uncommon Ground: Rethinking America's western past*, eds William Cronon et al., 28–51. New York and London: Norton, 1993

———. 'A place for stories: Nature, history, and narrative'. *Journal of American History*, vol. 78, no. 4 (1992): 1347–76

———. 'Modes of prophecy and production'. *Journal of American History*, vol. 76, no. 4 (1990): 1122–31

———. *Changes in the Land: Indians, colonists, and the ecology of New England*. New York: Hill and Wang, 1983

Crosby, Alfred. *Ecological Imperialism: The biological expansion of Europe, 900–1900*. 2nd edn. Cambridge: Cambridge University Press, 2004

———. 'Biotic change in nineteenth-century New Zealand'. In *Environmental History in the Pacific World*, ed. J.R. McNeill, 171–84. Aldershot, Burlington, Singapore, Sydney: Ashgate, 2001

———. 'The past and present of environmental history'. *American Historical Review*, vol. 100, no. 1 (1995): 1177–89

———. *Germs, Seeds & Animals: Studies in ecological history*. Armonk and London: M.E. Sharp, 1994

———. *Ecological Imperialism: The biological expansion of Europe, 900–1900*. Cambridge: Cambridge University Press, 1986

Crozier, Michael. 'Landslides and the Dunedin district'. *Science Record*, vol. 17 (1967): 9–11

Cumberland, Kenneth. 'A future for agriculture'. In *The Land Our Future: Essays on land use and conservation in New Zealand in honour of Kenneth Cumberland*, ed. A. Grant Anderson, 291–307. Auckland: NZ Geographical Society/ Longman Paul, 1980

———. 'A century's change: Natural to cultural vegetation in New Zealand'. *The Geographical Review*, vol. 31, no. 4 (1941): 529–54

———. *Soil Erosion in New Zealand: A geographical reconnaissance*. Wellington: Soil Conservation and Rivers Control Council, 1944

Cumpstone, J.H.L. *Health and Disease in Australia: A history*. Canberra: AGPS Press, 1989

Curson, P.H. *Times of Crisis: Epidemics in Sydney 1788–1900*. Sydney: Sydney University Press, 1985

Dacker, Bill. *Te Mamae Me Te Aroha – The Pain and the Love: A history of Kai Tahu whanui in Otago, 1844–1994*. Dunedin: University of Otago Press, 1994

Darby, John, R. Ewan Fordyce, Alan Mark, Keith Probert and Colin Townsend, eds. *The Natural History of Southern New Zealand*. Dunedin: University of Otago Press, 2003

Davidson, Janet. *The Prehistory of New Zealand*. Auckland: Longman Paul, 1984

Davies-Colley, R.J., G.W. Payne and M. van Elswijk. 'Microclimate gradients across a forest edge'. *New Zealand Journal of Ecology*, vol. 24, no. 2 (2000): 111–21

Day, Melvin. *Nicholas Chevalier Artist: His life and work with special reference to his career in Australia and New Zealand*. Wellington: Millwood Publications, 1981

Denoon, Donald, Stewart Firth, Jocelyn Linnekin, Malama Meleisea and Karen Nero, eds. *The Cambridge History of the Pacific Islanders*. Cambridge: Cambridge University Press, 1997

Department of Conservation and Te Runanga o Ngai Tahu. 'Te Waihora joint management plan: Mahere Tukutahi o te Waihora', ed. Department of Conservation and Te Runanga o Ngai Tahu. Christchurch: Department of Conservation and Te Runanga o Ngai Tahu, 2005

Devine, T.M. 'Industrialisation'. In *The Transformation of Scotland: The economy since 1700*, eds T.M. Devine et al., 34–70. Edinburgh: Edinburgh University Press, 2005

———. 'The transformation of agriculture: Cultivation and clearance'. In *The Transformation of Scotland: The economy since 1700*, eds T.M. Devine et al., 71–99. Edinburgh: Edinburgh University Press, 2005

———. *The Scottish Nation 1700–2000*. London: Penguin Books, 2000

———. *The Transformation of Rural Scotland: Social change and the agrarian economy, 1660–1815*. Edinburgh: Edinburgh University Press, 1994

———. 'Social responses to agrarian improvement: The highland and lowland clearances in Scotland, 1500–1850'. In *Scottish Society, 1500–1800*, eds R. Houston and I. Whyte, 148–68. Cambridge: Cambridge University Press, 1989

Donovan, J.W. 'Measles in Australia and New Zealand, 1834–1835'. *The Medical Journal of Australia*, vol. 1, no. 5 (1970): 5–10

Drayton, Richard. *Nature's Government: Science, imperialism, and the 'improvement of the world'*. New Haven: Yale University Press, 2000

Druett, Joan. *Exotic Intruders: The introduction of plants and animals into New Zealand*. Auckland: Heinemann Publishers, 1983

Drummond, James. *Our Feathered Immigrants: Evidence for and against introduced birds in New Zealand; Together with notes on the native fauna*. Wellington: John Mackay, Government Printer, 1907

Duckworth, Henry. *The Early Years of Andersons Bay and Tomahawk*. 2nd edn. Dunedin: Otago Heritage Books, 1982

Duff, Roger. *The Moa-hunter Period of Maori Culture*. 3rd edn. Wellington: E.C. Keating, Government Printer, 1977

Dunlap, Thomas. *Nature and the English Diaspora: Environment and history in the United States, Canada, Australia, and New Zealand*. New York: Cambridge University Press, 1999

Durward, Elizabeth. 'The Maori population of Otago'. *Journal of the Polynesian Society*, vol. 42, no. 166 (1933): 49–82

Eccles, Alfred, ed. *A Pakeha's Recollections: The reminiscences of Murray Gladstone Thomson*. Wellington: A.H. and A.W. Reed, 1944

Ellison, Edward. 'Maori life and leisure'. In *Work 'n' Pastimes: 150 years of pain and pleasure, labour and leisure*, ed. Norma Bethune, 65–81. Dunedin: New Zealand Society of Genealogists, 1998

Entwisle, Peter. *Behold the Moon: The European occupation of the Dunedin district 1770–1848*. 2nd edn. Dunedin: Port Daniel Press, 2010

———. *Taka: A vignette life of William Tucker 1784–1817*. Dunedin: Port Daniel Press, 2005

———. 'The Otago Peninsula: The historical case for its preservation'. Dunedin: Otago Peninsula Museum and Historical Society, 1980

———. 'Edward Weller'. In *The Advance Guard*, ed. G.J. Griffiths, 9–50. Dunedin: Otago Daily Times, 1974

Evans, Jeff. *Nga Waka O Nehera: The first voyaging canoes*. Auckland: Reed Books, 1997

Evison, Harry. *The Ngai Tahu Deeds*. Christchurch: Canterbury University Press, 2006

———. *The Long Dispute: European colonisation and Maori land rights in southern New Zealand*. Christchurch: Canterbury University Press, 1997

———. *Te Wai Pounamu*. Wellington and Christchurch: Aoraki Press, 1993

Ewan Fordyce, R. 'Fossils and the history of life'. In *The Natural History of Southern New Zealand*, eds John Darby, R. Ewan Fordyce, Alan Mark,

Keith Probert and Colin Townsend, 35–64. Dunedin: Otago University Press, 2003

Fairburn, Miles. 'Local community or atomized society: The social structure of nineteenth-century New Zealand'. *New Zealand Journal of History*, vol. 16, no. 2 (1982): 146–65

———. 'The rural myth and the new urban frontier: An approach to New Zealand social history, 1870–1940'. *New Zealand Journal of History*, vol. 9, no. 1 (1975): 3–21

Fankhauser, Barry. 'The nutritive value and cooking of *Cordyline australis* (ti kouka)'. In *Saying So Doesn't Make It So: Papers in honour of B. Foss Leach*, ed. D.G. Sutton, 199–221. Dunedin: New Zealand Archaeological Society, 1989

Fereday, R.W. 'On the direct injuries to vegetation in New Zealand by various insects, especially with reference to larvae of moths and beetles feeding upon the field crops; and the expediency of introducing insectivorous birds as a remedy'. *Transactions and Proceedings of the New Zealand Institute*, vol. 5 (1872): 289–94

Finney, Ben. 'Experimental voyaging and Maori settlement'. In *The Origins of the First New Zealanders*, ed. D.G. Sutton, 52–76. Auckland: Auckland University Press, 1994

Firth, Raymond. *Economics of the New Zealand Maori*. 2nd edn. Wellington: A.R. Shearer, Government Printer, 1972

Flannery, Tim. *The Future Eaters: An ecological history of the Australasian lands and people*. Sydney: Reed Books, 1994

Flores, Dan. 'Place: An argument for bioregional history'. *Environmental History Review*, vol. 18, no. 4 (1994): 1–18

Forrest, James. 'Locating the vegetation of early coastal Otago: A map and its sources'. *Transactions of the Royal Society of Botany*, vol. 2, no. 4 (1963): 49–63

Forsyth, Jane, and Glen Coates. *The Dunedin Volcano*. Dunedin: New Zealand Geological Survey, 1989

Frost, Alan. *The Global Reach of Empire: Britain's maritime expansion in the Indian and Pacific oceans 1764–1815*. Melbourne: Miegunyah Press, 2003

Fulton, Robert. *Medical Practice in Otago and Southland in the Early Days*. Dunedin: Otago Daily Times and Witness Newspapers, 1922

Furey, Louise. 'Material culture'. In *Change Through Time: 50 years of New Zealand archaeology*, eds Louise Furey and Simon Holdaway, 29–54. Auckland: New Zealand Archaeological Association, 2004

Galbreath, Ross. 'Displacement, conservation and customary use of native plants and animals in New Zealand'. *New Zealand Journal of History*, vol. 36, no. 1 (2002): 36–50

———. *Working for Wildlife: A history of the New Zealand Wildlife Service*. Wellington: Bridget Williams Books and Department of Internal Affairs, 1993

Gardner, W.G. 'A colonial economy'. In *The Oxford History of New Zealand*, 2nd edn., ed. Geofrey W. Rice, 70–77. Auckland: Oxford University Press, 1992

Gibb, Jeremy. 'A New Zealand regional holocene eustatic sea-level curve and its application to determination of vertical tectonic movements: A contribution to Igcp-project 200'. *Royal Society of New Zealand Bulletin*, vol. 24 (1986): 377–95

Gibbons, Peter. 'The far side of the search for identity'. *New Zealand Journal of History*, vol. 37, no. 1 (2003): 38–49

———. 'Cultural colonisation and national identity'. *New Zealand Journal of History*, vol. 36, no. 1 (2002): 5–17

Gibbs, George. *Ghosts of Gondwana: The history of life in New Zealand*. Nelson: Craig Potton Publishing, 2006

Gillies, Robert. 'Notes on some changes in the fauna of Otago'. *Transactions and Proceedings of the New Zealand Institute*, vol. 10 (1878): 306–24

Goldman, I. *Ancient Polynesian Society*. Chicago: Chicago University Press, 1970

Golson, Jack. 'Culture change in prehistoric New Zealand'. In *Anthropology in the South Seas: Essays presented to H.D. Skinner*, eds J.D. Freeman and W.R. Geddes, 29–74. New Plymouth: Thomas Avery & Sons, 1959

Gordon, Ross, ed. *Waikouaiti and Dunedin in 1850 – Reminiscences of John McLay an early settler*. Dunedin: Ross Gordon, 1998

Graham, David. *A Treasury of New Zealand Fishes*. Wellington: A.H. & A.W. Reed, 1974

Grant, Patrick. 'Late Holocene histories of climate, geomorphology and vegetation, and their effects on the first New Zealanders'. In *The Origins of the First New Zealanders*, ed. D.G. Sutton, 164–207. Auckland: Auckland University Press, 1994

Grey, Alan. *Aotearoa and New Zealand: A historical geography*. Christchurch: Canterbury University Press, 1994

Griffiths, Tom, and Libby Robin. 'Environmental history in Australasia'. *Environment and History*, vol. 10 (2004): 439–74

Griffiths, Tom, and Libby Robin, eds. *Ecology and Empire: Environmental history of settler societies*. Edinburgh: Keele University Press, 1997

Guthrie-Smith, Herbert. *Sorrows and Joys of a New Zealand Naturalist*. Wellington: A.H. & A.W. Reed, 1936

———. *Bird Life on Island and Shore*. Edinburgh and London: Blackwood and Sons, 1925
———. *Tutira: The story of a New Zealand sheep station*. Seattle and London: University of Washington Press, 1999 [first pub. 1921]
Haines, David. 'In search of the "Whaheen": Ngai Tahu women, shore whalers, and the meaning of sex in early New Zealand.' In *Moving Subjects: Gender, mobility and intimacy in an age of global empire*, eds Tony Balllantyne and Antoinette M. Burton, 49–66. Urbana and Chicago: University of Illinois Press, 2009.
Hainsworth, D.R. *Builders and Adventurers: The traders and the emergence of the colony 1788–1821*. Melbourne: Cassell Press, 1968
Hainsworth, D.R. 'Exploiting the Pacific frontier: The New South Wales sealing industry 1800–1821'. *Journal of Pacific History*, vol. 2, no. 1 (1967): 59–75
Hainsworth, D.R. 'Iron men in wooden ships: The Sydney sealers 1800–1820'. *Labour History*, vol. 13 (1967): 19–25
Hall, Marcus. 'True environmental history'. *Environmental History*, vol. 10, no. 1 (2005): 42–43
Hamel, G.E. *The Archaeology of Otago*. Wellington: Department of Conservation, 2001
Hancock, Lyndall. *Otago Harbour and Peninsula: A bibliography*. Dunedin: University of Otago Library, 1977
Harding, Jon. 'Historic deforestation and the fate of endemic invertebrate species in streams'. *New Zealand Journal of Marine and Freshwater Research*, vol. 37 (2003): 333–45
Harding, J.S. et al. 'Incorporation into stream food webs of marine-derived nutrients from petrel breeding colonies', *Freshwater Biology*, vol. 49 (2004): 576–86
Hargreaves, R.P. 'Farm fences in pioneer New Zealand'. *New Zealand Geographer*, vol. 21, no. 2 (1965): 144–55
Harper, G., K. Dickinson and P. Seddon. 'Habitat use by three rat species (*Rattus* spp.) on Stewart Island/Rakiura, New Zealand'. *New Zealand Journal of Ecology*, vol. 29, no. 2 (2005): 251–60
Harris, Graham. *Nga Riwai Maori – Maori potatoes*. Lower Hutt: The Open Polytechnic of New Zealand, 1999
Hawke, D.J., R.N. Holdaway, J.E. Causer and S. Ogden. 'Soil indicators of pre-European seabird breeding in New Zealand at sites identified by predator deposits'. *Australian Journal of Soil Research*, vol. 37 (1999): 103–13
Hawke, Gary. *The Making of New Zealand*. Wellington: Victoria University Press, 1981
Hay, James. *Reminiscences of Earliest Canterbury (Principally Banks Peninsula) and its Settlers*. Christchurch: Christchurch Press Company, 1915
Head, Lyndsay. 'Wiremu Tamihana and the *mana* of Christianity'. In *Christianity, Modernity and Culture*, ed. John Stenhouse, 58–86. Adelaide: ATF Press, 2005
Higham, T.F.G., R.E.M. Hedges, A.J. Anderson, C. Bronk Ramsey and B. Fankhauser. 'Problems associated with the AMS dating of small bone samples: The question of the arrival of Polynesian rats to New Zealand'. *Radiocarbon*, vol. 46, no. 1 (2004): 207–18
Higham, T.G.F., Atholl Anderson and C. Jacomb. 'Dating the first New Zealanders: The chronology of Wairau Bar'. *Antiquity*, vol. 73 (1999): 420–27
Hjarno, Jan. *Maori Fish-hooks in Southern New Zealand*. Dunedin: Otago Museum Trust Board, 1967
Hocken, Thomas. M. *Contributions to the Early History of New Zealand [Settlement of Otago]*. London: Sampson Low, Marston & Co., 1898
Holdaway, R.N. 'A spatio-temporal model for the invasion of the New Zealand archipelago by the Pacific rat *Rattus exulans*'. *Journal of the Royal Society of New Zealand*, vol. 29, no. 2 (1999): 91–105
———. 'Introduced predators and avifaunal extinction in New Zealand'. In *Extinctions in Near Time*, ed. R.D.E. McPhee, 189–238. New York: Kluwer Academic/Plenum, 1999
———. 'Arrival of rats in New Zealand'. *Nature*, vol. 384 (1996): 225–26
———. 'New Zealand's pre-human avifauna and its vulnerability'. *New Zealand Journal of Ecology*, vol. 12, supplement (1989): 11–25
Holdaway, R.N., and N.R. Beavan. 'Reliable 14c AMS dates on bird and Pacific rat *Rattus exulans* bone gelatin, from a $CaCO_3$-rich deposit'. *Journal of the Royal Society of New Zealand*, vol. 29 (1999): 185–211
Holland, Peter. *At Home in the Howling Wilderness: Settlers and the environment in southern New Zealand*. Auckland: Auckland University Press, 2013
———. 'Cultural landscapes as biogeographical experiments: A New Zealand perspective'. *Journal of Biogeography*, vol. 27, no. 1 (2000): 39–43
———. 'Plants and lowland South Canterbury landscapes'. *New Zealand Geographer*, vol. 44, no. 2 (1988): 50–60
Holland, Peter, and Ray Hargreaves. 'The trivial round, the common task: Work and leisure on a Canterbury hill country run in the 1860s and

1870s'. *New Zealand Geographer*, vol. 47, no. 1 (1991): 19–25

Hooker, Joseph, ed. *Journal of the Right Hon. Sir Joseph Banks*. London: Macmillan and Co., 1896

Howe, K.R. *The Quest for Origins*. 2nd edn. Auckland: Penguin Books, 2008

Igler, David. 'Longitudes and latitudes'. *Environmental History*, vol. 10, no. 1 (2005): 44–46

Ingold, Tim, David Riches and James Woodburn, eds. *Hunters and Gatherers: Property, power and ideology*. New York: Berg Publishers, 1988

Innes, John. 'Advances in New Zealand mammalogy 1990–2000: European rats'. *Journal of the Royal Society of New Zealand*, vol. 31, no. 1 (2001): 111–25

Jillett, John. 'Zooplankton associations off Otago Peninsula, south-eastern New Zealand, related to different water masses'. *New Zealand Journal of Marine and Fresh Water Research*, vol. 10, no. 4 (1976): 543–57

Johnson, David. *Hooked: The story of the New Zealand fishing industry*. Christchurch: Hazard Press, 2004

Johnson, Peter. *Otago Peninsula Plants: An annotated list of vascular plants growing in wild places*. Portobello: Save the Otago Peninsula (STOP), 2004

———. 'Okia Flat, Otago Peninsula: Botanical values and grazing'. In *Conservation Advisory Science Notes*. Wellington: Department of Conservation, 1993

———. 'Pingao on Otago Peninsula: Botanical report'. Landcare Research Contract Report LC 9293/29. Wellington: Department of Conservation, 1993

———. 'The sand dune and beach vegetation inventory of New Zealand II. South Island and Stewart Island'. Department of Scientific and Industrial Research Land Resources Scientific Report No. 16. Wellington: Department of Scientific and Industrial Research, 1992

———. 'Native bush conservation values, Turnbulls Bay, Otago Peninsula'. Department of Scientific and Industrial Research Land Resources Contract Report No. 91/113. Wellington: Department of Scientific and Industrial Research, 1991

Jones, Chris. 'Sooty shearwater (*Puffinus griseus*) breeding colonies on mainland South Island, New Zealand: Evidence of decline and predictors of persistence'. *New Zealand Journal of Zoology*, vol. 27 (2000): 327–34

Kawharu, Hugh. *Maori Land Tenure: Studies of a changing institution*. Oxford: Clarendon Press, 1977

———. 'New Zealand: Salvaging the remnant'. In *Land Tenure in the Pacific*, ed. Ron Crocombe, 143–63. Suva: University of the South Pacific Press, 1987

Keenan, Danny. 'Bound to the land: Maori retention and assertion of identity'. In *Environmental Histories of New Zealand*, eds Eric Pawson and Tom Brooking, 246–60. Oxford and New York: Oxford University Press, 2002

Kempthorne, Renatus. *Maori Christianity in Te Waipounamu: A history*. Christchurch: Te Hui Amorangi, 2000

King, Michael. *The Penguin History of New Zealand*. Auckland: Penguin Books, 2003

Kiple, Kenneth, ed. *Plague, Pox and Pestilence*. London: Weidenfield & Nicholson, 1997

Kirch, Patrick. *On the Road of the Winds: An archaeological history of the Pacific Islands before European contact*. Berkeley, LA, and London: University of California Press, 2000

Kitson, J.C., and H. Moller, 'Looking after your ground: Resource management practice by Rakiura Maori titi harvesters'. *Papers and Proceedings of the Royal Society of Tasmania*, vol. 142, no. 1 (2008): 161–76

Knight, Hardwicke. *The Ordeal of William Larnach*. Dunedin: The author, 1993

———. *Otago Peninsula: A local history*. Broad Bay, Dunedin: The author, 1979

———. 'Umu-ti'. *Journal of the Polynesian Society*, vol. 75 (1966): 332–47

Lalas, Chris. 'Recolonisation of Otago, southern New Zealand, by fur seals and sea lions: Unexpected patterns and consequences'. In *Proceedings of the Conserv-Vision Conference, 2–4 July 2007*, eds Bruce Clarkson et al. Hamilton: University of Waikato, 2008

Lalas, Chris, and Corey Bradshaw. 'Folklore and chimerical numbers: Review of a millenium of interaction between fur seals and humans in the New Zealand region'. *New Zealand Journal of Marine and Freshwater Research*, vol. 35 (2001): 477–97

le Guillou, Élie. *Voyage autour du monde de l'Astrolabe et de la Zélée sous les ordres du contre-amiral Dumont d'Urville pendant les années 1837, 38, 39 et 40 par Élie le Guillou, chirurgien major de la Zélée*. Trans. Basil Howard. Paris: J. Arago, Le Edition, 1844

Leach, B.F., and A.S. Boocock. *Prehistoric Fish Catches in New Zealand*. Oxford: Tempus Reparatum, 1993

Leach, B.F., and A. Boocook. 'The impact of pre-European Maori fishermen on the New Zealand snapper, *Pagrus auratus*, in the vicinity of Rotokura, Tasman Bay'. *New Zealand Journal of Archaeology*, vol. 16 (1994): 69–84

Leach, Foss. *Fishing in Pre-European New Zealand*. New Zealand Journal of Archaeology Special Publication: Archaeofauna Vol. 15. Wellington: New Zealand Journal of Archaeology, 2006

Leach, Helen. 'Fern consumption in Aotearoa and its oceanic precedents'. *Journal of the Polynesian Society*, vol. 112, no. 2 (2003): 141–56

———. 'The change from Archaic to Classic adze forms revisited'. *Archaeology in New Zealand*, vol. 37, no. 4 (1994): 248–54

———. *1,000 Years of Gardening in New Zealand*. Wellington: A.H. & A.W. Reed, 1984

———. *A Hundred Years of Otago Archaeology*. Records of the Otago Museum, Vol. 6. Dunedin: Otago Museum Trust Board, 1972

Leach, Helen, and G.E. Hamel. 'The place of Taiaroa Head and other Classic Maori sites in the prehistory of East Otago'. *Journal of the Royal Society of New Zealand*, vol. 8, no. 3 (1978): 239–51

Lee, Richard. *Forest Hydrology*. New York: Columbia University Press, 1980

Leslie, D.M. 'An interpretation of a section through Quaternary deposits and paleosols at Taiaroa Head, Otago Peninsula, New Zealand'. New Zealand Soil Bureau Scientific Report No. 34. Wellington: Department of Scientific and Industrial Research, 1978

———. 'Soils of Otago Peninsula'. New Zealand Soil Survey Report No. 28. Wellington: Department of Scientific and Industrial Research, 1976

———. 'Effects of basement lithology, regolith, and slope on landslide potential, Otago Peninsula, New Zealand'. New Zealand Soil Bureau Scientific Report No. 12. Wellington: Department of Scientific and Industrial Research, 1974

Lewthwaite, Gordon. 'The puzzle of Tupaia's map'. *New Zealand Geographer*, vol. 26 (1970): 1–19

Linklater, Andre. *Owning the Earth: The transforming history of land ownership*. London: Bloomsbury, 2014

McAloon, Jim. 'The New Zealand economy, 1792–1914'. In *The New Oxford History of New Zealand*, ed. Giselle Byrnes, 197–217. Melbourne and Auckland: Oxford University Press, 2009

———. 'Gentlemanly capitalism and settler capitalists: Imperialism, dependent development and colonial wealth in the South Island of New Zealand'. *Australian Economic History Review*, vol. 42, no. 2 (2002): 204–23

———. 'Resource frontiers, environment, and capitalism'. In *Environmental Histories of New Zealand*, eds Eric Pawson and Tom Brooking, 52–68. Oxford: Oxford University Press, 2002

McCahon, Colin. 'Beginnings'. *Landfall*, vol. 20, no. 4 (1966): 360–64

McCluskey, F.H. *Down the Bay: The history of the ferries on Otago Harbour*. Wellington: New Zealand Ship & Marine Society, 1995

McEvoy, Arthur F. *The Fisherman's Problem: Ecology and law in the California fisheries, 1850–1980*. New York: Cambridge University Press, 1986

McGlone, M.S. 'Goodbye Gondwana'. *Journal of Biogeography*, vol. 32, no. 5 (2005), 739–40

———. 'The origin of the indigenous grasslands of southeastern South Island in relation to pre-human woody ecosystems'. *New Zealand Journal of Ecology*, vol. 25, no. 1 (2001): 1–15

———. 'Polynesian deforestation of New Zealand: A preliminary synthesis'. *Archaeology in Oceania*, vol. 18 (1983): 11–25

McGlone, M.S., Atholl Anderson and R.N. Holdaway. 'An ecological approach to the settlement of New Zealand'. In *The Origins of the First New Zealanders*, ed. D.G. Sutton, 136–63. Auckland: Auckland University Press, 1994

McGlone, Matt, Peter Wardle and Trevor Worthy. 'Environmental change since the last glaciation'. In *The Natural History of Southern New Zealand*, eds John Darby, R. Ewan Fordyce, Alan Mark, Keith Probert and Colin Townsend, 105–28. Dunedin: University of Otago Press, 2003

McIntosh, P.D. *Soils for Horticulture in Coastal Otago*. Landuser Guide No. 3. Dunedin: Landcare Research New Zealand, Lincoln and Ravensdown Fertiliser Co-operative Limited, 1992

McKenzie, B.A. 'Processed and new crops'. In *New Zealand Pasture and Crop Science*, eds James White and John Hodgson, 263–68. Auckland: Oxford University Press, 1999

McLauchlan, Gordon. *The Farming of New Zealand*. Auckland: Australia and New Zealand Book Company, 1981

McLintock, A.H. *The History of Otago*. Christchurch: Capper Press, 1949

McNab, Robert, ed. *Historical Records of New Zealand*. 2 vols. Wellington: Government Printer, 1908

———. *Murihiku and the Southern Islands*. Invercargill: William Smith, 1907

———. *The Old Whaling Days*. Auckland: Golden Press, 1913. Repr., 1974

McNeill, J.R. 'Observations on the nature and culture of environmental history'. *History and Theory*, vol. 42 (2004): 39–41

———. ed. *Environmental History in the Pacific World. Vol. 2. The Pacific World: Lands, peoples and history of the Pacific, 1500–1900*. Aldershot, Burlington, Singapore, Sydney: Ashgate, 2001

———. 'Of rats and men: A synoptic environmental history of the island Pacific'. *Journal of World History*, no. 5 (1994): 299–349

McWethy, David B. et al. 'Rapid deforestation of South Island, New Zealand, by early Polynesian fires'. *The Holocene*, vol. 19, no. 6 (2009): 883–97

MacDiarmid, A.B. et al. 'Taking stock – The impacts of humans on New Zealand marine ecosystems since first settlement: Synthesis of major findings, and policy and management implications'. New Zealand Aquatic Environment and Biodiversity Report No. 170. Wellington: Ministry for Primary Industries, 2016

Maling, P.B. *Historic Charts and Maps of New Zealand 1642-1875*. Auckland: Reed Books, 1996

Matira, Tiaki Hikawera. *Takitimu*. Christchurch: Kiwi Publishers, 1997

Mead, Hirini. *Tikanga Māori: Living by Māori values*. Wellington: Huia Publishers, 2003

Merrington, Ernest Northcroft. *A Great Coloniser: The Rev. Dr. Thomas Burns*. Dunedin: The Otago Daily Times and Witness Newspapers Co., 1929

Middleton, Angela. 'Hereweka/Harbour Cone: A relict landscape on the Otago Peninsula'. *Australasian Historical Archaeology*, vol. 30 (2012): 34–42

———. 'Harbour Cone: A relic landscape on the Otago Peninsula'. *Archaeology in New Zealand*, vol. 52, no. 1 (2009): 32–45

Moller, Henrik, Jane C. Kitson and Theresa M. Downs, 'Knowing by doing: Learning for sustainable muttonbird harvesting'. *New Zealand Journal of Zoology*, vol. 36, no. 3 (2009): 243–58

Moller, H., and N. Alterio. 'Home range and spatial organisation of stoats (*Mustela erminea*), ferrets (*Mustela furo*) and feral house cats (*Felis catus*) on coastal grasslands, Otago Peninsula, New Zealand: Implications for yellow-eyed penguin (*Megadyptes antipodes*) conservation'. *New Zealand Journal of Zoology*, vol. 26 (1999): 165–74

Monro, D. 'Notes of a journey through a part of the Middle Island of New Zealand'. In Thomas M. Hocken, *Contributions to the Early History of New Zealand [Settlement of Otago]*, 230–63. London: Sampson Low, Marston & Co., 1898.

Morton, Harry. *The Whale's Wake*. Dunedin: University of Otago Press, 1982

Murdoch, R.C. 'The effects of a headland eddy on surface macro-zooplankton assemblages north of Otago Peninsula, New Zealand'. *Estuarine, Coastal and Shelf Science*, vol. 29 (1989): 361–83

Murdoch, R.C., R. Proctor, J.B. Jillett and J.R. Zeldis. 'Evidence for an eddy over the continental shelf in the downstream lee of Otago Peninsula, New Zealand'. *Estuarine, Coastal and Shelf Science*, vol. 30 (1990): 489–507

Nagaoka, Lisa. 'Explaining subsistence change in southern New Zealand using foraging theory models'. *World Archaeology*, vol. 34, no. 1 (2002): 84–102

Neal, Wallace. 'Otago Peninsula dairy farmers now shrunk to two: Survivors look back on an era'. *New Zealand Farmer*, October 1991, 16

Nunn, Patrick. 'The A.D. 1300 event in the Pacific Basin'. *Geographical Review*, vol. 97, no. 1 (2007): 1–23

———. 'Revising ideas about environmental determinism: Human–environment relations in the Pacific Islands'. *Asia Pacific Viewpoint*, vol. 44, no. 1 (2003): 63–72

Nunn, Patrick, and James Britton. 'Human–environment relationships in the Pacific Islands around A.D. 1300'. *Environment and History*, vol. 7, no. 1 (2001): 3–22

O'Malley, Vincent. *The Meeting Place: Māori and Pākehā encounters, 1642–1840*. Auckland: Auckland University Press, 2012

O'Regan, Tipene. 'Ngai Tahu and the Crown: Partnership promised'. In *Rural Canterbury: Celebrating its history*, eds Garth Cant and Russell Kirkpatrick. Wellington: Daphne Brasell Associates, 2001

———. 'Old myths and new politics'. In *The Shaping of History*, ed. Judith Binney, 15–37. Wellington: Bridget Williams Books, 2001

Oldstone, Michael. *Viruses, Plagues, and History*. New York and Oxford: Oxford University Press, 1998

Olssen, Erik. *A History of Otago*. Dunedin: John McIndoe, 1984

Orbell, Margaret. *The Natural World of the Maori*. Auckland: Collins, 1985

Park, Geoff. *Theatre Country: Essays on landscape & whenua*, Wellington: Victoria University Press, 2006

———. *Nga Uruora: The Groves of Life – Ecology and history in a New Zealand landscape*. Wellington: Victoria University Press, 1995

Patterson, Brad, Tom Brooking and Jim McAloon, *Unpacking the Kists: The Scots in New Zealand*. Dunedin: Otago University Press, 2003

Pawson, Eric. 'Plants, mobilities and landscapes: Environmental histories of botanical exchange'. *Geography Compass*, vol. 2, no. 5 (2008): 1464–77

———. 'Confronting nature'. In *Southern Capital: Christchurch: Toward a city biography 1850-2000*, eds John Cookson and Graeme Dunstall,

60–84. Christchurch: Canterbury University Press, 2000

Pawson, Eric, and Tom Brooking. 'Introduction'. In *Environmental Histories of New Zealand*, eds Eric Pawson and Tom Brooking, 1–16. Melbourne: Oxford University Press, 2002

———. 'Landscape change and environmental histories'. *New Zealand Geographer*, vol. 56, no. 2 (2000): 52–56

Pawson, Eric, and S. Dovers. 'Environmental history and the challenges of interdisciplinarity: An antipodean perspective'. *Environment and History*, vol. 9 (2003): 53–75

Perry, Virginia, ed. *Eliza's Journal – A gentlewoman's experiences in the late 1850s*. Dunedin: Virginia Perry, 2004

Petrie, Hazel. *Leaders of Industry: Maori tribal enterprise in early colonial New Zealand*. Auckland: Auckland University Press, 2006

Pool, D.I. *Te Iwi Maori: A New Zealand population past, present & projected*. Auckland: Auckland University Press, 1991

———. *The Maori Population of New Zealand 1769–1971*. Auckland: Auckland University Press, 1977

Potiki, Megan. 'The Otago Peninsula, a unique identity'. *Shima: The International Journal of Research into Island Cultures*, vol. 10, no. 1 (2016): 1–19

Potts, T.H. 'On the birds of NZ (ii)'. *Transactions and Proceedings of the New Zealand Institute*, vol. 3 (1870): 59–109

Prebble, Matiu, and David Mules. *To Hikoai Mai Hikaroroa Ki Waikouaiti – Kua te ra, ka te ahi*. Matauranga Kura Taiao/Nga Whenua Rahui Collaboration, 2004

Price, Una Shepherd. *My Family of Shepherds*. Scone (NSW): Privately Published, 1988

Probert, Keith, John Jillett and Sally Carson. *Southern Seas: Discovering marine life at 46 south*. Dunedin: University of Otago Press, 2005

Pybus, T.A. *The Maoris of the South Island*. Christchurch: Cadsonbury Publications, 2002

———. *Maori and Missionary: Early Christian missions in the South Island of New Zealand*. Christchurch: Cadsonbury Publications, 2002

Rawlence, Nicholas J., et al. 'Geographically contrasting biodiversity reductions in a widespread New Zealand seabird'. *Molecular Ecology*, vol. 24 (2015): 4612–13

Reay, Tony. 'Geology'. In *The Natural History of Southern New Zealand*, eds John Darby, R. Ewan Fordyce, Alan Mark, Keith Probert and Colin Townsend, 1–16. Dunedin: University of Otago Press, 2003

Reed, A.W. *The Reed Dictionary of New Zealand Place Names*. Auckland: Reed Books, 2002

Richards, Rhys. *Sealing in the Southern Oceans 1788–1833*. Porirua: Paremata Press, 2010

———. *Murihiku Re-viewed*. Wellington: Lithographic Services, 1995

Riley, Murdoch. *Maori Sayings and Proverbs*. Paraparaumu: Viking Sevenseas, 1990

Robertson, C.J., R.P. Hyvonen, M.J. Fraser and C.R. Pickard, eds. *Atlas of Bird Distribution in New Zealand*. Wellington: The Ornithological Society of New Zealand, 2007

Robertson, C.J.R., ed. *Complete Book of New Zealand Birds*. Sydney: Reader's Digest, 1985

Roman, Joe et al. 'Whales as marine ecosystem engineers'. *Frontiers in Ecology and the Environment*, vol. 12, no. 7 (2014): 377–85

Roper, D.S., and J.B. Jillett. 'Seasonal occurrence and distribution of flatfish (Pisces: Pleuronectiformes) in inlets and shallow water along the Otago Coast'. *New Zealand Journal of Marine and Freshwater Research*, vol. 15, no. 1 (1981): 1–13

Rose, Murray. 'What's new pussycat? A look at farms and farming life'. In *Work 'n' Pastimes: 150 years of pain and pleasure, labour and leisure*, ed. Norma Bethune. Dunedin: New Zealand Society of Genealogists, 1998

Ross, John O.C. *William Stewart: Sealing captain, trader and speculator*. Canberra: Roebuck Society, 1987

Salmond, Anne. *Between Worlds: Early exchanges between Maori and Europeans 1773–1815*. Auckland: Penguin Books, 1997

———. *Two Worlds: First meetings between Maori and Europeans 1642–1772*. London: Penguin, 1991

Sanders, G.H. *A general study of fifty dairy farmers of the Taieri Plain and the Otago Peninsula*. Dunedin: University of Otago, 1951

Schmidt, M. 'Radiocarbon dating the end of moa-hunting in New Zealand prehistory'. *Archaeology in New Zealand*, vol. 43 (2000): 324–29

Schwimmer, Eric, 'Rani Ellison: Maori fishing tycoon', *Te Ao Hou*, no. 20, 1957, 32–36

Shaffer, Scott A. et al. 'Migratory shearwaters integrate oceanic resources across the Pacific Ocean in an endless summer'. *Proceedings of the National Academy of Sciences of the United States of America*, vol. 103, no. 34 (2006): 12799–802

Shephard, Paul. *English Reaction to the New Zealand Landscape before 1850*. Pacific Viewpoint Monograph, vol. 4. Wellington: Victoria University Press, 1969

Shortland, Edward. *Traditions and Superstitions of the New Zealanders*. Christchurch: Kiwi Publishers, 2001. Repr.

———. *The Southern Districts of New Zealand; A journal, with passing notices of the customs of the aborigines*. London: Longman, Brown, Green & Longmans, 1851

Simmons, D.R. 'A New Zealand myth: Kupe, Toi, and the "fleet"'. *New Zealand Journal of History*, vol. 3, no. 1 (1969): 14–31

———. *Little Papanui and Otago Prehistory*. Records of the Otago Museum. Anthropology, No. 4. Dunedin: Otago Museum Trust Board, 1967

Simmons, I. G. *An Environmental History of Great Britain: From 10,000 years ago to the present*. Edinburgh: Edinburgh University Press, 2001

Sinclair, L., J. McCartney, J. Godfrey, M. Wakelin and G. Sherley. 'How did invertebrates respond to eradication of rats from Kapiti Island, New Zealand?' *New Zealand Journal of Zoology*, vol. 32 (2005): 293–315

Skinner, H.D. 'Excavations at Little Papanui, Otago Peninsula'. *Journal of the Polynesian Society*, vol. 69 (1960): 187–210

Smith, Ian J. *Hoopers Inlet: Located on the Otago Peninsula of New Zealand*. Dunedin: The author, 2015

Smith, I.W.G. 'Estimating the magnitude of pre-European Maori marine harvest in two New Zealand study areas'. New Zealand Aquatic Environment and Biodiversity Report No. 82. Wellington: Ministry of Fisheries, 2011

———. 'Retreat and resilience: Fur seals and human settlement in New Zealand'. In *The Exploitation and Cultural Importance of Sea Mammals*, ed. Gregory G. Monks, 6–18. Oxford: Oxbow Books, 2005

———. 'Nutritional perspectives on prehistoric marine fishing in New Zealand'. *New Zealand Journal of Archaeology*, vol. 24 (2004): 5–31

———. 'The exploitation and cultural importance of sea mammals'. Paper presented at the 9th Conference of the International Council of Archaeozoology. Durham, 2002

———. 'Historical documents, archaeology and 18th century seal hunting in New Zealand'. In *Oceanic Culture History: Essays in honour of Roger Green*, eds J.M. Davidson, G. Irwin, B.F. Leach, A. Pawley and D. Brown, 675–88. Wellington: New Zealand Journal of Archaeology Special Publication, 1996

———. 'Maori impact on the marine megafauna: Pre-European distributions of New Zealand sea mammals'. In *Saying So Doesn't Make It So: Papers in honour of B. Foss Leach*, ed. D.G. Sutton, 76–108. Dunedin: New Zealand Archaeological Society, 1989

———. 'Maori, Pakeha and Kiwi: Peoples, cultures and sequence in New Zealand archaeology'. *Manuscript in Review*, (n.d.): 1–17

Smith, I.W.G., and Helen Leach. 'Adzes from the excavation and museum collections'. In *Shag River Mouth: The archaeology of an early southern Maori village*, eds Atholl Anderson, Brian Allingham and I.W.G. Smith, 103–47. Canberra: ANH Publications, 1996

Smith, T.D. et al. 'Spatial and seasonal distribution of American whaling and whales in the age of sail', *PLoS ONE*, vol. 7, no. 4 (2012): e34905

Snedden, Fleur. *King of the Castle: A biography of William Larnach*. Auckland: David Bateman, 1997

Soper, Eileen. *The Otago of Our Mothers*. Christchurch: Whitcombe & Tombs, 1948

Stack, James. *Through Canterbury and Otago with Bishop Harper, 1859-60*. Christchurch: The Nag's Head Press, 1972

———. *More Maoriland Adventures of J.W. Stack*. Dunedin: A.H. and A.W. Reed, 1936

———. 'Sketch of the traditional history of the South Island Maoris'. *Transactions and Proceedings of the New Zealand Institute*, vol. 10 (1877): 57–92

Star, Paul. 'Environmental history and New Zealand history'. *Environment and Nature in New Zealand*, vol. 4, no. 1 (2014): http://environmentalhistory-au-nz.org/2014/04/environmental-history-and-new-zealand-history/

———. '"Doomed timber": Towards an environmental history of Seaward Forest'. In *Landscape/Community: Perspectives from New Zealand history*, eds Tony Ballantyne and Judith Bennett, 17–30. Dunedin: University of Otago Press, 2005

———. 'New Zealand environmental history: A question of attitudes'. *Environment and History*, vol. 9 (2003): 463–75

———. 'Native forest and the rise of preservation in New Zealand (1903–1913)'. *Environment and History*, vol. 8 (2002): 275–94

———. 'New Zealand's changing natural history: Evidence from Dunedin 1868–1875'. *New Zealand Journal of History*, vol. 32, no. 1 (1998): 59–69

Steadman, David. 'Extinctions of Polynesian birds: Reciprocal impacts of birds and people'. In *Historical Ecology in the Pacific Islands*, eds Patrick Kirch and Terry Hunt, 51–79. New Haven and London: Yale University Press, 1991

Frances Steel. 'Uncharted waters? Cultures of sea transport and mobility in New Zealand colonial history'. *The Journal of New Zealand Studies*, no. 12 (2011): 137–54

Steven, Margaret. 'Eastern trade'. In *India, China, Australia: Trade and society 1788–1850*, ed. James Broadbent, 31–61. Sydney: Historic Houses Trust of New South Wales, 2003

———. *Trade, Tactics and Territory: Britain in the Pacific, 1783–1823*. Melbourne: Melbourne University Press, 1983

Stevens, Michael J. '"What's in a name?": Murihiku, colonial knowledge-making and "thin-culture"'. *Journal of the Polynesian Society*, vol. 120, no. 4 (2011): 339–47

Stevens, Michael J. '"The ocean is our only highway and means of communication": Maritime culture in colonial southern New Zealand'. *The Journal of New Zealand Studies*, no. 12 (2011): 155–70

Stokes, Evelyn. *The Individualisation of Maori Interests in Land*. Hamilton: Te Maataahauraki Institute, 2002

Tau, Te Maire. *Ngā Pikitūroa o Ngāi Tahu: The oral traditions of Ngāi Tahu*. Dunedin: University of Otago Press, 2003

———. 'The death of knowledge: Ghosts on the plains'. *New Zealand Journal of History*, vol. 35, no. 2 (2001): 131–52

———. 'Ngai Tahu and the Canterbury landscape: A broad context'. In *Southern Capital: Christchurch: Toward a city biography 1850–2000*, eds John Cookson and Graeme Dunstall, 41–59. Christchurch: Canterbury University Press, 2000

Tau, Te Maire, and Atholl Anderson, eds. *Ngāi Tahu: A Migration History: The Carrington text*. Wellington: Bridget Williams Books, 2008

Taylor, W.A. *Lore and History of the South Island Maori*. Christchurch: Bascands, 1950

———. 'Some notes on early Otakou'. *Evening Star*, 21 January 1948

Tennyson, Alan, and Paul Martinson. *Extinct Birds*. Wellington: Te Papa Press, 2006

Teviotdale, David. 'The material culture of the moa hunters in Murihiku'. *Journal of the Polynesian Society*, vol. 40 (1932): 81–120

Thomson, A.S. *The Story of New Zealand*. 2 vols. London: John Murray, 1859. Repr., Capper Press, Christchurch

Thompson, H., and I. Thompson. *Clearwaters of New Zealand 1838–1986*. Invercargill: Sycamore Print, 1986

Thomson, G.M. *The Naturalisation of Animals and Plants in New Zealand*. Cambridge: Cambridge University Press, 1922

———. 'The natural history of Otago Harbour and the adjacent sea, together with a record of the researches carried on at the Portobello Marine Fish-hatchery: Part 1'. *Transactions and Proceedings of the New Zealand Institute*, vol. 45 (1913): 225–51

Thomson, Murray. *The Reminiscences of Murray Gladstone Thomson*. Wellington and Dunedin: A.H. and A.W. Reed, 1944

Thomson, Peter. 'Our fish supply'. *Transactions and Proceedings of the New Zealand Institute*, vol. 11 (1878): 380–89

———, 'The Dunedin fish supply'. *Transactions and Proceedings of the New Zealand Institute*, vol. 10 (1877): 324–30

———. 'Fish and their seasons'. *Transactions and Proceedings of the New Zealand Institute*, vol. 9 (1876): 484–90

———. 'Work for field naturalists'. *Transactions and Proceedings of the New Zealand Institute*, vol. 4 (1871): 138–41

———. 'On the sand hills, or dunes, in the neighbourhood of Dunedin'. *Transactions and Proceedings of the New Zealand Institute*, vol. 3 (1870): 263–69

Travers, W.T.L. 'Notes upon a New Zealand flesh-fly'. *Transactions and Proceedings of the New Zealand Institute*, vol. 3 (1870): 116–20

Tremewan, Peter. *Selling Otago*. Dunedin: Otago Heritage Books, 1994

Turner, Marianne. 'Functional and technological explanations for the variation among early New Zealand adzes'. *New Zealand Journal of Archaeology*, vol. 26 (2004): 57–101

Turvey, Samuel, and R.N. Holdaway. 'Postnatal ontogeny, populations structure, and extinction of the giant moa *Dinornis*'. *Journal of Morphology*, vol. 265, no. 1 (2005): 70–86

Wakefield, Edward Jerningham. *Adventure in New Zealand, from 1839 to 1844: With some account of the British colonisation of the islands*. 2 vols. London: John Murray, 1845

Walter, Richard, I.W.G. Smith and C. Jacomb. 'Sedentism, subsistence and socio-political organization in prehistoric New Zealand'. *World Archaeology*, vol. 38, no. 2 (2006): 274–90

Wanhalla, Angela. *Matters of the Heart: A history of interracial marriage in New Zealand*. Auckland: Auckland University Press, 2013

———. *In/Visible Sight: The mixed-descent families of southern New Zealand*. Wellington: Bridget Williams Books, 2009

———. '"My piece of land at Taieri": Boundary formation and contestation at Taieri Native Reserve, 1844–1868'. *The New Zealand Journal of History*, vol. 41, no. 1 (2007): 44–60

———. 'Marrying "in": The geography of intermarriage on the Taieri, 1830s–1920s'. In *Landscape/Community: Perspectives from New Zealand history*, eds Tony Ballantyne and Judith Bennett, 73–94. Dunedin: University of Otago Press, 2005

Ward, Alan. *National Overview: Waitangi Tribunal Rangahaua Whanui Series*. Vol. 1. Wellington: G.P. Publications, 1997

———. 'Land report for Ngai Tahu'. Wellington: Waitangi Tribunal, 1990

Weaver, John. *The Great Land Rush and the Making of the Modern World, 1650-1900*. Montreal & Kingston: McGill-Queen's University Press, 2003

Weiner, Douglas. 'A death-defying attempt to articulate a coherent definition of environmental history'. *Environmental History*, vol. 10, no. 3 (2005): 1–16

Weisler, Marshall I., Chris Lalas and Paul Rivett, 'New fish records from an Archaic midden South Island'. *Archaeology in New Zealand*, vol. 42, no. 1 (1999): 37–42

Wekey, S. *Otago as it is, its Goldmines and Natural Resources; Handbook for merchants, capitalists, and the general public, and a guide to intending emigrants*. Christchurch: Kiwi Publishers, 1998. Repr.

Weller, Richard. *A Fortune Lost: The Joseph Weller family in New South Wales and New Zealand 1824–1890*. Sheffield, UK: self-published, 2003

White, Richard. 'Environmental history: Watching a historical field mature'. *Pacific Historical Review*, vol. 70, no. 1 (2001): 105–11

———. *The Middle Ground: Indians, empires, and republics in the Great Lakes region 1650–1815*. Cambridge: Cambridge University Press, 1991

———. *Land Use, Environment, and Social Change: The shaping of Island County, Washington*. Seattle and London: University of Washington Press, 1980

Wightman, Andy. *The Poor have no Lawyers: Who owns Scotland and how they got it*. Edinburgh: Berlin, 2013

Wilkes, Owen. 'Were moas really hunted to extinction in less than 100 years?' *Archaeology in New Zealand*, vol. 43, no. 2 (2000): 112–20

Williams, Jim. '*Mahika kai*: The husbanding of consumables by Māori in precontact Te Wāipounamu'. *Journal of the Polynesian Society*, vol. 119, no. 2 (2010): 149–80

Williams, Jim. 'Papa-Tua-Nuku: Attitudes to land'. In *Ki te Whaiao: An introduction to Maori culture and society*, eds Tania M. Ka`ai, John C. Moorfield, Michael P.J. Reilly and Sharon Mosley, 50–60. Auckland: Pearson Education, 2004

Wilmshurst, J.M, A.J. Anderson, T.F.G Higham and T.H. Worthy. 'Dating the late prehistoric dispersal of Polynesians to New Zealand using the commensal Pacific rat'. *Proceedings of the National Academy of Sciences USA*, vol. 105, no. 22 (2008): 7676–768

Wilmshurst, Janet, and Thomas Higham. 'Using rat-gnawed seeds to independently date the arrival of Pacific rats and humans in New Zealand'. *The Holocene*, vol. 14, no. 6 (2004): 801–06

Wilmshurst, Janet, Matt McGlone and Dan Charman. 'Holocene vegetation and climate change in southern New Zealand: Linkages between forest composition and quantitative surface moisture reconstructions from an ombrogenous bog'. *Journal of Quaternary Science*, vol. 17, no. 7 (2002): 653–66

Wilson, Kerry-Jayne. *Flight of the Huia*. Christchurch: Canterbury University Press, 2004

Wood, Vaughan. 'Appraising soil fertility in early colonial New Zealand: The "biometric fallacy" and beyond'. *Environment and History*, vol. 9 (2003): 393–405

Worster, Donald. 'Nature and the disorder of history'. *Environmental History Review*, vol. 18, no. 2 (1994), 1–15

———. 'Doing environmental history'. In *The Ends of the Earth: Perspectives on modern environmental history*, ed. Donald Worster, 289–307. Cambridge: Cambridge University Press, 1988

———. *Rivers of Empire: Water, aridity, and the growth of the American west*. New York: Pantheon Books, 1985

Worthy, T.H. 'What was on the menu? Avian extinction in New Zealand'. *Archaeology in New Zealand*, vol. 19 (1997): 125–60

Worthy, T.H., and R.N. Holdaway. *The Lost World of the Moa*. Christchurch: Canterbury University Press, 2002

Wright, Olive. *The Voyage of the Astrolabe*. Wellington: A.H. & A.W. Reed, 1955

Yeates, G.W. 'Impact of historical changes in land use on the soil fauna'. *New Zealand Journal of Ecology*, vol. 15, no. 1 (1991): 99–106

Young, David. *Our Islands, Our Selves*. Dunedin: University of Otago Press, 2004

Index

Bold page numbers indicate illustrations, maps and information in captions.
Numbers in the form 297n69 refer to endnotes.

Abbot, Edward Immyns **170–71**
acclimatisation societies 236–38, 244, 246, 272, 276
Adam, James 180
adzes 48, 50, **52–53**, 297n69
agriculture *see* farming
Akapātiki Flat 50, 58, 61, 177, 214, 261
albatrosses 13, 14, 26–27, 35, 65, **245**, 278, 287, 347n4
alcohol 129, 137, 319nn117–18, 321n185
Allans Beach 273, **275**
Alligator, HMS 132
Anderson, Archibald 146, 147
Anderson, Atholl 41, 45, 47, 60, 66–67, 77, 94, 96, 134–35, 137–38, 140
Anderson, John and James 147, 327n67
Anderson, William 55
Andersons Bay 54, 147, **157–58**, 166, 182, **196**, 230, **256**, 270, 327n67; farming at 168–69, 173–74, 190, 200, 202, **248**, 252–53; market gardening at 255; recreation gardens 212; road, ferry and rail to 192–93, 195–97, **196**, 258
Anglem, William 131–32
Āraiteuru (waka) 46
Aramoana 77, 109, 112
archaeology 14, 44, 48–50, **49**, 56–57, 60–61, 64–70, **67**
artefacts 48–50, **52–53**, 56–57, **57**, **68–69**; in site dating 65
aruhe (fern root) 55, 80, 92–93

Ballantyne, Tony 169
Bank of Glasgow 254
Banks, Joseph 102, 104, 311n94
Barnicoat, John **83**, **123–25**, 126, 138–39, 143
Barr, James 161, 176
Bathgate, Alexander 178, 192, 237–38, 243–44, 277, 278
Beattie, Herries 44–47, 57, 70, 86, 140

Beattie, James 169, 274, 277, 284, 334n121
Begg, Alexander 228
Best, Elsdon 82, 93, 109
Binney, Judith 140
birds 235–38, 339n274; before human settlement 34–35; extinctions and collapses 59, 94–96, 178–79, 235, 267–68, 270–74, 276, 278; hunting 82–83, 90–92, **91**, 177, 179, 235
Blosseville, Jules de 44, 101
Boast, Richard 157
boats adopted by Māori 129–31, 215, 315nn47–48
Boultbee, John 16–17, 109, 116, 143
Bourke, Richard 131–32
Bowman, H.O. 264
Bradshaw, Corey 88
Brasch, Charles 70
Briden, Shar 49, 56
Britannia (ship) 103
British East India Company 16, 103, 111
Broad Bay 190, 195, 197, 200, 212–13, 330n19
Brooking, Tom 26
Brothers (ship) 16, 105, 106
Browne, Thomas Gore 214
Brunner, Thomas 80
Buchanan, John **33**, **280**
Buller, Walter 246
Burns, Thomas 163–64, 166, 168–73, 177–78, 181–82, 240, 270, 277, 286
Busby, James 122

Caddell, James 107, 109, 111–12, 117
canoe-building 70
Cape Saunders **6**, **13**, 15, **35**, **217**, 219, 261, 269, 272; farming at **211**, 253; naming by Cook 102, 182; seal hunting at 86, 88, 104–06
Carey, David 147
Carey, Hannah 147

369

Cargill, William 147–48, 163–64, 180
cats 177, 235
cattle 143, 146–47, 169–72, 176–77, 253–54, 332n60 *see also* dairy farming
Chapman, Frederick 86
cheese factories 209–11, 230, 262, 334n121
Chevalier, Nicholas **239**, 239–40, **240**
Chinese market gardeners 255
Christianity 136, 140–43, 283
Christie, James 182, 207, 322n188
church at Pukehiki 204, **205**, 209
Clarence (whaler) 118
Clark, Alexander 202
Clarke, George 154–55
Clearwater, Garrett Hopper 174, **200**, **211**
climate 14, 32–34, 47, 60, 64, 281–82
clothing 117–18
Codfish Island 118
Colleen (ferry) 195, **208**
conservation 243–44, 278, 341n327, 347n4 *see also* resource management
Cook, James 16, 102–03, 110, 151, 182, 310n84
creameries **262**, 263, 266, **267**, 279
crop growing 146, 169, 174–78, 188, 190, 198, 201, 327n94, 330n6; by Māori 148, 182; pest attacks 146, 177–78, 236, 238, 246 *see also* wheat
Crosby, Alfred 105, 110, 133–34
Crozier, Michael 233–34
Cumberland, Kenneth 25
curio hunting 48–50, 66–67, **68–69**, 70
curio trading 111, 311n94
Cutten, William Henry 220, 258, 326n63

Dacker, Bill 137, 181–82, 219, 264, 266
dairy farming 18, 188–92, 198–99, 207, **251**, 251–54, **252**, **262**, 262–63, 266, **267**, 279; decline 20, 287
Darwin, Charles 244
Dickson family 211, **253**, 253–54
diseases *see* infectious diseases
Drummond, James 237
ducks 34, 89–90, 270, 276
Dunedin 11, **170–71**; 1840s establishment 147, **157–59**, 165–67; in 1850s–1860s 18, **170–71**, 180–81, **186**, 186–88, **187**, **193**, 230, 329n146; in 1870s–1880s **191**, 193–95, 213, 254
Dunedin and Suburban Reserves Conservation Society 278
Dunedin Morning Herald 246
Dunedin Naturalists' Field Club 197, 229, 284
Dunedin Presbytery 181

East India Company *see* British East India Company
ecological control (by Māori) *see* resource management

Edina (ferry) 258
Edwardson, William 111
eels 85–86, 90–92
Elizabeth (ship) 122
Ellison, Edward 83, 86–87, 93
Ellison, Raniera 142, 217, 330n4
Ellison whānau 224
Endeavour (ship) 16, 102
Entwisle, Peter 134–35, 136–37, 241
environmental changes
 before 1840: 14, 41, 46, 48, 59–61; 1840s–1870s 188–90, 224–47, 283–84; 1880s–1890s 249–50, 254, 267–78; settlers' regrets 243–46, 276–79 *see also* extinctions and collapses
epidemics *see* infectious diseases
erosion 148, 224–27, 233–35, **234**, 274, 279, 284, 338n259
Evison, Harry 78, 134–35, 137, 155
extinctions and collapses 94–96, 111, 143–44; after Māori settlement 14, 16, 41, 46, 48, 59–61; from sealing and whaling 16–17, 104–05, 308n31; after European settlement 177–79, 214, 222, 235, 267–74, 284; settler interpretations 244–46; recoveries 26–27, 95, 223

Farley, Henry 212
farming
 by Europeans **24**, 145–48, 168–76, 188–92, 198–211, **211**, 260–63, 268–70; amalgamations 260; buildings **189**, 190, 198–99, **199**, **203**, 204, 230, **252**, **253**; by occupations **251**; retreat in twentieth century 287 *see also* crop growing; dairy farming
 by Māori 108–09, 117, 145, 148, 172, 182, 266, 279
Favourite (ferry) 194
fencing and walls **20**, 199–201, **200**, **201**, **210**, 341n328; by Māori 220, **221**
Fereday, R.M. 246
Ferens, Thomas 168, 179, 288
Ferguson, William Clarke **199**
ferrets 271–72
ferries 193–95, 212, 258–60, 263, 331n29, n31, 334n131
Firth, Raymond 95
fish 15, 36–37, **38–39**, 156, 284; introduced 276
Fish Protection Act 1877: 222
fishing
 by Māori 64–65, 70, 80, 82–83, **83**; after British settlement 214–17, 220–23, 264–65
 by settlers 19–20, 215–16, 264–65
Fitzroy, Robert 151–52, 156
flax 16, 111–13, 116, 211, 282, 311n91, 312n111, n116

foreshore and sea fishing rights 221–22, 224, 264–65, 286
forests
    before human settlement 32, 34, 292n9; clearing of 48, 59–61, 174, 185, 189, 229–30, **231**, 261, 284; settlers' regrets 243–44; in 1859 **175**; remnants 269–70, **271**
Foveaux Strait 88, 92, 95, 104, 116, 117, 133
Fowler, Samuel 106–07
French visits to Peninsula 134, 136–38, 145
fruit production 201–02, 255
Furneaux, Tobias 110

General Gates (ship) 113
geology 32, 233–34
Gill, Samuel 192–93, 197
Gillies, Robert 174, **175**, 188, 277
gold mining on Peninsula 211
gold rush 18, 186–88, 190
Golden Age (ferry) 194, 331n31, 334n131
Golson, Jack 66
Gondwana 13, 32
gorse 200, 244, 270, 276
Graham, David 37, 265
grasses and grassland 172, 174, 176, 190, 201, 237, 260–61, **261**, 338n236
Grey, George 156
Guard, Jacky 132
guns 17, 117, 118, 122–23, 313n145, 314n11, n14
Guthrie-Smith, Herbert 36, 281

Haast's eagle 35, 59
Haberfield, William 83
Halswell, Edmund Storr 131, 316n52
Hamel, Jill 56, 66–67
Hamilton, Andrew 192, **193**
Harbour Cone 182, 210, 230, **231**
Harbour Steam Company 194
Harbours Act 1878 222
Harwood 48, 50, 54, 58, 61
Harwood, Lucy Ann 50, **52**
Harwood, Octavius 50, **51**, 127–29, **128**, 138, 142, 145–46, 148, 151, 323n210; store at Ōtākou 123, **123**, 128–29, 137, 146, 225, 322n208
Hay, James 148
Heaphy, Charles 220
Herd, James 113, 116
Highcliff **33**, 182, 188, 195, 197, 199, **203**, **210**, 269; cheese factory and creamery 209, 262–63
Hobson, William 151
Hodgkins, William **25**
Holdaway, Richard 54, 94
Honekai 74, 113, 311n107
Hoopers Inlet **13**, **15**, 54, 156, 167, 202, 211, 233, **271**, 272, 290n21

Hoopers Inlet Gold Mining Company 211
horses 147, 176, 195, 207
Hughes, John 127
Hutton, Frederick **38**

Illustrated New Zealander 214
infectious diseases 110, 131–36, 140–42, 155, 310n84–85 *see also* measles
influenza 110, 133
insects 177–78, 235–38, 246, 286, 340n285
introduced species by Māori 96; natural arrival 235–36; by sealers and traders 105, 106, 108, 110–11; by settlers 174, 178, 229, 236–38, 244–46, 266–76, 284–86, 341n309, 346n132
Irving, Richard 200, 332n60, 334n121
Irwin, Jeff 41

Jane (ferry) 194, 331n31, n36
John Wickliffe (ship) 167–68
Johns, Dilys 56
Johnson, Peter 270
Jones, Johnny 127, 142, 146, 194

Kahukura (deity) 44, 142
Kai Huānga ('Eat Relation') feud 118, 122–23, 318n90
Kāi Tahu 14–15, 43, 71–78; land and fisheries claims 151, 223–24, 264–66, 329n146, 336n204; resistance to Ngāti Toa 17, 118, 122–23, 129, 131, 133; traditions 44–46
Kai Te Pahi 63, 78, 303n109
Kai Te Ruahikihiki 63, 73, 78, 303n109
kākā 34, 90, 94, 177, 178–79, 235, 284
kākāpō 34, 90
Kamautaurua (Quarantine Island) 116, 156
Karetai (chief) 118, 123, 129, 143, 215, 218, 225, 303nn108–09, 315n48; in land transactions 150–55, 219, 324n239; visits to Sydney 129, 131–33, 315n42, 316n56, n68
Karetai, Mrs 264, **265**
Karitāne *see* Waikouaiti
Kate (ferry) 258
Kāti Kurī 15, 72–74, 78
Kāti Māmoe 14–15, 46, 47, 71–78, 81, 154, 303nn107–09
Kāti Moki 63, 73, 78
Kāti Taoka 63, 73, 78
Kelly, James 107, 131
Kelvin Grove 146–47, 215, 322n191, nn194–97
Kemp Block sale 89, 157, 264
Kent, John Rudolphus 111–16, 282, 312n116
kererū (pigeons) 82, 235, 270, 287
Kettle, Charles 18, 147, **157–59**, **164–65**, 165–67, 190, 325n23, n26
King, James 176

King, Phillip Gidley 103–04
kiore 59, 61, 90, 96, 110–11, 177
kiwi 34, 90
Knight, Hardwicke 18, 50, **189**, 263
Kohi (at Ōtākou) 150
Korako (chief in 1817) 107
Korako, Hoani Wetere 214, 215, 225, 323n232
Koroko (chief) 151, 154

Lalas, Chris 88–89
land transactions 76, 217–20; between Māori and sealers and whalers 149–51, 218; between Māori and settlers 218, 220, 260, 266; New Zealand Company purchases 17–18, 149, 151–57, 323n234, 324n242
Larnach, William 11, 18, **24**, 195, 200, 206–08, 252, 275, 333n99; plantings and introductions 208, 238, 341n309; promotion of infrastructure 190, 197, 208
Larnach Castle 204, **206**, 206–08, 334n112
Le Breton, Louis **97–99**, 138, **139**
le Guillou, Élie 134
Leslie, D.M. 233
Leslie, William 146
Lewis, Richard 215
Liardet, Wilbraham **186**, **213**
lime kilns 204, **204**, 333n94
literacy 143
Little Papanui 48, 54, 66–70, **67–69**, 74, **91**
Long Beach 64
Lucy Ann (ship) 131

Macandrew, James 180–81, 206, 209, 222
Macandrew Bay 182, 195, 200
Mackay, Alexander 181, 224, 263–64, 265–66, 279
Mackenzie, Scobie 258
Makahoe/Mangahoe *see* Papanui Inlet
Maniototo plain 80
Mantell, Walter 181, 329n146
maps
    Dunedin and Peninsula **12**, **158–59**, **164–65**, **191**, **259**, **269**; Māori localities and knowledge **49**, **79**, **84**, **130**; Otago Harbour **12**, **114–15**, **153**, **259**; Peninsula **153**, **175**, **184**, **256–57**, **268**; settler landholdings **187**, **251**, **252**, **260**
market gardening 255
Marmon, John 113
Marsden, Samuel 131–32, 316n56
Mathieson, Alexander 199, 201, 332n60
Mathieson, John 201, 203, **203**, 209–11, 228, 236, 238, 274, 332n60, 334n121
Matilda (ship) 106, 309n61
McCahon, Colin 22
McClay, John 173, 174, 177, 180, 277
McDonald, James 203–04, **204**, 333n94

measles 132–35, 140, 155, 316n68, 317n69, n71, n74, n80
Mermaid (ship) 111
Middleton, Angela 20
Ministry for Culture and Heritage 56
missionaries 132, 136–37, 142–43
moa 14, 34, 46, 47–54, **51**, 59, **62**, 292n18, 295n34, 297n71, 299n105
Moki (chief) 73–74, 78
Molyneux plain 152, 168
Monro, David 144, 146, 148, 149
Monson, Mrs 144
Mt Charles 198, **207**, 234, 269, 290n21, 325n26
Muaupoko 46–47
Murdoch, J.W. 48–50
Murihiku 46
Murison, W.D. 244
muskets *see* guns
mustelids 267, 272–73
muttonbirds *see* tītī

Native Land Court 19, 219
Native Reserves Act 1856: 220
Neill, William Thompson 255–58, **256**, **257**, 268, **269**
New Edinburgh 151, **153**, 166
New South Wales 103–04, 111, 119
New Zealand Company 17–18, 116, 119, 146, 149, 151–57
New Zealand Dairy Supply Company 262
New Zealand Journal 174
Ngāi Tahu *see* Kāi Tahu
Ngāi Te Pahi *see* Kai Te Pahi
Ngāi Tuhaitara 72
Ngāti Irakehu 72
Ngāti Moki *see* Kāti Moki
Ngāti Ruahikihiki *see* Kai Te Ruahikihiki
Ngāti Ruanui prisoners 194
Ngāti Taoka *see* Kāti Taoka
Ngāti Toa 17, 142 *see also* Te Rauparaha
Nikūru 132
Noxious Weeds Act 1901: 275

O'Brien, George **207**, 241, **242**
Ocean Beach 32
Okia Flat **73**, **87**, 146, 261, 269
O'Malley, Vincent 157
Omate 123, 225
Onslow (ferry) 260
Otago Acclimatisation Society 236–38, 244, 246, 272, 276
Otago Block sale 17–18, 89, 146, 149, 151–57, **153**, 165–66
Otago Colonist 180
Otago Daily Times 223
Otago Harbour **15**, **25**, **33**, 112, 116, **139**, 152,

280; maps and charts 12, **114–15**, 153, 259; overfishing in 19–20, 222; whaling stations 17, 122–28, **123–25**
Otago Harbour Board 274
Otago Heads **41–42**, **242**
Otago Journal 172
Otago Museum **38–39**, 50, **51–53**, **69**
Otago News 177
Otago Peninsula Agricultural and Pastoral Society 207, 209, **210**
Otago Peninsula Cheese Factory **203**, 334n121
Otago Provincial Council 173, 180–81, 194 *see also* provincial government
Otago Witness 172, 176, 178, 181, 189, 197, 214, 229, 234, 237, 239, 246, 255
Ōtākou 263, 266, **267**, 274, 296n41
Ōtākou Māori 47, 77–87, 93, **97–99**; adjustment to 'people of the ships' 17, 105–09, 111–12, 116–19; in whaling period 122–46; effects of diseases on 132–36; in 1844 land sale 154–57; after British settlement 19, 179–82, 214–27, **218**, 263–66, 279, 286; pōhā bags 80–81, **81**

Palmer, Edwin 139–40, 312n118
Palmer, William 133
Papanui Beach 65, 66, 86–87
Papanui Inlet (Makahoe/Mangahoe) **15**, 48, **56**, 56–57, 86–87, **87**, **89**, 156, 167, 221–22, 263, 265, 272
Paparu 132
parakeets 34, 178, 238, 270, 272
parasites 110, 117, 310n80
Parata, Tame 76, 86, 263–64
Paratene, John 214
Parihaka prisoners 194, 195
Parihaumia 182
passerines 34
Patahi 139–40
Patrick, James 173, 176, 327n67
Patuki, Topi 180–81, 324n246, 329n146
Pawson, Eric 26
penguins 13–16, 26–27, 35, 48–49, 61, 65, 144, 270–72, 278, 287, 347n4
Peninsula (ferry) 194
Peninsula Agricultural and Pastoral Society 274
Peninsula County Council 192
Peninsula Farmers Association 255
Peninsula Steam Boat Company 194
Perseverance (schooner) 215
pests 105, 146, 178–79, 236–38, 246, 284–86, 340n285, 345n119
Phillip Laing (ship) 167–68
pigeons *see* kererū
pigs 16, 111, 117, 143–45, 177, 198, 214
Pikiwhara *see* Sandymount
Pilots Beach 74, 127

Pipikaretu Beach 54, 70, 80
Poatiri (Cape Saunders) 15, 70
Pohio, Horomona 154
Pokene (chief) 138, 151
Polynesian migrations 14, 40–41, 44–48, 60–61, 96–97
population
  Dunedin 254; Māori 134–35, 140, 181, 266, 318n90, 321nn185–86; Otago 186, 326n65, 330n2; Peninsula 188, 258
Port Chalmers 193–95, 216, 264
Port Chalmers District High School 260
Port Jackson *see* Sydney (Port Jackson)
Port Otago **139**
Port Oxley 112, **114–15**
Portobello 37, 146, 166, 173, 190–97 *passim*, 202, 208, 255, **256–57**, 258, 269, **280**, 327n66, 330n19; erosion at 233–34, **234**; forest clearance at 230, **231**, **232**; introduced species at 236, 237, 337n228; name 182, 322n188
Portobello (ferry) 194–95
Portobello Marine Fish Hatchery 222
potatoes 16, 108–09, 135–36, 145–48 *passim*, 172, 202, 215, 254–55, 283, 318n99, 319nn104–05, 321n171, 335n143
Potiki (chief) 225
poultry 143, 146, 176, 193, 198, 214, 321n178
pounamu 48, 50, **52–53**, 72
predators 59, 110–11, 267–68, 271–74
Preservation Inlet 118, 123
Pride of the Yarra (ferry) 193–94
property rights 19, 25–26, 149–52, 162–63, 167, 168, 281; traditional Māori 75–78, 93, 282; for farming settlers 190, 214, 279, 283–84, 322n198; Māori after British settlement 217–27, 286
provincial government 228, 236, 239, 286 *see also* Otago Provincial Council
Pukehiki 210
Pukehiki church 204, **205**, 209
Pukekura pā 72, 73–74, 77, 302n71
Purakaunui 64

rabbits 238, 244, 246, 272, 341n310
Rākaihautū 45
Rakihouia 45
Rakiriri (Goat Island) 156
Rangipipikao 74
Ratara, Teone 265–66
rats 110–11, 143, 144, 177, 267, 273–74
recreation 212, 331n31, 334n131
Reeves, William Pember 243
Renata, Aparata *see* Reynolds, Alfred
Rennie, George 163–64
resource management (Māori) 16, 92–97, 282
Reynolds, Alfred 69, 90, 270–72, 276–78, 287–88

Richdale, Lance 14, 287
Richmond, Mathew 156
Riddell, Walter 202–04, **205**, 209, 263, 334n121
Ridley, Captain 135, 317n69, 318n99
Riemenschneider, J.F. 181, 219
roads 18, 167, **184**, **186**, 192, 194–97, 212, 258, 263;
    road boards 192, 228, 263, 274–76
Rob Roy (ship) 118
Robertson, William 190, 211
Roebuck, Charles 147
Rowand, Andrew 146, 147, 322nn195–96
Royal Commission into the Middle Island Native
    Question 263–64, 265–66
Russell, Boyd 95
Russell, George Grey 206
Ryan family 254

Samson, James 67–70
sand drift 224–27, **226**, **227**, 274
Sandfly Bay 49, 54, 174, **184**, 211, 227, **239**, 240, **240**
Sandymount 83, 182, **199**, 230, 240, 253, 254, **262**,
    263, 272, **285**; bush remants at 261, 269; early
    settlement at 188, 202, 207; erosion at 227,
    234; stone for buildings 199, **199**
Sappho (ferry) 258
Schultze, Charles 146
Scottish Free Church 163–64, 167
Scottish settlers 140, 147–48, 149, 151, 163–69, 190,
    213, 228, 277–79, 283–84, 286, 330n15
sea lions 26–27, 54, 59, 86, **88**, **89**, 278, 287
seabirds 14, 35–37, 40–41, 47–49, 64–65, 111, 267,
    270, 272–73
Seal Point 190
seals 14–16, 26, **54**, **55**, 61, 96, 144, 278, 287,
    305n170; hunting by Māori 14, 47–48, 54, 59,
    64–65, 70, 86–89, 222; industrial hunting 16,
    88–89, 101, 103–08, 308n31
Seaton, David 260, 343n45
Selwyn, George 137
Shag River Mouth 48, 61
Sheehan, John 221–22
sheep 106, 146, 147, 172, 178, 192, 198, 253, 287
shellfish **38–39**, 64–65, 82, 94, 95, 156
Shepherd, Thomas 116–17, 119, 122
Shortland, Edward 45, 80–81, 117, 127, 129,
    144–45, 146, 148, 149–50, 181
Silverstream River 85
Sim, James 195, 197, 207, 209, **210**
Simmons, David 66
Skinner, Henry 66
Smith, Herbert Guthrie 277
Smith, Ian 64, 86
Smith, William Mein 166
Smith–Nairn Commission 89, 156, 224, 336n204
Snares Islands 35
Somerville, James 109, 173–74, 177, 178

sooty shearwaters *see* tītī
Soper, Eileen 22, 243
Sophia (ship) 107
Southland Current 36
Southland Front 15
Spain, William 154
Stack, James 132, 223, 329n140
Star, Paul 243, 246
Stevens, Michael 95, 140, 143
Stewart, William 122, **189**, 189–90, 332n60
Stewart Island 36, 92
stoats 271–73
Stokes, Edward 147, 322nn197
stone buildings and walls 20, **189**, **199**, 199–201,
    201, 207
Stuart, Alexander 201–02, 333n89, 334n121
Subtropical Front 15
Susannah (ship) 135
Sydney (Port Jackson) 16, 103–06 *passim*; Māori
    trade with 116, 126, 129, 135–36, 311n91–92,
    313n145, 318n99, 319n104; Māori visits to 111,
    126, 129, 131–32, 312n116, 315n42, 316n56
Sydney Cove (ship) 105, 106
Sydney Packet (ship) 133, 135, 317n69
Symonds, John Jermyn 152–54, 156

Tahakopa (village) 123, **124–25**, 225
Tahatu (chief) 113, 132, 134, 311n97, 315n42
Taiaroa, Hori Kerei 19, 82, 142, 156, 217–27, 263,
    264–65, 329n146, 336n203
Taiaroa, Te Matenga 123, 129, 132, 214, 219, 222,
    225, 303n108, 311n97, 315n42, 337n337; first
    meetings with Europeans 92, 111–12, 118,
    143; in land transactions 150–55, 324n239
Taiaroa Head 64, **71**, 72, 77, **83**, 273
Taiaroa Land Act 1883: 19, 220
Taiaroa whānau 224
Taieri and Peninsula Milk Supply Company 204,
    262–63
Taieri plain 84, 152, 168, 202, 214
Taieri River 85, 90, 264
takahē 94
Tākitimu (waka) 46
Taoka (chief) 73–74
Tarewai (ferry) 260
Tarewai (village) 116
Tarewai (war leader) 74–75, 302n71
Tau, Te Maire 46, 143
Taylor, Richard 93–94
Te Hautapunui-o-tu (Te Hau) 74, 302n71
Te Kahu, Tare Wetere 86, 224
Te Kohe, Piripi 142
Te Maiharanui (rangatira) 122
Te Maire, Rawiri 264
Te Matahaere 76, 107, 150
Te Pahi (Pahee) 113, 312n109

Te Rakiihia (chief) 74
Te Rakitauneke (chief) 72
Te Rapuwai (people) 14, 45, 47, 72–73
Te Rauone Beach 107, 127, 174, **221**, 225, **226**, **227**
Te Rauparaha 17, 118, 122–23, 129, 131, 155
Te Ruahikihiki (chief) 73
Te Ruatitiko (village) 116, 225
Te Taupō 225
Te Wahi (chief) 106
Te Wai Pounamu 72, 302n56
Te Wera (chief) **88**, 112, 302n73
Te Whakataupuka (chief) 113, 117–18, 123, 133, 311n107, 312n118, 314n14
Tees, HMS 113
Teviotdale, David 66–70, **67**
thistles 174, 228–29, 244, 275–76, 337n228, n230
Thomson, A.S. 244
Thomson, George Malcolm 20, 36, 222, 237, 249, 250, 276, 277, 279, 284
Thomson, John Turnbull **170–71**, 246
Thomson, Peter 177, 197, 215–16, 218, 222, 225, 227, 229, 241
tī (cabbage tree) and kāuru 55, 58, **58**, 86, 214, 298nn94–96
Tikao, Hone Taare 44, 86
timber mill 211, 230
timber trade 16, 103, 113, 129, 135, 311n92
Tiremorehu, Mataiha (Matthias) 45, 46
Titapu 138
tītī (muttonbirds) 14, 40, 92, 95, 288
tobacco 117, 129, 137, 313n135–136
Tokomairiro plain 153, 165
Tomahawk 173, 189–92, 199–200, 202, 228, 252–53, 274
Tomahawk Lagoon 156, 174, 177, 250, 275, 276
trade by Māori
　among Māori 57, 78, 81, 85, 92, 117; with 'people of the ships' 16–17, 105–09, 111–13, 117–19, 283, 311n92, 312n116; in whaling period 126, 129, 135–36, 311n92, 314n11; with British settlers 179–82, 214–16
transport 192–97, 230, 258, 343n45 *see also* roads
Treaty of Waitangi 151, 221–22
trees **35**, 116–17, 149, **201**, 267–70, **285**, 339n273; before human settlement 32, 34; conservation of 208 *see also* forests
tuberculosis/consumption 110, 117, 133–34, 138, 317n76
Tucker, William 106, 107, 311n94
Tuckett, Frederick 126, 140, 146, 149, 152–54, **153**, 157, 165–66
Tuhawaiki (chief) 111, 129, 131, 139, 151–55, 215, 315n48, 323n234, 324n239
tūī 34, 82, 90, 177, 179, 235, 270
Turner, Benjamin 54
tutu berries 86

University of Auckland 56
Uruao (waka) 45
Urville, Dumont d' 136, 144

Vauxhall 166, 258
Vauxhall Gardens 212, **212–13**
vegetable growing 147, 169–72, 201–02; by Māori 117, 214, 313n131 *see also* potatoes
venereal diseases 110
Victoria (ferry) 193–94
Victory Beach **87**
villages (Māori) 47–48, 56, 58, 64–67, 296n48, 297n51, 313n151
Vittoria (ship) 118
volcanic origins 32

Waikouaiti (Karitāne) 127, 133, 135, 143, 144, 147, 222–23
Waipapake (village) 116
Waitaha (people) 14, 45, 47, 57, 71, 72–73, 78, 81
Waitai (chief) 72
waka 56–57, **57**
Wakefield, Edward Gibbon 151, 162, 182, 183
Wakefield, Edward Jerningham 138
Wakefield, William 151, 154–56
Wallscott, Magda 263
Wanhalla, Angela 138
Ward, Alan 152
waterfowl 34
Watkin, James 133, 136–37, 138, 142–43, 150
Waverley 166, 195, **208**, 208, 258, 334n111
weasels 271–72
Weaver, John 219
weeds 105, 143, 228–29, 235, 275–76, 338n236
Weir, Cochrane 209
weka 80, 92, 214, 235, 276
Weller, Edward 123, 127, 132, 135, 148, 315n47, 316n62
Weller, George 127, 132, 135, 315n47
Weller, Joseph Brooks 122–23, 132, 134, 314n10
Weller Brothers/Weller and Co. 17, 118, 122–29, **123–25**, 131–32, 135, 140, 142, 145, 150–51, **226**, 315n32
whakapapa 44–47, 75, 142–43
Whakatakanewa (tohunga) 74
whales 26, 36–37, 143–44, 156, 222–23
whaling (commercial) 16–17, 118, 283, 314n21; resumption in 1869: 222–23, 336n197; shore stations 121–28, **123–25**, 150–51, **226**, 315n32
Whareakeake 106, 107, 313n142
wheat 117, 146, 169, 174–76, 178, 202
White, Joan 198
whitebait 85
Williams, Jim 90
Williams, Peter 118, 123

Williams, Robert 105, 108
Wohlers, Johann 134, 137
women settlers 22, 147, 173–74, 188, 200, 243, 252, 263
Worthy, Trevor 94

Young, David 94, 277, 278, 284
Zealandia 32
Zélée (ship) 134